WORLD TRADE ORGANIZATION

Dispute Settlement Reports

2001
Volume XIII

Pages 6479-6953

CAMBRIDGE
UNIVERSITY PRESS

PUBLISHED BY THE PRESS SYNDICATE OF THE UNIVERSITY OF CAMBRIDGE
The Pitt Building, Trumpington Street, Cambridge, United Kingdom

CAMBRIDGE UNIVERSITY PRESS
The Edinburgh Building, Cambridge CB2 2RU, UK
40 West 20th Street, New York, NY 10011–4211, USA
477 Williamstown Road, Port Melbourne, VIC 3207, Australia
Ruiz de Alarcón 13, 28014 Madrid, Spain
Dock House, The Waterfront, Cape Town 8001, South Africa

http://www.cambridge.org

First published 2004

Printed in the United Kingdom at the University Press, Cambridge

ISBN 0 521 83598 4 hardback

THE WTO DISPUTE SETTLEMENT REPORTS

The *Dispute Settlement Reports* of the World Trade Organization (the "WTO") include panel and Appellate Body reports, as well as arbitration awards, in disputes concerning the rights and obligations of WTO Members under the provisions of the *Marrakesh Agreement Establishing the World Trade Organization*. The *Dispute Settlement Reports* are available in English, French and Spanish. Starting with 1999, the first volume of each year contains a cumulative index of published disputes.

This volume may be cited as DSR 2001:XIII

TABLE OF CONTENTS

UNITED STATES - IMPORT PROHIBITION OF CERTAIN SHRIMP AND SHRIMP PRODUCTS

RECOURSE TO ARTICLE 21.5 OF THE DSU BY MALAYSIA

Report of the Appellate Body
WT/DS58/AB/RW

Adopted by the Dispute Settlement Body on 21 November 2001

Malaysia, *Appellant*	Present:
United States, *Appellee*	Bacchus, Presiding Member
Australia, *Third Participant*	Ganesan, Member
European Communities, *Third Participant*	Lacarte-Muró, Member
Hong Kong, China, *Third Participant*	
India, *Third Participant*	
Japan, *Third Participant*	
Mexico, *Third Participant*	
Thailand, *Third Participant*	

TABLE OF CONTENTS

I. INTRODUCTION

1. Malaysia appeals from certain issues of law and legal interpretations in the Panel Report, *United States - Import Prohibition of Certain Shrimp and Shrimp Products, Recourse to Article 21.5 of the DSU by Malaysia* (the "Panel Report").[1] In accordance with Article 21.5 of the *Understanding on Rules and Procedures Governing the Settlement of Disputes* (the "DSU"), Malaysia requested that the Dispute Settlement Body (the "DSB") refer to a panel its complaint with respect to whether the United States had complied with the recommendations and rulings of the DSB in *United States - Import Prohibition of Certain Shrimp and Shrimp Products* ("*United States - Shrimp*").

2. The background to this dispute is set out in detail in the Panel Report.[2] On 6 November 1998, the DSB adopted the reports of the original panel and the Appellate Body in *United States - Shrimp.*[3] The DSB recommended that the United States bring its import prohibition into conformity with its obligations under the *Marrakesh Agreement Establishing the World Trade Organization* (the "*WTO Agreement*"). On 6 December 1999, the period of time for implementation estab-

[1] WT/DS58/RW, 15 June 2001, DSR 2001:XIII, 6539.

[2] Panel Report, paras. 1.1-1.5 and 2.12-2.21.

[3] Appellate Body Report, WT/DS58/AB/R, adopted 6 November 1998, DSR 1998:VII, 2755; original panel report, WT/DS58/R and Corr.1, as modified by the Appellate Body Report, WT/DS58/AB/R, adopted 6 November 1998, DSR 1998:VII, 2755.

lished by the parties under Article 21.3(b) of the DSU expired. [4] At the DSB meeting of 23 October 2000, Malaysia informed the DSB that it was not satisfied that the United States had complied with the recommendations and rulings of the DSB, and announced that it wished to seek recourse to a panel under Article 21.5 of the DSU. [5] The DSB referred the matter to the original panel.

3. Malaysia's complaint relates to a measure taken by the United States in the form of an import prohibition to protect and conserve certain species of sea turtles, considered to be an endangered species. This original measure, Section 609 of the United States Public Law 101-162 ("Section 609"), and its application are described in detail in the Appellate Body Report in *United States - Shrimp*.[6] The Appellate Body found that Section 609 was provisionally justified under Article XX(g) of the *General Agreement on Tariffs and Trade 1994* (the "GATT 1994"). In implementing the recommendations and rulings of the DSB, the United States did not amend Section 609, with the result that the import prohibition is still in effect. However, the United States Department of State issued the Revised Guidelines for the Implementation of Section 609 of Public Law 101-162 Relating to the Protection of Sea Turtles in Shrimp Trawl Fishing Operations (the "Revised Guidelines").[7] These Revised Guidelines replace the guidelines issued in April 1996 that were part of the original measure. This dispute between Malaysia and the United States arises in relation to the import prohibition of shrimp and shrimp products provided for by Section 609, and its application by the United States.

4. Section 609, the Revised Guidelines, and their application, are described in the Panel Report. [8] In the following paragraphs, we set out those aspects of the Revised Guidelines that are pertinent to the consideration of the issues raised in this appeal.

5. Section 609(b)(2) provides that the import prohibition on shrimp does not apply to harvesting nations that are "certified" according to criteria set by the United States. The Revised Guidelines set forth the criteria for certification. The stated goal of the programme set out in the Revised Guidelines is the same as that set out in the programme of the original guidelines, namely, to protect endangered sea turtle populations from further decline by reducing their incidental mortality in commercial shrimp trawling. A central element of the United States programme is that commercial shrimp trawlers are required to use Turtle Excluder Devices ("TEDs") approved in accordance with standards established by

---

4 WT/DS58/15, 15 July 1999.

5 Malaysia's recourse to a panel was also in accordance with a bilateral agreement it had concluded with the United States in respect of the procedures to be followed under Articles 21.5 and 22 of the DSU. *See*, WT/DS58/16, 12 January 2000.

6 *Supra*, footnote 3, paras. 3-6.

7 United States Department of State, Federal Register Vol. 64, No. 130, 8 July 1999, Public Notice 3086, pp. 36946 - 36952. The Revised Guidelines are attached to the Panel Report.

8 Panel Report, paras. 2.5 - 2.11 and 2.22 - 2.32.

the United States National Marine Fisheries Service. Where the government of a harvesting country seeks certification on the basis of having adopted a programme that is based on TEDs, certification will be granted if this government's programme includes a requirement that commercial shrimp trawlers use TEDs that are "*comparable in effectiveness*" to those used in the United States, and a credible enforcement effort that includes monitoring for compliance.[9]

6. Under the original guidelines, the practice of the Department of State was to certify countries *only after* they had shown that they required the use of TEDs. Under the Revised Guidelines, countries may apply for certification even if they do not require the use of TEDs. In such cases, a harvesting country has to demonstrate that it has implemented, and is enforcing, a "*comparably effective*" regulatory programme to protect sea turtles without the use of TEDs. The Department of State is required "to take fully into account any demonstrated differences between the shrimp fishing conditions in the United States and those in other nations, as well as information available from other sources."[10]

7. An exporting country may also be certified if its shrimp fishing environment does not pose a threat of incidental capture of sea turtles. The Revised Guidelines provide that the Department of State shall certify a harvesting country pursuant to Section 609 if it meets any of the following criteria: the relevant species of sea turtles do not occur in waters subject to that country's jurisdiction; in that country's waters, shrimp is harvested exclusively by means that do not pose a threat to sea turtles, for example, any country that harvests shrimp exclusively by artisanal means; or, commercial shrimp trawling operations take place exclusively in waters in which sea turtles do not occur.[11]

8. Before the Panel, Malaysia argued that the United States had failed to comply with the recommendations and rulings of the DSB, and that, consequently, the United States continued to violate its obligations under the GATT 1994. In its Report circulated on 15 June 2001, the Panel found as follows:

(a) [t]he measure adopted by the United States in order to comply with the recommendations and rulings of the DSB violates Article XI.1 of the GATT 1994;

(b) in light of the recommendations and rulings of the DSB, Section 609 of Public Law 101-162, as implemented by the Revised Guidelines of 8 July 1999 and as applied so far by the [United States] authorities, is justified under Article XX of the GATT 1994 as long as the conditions stated in the findings of this Report, in particular

---

[9] Panel Report, para. 2.25.

[10] *Ibid.*, para. 2.28.

[11] *Ibid.*, para. 2.29.

the ongoing serious good faith efforts to reach a multilateral agreement, remain satisfied.[12]

9. The Panel urged "Malaysia and the United States to cooperate fully in order to conclude as soon as possible an agreement which will permit the protection and conservation of sea turtles to the satisfaction of all interests involved and taking into account the principle that States have common but differentiated responsibilities to conserve and protect the environment."[13] (footnote omitted)

10. On 23 July 2001, Malaysia notified the DSB of its intention to appeal certain issues of law covered in the Panel Report and certain legal interpretations developed by the Panel, pursuant to paragraph 4 of Article 16 of the DSU, and filed a Notice of Appeal pursuant to Rule 20 of the *Working Procedures for Appellate Review* (the "*Working Procedures*"). On 2 August 2001, Malaysia filed its appellant's submission.[14] On 17 August 2001, the United States filed an appellee's submission.[15] On the same day, Australia, the European Communities, Hong Kong, China, India, Japan, Mexico and Thailand each filed a third participant's submission.[16]

11. On 13 August 2001, the United States requested that the Division hearing this appeal change the date of the oral hearing set out in the working schedule for this appeal. After inviting the participants to make their views known with respect to this request, the Division ruled that it would not change the date of the oral hearing. Accordingly, the oral hearing in the appeal was held on 4 September 2001. The participants and third participants presented oral arguments and responded to questions put to them by the Members of the Division.

II. ARGUMENTS OF THE PARTICIPANTS AND THE THIRD PARTICIPANTS

A. *Claims of Error by Malaysia - Appellant*

1. *Terms of Reference*

12. Malaysia submits that the Panel erred in its examination of the new measure taken by the United States to comply with the recommendations and rulings of the DSB in *United States - Shrimp*.

---

[12] *Ibid.*, para. 6.1.

[13] Panel Report, para. 7.2.

[14] Pursuant to Rule 21 of the *Working Procedures*.

[15] Pursuant to Rule 22 of the *Working Procedures*.

[16] Pursuant to Rule 24 of the *Working Procedures*. Ecuador, a third party in the proceedings before the Panel, did not file a third participant's submission, but requested permission to attend the oral hearing as a "passive observer". After consulting the participants and third participants, the Division hearing this appeal granted Ecuador permission to attend the oral hearing in this capacity.

13. Malaysia submits that it is a legal principle that an implementing measure must be examined for conformity with the covered agreements rather than for conformity with the recommendations and rulings of the DSB. This principle is borne out in the case in *Canada - Measures Affecting the Export of Civilian Aircraft - Recourse by Brazil to Article 21.5 of the DSU* ("*Canada - Aircraft (21.5)*") [17], where the Appellate Body held that the scope of Article 21.5 dispute settlement proceedings is not limited to the issue of whether or not a WTO Member has implemented the recommendations and rulings of the DSB. The Appellate Body ruled that the task of the panel was to determine whether the new measure is consistent with the disputed provisions of the *WTO Agreement*.

14. Malaysia submits that, in carrying out its review under Article 21.5 of the DSU, a panel is not confined to examining the "measure taken to comply" only from the perspective of the claims, arguments and factual circumstances that relate to the measure that was the subject of the original proceedings. Although these may have some relevance in proceedings under Article 21.5 of the DSU, Malaysia submits that Article 21.5 proceedings involve, in principle, not the original measure, but rather a new and different measure that was not before the original panel. In Malaysia's view, the utility of the review envisaged under Article 21.5 of the DSU would be seriously undermined if a panel were restricted to examining the new measure from the perspective of the claims, arguments and factual circumstances that related to the original measure.

15. Malaysia argues that the Panel erred in its treatment of the Appellate Body Report in *United States - Shrimp*. First, Malaysia asserts that in relying solely on the reasoning of the Appellate Body, the Panel has in fact relied on the claims and arguments brought by the parties that related to the original measure. Second, Malaysia argues that the Panel erred in treating the Appellate Body Report in *United States - Shrimp* as having proposed alternative courses of conduct or alternative measures as *conditions* which, if fulfilled, would necessarily render the implementing measure consistent with the relevant covered agreement. In Malaysia's view, the alternative courses of conduct or alternative measures referred to by the Appellate Body were *dicta*, and, therefore, the Panel erred in interpreting these *dicta* as positive conditions for determining GATT-consistency.

2. *The Chapeau of Article XX of the GATT 1994*

16. Malaysia appeals certain of the Panel's conclusions under the chapeau of Article XX of the GATT 1994. In particular, Malaysia submits that the Panel erred in considering the obligation of the United States as an obligation to *negotiate*, as opposed to an obligation to *conclude* an international agreement.

[17] Appellate Body Report, WT/DS70/AB/RW, adopted 4 August 2000, DSR 2000:IX, 4299.

17. Malaysia notes that the Appellate Body made pertinent observations and comments in its analysis of the chapeau of Article XX of the GATT 1994 with respect to "arbitrary or unjustifiable discrimination". In its treatment of "unjustifiable discrimination" the Appellate Body stated "[a]nother aspect of the application of Section 609 that bears heavily in any appraisal of justifiable or unjustifiable discrimination is the failure of the United States to engage the appellees, as well as other Members exporting shrimp to the United States, in serious, across-the-board negotiations with the objective of concluding bilateral or multilateral agreements for the protection and conservation of sea turtles, before enforcing the import prohibition against the shrimp exports of those other Members".[18] In Malaysia's view, these remarks of the Appellate Body emphasize the need for the *conclusion* of an international agreement.

18. Malaysia submits that these remarks of the Appellate Body constitute *dicta*. The Panel misunderstood these remarks to mean that alternative actions, in particular a demonstration of prior good faith negotiation, would "insulate" a unilateral measure from being characterized as "unjustifiable discrimination". It is further submitted that in the context of the new measure, the Panel failed to examine whether, in the circumstances, the United States acted in a manner constituting "unjustifiable discrimination".

19. Malaysia further contends that if the conclusion of the Panel is allowed to stand, it will lead to the "incongruous" result that any WTO Member would be able to offer to negotiate in good faith an agreement incorporating its "unilaterally defined standards" before claiming that its measure is justified under the pertinent exceptions of Article XX of the GATT 1994. According to Malaysia, the conclusion of the Panel will thus lead to the result that if a WTO Member fails to *conclude* an agreement, it could still claim that its application of a unilateral measure does not constitute "unjustifiable discrimination".

20. In addition, Malaysia submits that the Panel erred in concluding that the Inter-American Convention for the Protection and Conservation of Sea Turtles (the "Inter-American Convention") can reasonably be considered as a benchmark of what can be achieved through multilateral negotiations in the field of protection and conservation. The Panel did not provide any reasoning for taking this view. The Appellate Body cited the Inter-American Convention merely as an "example" of efforts made by the United States to reach a multilateral solution in relation to the conservation of sea turtles. In no sense was that convention considered as a "legal standard" by the Appellate Body. Moreover, the Appellate Body stated that one of the obligations which the United States had to fulfill in order to avoid "unjustifiable discrimination" was to engage in serious efforts to negotiate in good faith *before* the enforcement of a "unilateral" import prohibition.

[18] Appellate Body Report, *United States - Shrimp*, *supra*, footnote 3, para. 166.

21. Malaysia submits that the Panel's legal interpretation is erroneous because the United States had not proven that the unilateral and non-consensual procedures of the import prohibition had been eliminated. On the contrary, the ongoing negotiations on the Memorandum of Understanding on the Conservation and Management of Marine Turtles and their Habitats of the Indian Ocean and South-East Asian Region (the "South-East Asian MOU") demonstrated that an alternative and less trade restrictive course of action for securing the legitimate goals of the United States measure, was available. The logical consequence of the above argument is that the negotiations are underway, and, therefore, the import prohibition should be lifted.

22. Malaysia also appeals the Panel's conclusions under the heading "[m]easures comparable in effectiveness to the United States measure". Malaysia submits that the Appellate Body spoke of measures comparable in effectiveness to the United States measures in the context of illustrating the difference between the design and the application of the original measure.[19] The Appellate Body noted that while the design of the measure permitted certification of countries with measures comparable in effectiveness to United States measures, this was not the way in which the measure was applied in fact. The Panel misread this observation of the Appellate Body to mean that a measure requiring that exporting countries adopt regulatory programmes that are comparable in effectiveness to that of an importing country could not constitute "unjustifiable discrimination".

23. Malaysia contends that the Appellate Body did not accept the legitimacy of "comparable measures" - either implicitly or otherwise. Rather, it was merely describing the intended operation of the original measure. This is evident, *inter alia*, from the fact that the term "comparable in effectiveness" is the language of the 1996 Guidelines, which implemented the original measure. The Appellate Body was in no way authorizing importing Members to impose unilateral measures conditioning market access on an exporting Member having measures "comparable in effectiveness" to their own measures. The Panel, therefore, erred in assuming that the new measure, which imposed this requirement of measures "comparable in effectiveness to the United States regulatory programme", could not constitute unjustifiable discrimination.

24. Malaysia also submits that the Panel erred in finding that the Revised Guidelines allowed for *flexibility*, as they take account of situations where sea turtles are not endangered by shrimp trawling. Malaysia submits that the Revised Guidelines address only the incidental capture of sea turtles in the course of shrimp trawl harvesting. Close scrutiny of the Revised Guidelines discloses that they do not address the fact that the same conditions do not prevail in Malaysia. Malaysia does not practise shrimp trawling and the incidental capture of sea tur-

---

[19] Appellate Body Report, *United States - Shrimp*, *supra*, footnote 3, para. 163.

tles in Malaysian waters is due to fish trawling and not shrimp trawling. Thus the Revised Guidelines fail to take into account the specific conditions prevailing in Malaysia and they, therefore, violate the chapeau of Article XX of the GATT 1994.

25. Malaysia appeals the Panel's treatment of the decision of the United States Court of International Trade (the "CIT") in *Turtle Island Restoration Network, et al. v. Robert L. Mallett, et al.*[20] (the "*Turtle Island* case"). Malaysia is of the view that, in declining to consider this decision, the Panel erred in taking the view that municipal law is insulated from scrutiny by panels. Malaysia submits that had the Panel scrutinized the decision in the *Turtle Island* case, and assessed the likelihood and consequences of the Revised Guidelines being modified in the future, it would have found that the "unjustifiable discrimination" under the chapeau of Article XX of the GATT 1994 has not been eliminated.

26. Finally, Malaysia requests that the Appellate Body recommend that the import prohibition be lifted so as to give effect to the recommendations and rulings of the DSB as per the Appellate Body Report.

B. Arguments of the United States - Appellee

1. Terms of Reference

27. The United States submits that Malaysia's argument that the Panel failed to apply the correct scope of review in accordance with Article 21.5 of the DSU is without merit. Malaysia's reliance in this regard on the Appellate Body Report in *Canada - Aircraft (21.5)* is misplaced. The issue in that appeal was whether the Panel's review was limited to issues considered in the original panel and Appellate Body proceedings. The Appellate Body found that the DSU imposed no such limitation. In the present case, however, the Panel's scope of review was fully consistent with the Appellate Body findings in *Canada - Aircraft (21.5).*

28. The United States observes that the Panel in this case quoted at length from the Appellate Body Report in *Canada - Aircraft (21.5).* The Panel then concluded that it was fully entitled to address *all* the claims of Malaysia under Article XI and Article XX of the GATT 1994, whether or not these claims, the arguments and the facts supporting them were made before the original panel and the Appellate Body proceedings.

29. The United States argues that Malaysia's argument is based solely on the Panel's use of the phrase "recommendations and rulings of the DSB". In the view of the United States, the Panel's use of the phrase "complied with the recommendations and rulings of the DSB", is entirely appropriate, and indicates no limitation in its scope of review. In the context of this case, the recommendations and

[20] 110 Fed. Supp. 2d 1005 (CIT, 2000).

rulings of the DSB are that the United States "bring its measure ... into conformity with the obligations of the United States under [the GATT 1994]". The GATT 1994 is the only covered agreement at issue in the dispute.

2. *The Chapeau of Article XX of the GATT 1994*

30. The United States submits that the Panel correctly found that the United States has remedied the aspect of discrimination relating to differences in efforts to negotiate a bilateral or multilateral agreement. In its previous ruling in *United States - Shrimp*, the Appellate Body found that certain aspects of the application of Section 609, in their "cumulative effect", amounted to unjustifiable discrimination between countries where the same conditions prevail. One of those aspects related to efforts to negotiate. The Appellate Body then cited, and relied upon, the factual findings of the original panel concerning the absence of serious efforts of the United States to negotiate a conservation agreement with the complaining WTO Members.

31. The United States contends that it has proceeded to remedy this aspect of unjustifiable discrimination identified by the Appellate Body. In particular, the United States has made substantial efforts to negotiate a sea turtle conservation agreement in the Indian Ocean and South-East Asia region. The Panel found that these efforts did remedy this aspect of unjustifiable discrimination.

32. The United States submits that Malaysia does not contest the core findings of the Panel, namely, that the United States has engaged in serious, good faith efforts to negotiate a sea turtle conservation agreement with the countries in the Indian Ocean and South-East Asia region. The Panel considered whether the United States had addressed the effort-to-negotiate aspect of "unjustifiable discrimination" identified by the Appellate Body, and properly found that the United States had indeed remedied this aspect of discrimination.

33. The United States submits that, instead of addressing the pertinent findings of the Panel, Malaysia makes a number of arguments that are either based on mischaracterization of the Panel Report, or that amount to a request for a reversal of the key findings of the Appellate Body Report in *United States - Shrimp*. Malaysia argues that the Panel found that "a demonstration of prior good faith negotiation would insulate a unilateral measure from being characterized as unjustifiable discrimination." [21] In the United States view, this argument fails to take into account the context of the Panel's discussions of efforts to negotiate, and thus amounts to a mischaracterization of the findings of the Panel.

34. The United States submits that the discussions by the Appellate Body and the Panel concerning negotiations arise in the context of applying the Article XX chapeau to the specific facts of this case. The language of the chapeau of Article

---

[21] Malaysia's appellant's submission, para. 3.11.

XX requires that the WTO Member imposing the measure demonstrates that a measure is not applied in a manner that constitutes a means of unjustifiable discrimination. In the view of the United States, no single aspect of the application of the measure can, as Malaysia puts it, "insulate" the measure from an examination of other aspects of alleged discrimination.

35. The United States contends that it has addressed the "unjustifiable discrimination" test of the chapeau by making the *prima facie* case that the United States measure does not result in unjustifiable discrimination between countries where the same conditions prevail. In particular, in the original panel and Appellate Body proceedings, the United States showed the absence of any "unjustifiable discrimination between countries where the same conditions prevail" by demonstrating that it applies the import restrictions even-handedly with respect to all countries that engage in shrimp trawl fishing in waters inhabited by endangered sea turtles.

36. The United States notes Malaysia's argument that the Panel "erred" in concluding that the Inter-American Convention on sea turtle conservation "can reasonably be considered as a benchmark of what can be achieved through multilateral negotiations." [22] The United States submits that Malaysia has cited the Panel Report out of context. The Panel properly considered the United States efforts to negotiate for the purpose of determining whether the United States had remedied this aspect of discrimination identified by the Appellate Body. In this context, the Panel examined the efforts to negotiate involved in concluding the Inter-American Convention, and compared them with the efforts made by the United States to negotiate a sea turtle conservation agreement for the Indian Ocean and South-East Asia region. It was only in this sense that the Panel considered the Inter-American Convention to be a "benchmark".

37. Regarding Malaysia's argument that the Panel erred in finding the United States measure to be consistent with the *WTO Agreement* because "the United States had not proven that the unilateral and non-consensual procedures of the import prohibition had been eliminated", the United States submits that this argument runs counter to the finding in the Appellate Body Report reaffirming that nothing in the text of Article XX requires the elimination of a measure simply by virtue of it being "unilateral".

38. The United States refers to Malaysia's argument that the Panel erred in finding the United States measure to be consistent with the *WTO Agreement* because the Indian Ocean and South-East Asia negotiations constitute an "alternative course of action for securing the legitimate goals of the United States measure which was less restrictive." According to the United States, this argument is based on the flawed premise that a WTO Member must exhaust all possibilities

[22] Malaysia's appellant's submission, para. 3.13.

for achieving its goals in other ways. The *WTO Agreement* contains no such requirement, and the Appellate Body made no such finding.

39. The United States submits that the Panel was correct in finding that the United States had remedied the aspect of unjustifiable discrimination identified in the Appellate Body Report relating to flexibility and consideration of local conditions.

40. The Appellate Body found that the most conspicuous flaw in the application of Section 609 was an apparent requirement that all other exporting Members adopt essentially the same policy as that applied to domestic shrimp trawlers of the United States. The Appellate Body noted that the statutory provisions of Section 609 do not, in themselves, require that other WTO Members adopt essentially the same policies and enforcement practices as the United States, but that the guidelines then in effect appeared to lack flexibility. The Appellate Body also found that the guidelines did not appear to allow for flexibility in the consideration of different conditions that may exist in different harvesting nations.

41. The United States argues that Malaysia does not take issue with the Panel's analysis of the language in the Revised Guidelines. In addition, Malaysia did not seek to test the flexibility of the guidelines in practice by seeking certification of the Malaysian programme for conserving sea turtles in shrimp trawl fisheries.

42. The United States refers to Malaysia's argument that the Revised Guidelines do not address Malaysia's claim that "Malaysia does not practise shrimp trawling and the incidental catch of sea turtles is due to fish trawling and not shrimp trawling."[23] According to the United States, this "vague, undeveloped argument" does not rebut the *prima facie* case that the revised United States guidelines do in fact allow for flexibility and consideration of local conditions.

43. In the view of the United States, Malaysia's argument that the Panel "erred in taking the view that the issue of municipal law is insulated from scrutiny by panels" mischaracterizes the Panel's findings, and is without merit. The Panel considered the record before it, and properly concluded that under the Revised Guidelines, the importation of shrimp harvested by vessels using TEDs is allowed, even if the exporting nation has not been certified pursuant to Section 609.

44. With respect to the *Turtle Island* case, the United States submits that Malaysia does not present any arguments as to why the Panel was incorrect in its reasoning with respect to the relevant domestic law. As the Panel noted, the domestic court expressly declined to order any change in the Revised Guidelines, and those provisions of the Revised Guidelines that allow the importation of TED-caught shrimp from non-certified countries remain in effect.

---

[23] Malaysia's appellant's submission, para. 3.21.

C. Arguments of the Third Participants

1. Australia

(a) Terms of Reference

45. Australia submits that, in accordance with the provisions of Article 21.5 of the DSU, a panel is required to examine the consistency with a covered agreement of measures taken to comply with the recommendations and rulings of the DSB. This requires the relevant panel to conduct a fresh factual and legal analysis of the revised or new measure.

46. It is Australia's view that the Panel in this case did not examine the measures taken to comply on that basis. Had it done so, Australia submits that the Panel would not have had sufficient grounds to arrive at the finding that Section 609 of Public Law 101-162, as implemented by the Revised Guidelines of 8 July 1999 and as applied so far by the United States authorities, is justified under Article XX of the GATT 1994.

(b) The Chapeau of Article XX of the GATT 1994

47. Australia argues that the Panel erred in its conclusion that engagement by the United States in good faith negotiations would, in itself, necessarily be sufficient to meet the requirement of the chapeau of Article XX that its measure not be applied in a manner involving unjustifiable discrimination. This approach is inconsistent with the text of the chapeau of Article XX, and misapplies the reasoning of the Appellate Body Report.

48. Australia is of the view that the Panel misconstrued the Appellate Body findings, and the requirements of the chapeau of Article XX, in concluding that the United States would be entitled to maintain the implementing measure if it were demonstrated that it was making serious, good faith efforts to conclude an international agreement on the protection and conservation of sea turtles. This interpretation would seriously impair the delicate balance of rights and obligations embodied in Article XX and open the door for WTO Members to justify unilaterally-imposed trade restrictions simply on the basis of simultaneous entry into international negotiations. Article XX does not proscribe unilateral trade restrictions, but a reasonable degree of limitation must be imposed on their use - in line with the wording of the chapeau - if the balance of rights and obligations is to be preserved.

49. Australia submits that it is for the United States to demonstrate what serious, good faith efforts it had undertaken to obviate or eliminate the unjustifiably discriminatory nature of the ban -including in the design, extent and implementation of the measure. The progress of the Indian Ocean initiative has demonstrated the existence of a viable, non-discriminatory alternative to the unilateral import restriction. Given this progress, the United States has not established why its unilateral import restriction is no longer a form of unjustifiable discrimination.

50. Australia argues that the Panel did not ensure that the United States effectively met its burden of proof in seeking to justify its measure pursuant to Article XX. In particular, the United States did not prove that its measure was consistent with the requirements of the chapeau of Article XX. The fact that the United States did not present sufficient evidence to demonstrate that the measure was not a means of unjustifiable discrimination meant that the Panel could not have found that the United States measure met the requirements of the chapeau.

2. *European Communities*

(a) Terms of Reference

51. The European Communities submits that, given that measures taken to comply with the recommendations and rulings of the DSB are, by definition, new and different measures that may be inconsistent with provisions of the *WTO Agreement* that were not examined by the original panel, it is correct that a panel acting pursuant to Article 21.5 of the DSU will, as a consequence, have to address a new and different factual and legal situation.

52. However, the European Communities submits that all panels are bound by their terms of reference that are determined, pursuant to Article 7.1 of the DSU, by the "request for the establishment of a panel". The European Communities observes that, in its "request for the establishment of a panel", Malaysia referred only to the GATT 1994, and to the recommendations and rulings of the DSB. On the basis of Malaysia's "request for the establishment of a panel", and on its subsequent submissions, the Panel found that the claims of Malaysia are exclusively based on the findings of the Appellate Body and on non-compliance with them. Malaysia does not make any new claim under Article XX.

53. Given that the terms of reference of a panel "established" pursuant to Article 21.5 of the DSU are based on the same claims and legal bases as the terms of reference of the original panel, the Panel's treatment of Malaysia's complaint pursuant to Article 21.5 of the DSU does not appear to be in error. The Panel was not at liberty to examine other issues.

(b) The Chapeau of Article XX of the GATT 1994

54. The European Communities believes that international cooperation and negotiation must be preferred over unilateral action, particularly in the area of the protection of the environment, for all the reasons set out in the original Appellate Body Report. The European Communities emphasizes that international cooperation by its own nature is a process and not a result. Such cooperation is necessarily based on reciprocal efforts to resolve a common concern in the mutual interest.

55. Under the circumstances of the present case, it appears to the European Communities that international cooperation requires as a minimum the exchange of data and readily available scientific knowledge between all interested parties.

Under the Revised Guidelines, the United States would admit Malaysian shrimp to the United States market provided that Malaysia shows, on the basis of relevant data, that either its turtle conservation programme is "comparable in effectiveness" to the conservation method chosen by the United States or, in the alternative, that such conservation methods are unnecessary under the conditions prevailing in the waters in which Malaysia's trawlers are operating. The United States is thus apparently seeking Malaysia's participation in international cooperation in the form of an exchange of available data.

56. The application of the new measure has become more flexible in comparison with the application of the original measure, and this is the basis for the Panel's finding that the contested United States measure is currently not in conflict with the prohibition of "unjustifiable discrimination" under the chapeau of Article XX of the GATT 1994.

57. With respect to the *Turtle Island* case, the European Communities submits that the Panel correctly concluded that it was not for it to second-guess the outcome of a domestic dispute on the correct interpretation of a United States statute where a certain interpretation had been chosen by a domestic court, and that interpretation was challenged by the United States administration on appeal in the domestic courts.

58. The European Communities contends that it flows from the findings of the Panel that the ruling of the domestic court did not oblige the United States to violate its WTO obligations under the circumstances of the present case, particularly because the ruling was not final and because requests for interim relief were rejected. This appears to be a correct reading of the situation under the domestic law of the United States. In particular, the Revised Guidelines continue to be fully applied and therefore represent the situation that prevails under United States law.

59. In conclusion, the European Communities reiterates its position before the Panel that the complaint by Malaysia in this case is somewhat premature. Malaysia has not yet applied for certification. It is, therefore, not yet clear how the contested legislation would apply to imports of shrimp and shrimp products from Malaysia.

3. Hong Kong, China

(a) Terms of Reference

60. Hong Kong, China recalls that in its submission to the Panel, it expressed the view that the issue before a panel acting pursuant to Article 21.5 of the DSU is whether a new measure is in itself consistent with the *WTO Agreement*, particularly with the specific provisions with which the original panel or Appellate Body found the original measure inconsistent.

61. In the view of Hong Kong, China, panels should limit their review to the new measure, that is the measure adopted after the original panel (or the Appel-

late Body, as the case may be) has pronounced on the WTO-inconsistency; examine the new measure's consistency with the *WTO Agreement*; and further, examine to what extent the WTO Member has adequately implemented the recommendations and rulings of the original panel or the Appellate Body in adopting the new measure.

62. With respect to the judgment of the CIT in the *Turtle Island* case, Hong Kong, China, notes that in the absence of a clear mandate given to international adjudicating bodies, they commonly interpret only international law and treat domestic law, whenever warranted, as a factual matter. The same approach seemed to have been adopted by the Panel in the present case. Accordingly, Hong Kong, China, is of the view that the Panel was not called upon to speculate on the results of the appeal of the CIT judgment and make a ruling on that basis. Further, Hong Kong, China is mindful that the CIT decision is under appeal and it could be upheld by the highest domestic United States court.

4. *India*

(a) Terms of Reference

63. India submits that, as the measures taken to comply with the recommendations and rulings of the DSB are, by definition, new and different measures, it is possible that the new implementing measures could be inconsistent with provisions of WTO covered agreements that were not examined by the original panel. Therefore, a panel "established" under Article 21.5 of the DSU would have to address a new and different factual and legal situation. India, therefore, agrees with Malaysia that a correct reading of Article 21.5 of the DSU required the Panel to examine the alleged inconsistency also with regard to WTO provisions that were not relevant for the resolution of the dispute in the original proceedings.

64. With respect to the *Turtle Island* case, India agrees with Malaysia that the Panel erroneously refrained from examining municipal law by treating it as a fact. In order to evaluate the WTO-consistency of municipal law, the interpretation given by a domestic court is of prime importance. India also concurs with Malaysia that the United States bears responsibility for the actions of all branches of its government, including the judiciary. The CIT is a judicial organ of the United States. Its interpretation that Section 609 did not permit the import of TED-caught shrimp from non-certified countries should be treated as an authoritative interpretation of United States law. In the light of the Appellate Body's finding in *United States - Shrimp*, the Panel should have concluded that Section 609 was inconsistent with the chapeau of Article XX of the GATT 1994.

5. *Japan*

(a) The Chapeau of Article XX of the GATT 1994

65. Japan is of the view that as the provisions in Article XX of the GATT 1994 are "exceptions" to the basic principles of the GATT 1994, they should be applied in a strict manner. This applies especially when a unilateral measure is claimed to be justified under this Article.

66. Although Japan agrees with most of the conclusions reached by the Panel, it is Japan's view that the Panel Report does not describe in detail the reasoning or process by which the Panel reached those conclusions. Considering the importance attached to the requirements of the chapeau of Article XX as a tool for prevention of abuse, the chapeau of Article XX must be applied in a manner that fully accounts for the strict standard required of the "General Exceptions" under Article XX.

67. Malaysia's argument that negotiations are not alternative actions for the United States to rectify and address the problem of "arbitrary and unjustifiable discrimination" is based on an incorrect reading of the original Appellate Body Report. As the lack of serious good faith negotiation was one of the reasons for the Appellate Body finding of "arbitrary or unjustifiable discrimination", it seems logical to assume that by engaging in sufficiently "serious good faith" negotiations and meeting other requirements, the United States has addressed the "arbitrary or unjustifiable discrimination". Thus, Japan agrees with the Panel's finding that the United States was not under the obligation to conclude an agreement for the protection and conservation of sea turtles before taking the measure.

68. Japan submits however, that as the notion of "serious" and "good faith" is subjective in nature, a more objective test, such as a common recognition by other negotiating countries on the necessity of the measure in question, may be needed in addition to the criterion of "serious good faith efforts". Japan considers that the Panel should have included explicitly in its Report such a test of support for, or recognition of, the measure in question by other negotiating countries as a part of the negotiation requirement.

6. *Mexico*

(a) Terms of Reference

69. Mexico agrees with Malaysia that the terms of reference of a panel "established" pursuant to Article 21.5 of the DSU are to examine whether the measures taken to comply with the recommendations and rulings are consistent with the covered agreements, rather than with its own recommendations and rulings.

70. Mexico submits that the Panel in this case should have paid particular attention to the question whether the United States measure could be justified under Article XX of the GATT 1994 because it was not applied in a manner that would constitute a means of "arbitrary or unjustifiable discrimination" between

countries where the same conditions prevail, or a disguised restriction on international trade. Mexico considers that the Panel should also have paid greater attention to the legal provisions themselves rather than to the Report of the Appellate Body which considered the original measure. In Mexico's view, it is not valid to argue that a WTO Member is authorized to adopt measures that would otherwise be inconsistent with Article XX of the GATT 1994, basing itself on an interpretation of Article XX limited to the circumstances and reasoning in a previous dispute settlement case.

7. *Thailand*

(a) Terms of Reference

71. Thailand is of the view that, in accordance with Article 21.5 of the DSU, the Panel was bound to evaluate the consistency of the "measures taken to comply" with the covered agreement concerned, which in the present case is the GATT 1994. Thailand agrees with the Panel that this was to be done in the light of the evaluation of the consistency of the original measure with a covered agreement undertaken by the original panel and subsequently by the Appellate Body.

72. However, Thailand's view differs from that of the Panel with respect to the scope of the "measures taken to comply" by the United States. Thailand disagrees with the approach of the Panel of examining only the consistency with the GATT 1994 of the Revised Guidelines, and disregarding Section 609.

73. Thailand submits that had the Panel examined the consistency of Section 609 as part of the United States implementing measure, the Panel would have found that, with regard to the import of TED-caught shrimp from non-certified countries, Section 609 is inconsistent with the chapeau of Article XX of GATT 1994, read in the light of the Appellate Body's finding in *United States - Shrimp*. To examine the consistency of Section 609 in this regard, had the Panel decided to do so, it would be necessary for the Panel to "seek a detailed understanding" of the legislation. As it is not for the Panel to interpret Section 609 itself, such understanding must be based on an authoritative interpretation of the legislation under the United States domestic legal system, at least in cases where authoritative interpretation is available.

74. Thailand argues that the fact that the Revised Guidelines have not been modified following the CIT judgment does not remove the current inconsistency of Section 609 with the GATT 1994. A breach of a treaty obligation does not necessarily involve an act of the executive branch. It can also involve an act of the legislature or the judiciary, or, as in this case, both of these branches of government.

III. PRELIMINARY PROCEDURAL MATTER

75. On 13 August 2001, we received a brief from the American Humane Society and Humane Society International (the "Humane Society brief"). This brief was also attached as an exhibit to the appellee's submission filed by the United States in this appeal.

76. As we have previously stated in our Report in *United States - Import Prohibition of Certain Shrimp and Shrimp Products* ("*United States - Shrimp*"), attaching a brief or other material to the submission of either an appellant or an appellee, no matter how or where such material may have originated, renders that material at least *prima facie* an integral part of that participant's submission.[24] In that Report, we stated further that it is for a participant in an appeal to determine for itself what to include in its submission.[25]

77. At the oral hearing in this appeal, held on 4 September 2001, we asked the United States to clarify the extent to which it adopted the arguments set out in the Humane Society brief. The United States stated: "[t]hose are the independent views of that organization. We adopt them to the extent they are the same as ours but otherwise they are their independent views. We submit them for your consideration but not like our arguments where, for example, the panel is expected to address each one." Accordingly, we focus our attention on the legal arguments in the appellee's submission of the United States.

78. On 20 August 2001, we received a brief from Professor Robert Howse, a professor of international trade law at the University of Michigan Law School in Ann Arbor, Michigan, in the United States. In rendering our decision in this appeal, we have not found it necessary to take into account the brief submitted by Professor Howse.

IV. ISSUES RAISED IN THIS APPEAL

79. The measure at issue in this dispute consists of three elements: Section 609 of the United States Public Law 101-162 ("Section 609"); the Revised Guidelines for the Implementation of Section 609 of Public Law 101-162 Relating to the Protection of Sea Turtles in Shrimp Trawl Fishing Operations (the "Revised Guidelines")[26]; and the application of both Section 609 and the Revised

---

[24] Appellate Body Report, WT/DS58/AB/R, adopted 6 November 1998, DSR 1998:VII, 2755, para. 89.

[25] *Ibid.*

[26] United States Department of State, Federal Register Vol. 64, No. 130, 8 July 1999, Public Notice 3086, pp. 36946 - 36952. The Revised Guidelines are attached to the Panel Report, *United States - Import Prohibition of Certain Shrimp and Shrimp Products, Recourse to Article 21.5 of the DSU by Malaysia* (the "Panel Report"), WT/DS58/RW, 15 June 2001.

Guidelines in the practice of the United States. Both the United States and Malaysia agree on this definition of the measure.[27] So does the Panel.[28] So do we.

80. With respect to this measure, the following issues are raised in this appeal:

(a) whether the Panel correctly fulfilled its mandate under Article 21.5 of the DSU of examining the consistency with the relevant provisions of the GATT 1994 of the United States measure that was taken to comply with the recommendations and rulings of the DSB in United States - Shrimp; and

(b) whether the Panel erred in finding that the measure at issue is now applied in a manner that no longer constitutes a means of "arbitrary or unjustifiable discrimination between countries where the same conditions prevail" and is, therefore, within the scope of measures permitted under Article XX of the GATT 1994.[29]

81. With respect to the measure at issue in this dispute, the United States has not appealed the conclusion of the Panel that the measure violates Article XI:1 of the GATT 1994.[30] Thus, we do not address that issue in this appeal.

82. Malaysia has not appealed the conclusion of the Panel that Section 609 is provisionally justified under subparagraph (g) of Article XX of the GATT 1994.[31] Also, Malaysia confirmed at the oral hearing in this appeal that it has also not appealed the conclusion of the Panel that the measure at issue is not applied in a manner that constitutes "a disguised restriction on international trade" under the chapeau of Article XX of the GATT 1994.[32] Thus, we do not address those issues in this appeal.

---

27 In response to our questions at the oral hearing, the United States submitted that:

> The measure at issue in this appeal would be Section 609 as currently applied through the [United States] guidelines currently in effect.

In response to the same question, Malaysia stated that:

> Malaysia's contention is that the measure at issue is the 1999 revised guidelines which are the guidelines to implement Section 609 and their application.

28 The Panel stated:

> The "implementing measure" is composed of Section 609 of Public Law 101-162, of the revised guidelines pursuant to Section 609, dated 8 July 1999, Federal Register, Vol. 64, No. 130, Public Notice 3086, p. 36946 (hereafter the "Revised Guidelines"), as well as of any practice under those Revised Guidelines.

(Panel Report, footnote 154 to para. 5.1)

29 Panel Report, para. 5.137.

30 *Ibid.*, para. 5.23.

31 *Ibid.*, para. 5.42.

32 The Panel's findings on this issue are set out in para. 5.144 of the Panel Report. At the oral hearing, we noted that Malaysia had made no reference in its appellant's submission to the findings of the Panel with respect to whether the United States measure was applied in a manner that constitutes "a disguised restriction on international trade". We asked Malaysia to confirm that it was not appealing those findings. Malaysia did so.

V. TERMS OF REFERENCE

83. The first issue raised by Malaysia in this appeal is whether the Panel properly examined the United States measure taken to comply with the recommendations and rulings of the DSB in *United States - Shrimp*. Malaysia argues that the Panel improperly limited its analysis to the recommendations and rulings of the DSB, and thus failed to fulfill its mandate under Article 21.5 of the DSU because it did not examine the consistency of the United States implementing measure with the relevant provisions of the GATT 1994. Malaysia argues as well that the Panel erroneously based its analysis entirely on our Report in *United States - Shrimp*.

84. Malaysia's appeal on this point goes to the heart of what a panel is required to do in proceedings under Article 21.5 of the DSU, which states, in pertinent part:

> Where there is disagreement as to the existence or consistency with a covered agreement of measures taken to comply with the recommendations and rulings such dispute shall be decided through recourse to these dispute settlement procedures, including wherever possible resort to the original panel.

85. In *Canada - Measures Affecting the Export of Civilian Aircraft - Recourse by Brazil to Article 21.5 of the DSU* ("*Canada - Aircraft (21.5)*"), we discussed one aspect of a panel's task under Article 21.5 of the DSU. In that case, the Panel declined to examine an argument by Brazil on the ground that the argument "did not form part" of the reasoning of the original panel and was "not relevant to the present dispute, which concerns the issue of whether or not Canada had implemented the DSB recommendation".[33] We disagreed with that ruling, and stated there that:

> It follows then that the task of the Article 21.5 Panel in this case is, in fact, to determine whether the new measure - the revised TPC programme - is consistent with Article 3.1(a) of the *SCM Agreement*.
>
> Accordingly, in carrying out its review under Article 21.5 of the DSU, a panel is not confined to examining the "measures taken to comply" from the perspective of the claims, arguments and factual circumstances that related to the measure that was the subject of the original proceedings. Although these may have some relevance in proceedings under Article 21.5 of the DSU, Article 21.5 proceedings involve, in principle, not the original measure, but rather

[33] Appellate Body Report, WT/DS70/AB/RW, adopted 4 August 2000, DSR 2000:IX, 4299, para. 39.

> a new and different measure which was not before the original panel. . . .[34]

We stated further that:

> Indeed, the utility of the review envisaged under Article 21.5 of the DSU would be seriously undermined if a panel were restricted to examining the new measure from the perspective of the claims, arguments and factual circumstances that related to the original measure, because an Article 21.5 panel would then be unable to examine fully the "consistency with a covered agreement of the measures taken to comply", as required by Article 21.5 of the DSU.[35]

86. As we ruled in our Report in *Canada - Aircraft (21.5)*, panel proceedings pursuant to Article 21.5 of the DSU involve, in principle, not the original measure, but a new and different measure that was not before the original panel. Therefore, "in carrying out its review under Article 21.5 of the DSU, a panel is not confined to examining the 'measure[] taken to comply' from the perspective of the claims, arguments and factual circumstances that related to the measure that was the subject of the original proceedings."[36]

87. When the issue concerns the consistency of a new measure "taken to comply"[37], the task of a panel in a matter referred to it by the DSB for an Article 21.5 proceeding is to consider that new measure in its totality. The fulfilment of this task requires that a panel consider both the measure itself and the measure's application. As the title of Article 21 makes clear, the task of panels under Article 21.5 forms part of the process of the "*Surveillance of Implementation of the Recommendations and Rulings*" of the DSB. Toward that end, the task of a panel under Article 21.5 is to examine the "consistency with a covered agreement of measures taken to comply with the recommendations and rulings" of the DSB. That task is circumscribed by the specific claims made by the complainant when the matter is referred by the DSB for an Article 21.5 proceeding. It is not part of the task of a panel under Article 21.5 to address a claim that has not been made.

88. Malaysia relies in this appeal on our ruling in *Canada - Aircraft (21.5).* We understand Malaysia to argue, based in part on our ruling in *Canada - Aircraft (21.5),* that the Panel in this case had a duty to review the *totality* of the United States measure, and to assess it for its consistency with the relevant provisions of the GATT 1994. That is indeed a panel's task under Article 21.5 of the DSU. Yet, as we have said, it is not part of a panel's task to go beyond the par-

---

34 Appellate Body Report, WT/DS70/AB/RW, *supra* footnote 33 paras. 40-41.

35 *Ibid.*, para. 41.

36 *Ibid.*, para. 41.

37 As opposed to a debate on the "existence ... of measures taken to comply", which is not at issue here.

ticular claims that have been made with respect to the consistency of a new measure with a covered agreement when a matter is referred to it by the DSB for an Article 21.5 proceeding. Thus, it would not have been appropriate in this case for the Panel to address a claim that was *not* made by Malaysia when requesting that this matter be referred by the DSB for an Article 21.5 proceeding.

89. With respect to a claim that *has* been made when a matter is referred by the DSB for an Article 21.5 proceeding, Malaysia seems to suggest as well that a panel must re-examine, for WTO-consistency, even those aspects of a new measure that were part of a previous measure that was the subject of a dispute, and were found by the Appellate Body to be *WTO - consistent* in that dispute, and that remain unchanged as part of the new measure.

90. In considering this argument, we examine what the Panel did in this case in fulfilling its task under the DSU. As we have said, the Panel was required to review the new measure in its totality and in its application when examining the matter referred by the DSB for the Article 21.5 proceeding. In this case, the question whether it did or did not fulfil this requirement arises from the treatment by the Panel of a particular part of the new measure that was also part of the original measure in the original proceedings - Section 609.

91. Section 609 - a United States statute enacted by the United States Congress - is a common aspect of both the original measure at issue in the previous case and appeal, and the new measure at issue in this case and appeal. As Section 609 is part of the new measure, it is not immune from scrutiny under Article 21.5. However, it will be recalled that, in the previous case, we found that Section 609 was entitled to "provisional justification" under subparagraph (g) of Article XX of the GATT 1994. It will be recalled as well that, in the previous case, the deficiencies we found in the *application* of the original measure by the United States that denied that original measure the benefit of the exception provided by Article XX of the GATT 1994 were unrelated to Section 609 itself. Those deficiencies related to the original guidelines that were promulgated by the United States Department of State for the purpose of implementing Section 609, and to the practice of the United States in applying those original guidelines to WTO Members.

92. In its analysis of the consistency of Section 609 in this new case, the Panel stated that:

> The Panel considers that two questions have to be addressed in order to determine whether the implementing measure meets the requirements of paragraph (g) of Article XX. First, the Panel notes that the Appellate Body found that Section 609 was "provisionally justified" under Article XX(g). We understand this to mean that, in the process of determining whether Section 609 was justified under Article XX, the Appellate Body concluded that Section 609 satisfied the first tier of the analysis defined in its report on *United States - Gasoline*, i.e. the *characterization* of the measure under Article XX(g). This implies that, as long as the implementing

> measure before us is identical to the measure examined by the Appellate Body in relation to paragraph (g), we should not reach a different conclusion from the Appellate Body.[38] (footnote omitted)

The Panel went on to conclude that:

> ... the United States did not amend Section 609, whereas it has issued revised implementing guidelines. We therefore conclude that since Section 609 as such has not been modified, the findings of the Appellate Body regarding paragraph (g) remain valid and the consistency of Section 609 as such with the requirements of paragraph (g) also remains valid, to the extent that the Revised Guidelines do not modify the *interpretation* to be given to Section 609 in that respect. We have no evidence that the Revised Guidelines have modified in any way the meaning of Section 609 *vis-à-vis* the requirements of paragraph (g), as interpreted by the Appellate Body.[39]

93. We agree. It is not disputed that the wording of Section 609 has not been changed since the first case. The Congress of the United States has not amended the statute. In addition, the meaning of Section 609 has not been changed by the decision of the United States Court of International Trade (the "CIT") in *Turtle Island Restoration Network, et al. v. Robert L. Mallett, et al.* (the "*Turtle Island* case").[40]

94. The CIT ruling in the *Turtle Island* case addressed the Revised Guidelines: that ruling made no change to the interpretation of Section 609. Moreover, as stated by the Panel, the ruling in the *Turtle Island* case is declaratory: the CIT has not ordered the United States Department of State to modify either the content or the interpretation of the Revised Guidelines; in the legal interpretation of the United States authorities entrusted with enforcing them, the Revised Guidelines remain the same.[41] Rightly, when examining the United States measure, the Panel took into account the status of municipal law at the time. In particular, the Panel took note of the fact that the CIT ruling in the *Turtle Island* case has not altered the content of the Revised Guidelines, and has not prevented the United States government from authorizing the importation of TED-caught shrimp from uncertified countries. In response to our questions at the oral hearing, the United States confirmed that the Department of State has received no order from the CIT to change its practice, and, therefore, the Department of State continues to apply the Revised Guidelines as before.[42] Malaysia has not shown otherwise.

---

38 Panel Report, para. 5.39.

39 Panel Report., para. 5.41.

40 110 Fed. Supp. 2d 1005 (CIT, 2000). *See*, Panel Report, para. 5.109.

41 Panel Report, para. 5.109.

42 The United States submitted that:

95. There is no way of knowing or predicting when or how that particular legal proceeding will conclude in the United States. The *Turtle Island* case has been appealed and could conceivably go as far as the Supreme Court of the United States.[43] It would have been an exercise in speculation on the part of the Panel to predict either when or how that case may be concluded, or to assume that injunctive relief ultimately would be granted and that the United States Court of Appeals or the Supreme Court of the United States eventually would compel the Department of State to modify the Revised Guidelines. The Panel was correct not to indulge in such speculation, which would have been contrary to the duty of the Panel, under Article 11 of the DSU, to make "an objective assessment of the matter ... including an objective assessment of the facts of the case".

96. As we see it, then, the Panel properly examined Section 609 as part of its examination of the totality of the new measure, correctly found that Section 609 had not been changed since the original proceedings, and rightly concluded that our ruling in *United States - Shrimp* with respect to the consistency of Section 609, therefore, still stands.

97. We wish to recall that panel proceedings under Article 21.5 of the DSU are, as the title of Article 21 states, part of the process of the "*Surveillance of Implementation of Recommendations and Rulings*" of the DSB. This includes Appellate Body Reports. To be sure, the right of WTO Members to have recourse to the DSU, including under Article 21.5, must be respected. Even so, it must also be kept in mind that Article 17.14 of the DSU provides not only that Reports of the Appellate Body "shall be" adopted by the DSB, by consensus, but also that such Reports "shall be ... unconditionally accepted by the parties to the dispute. ..." Thus, Appellate Body Reports that are adopted by the DSB are, as Article 17.14 provides, "... unconditionally accepted by the parties to the dispute", and, therefore, must be treated by the parties to a particular dispute as a final resolution to that dispute. In this regard, we recall, too, that Article 3.3 of the DSU states that the "prompt settlement" of disputes "is essential to the effective functioning of the WTO".

98. Therefore, so far as the examination of the measure at issue in this appeal is concerned, the task of the Panel with respect to Section 609, as part of that new measure, was limited to examining its *application*. More specifically, the task of the Panel as it related to Section 609 was to decide whether Section 609 has been *applied* by the United States in a way that constitutes "arbitrary or unjustifiable

---

> We do not believe that the court decision in the litigation changes the measure. The measure is the statute and the guidelines. There is litigation and controversy in the United States about what those guidelines might look like. However, for today and the foreseeable future, the guidelines stand. They are what governs. That is what happens at the ports.

(United States response to questioning at the oral hearing)

[43] Panel Report, para. 5.109.

discrimination between countries where the same conditions prevail" in violation of the chapeau of Article XX of the GATT 1994. Thus, given the structure of the new measure, the task of the Panel was to determine whether Section 609 has been *applied* by the United States, through the Revised Guidelines, either on their face, or in their application, in a manner that constitutes "arbitrary or unjustifiable discrimination".

99. This is precisely what the Panel did in this case. Therefore, we consider what the Panel did to be an appropriate fulfilment of its task under the DSU.

100. Malaysia argues with respect to the terms of reference that the Panel confined itself inappropriately to an examination of whether the new measure complied with the rulings and recommendations of the DSB, and, more specifically, with the rulings of the Appellate Body that were adopted by the DSB in the previous case relating to the original measure. In support of this argument, Malaysia quotes various selected passages from the Panel Report.[44]

101. In our view, a reading of the Panel Report as a whole does not provide support for Malaysia's contention. Indeed, the Panel appears to have done precisely the opposite of what Malaysia asserts. For example, we note that, in identifying its terms of reference, the Panel explicitly quoted the terms of Article 21.5 of the DSU[45] as well as our Report in *Canada - Aircraft (21.5)*.[46]

102. The Panel then stated:

> The terms of reference of this Panel do not differ from the standard terms of reference applied in other Article 21.5 cases. In light of the reasoning of the Appellate Body mentioned above, the Panel considers that it is fully entitled to address all the claims of Malay-

---

[44] Malaysia's appellant's submission, para. 3.2. Malaysia refers to footnote 211 of para. 5.66 and paras. 5.116, 5.120, 5.125 and 5.134 of the Panel Report.

[45] Panel Report, para. 5.7.

[46] *Ibid.*, para. 5.8. After quoting our Report in *Canada - Aircraft (21.5)*, the Panel concluded that:

> In light of the reasoning of the Appellate Body [in *Canada - Aircraft (21.5)]*, the Panel considers that it is fully entitled to address all the claims of Malaysia under Article XI and Article XX of the GATT 1994, whether or not these claims, the arguments and the facts supporting them were made before the Original Panel and in the Appellate Body proceedings...

(*Ibid.*, para. 5.9)

We agree with the Panel. However, we do not agree with Malaysia's reading of our Report in *Canada - Aircraft (21.5)*. As the United States submits: "[t]he issue in *Canada Aircraft* was whether the Article 21.5 Panel's review was limited to issues considered in the original panel and Appellate Body proceedings, and the Appellate Body found that the DSU provides no such limitation". (footnote omitted) (United States appellee's submission, para. 11) With respect to this case, the United States notes: "[t]he Panel's report makes no limitations on its consideration of Malaysia's arguments". (United States appellee's submission, para.13) On this, we agree with the United States. The Panel in this case examined all of Malaysia's arguments, and did not decline to consider an argument on its merits on the ground that such argument had not been raised before the original panel or the Appellate Body.

> sia under Article XI and Article XX of the GATT 1994, whether or not these claims, the arguments and the facts supporting them were made before the Original Panel and in the Appellate Body proceedings *provided*, as recalled by the panel on *Australia - Measures Affecting Importation of Salmon - Recourse by Canada to Article 21.5 of the DSU,* that the claims are identified in the request for referring the matter to a panel under Article 21.5 of the DSU.[47] (footnotes omitted)

103. Furthermore, in its analysis, the Panel examined Malaysia's claim that the new measure taken by the United States continued to violate Article XI:1 of the GATT 1994, and stated as follows:

> The Panel notes that the elements of the original measure found to be incompatible with Article XI:1 in the Original Panel Report are still part of the implementing measure, i.e. Section 609 as currently applied by the United States. In particular, the United States continues to apply an import prohibition on shrimp and shrimp products harvested in a manner determined to be harmful to sea turtles. We note that the United States does not contest the fact that it applies such a prohibition of import. We consider that the prohibition at issue falls within the "prohibitions or restrictions, other than duties, taxes or other charges" maintained by a Member on the importation of a product from another Member, in contravention of Article XI:1.
>
> The Panel therefore concludes that the measure taken by the United States to comply with the recommendations and rulings of the DSB in this case *violates Article XI:1 of the GATT 1994.*[48] (emphasis added)

104. The Panel then examined the provisional justification under Article XX(g) of the GATT 1994 of Section 609, which it had correctly found to be unchanged, in the following terms:

> As a result, when considering the arguments of the United States, we shall first determine the consistency of the implementing measure under paragraph (g) of Article XX. If we find the implementing measure to be "provisionally justified" under paragraph (g), we shall proceed to determine whether it is applied in *conformity with the chapeau of Article XX.*[49] (emphasis added)
>
> ...

---

[47] Panel Report, para. 5.9.

[48] Panel Report, paras. 5.22-5.23.

[49] *Ibid.*, para. 5.28.

> We therefore conclude that the implementing measure is provisionally justified *under paragraph (g) of Article XX*. We proceed with the second tier of the method applied by the Appellate Body in this case, i.e. the "further appraisal of the *same measure* under the introductory clause of Article XX."[50] (emphasis added, footnote omitted)

105. This analysis shows clearly that the Panel properly understood the scope of its mandate. Furthermore, the Panel's examination of whether the measure applied by the United States constitutes a "disguised restriction on international trade" under the chapeau of Article XX of the GATT 1994 demonstrates that the Panel understood very well the scope of its mandate. The Panel stated:

> The Panel notes that it is instructed by Article 21.5 of the DSU to review "the existence or consistency with a covered agreement of measures taken to comply with the recommendations and rulings" of the DSB. The fact that the Appellate Body did not have to make a finding that the original measure was a disguised restriction on trade does not mean that the measure adopted to implement the DSB recommendations and rulings is not a disguised restriction on trade. The Panel also recalls that, as the party invoking Article XX, the United States bears the burden of proving that its implementing measure meets *all* the relevant requirements of the chapeau. This implies that the United States make a *prima facie* case that the implementing measure is not a disguised restriction on trade.[51]

106. Thus, the Panel examined the measure in the light of the relevant provisions of the GATT 1994, and, in doing so, made numerous references both to whether a violation of the GATT 1994 had occurred and to whether such a violation was nonetheless justified under Article XX. Accordingly, in reading the Panel Report as a whole, we find no support for Malaysia's argument that the Panel examined the new measure applied by the United States *only* in the light of the recommendations and rulings of the DSB.

107. Malaysia also objects to the frequent references made by the Panel to our reasoning in our Report in *United States - Shrimp*. The reasoning in our Report in *United States - Shrimp* on which the Panel relied was not *dicta*; it was essential to our ruling. The Panel was right to use it, and right to rely on it. Nor are we surprised that the Panel made frequent references to our Report in *United States - Shrimp*. Indeed, we would have expected the Panel to do so. The Panel had, necessarily, to consider our views on this subject, as we had overruled certain aspects of the findings of the original panel on this issue and, more important, had provided interpretative guidance for future panels, such as the Panel in this case.

---

50 Panel Report, para. 5.42.

51 Panel Report, para. 5.138.

108. In this respect, we note that in our Report in *Japan - Taxes on Alcoholic Beverages*, we stated that:

> Adopted panel reports are an important part of the GATT *acquis*. They are often considered by subsequent panels. They create legitimate expectations among WTO Members, and, therefore, should be taken into account where they are relevant to any dispute.[52]

109. This reasoning applies to adopted Appellate Body Reports as well. Thus, in taking into account the reasoning in an adopted Appellate Body Report - a Report, moreover, that was directly relevant to the Panel's disposition of the issues before it - the Panel did not err. The Panel was correct in using our findings as a tool for its own reasoning. Further, we see no indication that, in doing so, the Panel limited itself merely to examining the new measure from the perspective of the recommendations and rulings of the DSB.

110. We find, therefore, that the Panel correctly fulfilled its mandate under Article 21.5 of the DSU of examining the consistency, with the relevant provisions of the GATT 1994, of the United States measure taken to comply with the recommendations and rulings of the DSB in *United States - Shrimp*.

VI. THE CHAPEAU OF ARTICLE XX OF THE GATT 1994

111. The second issue raised in this appeal is whether the Panel erred in finding that the new measure at issue is applied in a manner that no longer constitutes a means of "arbitrary or unjustifiable discrimination between countries where the same conditions prevail" and is, therefore, within the scope of measures permitted under Article XX of the GATT 1994.[53]

112. In its Notice of Appeal, Malaysia appeals the finding of the Panel that "Section 609 of Public Law 101-162, as implemented by the Revised Guidelines of 8 July 1999 and as applied so far by the [United States] authorities, is justified under Article XX of the GATT 1994 as long as the conditions stated in the findings of this Report, in particular the ongoing serious, good faith efforts to reach a multilateral agreement, remain satisfied."[54] In its appellant's submission, Malaysia has put forward six points of disagreement with respect to the reasoning and findings of the Panel that lead Malaysia to conclude that, despite the changes made by the United States to the original measure, elements of "arbitrary or unjustifiable discrimination" still remain in the manner in which the new measure is applied by the United States.

---

[52] Appellate Body Report, ("*Japan - Alcoholic Beverages* "), WT/DS8/AB/R, WT/DS10/AB/R, WT/DS11/AB/R, adopted 1 November 1996, DSR 1996:I, 97, at 108.

[53] Panel Report, para. 5.137.

[54] *Ibid.*, para. 6.1.

113. Malaysia argues that:

- the Panel erred in interpreting our previous ruling in *United States - Shrimp* as imposing upon the United States an obligation to *negotiate* rather than an obligation to *conclude* an international agreement[55];
- the Panel's finding results in "the absurd situation where any WTO Member would be able to offer to negotiate in good faith on an agreement incorporating its unilaterally defined standards before claiming that its measure is justified under Article XX of the GATT 1994 and in the event of failure to conclude an agreement, claim that the measure applying the unilateral standards could not constitute unjustifiable discrimination"[56];
- the Panel erred in concluding that the Inter-American Convention can reasonably be regarded as a "benchmark" of what can be achieved through multilateral negotiations in the field of protection and conservation[57];
- the Panel misconstrued the usage of the term "measures comparable in effectiveness to United States measures" by the Appellate Body to mean that the Appellate Body accepted the legitimacy of such "comparable measures"[58];
- the Panel erred in concluding that the Revised Guidelines are sufficiently flexible, even though the Revised Guidelines do not provide explicitly for the particular conditions prevailing in Malaysia [59]; and
- the Panel erred in its treatment of the CIT ruling in the *Turtle Island* case and, thus, in its conclusion about the legal validity of those portions of the Revised Guidelines that permit the importation of TED-caught shrimp from non-certified harvesting countries.[60]

114. Malaysia's first three arguments relate to the nature and extent of the duty of the United States to pursue international cooperation in protecting and conserving endangered sea turtles. Malaysia's last three arguments relate to the flexibility of the Revised Guidelines. Our analysis will address each of these arguments made by Malaysia.

---

55 Malaysia's appellant's submission, para 3.10(b)(i).

56 Executive summary of Malaysia's appellant's submission, para. 2(b)(ii).

57 Malaysia's appellant's submission, para 3.13.

58 *Ibid.*, paras. 3.17-3.18. *See also*, Executive summary of Malaysia's appellant's submission, para. 2(iv);

59 Malaysia's appellant's submission, paras. 3.20-3.21.

60 *Ibid.*, paras. 3.22-3.25.

A. *The Nature and the Extent of the Duty of the United States to Pursue International Cooperation in the Protection and Conservation of Sea Turtles*

115. Before the Panel, Malaysia asserted that the United States should have negotiated and *concluded* an international agreement on the protection and conservation of sea turtles before imposing an import prohibition. Malaysia argued that "by continuing to apply a unilateral measure after the end of the reasonable period of time pending the conclusion of an international agreement, the United States failed to comply with its obligations under the GATT 1994".[61] The United States replied that it had in fact made serious, good faith efforts to negotiate and *conclude* a multilateral sea turtle conservation agreement that would include both Malaysia and the United States, and that these efforts, as detailed and documented before the Panel, should, in view of our previous ruling, be seen as sufficient to meet the requirements of the chapeau of Article XX. The Panel found as follows:

> ... The Panel first recalls that the Appellate Body considered "the *failure of the United States to engage the appellees*, as well as other Members exporting shrimp to the United States, in serious across-the-board negotiations *with the objective of concluding bilateral or multilateral agreements* for the protection and conservation of sea turtles, *before* enforcing the import prohibition against the shrimp exports of those other Members" bears heavily in any appraisal of justifiable or unjustifiable discrimination within the meaning of the chapeau of Article XX. From the terms used, it appears to us that the Appellate Body had in mind a negotiation, not the conclusion of an agreement. If the Appellate Body had considered that an agreement had to be concluded before any measure can be taken by the United States, it would not have used the terms "with the objective"; it would have simply stated that an agreement had to be concluded.
>
> ...
>
> We are consequently of the view that the Appellate Body could not have meant in its findings that the United States had the obligation to conclude an agreement on the protection and conservation of sea turtles in order to comply with Article XX. However, we reach the conclusion that the United States has an obligation to make serious good faith efforts to reach an agreement before resorting to the type of unilateral measure currently in place. We also consider that those efforts cannot be a "one-off" exercise. There must be a continuous process, including once a unilateral measure has been

---

[61] Panel Report, para. 5.1.

> adopted pending the conclusion of an agreement. Indeed, we consider the reference of the Appellate Body to a number of international agreements promoting a multilateral solution to the conservation concerns subject to Section 609 to be evidence that a multilateral, ideally non-trade restrictive, solution is generally to be preferred when dealing with those concerns, in particular if it is established that it constitutes "an alternative course of action reasonably open".
>
> ...
>
> We understand the Appellate Body findings as meaning that the United States has an obligation to make serious good faith efforts to address the question of the protection and conservation of sea turtles at the international level. We are mindful of the potentially subjective nature of the notion of serious good faith efforts and of how difficult such a test may be to apply in reality.[62] (footnotes omitted)

116. Malaysia appeals these findings of the Panel. According to Malaysia, demonstrating serious, good faith efforts to *negotiate* an international agreement for the protection and conservation of sea turtles is not sufficient to meet the requirements of the chapeau of Article XX.[63] Malaysia maintains that the chapeau requires instead the *conclusion* of such an international agreement. As Malaysia sees it, the "pertinent observations and comments" that we made in *United States - Shrimp* that could be construed to suggest otherwise "constitute dicta" in our previous Report.[64] On this basis, Malaysia argues that the Panel used that Report improperly in attempting to justify its reasoning that serious, good faith efforts alone would be enough to meet the requirements of the chapeau.[65] Further, Malaysia submits that the Panel misread our Report with respect to the Inter-American Convention, and, consequently, did not use that Convention properly in its analysis.[66]

117. The chapeau of Article XX states:

> Subject to the requirement that such measures are not applied in a manner which would constitute a means of arbitrary or unjustifiable discrimination between countries where the same conditions prevail, or a disguised restriction on international trade, nothing in this Agreement shall be construed to prevent the adoption or enforcement by any contracting party of measures: ...

---

62 Panel Report, paras. 5.63, 5.67 and 5.76.
63 Malaysia's appellant's submission, para. 3.11.
64 *Ibid.*, paras. 3.10-3.11.
65 *Ibid.*, para. 3.11.
66 *Ibid.*, para. 3.13.

118. The chapeau of Article XX establishes three standards regarding the *application* of measures for which justification under Article XX may be sought: first, there must be no "arbitrary" discrimination between countries where the same conditions prevail; second, there must be no "unjustifiable" discrimination between countries where the same conditions prevail; and, third, there must be no "disguised restriction on international trade".[67] The Panel's findings appealed by Malaysia concern the first and second of these three standards.[68]

119. It is clear from the language of the chapeau that these two standards operate to prevent a Member from applying a measure provisionally justified under a sub-paragraph of Article XX in a manner that would result in "arbitrary or unjustifiable discrimination".[69] In *United States - Shrimp*, we stated that the measure at issue there resulted in "unjustifiable discrimination", in part because, as applied, the United States treated WTO Members differently. The United States had adopted a cooperative approach with WTO Members from the Caribbean/Western Atlantic region, with whom it had concluded a multilateral agreement on the protection and conservation of sea turtles, namely the Inter-American Convention. Yet the United States had not, we found, pursued the negotiation of such a multilateral agreement with other exporting Members, including Malaysia and the other complaining WTO Members in that case.

120. Moreover, we observed there that Section 609, which was part of that original measure and remains part of the new measure at issue here, calls upon the United States Secretary of State to "initiate negotiations as soon as possible for the development of bilateral or multilateral agreements with other nations for the protection and conservation of ... sea turtles" and to "initiate negotiations as soon as possible with all foreign governments which are engaged in commercial fishing operations ... for the purpose of entering into bilateral and multilateral treaties with such countries to protect such species of sea turtles."[70] We concluded in that appeal that the United States had failed to comply with this statutory requirement in Section 609.

121. As we pointed out there:

> Apart from the negotiation of the Inter-American Convention for the Protection and Conservation of Sea Turtles ... which concluded in 1996, the record before the Panel does not indicate any serious,

---

[67] Appellate Body Report, *United States - Shrimp*, *supra*, footnote 24, para. 150; Appellate Body Report, *United States - Standards for Reformulated and Conventional Gasoline* ("*United States - Gasoline* "), WT/DS2/AB/R, adopted 20 May 1996, DSR 1996:I, 3, at 21-22.

[68] The Panel also made findings regarding disguised restriction on trade but these are not appealed. Panel Report, paras. 5.138-5.144.

[69] Appellate Body Report, *United States - Shrimp*, *supra*, footnote 24, paras. 156 and 160; Appellate Body Report, *United States - Gasoline*, *supra*, footnote 67 at 21-22.

[70] Section 609(a). *See also*, Appellate Body Report, *United States - Shrimp*, *supra*, footnote 24, para. 167.

> substantial efforts to carry out these express directions of Congress.[71] (footnotes omitted)

122. We also stated:

> Clearly, the United States negotiated seriously with some, but not with other Members (including the appellees), that export shrimp to the United States. The effect is plainly discriminatory and, in our view, unjustifiable.[72]

123. We concluded in *United States - Shrimp* that, to avoid "arbitrary or unjustifiable discrimination", the United States had to provide all exporting countries "similar opportunities to negotiate" an international agreement. Given the specific mandate contained in Section 609, and given the decided preference for multilateral approaches voiced by WTO Members and others in the international community in various international agreements for the protection and conservation of endangered sea turtles that were cited in our previous Report, the United States, in our view, would be expected to make good faith efforts to reach international agreements that are comparable from one forum of negotiation to the other. The negotiations need not be identical. Indeed, no two negotiations can ever be identical, or lead to identical results. Yet the negotiations must be *comparable* in the sense that comparable efforts are made, comparable resources are invested, and comparable energies are devoted to securing an international agreement. So long as such comparable efforts are made, it is more likely that "arbitrary or unjustifiable discrimination" will be avoided between countries where an importing Member concludes an agreement with one group of countries, but fails to do so with another group of countries.

124. Under the chapeau of Article XX, an importing Member may not treat its trading partners in a manner that would constitute "arbitrary or unjustifiable discrimination". With respect to this measure, the United States could conceivably respect this obligation, and the conclusion of an international agreement might nevertheless not be possible despite the serious, good faith efforts of the United States. Requiring that a multilateral agreement be *concluded* by the United States in order to avoid "arbitrary or unjustifiable discrimination" in applying its measure would mean that any country party to the negotiations with the United States, whether a WTO Member or not, would have, in effect, a veto over whether the United States could fulfill its WTO obligations. Such a requirement would not be reasonable. For a variety of reasons, it may be possible to conclude an agreement with one group of countries but not another. The conclusion of a multilateral agreement requires the cooperation and commitment of many countries. In our view, the United States cannot be held to have engaged in "arbitrary or unjustifi-

---

71 Appellate Body Report, *supra*, footnote 24, para. 167.

72 *Ibid.*, para. 172.

able discrimination" under Article XX solely because one international negotiation resulted in an agreement while another did not.

125. As we stated in *United States - Shrimp*, "the protection and conservation of highly migratory species of sea turtles ... demands concerted and cooperative efforts on the part of the many countries whose waters are traversed in the course of recurrent sea turtle migrations".[73] Further, the "need for, and the appropriateness of, such efforts have been recognized in the WTO itself as well as in a significant number of other international instruments and declarations".[74] For example, Principle 12 of the Rio Declaration on Environment and Development states, in part, that "[e]nvironmental measures addressing transboundary or global environmental problems should, as far as possible, be based on international consensus".[75] Clearly, and "as far as possible", a multilateral approach is strongly preferred. Yet it is one thing to *prefer* a multilateral approach in the application of a measure that is provisionally justified under one of the subparagraphs of Article XX of the GATT 1994; it is another to require the *conclusion* of a multilateral agreement as a condition of avoiding "arbitrary or unjustifiable discrimination" under the chapeau of Article XX. We see, in this case, no such requirement.

126. Malaysia also disagrees with certain statements made by the Panel with respect to the Inter-American Convention. The Panel found that:

> With respect to the absence of or insufficient negotiation with some Members compared with others, the reference of the Appellate Body to the Inter-American Convention is evidence that the efforts made by the United States to negotiate with the complainants before imposing the original measure were largely insufficient. The Inter-American Convention was negotiated as a binding agreement and has entered into force on 2 May 2001. We conclude that the Inter-American Convention can reasonably be considered as a benchmark of what can be achieved through multilateral negotiations in the field of protection and conservation. While we agree that factual circumstances may influence the duration of the process or the end result, we consider that any effort alleged to be a "serious good faith effort" must be assessed against the efforts made in relation to the conclusion of the Inter-American Convention.[76]

127. Malaysia maintains that the word "benchmark", as used by the Panel, has the connotation of a "legal standard", and asserts that nothing in the Appellate Body Report in *United States - Shrimp* suggests that the Inter-American Conven-

---

[73] Appellate Body Report, *supra*, footnote 24, para. 168.
[74] *Ibid*.
[75] *Ibid*.
[76] Panel Report, para. 5.71.

tion has the status of a legal standard.[77] Malaysia sees a distinction between a "benchmark", which would have the value of a "legal standard", and an "example", which would not have such a value.[78]

128. It should be recalled how we viewed the Inter-American Convention in *United States - Shrimp*. We stated there:

> The Inter-American Convention thus provides convincing demonstration that an alternative course of action was reasonably open to the United States for securing the legitimate policy goal of its measure, a course of action other than the unilateral and non-consensual procedures of the import prohibition under Section 609. It is relevant to observe that an import prohibition is, ordinarily, the heaviest "weapon" in a Member's armoury of trade measures. The record does not, however, show that serious efforts were made by the United States to negotiate similar agreements with any other country or group of countries before (and, as far as the record shows, after) Section 609 was enforced on a world-wide basis on 1 May 1996. Finally, the record also does not show that the appellant, the United States, attempted to have recourse to such international mechanisms as exist to achieve cooperative efforts to protect and conserve sea turtles before imposing the import ban.[79]

129. Thus, in the previous case, in examining the original measure, we relied on the Inter-American Convention in two ways. First, we used the Inter-American Convention to show that "consensual and multilateral procedures are available and feasible for the establishment of programmes for the conservation of sea turtles."[80] In other words, we saw the Inter-American Convention as evidence that an alternative course of action based on cooperation and consensus was reasonably open to the United States. Second, we used the Inter-American Convention to show the existence of "unjustifiable discrimination". The Inter-American Convention was the result of serious, good faith efforts to negotiate a regional agreement on the protection and conservation of turtles, including efforts made by the United States. In the original proceedings, we saw a clear contrast between the efforts made by the United States to conclude the Inter-American Convention and the absence of serious efforts on the part of the United States to negotiate other similar agreements with other WTO Members. We concluded there that such a disparity in efforts to negotiate an international agreement amounted to "unjustifiable discrimination".[81]

---

77 Malaysia's appellant's submission, para. 3.13.

78 *Ibid.*

79 Appellate Body Report, *supra*, footnote 24, para. 171.

80 *Ibid.*, para. 170.

81 *Ibid.*, para. 172.

130. With this in mind, we examine what the Panel did here. In its analysis of the Inter-American Convention in the context of Malaysia's argument on "unjustifiable discrimination", the Panel relied on our original Report to state that "the Inter-American Convention is evidence that the efforts made by the United States to negotiate with the complainants before imposing the original measure were largely insufficient".[82] The Panel went on to say that "the Inter-American Convention can reasonably be considered as a benchmark of what can be achieved through multilateral negotiations in the field of protection and conservation."[83]

131. At no time in *United States - Shrimp* did we refer to the Inter-American Convention as a "benchmark". The Panel might have chosen another and better word - perhaps, as suggested by Malaysia, "example".[84] Yet it seems to us that the Panel did all that it should have done with respect to the Inter-American Convention, and did so consistently with our approach in *United States - Shrimp*. The Panel compared the efforts of the United States to negotiate the Inter-American Convention with one group of exporting WTO Members with the efforts made by the United States to negotiate a similar agreement with another group of exporting WTO Members. The Panel rightly used the Inter-American Convention as a factual reference in this exercise of comparison. It was all the more relevant to do so given that the Inter-American Convention was the only international agreement that the Panel could have used in such a comparison. As we read the Panel Report, it is clear to us that the Panel attached a relative value to the Inter-American Convention in making this comparison, but did not view the Inter-American Convention in any way as an absolute standard. Thus, we disagree with Malaysia's submission that the Panel raised the Inter-American Convention to the rank of a "legal standard". The mere use by the Panel of the Inter-American Convention *as a basis for a comparison* did not transform the Inter-American Convention into a "legal standard". Furthermore, although the Panel could have chosen a more appropriate word than "benchmark" to express its views, Malaysia is mistaken in equating the mere use of the word "benchmark", as it was used by the Panel, with the establishment of a legal standard.

132. The Panel noted that while "factual circumstances may influence the duration of the process or the end result, ... any effort alleged to be a 'serious good faith effort' must be assessed against the efforts made in relation to the conclusion of the Inter-American Convention."[85] Such a comparison is a central element of the exercise to determine whether there is "unjustifiable discrimination". The Panel then analyzed the negotiation process in the Indian Ocean and South-East Asia region to determine whether the efforts made by the United States in those negotiations were serious, good faith efforts comparable to those made in relation

82 Panel Report, para. 5.71.
83 Panel Report, para. 5.71.
84 Malaysia's appellant's submission, para. 3.13.
85 Panel Report, para. 5.71.

with the Inter-American Convention. In conducting this analysis, the Panel referred to the following elements:

- A document communicated on 14 October 1998 by the United States Department of State to a number of countries of the Indian Ocean and the South-East Asia region. This document contained possible elements of a regional convention on sea turtles in this region.[86]
- The contribution of the United States to a symposium held in Sabah on 15-17 July 1999. The Sabah Symposium led to the adoption of a Declaration calling for the negotiation and implementation of a regional agreement throughout the Indian Ocean and South-East Asia region.[87]
- The Perth Conference in October 1999, where participating governments, including the United States, committed themselves to developing an international agreement on sea turtles for the Indian Ocean and South-East Asia region.[88]
- The contribution of the United States to the Kuantan round of negotiations, 11-14 July 2000. This first round of negotiations towards the conclusion of a regional agreement resulted in the adoption of the Memorandum of Understanding on the Conservation and Management of Marine Turtles and their Habitats of the Indian Ocean and South-East Asia (the "South-East Asian MOU"). The Final Act of the Kuantan meeting provided that before the South-East Asian MOU can be finalized, a Conservation and Management Plan must be negotiated and annexed to the South-East Asian MOU.[89] At the time of the Panel proceedings, the Conservation and Management Plan was still being drafted.[90]

133. On this basis and, in particular, on the basis of the "contribution of the United States to the steps that led to the Kuantan meeting and its contribution to the Kuantan meeting itself"[91], the Panel concluded that the United States had made serious, good faith efforts that met the "standard set by the Inter-American Convention."[92] In the view of the Panel, whether or not the South-East Asian MOU is a legally binding document does not affect this comparative assessment

---

86 Panel Report, para. 5.79.
87 *Ibid.*
88 *Ibid.*
89 *Ibid.*, para. 5.81.
90 *Ibid.*, para. 5.84.
91 *Ibid.*, para. 5.82.
92 *Ibid.*

because differences in "factual circumstances have to be kept in mind".[93] Furthermore, the Panel did not consider as decisive the fact that the final agreement in the Indian Ocean and South-East Asia region, unlike the Inter-American Convention, had not been concluded at the time of the Panel proceedings. According to the Panel, "at least until the Conservation and Management Plan to be attached to the MOU is completed, the United States efforts should be judged on the basis of its active participation and its financial support to the negotiations, as well as on the basis of its previous efforts since 1998, having regard to the likelihood of a conclusion of the negotiations in the course of 2001." [94]

134. We note that the Panel stated that "any effort alleged to be a 'serious good faith effort' must be assessed against the efforts made in relation to the conclusion of the Inter-American Convention."[95] In our view, in assessing the serious, good faith efforts made by the United States, the Panel did not err in using the Inter-American Convention as an *example*. In our view, also, the Panel was correct in proceeding then to an analysis broadly in line with this principle and, ultimately, was correct as well in concluding that the efforts made by the United States in the Indian Ocean and South-East Asia region constitute serious, good faith efforts comparable to those that led to the conclusion of the Inter-American Convention. We find no fault with this analysis. [96]

135. In sum, Malaysia is incorrect in its contention that avoiding "arbitrary and unjustifiable discrimination" under the chapeau of Article XX requires the *conclusion* of an international agreement on the protection and conservation of sea turtles. Therefore, we uphold the Panel's finding that, in view of the serious, good faith efforts made by the United States to negotiate an international agreement, "Section 609 is now applied in a manner that no longer constitutes a means of

---

[93] Panel Report. It appears that the United States was in favour of a legally binding agreement for the Indian Ocean and South-East Asia region, but a number of other parties were not, and the latter view prevailed. *See*, Panel Report, para. 5.83.

[94] Panel Report, para. 5.84.

[95] *Ibid.*, para. 5.71.

[96] We note that a multilateral conference on sea turtles was held in Manila and resulted in the adoption of the Conservation and Management Plan to be annexed to the South-East Asian MOU. We also note that the South-East Asian MOU came into effect on 1 September 2001. To our mind, these events only reinforce the finding of the Panel that the efforts made by the United States to negotiate an international agreement in the Indian Ocean and South-East Asia region constitute serious, good faith efforts comparable to those made in relation to the Inter-American Convention. The Inter-American Convention, in Article IV.2(h), provides for the use of TEDs to reduce the incidental capture and mortality of sea turtles in the course of fishing activities. Objective 1.4 of the Conservation and Management Plan attached to the South-East Asian MOU requires signatory states to "[r]educe to the greatest extent practicable the incidental capture and mortality of marine turtles in the course of fishing activities". In this respect, signatory states are directed to "[d]evelop and use gear, devices and techniques to minimise incidental capture of marine turtles in fisheries, such as devices that effectively allow the escape of marine turtles, and spatial and seasonal closures".

unjustifiable or arbitrary discrimination, as identified by the Appellate Body in its Report".[97]

B. The Flexibility of the Revised Guidelines

136. We now turn to Malaysia's arguments relating to the flexibility of the Revised Guidelines. Malaysia argued before the Panel that the measure at issue results in "arbitrary or unjustifiable discrimination" because it conditions the importation of shrimp into the United States on compliance by the exporting Members with policies and standards "unilaterally" prescribed by the United States.[98] Malaysia asserted that the United States "unilaterally" imposed its domestic standards on exporters.[99] With respect to this argument, the Panel found:

> It seems that whereas the Appellate Body found that requiring the adoption of essentially the same regime constituted arbitrary discrimination, it accepted - at least implicitly - that a requirement that the US and foreign programmes be "comparable in effectiveness" would be compatible with the obligations of the United States under the chapeau of Article XX. This is because it would "permit a degree of discretion or flexibility in how the standards for determining comparability might be applied, in practice, to other countries." We therefore conclude that if, *in practice*, the implementing measure provides for "comparable effectiveness", the finding of the Appellate Body in terms of lack of flexibility will have been addressed.[100] (footnote omitted)

137. Malaysia disagrees with the Panel that a measure can meet the requirements of the chapeau of Article XX if it is flexible enough, both in design and application, to permit certification of an exporting country with a sea turtle protection and conservation programme "comparable" to that of the United States.

---

[97] Panel Report, para. 5.137. We do wish to note, though, that there is one observation by the Panel with which we do not agree. In assessing the good faith efforts made by the United States, the Panel stated that:

> The United States is a *demandeur* in this field and given its scientific, diplomatic and financial means, it is reasonable to expect rather more than less from that Member in terms of serious good faith efforts. Indeed, the capacity of persuasion of the United States is illustrated by the successful negotiation of the Inter-American Convention.

(Panel Report, para. 5.76)

We are not persuaded by this line of reasoning. As we stated in our previous Report, the chapeau of Article XX is "but one expression of the principle of good faith". (Appellate Body Report, *United States - Shrimp, supra*, footnote 24, para. 158) This good faith notion applies to all WTO Members equally.

[98] Panel Report, para. 3.131.

[99] *Ibid.*, paras. 3.125 and 3.127.

[100] *Ibid.*, para. 5.93.

According to Malaysia, even if the measure at issue allows certification of countries having regulatory programs "comparable" to that of the United States, and even if the measure is applied in such a manner, it results in "arbitrary or unjustifiable discrimination" because it conditions access to the United States market on compliance with policies and standards "unilaterally" prescribed by the United States. Thus, Malaysia puts considerable emphasis on the "unilateral" nature of the measure, and Malaysia maintains that our previous Report does not support the conclusion of the Panel on this point.[101]

138. We recall that, in *United States - Shrimp*, we stated:

> It appears to us ... that conditioning access to a Member's domestic market on whether exporting Members comply with, or adopt, a policy or policies unilaterally prescribed by the importing Member may, to some degree, be a common aspect of measures falling within the scope of one or another of the exceptions (a) to (j) of Article XX. Paragraphs (a) to (j) comprise measures that are recognized as exceptions to substantive obligations established in the GATT 1994, because the domestic policies embodied in such measures have been recognized as important and legitimate in character. It is not necessary to assume that requiring from exporting countries compliance with, or adoption of, certain policies (although covered in principle by one or another of the exceptions) prescribed by the importing country, renders a measure a priori incapable of justification under Article XX. Such an interpretation renders most, if not all, of the specific exceptions of Article XX inutile, a result abhorrent to the principles of interpretation we are bound to apply.[102] (emphasis added)

139. In our view, Malaysia overlooks the significance of this statement. Contrary to what Malaysia suggests, this statement is not "*dicta*". As we said before, it appears to us "that conditioning access to a Member's domestic market on whether exporting Members comply with, or adopt, a policy or policies unilaterally prescribed by the importing Member may, to some degree, be a common aspect of measures falling within the scope of one or another of the exceptions (a) to (j) of Article XX." This statement expresses a principle that was central to our ruling in *United States - Shrimp*.

140. A separate question arises, however, when examining, under the chapeau of Article XX, a measure that provides for access to the market of one WTO Member for a product of other WTO Members *conditionally*. Both Malaysia and the United States agree that this is a common aspect of the measure at issue in the original proceedings and the new measure at issue in this dispute.

---

[101] Malaysia's appellant's submission, paras. 3.17-3.19.
[102] Appellate Body Report, *supra*, footnote 24, para. 121.

141. In *United States - Shrimp*, we concluded that the measure at issue there did not meet the requirements of the chapeau of Article XX relating to "arbitrary or unjustifiable discrimination" because, through the application of the measure, the exporting members were faced with "a single, rigid and unbending requirement"[103] to adopt *essentially the same* policies and enforcement practices as those applied to, and enforced on, domestic shrimp trawlers in the United States. In contrast, in this dispute, the Panel found that this new measure is more flexible than the original measure and has been applied more flexibly than was the original measure. In the light of the evidence brought by the United States, the Panel satisfied itself that this new measure, in design and application, does *not* condition access to the United States market on the adoption by an exporting Member of a regulatory programme aimed at the protection and the conservation of sea turtles that is *essentially the same* as that of the United States.

142. As the Panel's analysis suggests, an approach based on whether a measure requires "essentially the same" regulatory programme of an exporting Member as that adopted by the importing Member applying the measure is a useful tool in identifying measures that result in "arbitrary or unjustifiable discrimination" and, thus, do *not* meet the requirements of the chapeau of Article XX. However, this approach is not sufficient for purposes of judging whether a measure *does* meet the requirements of the chapeau of Article XX. Therefore, in construing our previous Report, the Panel inferred from our reasoning there that a measure requiring United States and foreign regulatory programmes to be "comparable in effectiveness", as opposed to being "essentially the same", would, absent some other shortcoming, comply with the chapeau of Article XX. On this, the Panel stated:

> It seems that whereas the Appellate Body found that requiring the adoption of essentially the same regime constituted arbitrary discrimination, it accepted - at least implicitly - that a requirement that the US and foreign programmes be "comparable in effectiveness" would be compatible with the obligations of the United States under the chapeau of Article XX. This is because it would "permit a degree of discretion or flexibility in how the standards for determining comparability might be applied, in practice, to other countries." We therefore conclude that if, *in practice*, the implementing measure provides for "comparable effectiveness", the finding of the Appellate Body in terms of lack of flexibility will have been addressed.[104] (footnote omitted)

143. The Panel reads our previous Report to state that a major deficiency of the original measure was its lack of flexibility, in both design and application. The Panel sees our previous Report as suggesting that the original measure was ap-

---

[103] Appellate Body Report, *supra*, footnote 24, para. 177.

[104] Panel Report, para. 5.93.

plied in a manner which constituted "unjustifiable discrimination" essentially "because the application of the measure at issue did not allow for any inquiry into the appropriateness of the regulatory program for the conditions prevailing in the exporting countries."[105] The Panel reasons that a measure that, in its design and application, allows certification of exporting Members having regulatory programmes "comparable in effectiveness" to that of the United States does take into account the specific conditions prevailing in the exporting WTO Members and is, therefore, flexible enough to meet the requirements of the chapeau of Article XX.

144. Given that the original measure in that dispute required "essentially the same" practices and procedures as those required in the United States, we found it necessary in that appeal to rule only that Article XX did not allow such inflexibility. Given the Panel's findings with respect to the flexibility of the new measure in this dispute, we find it necessary in this appeal to add to what we ruled in our original Report. The question raised by Malaysia in this appeal is whether the Panel erred in inferring from our previous Report, and thereby finding, that the chapeau of Article XX permits a measure which requires only "comparable effectiveness".

145. In our view, there is an important difference between conditioning market access on the adoption of essentially the same programme, and conditioning market access on the adoption of a programme *comparable in effectiveness*. Authorizing an importing Member to condition market access on exporting Members putting in place regulatory programmes *comparable in effectiveness* to that of the importing Member gives sufficient latitude to the exporting Member with respect to the programme it may adopt to achieve the level of effectiveness required. It allows the exporting Member to adopt a regulatory programme that is suitable to the specific conditions prevailing in its territory. As we see it, the Panel correctly reasoned and concluded that conditioning market access on the adoption of a programme *comparable in effectiveness*, allows for sufficient flexibility in the application of the measure so as to avoid "arbitrary or unjustifiable discrimination". We, therefore, agree with the conclusion of the Panel on "comparable effectiveness".

146. Malaysia also argues that the measure at issue is not flexible enough to meet the requirement of the chapeau of Article XX relating to "unjustifiable or arbitrary discrimination" because the Revised Guidelines do not provide explicitly for the specific conditions prevailing in Malaysia.[106]

---

[105] Panel Report, para. 5.92.

[106] According to Malaysia, the specificity of its case rests on the fact that shrimp trawling is not practised in Malaysia; shrimp is a by-catch from fish trawling and therefore, the incidental catch of sea turtles is due to fish trawling, not shrimp trawling. *See*, Malaysia's appellant's submission, para. 3.21 and Panel Report, para. 3.128. In addition, Malaysia stated:

> Malaysia is a nesting ground but it is not known to be a feeding ground for sea turtles and the nesting season in Malaysia does not overlap with the shrimp season.

147. We note that the Revised Guidelines contain provisions that permit the United States authorities to take into account the specific conditions of Malaysian shrimp production, and of the Malaysian sea turtle conservation programme, should Malaysia decide to apply for certification. The Revised Guidelines explicitly state that "[if] the government of a harvesting nation demonstrates that it has implemented and is enforcing a comparably effective regulatory program to protect sea turtles in the course of shrimp trawl fishing without the use of TEDs, that nation will also be eligible for certification."[107] Likewise, the Revised Guidelines provide that the "Department of State will take fully into account any demonstrated differences between the shrimp fishing conditions in the United States and those in other nations as well as information available from other sources."[108]

148. Further, the Revised Guidelines provide that the import prohibitions that can be imposed under Section 609 do not apply to shrimp or products of shrimp "harvested in any other manner or under any other circumstances that the Department of State may determine, following consultations with the [United States National Marine Fisheries Services], does not pose a threat of the incidental taking of sea turtles."[109] Under Section II.B(c)(iii) of the Revised Guidelines (*Additional Sea Turtle Protection Measures*), the "Department of State recognizes that sea turtles require protection throughout their life-cycle, not only when they are threatened during the course of commercial shrimp trawl harvesting."[110] Additionally, Section II.B(c)(iii) states that "[i]n making certification determinations, the Department shall also take fully into account other measures the harvesting nation undertakes to protect sea turtles, including national programmes to protect nesting beaches and other habitat, prohibitions on the direct take of sea turtles, national enforcement and compliance programmes, and participation in any in-

---

The Loggerheads and the Kemps released rarely nested on Malaysian beaches and did not occur in Malaysian waters respectively and the high mortality of sea turtles that is reported in the shrimp trawls in the United States relate to both these sea turtles. The Green Turtle, the Hawksbill, Leatherback and Olive Ridley are the major sea turtle species in Malaysia. Green turtles were resident in sea grass beds which were found in shallow coastal waters, whilst the Hawksbills were found in coral reef. Trawling was prohibited in these areas. During the nesting season, the Green turtles remain close to the shore in areas where trawling was also prohibited. During long distance migrations between feeding and nesting grounds, turtles were actively swimming close to the surface of the water which made them more vulnerable to drift nets and long lines rather than trawl nets. In Malaysia, trawling targeted fish for the most part of the year and thus the incidental capture of sea turtles was due to fish trawls and not shrimp trawls.

(Malaysia's response to questioning at the oral hearing)

107 Revised Guidelines, Section II.B; *see*, Panel Report, p. 105.

108 *Ibid.*

109 Revised Guidelines, Section I.B; *see*, Panel Report, p. 103.

110 Revised Guidelines, Section II.B(c)(iii); *see*, Panel Report, p. 106.

ternational agreement for the protection and conservation of sea turtles."[111] With respect to the certification process, the Revised Guidelines specify that a country that does not appear to qualify for certification will receive a notification that "will explain the reasons for this preliminary assessment, suggest steps that the government of the harvesting nation can take in order to receive a certification, and invite the government of the harvesting nation to provide ... any further information." Moreover, the Department of State commits itself to "actively consider any additional information that the government of the harvesting nation believes should be considered by the Department in making its determination concerning certification."[112]

149. These provisions of the Revised Guidelines, on their face, permit a degree of flexibility that, in our view, will enable the United States to consider the particular conditions prevailing in Malaysia if, and when, Malaysia applies for certification. As Malaysia has not applied for certification, any consideration of whether Malaysia would be certified would be speculation.[113]

150. We need only say here that, in our view, a measure should be designed in such a manner that there is sufficient flexibility to take into account the specific conditions prevailing in *any* exporting Member, including, of course, Malaysia.[114] Yet this is not the same as saying that there must be specific provisions in the measure aimed at addressing specifically the particular conditions prevailing in *every individual* exporting Member. Article XX of the GATT 1994 does not require a Member to anticipate and provide explicitly for the specific conditions prevailing and evolving in *every individual* Member.

151. We are, therefore, not persuaded by Malaysia's argument that the measure at issue is not flexible enough because the Revised Guidelines do not explicitly address the specific conditions prevailing in Malaysia.

152. Malaysia argues, finally, that the Panel should have scrutinized the decision of the CIT in the *Turtle Island* case and assessed, in the light of that decision, the likelihood and consequences of the Revised Guidelines being modified in the future. According to Malaysia, the Panel should have come to the conclusion that the Revised Guidelines are not flexible enough because the CIT ruled that the part of the Revised Guidelines allowing TED-caught shrimp from non-certified harvesting countries to be imported into the United States is contrary to

---

[111] Revised Guidelines, Section II.B(c)(iii); *see*, Panel Report, p. 106.

[112] Revised Guidelines, Section II.C, Panel Report, p. 107. *See also*, Revised Guidelines, Section II.D, Panel Report, p. 108.

[113] In this respect, we note that the European Communities stated that:

> ... the complaint by Malaysia in this case is somewhat premature. As it appears Malaysia has not yet applied for certification and it is therefore not yet clear how the contested legislation would apply to imports of shrimp and shrimp products from Malaysia.
>
> (European Communities' third participant's submission, para. 27)

[114] Appellate Body Report, *United States - Shrimp*, *supra*, footnote 24, para. 164.

Section 609.[115] As we have already ruled[116], we are of the view that, when examining the United States measures, the Panel took into account the status of municipal law at the time, and reached the correct conclusion. The CIT decision in the *Turtle Island* case has not modified the legal effect or the application of the Revised Guidelines; hence, we are not persuaded by this argument of Malaysia.

153. For all these reasons, we uphold the finding of the Panel, in paragraph 6.1 of the Panel Report, that "Section 609 of Public Law 101-162, as implemented by the Revised Guidelines of 8 July 1999 and as applied so far by the [United States] authorities, is justified under Article XX of the GATT 1994 as long as the conditions stated in the findings of this Report, in particular the ongoing serious, good faith efforts to reach a multilateral agreement, remain satisfied".[117]

VII. FINDINGS AND CONCLUSIONS

154. For the reasons set out in this Report, the Appellate Body:

(a) *finds* that the Panel correctly fulfilled its mandate under Article 21.5 of the DSU of examining the consistency, with the relevant provisions of the GATT 1994, of the United States measure taken to comply with the recommendations and rulings of the DSB in *United States - Shrimp*; and

(b) *upholds* the finding of the Panel, in paragraph 6.1 of its Report, that "Section 609 of Public Law 101-162, as implemented by the

115 Malaysia's appellant's submission, para. 3.25.

116 *See, supra*, footnote 114, para. 95.

117 Panel Report, para. 6.1. The Panel stated that its findings of justification stand, "*as long as*" certain conditions it set out in its Report, in particular, the good faith efforts to reach a multilateral agreement, continue to be met. In this respect, we note that the United States negotiated and concluded a Memorandum of Understanding with certain countries in the Indian Ocean and South-East Asia region, the South-East Asian MOU. *See, supra,* footnote 96. This agreement took effect on 1 September 2001, almost two and a half months after the circulation of the Panel Report. The participants have not disputed the existence of this agreement. There was some dispute at the oral hearing as to the legally binding nature of this agreement. Basic Principle 4 of that agreement states:

> This Memorandum of Understanding, including the Conservation and Management Plan, may be amended by consensus of the signatory States. When appropriate, the signatory States will consider amending this Memorandum of Understanding to make it legally binding.

At the oral hearing, the United States stated that "[The South-East Asian MOU] is considered a political undertaking that does not have binding consequences under international law". Malaysia stated that "The [South-East Asian] MOU ... would have the status of a treaty under the Vienna Convention of the law of treaties, because "treaty" has been defined as an international agreement that is concluded between States in written form and governed by international law, whether embodied in a single instrument or in two or more related instruments, whatever its particular designation." We need not judge this issue, and we do not. Even so, we note that, whether legally binding or not, the Memorandum of Understanding reinforces the Panel's finding that the United States had indeed made serious good faith efforts to negotiate a multilateral agreement.

> Revised Guidelines of 8 July 1999 and as applied so far by the [United States] authorities, is justified under Article XX of the GATT 1994 as long as the conditions stated in the findings of this Report, in particular the ongoing serious good faith efforts to reach a multilateral agreement, remain satisfied".

155. As we have upheld the Panel's finding that the United States measure is now applied in a manner that meets the requirements of Article XX of the GATT 1994, we do not make any recommendation to the DSB pursuant to Article 19.1 of the DSU.

UNITED STATES - IMPORT PROHIBITION OF CERTAIN SHRIMP AND SHRIMP PRODUCTS

RECOURSE TO ARTICLE 21.5 OF THE DSU BY MALAYSIA

Report of the Panel

WT/DS58/RW

Adopted by the Dispute Settlement Body on 21 November 2000 as upheld by the Appellate Body Report

TABLE OF CONTENTS

I. INTRODUCTION

1.1 On 6 November 1998, the Dispute Settlement Body (DSB) adopted the Appellate Body Report on *United States - Import Prohibition of Certain Shrimp and Shrimp Products* (WT/DS58/AB/R) and the Panel Report (WT/DS58/R), as modified by the Appellate Body Report, requesting that the United States bring its measure found to be inconsistent with Article XI of the GATT 1994, and not justified under Article XX of the GATT 1994 into conformity with the obligations of the United States under that Agreement.

1.2 On 21 January 1999, the United States and the other parties to the dispute agreed to a 13-month reasonable period of time for the United States to comply with the recommendations and rulings of the DSB.[1]

1.3 In a communication dated 12 January 2000, Malaysia and the United States informed the DSB of the understanding reached between Malaysia and the United States regarding possible proceedings pursuant to Articles 21 and 22 of the Understanding on Rules and Procedures Governing the Settlement of Disputes (DSU) concerning the implementation of the DSB recommendations and rulings in this case. This communication confirms the understanding reached between Malaysia and the United States, pursuant to an exchange of letters dated 22 December 1999, whereby they agreed that if Malaysia at some future date decided that it may wish to initiate proceedings under Article 21.5 and Article 22 of the DSU, Malaysia would initiate proceedings under Article 21.5 prior to any proceedings under Article 22; for this purpose Malaysia would provide the United States advance notice of any proposal to initiate proceedings under Article 21.5 and hold consultations with the United States before requesting the establishment of a panel under Article 21.5.[2]

1.4 On 12 October 2000, Malaysia requested the DSB, pursuant to Article 21.5 of the DSU, to establish a Panel to "find that by not lifting the import prohibition and not taking the necessary measures to allow the importation of certain shrimp and shrimp products in an unrestrictive manner, the United States has failed to comply with the 6 November 1998 recommendations and rulings of the Dispute Settlement Body." Malaysia further requested that "the Panel suggest that the United States should lift the import prohibition immediately and allow the importation of certain shrimp and shrimp products in an unrestrictive manner in order to comply with the said recommendations and rulings of the Dispute Settlement Body."[3]

1.5 At its meeting on 23 October 2000, the DSB decided, in accordance with Article 21.5 of the DSU, to refer to the original panel the matter raised by Malaysia in WT/DS58/17. Australia, Canada, Ecuador, the European Communities, India, Japan, Mexico, Pakistan, Thailand and Hong Kong, China reserved their third-party rights.

A. *Terms of Reference*

1.6 At the meeting of the DSB on 23 October 2000, it was agreed that the Panel should have standard terms of reference as follows:

> "To examine, in the light of the relevant provisions of the covered agreements cited by Malaysia in document WT/DS58/17, the mat-

[1] WT/DS58/15, 15 July 1999.
[2] WT/DS58/16, 12 January 2000.
[3] WT/DS58/17, 13 October 2000.

ter referred to the DSB by Malaysia in that document and to make such findings as will assist the DSB in making the recommendations or in giving the rulings provided for in those agreements."[4]

B. Panel Composition

1.7 The Panel was composed of the original panellists as follows:

Chairperson: Mr. Michael Cartland

Members: Mr. Carlos Márcio Cozendey

Mr. Kilian Delbrück

1.8 The Panel met with the parties on 23 January 2001 and with the parties and third parties on 24 January 2001. In a communication dated 15 February 2001, the Chairperson of the Panel informed the DSB that the Panel would not be able to issue its report within 90 days after the date of referral of the matter to it. The reasons for that delay are stated in WT/DS58/19. The Panel issued its report to the parties on 16 May 2001[5] and circulated the report to Members on 15 June 2001.

II. FACTUAL ASPECTS

A. Conservation Issues

2.1 As described during the consultations of the Original Panel with scientific experts[6], most populations of sea turtles are considered to be threatened or endangered, due to human activity, either directly (sea turtles have been exploited for their meat, shells and eggs), or indirectly (incidental capture in fisheries, destruction of their habitats, pollution of the oceans). Seven species of sea turtles have been identified[7] and are distributed mainly in subtropical or tropical areas of the world. Marine turtles are highly migratory animals, which make use of resources available in different parts of the globe only during part of the year or of their life cycles. Sea turtles migrate between their foraging and nesting grounds, but come ashore to lay their eggs. After approximately two to three months of incubation, the sea turtle hatchlings emerge and head for the sea. The survival rate of these hatchlings is low, with few reaching the age of reproduction (10-50

---

4 WT/DS58/18, 8 November 2000.

5 It was agreed between the parties that the Panel would not issue an interim report.

6 Panel Report, *United States - Import Prohibition of Certain Shrimp and Shrimp Products*, adopted on 6 November 1998, WT/DS58/R and Corr.1 (hereafter the "Panel Report"), DSR 1998:VII, 2821, paras. 5.1-5.312 and Annex IV, Transcript of the Meeting with the Experts. In its consultation with scientific experts, the Panel focused its questions on: (i) approaches to sea turtle conservation in light of local conditions; and (ii) habitat and migratory patterns of sea turtles.

7 Green turtle (*Chelonia mydas*), loggerhead (*Caretta caretta*), flatback (*Natator depressus*), hawksbill (*Eretmochelys imbricata*), leatherback (*Dermochelys coriacea*), olive ridley (*Lepidochelys olivacea*), and Kemp's ridley (*Lepidochelys kempi*).

years, depending on the species). As confirmed by the scientific experts, during their lifetime, marine turtles migrate through a variety of habitats and across or outside national jurisdictional boundaries.

2.2 The 1973 Convention on International Trade in Endangered Species of Wild Fauna and Flora (CITES) recognizes all seven species of marine turtles as threatened with extinction and lists these species in Appendix I of CITES.[8] All species except the Australian flatback are listed in Appendices I and II of the 1979 Convention on the Conservation of Migratory Species of Wild Animals (CMS or the Bonn Convention).[9] These species are also included in the World Conservation Union (IUCN) Red List of Threatened Species 2000.[10]

2.3 Given their highly migratory nature, the protection and conservation of threatened marine turtles requires the concerted action of all States within the national jurisdictions in which such species spend any part of their life cycle. An Inter-American Convention for the Protection and Conservation of Sea Turtles was negotiated between 1993 and 1996 with countries of the Caribbean and Western Atlantic region.[11] The Inter-American Convention entered into force on 2 May 2001, 90 days after the eighth instrument of ratification was deposited with the Government of Venezuela.[12]

2.4 Recent international cooperative efforts in the South-East Asian region include the following: the adoption of the Sabah Declaration at the 2nd ASEAN Symposium and Workshop on Sea Turtle Biology and Conservation in Sabah, Malaysia in July 1999[13]; a Resolution on Developing an Indian Ocean and South-East Asian Regional Agreement on the Conservation and Management of Marine Turtles and their Habitats at a workshop in Perth, Australia in October 1999[14];

---

8 Adopted on 3 March 1973 and entered into force on 1 July 1975, with 152 parties as of 15 May 2001. CITES regulates trade in endangered species by defining conditions under which import and export permits may be issued. The conditions are differentiated according to a classification system based on three appendices of protected species. Appendix I includes all species threatened with extinction which are or may be affected by trade. Trade in these species is subject to strict regulation through both import and export permits. *See* www.cites.org.

9 Adopted on 23 June 1979 and entered into force on 1 November 1983, with 74 parties as of 1 March 2001. *See* www.unep-wcmc.org/cms.

10 Scientific criteria are used to classify species into one of eight categories in this Red List system: Extinct, Extinct in the Wild, Critically Endangered, Endangered, Vulnerable, Lower Risk, Data Deficient and Not Evaluated. A species is classed as threatened if it falls in the Critically Endangered, Endangered or Vulnerable categories. *See* www.iucn.org/redlist/2000/species.html.

11 Hereafter the "Inter-American Convention". The Latin American Fisheries Development Organization (*Oldepesca*), an intergovernmental regional fisheries body, acts as the provisional secretariat for the Convention. *See* the text of the Convention at www.seaturtle.org/iac/convention.shtml.

12 As of 15 May 2001, the Convention has nine parties: Brazil, Costa Rica, Ecuador, Honduras, Mexico, The Netherlands, Peru, Venezuela, and the United States.

13 Including concerned scientists and participants from the Indo-Pacific and Indian Ocean regions, including South-East Asian member nations. See www.arbec.com.my/turtle.htm.

14 With participation from Australia, Bangladesh, Cambodia, Comoros, India, Iran, Kenya, Madagascar, Malaysia, Maldives, Mauritius, Mozambique, Oman, Pakistan, Philippines, Reunion (France), Seychelles, Sri Lanka, Tanzania, Thailand, United Arab Emirates and Vietnam.

and the adoption of a Memorandum of Understanding on the Conservation and Management of Marine Turtles and their Habitats of the Indian Ocean and South-East Asia at an intergovernmental meeting of 24 States in Kuantan, Malaysia in July 2000.[15] This Memorandum was concluded under the auspices of the Bonn Convention on the Conservation of Migratory Species of Wild Animals. Agreement was reached to work towards finalizing a Conservation and Management Plan at the next intergovernmental session scheduled to be held in 2001, at which time the Memorandum of Understanding will be open for signature.

B. *History of the Case*

1. *Section 609: the 1996 Guidelines*

2.5 Pursuant to the United States Endangered Species Act (ESA) of 1973, all sea turtles that occur in US waters are listed as endangered or threatened species. In 1987, the United States issued regulations pursuant to the ESA that required all United States shrimp trawlers to use Turtle Excluder Devices ("TEDs") or tow-time restrictions in specified areas where there was a significant mortality of sea turtles associated with shrimp harvesting.[16] Developed over the past two decades in the southeast shrimp fisheries of the United States, TEDs are considered to be an effective way in which to exclude by-catch during shrimp trawling. The 1987 Regulations became fully effective in 1990 and were modified to require the use of TEDs at all times and in all areas where shrimp trawling interacts in a significant way with sea turtles.

2.6 As described in our Original Panel Report on *United States - Import Prohibition of Certain Shrimp and Shrimp Products*[17], this case concerns Section 609 of the United States Public Law 101-162 Relating to the Protection of Sea Turtles in Shrimp Trawl Fishing Operations enacted in 1989 pursuant to the ESA and its implementing measures.[18] Section 609 calls upon the US Secretary of State, in consultation with the US Secretary of Commerce, *inter alia*, to initiate negotiations for the development of bilateral or multilateral agreements for the protection and conservation of sea turtles, in particular with governments of countries engaged in commercial fishing operations likely to have a negative impact on sea turtles.

2.7 Section 609 further provides that shrimp harvested with technology that may adversely affect certain species of sea turtles protected under US law may not be

---

[15] With representation from Australia, Bangladesh, Comores, Egypt, Reunion (France), India, Indonesia, Iran, Kenya, Malaysia, Mauritius, Myanmar, Oman, Pakistan, Papua New Guinea, Philippines, South Africa, Sri Lanka, Thailand, United Arab Emirates, Tanzania, United States of America, Vietnam and Yemen. *See* www.unep-wcmc.org/cms.

[16] Hereafter the "1987 Regulations" (52 Federal Register 24244, 29 June 1987). TEDs are trapdoors installed inside shrimp trawling nets that allow sea turtles and other unintentional, large by-catch to escape.

[17] Panel Report, paras. 2.1-2.26.

[18] Hereafter "Section 609", 16 United States Code (U.S.C.) 1537.

imported into the United States, unless the President annually certifies to the Congress: (a) that the harvesting country concerned has a regulatory programme governing the incidental taking of such sea turtles in the course of such harvesting that is comparable to that of the United States, and that the average rate of that incidental taking by the vessels of the harvesting country is comparable to the average rate of incidental taking of sea turtles by United States vessels in the course of such harvesting; or (b) that the fishing environment of the harvesting country does not pose a threat of incidental taking to sea turtles in the course of such harvesting.

2.8 The United States issued guidelines in 1991 and 1993 for the implementation of Section 609.[19] Pursuant to these guidelines, Section 609 was applied only to countries of the Caribbean/Western Atlantic. In September 1996, the United States concluded the Inter-American Convention for the Protection and Conservation of Sea Turtles with a number of countries of that region. In December 1995, the US Court of International Trade ("CIT") found the 1991 and 1993 Guidelines inconsistent with Section 609 insofar as they limited the geographical scope of Section 609 to shrimp harvested in the wider Caribbean/Western Atlantic area. The CIT directed the US Department of State to prohibit, no later than 1 May 1996, the importation of shrimp or products of shrimp wherever harvested in the wild with commercial fishing technology which may affect adversely those species of sea turtles the conservation of which is the subject of regulations of the Secretary of Commerce.

2.9 In April 1996, the Department of State published revised guidelines to comply with the CIT order of December 1995. The new guidelines extended the scope of Section 609 to shrimp harvested in all countries. The Department of State further determined that, as of 1 May 1996, all shipments of shrimp and shrimp products into the United States must be accompanied by a declaration attesting that the shrimp or shrimp product in question has been harvested either under conditions that do not adversely affect sea turtles or in waters subject to the jurisdiction of a nation currently certified pursuant to Section 609.[20]

2.10 The 1996 Guidelines define shrimp or shrimp products harvested in conditions that do not affect sea turtles to include:

(a) Shrimp harvested in an aquaculture facility;

(b) shrimp harvested by commercial shrimp trawl vessels using TEDs comparable in effectiveness to those required in the United States;

(c) shrimp harvested exclusively by means that do not involve the retrieval of fishing nets by mechanical devices or by vessels using gear that, in accordance with the US programme, would not require TEDs; and

---

19 Hereafter the "1991 Guidelines" (56 Federal Register 1051, 10 January 1991); and the "1993 Guidelines" (58 Federal Register 9015, 18 February 1993).

20 Hereafter the "1996 Guidelines" (61 Federal Register 17342, 19 April 1996), Section 609(b)(2).

(d) species of shrimp, such as the *pandalid* species, harvested in areas in which sea turtles do not occur.[21]

2.11 The 1996 Guidelines provided that certification could be granted by 1 May 1996, and annually thereafter to harvesting countries other than those where turtles do not occur or that exclusively use means that do not pose a threat to sea turtles "only if the government of [each of those countries] has provided documentary evidence of the adoption of a regulatory programme governing the incidental taking of sea turtles in the course of commercial shrimp trawl harvesting that is comparable to that of the United States and if the average take rate of that incidental taking by vessels of the harvesting nation is comparable to the average rate of incidental taking of sea turtles by United States vessels in the course of such harvesting." For the purpose of these certifications, a regulatory programme must include, *inter alia*, a requirement that all commercial shrimp trawl vessels operating in waters in which there is a likelihood of intercepting sea turtles use TEDs at all times. TEDs must be comparable in effectiveness to those used by the United States. Moreover, the average incidental take rate will be deemed comparable to that of the United States if the harvesting country requires the use of TEDs in a manner comparable to that of the US programme.

2. *Panel Proceedings*

2.12 Following a joint request for consultations by India, Malaysia, Pakistan and Thailand on 8 October 1996[22], Malaysia and Thailand requested in a communication dated 9 January 1997[23], and Pakistan asked in a communication dated 30 January 1997[24], that the Dispute Settlement Body (DSB) establish a panel to examine their complaint regarding a prohibition imposed by the United States on the importation of certain shrimp and shrimp products by Section 609 and associated regulations and judicial rulings. On 25 February 1997, the DSB established two panels in accordance with these requests and agreed that these panels would be consolidated into a single Panel, pursuant to Article 9 of the Dispute Settlement Understanding (DSU), with standard terms of reference.[25]

2.13 On 10 April 1997, the DSB established another panel with standard terms of reference in accordance with a request made by India in a communication dated 25 February 1997[26], and agreed that this third panel, too, would be merged into the earlier Panel established on 25 February 1997.[27] The Report of the con-

---

[21] Hereafter the "1996 Guidelines" (61 Federal Register 17342, 19 April 1996), Section 609(b)(2), p. 17343.

[22] WT/DS58/1, 14 October 1996.

[23] WT/DS58/6, 10 January 1997.

[24] WT/DS58/7, 7 February 1997.

[25] WT/DSB/M/29, 26 March 1997.

[26] WT/DS58/8, 4 March 1997.

[27] WT/DSB/M/31, 12 May 1997.

solidated Panel, *United States - Import Prohibition of Certain Shrimp and Shrimp Products,* was circulated to WTO Members on 15 May 1998. [28]

2.14 On 13 July 1998, the United States appealed certain issues of law and legal interpretations in the Original Panel Report.[29] The Appellate Body issued its Report on 12 October 1998.[30] The Appellate Body Report found that the United States measure at issue, Section 609, qualified for provisional justification under Article XX(g), but that it failed to meet the requirements of the chapeau of Article XX, as it was applied in a manner that constituted arbitrary and unjustifiable discrimination.

2.15 On 8 October 1996, the US Court of International Trade ruled that the embargo on shrimp and shrimp products enacted by Section 609 applies to "all shrimp and shrimp products harvested in the wild by citizens or vessels of nations which have not been certified."[31] The CIT found the 1996 Guidelines to be contrary to Section 609 when allowing, with a Shrimp Exporter's Declaration form, imports of shrimp from non-certified countries, if the shrimp were harvested with commercial fishing technology that did not adversely affect sea turtles.

2.16 On 25 November 1996, the CIT clarified that shrimp harvested by manual methods which do not harm sea turtles, by aquaculture and in cold water, could continue to be imported from non-certified countries.[32]

2.17 On 4 June 1998, the US Court of Appeals for the Federal Circuit issued a ruling that vacated the CIT decision of 8 October 1996 and 25 November 1996. On 28 August 1998, the Department of State reinstated the policy of permitting importation of shrimp harvested with TEDs in countries not certified under Section 609.[33]

2.18 On 19 July 2000, the CIT issued a decision that found that the current policy of the Department of State to allow shipments of shrimp caught with TEDs from countries not formally certified pursuant to Section 609 to be imported into the United States, violates that statute on its face.[34] In its ruling, however, the CIT refused to issue an injunction to reverse that policy as it deemed that the evidence was insufficient to show that the policy was harming sea turtles. This CIT decision has been appealed and is currently under review by the US Court of Appeals of the Federal Circuit.

---

[28] Adopted on 6 November 1998, WT/DS58/R.

[29] WT/DS58/11, 13 July 1998.

[30] Appellate Body Report, *United States - Import Prohibition of Certain Shrimp and Shrimp Products*, adopted on 6 November 1998, WT/DS58/AB/R, DSR 1998:VII, 2755 (hereafter the "Appellate Body Report").

[31] *Earth Island Institute v. Warren Christopher*, 942 Fed. Supp. 597 (CIT 1996).

[32] *Earth Island Institute v. Warren Christopher*, 948 Fed. Supp. 1062 (CIT 1996).

[33] Notice of Proposed Revisions the Guidelines for the Implementation of Section 609 of Public Law 101-162, Relating to the Protection of Sea Turtles in Shrimp Trawl Fishing Operations, US Department of State, Federal Register Vol. 64, No. 57, 25 March 1999, Public Notice 3013, pp. 14481-14485 (hereafter the "Proposed Revisions to the Guidelines").

[34] *Turtle Island Restoration Network v. Robert Mallett*, 110 Fed. Supp. 2d 1005 (CIT 2000).

C. *Reasonable Period of Time*

2.19 On 25 November 1998, the United States informed the DSB of its intention to implement the recommendations and ruling of the DSB within a "reasonable period of time."

2.20 On 21 January 1999, the United States and the other parties to the original dispute agreed to a 13-month reasonable period of time for the United States to comply with the recommendations and rulings of the DSB.[35] This reasonable period of time expired on 6 December 1999.

D. *Implementation*

2.21 Pursuant to Article 21.6 of the DSU, the United States submitted regular status reports regarding the implementation of the recommendations and rulings of the DSB in this dispute, on 15 July 1999, 8 September 1999, 15 October 1999, 9 November 1999 and 17 January 2000.[36] These reports set out that the intention of the revision of the 1996 Guidelines pursuant to Section 609 was "to: (1) introduce greater flexibility in considering the comparability of foreign programs and the US programme and (2) elaborate a timetable and procedures for certification decisions, including an expedited timetable to apply in 1999 only. These latter changes are designed to increase the transparency and predictability of the certification process and to afford foreign governments seeking certification a greater degree of due process." The reports also explained that the United States was engaged in efforts to negotiate an agreement on the conservation of sea turtles with the Governments of the Indian Ocean region, and that the United States had offered and was providing technical assistance on the design, construction, installation and operation of TEDs.

1. *Section 609: the 1999 Revised Guidelines*

2.22 On 25 March 1999, the United States Department of State published a notice in the US Federal Register that summarized the Appellate Body Report, proposed measures by which the United States would implement the recommendations and rulings of the DSB, and sought comments from interested parties.[37] On 8 July 1999, the United States Department of State issued Revised Guidelines for the Implementation of Section 609 of Public Law 101-162 Relating to the Protection of Sea Turtles in Shrimp Trawl Fishing Operations.[38] The Revised

---

[35] WT/DS58/16, 12 January 2000.

[36] WT/DS58/15, 15 July 1999 and Addenda 1-4.

[37] Proposed Revisions to the Guidelines.

[38] Revised Guidelines for the Implementation of Section 609 of Public Law 101-162 Relating to the Protection of Sea Turtles in Shrimp Trawl Fishing Operations, US Department of State, Federal Register Vol. 64, No. 130, 8 July 1999, Public Notice 3086, pp. 36946-36952 (hereafter the "Revised Guidelines"). The text of the Revised Guidelines (pp. 36949-36952) is reproduced as the An-

Guidelines summarize the comments received and set forth the measures that the United States would take to implement the recommendations and rulings of the DSB. For ease of reference, the Revised Guidelines in their entirety are attached as the Annex to this report.

2.23 The Revised Guidelines issued pursuant to Section 609 set forth the criteria for certification.[39] First, since certification decisions are based on comparability with the US regulatory programme governing the incidental taking of sea turtles in the course of shrimp harvesting, there is an explanation of the components of that programme. The stated goal of this programme is to protect sea turtles populations from further decline by reducing their incidental mortality in commercial shrimp trawling. The US programme requires that commercial shrimp trawlers use TEDs approved in accordance with standards established by the US National Marine Fisheries Service (NMFS), in areas and at times when there is a likelihood of intercepting sea turtles, with very limited exceptions.[40]

2.24 Second, the Department of State determined that the import prohibitions imposed pursuant to Section 609 do not apply to shrimp or products of shrimp harvested under the following conditions in which harvesting does not adversely affect sea turtles:

(a) Shrimp harvested in aquaculture;

(b) shrimp harvested by trawlers using TEDs comparable in effectiveness to those required in the United States;

(c) shrimp harvested exclusively by means that do not involve the retrieval of fishing nets by mechanical devices, or by vessels using specified gear, in accordance with the US programme; or

(d) shrimp harvested in any other manner or under any other circumstances that the Department of State may determine, following consultation with the NMFS, does not pose a threat of the incidental taking of sea turtles. In the latter case, the Department of State is to publish these determinations in the Federal Register and notify the foreign governments and interested parties.[41]

2.25 Moreover, if the government of the harvesting nation seeks certification on the basis of having adopted a TEDs programme, certification pursuant to Section 609(b)(2)(A) or (B) shall be made if a programme includes:

(a) A requirement that all commercial shrimp trawl vessels operating in waters in which there is a likelihood of intercepting sea turtles use TEDs at all times. TEDs must be comparable in effectiveness

---

nex of this Report. For ease of reference, the paras. of the Revised Guidelines have been numbered in the attached Annex.

39 Revised Guidelines, Annex to this Report: paras. 2-5.

40 Revised Guidelines, Annex to this Report: para. 2.

41 Revised Guidelines, Annex to this Report: para. 5

to those used in the United States. Any exceptions to this requirement must be comparable to those of the US programme described above; and

(b) a credible enforcement effort that includes monitoring for compliance.[42]

2.26 Third, the Revised Guidelines confirm the requirement, effective as of 1 May 1996, that all shipments of shrimp and shrimp products imported into the United States must be accompanied by an Exporter's/Importer's Declaration attesting that the shrimp accompanying the declaration were harvested either under conditions that do not adversely affect sea turtles (as defined above) or in waters subject to the jurisdiction of a nation currently certified pursuant to Section 609.[43]

2.27 Fourth, provision is made for the government of any harvesting nation to request that the Department of State review information regarding the shrimp fishing environment and conditions in that nation in making decisions pursuant to Section 609. Information, based on empirical data supported by objective scientific studies of sufficient duration and scope to provide the necessary information for a reliable determination, may be presented to demonstrate, *inter alia*:

(a) That some portion of the shrimp intended for export to the United States is harvested under one of the conditions identified above as not adversely affecting sea turtles;

(b) that the government of that nation has adopted a regulatory programme governing the incidental taking of sea turtles during shrimp fishing that is comparable to the US programme and, therefore, that the nation is eligible for certification; or

(c) that the fishing environment in that nation does not pose a threat of the incidental taking of sea turtles and, therefore, that the nation is eligible for certification.[44]

2.28 A country may be certified on the basis of having a regulatory programme not involving the use of TEDs. The criteria used in comparing such a programme are "[i]f the government of a harvesting nation demonstrates that it has implemented and is enforcing a comparably effective regulatory program to protect sea turtles in the course of shrimp trawl fishing without the use of TEDs, that nation will also be eligible for certification." Such a finding is to be based on empirical data supported by objective scientific studies of sufficient duration and scope to provide the information for a reliable determination. In reviewing this information, the Department of State is "to take fully into account any demonstrated dif-

[42] Revised Guidelines, Annex to this Report: paras. 18-19.

[43] Revised Guidelines, Annex to this Report: para. 6.

[44] Revised Guidelines, Annex to this Report: para. 10.

ferences between the shrimp fishing conditions in the United States and those in other nations, as well as information available from other sources."[45]

2.29 As noted above, countries may seek to be certified on the basis of having a shrimp fishing environment that does not pose a threat of the incidental taking of sea turtles. The Revised Guidelines provide that the Department of State shall certify any harvesting nation pursuant to Section 609(b)(2)(C) on this basis that meets any of the following criteria:

(a) Any harvesting nation without any of the relevant species of sea turtles occurring in waters subject to its jurisdiction;

(b) any harvesting nation that harvests shrimp exclusively by means that do not pose a threat to sea turtles; e.g., any nation that harvests shrimp exclusively by artisanal means; or

(c) any nation whose commercial shrimp trawling operations take place exclusively in waters subject to its jurisdiction in which sea turtles do not occur.[46]

2.30 There is also recognition in the Revised Guidelines that sea turtles require protection throughout their life cycle, not only when they are threatened during shrimp harvesting. Thus, in certifying, the Department "shall also take fully into account other measures the harvesting nation undertakes to protect sea turtles, including national programs to protect nesting beaches and other habitat, prohibitions on the directed take of sea turtles, national enforcement and compliance programs, and participation in any international agreement for the protection and conservation of sea turtles." The Department of State is also to engage in consultations with harvesting nations.[47]

2.31 Each year the Department of State considers for certification any nation that is currently certified and any other harvesting nation who requests certification prior to 1 September of the preceding year. In addition, "any harvesting nation that is not certified on 1 May of any year may be certified prior to the following 1 May at such time as the harvesting nation meets the criteria necessary for certification. Conversely, any harvesting nation that is certified on 1 May of any year may have its certification revoked prior to the following 1 May at such time as the harvesting nation no longer meets those criteria."[48]

2.32 There is recognition that the Revised Guidelines may be revised in the future to take into consideration additional information on the interaction between sea turtles and shrimp fisheries; changes in the US programme; and considering the pending domestic litigation in the United States.

---

45 Revised Guidelines, Annex to this Report: Section II.B.(a)(2).

46 Revised Guidelines, Annex to this Report: para. 14.

47 Revised Guidelines, Annex to this Report: para. 23.

48 Revised Guidelines, Annex to this Report: para. 40.

III. MAIN ARGUMENTS OF THE PARTIES

A. *Procedural Issues*

1. *Terms of Reference*

3.1 According to **Malaysia**, the mandate of the Panel is to examine the consistency with Articles XI and XX of the GATT 1994 of measures taken by the United States to comply with the recommendations and rulings of the Dispute Settlement Body (DSB). Such an approach is consistent with the views expressed by the Appellate Body with regard to the scope of an Article 21.5 dispute settlement proceeding in *Canada - Measures Affecting The Export of Civilian Aircraft.*[49] Essentially, the Article 21.5 Panel, in reviewing the "consistency" under Article 21.5 of the Dispute Settlement Understanding (DSU), is entrusted with the task of determining that the "measures taken to comply with the recommendations and ruling of the DSB was in "conformity with", "adhering to the same principles" or "compatible" with the obligations of the implementing party under the relevant provisions of the WTO Agreement. Malaysia thus argues that the steps taken by the United States did not remove the elements of "unjustifiable discrimination" and "arbitrary discrimination". Therefore, Malaysia argues that the measure of the United States remains inconsistent with Article XI and is not justified under Article XX of the GATT 1994.

3.2 Malaysia further argues that it does not limit itself in this dispute to contesting whether the United States has complied with the DSB recommendations and rulings. Malaysia is thus exercising its rights under Article 21.5 of the DSU.

3.3 Malaysia also submits that the Panel should find that in order to comply with the recommendations and rulings of the DSB, the import prohibition pursuant to Section 609 should be removed. This is a component of Malaysia's request for the establishment of a panel.[50]

3.4 In the view of the **United States**, the issue in this proceeding is to determine whether the United States has complied with the rulings and recommendations of the DSB by modifying the application of Section 609 of Public Law 101-162 ("Section 609")[51] in accordance with the findings in the Appellate Body Report.

---

[49] Adopted on 4 August 2000, WT/DS70/AB/RW (hereafter "*Canada - Aircraft - Recourse by Brazil to Article 21.5 of the DSU*"), DSR 2000:IX, 4299, paras. 36-37 and 40-41.

[50] WT/DS58/17, 13 October 2000.

[51] Revised Guidelines for the Implementation of Section 609 of Public Law 101-162 Relating to the Protection of Sea Turtles in Shrimp Trawl Fishing Operations, US Department of State, Federal Register Vol. 64, No. 130, 8 July 1999, Public Notice 3086, pp. 36946-36952 (hereafter the "Revised Guidelines"). The text of the Revised Guidelines (pp. 36949-36952) is reproduced as the Annex of this Report. For ease of reference, the paras. of the Revised Guidelines have been numbered in the attached Annex.

2. *Submissions from Non-Governmental Organizations*

3.5 The Panel received two submissions from non-governmental organizations (NGOs) in this case. One was submitted on 12 November 2000 by Earth Justice Legal Defense Fund on behalf of *the Turtle Island Restoration Network, the Human Society of the United States, the American Society for the Prevention of Cruelty to Animals, Defenders of Wildlife, and the Fiscalia Del Medio Ambiente (Chile)* (hereafter "Earthjustice Submission").

3.6 The second was submitted on 13 December 2000 by the National Wildlife Federation on behalf of *the Center for Marine Conservation, Centro Ecoceanos, Defenders of Wildlife, Friends of the Earth, Kenya Sea Turtle Committee, Marine Turtle Preservation Group of India, National Wildlife Federation, Natural Resources Defense Council, Operation Kachhapa, Project Swarajya, Visakha Society for Prevention of Cruelty to Animals* (hereafter "National Wildlife Federation Submission").

3.7 These submissions were respectively communicated to the parties on 15 and 18 December 2000. In a letter accompanying these submissions, the Panel informed the parties that they may comment in their submissions on the admissibility and relevance of these submissions. The Panel also informed the parties that it would address this matter in its report.

3.8 **Malaysia** holds the view that the Panel does not have the right to accept, or consider any unsolicited briefs. Moreover, Malaysia submits that the finding in the Original Panel that Article 13 of the DSU did not confer any right on a Panel to accept unsolicited briefs. Article 13 gives a panel the right to "seek" information and technical advice from any individual or body that it deemed appropriate. Articles 10 and 12 and Appendix 3 of the DSU provide that only Members who are parties to a dispute, or who have notified the DSB of their interest in becoming third parties have the legal right to make submissions to a panel and to have those submissions considered by a panel. To the contrary, the Appellate Body's interpretation in *United States - Import Prohibition of Certain Shrimp And Shrimp Products*[52] had the effect of providing greater rights to those who were not WTO Members.

3.9 Malaysia argues that, of prime importance for the Panel's consideration, is that the practice of admission and acceptance of unsolicited submissions by panels and the Appellate Body has been the subject of intense debate at a special meeting of the General Council on 22 November 2000. The overwhelming view of the WTO Members at the meeting was that panels and the Appellate Body did not have the authority to receive or consider unsolicited briefs. This view was conveyed to, and noted by the Chairperson of the Appellate Body.

[52] Adopted on 6 November 1998, WT/DS58/AB/R, *United States - Import Prohibition of Certain Shrimp and Shrimp Products* (hereafter the "Appellate Body Report"), DSR 1998:VII, 2755.

3.10 The **United States** argues that under the findings of the Appellate Body in this case, the Panel has the discretion to consider either or both of the submissions from NGOs. The Appellate Body wrote that: "[a] panel has the discretionary authority either to accept and consider or to reject information and advice submitted to it, whether requested by a panel or not."[53]

3.11 According to the United States, the National Wildlife Federation Submission was directly relevant to the issues in this dispute. It addresses the issue of US compliance with the recommendations and rulings of the DSB. Moreover, it presents the views of the submitters on the status under international environmental law of consensual versus unilateral environmental measures, an issue raised to varying extents by Malaysia and certain third parties.

3.12 Accordingly, the United States submits that the Panel should exercise its discretion to consider the National Wildlife Federation Submission. At the same time, however, the United States decided to attach the National Wildlife Federation brief to its submission in this case. The United States submits that this ensures that a relevant and informative document is before the Panel, regardless of whether the Panel decides to exercise its discretion to accept the National Wildlife Federation Submission directly from the submitters. On the other hand, the United States argues that the Earthjustice Submission does not appear to be as relevant to the issues in this dispute as it addresses a hypothetical issue that is not before the Panel. The United States notes, however, that the Panel does have the discretion to accept the Earthjustice Submission directly from the submitters according to the Appellate Body's ruling.[54]

3.13 In response to a question by the Panel[55], the United States argues that the "*amicus*" brief attached to its rebuttal submission reflected the independent views of the organizations that signed on to that brief. These organizations have a great interest, and specialized expertise, in sea turtle conservation and related matters. The views of these organizations should be of value to the Panel in resolving the matters at issue in this dispute. The United States notes, however, that the "*amicus*" brief included certain procedural and substantive defenses not advanced in the submission of the United States, and thus that these matters are not before the panel.

3.14 The United States also argues that Malaysia makes the rather extraordinary argument that the Appellate Body was wrong and the Panel should ignore the Appellate Body finding. Nowhere does the DSU grant dispute settlement

---

53 Appellate Body Report, para. 108.

54 Appellate Body Report, paras. 108 and 110.

55 The question reads as follows: "The Panel takes note of the fact that the United States attached to its rebuttals, as [an] exhibit, one of the "*amicus* briefs" submitted directly to the Panel. Having been submitted by the United States, this document becomes part of the US submissions in this case. Could the United States clarify whether, by doing so, it intends to fully endorse the content of the document contained in [this] Exhibit or whether [this] Exhibit is submitted for the information of the Panel, without the United States endorsing part or all of the views expressed in it?"

panels the authority to overrule the Appellate Body. In addition, Malaysia's only rationale for its position is that the Appellate Body finding gives greater rights to "*amici*" than to WTO Member governments. This claim is demonstrably false. Under the DSU, any WTO Member may preserve its third-party rights and have its views considered by a panel. In stark contrast, the Appellate Body findings simply provide panels with the *discretion* to consider unsolicited submissions. The differences between the rights afforded to third parties and "*amici*" is dramatically illustrated by events in the recent proceedings in the case on *European Communities - Measures Affecting Asbestos and Asbestos-Containing Products.*[56] In that case, the Appellate Body accepted and considered all submissions filed by third parties. By contrast, the Appellate Body considered nearly twenty applications for leave to file unsolicited submissions, and rejected each one of those applications.

3.15 **Malaysia** argues that it is not suggesting that the Panel should overturn the Appellate Body's decision on this issue. However, in the light of the development in the special meeting of the General Council on 22 November 2000, Malaysia submits that the Panel should exercise extreme caution when dealing with unsolicited "*amicus curiae*" briefs.

3. *Burden of Proof*

3.16 **Malaysia** submits that the burden of proof is on the United States, as the party invoking Article XX, to justify its invocation.[57] This approach has been adopted by the Appellate Body in *Brazil - Export Financing Programme for Aircraft - Recourse by Canada To Article 21.5 of the DSU.*[58] It was held in that case that since it was Brazil that asserted the "affirmative defence," the burden of proof rested on Brazil.[59] The issue of the burden of proof also has been dealt with in the Appellate Body's decision in *United States - Measure Affecting Imports of Woven Wool Shirts and Blouses from India.*[60] The Appellate Body held that " [...] the burden of proof rests upon the party, whether complaining or defending, who asserts the affirmative of the particular claim or defence."[61]

3.17 However, Malaysia argues, the pertinent point in the Appellate Body's decision is that it acknowledges the fact that several GATT 1947 and WTO pan-

---

[56] Adopted on 5 April 2001, WT/DS135/AB/R, DSR 2001:VII, 3243 (hereafter "*EC - Asbestos*").

[57] Malaysia refers to *United States - Restrictions on Imports of Tuna* (DS21/R, not adopted, circulated on 3 September 1991, BISD 39S/155) in which the panel held that "the practice of Panels has been to interpret Article XX narrowly, to place the burden on the party invoking Article XX *to justify its invocation* [...]" (para. 5.22, emphasis added by Malaysia).

[58] Adopted on 4 August 2000, WT/DS46/AB/RW (hereafter "*Brazil - Aircraft - Recourse by Canada To Article 21.5 of the DSU*"), DSR 2000:VIII, 4067.

[59] *Ibid.* para. 65.

[60] Adopted on 23 May 1997, WT/DS33/AB/R, DSR 1997:I, 323 (hereafter "*United States - Wool Shirts*").

[61] *Ibid.*, DSR 1997:I, 323, at p. 335 .

els have required such proof of a party invoking a defence, such as those found in Article XX. The Appellate Body clearly stated that the sub-paragraphs in Article XX are " [...] limited exceptions from obligations under certain other provisions of GATT 1994, not positive rules establishing obligations in themselves. They are in the nature of affirmative defences. It is only reasonable that the burden of establishing such a defence should rest on the party asserting it."[62]

3.18 Hence, Malaysia submits that, as the party who is asserting the affirmative defence under Article XX, the burden is on the United States to show that its measures are justified under Article XX. In this respect, the United States has failed to show that the steps taken by the United States to implement the DSB recommendations and rulings render Section 609 justified under Article XX. As such, the United States has failed to comply with the recommendations and rulings of the DSB.

3.19 Malaysia argues that the United States has to prove to the Panel that the implementation measures that have been undertaken fully satisfy the requirements of the chapeau of Article XX of the GATT 1994 and that there is no longer any inconsistency with Article XI of the GATT 1994.

3.20 Malaysia substantiates this argument with reference to the Appellate Body's assessment that the US measure has been "provisionally justified." This means that the United States has to prove that this measure is now fully justified under Article XX. Accordingly, the United States has to address each and every aspect stipulated by the Appellate Body in order to satisfy the elements of "unjustifiable discrimination" and "arbitrary discrimination" where the same conditions prevail. If the United States does not fulfill these standards, the US measure would not qualify as an exception under Article XX.

3.21 In its response to a question of the Panel, the **United States** agrees that it had the initial burden of showing that the US measure falls within the scope of Article XX. In this proceeding, Malaysia has the initial burden of showing that the US measure is inconsistent with one or more obligations under a covered agreement. However, as Malaysia notes, the United States has not contested that its measure is an import prohibition under GATT Article XI.

3.22 The United States claims that it is asserting as an affirmative defense that its measure falls, as modified, within the scope of Article XX. As the Appellate Body explained in its Report on *United States - Wool Shirts,* the burden of establishing such a defense rests on the party asserting it.[63] As the Appellate Body also explained in *United States - Wool Shirts,* "If [the party asserting a particular claim or defense] adduces sufficient evidence to raise a presumption that what is claimed is true, the burden then shifts to the other party, who will fail unless it

---

[62] Adopted on 23 May 1997, WT/DS33/AB/R, DSR 1997:I, 323, at p. 337 (hereafter "*United States - Wool Shirts*")

[63] *United States - Wool Shirts*, p. 337.

adduces sufficient evidence to rebut the presumption."[64] The United States submits that it has presented a *prima facie* case that its measure, as modified, falls within the scope of Article XX, and that the burden has thus shifted to Malaysia to present evidence and legal argument to the contrary. In particular, the United States has fully explained the manner in which it has modified the aspects of the application of the measure that the Appellate Body found to result in arbitrary or unjustifiable discrimination. Therefore, the United States has made a *prima facie* case that the US measure, as modified, indeed falls within the scope of Article XX.

3.23 In the view of the United States, this burden shifting analysis is particularly pertinent to the issue of whether the United States has modified the guidelines implementing Section 609 of the United States Public Law 101-162 ("the Revised Guidelines") to make them more flexible and to take account of local conditions. The United States contends it has shown that the Guidelines have been modified to provide for more flexibility. The United States further submits that it has also shown specific instances where these more flexible Guidelines have been applied in the cases of Pakistan and Australia. The United States claims that these facts are more than sufficient to meet its burden of establishing a *prima facie* case that it has complied with the aspects of the DSB recommendations and rulings relating to flexibility in the application of the measure. Therefore, the United States argues that the burden thus shifts to Malaysia to show that in fact the United States has not introduced such flexibility.

3.24 The United States submits that Malaysia has not presented any valid reasons why, as it claims, the Revised Guidelines do not provide the degree of flexibility envisioned in the DSB recommendations. This point is reinforced, the United States argues, when one considers that, first, under the Appellate Body's burden-shifting analysis, the burden now resides with Malaysia to rebut the *prima facie* case of the United States, and, second, that Malaysia has never even sought to test the Revised Guidelines by applying for certification. In other words, where the Revised Guidelines on their face provide for more flexibility, and where Malaysia has never tested these Guidelines and simply asserts that the Guidelines are insufficiently flexible, Malaysia cannot be found to have prevailed on this key issue in the proceeding.

3.25 A related issue in the view of the United States is that the Appellate Body finding was based on certain aspects of the US measure "in their cumulative effect". The United States argues that this issue should not arise because it has in fact responded to all aspects of the discrimination identified by the Appellate Body. Thailand, as a third party, spent a great deal of time addressing this issue, and claims that the United States would be in violation of its treaty obligations unless it addressed *each* aspect of discrimination identified by the Appellate Body. According to the United States, Thailand's reasoning is circular and re-

---

64 *United States - Wool Shirts*, p. 335.

flects a misunderstanding of the Appellate Body Report. The Appellate Body did *not* find, as Thailand assumes, that each and every element of differential treatment among Members rises to the level of a violation of the Article XX chapeau. To the contrary, the Appellate Body carefully wrote that all five of the aspects of differential treatment, in their cumulative effect - that is in the aggregate, when added together - amounted to a violation. The United States thus argues that the Appellate Body, conservatively and properly, did not specify how it would have decided the case if some, but not other, aspects of differential treatment were corrected.

3.26 The United States submits that it has addressed all aspects of differential treatment, and thus that the Panel should not be presented with this issue. However, if the Panel finds otherwise, the United States notes that the Appellate Body Report does provide some guidance. For example, "the most conspicuous" flaw, the Appellate Body said, was the failure of the measure to be applied in a flexible manner. On the other hand, it would be fair to say that the Appellate Body Report placed less emphasis on the aspect of differential treatment arising from differing phase-in periods.

3.27 **Malaysia** agrees with the statement of the United States that the Appellate Body's use of the term "cumulative effect" is important in the Panel's examination of United States compliance with the Appellate Body's findings. The term "cumulative" is defined as "forming an aggregate; the word signifies that two things are to be added together, instead of one being a repetition or in substitution of the other." [65] However, Malaysia claims that it does not agree with the United States' contention that it "need not necessarily address each one of those aspects [of the United States application of Section 609 which constituted "unjustifiable discrimination"] in order to comply with the Appellate Body's findings." Neither can Malaysia agree with the United States that "it has addressed all of the defects in the application of Section 609." Malaysia submits that the United States has to address each and every aspect in satisfying the elements of "unjustifiable discrimination".

B. *Violation of Article XI*

3.28 **Malaysia** argues that the prolonged enforcement of Section 609, which has the effect of an import prohibition, continues to undermine the Malaysian shrimp export industry to the United States' market. As submitted by Malaysia in the Original Panel[66], Malaysia's exports declined from US$9.1 million in 1995 to US$4.86 million in 1996. Exports had declined by a significant 38 per cent from US$2.87 million for the period (May - October 1995) to US$1.8 million for the

65 *Black's Law Dictionary*, 6th Ed., p. 380.

66 *United States - Import Prohibition of Certain Shrimp and Shrimp Products*, adopted on 6 November 1998, WT/DS58/R (hereafter the "Panel Report"), DSR 1998:VII, 2821, paras. 3.120 and 3.126.

corresponding months of 1996. Since then, Malaysian companies have ceased exporting to the United States and have had to develop other export markets in Europe, Hong Kong, Australia, Japan and China. As a result, Malaysia argues that its exporters continue to suffer a loss of export opportunities and market share in the United States for wild-harvested shrimp due to the prolonged import prohibition.

3.29 The **United States** claims that during the 13-month period agreed to by the parties to the dispute, it proceeded to modify its application of the measure in order to address the specific problems identified by the Appellate Body. The United States compliance includes: Revised Guidelines that provide more flexibility in decision-making; enhanced due process protections for exporting countries; efforts to negotiate a sea turtle conservation agreement in the Indian Ocean region; and enhanced offers of technical assistance.

3.30 Nevertheless, with regard to Section 609, the United States does not claim that the import prohibition is now compatible with Article XI of the GATT 1994, nor does it contend that the prohibition in question is not in force. Furthermore, in its reply to a question by the Panel[67], the United States expressly states that, as noted by Malaysia, the United States does not contest that its measure is an import prohibition under GATT Article XI.

C. Justification under Article XX

1. General Comments

3.31 The **United States** mentions that in detailed and exhaustive findings, the Appellate Body confirmed that the US measure which has the effect of an import prohibition was provisionally justified under GATT Article XX(g) as a measure relating to the conservation of an exhaustible natural resource. However, the Appellate Body Report also found that certain specifically-identified aspects of the application of the US measure amounted to unjustifiable or arbitrary discrimination under the chapeau of Article XX.

3.32 The United States claims that implementation of the recommendations and rulings of the DSB in this matter has several distinct elements. These elements respond to the several distinct findings contained in the Appellate Body Report relating to the way in which the United States formerly applied Section 609.

3.33 According to the United States, compliance steps include:

(a) Revised Guidelines that provide more flexibility in decision-making;

(b) enhanced due process protections for exporting countries;

---

67 The question reads as follows: "Do you agree with Malaysia's statement that the burden of proof lies with the United States to demonstrate that the measures taken to comply with the recommendations and rulings of the DSB are justified under Article XX of the GATT 1994?"

(c) efforts to negotiate a sea turtle conservation agreement in the Indian Ocean region; and

(d) enhanced offers of technical assistance.

3.34 **Malaysia** argues that in its findings and conclusions, in paragraph 187, the Appellate Body:

> "concludes that the United States measure, while qualifying for provisional justification under Article XX(g), fails to meet the requirements of the chapeau of Article XX, and, therefore, is not justified under Article XX of the GATT 1994."

3.35 Malaysia submits that this explicitly means that the measure concerned, i.e. the import prohibition contained in Section 609, although provisionally justified under the GATT Article XX (g), is however not justified under Article XX because it fails to meet the requirements of the chapeau.

3.36 Malaysia submits that since the imposition of the import prohibition is not justified under Article XX of the GATT 1994, it should be removed in order for the United States to bring the measure into conformity with its obligations under that Agreement.

3.37 Thus, Malaysia claims that in order to comply with the recommendations and rulings of the DSB, the import prohibition contained in Section 609 should be removed instead of being modified.

2. *Article XX(g)*

3.38 With regard to Section 609 and its consistency with paragraph (g) of Article XX of the GATT 1994, the **United States** claims that the Appellate Body separately found that endangered sea turtle species covered by Section 609 were "exhaustible natural resources" under Article XX(g)[68], and that the United States made Section 609 "effective in conjunction with restrictions on domestic production or consumption" under Article XX(g).[69]

3.39 The United States claims that the Appellate Body clearly, and at length, explained that the general design of the Section 609 import prohibition was provisionally justified under Article XX(g). The United States quotes the relevant paragraphs of the Appellate Body Report:

> "137. In the present case, we must examine the relationship between the general structure and design of the measure here at stake, Section 609, and the policy goal it purports to serve, that is, the conservation of sea turtles.
>
> 138. *Section 609(b)(1) imposes an import ban on shrimp that have been harvested with commercial fishing technology which*

[68] Appellate Body Report, paras. 127-134.

[69] Appellate Body Report, paras. 143-145

may adversely affect sea turtles. This provision is designed to influence countries to adopt national regulatory programs requiring the use of TEDs by their shrimp fishermen. In this connection, it is important to note that the general structure and design of Section 609 *cum* implementing guidelines is fairly narrowly focused.

[…]

141. In its general design and structure, therefore, Section 609 is not a simple, blanket prohibition of the importation of shrimp imposed without regard to the consequences (or lack thereof) of the mode of harvesting employed upon the incidental capture and mortality of sea turtles. *Focusing on the design of the measure here at stake, it appears to us that Section 609, cum implementing guidelines, is not disproportionately wide in its scope and reach in relation to the policy objective of protection and conservation of sea turtle species. The means are, in principle, reasonably related to the ends. The means and ends relationship between Section 609 and the legitimate policy of conserving an exhaustible, and, in fact, endangered species, is observably a close and real one, a relationship that is every bit as substantial as that which we found in United States - Gasoline between the EPA baseline establishment rules and the conservation of clean air in the United States.*

142. *In our view, therefore, Section 609 is a measure "relating to" the conservation of an exhaustible natural resource within the meaning of Article XX(g) of the GATT 1994.*"[70]

3.40 The United States also claims that the Appellate Body emphasized the distinction between the issues of whether the general design of a measure is provisionally justified under one of the specific Article XX paragraphs, and whether the application of the measure is consistent with the requirements of the chapeau of Article XX.

3.41 **Malaysia** claims that in its findings and conclusions the Appellate Body modified the Panel Report and, *inter alia*, found that the US measure, though provisionally justified under Article XX(g), had failed to meet the requirements of the chapeau of Article XX, and, therefore, was not justified under Article XX of the GATT 1994.[71]

3.42 Malaysia submits that this explicitly means that the measure concerned, i.e. the import prohibition contained in Section 609, although provisionally justified under Article XX(g) is however not justified under Article XX because it failed to meet the requirements of the chapeau.

---

70 Emphasis added and footnotes omitted by the United States.

71 Appellate Body Report, para. 187

3.43 Moreover, Malaysia notes that it does not dispute the finding of the Appellate Body Report with regard to the provisional justification of Section 609 under Article XX(g).

3. *Chapeau*

(a) General Compliance Issues

3.44 The **United States** claims, as stated above, that the Appellate Body emphasized the distinction between the issues of whether the general design of a measure is provisionally justified under one of the specific Article XX subparagraphs, and whether the application of the measure is consistent with the requirements of the chapeau of Article XX. In support of this, the United States calls attention to the Appellate Body's citation to its earlier Report in *United States - Standards for Reformulated and Conventional Gasoline*, where it points out that the chapeau of Article XX "by its express terms addresses, not so much the questioned measure or its specific contents as such, but rather the manner in which that measure is applied."[72]

3.45 The United States recalls that the Appellate Body Report, after finding that the US measure was provisionally justified under Article XX(g), considered the criteria in the chapeau of Article XX. The United States considers that the Appellate Body's detailed findings under the chapeau of Article XX are addressed not to the Section 609 statute itself, but to the United States' application of the measure.

3.46 The United States claims that it has addressed all of the defects in the application of Section 609 found and identified by the Appellate Body: unjustifiable discrimination and arbitrary discrimination. Thus, the United States claims that it has complied with the recommendations and rulings of the DSB.

3.47 The United States observes that the Appellate Body found that while Section 609 requires as a condition of certification that foreign programmes for the protection of sea turtles in the course of shrimp trawl fishing be comparable to the United States' programme, the practice of the Department of State in making certification decisions was to require foreign programmes to be essentially the same as the United States' programme. In assessing foreign programmes, the Department of State should have been more flexible in making such determinations and, in particular, should have taken into consideration different conditions that may exist in the territories of those other nations.

3.48 The United States claims that, in response to this recommendation, the Department of State now considers any evidence that another nation may present that its programme to protect sea turtles in the course of shrimp trawl fishing is

[72] Appellate Body Report, para. 115 (citing its report on *United States - Standards for Reformulated and Conventional Gasoline*, WT/DS2/AB/R (hereafter "*United States - Gasoline*"), DSR 1996:I, 3, at p. 20.

comparable to the US programme.[73] In reviewing such evidence, the Department of State takes into account any demonstrated differences in foreign shrimp fishing conditions, insofar as such differences may affect the extent to which sea turtles are subject to capture and drowning in the commercial shrimp trawl fisheries.[74]

3.49 It is also the view of the United States that the DSB found that the certification process under Section 609 was neither transparent nor predictable and denied to exporting nations basic fairness and due process. There was no formal opportunity for an applicant nation to be heard or to respond to arguments against it. There was no formal written, reasoned decision. But for notice in the United States Federal Register, nations were not notified of decisions specifically. There was no procedure for review of, or appeal from, a denial of certification.

3.50 In response to this finding, the United States claims that it has instituted a broad range of procedural changes in the manner in which it makes certification decisions under Section 609. The process is now transparent and predictable. For example, the Department of State now notifies governments of shrimp harvesting nations on a timely basis of all pending and final decisions and provides them with a meaningful opportunity to be heard and to present any additional information relevant to the certification decision. The Department of State also gives the governments of harvesting nations that are not certified a full explanation of the reasons that the certification was denied and clearly identifies steps that such governments may take to receive a certification in the future.[75]

3.51 The United States considers that the Appellate Body found that at the time the WTO complaint first arose, the United States did not permit imports of shrimp harvested by vessels using Turtle Excluder Devices ("TEDs") that were comparable in effectiveness to those used in the United States, unless the harvesting nation was certified pursuant to Section 609. In other words, shrimp caught using methods identical to those employed in the United States were excluded from the United States market solely because they had been caught in waters of uncertified nations.

3.52 In response the United States claims that even before the Appellate Body issued its Report, the United States revised the policy at issue. Since August 1998, the United States has permitted the importation of shrimp harvested by vessels using TEDs, even if the exporting nation is not certified pursuant to Section 609.

3.53 With regard to this finding, the United States also argues that on 19 July 2000, the US Court of International Trade ("CIT") issued a decision which found that the current policy of the United States to permit the importation of shrimp harvested by TEDs from countries that are not certified pursuant to Section 609 "violates that statute on its face." However, the Court also expressly refused to

73 Revised Guidelines.

74 Revised Guidelines, Annex to this Report: paras. 10-13, 16-19 and Section II.B.(a)(2).

75 Revised Guidelines, Annex to this Report: paras. 27, 29, 30, 35, 37 and 38.

issue an injunction to reverse that policy, finding that there was insufficient evidence to show that the policy was harming sea turtles. An appeal of this decision has been lodged with the United States Court of Appeals for the Federal Circuit. Pending the outcome of this appeal, the current policy remains in effect.

3.54 The United States therefore claims that during the 13-month implementation period it has addressed all the recommendations and rulings of the DSB identified above.

3.55 **Malaysia** submits that the United States has mischaracterized the Appellate Body's finding and analysis by erroneously stating that the Appellate Body's detailed findings under the Article XX chapeau are addressed not to the Section 609 statute itself, but to the United States' application of the measure.

3.56 Malaysia argues that the dichotomy proposed by the United States is fallacious in light of the fact that the application of the measure by the United States in the context of satisfying the three requirements of the chapeau is an integral part of the Section 609 statute, which had been found by the Appellate Body to be only provisionally justified. Failure by the United States to fulfil the required standards under the chapeau would render Section 609 unjustified under GATT Article XX.

3.57 Malaysia also argues that in determining whether the United States has fulfilled the chapeau requirements of Article XX of the GATT 1994, the Appellate Body had examined the manner in which Section 609 had been applied. The Appellate Body opined that there were three standards to be fulfilled, namely arbitrary discrimination between countries where the same conditions prevail; unjustifiable discrimination between countries where the same conditions prevail; and disguised restriction on international trade. It should be noted that the Appellate Body, in its analysis of these standards, had faulted the United States in the manner of its application of Section 609 on several counts and had simultaneously made pertinent observations and comments.

3.58 Moreover, Malaysia considers that in order to give effect to the DSB recommendations and rulings, the import prohibition contained in Section 609 instead of being modified should have been removed to allow the importation of certain shrimp and shrimp products without any restriction. Malaysia insists that the Appellate Body in its Report had instead amplified the discriminatory elements of "unjustifiable discrimination" and "arbitrary discrimination" that need to be removed in order to comply with the recommendations and rulings of the DSB.

3.59 It is the view of Malaysia that in spite of the steps taken by the United States, these discriminatory elements still remain and the United States has to prove to the Panel that the implementation it has undertaken has fully satisfied the requirements of the chapeau of Article XX of the GATT 1994 and there is no longer any inconsistency with GATT Article XI. Thus, Malaysia claims and insists that the United States has to address each and every aspect in satisfying the elements of "unjustifiable discrimination" and "arbitrary discrimination" where the same conditions prevail.

3.60 With regard to the chapeau, Malaysia submits that what is at issue here is not Article XX(g), as claimed by the United States, but whether the requirements of the chapeau of Article XX have been met, particularly whether the United States has demonstrated a justification to continue the import prohibition based on unilateral and non-consensual measures sufficient to meet the requirements of the chapeau of Article XX.

3.61 The **United States** claims that compliance with the DSB recommendations and rulings does not require that the United States lift its import prohibition on shrimp and shrimp products harvested in a manner harmful to endangered sea turtles.

3.62 The United States argues that the Appellate Body affirmatively found that the general design and structure of Section 609 - a fundamental element of which is an import prohibition on certain shrimp and shrimp products - is provisionally justified under Article XX(g) of the GATT 1994.[76] The United States claims that the Appellate Body's detailed findings under the Article XX chapeau are addressed not to the Section 609 statute itself, but to the United States' application of the measure. The United States also argues that by its very terms, the chapeau of Article XX deals with the manner in which a measure is applied.

3.63 Thus, in the view of the United States, Malaysia cannot be correct in asserting that the only way to comply with the DSB recommendations and rulings is to lift the import prohibition under Section 609. The United States also argues that the Appellate Body Report provided the United States with the compliance option of modifying the United States' application of the measure and therefore states that it chose this option, and proceeded to comply based on a careful consideration of the Appellate Body Report. The United States recalls that the European Communities (EC), in its third-party submission, agrees with the United States that Malaysia's position is inconsistent with the findings of the Appellate Body.

(b) Unjustifiable Discrimination

(i) Cumulative Assessment of the Aspects Found to Constitute Unjustifiable Discrimination

3.64 The **United States** notes that the Appellate Body found that the "cumulative effect" of certain aspects of its application of Section 609 constituted "unjustifiable discrimination" between countries where the same conditions prevail. The United States considers that the Appellate Body's use of the term "cumulative effect" is important in the Panel's examination of the United States' compliance with the Appellate Body findings. This carefully considered phrase means that

[76] Appellate Body Report, paras. 125-146.

the Appellate Body's findings of unjustifiable discrimination depended on a combination of aspects of the application of Section 609, and that the United States need not necessarily address each one of those aspects in order to comply with the Appellate Body findings. However, the United States claims that it has addressed all of the defects in the application of Section 609 identified by the Appellate Body and the Panel is not required in this proceeding to consider and apply the Appellate Body's finding on "cumulative effects".

3.65 The United States also notes that Hong Kong, China takes issue with its position that the Appellate Body's use of the term "cumulative effect" was purposeful and potentially important; that the Appellate Body's findings of unjustifiable discrimination depended on a *combination* of aspects of the application of Section 609, and the United States need not necessarily address *each one* of those aspects in order to comply with the Appellate Body findings. However, since none of the aspects of unjustifiable discrimination identified by the Appellate Body remain under the modified US measure, the Panel is not required in this proceeding to consider and apply the Appellate Body's finding on "cumulative effects."

3.66 **Malaysia** agrees with the United States' statement that the Appellate Body's use of the term "cumulative effect" is important in the Panel's examination of United States compliance with the Appellate Body's findings. The term "cumulative" is defined as "forming an aggregate; the word signifies that two things are to be added together, instead of one being a repetition or in substitution of the other." [77] However, Malaysia claims that it does not agree with the United States' contention that it "need not necessarily address each one of those aspects [of the United States application of Section 609 which constituted "unjustifiable discrimination"] in order to comply with the Appellate Body's findings." Neither can Malaysia agree with the United States that "it has addressed all of the defects in the application of Section 609." Malaysia submits that the United States has to address each and every aspect in satisfying the elements of "unjustifiable discrimination".

(ii) Efforts to Negotiate and Whether a WTO Member is Obliged to Seek or Obtain International Consensus

(a) Efforts to Negotiate

3.67 The **United States** recalls that the Appellate Body found that the differences among exporting nations in the extent of the United States' efforts to negotiate conservation agreements contributed to the finding of unjustifiable discrimination. The Appellate Body found that the United States negotiated seriously with some, but not with other Members (including the appellees) that export

---

[77] *Black's Law Dictionary*, 6th Ed., p. 380.

shrimp to the United States and the Appellate Body stated that the effect is plainly discriminatory and unjustifiable. In other words, according to the Appellate Body findings, the United States failed to engage the other parties to this dispute, as well as other WTO Members exporting shrimp to the United States, in serious across-the-board negotiations, apart from negotiations on the Inter-American Convention for the Protection and Conservation of Sea Turtles ("The Inter-American Convention"), for the purpose of concluding agreements to conserve sea turtles.

3.68 With regard to this finding the United States clarifies that it is true that it negotiated the Inter-American Convention before embarking on negotiations toward the Memorandum of Understanding on the Conservation and Management of Marine Turtles and their Habitats of the Indian Ocean and South-East Asian Region ("MOU"), largely because Section 609 was originally interpreted to apply to countries in the Inter-American region much earlier. Nevertheless, the United States has since undertaken negotiations with countries in the Indian Ocean and South-East Asian region that are as serious as the earlier negotiations.

3.69 The United States also recalls that seven nations have now ratified the Inter-American Convention for the Protection and Conservation of Sea Turtles. That Convention will enter into force 90 days after the eighth instrument of ratification is deposited with the Government of Venezuela. The United States also notes that the negotiation of that Convention took place from 1993 to 1996, after nations in the Caribbean and Western Atlantic were first affected by the import restrictions of Section 609.

3.70 The United States claims that as early as 1996, it proposed to governments in the Indian Ocean region the negotiation of an agreement to protect sea turtles in that region, but received no positive response. In 1998, even before the Appellate Body issued its Report, the United States reiterated its desire to enter into such negotiations with affected governments, including Malaysia. During the summer of 1998, the United States informally approached several governments in the Indian Ocean region, as well as numerous non-governmental organizations, in an effort to get such negotiations under way.

3.71 The United States also recalls that on 14 October 1998, following the issuance of the Appellate Body Report, but before its adoption by the DSB, it formally renewed this proposal to representatives of the embassies of the four complainants in Washington, D.C. United States embassies delivered the same message to a wide range of nations in the Indian Ocean region. In each case, the United States presented a list of "elements" that the United States believed could form the basis of such an agreement. The United States also made clear its willingness to support the negotiating process in a number of ways.[78]

[78] US Department of State, Possible Elements of a Regional Convention for the Conservation of Sea Turtles in the Indian Ocean.

3.72 The United States highlights in its submissions that, in a continuing effort to launch such negotiations, the United States actively participated in a Symposium and Workshop on Sea Turtle Conservation and Biology, held in Sabah, Malaysia on 15-17 July 1999. The Symposium concluded with the adoption of the Sabah Declaration, which called for "the negotiation and implementation of a wider regional agreement for the conservation and management of marine turtle populations and their habitats throughout the Indo-Pacific and Indian Ocean region."[79]

3.73 The United States also recalls that in October 1999, the Government of Australia hosted a follow-up conference in Perth, Australia, to consider the conservation of sea turtles throughout the Indian Ocean and South-East Asian region. The United States again participated actively and contributed funding to defray the costs of the conference and to facilitate the participation of representatives from developing countries. At the Perth Conference, participating governments committed themselves to develop an international agreement on sea turtle conservation for that region[80], and the Government of Malaysia subsequently hosted the first round of negotiations toward such an agreement in Kuantan, Malaysia, from 11-14 July 2000. The United States again participated actively and contributed significant funding to cover the costs of the meeting and to facilitate the participation of representatives from developing countries. In all, 24 countries participated in the negotiations, along with a number of intergovernmental organizations and non-governmental organizations.

3.74 The Kuantan meeting, the United States notes, adopted language for the non-binding Memorandum of Understanding. The meeting also produced a Final Act, indicating that, before the MOU can be finalized, a Conservation and Management Plan must first be negotiated and appended as an annex to the MOU. Negotiations on the Conservation and Management Plan are anticipated to take place in 2001.

3.75 Thus, the United States claims that it has, in fact, addressed this finding of the Appellate Body, by engaging in negotiations not only with Malaysia but also with other nations of the Indian Ocean region on a sea turtle conservation agreement and that those negotiations have achieved considerable, and indeed remarkable, progress in the last two years.

---

79 Sabah Declaration, July 1999.

80 Resolution on Developing an Indian Ocean and South-East Asian Regional Agreement on the Conservation and Management of Marine Turtles and their Habitats, October 1999.

3.76 Moreover, in response to a question of the Panel[81] concerning the efforts of the United States to resort to international mechanisms to protect sea turtles to which the Appellate Body referred in its Report, the United States replies that perhaps the primary international mechanism mentioned by the Appellate Body is the Convention on International Trade in Endangered Species of Wild Fauna and Flora (CITES). The United States is a party to CITES and plays a leading role in CITES bodies, in particular the CITES Conferences of the Parties (COP).

3.77 For quite some time, the United States notes, all species of sea turtles covered by Section 609 have been listed in Appendix I to CITES. The United States fully supports these listings, which have essentially banned international trade in sea turtles and sea turtle products. The United States has also firmly and successfully resisted efforts at a recent CITES COP to "downlist" a particular population of hawksbill sea turtles to Appendix II, which would reopen trade in the sea turtles in question.

3.78 The United States also explains that by listing all these sea turtle species in Appendix I and by maintaining those listings, CITES has essentially done all it can to protect endangered sea turtles. CITES has no explicit mandate to manage wildlife populations; it only regulates international trade in the species themselves. In particular, CITES does not have responsibility for adopting measures to protect sea turtles from other types of harm, including their incidental drowning in shrimp trawl nets.

3.79 With regard to sea turtle species, the United States submits that unfortunately their listing in Appendix I to CITES has not secured their survival. Indeed, argues the United States, most species of sea turtles, including most species in the Indian Ocean and South-East Asian region, have continued to decline precipitously since their CITES listings, some to the brink of extinction.

3.80 Accordingly, while the United States has actively supported and promoted all CITES efforts to protect sea turtles, both before and after the Appellate Body Report, the United States does not feel that it can rely on those efforts alone to achieve its goal of effective sea turtle conservation.

3.81 The United States notes that another international mechanism mentioned in the Appellate Body Report is the Convention on the Conservation of Migratory Species of Wild Animals (CMS), also known as the Bonn Convention. Since the issuance of the Appellate Body Report, the United States has successfully worked with the CMS Secretariat in advancing the negotiations toward the MOU.

---

[81] The question reads as follows: "With reference to the Appellate Body finding (WT/DS58/AB/R, para. 171) that the United States did not attempt to have recourse to such international mechanisms as exist to achieve cooperative efforts to protect and conserve sea turtles before imposing the import ban, could the United States specify if, since the issuance of the Appellate Body Report, the United States had recourse to those international mechanisms? If yes, please specify the agreements, the bodies and the procedures applied. If no, please explain why it was found impossible, inappropriate or irrelevant."

CMS is contributing its recognized expertise in these negotiations and serves as the interim secretariat for the MOU.

3.82 Finally, the United States argues that it has had considerable recourse to the World Conservation Union (IUCN) since the issuance of the Appellate Body Report in furtherance of its goal to conserve sea turtles. With financial support from the United States and like-minded members, IUCN has adopted an active programme to support sea turtle conservation efforts in various regions. IUCN is working with the United States and other countries in the Inter-American region to prepare for the entry into force of the Inter-American Convention. IUCN has also actively supported the negotiating process toward the MOU. At the most recent IUCN Conservation Congress in Amman, Jordan, the United States worked with other delegations to ensure passage of resolutions calling for sea turtle conservation efforts worldwide.

3.83 Arguing that there was a lack of cooperative efforts by the United States prior to the imposition of the unilateral ban, **Malaysia** submits that the Appellate Body Report emphasized the "failure of the United States to engage [...] Members exporting shrimp to the United States in serious across-the-board negotiations with the objective of concluding bilateral or multilateral agreements for the protection and conservation of sea turtles before enforcing the import prohibition against the shrimp exports of those Members" as bearing heavily on any appraisal of unjustifiable discrimination.[82]

3.84 Malaysia submits that with regard to this failure of the United States "*to have prior consistent recourse to diplomacy* as an instrument of environmental protection policy, which produces discriminatory impacts on countries exporting shrimp to the United States *with which no international agreements are reached or even seriously attempted*,"[83] the Appellate Body stressed three very substantive points regarding the importance of international consensus for addressing environmental measures rather than resorting to unilateral actions. The Appellate Body firstly noted that the Congress of the United States expressly recognised the importance of securing *international agreements* for the protection and conservation of the sea turtles species in enacting Section 609, but apart from the negotiation of the Inter-American Convention, the United States did not indicate any serious substantial efforts to carry out the express directions of Congress.

3.85 Secondly the Appellate Body opined that the protection and conservation of highly migratory species of sea turtles demands concerted and *cooperative efforts* on the part of the many countries whose waters are traversed in the course of recurrent sea turtle migrations. It noted that the need for such efforts have been recognised in the WTO itself and in a significant number of other international instruments and declarations, such as Principle 12 of the *Rio Declaration on Environment and Development*, paragraph 2.22(i) of *Agenda 21*, Article 5 of the

[82] Appellate Body Report, para. 166.

[83] Appellate Body Report, para. 167 (emphasis added by Malaysia).

Convention on Biological Diversity, the Convention on the Conservation of Migratory Species of Wild Animals, and in the Report of the WTO Committee on Trade and Environment on the occasion of the Singapore Ministerial Conference.[84]

3.86 Thirdly, the Appellate Body found that successful negotiation of the Inter-American Convention provides "convincing demonstration that an alternative course of action was reasonably open to the United States for securing the legitimate policy goal of its measure, a course of action other than the unilateral and non-consensual procedures of the import prohibition under Section 609".[85] According to Malaysia, the well advanced state of negotiations in the Indian Ocean and South-East Asian Region, and the recognition of the effectiveness of Malaysia's sea turtle conservation programme also show that there are alternative courses of action reasonably open to the United States to protect sea turtles in Malaysia. Thus, Malaysia reiterates that as the country invoking the "exceptions" of Article XX, the United States bears the burden of proving otherwise.

3.87 Malaysia notes that the Original Panel Report concluded that "the best way for the parties to this dispute to contribute effectively to the protection of sea turtles in a manner consistent with WTO objectives, including sustainable development, would be to reach cooperative agreements on integrated conservation strategies,"[86] and notes that this finding by the Panel was not overruled by the Appellate Body.

3.88 With regard to Malaysia's cooperation efforts, Malaysia claims that, since 1999, it has participated in discussions with the United States and other Asian countries and has agreed, as stated in the Sabah Declaration of July 1999 as well as in the Perth Resolution of October 1999, to develop an MOU. At the Kuantan conference hosted by Malaysia in July 2000, Malaysia, the United States and 22 other countries adopted a Memorandum of Understanding on the Conservation and Management of Marine Turtles and their Habitats of the Indian Ocean and South-East Asian Region ("MOU") and, in the Final Act, agreed to hold negotiations in 2001 on a Conservation and Management Plan to be appended to this MOU.

3.89 Malaysia refers to the Conservation and Management Plan (CMP) under the MOU, the details of which have yet to be finalized. It is believed that the United States volunteered to prepare a draft of the CMP. This draft is expected to be discussed during the next negotiations scheduled to be held in the first quarter of 2001. Malaysia believes that the Philippines has indicated its interest in hosting this meeting. The CMP is expected to cover, *inter alia*, protection of sea turtles, sale and trade in sea turtles, reducing the threats to sea turtles, research and education, exchange of information, capacity building and harmonization of do-

[84] Appellate Body Report, para. 168.
[85] Appellate Body Report, para. 171.
[86] Panel Report, para. 9.1.

mestic laws on the protection of sea turtles. The two main issues that remain unresolved are funding and the setting up of a Secretariat. Of particular concern is where the Secretariat should be based.

3.90 Malaysia does not agree with the United States that the MOU will not be legally binding even when the Conservation and Management Plan has been adopted. Malaysia states that signatories to the MOU had expressed their willingness to make it legally binding in Clause 4 of the Basic Principles of the MOU, where signatory States expressly demonstrated that they "[w]hen appropriate [...]*will* consider amending this MOU to make it legally binding" (emphasis added). The fact that the signatory States *will* rather than *may* consider making the MOU legally binding is a manifestation of their intention to make it legally binding. This illustrates that there is a real likelihood that the MOU will be made legally binding. It is ironic that the United States makes this assumption when the clause was actually inserted at its request.

3.91 Malaysia notes that the MOU also recognises the importance of *involving all States* in cooperative conservation and management of marine turtles and their habitats. Therefore the continuous unilateral action by the United States in the imposition of the import prohibition and the application of unilaterally determined standards is an act contrary to its obligation to refrain from acts which would defeat the object and purpose of the MOU, as per Article 18 of the Vienna Convention on the Law of Treaties.

3.92 Malaysia also argues that the MOU is attached to the Final Act of the Negotiation meeting to adopt the text of the MOU, signed on 14 July 2000; that it is an international agreement signed by the representatives of several countries, including the United Sates. Article 2 of the Vienna Convention defines a "treaty" as "an international agreement concluded between States in written form and governed by international law, whether embodied in a single instrument or in two or more related instruments." Further, there is also a direct reference to the Convention on Migratory Species and other international instruments in the Final Act and the MOU.

3.93 Malaysia's intentions with respect to the MOU are reflected in the fact that Malaysia is a signatory to the Final Act of the Negotiation Meeting to adopt the text of the MOU in which Clause 4 of the Basic Principles of the MOU states that the signatory States, when appropriate, will consider amending the MOU to make it legally binding.

3.94 It is the view of Malaysia that, even though the MOU will become legally binding only after the Conservation and Management Plan has been finalized and annexed to the MOU in 2001, there is a good faith obligation of the United States to refrain from unilateral acts that would defeat the purpose of this MOU to recognize the right of exporting countries, including Malaysia, to continue its conservation programme for sea turtles. Malaysia's turtle conservation programme has been confirmed as "one of the best conservation programmes for marine turtles anywhere in the world".[87] The unilateral import prohibition of the United States, by ignoring the internationally recognised effectiveness of Malaysia's existing conservation programme for sea turtles and by acting contrary to the declared United States' commitment to finalize the multilateral agreement on the conservation of marine turtles in 2001, continues to constitute "arbitrary or unjustifiable discrimination between countries" as prohibited by Article XX of the GATT 1994.

3.95 In the view of the **United States**, the application of the US measure does not defeat the purpose of the MOU. By its own terms, the objective of the MOU is "to protect, conserve, replenish and recover marine turtles and their habitats, based on the best scientific evidence, taking into account the environmental, socio-economic and cultural characteristics of the signatory States." Section 609 does not in any way undermine this objective. Indeed, Section 609 has the same basic objective as the MOU - to conserve sea turtles. Moreover, since the MOU does not regulate international trade in shrimp and shrimp products, the maintenance of the trade restrictions at issue in this dispute cannot be said to conflict with the provisions of the MOU in any way. The United States recalls that at its request, a clause was added to paragraph 4 of the "Basic Principles" section of the MOU, providing that "[w]hen appropriate, the signatory States will consider amending this Memorandum of Understanding to make it legally binding".

3.96 **Malaysia** submits that its efforts to reach a negotiated solution in relation to the issue of conservation of sea turtles in its region encompass participation in various negotiations and related activities on the conservation of nature, natural resources and environment. In this respect, Malaysia:

(a) Is a party to the ASEAN Agreement on the Conservation of Nature and Natural Resources signed in 1985;

(b) participated in the 1st ASEAN Symposium and Workshop on Sea Turtle Biology and Conservation;

(c) is a party to the ASEAN Memorandum of Understanding on Sea Turtle Conservation and Protection;

(d) is a signatory to the Langkawi Declaration on the Environment, 1989;

(e) participated in bilateral and regional turtle conservation programmes through the ASEAN Working Group for Nature Conservation; and

(f) is a party to the Convention on International Trade and Endangered Species of Wild Fauna and Flora (CITES).

---

[87] Panel Report, Annex IV, Transcript of the Meeting with the Experts held on 21-22 January 1998, para. 69.

3.97 With regard to its multilateral and bilateral negotiations since 1996, Malaysia submits that those include the following:

(a) In 1996, Malaysia launched the Turtle Island Heritage Protected Area in cooperation with the Philippines to develop uniform conservation measures for turtles on the islands;

(b) in the same year Malaysia hosted the first South-East Asian Fisheries Development Centre (SEAFDEC) workshop on marine turtle research and conservation;

(c) Malaysia participated in discussions with the United States and other Asian countries to develop the Indian Ocean and South-East Asian Region Agreement on the Conservation and Management of Marine Turtles and their Habitats as *per* the Sabah Declaration of July 1999 and the Perth Resolution of October 1999;

(d) in July 2000, Malaysia hosted negotiations on an Indian Ocean and South-East Asian Regional Agreement on the Conservation and Management of Marine Turtles and their Habitats, where a Memorandum of Understanding on the Conservation and Management of Marine Turtles and their Habitats of the Indian Ocean and South-East Asian Region was adopted (the Conservation and Management Plan is expected to be finalised soon);

(e) Malaysia agreed to host jointly with Thailand the Regional Millennium Conference on Sustainable Fisheries Development under ASEAN and SEAFDEC, scheduled for November 2001. Topics to be covered are fisheries management, aquaculture, and post harvest and fisheries trade;

(f) in April 2001, Malaysia will hold a national conference on fisheries management and conservation. Among the topics to be covered is conservation of endangered species which includes marine turtles;

(g) Malaysia is in the process of acceding to the Convention on the Conservation of Migratory Species of Wild Animals; and

(h) Malaysia has bilateral and regional turtle conservation programmes through the ASEAN Working Group for Nature Conservation.

3.98 The above elements, Malaysia submits, reflect the efforts of Malaysia to act to conserve and protect sea turtles.

(b) Whether a WTO Member is Obliged to Seek or Obtain International Consensus Before Resorting to the Measure at Issue

3.99 **Malaysia** submits that in order to comply with the Appellate Body's recommendations and rulings, on the expiry of the reasonable time period, the

United States should lift the import prohibition whilst it engages in negotiations for the conservation of marine turtles. As mentioned earlier, the United States participation in the development of an Indian Ocean and South-East Asian Regional Agreement on the Conservation and their Habitats provides concrete evidence that an alternative course of action was reasonably open to the United States for securing the policy goal of its measure rather than imposing an import prohibition.

3.100 When arguing that cooperative efforts to protect and conserve sea turtles must be undertaken the imposition of the import ban, Malaysia submits that the efforts made by the United States, set out in its Status Reports to the DSB[88] cannot be deemed to have prior to any retrospective effect in eliminating the existence of the import prohibition which was present even before the actions taken by the United States.

3.101 In support of its claims, Malaysia recalls the following finding and conclusion in the Original Panel Report:

> "9.1. In our view, and based on the information provided by the experts, the protection of sea turtles throughout their life stages is important and TEDs are one of the recommended means of protection within an integrated conservation strategy. We consider that the best way for the parties to this dispute to contribute effectively to the protection of sea turtles in a manner consistent with WTO objectives, including sustainable development, would be to reach cooperative agreements on integrated conservation strategies, covering, *inter alia*, the design, implementation and use of TEDs while taking into account the specific conditions in the different geographical areas concerned."[89]

3.102 The **United States** claims that Malaysia's argument in the sense that "co-operative efforts to protect and conserve sea turtles must be undertaken prior to the imposition of the import ban", is incorrect for three reasons:

(a) First, the issue in this proceeding is not what steps the United States should have taken during the past decade to ensure comparable treatment between exporting nations, but whether or not the United States has taken appropriate steps to address the aspects of the application of Section 609 that the Appellate Body found inconsistent with the Article XX chapeau. The United States could not travel back in time and conduct negotiations with the complaining countries. Rather, the United States appropriately used the reasonable period of time to engage in serious sea turtle conservation negotiations with Malaysia and the other complaining countries. As a result, by the *end* of the reasonable period of time the United

88 WT/DS58/15 and Add. 1-4.

89 Panel Report, para. 9.1.

States had complied with the recommendations and rulings relating to discrimination in the level of negotiations. Moreover, by the present time - one year after the December 1999 end of the reasonable period of time - even further progress has been made in those negotiations.

(b) Second, if Malaysia is arguing that the Panel must ignore the negotiations conducted during the reasonable period of time because the import restrictions remained in effect, such an argument is inconsistent with the Dispute Settlement Understanding. In particular, Article 21.3 provides that "if it is impracticable to comply immediately with the recommendations and rulings, the Member concerned shall have a reasonable period of time to do so." In this case, the United States and the four complainants agreed on a 13-month reasonable period of time. The United States was within its rights under the DSU to maintain the import restrictions during the reasonable period of time, and the United States complied with its obligations under the DSU by using this period to amend the Revised Guidelines, to offer and provide technical assistance, and to engage in serious, good faith negotiations on sea turtle conservation. Thus, the measure as modified by the end of the reasonable period of time complies with the DSB recommendations and rulings.

(c) Third, nowhere in the Appellate Body Report does the Appellate Body indicate that the United States should lift its import prohibition. In fact, the import prohibition on shrimp harvested in a manner harmful to endangered species of sea turtles is part of the general design and structure of the US measure, which the Appellate Body found to be provisionally justified under Article XX(g). As noted, the Appellate Body instead expressed concerns with respect to the *application* of Section 609, one element of which was the extent of efforts to negotiate with differing countries. By addressing this aspect of the *application* of Section 609, without removing the ban on certain shrimp imports, the United States has directly and fairly complied with the DSB recommendations and rulings.

3.103 The United States also notes that in its third-party submission, the European Communities agrees [with the United States] that it would be unreasonable to interpret the finding of the Appellate Body to require the United States "to travel back in time" and hold negotiations some time in the past.

3.104 As a "corollary" to its submissions on the need for preliminary international consensus, **Malaysia** claims that no unilateral actions to deal with environmental measures may be imposed before any international consensus is reached. This is, according to Malaysia, particularly borne out by the references cited by the Appellate Body to the various international instruments and declarations. In the absence of any mutually agreed international standard to conserve and protect sea turtles, recognition of each country's sovereign right to manage and maintain its own conservation programme for sea turtles should be respected. This is consonant with the principle of national sovereignty which is accorded recognition in several multilateral environmental treaties, in particular, Articles XIII and XIV of the Convention on International Trade and Endangered Species of Wild Fauna and Flora (CITES), Articles 3 and 5 and the Preamble of the Convention on Biological Diversity (CBD), and Article 3 and the Preamble of the United Nations Framework Convention on Climate Change (UNFCCC).[90]

3.105 The **United States** argues that the rule proposed by Malaysia is most definitely not a corollary of any Appellate Body findings. To the contrary, such a rule is flatly inconsistent with the Appellate Body Report and would effectively eviscerate the Article XX(g) exception. In fact, Malaysia presented this very same argument to the Appellate Body, and the Appellate Body declined to adopt it.[91]

3.106 The United States recalls that the Appellate Body found that the general design and structure of Section 609 was provisionally justified under Article XX(g), but that certain aspects of the *application* of Section 609 were inconsistent with the chapeau of Article XX. Part of the general design and structure of Section 609 was for the United States to *initiate* sea turtle conservation negotiations with affected countries. The United States argues that the law, however, does not contemplate the *completion* of such negotiations before the effective date of the selective import prohibition. And, in fact, the import prohibition under Section 609 went into effect before such negotiations were completed with any exporting country. The Appellate Body found no defect with this fundamental aspect of the US measure. The Appellate Body thus approved of a measure that, by its general design and structure, was inconsistent with the purported "corollary" proposed by Malaysia.

3.107 With regard to Malaysia's argument on this particular issue, the United States finds that such a "corollary" in the Appellate Body Report would amount to grave legal error. The United States argues that Malaysia's "corollary" is inconsistent with the Appellate Body's reasoning with respect to negotiations. The unjustifiable discrimination found by the Appellate Body was that the United States' efforts to negotiate with Western Hemisphere nations were more extensive than the negotiations with the complaining, Indian Ocean nations. Since the United States did not complete negotiations with Western Hemisphere nations before imposing the import prohibition, the fact that the United States has similarly not yet completed negotiations with Indian Ocean countries is not an instance of "unjustifiable discrimination." To the contrary, this aspect of Section

[90] Panel Report, para. 3.99.

[91] Panel Report, para. 3.275 (summarizing Malaysia's argument that conservation measures may only be adopted on a cooperative basis); Appellate Body Report, para. 52 (incorporating by reference Malaysia's argument to the Panel on this issue).

609 results in the *same* treatment for both Indian Ocean nations and Western Hemisphere nations.

3.108 The United States also argues that in comparing the length of time it took to negotiate the Inter-American Convention with the time it is taking to negotiate the MOU, one must also keep in mind that the former is a legally binding instrument, while the latter is not. Legally binding instruments almost always take longer time to negotiate and conclude than non-legally binding instruments, if only because the former are subject to higher levels of scrutiny. Governments often tend to take greater care in crafting provisions of legally binding instruments, which must be approved at the highest levels, than they take in crafting provisions of non-legally binding instruments. This heightened degree of care usually translates into longer negotiating periods.

3.109 **Malaysia** submits that the United States has misunderstood the Malaysian submission. The "corollary" that no unilateral actions to deal with environmental measures *may be* imposed before any international consensus is reached is premised on Malaysia's submission that cooperative efforts to protect sea turtles must be undertaken prior to the imposition of the import ban, after an analysis of the Appellate Body's examination of the standard of "unjustifiable discrimination". It is significant to note that the words "may be" have been used and not "shall". The elements of "cooperative efforts", "international mechanisms" and "international consensus" with the objective concluding bilateral or multilateral agreements for the protection and conservation of sea turtles before imposing the import prohibition has been considered vital by the Appellate Body whilst examining the standard of "unjustifiable discrimination." This deduction is made based on the Appellate Body's decision wherein it had acknowledged that the WTO itself and a host of international instruments and declarations essentially state that environmental measures addressing transboundary or global environmental problems should as far as possible be based on an international consensus and unilateral actions to deal with environmental challenges outside the jurisdiction of the importing country should be avoided.[92] Based on the reasoning above, it is not correct for the United States to state that Malaysia seems to step back from this argument. Malaysia submits that the statement that the Appellate Body Report did not exclude the legal justifiability of unilateral import restrictions based on Article XX *if international agreements for the protection of sea turtles cannot be secured*, is consistent with the aforesaid reasoning.

3.110 The **United States** notes that Australia, in its third-party submission, is concerned about the continuation of an import ban based on a unilaterally determined conservation standard to address a transboundary or global environmental issue. Australia presents a legal argument to support its policy concern. The United States submits that this argument, however, is based on an unsupported leap from a description of the Appellate Body findings to the flawed premise that

---

[92] Appellate Body Report, para. 168.

the United States must show that its import ban is now based on "consensual and multilateral procedures". Australia does not cite any Appellate Body finding that environmental measures must be based on "consensual and multilateral procedures," and, in fact, the Appellate Body made no such finding.

3.111 The United States argues that the Appellate Body uses the phrase "consensual and multilateral procedures" only once, in a discussion of the Inter-American Convention on Sea Turtle Conservation. Specifically, the Appellate Body notes that: "[t]he Inter-American Convention demonstrates the conviction of its signatories, including the United States, that *consensual and multilateral procedures* are available and feasible for the establishment of programs for the conservation of sea turtles."[93] From this observation, claims the United States, the Appellate Body does not jump, as Australia does, to the conclusion that all environmental measures must be based on "consensual and multilateral procedures," nor that all countries that participated in similar negotiations would share such convictions. Indeed, such conclusions would be illogical and untenable, since, depending on the positions of the Parties to the negotiation, it may not be possible to reach consensus.

3.112 The United States notes that Australia also makes a related argument that the progress in the ongoing Indian Ocean and South-East Asian regional negotiations proves that the United States has an alternative avenue for addressing its sea turtle conservation concerns. In the opinion of the United States, this argument is based on two flawed premises. First, Australia implies that prior to invoking the Article XX(g) exception, a WTO Member must exhaust all possibilities for achieving its goals in other ways. The WTO Agreement contains no such requirement, and the Appellate Body made no such finding in this regard. In fact, the Appellate Body affirmatively found that the means of the US measure were reasonably related to its ends (i.e., sea turtle conservation).

3.113 Second, continues the United States, the progress made in multilateral negotiations in the Indian Ocean and South-East Asian region will not necessarily translate into the achievement of the environmental goal of the US measure. In other words, the negotiations may, or may not, result in multilaterally-agreed steps that will save sea turtles from extinction. One fact, however, is more certain: if insufficient steps are taken to reduce incidental sea turtle mortality in shrimp trawling operations, sea turtles will be subject to irrevocable and permanent extinction. In short, the fact that the United States has engaged in multilateral negotiations cannot, as Australia suggests, be used as a basis for finding that the United States has not complied with the DSB recommendations and rulings.

3.114 Third, the United States also recalls that the Appellate Body uses this observation to support its finding that the failure of the United States to negotiate seriously with some countries but not with other Members that export shrimp to the United States, resulted in unjustifiable discrimination under the chapeau of

[93] Appellate Body Report, para. 170 (emphasis added by the United States).

Article XX(g). The United States claims that the Appellate Body repeatedly mentions that the issue was whether or not the United States *pursued* negotiations with the appellees; nowhere did the Appellate Body purport to impose a requirement that the parties to such negotiations must reach an agreement. Indeed, such an *a priori* requirement, as the Appellate Body wrote, would render Article XX "*inutile*." If the importing and exporting nation reach agreement on a particular conservation measure, neither WTO Member would likely need recourse to WTO dispute settlement procedures. The Appellate Body Report expressly rejected the creation of such *a priori* tests for the application of Article XX exceptions, and did so in the strongest possible terms:[94]

> "The Panel, in effect, constructed an *a priori* test that purports to define a category of measures which, *ratione materiae*, fall outside the justifying protection of Article XX's chapeau. In the present case, the Panel found that the US measure at stake fell within that class of excluded measures because Section 609 conditions access to the domestic shrimp market of the United States on the adoption by exporting countries of certain conservation policies prescribed by the United States. *It appears to us, however, that conditioning access to a Member's domestic market on whether exporting Members comply with, or adopt, a policy or policies unilaterally prescribed by the importing Member may, to some degree, be a common aspect of measures falling within the scope of one or another of the exceptions (a) to (j) of Article XX.* Paragraphs (a) to (j) comprise measures that are recognized as *exceptions to substantive obligations* established in the GATT 1994, because the domestic policies embodied in such measures have been recognized as important and legitimate in character. It is not necessary to assume that requiring from exporting countries compliance with, or adoption of, certain policies (although covered in principle by one or another of the exceptions) prescribed by the importing country, renders a measure *a priori* incapable of justification under Article XX. *Such an interpretation renders most, if not all, of the specific exceptions of Article XX inutile, a result abhorrent to the principles of interpretation we are bound to apply.*"

3.115 In response to Malaysia's disagreement with the unilateral determinations of the United States under Section 609, the United States explains that neither the Appellate Body Report nor the terms of the Article XX chapeau exclude the possibility that an importing Member may make certain determinations regarding imported goods. The test of the Article XX chapeau is whether a measure is applied in a manner that results in arbitrary or unjustifiable discrimination, not whether determinations are made by a Member itself or in conjunction with other

[94] Appellate Body Report, para. 121 (emphasis added by the United States).

Members. Individual Members have the capacity to act fairly and without discrimination; conversely, multilateral action is no guarantee against discrimination.

3.116 Moreover, the chapeau of Article XX makes clear that any single Member of the WTO may invoke its provision. In that regard, it is worth recalling the precise words of the chapeau of Article XX:

> "Subject to the requirement that such measures are not *applied in a manner* which would constitute a means of arbitrary or unjustifiable discrimination between countries where the same conditions prevail, or a disguised restriction on international trade, nothing in this Agreement shall be construed to prevent the adoption or enforcement ba *any Member* of measures [described in paragraphs (a) through (j)]." (Emphasis added by the United States).

3.117 Finally, the United States explains that the Panel is to examine whether the measure - that is the actions of the United States - is consistent with the chapeau of Article XX. The United States can control, and is responsible, for its actions. Thus, the United States can take steps to meet the requirements of the chapeau by expending *efforts* to negotiate. However, the United States cannot control, and cannot be held responsible, for the actions of its negotiating partners. It would not make sense if the issue of US compliance turned on the actions of other WTO Members, including the complaining parties. This would be the precise result if, as Malaysia suggests, the United States must reach agreement with other parties before applying the measure.

(iii) Other Aspects

(a) Consideration of the Situation of Exporting Countries in the Revised Guidelines

3.118 The **United States** claims that, in order to comply with the recommendations and rulings of the DSB, it introduced modifications to the 1996 Guidelines governing the application of Section 609. For that purpose, on 25 March 1999, the US Department of State published a notice in the US Federal Register that summarized the Appellate Body Report, proposed measures by which the United States would implement the recommendations and rulings of the DSB, and sought comments from any interested parties.[95] On July 8, 1999, the Department of State published a second notice in the US Federal Register that summarized the comments received and set forth the measures that the United States would

[95] Notice of Proposed Revisions to the Guidelines for the Implementation of Section 609 of Public Law 101-162, Relating to the Protection of Sea Turtles in Shrimp Trawl Fishing Operations, US Department of State, Federal Register Vol. 64, No. 57, 25 March 1999, Public Notice 3013, pp. 14481-14485

take to implement the recommendations and rulings of the DSB, taking into account those comments.[96]

3.119 The United States also mentions that the Appellate Body found that the most conspicuous flaw in the application of Section 609 is an apparent requirement that "all other exporting Members [...] adopt essentially the same policy (together with an approved enforcement programme) as that applied to, and enforced on, United States domestic shrimp trawlers."[97]

3.120 The United States claims that it directly addressed this "most conspicuous flaw" through the adoption of Revised Guidelines governing the application of Section 609. Those Revised Guidelines introduce added flexibility in a wide variety of ways. Notably, a country may be certified as having a comparable sea turtle conservation programme even if such country does not adopt a TEDs programme, and that the United States "will take fully into account any demonstrated differences between the shrimp fishing conditions in the United States and those in other nations."[98]

3.121 The United States also recalls that another aspect of the application of Section 609 which contributed to the Appellate Body's finding of unjustifiable discrimination was that "when this dispute was before the Panel and before us, the United States did not permit imports of shrimp harvested by commercial shrimp trawl vessels using TEDs comparable in effectiveness to those required in the United States if those shrimp originated in waters of countries not certified under Section 609."[99] The United States, however, modified this aspect of the application of Section 609 even prior to the release of the Appellate Body Report. Specifically, since August 1998, the United States has permitted the importation of shrimp harvested by TEDs, even if the exporting nation is not certified pursuant to Section 609.

3.122 **Malaysia** submits that an examination of the Revised Guidelines reveals they are still very biased towards meeting the United States' shrimping conditions even in cases where the fishing environment of a harvesting nation does not pose a threat to sea turtles or the harvesting nation adopts a regulatory programme bearing the common feature of "incidental taking of sea turtles *in the course of commercial shrimp trawl harvesting*" (emphasis added by Malaysia). This is evident from the part entitled "Guidelines for Making Certification Decisions."

3.123 Malaysia claims that the United States has failed to address other aspects of the application of the United States' measure which constitutes the unjustifiable discrimination faulted by the Appellate Body. The Appellate Body held that Section 609 is "in effect an economic embargo which requires *all other exporting Members*, if they wish to exercise their GATT rights, to adopt *essentially the*

[96] Revised Guidelines, Annex to this Report.

[97] Appellate Body Report, para. 161.

[98] Revised Guidelines, Annex to this Report: Section II.B.(a)(2).

[99] Appellate Body Report, para. 165.

same policy (together with an approved enforcement programme) as that applied to, and enforced on United States domestic shrimp trawlers."[100] Malaysia claims that this element requiring *"all other exporting Members"* to adopt *"essentially the same"* policy is still present in the Revised Guidelines. In spite of the Revised Guidelines, Section 609 only allows import of shrimp harvested by commercial shrimp trawl vessels using TEDs comparable in effectiveness to those required in the United States.[101] Therefore Malaysia insists that this only allows import of shrimps harvested exclusively by means in accordance with the United States programme.[102]

3.124 Malaysia also claims that by setting out this condition, the United States is subjecting exporting nations to its own unilaterally determined standard as to what constitute "means that do not pose a threat to sea turtles". Therefore, in order to enable its shrimp to enter into the United States, a harvesting nation will have to adopt a means of harvesting shrimps that the United States will consider as not posing "a threat to sea turtles". Hence, the harvesting nations will have to adopt "*essentially the same* policy" as that of the United States if they wish to exercise their GATT rights. This, Malaysia submits, is the "intended and actual coercive effect on the specific policy decisions made by foreign governments" which the Appellate Body has ruled to be the "most conspicuous flaw"[103] of the US measure.

3.125 Malaysia submits that what Malaysia is complaining about is the fact that the Revised Guidelines require harvesting nations to have conservation measures comparable to that of the United States before the product can be exported into the United States. In other words, before it can be brought into the United States, the harvesting nation must have a turtle conservation programme that is comparable to that of the United States. The effect is, sovereign harvesting nations are coerced into adopting sea turtle conservation measures comparable to the one that has been unilaterally determined by the United States.

3.126 Moreover, Malaysia submits that there is no compliance by virtue of the fact that it is Malaysia's sovereign right to monitor its own conservation programme for protection of sea turtles and it is not for the United States to examine the effectiveness of Malaysia's programme *vis-à-vis* its own in the absence of any mutually agreed standards to govern the effectiveness of such a conservation programme. Furthermore, the heavy burden imposed on Malaysia to demonstrate to the United States that it is enforcing a "comparably effective regulatory program" (even though without the use of TEDs) through empirical data supported by objective scientific studies of sufficient duration and scope is "[an] abuse and misuse of an exception of Article XX [as] the detailed operating provisions of the

[100] Appellate Body Report, para. 161.
[101] Revised Guidelines, Annex to this Report: para. 2.
[102] *Ibid.*
[103] Appellate Body Report, para. 161.

measure [the Revised Guidelines] prescribe the arbitrary or unjustifiable activity."[104]

3.127 In response to the question from the Panel concerning a situation where Malaysia would apply for certification to the United States[105], Malaysia contends that it should not be subjected to the application of provisions that have been determined to be flawed. The flaw in these provisions has been maintained in spite of the modifications made to Section 609. Further, Malaysia maintains that no sovereign nation should be subjected to the United States' own unilaterally determined standard on how conservation of sea turtles is to be carried out, the very element that has been faulted by the Appellate Body.

3.128 Since the Original Panel, Malaysia has submitted that it does not have the same shrimp harvesting conditions as those in the United States. The fact that the Revised Guidelines address "incidental taking of sea turtles in the course of commercial *shrimp trawl harvesting*" (emphasis added) completely ignores the fact that other harvesting nations, like Malaysia, do not practise commercial shrimp trawl harvesting like the United States. From the outset, therefore, Malaysia is already at a disadvantage as a result of this fact. Since Malaysia does not practise shrimp trawling, it does not have recourse to the Revised Guidelines as the Guidelines deal only with commercial shrimp trawl harvesting, whereas in Malaysia shrimp is a by-catch from fish trawling activities. Therefore, the incidental capture of sea turtles in Malaysia is due to fish trawling. That is why Malaysia claims that it is clear that Malaysia's programme for turtle conservation would never be comparable to the United States. Malaysia's turtle conservation measures have been found to be one of the best in the world, but it would never be comparable to the United States programme as it is tailored to address the conditions unique and peculiar to Malaysia.

3.129 Malaysia notes the claim of the United States that it has yet to have the opportunity to take into account the peculiar and unique circumstances of Malaysia because Malaysia has not sought certification, hence these unique and peculiar circumstances have not been presented to them. Malaysia submits that it is not for to the United States to unilaterally examine the conditions prevailing in Malaysia, and then make a unilateral decision as to whether Malaysia's pro-

---

[104] Appellate Body Report, para. 160.

[105] The question reads as follows: "Should Malaysia apply for certification to the United States, would there be elements in the Malaysian programme [for sea turtle conservation] [...] which would make it impossible for the United States to certify it? Why?" In response to this question, the United States replies that "there are no elements in the Malaysian program [...] that would make it impossible for the United States to certify Malaysia pursuant to Section 609. As set forth in the implementing guidelines for Section 609 [the Revised Guidelines] [...], the United States would review any documentary evidence that Malaysia may wish to provide to demonstrate that its regulatory program to protect sea turtles in the course of shrimp fishing is comparable to the US program. The fact that Malaysia is choosing to protect sea turtles through means that do not involve the use of TEDs is not a bar to certification, in light of the modifications made to the guidelines in implementation of the DSB recommendations and rulings."

gramme is comparable to the United States' unilaterally determined programme. No sovereign nation should be subjected to such scrutiny. This is also one of the reasons why Malaysia has not chosen to seek certification.

3.130 Clarifying this point in its response to a question from the Panel as to whether there are any turtles caught as incidental by-catch in the course of shrimp trawling, Malaysia responds that in Malaysia, turtles caught as incidental by-catch are only in fish trawling. Malaysia does not practise shrimp trawling. Further, in Malaysia, sea turtle mortality is not due to fishery activities, but is attributed to other causes, for instance pollution. Some incidents of death result from choking due to the consumption by turtles of plastic materials, which have been thrown into the sea, that the turtles mistake for food.

3.131 In short, Malaysia recalls the unilateral imposition by the United States of a ban on imports of certain shrimp and shrimp products from Malaysia, and the unilateral imposition by the United States of a certification system that does not take into account the internationally recognized effectiveness of Malaysia's conservation programme for marine turtles without the use of TEDs, nor the particular circumstances that prevail in Malaysia. Malaysia claims that this results in continued "unjustifiable discrimination between countries" prohibited by the chapeau of Article XX.

3.132 In the view of the **United States**, Malaysia argues that the Revised Guidelines are not more flexible because they still require "comparability" with the United States' TEDs programme. This argument, however, reflects a fundamental misreading of the Appellate Body Report. Section 609, as part of its essential structure noted by the Appellate Body, requires a comparison between the programmes of the United States and those of other countries. The Appellate Body, claims the United States, found that this aspect of Section 609 was reasonably related to sea turtle conservation and provisionally within the scope of Article XX(g). The flaw found by the Appellate Body was that the US Guidelines appeared to require exporting nations to adopt a *specific* policy to achieve a particular take rate of sea turtles in shrimp fisheries. And this flaw has been explicitly addressed in the Revised Guidelines. The Revised Guidelines are very clear that countries seeking certification may select any policy, so long as the result is comparable to the US programme in terms of sea turtle conservation.

3.133 To explain the particularities of the Revised Guidelines and its compliance with the recommendations and ruling of the DSB, the United States, in its answer to a question [106]by the Panel, highlights the manner in which the Revised Guidelines are applied and how the different policies are compared, granting enough flexibility to the applicants.

[106] The text of the question reads: "Could the United States describe the methodology used to assess the comparability of foreign regulatory programmes with the US programme? For instance, could the United States provide the Panel with materials describing how this assessment was made in the cases of Australia and Pakistan?"

3.134 The United States explains that with respect to any country that expresses interest in this matter (i.e. applies for certification), the Department of State solicits any information that a country may have to indicate it has adopted a regulatory programme for the protection of sea turtles in its commercial shrimp fisheries comparable to the US programme. The Department of State closely reviews such information in consultation with the United States National Marine Fisheries Service (NMFS) in light of the provisions of Section 609 and the attendant Revised Guidelines

3.135 The United States claims that it not only considers the regulatory programme for the conservation of sea turtles; it also takes into consideration all other available information about the fishing environment and sea turtle populations of the country, as provided by the country in question, and as may be produced by other reputable sources, including established scientific, fishery, industrial and environmental organizations.

3.136 The United States clarifies that officials of the Department of State and NMFS also travel to the country in question to engage in a face-to-face dialogue with its governmental counterparts. The purpose of these visits is to discuss the regulatory programme of the country, answer questions about its comparison to the US programme, and to review aspects of the former programme in practice. For example, if a country's programme requires the use of TEDs, US officials work with foreign officials to review the design and installation of those TEDs, as well as the efforts made to ensure at least adequate enforcement. The visits almost always include the provision of hands-on technical assistance with fishermen and fisheries managers.

3.137 The United States gives two particular examples of countries whose shrimp and shrimp products are exported to the United States after having applied for certification since the adoption of the Revised Guidelines: Australia and Pakistan. With regard to Australia, the United States mentions that Australia has not sought certification pursuant to Section 609, but has rather sought to export shrimp harvested in two areas of Australia (the Spencer Gulf and the Northern Prawn Fisheries), on grounds that the harvesting of those shrimp does not harm endangered sea turtles. In the case of the Spencer Gulf, Australia provided comprehensive information indicating that there was virtually no interaction between sea turtles and shrimp fisheries in that cold-water area. Following careful review of that information by the Department of State and NMFS, the United States readily agreed to permit the importation of shrimp from the Spencer Gulf. Similarly, Australia sought to export shrimp from its Northern Prawn Fishery following its imposition of a mandatory use of TEDs in that area. The Department of State and the NMFS reviewed information provided by Australia demonstrating that the TEDs were comparable to those required for use in the United States. United States' officials from these agencies also visited the shrimp fishing grounds in the Northern Prawn Fishery and engaged in a cordial and informative exchange of information with their Australian counterparts. As a result of these undertakings, the United States agreed to permit the importation of this shrimp as well. Australia in its third-party submission acknowledges that the United States has made changes in the application of its measure. In particular, Australia confirms that under the Revised Guidelines, the United States now permits imports from Australia's Spencer Gulf region and Northern Prawn Fishery.

3.138 Pakistan, in contrast, explains the United States, sought to be certified pursuant to Section 609 on the grounds that it had implemented a comprehensive programme that was comparable to the US programme. The process followed by the United States to review this request was nevertheless similar to the process followed in reviewing the Australian requests. The Department of State and NMFS reviewed information provided by Pakistan, which showed that, in one of its two coastal provinces it had banned trawl fishing outright, while in the other it had begun requiring TEDs. Following a visit by US officials to Pakistan and further exchanges of information, the Department of State certified that Pakistan had indeed adopted a programme that was comparable to the US programme.

3.139 Furthermore, the United States' answer to the complementary question of the Panel on the description of the precise criteria used in the comparison of the regulatory programmes provides a clear and better comprehension of the passages from the Revised Guidelines that set forth the criteria for certification on the basis of having a comparable regulatory programme.[107]

3.140 The United States, when referring to the precise criteria used in comparing a foreign regulatory programme based on TEDs usage, explains that if the government of the harvesting nation seeks certification on the basis of having adopted a TEDs programme, certification shall be made if a programme includes the following:

(a) Required use of TEDs - a requirement that all commercial shrimp trawl vessels operating in waters in which there is a likelihood of intercepting sea turtles use TEDs at all times. TEDs must be comparable in effectiveness to those used in the United States. Any exceptions to this requirement must be comparable to those of the US programme described above; and

(b) Enforcement - a credible enforcement effort that includes monitoring for compliance and appropriate sanctions.

3.141 The United States adds that a country may also be certified on the basis of having a regulatory programme not involving the use of TEDs. If the government of a harvesting nation demonstrates that it has implemented and is enforcing a comparably effective regulatory programme to protect sea turtles in the course of shrimp trawl fishing without the use of TEDs, that nation will also be eligible for certification. Such a demonstration, explains the United States, would need to be based on empirical data supported by objective scientific studies of sufficient duration and scope to provide the information for a reliable determination. In

[107] The question reads as follows: "[...] can [the United States] give a clear description of the precise criteria used in the comparison of regulatory programmes of the applicant countries with the United States programme?"

reviewing any such information, the Department of State will take fully into account any demonstrated differences between the shrimp fishing conditions in the United States and those in other nations, as well as information available from other sources.

3.142 In addition, explains the United States, countries may also seek to be certified on the basis of having a shrimp fishing environment that does not pose a threat of incidental taking of sea turtles. The Revised Guidelines provide that the Department of State shall certify any harvesting nation on this basis that meets any of the following precise criteria:

(a) Any harvesting nation without any of the relevant species of sea turtles occurring in waters subject to its jurisdiction;

(b) any harvesting nation that harvests shrimp exclusively by means that do not pose a threat to sea turtles; e.g., any nation that harvests shrimp exclusively by artisanal means; or

(c) any nation whose commercial shrimp trawling operations take place exclusively in waters subject to its jurisdiction in which sea turtles do not occur.

3.143 The United States also refers to the particular situation of uncertified countries that may also export shrimp to the United States if such shrimp is harvested in a manner that does not pose a threat to sea turtles. According to the Revised Guidelines, the import prohibitions imposed pursuant to Section 609 do not apply to shrimp or products of shrimp harvested under the following conditions, since such harvesting does not adversely affect sea turtles:

(a) Shrimp harvested in an aquaculture facility in which the shrimp spend at least 30 days in pond prior to being harvested.

(b) Shrimp harvested by commercial shrimp trawl vessels using TEDs comparable in effectiveness to those required in the United States.

(c) Shrimp harvested exclusively by means that do not involve the retrieval of fishing nets by mechanical devices, such as winches, pulleys, power blocks or other devices providing mechanical advantage, or by vessels using gear that, in accordance with the US programme described above, would not require TEDs.

(d) Shrimp harvested by any other means or under any other circumstances that the Department of State may determine, following consultation with the NMFS, does not pose a threat of the incidental taking of sea turtles. The Department of State shall publish any such determinations in the Federal Register and shall notify affected foreign governments and other interested parties directly.

3.144 The United States also mentions that in accordance with the current policy, shrimp harvested in the northern shrimp fishery in Brazil, where the Government of Brazil is enforcing a requirement to use TEDs, is being imported into the United States, even though Brazil does not qualify for certification due to the lack of TEDs use in the southern Brazilian fishery.

3.145 Finally, the United States argues that with regard to Malaysia's concerns with the implications of the US measure for Malaysian sovereignty, such issues of sovereignty were fully discussed during the Original Panel proceeding. At that time, the United States pointed out that the US measure did not affect Malaysia's sovereignty - the United States could not force any nation to adopt any particular environmental policy. In contrast, claims the United States, control of a nation's borders is a fundamental aspect of sovereignty, and the US measure is simply an application of its sovereign right to exclude certain products from importation. Whether or not the United States, in acceding to the WTO Agreement, agreed to refrain from such actions is the subject of this dispute. And, in any event, the Appellate Body Report addresses and resolves these issues. The Appellate Body found that the United States has a jurisdictional nexus with respect to the sea turtles found in the complainants' waters, and the Appellate Body found that the general design and structure of Section 609 falls within the scope of Article XX(g).

(b) The Ruling of the United States Court of International Trade

3.146 **Malaysia** submits that since the United States Court of International Trade ("CIT") in the case of *Turtle Island Restoration Network and Anor. v. Robert L. Mallett, Acting Secretary of Commerce and Anor. and National Fisheries Institute Inc.* ruled that the United States Administration is ordered immediately from relying on the part of the Revised Guidelines which violates Section 609, it would appear that the relevant part of the revision made to the Revised Guidelines is null and void since the Revised Guidelines are *ultra vires* Public Law 101-162, in particular Section 609. Since a part of the Revised Guidelines which the United States seeks to rely upon as an element of its implementation process is being rendered a nullity *vis-à-vis* its parent legislation, Malaysia submits that there is therefore no compliance of the recommendation and rulings of the DSB by the United States.

3.147 Malaysia argues that the CIT held that the United States Administration determination(s) to grant United States entry to shrimp or products from shrimp which have been harvested with trawls equipped with US-comparable TEDs in waters of nations not duly certified by the President to the US Congress pursuant to Section 609 (on a shipment-by-shipment basis) violate that statute on its face.[108] On page 44 of its judgement, the CIT also held that the United States Administration "[defendants] be enjoined immediately from relying on that part of their guidelines which is violative of Section 609 on its face […]".

3.148 Malaysia claims that according to Article 27 of the Vienna Convention on the Law of Treaties, "A party may not invoke the provisions of its internal law as

---

108 *Turtle Island Restoration Network, v. Robert Mallett,* 110 Fed. Supp. 2d 1005 (CIT 2000).

justification of its failure to perform a treaty". This was also the legal position adopted by the Appellate Body when it opined that "the United States bears responsibility for acts of all its departments of government, including its judiciary"[109]. On this score Malaysia submits that the United States bears responsibility for the CIT decision. Neither can the United States excuse itself that just because the CIT did not restrain it by the non-issuance of an injunctive relief, it is in a position to maintain its current policy. Malaysia submits that pending the outcome of the appeal the CIT decision stands.

3.149 The **United States** notes that the Appellate Body explained that another aspect of the application of Section 609 which contributed to the finding of unjustifiable discrimination was that "when this dispute was before the Panel and before us" - that is, the Appellate Body - "the United States did not permit imports of shrimp harvested by commercial shrimp trawl vessels using TEDs comparable in effectiveness to those required in the United States if those shrimp originated in waters of countries not certified under Section 609." The United States, however, modified this aspect of the application of Section 609 even prior to the release of the Appellate Body Report. Specifically, since August 1998, the United States has permitted the importation of shrimp harvested by TEDs, even if the exporting nation is not certified pursuant to Section 609.

3.150 With regard to the Malaysian submission referring to the judgement of the CIT, the United States claims that Malaysia's argument, however, is incorrect, and is based on a misunderstanding of the ruling. The CIT did find, as Malaysia notes, that in its view Section 609 did not allow the importation from non-certified nations of shrimp harvested by TEDs. The court did not, however, order the US Department of State to change its current policy. The US Executive Branch does not agree with the court's interpretation, and the issue is currently under review by an appellate court. This appellate process will take considerable time to reach any conclusion. In the meantime, the United States plans to maintain its current policy. Thus, the ongoing legal proceedings have not resulted in any change in the US measure which is at issue and within the Panel's terms of reference. In short, the United States permits the importation of shrimp harvested by TEDs, even if the exporting nation is not certified pursuant to Section 609, in accordance with the recommendations and rulings of the DSB.

3.151 The United States mentions that it does not expect a decision in that case for at least eight months or more, as the parties are still in the process of exchanging written briefs. In addition, there is always the possibility that the dates for submitting briefs may be extended. After the parties have completed exchanging written briefs, the court must set a date for oral arguments. Usually the court sets an oral argument date at least three months ahead of time. Its best estimate is that a date for the oral hearing would be set at the end of June or early July 2001, at the earliest. Following the oral hearing, the court may issue its decision. The

109 Appellate Body Report, para. 173.

court is not required by law to issue its decision by any particular date. Normally decisions are issued within three to nine months after argument, but it could be longer. Furthermore, there remains the possibility of another round of review within the court of appeals itself (i.e. either party may request a review by all of the judges on the court of appeals rather than a review by a subgroup of judges). In addition, notes the United States, there remains the possibility that the case could be appealed to the US Supreme Court. As a result, it may take considerable time before the *Turtle Island Restoration Network* case finishes working its way through the US judicial system.

3.152 With regard to the possible outcome of the appeal, the United States is of the opinion that the outcome of this litigation will likely be one of two possibilities. First, the Court of Appeals could reverse the decision by the CIT that the determination of the Department of State to permit the importation of TED-caught shrimp from countries not certified pursuant to Section 609 violates that law. If this were the case, the United States would be able to continue to import TED-caught shrimp from uncertified nations, as long as the shipments were accompanied by the appropriate customs documentation.

3.153 The second possible outcome, explains the United States, would be for the US Court of Appeals to affirm the lower court's decision, in which case the Court of Appeals probably also would enforce the prohibition against importing any shrimp or shrimp products from non-certified countries. Such a prohibition might not be enforced until after all appellate options had been exhausted. Such options would include consideration of whether to request review by the US Supreme Court.

3.154 The United States considers that the Court of Appeals may render any number of other decisions that it cannot predict at this point. But these two outcomes are the most likely at this time.

3.155 The United States also argues that it is also worth noting that it was precisely this aspect of the US measure upon which the Panel Report was based. In particular, this Panel reasoned that the country-wide application of the import prohibition, including with respect to TED-caught shrimp, raised the possibility that exporting nations might be subject to inconsistent requirements, resulting in a threat to the multilateral trading system. Since the US import prohibition no longer applies to TED-caught shrimp, the reason why this Panel originally found the US measure outside the scope of Article XX would no longer apply.

3.156 Finally, the United States argues that the Mexican submission notes Mexico's view that a definitive court ruling regarding TED-harvested shrimp imported from non-certified countries would be a "serious setback" to US implementation. However, the US measure at issue in this proceeding does allow the importation of TED-caught shrimp from non-certified countries. In any proceeding, it would be possible for one or more parties to speculate on future changes in the measure at issue. However, such hypothetical scenarios are not before the Panel. Rather, the issue here is whether the US measure currently in effect is consistent with the obligations of the United States under the WTO Agreement.

(c) Technical Assistance

3.157 The **United States** mentions that the Appellate Body also found that differences in levels of available technical assistance contributed to its finding of unjustifiable discrimination, because far greater efforts to transfer TEDs technology successfully were made to certain exporting countries than to others. The United States provided less technical assistance to those nations that first became affected by the law at the end of 1995 as a result of the decision of the US Court of International Trade.

3.158 The United States argues that it has reiterated many times its offer of technical assistance and training in the design, construction, installation and operation of TEDs to any government that requests it. The United States has made clear that any government wanting to receive such training need only make a formal request to the United States.

3.159 The United States also submits that it has provided such assistance and training to a number of governments and other organizations in the Indian Ocean and South-East Asian region since the DSB adopted the Appellate Body Report in this matter. For example, in July 1999, the US National Marine Fisheries Service (NMFS) presented a paper on TEDs and technology transfer at the sea turtle symposium in Sabah, Malaysia, discussed above. In September 1999, NMFS officials travelled to Bahrain to assist that government in the development of its TEDs programme. In July 2000, the NMFS hosted a visit to the United States by the Bahrain Director of Fisheries for discussions on TEDs and other fishery management subjects. The NMFS also conducted a TEDs workshop in Karachi, Pakistan in January 2000, focusing on evaluation and training issues. The United States believes that this workshop assisted the Government of Pakistan in its adoption of a successful TEDs programme. The NMFS conducted similar training in three places in Australia in July 2000 (Karumba, Cairns and Darwin) relating to the Australian Northern Prawn Fishery. In April 2000, the NMFS hosted a training seminar relating to TEDs for technical experts from the South-East Asian Fisheries Development Center.

3.160 The United States recalls that one of the complaining countries, Pakistan, accepted this offer, and Pakistan now has been certified under Section 609. The United States claims that Malaysia does not contest that the United States has made such good faith offers of technical assistance, nor the fact that Malaysia has not availed itself of such assistance.

3.161 **Malaysia** submits that the offer of technical assistance to the complaining parties, including Malaysia, does not eliminate the unjustifiable discrimination because it is not incumbent on Malaysia to use TEDs as a means of conserving turtles, in the absence of any multilaterally agreed standard on the use of TEDs and besides TEDs is not the sole measure to protect sea turtles. Furthermore Malaysia claims that it has been reported to have one of the best conservation programmes for marine turtles anywhere in the world and this programme has been maintained without the need to use TEDs.

3.162 Thus, with respect to the claim of the United States of its offer of technical training in the design, construction, installation and operation of TEDs to any government that requests it, Malaysia submits that it is of no consequence to Malaysia because, as in the words of Dr. Eckert, one of the scientific experts called by the Panel:[110] "[Malaysia] has one of the best conservation programmes for marine turtles anywhere in the world. They have really taken hold of the situation relative to the conservation of their nesting stocks, and done very, very well. It's been a very admirable effort".[111] The conservation programmes in Malaysia have been sustained at such a remarkable level even without resorting to the use of TEDs.[112] Nevertheless, Malaysia argues, its turtle conservation measures would never be comparable to the United States' programme as they are tailored to address the conditions unique and peculiar to Malaysia. Although the United States claims that it has yet to have the opportunity to take into account the peculiar and unique circumstances because Malaysia has not sought certification, Malaysia submits that it is not for the United States to unilaterally examine the conditions prevailing in Malaysia, and then make a unilateral decision on whether Malaysia's programme is comparable to the United States' unilaterally determined programme. No sovereign nation should be subjected to such scrutiny. This is also one of the reasons why Malaysia has chosen not to seek certification.

3.163 The **United States** claims that Malaysia's only comment on the offers of technical assistance by the United States is that Malaysia needs no such assistance because it has already established certain sea turtle conservation programmes. However, the programmes to which Malaysia refers relate to the protection of sea turtle eggs, while the US conservation measure is aimed at reducing the mortality of juvenile and adult sea turtles in shrimp trawling operations. The expert quoted by Malaysia, Dr. Scott Eckert, was very clear in stating that programmes to protect sea turtle eggs are not sufficient to conserve sea turtles. The United States notes that Dr. Eckert stated that "there are quite a few different possible threats faced by sea turtle populations but the most significant ones are the incidental take of sea turtles by fishing industries" and that "I do not believe that it is possible to mitigate incidental take in fisheries if that is your problem by simply trying to enhance production on a nesting beach. The data we have so far to date suggests that this is simply not a valid mitigation measure. You must take a multifaceted approach to all of your conservation."[113]

3.164 **Malaysia** further submits that evidence accepted by the Original Panel shows that the threats faced by sea turtles in Malaysia are different from those in the United States. As such, Malaysia addresses the situation differently. The ex-

[110] Panel Report, Annex IV, Transcript of the Meeting with the Experts held on 21-22 January 1998.

[111] *Ibid*, para. 69 of Annex IV.

[112] Panel Report, para. 3.7.

[113] Panel Report, Annex IV, Transcript of the Meeting with the Experts held on 21-22 January 1998, paras. 12-13.

tinction of sea turtles is not solely due to incidental take. In Malaysia, commercial exploitation of turtle eggs is a major problem; hence Malaysia's emphasis on the protection of turtle eggs as a conservation strategy. Malaysia notes that there is no evidence that the use of TEDs is the only way to address incidental take. Thus, insisting on the use of TEDs when the situation does not warrant it shows the inflexibility of the US measure. Malaysia also reiterates its stand that the Panel should not dwell on facts that were accepted in the Original Panel deliberations.[114] At this stage, the focus is on whether the United States has complied with the recommendations and rulings of the DSB. Malaysia's turtle conservation programme has been found to be one of the best in the world. However, Malaysia has been compelled to prove to the United States that its turtle conservation programme is comparable to that of the United States in order to be certified, so that its shrimp could gain entry into the United States. This has served to amplify the non-compliance of the United States with the DSB rulings and recommendations.

(d) Phase-in Period

3.165 **Malaysia** argues that the unilateral import prohibition of the United States, by ignoring the internationally recognized effectiveness of Malaysia's existing conservation programme for sea turtles and by acting contrary to the declared commitment of the United States to finalize the multilateral agreement on the conservation of marine turtles in 2001, continues to constitute arbitrary and unjustifiable discrimination between countries as prohibited by Article XX of the GATT 1994. This discrimination, continues Malaysia, also becomes evident when one compares the more than five years of US negotiations, in the early 1990s, for the Inter-American Convention for the Protection and Conservation of Sea Turtles of 1996, with a corresponding Indian Ocean and South-East Asian Regional Agreement on the Conservation and Management of Marine Turtles and their Habitats.

3.166 The **United States**, in response to Malaysia's claim and Australia's comment, in its third-party submission, argues that the difference in phase-in periods has been corrected by the passage of time. The Appellate Body noted that Western Hemisphere countries had a three-year phase-in period before the import prohibition went into effect, while other nations - due to a domestic court ruling - only had a four-month period. By this point, however, Malaysia has had more than sufficient time to adopt a TEDs or comparable conservation programme. The United States argues that the Appellate Body started counting the phase-in period from December 1995, when the domestic court first ruled on the geographic scope of the measure. The reasonable period of time ended in December 1999 - four years after the domestic court ruling. And, by this time, more than five years have elapsed.

---

[114] Panel Report, para. 3.73.

3.167 It is the view of the United States that these periods provide more than sufficient time for Malaysia to have adopted a TEDs or comparable programme, had it chosen to do so. For example, Thailand adopted a TEDs programme, and was certified by the US Department of State, in less than one year after the December 1995 domestic court ruling. Similarly, Pakistan made use of the Revised Guidelines adopted during the reasonable period of time, as well as the enhanced US offers of technical assistance, and has now also been certified.

3.168 Finally, the United States argues that since Malaysia has indicated no intention of adopting TEDs or other comparable measures to reduce sea turtle mortality in shrimp trawling operations, this is a non-issue.

(c) Arbitrary Discrimination

(a) Lack of Flexibility

3.169 The **United States** claims that it has addressed the two distinct aspects of the US application of Section 609 that the Appellate Body found constituted "arbitrary discrimination" between countries where the same conditions prevail. The United States recalls that the Appellate Body found:

(a) That the lack of flexibility in applying the guidelines not only contributed to a finding of "unjustifiable discrimination", but also resulted in "arbitrary discrimination" under the Article XX chapeau. The Revised Guidelines responded to this finding by increasing the flexibility in its application; and

(b) that the US certification process lacked transparency and due process protections for exporting WTO Members. The Revised Guidelines responded to these findings by providing extensive new procedures to ensure that every exporting country was fairly treated in the certification process.

3.170 The United States claims that, as explained above, the Revised Guidelines introduce added flexibility in a wide variety of ways. Notably, a country may be certified as having a comparable sea turtle conservation programme even if such country does not adopt a TEDs programme, and that the United States "will take fully into account any demonstrated differences between the shrimp fishing conditions in the United States and those in other nations."[115]

3.171 **Malaysia** submits and recalls that the flexibility in considering the comparability of foreign programmes and the United States' programme, the increased transparency and predictability of the certification process, and greater degree of due process alleged to be provided through the Revised Guidelines have not eliminated the elements of unjustifiable and arbitrary discrimination, which continue to persist and which are prohibited by Article XX of the GATT 1994. Ma-

[115] Revised Guidelines, Annex to this Report: Section II.B.(a)(2).

laysia considers that the alleged flexibility, as claimed by the United States, that takes fully into account any demonstrated differences between the shrimp fishing conditions in the United States and in other nations is negated if one examines how the Revised Guidelines are structured; an examination of the Revised Guidelines reveals they are still very biased towards meeting the shrimp trawling conditions in the United States. Malaysia observes that throughout the part of the Revised Guidelines entitled "II. Guidelines for Making Certification Decisions", the slant adopted by the United States is geared towards the scenario where the harvesting nation adopts a regulatory programme that addresses the incidental taking of sea turtles in the course of commercial shrimp trawl harvesting.

3.172 Malaysia also submits that by limiting importation only to shrimp that meet the unilaterally determined conditions, the United States has failed to remove the "rigidity and inflexibility" that the Appellate Body held to constitute "arbitrary discrimination". The certification process subjects shrimp exporting nations to the sole discretion of the United States, which is the sole determinant of whether the exported shrimps meet the unilaterally determined standards set by the US Department of State.

3.173 Malaysia submits that, even though the US Department of State now takes into consideration any evidence that an exporting nation may present, the programme to protect sea turtles in the course of shrimp trawl fishing practised by that exporting nation still has to be "comparable to the United States' program". The actual coercive effect on the specific policy decisions made by foreign governments is still maintained in spite of the Revised Guidelines. Member countries are still subjected to the discretion of the US Department of State which can refuse certification if it finds that the turtle protection programme is not comparable to that of United States. The United States' failure to remove this "coercive effect" amounts to blatant non-compliance of the recommendations and rulings of the DSB.

3.174 Malaysia argues that from an examination of the Revised Guidelines, it is clear that the United States has no intention of removing the "unilateral character" of Section 609. Clearly the United States still intends to maintain an economic embargo that enforces the unilaterally determined environmental standard. Failure of the United States to remove the "unilateral character" embedded in Section 609 is a clear manifestation of the United States' intention to maintain the disruptive and discriminatory influence of the import prohibition. In doing so, the United States fails to comply with recommendations and rulings of the DSB.

3.175 Furthermore, Malaysia claims that it has demonstrated that the same conditions do not prevail in Malaysia and that the United States has not considered those unique and peculiar conditions. Malaysia also submits that the following characterization made by Malaysia was accepted by the Panel and that the Appellate Body did not overrule it:

(a) Malaysia was a nesting ground but was not known to be a feeding ground for sea turtles;

(b) the nesting season in Malaysia did not overlap with the shrimp season;

(c) the loggerhead and Kemp's ridley sea turtles rarely nested on Malaysian beaches and did not occur in Malaysian waters respectively and the high mortality of sea turtles reported in shrimp trawls in the United States relate to both these sea turtles;

(d) the green turtle, hawksbill, leatherback and olive ridley were the major sea turtle species in Malaysia. Green turtles were resident in sea grass beds which were found in shallow coastal waters whilst hawksbills were found in coral reef; trawling was prohibited in these areas. During the nesting season, green turtles remained close to shore, in areas where trawling was also prohibited;

(e) during long-distance migrations between feeding and nesting grounds, turtles were actively swimming close to the surface of the water, which made them more vulnerable to the driftnets and longlines rather than trawlnets; and

(f) in Malaysia trawling targeted fish for most of the year and thus the incidental capture of sea turtles was due to fish trawls and not shrimp trawls.[116]

3.176 Malaysia considers that the Revised Guidelines are "saddled with detailed operating provisions"; Malaysia therefore submits that the heavy burden imposed on Malaysia to demonstrate to the United States that it is enforcing a comparably effective regulatory programme through empirical data supported by objective scientific studies of sufficient duration and scope is an abuse and misuse of an exception of Article XX.

3.177 The **United States** argues that it has not yet had the opportunity to take such circumstances into account since Malaysia has never sought to be certified under Section 609.

3.178 As stated above, the United States argues that Section 609, as part of its essential structure noted by the Appellate Body, requires a comparison between the programmes of the United States and those of other countries and recalls that the Appellate Body found that this aspect of Section 609 *was* reasonably related to sea turtle conservation and provisionally within the scope of Article XX(g). The flaw found by the Appellate Body was that the Revised Guidelines appeared to require exporting nations to adopt a *specific* policy to achieve a particular take rate of sea turtles in shrimp fisheries, a matter addressed in the Revised Guidelines and its current application.

---

[116] Panel Report, paras. 3.273 and 3.287.

(b) Due Process

3.179 The **United States** recalls that another finding of the Appellate Body was that the certification process under Section 609 was neither transparent nor predictable and denied to exporting nations basic fairness and due process. There was no formal opportunity for an applicant nation to be heard or to respond to arguments against it. There was no formal written, reasoned decision. Except for notice in the US Federal Register, nations were not notified of decisions specifically. There was no procedure for review of, or appeal from, a denial of certification.

3.180 In response to this finding, the United States explains that it has instituted a broad range of procedural changes in the manner in which it makes certification decisions under Section 609. The process is now transparent and predictable. For example, the Department of State now notifies governments of shrimp harvesting nations on a timely basis of all pending and final decisions and provides them with a meaningful opportunity to be heard and to present any additional information relevant to the certification decision. The Department of State also gives the governments of harvesting nations that are not certified a full explanation of the reasons why the certification was denied and clearly identifies steps that such governments may take to receive a certification in the future.[117]

3.181 The United States claims that many procedures have been established to ensure that the certification determinations will be both more predictable and transparent. The section of the Revised Guidelines entitled "Timetable and Procedures for Certification Decisions" provides, *inter alia*, for the considerable information exchange that is intended to allow the foreign government to predict the likely result.

3.182 The United States explains that the Revised Guidelines, as stated in Public Notice 3086[118], stipulate that:

> "By March 15, the Department of State will notify in writing through diplomatic channels the government of each nation that, on the basis of available information [...], does not appear to qualify for certification. Such notification will explain the reasons for this preliminary assessment, suggest steps that the government of the harvesting nation can take in order to receive a certification and invite the government of the harvesting nation to provide, by April 15, any further information. If the government of the harvesting nation so requests, the Department of State will schedule face-to-face meetings between relevant US officials and officials of the harvesting nation to discuss the situation."

[117] Revised Guidelines, Annex to this Report: para. 27.
[118] *Ibid.*

3.183 Furthermore, according to the Revised Guidelines, between 15 March and 1 May, the Department of State will actively consider any additional information that the government of the harvesting nation believes should be considered by the Department in making its determination concerning certification.

3.184 The United States argues that when applying the Revised Guidelines, the Department of State makes formal decisions on certification by 1 May of each year and, moreover, the governments of all nations that have requested certification are notified in writing of the decision promptly through diplomatic channels.

3.185 The United States explains that according to the Revised Guidelines, in the case of those nations for which certification is denied, such notifications will again state the reasons for such denial as well as the necessary steps to receive a certification in the future.

3.186 Finally, the Revised Guidelines establish that the government of any nation that is denied a certification by 1 May may, at any time thereafter, request reconsideration of that decision.

3.187 Another important improvement of the Revised Guidelines, explains the United States, is that when the United States receives information from that government demonstrating that the circumstances that led to the denial of the certification have been corrected, US officials will visit the exporting nation as early as a visit can be arranged. If the visit demonstrates that the circumstances that led to the denial have indeed been corrected, the United States will certify that nation immediately thereafter.

3.188 With regard to a question of the Panel about whether and under which conditions the administrative decisions taken in the certification process under Section 609 could be appealed before a domestic court in the United States by an exporting member [119], the United States responds that administrative regulations often do not expressly address whether judicial appeal is possible. As a general matter, judicial review of a final decision by the US State Department regarding certification of a country may be had in the US court system pursuant to the Administrative Procedure Act, (5 USC. 701 *et. seq.).*

3.189 **Malaysia** submits that it had chosen not to make use of the Revised Guidelines and technical assistance offered because it considers that in order to comply with the DSB recommendations and rulings, the import prohibition contained in Section 609 should be removed instead of being modified in the way that it has been.

[119] The question reads: "The Revised Guidelines do not expressly provide for judicial appeal. Could the United States specify whether and under which conditions the administrative decisions taken in the certification process under Section 609 could be appealed before a domestic court in the United States by an exporting member?"

(d) Disguised Restriction on International Trade

3.190 The **United States,** argues that the parties fully briefed the issue of "disguised restriction on international trade" in the Original Panel proceeding. The United States recalls its main arguments to demonstrate that its measure is not a disguised restriction on international trade are mentioned in the Panel Report.[120]

3.191 The United States points out that a number of factors showed that the United States measure was a *bona fide* conservation measure, not a disguised trade restriction. Those factors include the facts that: (1) the international community, as reflected in CITES, agrees that sea turtles are endangered; (2) TEDs have been adopted by dozens of countries worldwide as an important sea turtle conservation measure; (3) the United States has made extensive efforts to disseminate TED technology; and (4) the import prohibition is narrowly crafted to affect only shrimp harvested in manners harmful to sea turtles.

3.192 Moreover, continues the United States, although this issue was not directly addressed by the Appellate Body, several Appellate Body findings support the United States position that the measure is not a disguised restriction on international trade. The Appellate Body acknowledged that TEDs are an effective tool for sea turtle conservation.[121] The Appellate Body affirmatively found that the measure, which exempts types of shrimp harvested in manners not harmful to sea turtles, "is not disproportionately wide in scope and reach in relation" to its policy objective.[122] And, it found that, as between domestic and foreign shrimpers, the measure in principle was "even-handed."[123]

3.193 In short, concludes the United States, the record plainly shows that the US measure is not a disguised restriction on international trade. Neither Malaysia in its submissions, nor, indeed, Mexico in its third-party submission, has presented any evidence or arguments to the contrary.

3.194 **Malaysia** is of the view that the issue of the US measure being a disguised restriction on international trade under the Article XX chapeau was not dealt with by the Appellate Body. Malaysia mentions that upon deciding that the measure was not entitled to the justifying protection of Article XX of GATT 1994, the Appellate Body did not even consider it necessary to examine whether the measure was applied in a manner that constitutes a disguised restriction on international trade. The issue was not even considered, let alone decided. The Appellate Body held that it was not necessary to do so after having found that the application of the US measure constituted "unjustifiable discrimination" and "arbitrary discrimination". On this score Malaysia does not deem it necessary to deal likewise with this issue.

---

[120] Panel Report, paras. 3.277-3.281.

[121] Appellate Body Report, para. 140.

[122] *Ibid.*, para. 141.

[123] *Ibid.*, paras. 144-145.

IV. SUMMARY OF THIRD PARTY SUBMISSIONS[124]

1. Australia

4.1 Australia submits that the United States continues to apply an import prohibition inconsistent with Article XI of the GATT 1994. In these circumstances, the United States needs to demonstrate that its measure now meets the requirements of the general exceptions provision of Article XX of the GATT 1994, if it is to demonstrate compliance with the recommendations and rulings of the DSB in this dispute.

4.2 Australia notes the Appellate Body found that the United States measure, Section 609 of Public Law 101-162, qualified for provisional justification under Article XX(g), but that it failed to meet the requirements of the chapeau of Article XX, as it was applied in a manner that constituted arbitrary and unjustifiable discrimination. This finding that the US measure was provisionally justified under Article XX(g) recognized that there might well be circumstances in which the import prohibition contained in Section 609 could be applied in a manner consistent with the requirements of the chapeau of Article XX. Australia notes that this could be the case if the import prohibition was applied as part of a cooperative approach to addressing sea turtle conservation based on intergovernmental consensus.

4.3 It is pointed out by Australia that the preamble to the WTO Agreement recognizes the need for the trading relations of WTO Members to be conducted in accordance with the objective of sustainable development. Through the work of the Committee on Trade and Environment (CTE), WTO Members have specifically sought to ensure that trade and environment policies are mutually supportive in promoting sustainable development. They have recognized that trade measures may be needed in some circumstances to achieve environmental objectives, and the scope for WTO provisions, including Article XX of the GATT 1994, to accommodate such measures. In particular, WTO Members have recognized the complementarity between the work of the WTO and multilateral environmental agreements.

4.4 Australia's participation as a third party throughout this dispute has reflected both substantive trade interests and concerns with important issues of principle. In relation to its substantive trade interests, Australia had immediate access concerns for shrimp from the Spencer Gulf region and the Northern Prawn Fishery. Australia welcomes changes in the application of the US measure which have restored this access. However, access for shrimp from other Australian fisheries remains prohibited.

---

[124] Canada and Pakistan reserved their rights as third parties but did not make any submissions to the Panel.

4.5 On the issues of principle, Australia shares the concerns of the United States in relation to sea turtle conservation and has welcomed and supported the efforts of the United States and other countries, including Malaysia, to address these concerns through cooperative initiatives in the Indian Ocean and South-East Asian region. In October 1999 Australia hosted a workshop aimed at addressing the need for a "regional agreement for the conservation and management of marine turtle populations and their habitats throughout the Indo-Pacific and the Indian Ocean region." The outcomes of the Workshop provided a building block leading to the adoption by consensus of the Memorandum of Understanding on the Conservation and Management of Marine Turtles and their Habitats of the Indian Ocean and South-East Asia at the meeting in Kuantan, Malaysia in July 2000. The Memorandum of Understanding acknowledges and seeks to address the wide range of threats to sea turtles, including habitat destruction, direct harvesting and trade, fisheries by-catch, pollution and other man-induced sources of mortality.

4.6 However, Australia remains concerned at the continuation of an import ban by the United States based on a unilaterally determined conservation standard to address a transboundary or global environmental issue. In particular, Australia considers that the progress in recent efforts to promote sea turtle conservation in the Indian Ocean and South-East Asian region demonstrates the existence of alternative avenues to achieve the important objective of sea turtle conservation. Australia considers that such cooperative efforts are an appropriate and effective means of dealing with an issue such as sea turtle conservation. Not only do they allow the full range of issues involved in sea turtle conservation to be identified and addressed, but they also provide a means of avoiding inappropriate or unnecessarily trade restrictive action.

4.7 As its legal argument, Australia submits that the Appellate Body found that the US measure qualified for provisional justification under Article XX(g), but that it failed to meet the requirements of the chapeau of Article XX. In particular, the Appellate Body found that the measure had been applied by the United States in a manner that constituted arbitrary and unjustifiable discrimination between Members of the WTO due to the following problems:

(a) The rigidity and inflexibility in the administration of the import ban;

(b) the unilateral and non-consensual procedures of the import measure;

(c) the differential phase-in periods and differential approaches to technology transfer for different groups of countries; and

(d) the denial of transparency, procedural fairness and due process in the administration of the import ban.

4.8 Australia considers that the legal issue of whether the United States has rectified the problem identified in (a) and (d) requires an analysis of the changes to the US Guidelines and US practice in their administration. In this regard, Australia welcomes certain changes to the US Guidelines which have subsequently allowed the US to make determinations granting import access to shrimp from the Spencer Gulf region and the Northern Prawn Fishery. Australia notes that certain of the changes are subject to continuing domestic court action in the United States and will be following closely developments in this regard.

4.9 Australia considers that the legal issue of whether the United States has rectified the problems identified in (c) above requires, at least in part, an analysis of current US practice in relation to the provision of technical assistance and training in the design, construction, installation and operation of Turtle Excluder Devices (TEDs). Australia notes that the US does not appear to have expressed a view on what actions it has taken, or was required to take, to address the issue of differential phase-in periods for TEDs which the Appellate Body also found to constitute unjustifiable discrimination.

4.10 In relation to (b), Australia notes the argument of the United States that one of the elements needed for it to achieve compliance was "to engage in serious, good faith negotiations on sea turtle conservation". Australia agrees with the United States that such negotiations may have provided it with one means of bringing its measure into compliance with the requirements of the chapeau of Article XX, specifically to address problem (b).

4.11 Australia notes that many of the points raised by the Appellate Body in relation to problem (b) concern actions which the United States failed to take before moving to impose or enforce the import ban. If these actions had been taken they could have obviated the need for an import ban, through achievement of intergovernmental agreement or consensus on a range of actions to address sea turtle conservation, or ensured that a ban would have been implemented in accordance with a multilaterally agreed approach. Indeed, the key objective of "serious, good faith negotiations", from the perspective of the chapeau of Article XX, is that they should be aimed at seeking to avoid any discrimination at all, to the extent that was possible, or limiting any unavoidable discrimination to that which was not "arbitrary" or "unjustifiable", while also avoiding any disguised restrictions on international trade.

4.12 Australia notes that the United States is largely silent on the content, objectives or nature of the negotiations required for them to be "serious, good faith negotiations" and to repair the unjustifiable discrimination found by the Appellate Body. Furthermore, the United States has presented no evidence that indicates any change to the "unilateral and non-consensual procedures" of the import ban it maintained after the end of the reasonable period of time, or that the ban is now based on "consensual and multilateral procedures".

4.13 Preserving the delicate balance of Article XX, Australia puts forward, is essential if it is to achieve its aim of allowing WTO Members to take measures otherwise inconsistent with the GATT 1994 for a range of important public policy objectives, while preventing it from being used to inappropriately escape from treaty obligations owed to other Members.

4.14 Australia argues that Article XX of the GATT 1994 is central to this dispute. Australia considers that the findings of the Appellate Body have confirmed the vitality of the balance of rights and obligations in Article XX, and its continuing relevance to the current concerns of the international community to reconcile economic growth and environmental protection.

4.15 Australia refers to the Indian Ocean and South-East Asian Regional Initiative in its response to the request by the panel for a description of efforts made to reach a multilateral solution in relation to the conservation of marine turtles.[125]

4.16 Australia notes the technical workshop that it hosted from 19 to 22 October 1999 in Perth. This adopted a resolution on the value of a new regional instrument to facilitate closer collaboration to improve the conservation of marine turtles and their habitats. The participants also agreed on further consultations aimed at concluding such an instrument. The meeting welcomed Australia's offer to prepare a draft text.

4.17 Australia also notes that the endorsement at the workshop of the need for a new regional instrument built upon the agreement at the 2nd ASEAN Symposium and Workshop on Sea Turtle Biology and Conservation, held from 15 to 17 July 1999. The cooperative efforts advanced by these meetings resulted in the adoption of the *Memorandum of Understanding on the Conservation and Management of Marine Turtles and their Habitats of the Indian Ocean and South-East Asia* at an intergovernmental meeting of 24 States hosted by Malaysia in Kuantan in July 2000.

4.18 Australia notes that the Memorandum of Understanding requires the completion of a Conservation and Management Plan prior to being opened for signature. Australia had prepared a draft Conservation and Management Plan based on the consultations held at the Perth Workshop as part of its preparation of a draft text of the Memorandum. The Kuantan meeting agreed to develop further the Plan with a view to having it adopted at the next intergovernmental meeting which should be held in the first quarter of 2001.

4.19 Australia puts forward that the discussion at the Perth workshop was wide ranging in its scope. The discussions identified the need for action in relation to a number of areas: the protection of marine turtle habitat; the management of direct harvesting and trade; reduction in the incidental capture and mortality of marine turtles in the course of fishing activities; and promotion of research, information exchange, and capacity building.

4.20 Australia notes that the Memorandum of Understanding provides for all of these issues to be addressed in the Conservation and Management Plan. This will provide a comprehensive basis for cooperative efforts to address the range of threats faced by marine turtles and their habitats within the region. In particular, Australia notes that the threat posed to marine turtles by fisheries by-catch is ex-

---

[125] Australia submitted to the Panel the *Report of the Consultation on Needs and Mechanisms for Regional Conservation and Management of Marine Turtles*, Perth, Western Australia, 19-22 October 1999.

plicitly identified as one of the issues that will continue to be pursued through this process.

4.21 Australia argues that it has not claimed, as asserted by the United States, that "all environmental measures must be based on 'consensual and multilateral procedures'." However, the Appellate Body has clearly indicated that these considerations are directly relevant to examination of whether the US measure conforms to the requirements of the chapeau of Article XX. In particular, the Appellate Body emphasized that "[t]he unilateral character of the application of Section 609 heightens the disruptive and discriminatory influence of the import prohibition and underscores its unjustifiability." In this regard, Australia considers that three issues are particularly relevant.

4.22 Australia is of the view that first, "multilateral and consensual procedures" have been and are available for pursuing concerns about marine turtle conservation, including fisheries by-catch. Second, the US has not presented any evidence to indicate that its import measure is now based on 'multilateral and consensual procedures'. Third, in these circumstances, the question which the panel must address is whether the US had demonstrated a justification for the continuance of import measures based on 'unilateral and non-consensual procedures' sufficient to meet the requirements of the chapeau of Article XX.

4.23 Australia notes that the United States has claimed that Australia's argument about the existence of an alternative avenue for addressing sea turtle conservation concerns "is based on two flawed premises". On the first of these, Australia has not claimed, as asserted by the United States, that "a WTO Member must exhaust all possibilities for achieving its goals in other ways." In Australia's view the question is whether the US measure meets the specific requirements of the chapeau of Article XX. In this regard, Australia notes that the Appellate Body drew attention to four specific points relating to the failure of the United States to engage other countries in serious negotiations on marine turtle conservation before enforcing its import prohibition. These points have been strengthened by progress with the current cooperative initiative in the Indian Ocean and South-East Asian region.

4.24 The second of the "flawed premises" that the United States identified in Australia's argument is that "the progress made in multilateral negotiations in the Indian Ocean and South-East Asian region will not necessarily translate into the achievement of the environmental goal of the US measure." However, it is difficult to see how the regional initiative could be substantively inferior to the import prohibition imposed by the United States in this regard. The import prohibition only addresses one of the threats posed to marine turtles, whereas the current cooperative initiative in the Indian Ocean region provides for a comprehensive approach. The current cooperative initiative provides a framework for addressing all fisheries by-catch issues relevant to marine turtle conservation, whereas the import prohibition will only directly affect export oriented fisheries. Furthermore, the import prohibition will only be effective if it induces the adoption of TEDs, an outcome that it clearly cannot guarantee.

4.25 In concluding, Australia submits that a key argument of the United States in support of its claimed compliance with the Appellate Body's findings is that it has engaged in serious, good faith negotiations. From the perspective of Article XX, the key objective of serious, good faith negotiations, in the context of this dispute, is that they should be aimed at seeking to avoid any discrimination at all, to the extent that was possible, or limiting any unavoidable discrimination to that which was not "arbitrary" or "unjustifiable". At the same time, the negotiations would need to avoid any disguised restrictions on international trade to ensure compliance with all the requirements of the chapeau of Article XX.

4.26 In short, Australia is of the view that the United States must demonstrate what serious efforts it has taken aimed at obviating or eliminating the discriminatory impact of the import ban. In particular, good faith negotiations, aimed at addressing the defects in the application of Section 609 identified by the Appellate Body, would require the United States to engage in discussions that could involve changes in the existence or nature of the import ban, as well as changes in aspects of its implementation. It would be a serious misconstruction of the Appellate Body's findings to suggest that these should be interpreted in a manner that could never require the lifting of the import prohibition.

2. *Ecuador*

4.27 Ecuador submits that it is participating as a third party given its trade interest and the systemic implications of the case. Ecuador is one of the main suppliers of shrimp to the United States' market and Ecuadorian exports could be affected by the scope of Article XX of the GATT 1994.

4.28 Ecuador considers that the Panel has before it a very delicate case requiring careful evaluation of the arguments submitted by all the parties. While in principle the Panel's terms of reference are to ascertain whether the United States has applied the conclusions and recommendations adopted by the Dispute Settlement Body (DSB), the practical consequences of this Panel's decisions will send a clear signal regarding proper compliance with Article XX of the GATT so as to prevent the possible use of environmental policies to disguise protectionist trade measures.

4.29 Ecuador shares the genuine concern of the United States, Malaysia and other Members of the WTO regarding the need to preserve marine species which may be endangered by economic activity not guided by considerations of environmental sustainability. However, these genuine concerns are not now under discussion. What the Panel has to determine is whether the United States has complied with the conclusions and recommendations adopted by the DSB and whether the measures it has taken to protect sea turtles are compatible with its obligations under the WTO Agreements.

4.30 Ecuador's view is that the United States maintains an import prohibition inconsistent with Article XI of the GATT 1994. The United States did not appeal against this conclusion by the Original Panel, nor does it now contend that the prohibition in question is not in force. It is therefore easier, in these circumstances, to establish that the issue for this Panel is to determine whether the changes which the United States claims to have introduced in the application of Section 609 are sufficient to take advantage of the general exception provided for in GATT Article XX.

4.31 Ecuador takes the view that the burden of proof in this matter is on the United States, despite its being the responding party, since the issue here concerns the application of an exception to a measure inconsistent with the GATT 1994. It is the United States which must justify such inconsistency by responding to all the points raised by the Panel and, in particular, by the Appellate Body in this matter.

4.32 Ecuador does not agree with the United States that, pursuant to the Appellate Body's findings, it is not necessarily obliged to lift its prohibition on shrimp imports. On the contrary, if the United States cannot show that it has complied with all the conditions laid down by the Appellate Body in determining that the measure constitutes arbitrary and unjustifiable discrimination and that the exception under Article XX of the GATT is not, therefore, applicable, then the United States should withdraw the prohibition on shrimp imports by amending Section 609.

4.33 Ecuador considers that it is inadmissible that a violation of Article XI of the GATT should be countenanced pending modification of the application of Section 609 of the Trade Act by the United States. That line of reasoning, which was adopted by the United States during the reasonable period of time, is no longer applicable. In the event that the Panel finds that the United States has not fully applied the conclusions and recommendations adopted by the DSB, the United States is not entitled to a further reasonable period of time.

3. *European Communities*

4.34 The European Communities notes with considerable concern that, contrary to the requirement contained in Article 6.2 of the Dispute Settlement Understanding (DSU), the request for the establishment of a panel in the present proceedings does not mention whether consultations were held between Malaysia and the United States before the disagreement on the compatibility of the US measures with a covered agreement was referred to the Panel.[126] While the parties to the present dispute have agreed, by an exchange of letters dated 22 December 1999[127], to hold consultations before requesting the establishment of a panel[128], the notice concerning the request for consultations foreseen in Article 4.4 of the DSU was not provided to the DSB and was not circulated to WTO

[126] WT/DS58/17, 13 October 2000.
[127] WT/DS58/16, 12 January 2000.
[128] *Ibid.* para. 2.

Members. There is thus no indication whether such consultations were held in the present case.

4.35 The European Communities notes in this context that an inconsistent and contradictory practice has developed in a number of cases in which parties had recourse to procedures pursuant to Article 21.5 of the DSU without regard for the requirement of first entering into consultations under Article 4 of the DSU before filing a request for the establishment of a panel. In certain cases, parties have agreed bilaterally to dispense with recourse to formal consultations under Article 4 of the DSU. Even though the bilateral agreement in this case provides explicitly that consultations are required before the disagreement could be referred to the Panel pursuant to Article 21.5 of the DSU, as already mentioned there is no indication that consultations were indeed held and, even if they were, such consultations were certainly not held in accordance with the procedural requirements of Article 4 of the DSU.

4.36 The procedural step of holding consultations is however of fundamental importance for the dispute settlement system, in the view of the European Communities. Consultations give the parties an opportunity to resolve their differences without an adjudication of the dispute and will, at the very least, allow the parties to clarify the precise issues on which they continue to disagree. In this way, consultations contribute to ensuring that panel proceedings are limited to issues on which there is real and serious disagreement. In addition, any request for consultations under Article 4 of the DSU must be circulated to the entire WTO membership in order to identify and circumscribe the dispute, thus allowing potential third parties to prepare their request to participate in the procedure. In this regard, it must be recalled that third parties may participate in consultations requested under any of the provisions cited in Article 4.11 and footnote 4 of the DSU. Thus, third party rights are clearly impaired by the omission of the formal consultation stage in a dispute settlement procedure.

4.37 In the context of the *European Communities - Bananas* dispute, the European Communities has made it clear[129] that it considers consultations pursuant to Article 4 of the DSU to be necessary before the establishment of a panel can be requested pursuant to Article 21.5 of the DSU. The reason is the reference contained in Article 21.5 that any dispute on implementation "shall be decided through recourse to these dispute settlement procedures." In the view of the European Communities, "these dispute settlement procedures" include consultations and a right to an appeal. This is so for reasons related to the multilateral character of the procedures, which include procedural rights of other WTO Members, particularly potential third parties, and a standardised dispute settlement procedure the basic features of which may not be amended simply because that pleases the parties in an individual case.

[129] Statement of the EC at the DSB meeting of 22 September 1998, WT/DSB/M/48, p. 7.

4.38 If the parties to a dispute were entirely free to develop procedures of their own choice (*quod non*), the European Communities submits this would jeopardise third party rights enshrined in the DSU (particularly in Articles 4.11 and 10). Nothing would stop the parties from agreeing bilaterally not only to omit the procedural step of consultations, but also to avoid other procedural steps such as the panel stage and to submit their dispute to the Appellate Body straight away (e.g. in order to "gain time" and to exclude third parties who cannot participate in Appellate Body procedures if they did not reserve their right to participate in the preceding panel procedure). It would also mean that the parties would be free to agree among themselves that a panel report pursuant to Article 21.5 of the DSU is not binding and that it may be subjected to some kind of review by another international body outside the WTO.

4.39 The European Communities believes these scenarios are not compatible with the multilateral nature of the procedures under the DSU, the procedural rights of third parties and indeed the general matrix of procedural checks and balances built into the dispute settlement system. The DSU contains sufficient flexibility to adapt the basic procedural requirements to the needs of the parties in individual disputes. As an example, Article 4.7 (second sentence) of the DSU allows the parties to shorten the 60-day period on the basis of a bilateral agreement. If the parties to the dispute agree, a panel under Article 21.5 of the DSU may be established at the first meeting where the request is considered by the DSB (Article 6.1 of the DSU). Panels may propose special working procedures after consultations with the parties (Article 12.1 of the DSU). All these provisions indicate that there is some flexibility in the procedures, which is largely dependent on the agreement of the parties to the dispute. None of these provisions however allows the parties to the dispute to simply omit one of the essential procedural steps before requesting the next one.

4.40 The European Communities considers that all the important functions of the consultations are undermined if the parties to the dispute are considered to be free to "jump the gun" and go to a panel procedure without holding formal consultations under Article 4 of the DSU first. Moreover, consultations must in any event take place in order to agree on the procedure to be followed, and it is obvious that this is also an occasion to consult on substantive issues. Thus, in reality no time is gained in omitting this procedural step; the only consequence is that third parties are put at a disadvantage and that the panel may have to address issues on which there is no real disagreement.

4.41 In conclusion, the European Communities is firmly of the view that the existing rules of the DSU do not allow parties to a dispute to agree bilaterally simply to dispense with consultations under Article 4. Any other approach leads to unacceptable procedural uncertainty about the limits of the procedural guarantees for both parties and to curtailing third party rights clearly enshrined in the DSU. If the parties to the dispute do not respect their obligations under Article 4 of the DSU, the Panel should draw the consequence of this failure of the parties and make a ruling that the dispute is not properly before it (or inadmissible, to use a term of art), since all the procedural steps that are required before a dispute may be submitted to a panel have not been followed in the present case.

4.42 In the event that the Panel concludes that it is nonetheless necessary to enter into the consideration of the merits of the present case, the European Communities raises the following points.

4.43 The European Communities notes that the parties to the present dispute seem to agree that the United States has engaged into serious negotiations concerning conservation measures aiming at the protection of sea turtles in the Indian Ocean. Malaysia recognises that substantial progress has been made toward the conclusion of an agreement on standards for such fishing techniques in the Indian Ocean. However, Malaysia claims that as long as an agreement on these fishing techniques has not been concluded, the United States is obliged, by virtue of the recommendations and rulings of the DSB in this case, to discontinue the application of Section 609 of its law Relating to the Protection of Sea Turtles in Shrimp Trawl Fishing Operations to shrimps and shrimp products imported from Malaysia.

4.44 The European Communities notes that Malaysia claims that the 1999 amendments to the Guidelines for the application of Section 609 (the Revised Guidelines) are insufficient for the purpose of bringing the United States measure into compliance with the US obligations under the WTO in accordance with the recommendations and rulings of the DSB in this case. Malaysia argues that it cannot be compelled to submit its own conservation measures to scrutiny of their equivalence with the US standards because that would mean that it has to bow to standards unilaterally determined by the United States. The European Communities shares Malaysia's concern regarding the unilateral application of domestic standards outside the territory of the state that originally developed them.

4.45 In this context, the European Communities notes that the Revised Guidelines satisfy themselves with standards that are "equivalent" in their effectiveness to the standards applicable to US shrimp trawlers. The United States thus does not apply its domestic standards as such to foreign fishing activities. It is only the effectiveness of the measures taken by Malaysia that is the United States wishes to be able to ascertain.

4.46 The European Communities notes that the Appellate Body specifically underlined in the *United States - Shrimp* case that the United States is required by the chapeau of Article XX GATT to apply its conservation measures in a manner that is compatible with the need for international cooperation and negotiation. The European Communities further notes that international cooperation, which is the opposite of unilateral action, cannot take place in any meaningful way without an exchange of information before more far-reaching cooperative efforts may be envisaged.

4.47 The European Communities therefore considers that a request for information relating to readily available empirical data and objective scientific studies on the effectiveness of conservation measures taken by a foreign country is a necessary part of a cooperative effort. Of course, to require burdensome research of data that are not easily available may not be part of a reasonable effort for cooperation in good faith. The European Communities cannot judge whether it would be difficult for Malaysia to demonstrate the effectiveness of its own conservation measures or, in the absence of such measures, whether it is able to show with readily available empirical data that there is no need for such measures under the specific conditions prevailing in the waters in which Malaysian shrimp trawlers operate. The European Communities notes that there is some reference to these conditions in Malaysia's written submissions.

4.48 Malaysia's claim that the United States is applying unilateral effectiveness standards cannot stand, the European Communities submits, if it is Malaysia that refuses to enter into a cooperative effort by communicating to the United States and other interested nations, on the basis of readily available empirical data and scientific studies, the conservation situation for sea turtles threatened by shrimp trawling in the waters of the Indian Ocean. After all, there can be no doubt that sea turtles of the species to which Section 609 refers are among the species that are threatened by extinction according to CITES and that these sea turtles form part of the "global commons" which cannot be adequately protected by a single state without some form of international cooperation. International cooperation means, as a minimum, communication of relevant available data between the nations that participate in such cooperation.

4.49 In the view of the European Communities, the United States was required by the recommendations and rulings of the DSB to enter into negotiations during the reasonable period of time in order to be able to apply Section 609 in a non-discriminatory manner. Malaysia confirms that such negotiations have indeed been initiated by the United States and that they are "well advanced" at present. It would be difficult to claim that there is an obligation of result with regard to international negotiations. Rather, to paraphrase the third sentence of Article 3.7 of the DSU, it would be clearly preferable if the parties to the present dispute could find a mutually acceptable solution to the dispute that is consistent with the covered agreements. Such a solution could best be achieved by the conclusion of an international agreement on the conservation of sea turtles in the Indian Ocean. Of course, since the conclusion of such an international agreement depends on the consent of both parties, it would not be possible to require that the parties enter into such an agreement at a particular point in time, such as the end of the reasonable period of time in the present case.

4.50 The EC notes that, as a separate matter, Malaysia draws the Panel's attention to the fact that the Revised Guidelines have been found inconsistent with Section 609 by a domestic court in the United States. Malaysia claims in this context that, even though the court ruling in that case is presently under appeal and that in the meantime the ruling has not led to a change in the way in which the Revised Guidelines are applied, the United States must assume international responsibility for the rulings taken by its courts.

4.51 It is true, the European Communities argues, that the domestic court ruling in the present case casts a doubt on the ability of the United States to continue the application of the Revised Guidelines without an amendment to Section 609. This is at present an open issue and may make it more difficult to make informed decisions on the prospect for the access of shrimp and shrimp products from non-certified nations to the market of the United States. On the other hand, it does not appear that the domestic court ruling has any immediate effect on the ability of the United States to take a more flexible approach to the imports of shrimp and shrimp products, as required by the Appellate Body.

4.52 Thus, in conclusion the European Communities finds the present complaint by Malaysia somewhat premature. However, since the European Communities is not in possession of all the factual elements that may be relevant to the resolution of the present dispute, the European Communities will abstain from making a more detailed suggestion on how the Panel should dispose of this dispute.

4.53 In response to the question of the Panel concerning efforts to reach a multilateral solution in relation to the conservation of sea turtles, the EC considers that the *Report of the Consultations on Needs and Mechanisms for Regional Conservation and Management of Marine Turtles* held in Perth, Western Australia, from 19 to 22 October 1999 gives the full picture of the efforts undertaken to develop multilateral conservation methods for sea turtles in the Indian Ocean region. The European Communities cannot add any further information on these negotiations (nor on the negotiations of the Inter-American Convention for the Protection and Conservation of Sea Turtles, in which it did not participate) beyond the material that is already before the Panel.

4.54 In response to the question posed by Malaysia on the burden of proof, the European Communities makes reference to the following finding of the Appellate Body in *United States - Standards for Reformulated and Conventional Gasoline*:

> "The burden of demonstrating that a measure provisionally justified as being within one of the exceptions set out in the individual paragraphs of Article XX does not, in its application, constitute abuse of such exception under the chapeau, rests on the party invoking the exception. That is, of necessity, a heavier task than that involved in showing that an exception, such as Article XX(g), encompasses the measure at issue."[130]

4.55 In addition, as is apparent from its answer to the same question, the United States accepts that it "is asserting as an affirmative defense that its measure falls, as modified, within the scope of Article XX. As the Appellate Body explained in *United States - Wool Shirts*, the burden of establishing such a defence rests on the party asserting it." It appears, therefore, that there is no dispute with regard to the issue raised by Malaysia's question concerning the burden of proof.

---

[130] Adopted on 20 May 1996, WT/DS2/AB/R, p. 22 *et seq*.

4. *Hong Kong, China*

4.56 Hong Kong, China makes its submission as a third party in this case out of legal and systemic interest. Hong Kong, China also notes that it took part as respectively a third party and a third participant in the Original Panel and the Appellate Body proceedings.

4.57 In summary, the aim of Hong Kong, China's written submission is first to set out what is the appropriate legal framework to consider the question of whether or not the United States has implemented the DSB recommendations and rulings. In this connection, Hong Kong, China provides its understanding of the mandate of "compliance panels" and identifies the recommendations and rulings of the DSB which the present compliance panel should examine. The submission also aims to answer a question raised, i.e. in case the implementing actions of a WTO Member are overturned by its domestic court.

4.58 With respect to the mandate of a 21.5 panel, Hong Kong, China refers to a recent Appellate Body case and argues that what is at stake before a compliance panel is whether a new (in comparison to the original dispute) measure is in itself consistent with the WTO Agreements, particularly with the specific provisions with which the panel or Appellate Body found the original measure inconsistent. The new measure must also be a measure which is related to the original dispute, that is, it must be a measure which is adequate for the WTO Member concerned to be deemed to have complied with the recommendations and rulings of the DSB.

4.59 Hong Kong, China recalls the relevant rulings of the Appellate Body and states that the compliance panel must examine whether the US actions taken consequent to the rulings of the DSB and taken to comply with the said rulings are in conformity with the relevant GATT provisions.

4.60 Hong Kong, China recalls the statement of the United States in its written submission that it "need not necessarily address each one of those aspects in order to comply with the Appellate Body findings" on the grounds that the term "cumulative effect" used in paragraph 176 of the Appellate Body Report in *United States - Shrimp*, as read by the United States, means that the Appellate Body's findings of unjustifiable discrimination depended on a combination of aspects of the application of Section 609. Hong Kong, China disagrees with this reading although it notes that the United States, notwithstanding its assertion above, also states that it has indeed addressed all of the defects in the application of Section 609.

4.61 In case the implementing actions are overturned by a domestic court, Hong Kong, China touches upon a decision by the US Court of International Trade (CIT), attached to Malaysia's written submission. The legal question that arises is whether, in view of the mentioned CIT decision, the United States can be deemed to have complied with its WTO obligations. Hong Kong, China considers that the other issues before the compliance panel are whether implementation occurs once legislative/administrative actions have been taken, and the effects of subsequent judiciary action that put into jeopardy the mentioned legislative/administrative implementing actions.

4.62 In concluding, Hong Kong, China reiterates that environmental protection in general and conservation of sea turtles in particular is not in dispute in this case. Indeed, all parties and third parties to the dispute fully endorsed these causes. What is at issue is whether the specific measures taken by the United States to comply with the recommendation and rulings of the DSB are consistent with the WTO provisions, particularly the chapeau of GATT Article XX.

4.63 In response to the question of the Panel on efforts to reach a multilateral solution in relation to the conservation of sea turtles, Hong Kong, China replies that it has not been involved in any negotiations with the United States in this respect.

5. *India*

4.64 India submits that Section 609, in its present form and manner of application would amount to a unilateral economic embargo. It requires other Members, which want to have access to the US market, to adopt essentially the same shrimp/turtle policy as that of the United States without taking into account the different conditions of other countries. The unilateral character of the measure heightens its disruptive and discriminatory effects. This measure ought to be multilateral and consensual. In this regard, India urges the Panel to take into account Principles 7, 11 and 12 of the Rio Declaration on Environment and Development. India also joins Malaysia and others in calling upon the United States to remove the measure, i.e. Section 609 and the import prohibition under that Section.

4.65 In response to Malaysia's question with respect to the burden of proof in this case, India agrees with Malaysia that the burden of proof lies with the United States to demonstrate that the measures taken by it to comply with the DSB recommendations and rulings are justified under GATT Article XX.

4.66 In response to the Panel's question concerning efforts to reach a multilateral solution in relation to the conservation of sea turtles, India notes that it participated in the Perth Seminar held on 19-22 October 1999. The needs and mechanisms for regional cooperation in the conservation and management of marine turtles was discussed at this seminar, and a resolution on developing a regional agreement on Conservation and Management of Marine Turtles and their Habitats in the Indian Ocean and South-East Asian Region was adopted. India also was represented at the follow-up meeting held in Malaysia on 11-14 July 2000. Various aspects of marine turtle conservation were discussed at this meeting and the draft agreement was further modified. The draft agreement was circulated to the different state parties for consideration and signature. India notes that it is still studying this draft agreement. India confirms that it is a signatory to the Bonn Convention on Migratory Species of Wild Animals.

6. *Japan*

4.67 Japan believes that preserving the global environment is important and that protecting endangered species is essential. At the same time, it is also necessary to ensure that both trade and environment policies are mutually supportive. As mentioned by Japan during the CTE discussions, when a trade measure is applied for environmental purposes, it is necessary to ensure that such measures are not used: (a) to disguise protectionism; nor (b) in an arbitrary manner. Japan believes the extraterritorial use of unilateral trade measures could raise concerns over arbitrary and discriminatory implementation. When such measures are used for environmental policy, their legal consistency must be checked carefully.

4.68 In Japan's view, the key legal issue in this panel is whether the measures taken by the United States in order to comply with the recommendations and rulings of the DSB are sufficient to justify the import ban under GATT Article XX (in particular, the chapeau of Article XX). While the United States could have fully implemented the recommendations and rulings of the DSB by lifting the import ban under Section 609, Japan does not agree with the arguments that the DSB recommendations necessarily require the United States to lift the import ban itself.

4.69 Japan considers that as the provisions in Article XX are "exceptions" to the basic principles of the GATT, they should be applied in a strict manner. Japan fully agrees with the Appellate Body Report that "the purpose and object of the introductory clauses of Article XX is generally the prevention of 'abuse of the exceptions of [Article XX]'."[131] Therefore, Japan believes that if the United States maintains the import ban, all the aspects examined by the Appellate Body in the original dispute should be carefully examined again in order to find out if the US measure is now justifiable under Article XX. In this regard, Japan cannot accept the argument of the United States that "the United States need not necessarily address each one of those aspects in order to comply with the Appellate Body findings." Japan considers that the arguments presented by Australia are important, for example: (a) that "the US does not appear to have expressed a view on what actions it has taken, or was required to take, to address the issue of differential phase-in periods for TEDs"; and (b) that "the US has not presented any evidence in its first submission that indicates any change to the 'unilateral and consensual procedures' of the import ban, or that the ban is now based on 'consensual and multilateral procedures'."

4.70 In response to the question of the Panel concerning efforts for the conservation of sea turtles, Japan submits that it has not been involved in any bilateral or multilateral negotiations with the United States. Regarding the conservation of sea turtles in general, however, their conservation has been on the agenda of the Conference of the Parties to CITES, in which both Japan and the United States have participated. In its meeting in 2000, CITES considered a proposal to down-

---

[131] Appellate Body Report, para. 116.

list or transfer a particular species of sea turtles (the hawksbill turtle) from Appendix I to Appendix II, i.e. in order to change the import/export regulations applied by CITES.

4.71 The view of Japan in response to Malaysia's question concerning the burden of proof is that the key legal issue in this Panel is whether the measures taken by the United States in order to comply with the recommendations and rulings of the DSB are sufficient for making the import ban justifiable under GATT Article XX. Japan's understanding of the argument of the United States in this proceeding is, essentially, that the United States has rectified all the problems identified in the recommendations and rulings of the DSB, and that now the import ban under Section 609 is justified under the provisions of Article XX.

4.72 Generally speaking, since the provisions of Article XX are "exceptions" to the basic GATT principles, Japan considers that the burden of establishing an affirmative defence based on these provisions should rest on the party asserting it. This is a well-established principle and was confirmed by the Appellate Body in *United States - Measure Affecting Imports of Woven Wool Shirts and Blouses from India.*[132] Japan also considers the finding of the Appellate Body in *Brazil - Export Financing Programme for Aircraft*[133] lead to the conclusion in this context that the above-mentioned allocation of burden of proof would not be altered even before an Article 21.5 panel.

7. *Mexico*

4.73 As a general observation, Mexico submits that it does not believe this case concerns an environmental dispute. The WTO is not the appropriate forum for raising such issues. Moreover, neither the parties nor the third parties question the appropriateness of protecting the environment in general or migratory species such as sea turtles in particular. Mexico reiterates its substantial interest in this case, *inter alia*, because of its systemic implications for the interpretation of the general exceptions to the GATT 1994.

4.74 With reference to the terms of reference of the Panel, Mexico agrees with the line of reasoning followed by the Appellate Body in *Canada - Measures Affecting the Export of Civilian Aircraft - Recourse by Brazil to Article 21.5 of the DSU*[134], inasmuch as the present Panel's terms of reference are not confined to determining whether or not the United States has complied with the DSB recommendations and rulings, but rather to determining whether the United States' measure is consistent with a covered agreement, in this case the GATT 1994.

---

[132] Adopted on 23 May 1997, WT/DS33/AB/R (hereafter "*United States - Wool Shirts*"), DSR 1997:I, 323.

[133] Adopted on 4 August 2000, WT/DS46/AB/RW (hereafter "*Brazil - Aircraft - Recourse by Canada to Article 21.5 of the DSU*"), DSR 2000:VIII, 4067, para. 66.

[134] Adopted on 4 August 2000, WT/DS70/AB/RW (hereafter *"Canada - Aircraft - Recourse by Brazil to Article 21.5 of the DSU"*), DSR 2000:IX, 4299, para. 41.

4.75 In view of the fact that the parties appear to agree that the United States' measure continues to constitute a "prohibition or restriction" within the meaning of Article XI:1 of the GATT 1994,[135] Mexico argues that the scope of this dispute is confined to determining whether that measure is justified under GATT Article XX[136] and, specifically, under the chapeau of that article.

4.76 Mexico agrees with the Panel that Article XX is a limited and conditional exception to the obligations imposed by other provisions of the General Agreement, *not a positive rule establishing obligations in itself*, and that it has therefore been interpreted narrowly.

4.77 With respect to the actions of the United States to bring its measure into conformity with the recommendations and rulings of the DSB, Mexico argues that the United States confined itself to modifying the *application* of its law on the basis of the Appellate Body's findings.

4.78 Thus, in referring to the differences of treatment which constituted "unjustifiable discrimination", the United States indicates that:

(a) It has introduced greater flexibility in the application of Section 609;

(b) it no longer prohibits the importation of shrimp harvested by vessels using TEDs even where they originated in non-certified countries. (The United States recognizes that this aspect is the subject of domestic judicial proceedings);

(c) it has endeavoured to conduct negotiations with the complaining parties, in particular with Malaysia and other Indian Ocean nations; and

(d) it has offered and provided technical assistance services.

4.79 In referring to the United States' measure that has been considered to constitute a means of arbitrary discrimination, Mexico points out the observation by the United States that it has resolved the two main problems, namely lack of flexibility and lack of transparency (concepts identified in sub-paragraphs (a) and (b) above).

4.80 With respect to whether the United States has complied with the recommendations and rulings of the DSB, Mexico considers that the United States' argument that it only needed to modify specific aspects of the *application* of its

[135] According to Mexico, para. 7.17 of the Panel Report in this case (WT/DS58/R) stated that: "the wording of Section 609 and the interpretation of it made by the CIT are sufficient evidence that the United States imposes a "prohibition or restriction" within the meaning of Article XI:1. We therefore find that Section 609 violates Article XI:1 of GATT 1994." Mexico notes that no appeal was made against that finding.

[136] Mexico refers to para. 187(c) of the Appellate Body Report that states that the United States measure "while qualifying for provisional justification under Article XX(g), fails to meet the requirements of the chapeau of Article XX, and, therefore, is not justified under Article XX of the GATT 1994."

legislation is excessively minimalist, particularly when it comes to justifying a measure under the general exceptions to the GATT 1994. In Mexico's opinion, in order to determine whether the United States' measure is now in conformity with the GATT 1994, the Panel should consider the following:

(a) Whether the United States measure can be justified under Article XX.

(b) Whether the judicial proceeding in the case concerning *Turtle Island Restoration Network and Anor. v. Robert L. Mallett Acting Secretary of Commerce and Anor. and National Fisheries Institute Inc.* constitutes in itself non-compliance with the DSB recommendations and rulings.

4.81 Concerning the justification of the measure under Article XX, Mexico's argument on this subject may be set forth as follows:

(a) The Panel determined that the US measure constitutes a violation of Article XI:1 of the GATT 1994. This was not appealed.

(b) The Appellate Body found that the measure is not justifiable under Article XX of the GATT 1994 because it was applied in a manner which constituted arbitrary discrimination, as well as unjustifiable discrimination.

(c) The Appellate Body did not rule on the third element of the chapeau to Article XX (disguised restriction on international trade).[137]

(d) The United States decided to maintain a prohibition on importation, which had been declared inconsistent with Article XI of the GATT 1994, and alleges that, by merely following the findings of the Appellate Body, it brought its measure into conformity.

(e) Mexico maintains that it is not enough for the United States to demonstrate that it followed the findings of the Appellate Body; rather, it must show that its measure no longer constitutes a means of arbitrary or unjustifiable discrimination and, *in addition,* that it is not applied in a manner which would constitute a disguised restriction on international trade.

(f) The United States has not demonstrated that its measure is not applied in a manner that constitutes a disguised restriction on international trade. In fact, Mexico considers that the Panel could only examine this aspect if the United States were to submit arguments on the subject. As it has not done so, Mexico does not see how the Panel could justify the United States' measure under Article XX.

[137] Mexico notes that in para 184 of its Report, the Appellate Body stated that "[h]aving made this finding, it is not necessary for us to examine also whether the United States measure is applied in a manner that constitutes a "disguised restriction on international trade" under the chapeau of Article XX."

(g) As the measure cannot be justified under Article XX of the GATT, the finding that the United States' measure is inconsistent with Article XI of the GATT prevails.

4.82 Mexico recalls that the United States asserted that Mexico was disregarding the fact that the parties had discussed the matter of a disguised restriction in the Original Panel proceeding, apart from which the Appellate Body supported the United States' position that its measure was not a disguised restriction on international trade. However, Mexico observes that, in referring to the Panel Report, the United States confined itself to repeating the arguments that it had itself submitted, which were clearly not endorsed by the Panel. In addition, the United States referred to two paragraphs (140 and 141) of the Appellate Body Report, without mentioning that those paragraphs referred to sub-paragraph (g) of Article XX, not its chapeau.

4.83 Mexico comments on the judicial proceedings in the case concerning *Turtle Island Restoration Network and Anor. v. Robert L. Mallett Acting Secretary of Commerce and Anor. and National Fisheries Institute Inc.* Malaysia maintains that the CIT determined that the fact of granting entry to shrimp or shrimp products harvested by vessels using TEDs, but from non-certified nations, resulted in a violation of the letter of Section 609, for which reason the US Administration should not apply the Revised Guidelines, and that the United States had, therefore, not complied with the recommendations and rulings of the DSB. Mexico notes that the response of the United States is that Malaysia had misunderstood the Court's ruling, which did not oblige the US Department of State to change its current policy, and that, in fact, the issue is currently under review by an appellate court, for which reason there has been no modification of the measure for the time being.

4.84 Mexico takes note of the arguments and considers that a prohibition on importation of shrimp harvested by TEDs merely because of a lack of certification would be harmful.

4.85 In its response to the Panel's question with respect to efforts to achieve multilateral agreement, Mexico points out that the efforts to achieve a multilateral settlement are irrelevant for determining compliance or non-compliance with the requirements of Article XX because otherwise the implication would be that a level of effort is required as a threshold for determining whether a measure is justified or unjustified. In Mexico's opinion, no such threshold requirement is contained, either explicitly or implicitly, in Article XX, apart from which it would be necessary to specify which party or parties would be responsible for that effort: the party which imposes the measure, or the one which suffers the consequences of the measure? Nor is an import prohibition justifiable on the grounds that the negotiations for an international agreement have not been concluded, since the success or failure of a multilateral negotation is also no guarantee of compliance with all the requirements of Article XX.

4.86 An import prohibition, Mexico argues, may be applied in a manner which constitutes a means of arbitrary or unjustifiable discrimination even where the

Member imposing the prohibition or the other Members involved have made serious efforts, in good faith, to achieve a multilateral settlement. Moreover, irrespective of whether negotiations have taken place, all WTO Members must comply in the first instance with their substantive obligations under the covered agreements, including Article XI of the GATT. When that is not possible and the Member concerned decides to avail itself of the general exceptions, that Member must comply with each and all of the requirements laid down in Article XX. Otherwise, that Member will not be entitled to impose a prohibition or quantitative restriction on the importation of products, regardless of the aim pursued and whether or not it has entered into negotiations with other Members.

4.87 Regarding submissions to the Panel from non-governmental organizations, Mexico makes the following observations:

(a) In Spanish, the normal meaning of the verb "recabar" (to seek) as used in Article 13 of the DSU is: "*alcanzar, conseguir con instancias o súplicas lo que se desea*" (to get what one wants by formal request or entreaty), or "*pedir, solicitar*" (to ask for, request). The Panel's authority is restricted to "asking or requesting" or to "getting what it wants by formal request or entreaty". Therefore, if the Panel does not take that initiative, Article 13 is not applicable.

(b) The United States attached to its submission a communication from an entity called the Center for Marine Conservation ("CMC"). In Mexico's opinion, that communication should not have been accepted when it was initially submitted unless it had been sought, i.e. "asked for or requested", by the Panel.

4.88 Moreover, Mexico notes the fact that the United States attached the communication to its submission at a later stage does not give it the right to have it taken into account by the Panel, unless the United States assumes responsibility for it, in which case it would no longer be a CMC communication but the official position of the Government of the United States. In that case, this status would be applicable to the entire document originally submitted by the CMC, since if one or more parts of that communication did not conform to the official position of the United States Government, the part or parts in question would not have been included in the second written submission of the United States. Finally, the document in question had not been transmitted to Mexico or, presumably, to any of the parties to this proceeding. Mexico was therefore unable to refer to the content of the communication.

4.89 In concluding, Mexico is of the opinion that the United States bears the burden of proving that its measure is justified under Article XX of the GATT 1994. The United States has not succeeded in doing so, in particular because it has not taken the trouble to demonstrate that its measure is not applied in a manner which would constitute a disguised restriction on international trade.

4.90 Moreover, taking into account the findings of the Panel, to the effect that the United States' measure constituted a violation of Article XI:1 of the GATT

1994, Malaysia has a presumption in its favour, which has not been effectively refuted by the United States.

4.91 In view of the fact that the United States attached the CMC communication to its submission as an integral part thereof, Mexico considers that it should be treated as the official position of the United States and not as a CMC communication or an "*amicus curiae*" brief. Furthermore, any reference to that communication in the Panel Report should be made as a reference to the written submission of the United States, without mentioning the CMC. Otherwise, recognition would be given to a communication from a non-member of the WTO, which was not requested by the Panel.

4.92 On Malaysia's question concerning the burden of proof, Mexico considers that it is the responsibility of the party which invokes the general exception under Article XX to justify the invocation of that exception. This has been the approach adopted by various panels.[138]

4.93 In this Panel, Mexico considers that the burden is on the United States to prove that its measure is consistent with the three requirements of the Article XX chapeau, i.e. that the measure is not applied in a manner which would constitute: (i) a means of unjustifiable discrimination; (ii) a means of arbitrary discrimination; or (iii) a disguised restriction on international trade.

4.94 In Mexico's opinion, the United States has put forward arguments concerning the first two elements, but not the third. Accordingly, it is not possible for the United States' measure to be justified under Article XX of the GATT 1994.

8. *Thailand*

4.95 Thailand submits that the issue at hand is whether the United States has taken measures to comply with the DSB recommendations and rulings that remove the inconsistencies with the covered agreements as identified in the Panel and Appellate Body Reports adopted by the DSB. In Thailand's view, the United States has not done so.

4.96 First, Thailand argues that the US statutory prohibition may be justified under GATT Article XX only if it is applied in a manner that does not constitute "a means of arbitrary or unjustifiable discrimination between countries where the

---

[138] Mexico refers to the Panel in *Canada - Administration of the Foreign Investment Review Act* (L/5504, adopted on 7 February 1984, BISD 30S/140) that held that: "(s)ince Article XX(d) is an exception to the General Agreement, it is up to Canada, as the party invoking the exception, to demonstrate that the purchase undertakings are necessary to secure compliance with the Foreign Investment Review Act". See *Analytical Index to the GATT*, Vol. I, p. 621. Similarly, the Panel in *United States - Restrictions on Imports of Tuna* (WT/DS21/R, not adopted, circulated on 3 September 1991, BISD 39S/155) pointed out that "Article XX is a limited and conditional exception from obligations under other provisions of the General Agreement, and not a positive rule establishing obligations in itself. Therefore, the practice of panels has been to interpret Article XX narrowly, to place the burden on the party invoking Article XX to justify its invocation, and not to examine Article XX exceptions unless invoked" (para 5.22, references deleted).

same conditions prevail." According to the DSB recommendations and rulings, the United States is requested to bring its measure found by the Panel to be inconsistent with Article XI and found by the Appellate Body not to be justified under Article XX into conformity with its obligations under the GATT 1994.[139]

4.97 In Thailand's view, it is the statutory prohibition, as applied, not its "application" that violates the obligations of the United States under the GATT 1994. The term "measure" used in the Appellate Body Report paragraph 188 can only be understood to refer to *the import prohibition* as mandated by Section 609 and applied by the Department of State through its Guidelines, not the application of this prohibition as suggested by the United States. Careful reading of the Appellate Body Report, paragraphs 184 (4th line), 186 (6th line), and 187(c), confirms Thailand's understanding of the ruling: the Appellate Body mentions the word "measure" and not "application." The *measure at issue* in this dispute has been identified by the panel as *"the embargo applied by the United States on the basis of Section 609."*[140] The Appellate Body confirms that it is this measure, not its application, which is at issue in the appeal.[141] Thailand is of the view that as long as its application by the United States Government is inconsistent with a covered agreement, the prohibition, as applied, violates the US obligations under the WTO Agreement. If the United States cannot or does not apply the prohibition in a manner consistent with Article XX, it must stop applying the import prohibition and consequently review and amend Section 609 in order to comply with the DSB recommendations and rulings.

4.98 In order that the statutory prohibition of the United States is justified, Thailand submits that *all* the aspects of inconsistency with GATT 1994 Article XX must be removed. The Appellate Body has identified a number of discriminatory elements in the US measure. Any of these elements constitute in itself a breach of treaty obligation. The United States must remove *all* of these discriminatory elements in order to comply with the ruling and conform to the principle *pacta sunt servanda* - the rule that treaties are binding on the parties and must be performed in good faith, which is a fundamental principle of the law of treaties well enshrined in Article 26 of the Vienna Convention on the Law of Treaties.

4.99 Thailand disagrees with the suggestion of the United States that it need not necessarily address each one of the aspects of discrimination in order to comply with the Appellate Body findings. On the contrary, the principle of good faith treaty performance dictates that any and each breach of treaty obligation by the United States must be removed.

---

[139] Appellate Body Report, para. 188. According to the Original Panel, the import ban as applied by the United States on the basis of Section 609 is not consistent with Article XI of the GATT 1994 and is not justified under Article XX of the same Agreement (Panel Report, para. 8.1). The Appellate Body confirmed that the US "measure" is not justified under Article XX (Appellate Body Report, para. 187(c)).

[140] Panel Report, para. 7.11. *See* also paras. 7.17 and 8.1.

[141] Appellate Body Report, para. 98(b).

4.100 Thailand considers that the Panel should examine whether each and every aspect of the discrimination identified by the Appellate Body has been removed, notwithstanding the US claim that the Panel is not required to do so because the United States has addressed all the aspects of discrimination found by the Appellate Body. Only *one* of these aspects that remains after the expiry of the reasonable period of time constitutes in itself a violation by the United States of its obligations under the GATT 1994.

4.101 Second, Thailand is of the view that the United States still applies the statutory prohibition in a manner that constitutes "a means of arbitrary or unjustifiable discrimination between countries where the same conditions prevail." The reasonable period of time has expired, but the United States still has not removed some of the aspects of the discrimination found by the Appellate Body to be inconsistent with Article XX of the GATT 1994. Two of these aspects are addressed as follows.

4.102 The first aspect Thailand considers is that the United States Government cannot implement the DSB ruling that it must permit importation of shrimps harvested using TEDs from non-certified countries because such permission violates Section 609 as interpreted by the US judiciary.

4.103 Thailand notes that, according to the DSB recommendations and rulings, the United States must permit importation of shrimps harvested by vessels using TEDs comparable in effectiveness to those required in the United States, even if the harvesting nation is not certified pursuant to Section 609. Failure to do so constitutes an unjustifiable discrimination in the sense of the Article XX chapeau.[142]

4.104 Thailand notes that in July 2000, however, the US Court of International Trade ruled that allowing such importation is inconsistent with Section 609 ("the CIT ruling").[143] The CIT ruling means that Section 609, as interpreted by the US judiciary, mandates action that is inconsistent with paragraph 165 of the Appellate Body Report and the relevant provision of the covered Agreement (i.e. the chapeau of Article XX of the GATT 1994). Section 609, therefore, cannot be reconciled with, as the Appellate Body puts it, "the declared policy objective of protecting and conserving sea turtles"[144] and, consequently, is not justified under Article XX(g), provisionally or otherwise.

4.105 Pursuant to the legal system of the United States, Thailand notes, it is the Judiciary that has the authority to adopt interpretations of legal provisions. The US judiciary is *not* bound by interpretations given by the Executive Branch of legal provisions. It is the meaning of the law as ascertained by the US courts that must be retained by the Panel. Previous panels and the Appellate Body have un-

---

[142] Appellate Body Report, para. 165.
[143] *Turtle Island Restoration Network v. Robert Mallett*, 110 Fed. Supp. 2d 1005 (CIT 2000).
[144] Appellate Body Report, para. 165.

derlined this point in *United States - Anti-Dumping Act of 1916*[145] and *United States - Sections 301-310 of the Trade Act of 1974*.[146] The Appellate Body also ruled in the *United States - Shrimp* report that "the United States, like all other Members of the WTO and of the general community of States, bears responsibility for acts of all its departments of government, including its judiciary."[147]

4.106 It is Thailand's view, therefore, that Section 609 as currently interpreted by the US Judiciary is inconsistent with the obligations of the United States under the WTO Agreement. Contrary to the claim of the United States, this is not a matter of speculation. Section 609 *currently* stands in violation of the obligations of the United States. Under customary international law and under the WTO Agreement, Article XVI:4, the United States must amend this Act in order to comply with its obligations.

4.107 The second aspect Thailand argues is that the United States has failed to remove the inconsistency regarding the "lack of flexibility" issue. The US measure at issue in the original dispute requires other WTO Members to adopt essentially the same conservation programme as that applied by the United States. The use of approved TEDs at all times is required regardless of possible different conditions in other countries. According to the Appellate Body, this "rigidity and inflexibility" constitutes an unjustifiable and arbitrary discrimination within the meaning of the chapeau of Article XX.[148] The Revised Guidelines are not sufficient to remove the discrimination found by the Appellate Body, since:

(a) TEDs remains the requirement or *the standard of judgment* regardless of any different conditions prevailing in the territories or jurisdiction areas of other Members.[149]

(b) The US Department of State remains the sole authority to assess the effectiveness of other Members' programmes to protect sea turtles in the course of shrimp trawl fishing, on the basis of a standard decided by the US authorities alone.

---

[145] Both panels and the Appellate Body Reports WT/DS136/AB/R, WT/DS162/AB/R were adopted on 26 September 2000. *See* para. 101 of the Appellate Body Report, para. 6.84 of the Panel Report in WT/DS136/R, and para. 6.97 of the Panel Report in WT/DS162/R.

[146] Adopted on 27 January 2000, WT/DS152/R. *See* para. 8.1(d), which should be read in conjunction with footnote 700 on p. 337 of that Report.

[147] Appellate Body Report, para. 173. The Appellate Body rightly quoted doctrinal writings in support of this ruling in footnote 177 on p. 71 of the Report. In this respect, it is pertinent to note the view of Lord McNair, an authority on the law of treats in *The Law of Treaties*, Oxford University Press, 1961, p. 346. Therefore, the fact that the US Government (the Department of State) has not, as of now, modified the 1999 Revised Guidelines in order to comply with the CIT ruling does not remove the inconsistency of Section 609 with the DSB recommendations and rulings.

[148] Appellate Body Report, paras. 161-164, 172 and 177.

[149] The differences in fishing conditions are taken into account only to the extent relevant to determining whether a non-TED programme is as effective as the US TED-based programme, and not to determining whether it is effective on its own merit as a turtle conservation programme for shrimp fishing.

(c) The applying nations have the burden of demonstrating that they apply comparably effective regulatory programmes. This amounts to a presumption that only a TED-based programme is effective for sea turtle conservation in shrimp trawl fishing, unless proven otherwise.

(d) The apparent, newly introduced "flexibility" of allowing non-TED users to be certified is rendered meaningless by the statement (Section II.B(a) of the Revised Guidelines) that the Department of State is "aware of no measures or series of measures that can minimize the capture and drowning of sea turtles [...] that is comparable in effectiveness to the required use of TEDs." Since the sole judge (i.e. the US Department of State) is not aware of anything else that may be as effective as TEDs, it becomes quite impossible to prove otherwise.

4.108 Therefore, Thailand submits that the Revised Guidelines still impose *de facto* the use of TEDs as the only basis for certification. The Appellate Body has ruled, however, that the United States must not require other nations to adopt essentially the same programme as that applied by the United States because this violates the chapeau of Article XX.[150] Under the Revised Guidelines, the United States "system and processes of certification", as the Appellate Body puts it, are still "established and administered by the United States Agencies alone" and decision making by the US authorities in this regard is still "unilateral."[151]

4.109 In conclusion, Thailand submits that the United States has not taken measures to comply with the DSB recommendations and rulings consistent with the GATT 1994. The measures taken by the United States to comply with the DSB recommendations and rulings in this case are still *inconsistent* with the provisions of the relevant covered Agreement, i.e. Article XX of the GATT 1994.[152] Consequently, the United States has failed to bring its prohibition measure into conformity with its WTO obligations as recommended by the DSB. Since the discrimination has not been removed, it is the statutory prohibition itself, i.e. Section 609, as applied, that *remains* in violation of the US obligations under the WTO Agreement and unjustified by GATT Article XX.

4.110 In response to Malaysia's request, Thailand submits that the Panel should recommend that the United States bring its measure into conformity with the WTO Agreement and suggest that the United States stop applying the import prohibition mandated by Section 609 immediately.

---

150 Appellate Body Report, paras. 161-164.

151 Appellate Body Report, para. 172.

152 As demonstrated above, the United States still applies the import prohibition under Section 609 in a manner that constitutes "a means of arbitrary or unjustifiable discrimination between countries where the same conditions prevail."

4.111 In response to the question posed by Malaysia, Thailand considers that it is well-established GATT/WTO practice that when an affirmative defence, such as GATT Article XX, is invoked, the burden of proof rests on the party asserting it.[153]

V. FINDINGS

A. *General Approach to the Issues Before the Panel*

5.1 This Panel was established pursuant to Article 21.5 of the Understanding on Rules and Procedures Governing the Settlement of Disputes ("DSU") to examine the claims raised by Malaysia with respect to the consistency with the GATT 1994 of the measures taken by the United States to comply with the recommendations and rulings of the Dispute Settlement Body ("DSB") in the case *United States - Import Prohibition of Certain Shrimp and Shrimp Products* (hereafter "the implementing measure").[154] Malaysia claims that the United States did not comply with the findings contained in the Original Panel Report and with the findings of the Appellate Body for the following main reasons:

(a) Malaysia argues that the United States was not entitled, further to the Appellate Body findings, unilaterally to adopt an import ban outside the framework of an international agreement.

(b) Malaysia also argues that the United States should have negotiated an agreement on the protection and conservation of sea turtles before the eventual imposition of an import ban. Thus, by continuing to apply a unilateral measure[155] after the end of the reasonable period of time pending the conclusion of an international agreement, the United States failed to comply with its obligations under the GATT 1994.

(c) Malaysia also claims that the Revised Guidelines adopted by the United States do not comply with the recommendations and rulings

[153] Panel Report, para. 7.30; Appellate Body Report, *United States - Measure Affecting Imports of Woven Wool Shirts and Blouses from India* (adopted on 23 May 1997, WT/DS33/AB/R), DSR 1997:I, 323, at 335 and footnote 23.

[154] The "implementing measure" is composed of Section 609 of Public Law 101-162, of the revised guidelines pursuant to Section 609, dated 8 July 1999, Federal Register, Vol. 64, No. 130, Public Notice 3086, p. 36946 (hereafter the "Revised Guidelines"), as well as of any practice under those Revised Guidelines. The measure reviewed by the Panel in its report (WT/DS58/R), hereafter respectively the "Original Panel" and the "Original Panel Report", and in the Appellate Body Report (WT/DS58/AB/R) will be referred to hereafter as the "original measure".

[155] Throughout these findings and unless stated otherwise, the term "unilateral measure(s)" shall be deemed to refer to a measure which has been designed and is applied without being expressly mandated or permitted by a multilateral agreement, without prejudice to the question of its justification under Article XX of the GATT 1994 or any other provision of the Marrakesh Agreement Establishing the World Trade Organization (hereafter the "WTO Agreement").

of the DSB. In particular, Malaysia is of the view that the United States imposes its own conservation policy and standards on other Members and that such a practice is contrary to the sovereign right of Malaysia to define its own environmental policies and standards.

5.2 The United States does not contest the fact that it imposes an import ban that falls within the scope of Article XI of the GATT 1994. However, the United States argues that:

(a) Section 609 has been found to be provisionally justified under paragraph (g) of Article XX of the GATT 1994; and

(b) as far as the other recommendations and rulings of the DSB are concerned, the United States has made efforts to negotiate a sea turtle conservation agreement and has modified the guidelines implementing Section 609 in order to comply with those recommendations and rulings.

5.3 In light of the claims and arguments of the parties and of the recommendations and rulings of the DSB, the Panel is of the view that the matter before it should be addressed as follows. First, the Panel should determine a number of preliminary issues such as: (i) the exact scope of its terms of reference; (ii) the burden of proof and the date at which the Panel should consider the evidence before it; and (iii) the treatment of unsolicited submissions from non-governmental organizations.

5.4 Second, since an Article 21.5 panel is supposed to review the existence and consistency of the measures taken to implement the DSB recommendations and rulings with a covered agreement, we shall proceed with determining if, as claimed by Malaysia, the implementing measure violates Article XI:1 of the GATT 1994. If we find that to be the case, we shall proceed to address the defence put by the United States under Article XX of the GATT 1994. In this context we will review the specific arguments raised by both parties as well as the general issue, invoked by Malaysia, of the sovereign right of a country to determine its own environmental policies and standards.

5.5 In doing so, we shall take into account the fact that Malaysia's claims are concentrated on the findings of the Appellate Body in this case, which will require us to start our analysis from the Appellate Body findings and the Original Panel findings. In other words, although we are entitled to analyse fully the "consistency with a covered agreement of measures taken to comply", our examination is not done from a completely fresh start. Rather, it has to be done in the light of the evaluation of the consistency of the original measure with a covered agreement undertaken by the Original Panel and subsequently by the Appellate Body. In particular, we note that some of the basic assessments of the Original Panel were reversed by the Appellate Body and, consequently, our evaluation of the consistency of the "measures taken to comply" has to respect the Appellate Body analysis as stated in the Report adopted by the DSB.

B. Preliminary Issues

1. Terms of Reference of the Panel

5.6 We note that, as confirmed by the Appellate Body[156], a panel has the responsibility to determine its jurisdiction and that assessing the scope of its terms of reference is an essential part of this determination. We note that Malaysia argues that it does not limit itself in this dispute to contesting whether the United States has complied with the DSB recommendations and rulings. It states that it is exercising its rights under Article 21.5 of the DSU. Malaysia adds that the mandate of the Panel under Article 21.5 of the DSU is to examine the existence or the consistency with Articles XI and XX of the GATT 1994 of measures taken by the United States to comply with the recommendations and rulings of the DSB. Malaysia further argues that the steps taken by the United States did not remove the elements of "unjustifiable discrimination" and "arbitrary discrimination" that existed in the original measure. The implementing measure remains inconsistent with Article XI and not justified under Article XX. We note that the United States does not argue that Malaysia's claims are insufficiently specific or that its request for establishment of an Article 21.5 panel otherwise fails to meet the requirements of Article 6.2 of the DSU.

5.7 The first sentence of Article 21.5 of the DSU reads in relevant parts as follows:

> "Where there is disagreement as to the *existence* or *consistency with a covered agreement* of *measures taken to comply with the recommendations and rulings* [of the DSB] such dispute shall be decided through recourse to these dispute settlement procedures, [...]" (Emphasis added).

5.8 We recall that, *in Canada - Measures Affecting The Export of Civil Aircraft - Recourse by Brazil to Article 21.5 of the DSU*[157], the Appellate Body stated that:

> "[...] a panel [under Article 21.5] is not confined to examining the measures taken to comply from the perspective of the claims, arguments and factual circumstances that related to the measure that was subject to the original proceedings. [...] Article 21.5 proceedings involve, in principle, not the original measure, but rather a new and different measure which was not before the original panel [...] It is natural, therefore, that the claims, arguments and factual circumstances which are pertinent to the "measure taken to comply" will not, necessarily, be the same as those which were perti-

---

[156] See, e.g., Report of the Appellate Body on *United States - Anti-Dumping Act of 1916*, adopted on 26 September 2000, WT/DS136; 162/AB/R, DSR 2000:X, 4793, para. 54.

[157] Adopted on 4 August 2000, WT/DS70/AB/RW (hereafter "*Canada - Aircraft - Recourse by Brazil to Article 21.5 of the DSU*"), DSR 2000:IX, 4299.

nent in the original dispute. Indeed, the utility of the review envisaged under Article 21.5 of the DSU would be seriously undermined if a panel were restricted to examining the new measure from the perspective of the claims, arguments and factual circumstances that related to the original measure, because an Article 21.5 panel would then be unable to examine fully the "consistency with a covered agreement of the measure taken to comply", as required by Article 21.5 of the DSU."[158]

5.9 The terms of reference of this Panel[159] do not differ from the standard terms of reference applied in other Article 21.5 cases. In light of the reasoning of the Appellate Body mentioned above, the Panel considers that it is fully entitled to address all the claims of Malaysia under Article XI and Article XX of the GATT 1994, whether or not these claims, the arguments and the facts supporting them were made before the Original Panel and in the Appellate Body proceedings *provided*, as recalled by the panel on *Australia - Measures Affecting Importation of Salmon - Recourse by Canada to Article 21.5 of the DSU*[160], that the claims are identified in the request for referring the matter to a panel under Article 21.5 of the DSU.

5.10 In this respect, we reviewed the recourse by Malaysia to Article 21.5 of the DSU.[161] We are mindful of the requirements of Article 6.2 of the DSU and of the reasoning of the Appellate Body in *European Communities - Regime for the Importation, Sale and Distribution of Bananas* [162]and *Korea - Definitive Safeguard Measure on Imports of Certain Dairy Products.*[163] We do not intend, however, to take a position on the application of Article 6.2 in Article 21.5 proceedings. We simply note at this stage that the United States did not argue that any claim made by Malaysia was insufficiently specific in the light of Article 6.2 of the DSU and, therefore, we will proceed to address all of them, to the extent necessary for the fulfilment of our mandate.

5.11 The Panel finally notes that third parties also have formulated a number of claims and arguments in their submissions and at the hearing. In accordance with the practice of other panels under the GATT 1947 and the WTO Agreement[164],

---

158 Adopted on 4 August 2000, WT/DS70/AB/RW (hereafter "*Canada - Aircraft - Recourse by Brazil to Article 21.5 of the DSU*"), DSR 2000:IX, 4299, para. 41.

159 WT/DS58/18.

160 Adopted on 20 March 2000, WT/DS18/RW (hereafter "*Australia - Salmon - Recourse by Canada to Article 21.5 of the DSU*"), DSR 2000:IV, 2301,para. 7.10, sub-paras. 11 and 12.

161 WT/DS58/17.

162 Adopted on 25 September 1997, WT/DS27/AB/R, DSR 1997:II, 591, paras. 141 and, mostly, 142.

163 Adopted on 12 January 2000, WT/DS98/AB/R, DSR 2000:I, 3, paras. 127-128 and 130-131.

164 See the report of the panel on Japan - *Trade in Semiconductors*, adopted on 4 May 1988, BISD 35S/116, para. 98, where the panel stated that a panel is not required to make findings on issues raised solely by interested third parties. See also the report on *Australia - Salmon - Recourse by Canada to Article 21.5 of the DSU, Op. Cit.*, where the panel did not formally address the question

we have decided to consider only those claims of third parties that have been raised by the parties themselves.

2. *Date on which the Panel Should Assess the Facts*

5.12 The Panel notes that the 13-month reasonable period of time agreed upon by the parties expired on 6 December 1999. However, the DSB only established this Article 21.5 Panel at its meeting on 23 October 2000. The Panel notes that the DSU is silent as to the date on which the existence or consistency of the implementing measure must be assessed. On the one hand, it could be argued that such a date must be logically the day following the end of the reasonable period of time referred to in Article 21.3 of the DSU. On the other hand, keeping in mind that a prompt settlement of disputes is, pursuant to Article 3.3 of the DSU, essential to the effective functioning of the WTO and the maintenance of a proper balance between the rights and obligations of Members, it may be appropriate for the Panel to take into account events subsequent to the end of the reasonable period of time.[165]

5.13 The Panel takes the view that it should take into account all the relevant facts occurring until the date the matter was referred to it. By applying this approach, an Article 21.5 panel can reach a decision that favours a prompt settlement of the dispute. Indeed, it avoids situations where implementing measures allowing for compliance with the DSB recommendations and rulings would be disregarded simply because they occur after the end of the reasonable period of time. The Panel, while mindful of the obligation of the United States to bring its legislation into conformity by the end of the reasonable period of time, considers that it is consistent with the spirit of Article 3.3 of the DSU to take into account any relevant facts until the date on which the matter was referred to the Panel.[166]

3. *Admissibility of Submissions from Non-Governmental Organizations*

5.14 In the course of the proceedings, the Panel received two unsolicited submissions from non-governmental organizations. One was submitted by *Earthjustice Legal Defense Fund* on behalf of *Turtle Island Restoration Network, The Humane Society of the United States, The American Society for the Prevention of Cruelty to Animals, Defenders of Wildlife,* and *Fiscalia del Medio Ambiente*

---

of the absence of consultations pursuant to Article 4 of the DSU raised by the European Communities as a third party.

[165] We note that similar premises seem to have been at the origin of the approach followed by the panel in *Australia - Salmon - Recourse by Canada to Article 21.5 of the DSU, Op. Cit*. See para. 7.21.

[166] The Panel notes that, in the case on *Australia - Salmon - Recourse by Canada to Article 21.5 of the DSU, Op. Cit.*, para. 7.10, sub-para. 24, the panel took into account, in relation to the definition of its terms of reference, facts that occurred after the end of the reasonable period of time.

(Chile).[167] The other submission was filed by the *National Wildlife Federation* on behalf of the *Center for Marine Conservation, Centro Ecoceanos, Defenders of Wildlife, Friends of the Earth, Kenya Sea Turtle Committee, Marine Turtle Preservation Group of India, National Wildlife Federation, Natural Resources Defense Council, Operation Kachhapa, Project Swarajya, Visakha Society for Prevention of Cruelty to Animals.*[168] Those submissions were respectively communicated to the parties on 15 and 18 December 2000. In a letter accompanying these submissions, the Panel informed the parties that they were free to comment in their rebuttals on the admissibility and relevance of these submissions. The Panel also informed the parties that it would set out in its report its decision as to how it would address these submissions.

5.15 The parties discussed the above-mentioned submissions in their rebuttals, at the hearing and in replies to questions of the Panel.[169] The Panel notes that Malaysia considers in substance that the Panel has no right under the DSU to accept or consider any unsolicited briefs, whereas the United States argues that the Earthjustice Submission, which addresses a hypothetical question not before the Panel, does not appear to be as relevant to the issue in this dispute as the National Wildlife Federation Submission. As far as the National Wildlife Federation Submission is concerned, the United States considers that it raises issues directly relevant to the matter before the Panel and decided to attach it as an exhibit to its submissions "to ensure that a relevant and informative document [would be] before the Panel, regardless of whether the Panel decid[ed] to exercise its discretion to accept [that submission] directly from the submitters." However, we take note of the fact that the United States does not endorse some of the legal arguments contained in the "amicus brief" submitted by the National Wildlife Federation.[170]

5.16 As far as the Earthjustice Submission is concerned, the Panel takes note of the arguments of the parties and decides not to include it in the record of this case. Regarding the National Wildlife Federation Submission, the Panel notes that it is part of the submissions of the United States in this case and, as a result, is already part of the record.

4. *Burden of Proof*

5.17 Malaysia refers to the Appellate Body Report in *United States - Measures Affecting Imports of Woven Wool Shirts and Blouses from India*[171] to claim that a

---

[167] Hereafter the "Earthjustice Submission".

[168] Hereafter the "National Wildlife Federation Submission".

[169] See paras. 3.5 to 3.15 above.

[170] The United States specified that "[t]he amicus brief attached to the US rebuttal submission reflects the independent views of the organizations that signed on to the amicus brief. [...] We would note, however, that the amicus brief includes certain procedural and substantive defences not advanced in the US submission [...], and thus that these matters are not before the Panel."

[171] Adopted 23 May 1997, WT/DS33/AB/R (hereafter "*United States - Shirts and Blouses*"), DSR 1997:I, 323.

defence such as that invoked by the United States under Article XX of the GATT 1994 is an affirmative defence. The burden is on the United States to prove that its implementing measure complies with the requirements of Article XX of the GATT 1994. The United States argues that Malaysia has the initial burden of showing that the implementing measure is inconsistent with one or more obligations under a covered agreement. However, the United States does not contest that the implementing measure is an import prohibition under Article XI. The United States also agrees that it has the initial burden of proof of showing that the implementing measure falls within the scope of Article XX.

5.18 We recall that, in *Brazil - Export Financing Programme For Aircraft - Recourse by Canada to Article 21.5 of the DSU*[172], the Appellate Body confirmed the finding of the Article 21.5 panel that Brazil had invoked item (k) of the Illustrative List of Export Subsidies[173] as an "affirmative defence". The Appellate Body also considered that the fact that the measure at issue was taken to comply with recommendations and rulings of the DSB did not alter the allocation of the burden of proving Brazil's defence under item (k). The Appellate Body then stated that:

> "In *United States - Measures Affecting Imports of Woven Wool Shirts and Blouses from India*, we said: "It is only reasonable that the burden of establishing [an affirmative] defence should rest on the party asserting it." [Footnote omitted] As it is Brazil asserting this "defence" using item (k) in these proceedings, we agree with the Article 21.5 Panel that Brazil has the burden of proving that the revised PROEX is justified under the first paragraph of item (k)".[174]

5.19 We therefore conclude that it is up to Malaysia to establish a *prima facie* case that its claims under Article XI:1 of GATT 1994 are founded. We also conclude that, even though this is a compliance case and even though good faith application of treaty obligations is to be presumed[175], the United States still has to establish a *prima facie* case that the implementing measure is justified under Article XX, since it is an affirmative defence. If the United States establishes a *prima facie* case, the burden of proof will shift onto Malaysia. If the evidence on a particular claim or defence remains in equipoise, the party bearing the initial burden of proof will be deemed to have failed to provide sufficient evidence in support of its claim.

---

[172] Adopted on 4 August 2000, WT/DS46/AB/RW (hereafter "*Brazil - Aircraft - Recourse by Canada to Article 21.5 of the DSU*"), DSR 2000:VIII, 4067.

[173] WTO Agreement on Subsidies and Countervailing Measures, Annex I.

[174] *Brazil - Aircraft - Recourse by Canada to Article 21.5 of the DSU*, para. 66.

[175] See Article 26 of the Vienna Convention on the Law of Treaties, UN Doc. A/CONF.39/27 (1969), (hereafter the "Vienna Convention").

C. Violation of Article XI:1 of the GATT 1994

5.20 The Panel notes that Malaysia claims that Section 609 as it is currently applied by the United States continues to violate Article XI:1 of the GATT 1994. The United States does not claim that the implementing measure is compatible with Article XI:1.

5.21 Article XI:1 of the GATT 1994 provides as follows:

> "No prohibitions or restrictions other than duties, taxes or other charges, whether made effective through quotas, import or export licences or other measures, shall be instituted or maintained by any Member on the importation of any product of the territory of any other Member or on the exportation or sale for export of any product destined for the territory of any other Member."

5.22 The Panel notes that the elements of the original measure found to be incompatible with Article XI:1 in the Original Panel Report are still part of the implementing measure, i.e. Section 609 as currently applied by the United States. In particular, the United States continues to apply an import prohibition on shrimp and shrimp products harvested in a manner determined to be harmful to sea turtles. We note that the United States does not contest the fact that it applies such a prohibition of import. We consider that the prohibition at issue falls within the "prohibitions or restrictions, other than duties, taxes or other charges" maintained by a Member on the importation of a product from another Member, in contravention of Article XI:1.

5.23 The Panel therefore concludes that the measure taken by the United States to comply with the recommendations and rulings of the DSB in this case violates Article XI:1 of the GATT 1994.

D. Application of Article XX of the GATT 1994

1. Preliminary Remarks

5.24 We note that the United States claims that the Revised Guidelines respond to all the inconsistencies identified by the Appellate Body under the chapeau of Article XX of the GATT 1994 and thus its import prohibition on certain shrimp and shrimp products is justified. Malaysia, on the contrary, claims that the United States is not entitled to impose any prohibition in the absence of an international agreement allowing it to do so. Malaysia also claims that the United States should have withdrawn the import prohibition pending the conclusion of an international agreement. Malaysia adds that the Revised Guidelines are still biased and that the United States has failed to address the aspects of the original measure faulted by the Appellate Body.[176]

[176] A more detailed account of the arguments of the parties is found in Section III above.

5.25 We first note that the United States invokes Article XX as a "defence" for the violation of Article XI:1. We recall what we said above about the burden of proof with respect to "affirmative defences" in Article 21.5 cases. The United States chose to demonstrate the consistency of the implementing measure with Article XX by proving that it satisfactorily responded to all the findings of the Appellate Body. We also note that, when Malaysia contests that the implementing measure is consistent with Article XX, it also claims that the United States did not satisfy the requirements contained in the Appellate Body findings. The Panel notes in this respect that the claims of Malaysia are exclusively based on the findings of the Appellate Body and on non-compliance with them. Malaysia does not make any new claim under Article XX.

5.26 The Panel is mindful that the United States bears the burden of proving that the implementing measure is compatible with *all* the requirements of the chapeau of Article XX. The Panel notes in this respect that the Appellate Body did not discuss whether the original measure was a disguised restriction on international trade. As a result, this aspect will have to be addressed separately and without referring to any finding in the Appellate Body Report. However, as far as unjustifiable and arbitrary discrimination is concerned, the Panel is of the view that, in the absence of new claims, it is not required to go beyond reviewing the conformity of the implementing measure of the United States *with the findings of the Appellate Body*. In that context, the Panel considers it appropriate to apply the following approach: (i) present its understanding of the Appellate Body findings; and (ii) address the defence of the United States and Malaysia's arguments with respect to Article XX.

5.27 The Panel notes that, in its Report, the Appellate Body recalled the approach which it considered to be appropriate when assessing the conformity of an affirmative defence under Article XX:

> "In order that the justifying protection of Article XX may be extended to it, the measure at issue must not only come under one or another of the particular exceptions - paragraphs (a) to (j) - listed in Article XX; it must also satisfy the requirements imposed by the opening clauses of Article XX. The analysis is, in other words, two-tiered: first, provisional justification by reason of characterization of the measure under Article XX(g); second, further appraisal of the same measure under the introductory clauses of Article XX."[177]

5.28 As a result, when considering the arguments of the United States, we shall first determine the consistency of the implementing measure under paragraph (g) of Article XX. If we find the implementing measure to be "provisionally justi-

---

[177] Appellate Body Report, para. 118, quoting the Appellate Body Report on *United States - Standards for Reformulated and Conventional Gasoline,* adopted 20 May 1996, WT/DS2/AB/R (hereafter "*United States - Gasoline*"), DSR 1996:I, 3, p. 20.

fied" under paragraph (g), we shall proceed to determine whether it is applied in conformity with the chapeau of Article XX.

5.29 In this respect, we recall that both the Original Panel and the Appellate Body expressly addressed the question of the negotiation of a multilateral agreement for the protection of sea turtles. Both considered the absence of negotiations with the complaining parties to be evidence of "unjustifiable discrimination" within the meaning of the chapeau of Article XX. We also note that the Appellate Body presented the "failure of the United States to engage the appellees, as well as other Members exporting shrimp to the United States, in serious, across-the-board negotiations with the objective of concluding bilateral or multilateral agreements for the protection and conservation of sea turtles" as "another aspect of the application of Section 609 that bears heavily in any appraisal of justifiable or unjustifiable discrimination".[178] We also note that the Appellate Body insisted on the fact that such negotiations had not taken place *before* the United States enforced its import prohibition.[179]

5.30 Without taking a definitive position at this stage on the actual scope and consequences of these statements of the Appellate Body[180], we assume, for the sake of the structure of our findings, that the Appellate Body, like the Original Panel, considered that negotiations should have taken place *before* an import prohibition was applied. This, in our opinion, implies that, *as part of our analysis of the implementing measure before us*, we must first determine whether the United States engaged in serious negotiating efforts. Therefore, it seems appropriate for us first to determine the actual scope of the Original Panel and Appellate Body findings, as adopted by the DSB, in respect of the negotiation of an international agreement before reviewing the modifications made by the United States to its original measure. Indeed, if we were to conclude that the United States may not impose any measure of the type currently applied except pursuant to an international agreement, it would not be necessary to review any further the compatibility of the implementing measure, unless such an international agreement exists and actually allows the implementing measure currently in place.[181]

5.31 This is why, as part of our analysis of whether the US implementing measure constitutes or not unjustifiable discrimination, we shall first seek to determine the extent of the obligations of the United States with respect to the negotiation of an international agreement, as identified by the Appellate Body. Thereafter, as necessary, we will pursue our analysis of the compatibility of the implementing measure with the chapeau of Article XX by determining whether, on the

---

178 Appellate Body Report, para. 166.

179 *Ibid.*

180 See section V.D.3(a) below on the question of the actual scope of the findings of the Appellate Body with respect to the issue of bilateral or multilateral negotiations with the objective of reaching an agreement on the protection and conservation of sea turtles.

181 This approach is consistent with the principle of judicial economy as recalled by the Appellate Body, *inter alia*, in *United States - Shirts and Blouses, Op. Cit.*, p. 339.

basis of the other requirements identified in the DSB recommendations and rulings, the implementing measure meets the "unjustifiable discrimination" and "arbitrary discrimination" tests of the chapeau of Article XX.

5.32 Finally, since we are called upon to examine the compatibility of the implementing measure with all the relevant provisions of Article XX, we shall determine, as appropriate, whether or not that measure constitutes or not a disguised restriction on international trade.

2. *Consistency of the Implementing Measure with Paragraph (g) of Article XX of the GATT 1994*

5.33 Paragraph (g) of Article XX of the GATT 1994 provides that, subject to the requirement that such measure not be applied in a manner contrary to the chapeau of Article XX, nothing in the GATT 1994 shall be construed to prevent the adoption or enforcement by any Member of measures:

> "relating to the conservation of exhaustible natural resources if such measures are made effective in conjunction with restrictions on domestic production or consumption".

5.34 The Panel notes that it is instructed by Article 21.5 of the DSU to review "the existence or consistency with a covered agreement of measures taken to comply with the recommendations and rulings" of the DSB. The Panel notes that the Appellate Body found that:

> "134. For all the forgoing reasons [developed in paragraphs 127 to 133 of the Appellate Body Report], we find that the sea turtles here involved constitute "exhaustible natural resources" for purposes of Article XX(g) of the GATT 1994."[182]

5.35 The Appellate Body also found that:

> "141. In its general design and structure, therefore, Section 609 is not a simple, blanket prohibition of the importation of shrimp imposed without regard to the consequences (or lack thereof) of the mode of harvesting employed upon the incidental capture and mortality of sea turtles. Focusing on the design of the measure here at stake [footnote omitted], it appears to us that Section 609, *cum* implementing guidelines, is not disproportionately wide in its scope and reach in relation to the policy objective of protection and conservation of sea turtle species. The means are, in principle, reasonably related to the ends. The means and ends relationship between Section 609 and the legitimate policy of conserving an exhaustible, and, in fact, endangered species, is observably a close and real one, a relationship that is every bit as substantial as that

[182] Appellate Body Report, para. 134.

which we found in *United States - Gasoline* between the EPA baseline establishment rules and the conservation of clean air in the United States.

142. In our view, therefore, Section 609 is a measure "relating to" the conservation of an exhaustible natural resource within the meaning of Article XX(g) of the GATT 1994."

5.36 Finally, the Appellate Body found that:

"145. Accordingly, we hold that Section 609 is a measure made effective in conjunction with the restriction on domestic harvesting of shrimp, as required by Article XX(g)".

5.37 The Panel recalls that, as the party invoking Article XX, the United States bears the burden of proving that its implementing measure meets *all* the relevant requirements of that Article, including those of paragraph (g). This implies that the United States must make a *prima facie* case that the implementing measure relates to the conservation of exhaustible natural resources if such a measure is made effective in conjunction with restrictions on domestic production or consumption.

5.38 The United States has argued that Section 609 was found to be "provisionally justified" by the Appellate Body under paragraph (g). Malaysia does not raise any claims or arguments on the specific issue of the compatibility of Section 609 with paragraph (g) as such.[183]

5.39 The Panel considers that two questions have to be addressed in order to determine whether the implementing measure meets the requirements of paragraph (g) of Article XX. First, the Panel notes that the Appellate Body found that Section 609 was "provisionally justified" under Article XX(g).[184] We understand this to mean that, in the process of determining whether Section 609 was justified under Article XX, the Appellate Body concluded that Section 609 satisfied the first tier of the analysis defined in its report on *United States - Gasoline*[185], i.e. the *characterization* of the measure under Article XX(g). This implies that, as long as the implementing measure before us is identical to the measure examined by the Appellate Body in relation to paragraph (g), we should not reach a different conclusion from the Appellate Body.

5.40 This leads us to the second question, i.e. what exactly did the Appellate Body find to be "provisionally justified" under Article XX(g)?[186] We note that

---

[183] A more detailed account of the arguments of the parties can be found in Section III above.

[184] Appellate Body Report, para. 147.

[185] *Op. Cit.*, DSR 1996:3, at p. 20. See also Appellate Body Report, para. 118.

[186] We are mindful that, as mentioned by the Appellate Body in *Australia - Measures Affecting Importation of Salmon* (adopted on 6 November 1998, WT/DS18/AB/R, DSR 1998:VIII, 3327, para. 223), our findings must be complete enough to enable the DSB to make sufficiently precise recommendations and rulings so as to allow for prompt compliance in order to ensure effective resolution of disputes to the benefit of all Members.

the Appellate Body stated that it had to "examine the relationship between the general structure and design of the measure here at stake, Section 609, and the policy goal it purports to save, that is, the conservation of sea turtles."[187] We also recall that, in footnote 76 of its report, the Appellate Body stated that the United States measure at issue was referred to as "Section 609" or "the measure" and that, by these terms, the Appellate Body meant Section 609 *and* the 1996 Guidelines. While we have no doubt that the Appellate Body actually considered the measure as a whole, our reading of the relevant paragraphs of the Appellate Body Report nonetheless leads us to believe that the Appellate Body essentially based its finding of "provisional justification" on the features of Section 609 as such. This is because, according to the Appellate Body interpretation, the elements to be considered in order to determine the compatibility of the measure with paragraph (g) are essentially found in the text of Section 609 as such. In our view, references to the implementing guidelines are there to confirm that the content of those guidelines does not affect the interpretation of Section 609 as such in that respect.

5.41 As already mentioned above, the United States did not amend Section 609, whereas it has issued revised implementing guidelines. We therefore conclude that since Section 609 as such has not been modified, the findings of the Appellate Body regarding paragraph (g) remain valid and the consistency of Section 609 as such with the requirements of paragraph (g) also remains valid, to the extent that the Revised Guidelines do not modify the *interpretation* to be given to Section 609 in that respect. We have no evidence that the Revised Guidelines have modified in any way the meaning of Section 609 *vis-à-vis* the requirements of paragraph (g), as interpreted by the Appellate Body.

5.42 We therefore conclude that the implementing measure is provisionally justified under paragraph (g) of Article XX. We proceed with the second tier of the method applied by the Appellate Body in this case, i.e. the "further appraisal of the *same measure* under the introductory clause of Article XX."[188]

3. *Arbitrary or Unjustifiable Discrimination Between Countries where the Same Conditions Prevail: the Question of International Negotiations*

(a) Extent of the US Obligation to Negotiate and/or Reach an International Agreement on the Protection and Conservation of Sea Turtles

(i) Abuse or Misuse of Rights under Article XX as a Standard for Determining the

[187] Appellate Body Report, para. 137.
[188] Appellate Body Report, para. 118.

Extent of an Obligation to Negotiate and/or Enter into an International Agreement

5.43 As mentioned above, the Appellate Body, as part of its process of determining whether the original measure had been applied in a manner that constituted a means of "unjustifiable discrimination", addressed the issue of international negotiations, an issue which is raised by Malaysia before this Panel. After having considered that the lack of flexibility to take into account the different situations in different countries amounted to unjustifiable discrimination[189], the Appellate Body added that:

> "166. Another aspect of the application of Section 609 that bears heavily in any appraisal of justifiable or unjustifiable discrimination is the failure of the United States to engage the appellees, as well as other Members exporting shrimp to the United States, in serious, across-the-board negotiations with the objective of concluding bilateral or multilateral agreements for the protection and conservation of sea turtles, before enforcing the import prohibition against the shrimp exports of those other Members."

5.44 As underlined by the Appellate Body itself, Section 609(a) directs the US Secretary of State *inter alia* to initiate negotiations as soon as possible for the development of bilateral or multilateral agreements with other nations for the protection and conservation of sea turtles. This as such is not a ground for a finding of unjustifiable discrimination unless, in implementing Section 609(a), the United States authorities have discriminated between exporting countries by negotiating seriously with some and less seriously or not at all with others.

5.45 However, the Appellate Body did not conclude its analysis at that point. It also noted that "the protection and conservation of highly migratory species [...] demand concerted and cooperative efforts on the part of the many countries whose waters are traversed in the course of recurrent sea turtle migrations."[190] The Appellate Body went on to recall that the need for and the appropriateness of such efforts had been recognized by the WTO itself as well as in a significant number of other international instruments and declarations.[191] In addition, the Appellate Body recalled that the United States had actually succeeded in negotiating an international agreement for the protection and conservation of sea turtles, namely the Inter-American Convention.[192] In the conclusion to its analysis, the Appellate Body also stated that "The unilateral character of the application of Section 609 heightens the disruptive and discriminatory influence of the import prohibition and underscores its unjustifiability."[193]

---

[189] See para. 5.90 below.

[190] Appellate Body Report, para. 168.

[191] *Ibid.*

[192] Appellate Body Report, paras. 169-171.

[193] Appellate Body Report, para. 172 *in fine*.

5.46 The approach of the Appellate Body leads us to conclude that it is not solely the fact that the United States negotiated seriously with some Members and less seriously with others which is at the origin of its finding of unjustifiable discrimination in relation to negotiations, even though it would have been sufficient in itself to justify such a conclusion. We believe that another reason for the Appellate Body finding is that the United States, by unilaterally defining and implementing criteria for applying Section 609, failed to take into account the different situations which may exist in the exporting countries. In other words, the United States failed to pass the "unjustified discrimination" test by applying the same regime to domestic and foreign shrimp.

5.47 This second requirement is, however, insufficient on its own to explain the findings of the Appellate Body. We believe the reason for such findings on this issue by the Appellate Body flows from the context. The protection and conservation of sea turtles is a field where a multilateral approach is appropriate because of the highly migratory nature of sea turtles. Moreover, this is a field where international cooperation is clearly favoured under the applicable norms of international law. Finally, the successful negotiation and the content of the Inter-American Convention are evidence that a multilateral agreement is a reasonably open alternative course of action for securing the legitimate goals of the US measure.[194]

5.48 Having determined that the United States *had* to engage in negotiations does not suffice to determine whether the United States has complied with the recommendations and rulings of the DSB in this respect. It is also necessary to assess the extent of the efforts required. In this regard, we consider that the findings of the Appellate Body concerning the nature of the chapeau of Article XX and, in particular, the notion of abuse or misuse of rights under Article XX provide clear guidance as to how to assess the degree of efforts required from the United States in relation to the negotiation of an international agreement.

5.49 We note that the Appellate Body stated in its Report that:

> "156. Turning then to the chapeau of Article XX, we consider that it embodies the recognition on the part of WTO Members of the need to maintain a balance of rights and obligations between the right of a Member to invoke one or another of the exceptions of Article XX, specified in paragraphs (a) to (j), on the one hand, and the substantive rights of the other Members under the GATT 1994, on the other hand. *Exercise by one Member of its right to invoke an exception, such as Article XX(g), if abused or misused, will, to that extent, erode or render naught the substantive treaty rights in, for example, Article XI:1, of other Members.* […] thus, a balance must be struck between the *right* of a Member to invoke an exception under Article XX and the *duty* of that same Member to respect the

[194] Appellate Body Report, para. 171.

treaty rights of the other Members. To permit one Member to abuse or misuse its right to invoke an exception would be effectively to allow that Member to degrade its own treaty obligations as well as to devalue the treaty rights of other Members. If the abuse or misuse is sufficiently grave or extensive, the Member, in effect, reduces its treaty obligation to a merely facultative one and dissolves its juridical character, and, in so doing, negates altogether the treaty rights of other Members." [195]

5.50 The Appellate Body also considered that:

"159. The task of interpreting and applying the chapeau is, hence, essentially the delicate one of locating and marking out a *line of equilibrium* between the right of a Member to invoke an exception under Article XX and the rights of the other Members under varying substantive provisions (e.g., Article XI) of the GATT 1994, so that neither of the competing rights will cancel out the other and thereby distort and nullify or impair the balance of rights and obligations constructed by the Members themselves in that Agreement. *The location of the line of equilibrium, as expressed in the chapeau, is not fixed and unchanging; the line moves as the kind and the shape of the measures at stake vary and as the facts making up specific cases differ.*"[196]

We conclude that, in order for us to determine what is actually required from the United States in relation to engaging in serious "across-the-board" negotiations with the objective of concluding bilateral or multilateral agreements for the protection and conservation of sea turtles, we need to assess what is required to avoid abuse or misuse of the rights of the United States under Article XX in the present case.

5.51 The existence of an abuse or misuse of those rights is dependent on a "line of equilibrium" between the right of a Member to invoke an exception under Article XX and the rights of the other Members under varying substantive provisions (e.g., Article XI) of the GATT 1994. As mentioned by the Appellate Body, "the location of the line of equilibrium, as expressed in the chapeau, is not fixed and unchanging; the line moves as the kind and the shape of the measures at stake vary and as the facts making up specific cases differ." In other words, the position of the line itself depends on the type of measure imposed and on the particular circumstances of this case. The measure at issue - an import prohibition - has been described by the Appellate Body as "ordinarily, the heaviest 'weapon' in a Member's armoury of trade measures."[197] In making this analogy, it seems that the Appellate Body meant to imply that other, less trade restrictive measures ex-

[195] Italics in the original, underlining added.
[196] Underlining added.
[197] Appellate Body Report, para. 171.

isted and also that import prohibitions, because of their impact, had to be subject to stricter disciplines. We believe that, in order to determine the position of the line, we need not only to identify the facts making up this specific case, i.e. the factual context, but also to consider the legal framework influencing the interpretation to be given to the notion of "unjustifiable discrimination" in the factual context of the protection and conservation of sea turtles.

5.52 The *factual context* is essentially related to the biology of sea turtles and, more particularly, the fact that the sea turtles covered by Section 609 are highly migratory species, as was confirmed by the experts consulted by the Original Panel.[198] We also note that the Appellate Body stated that this objective - the protection and conservation of sea turtles as highly migratory species - "demands concerted and cooperative efforts on the part of the many countries whose waters are traversed in the course of recurrent sea turtle migrations."[199] It is also important to keep in mind, as implicitly noted by the Appellate Body, that the situation of each Member may be different in terms of sea turtle protection and conservation.[200]

5.53 As far as the *legal framework* is concerned, we recall that the Appellate Body also noted that "the need for, and the appropriateness of, such efforts [to protect migratory species] have been recognized in the WTO itself as well as in a significant number of international instruments and declarations."[201] Inevitably, when considering this legal framework, we will have to rely on the customary norms of international law on treaty interpretation, as embodied in the Vienna Convention.

5.54 In that framework, assessing first the *object and purpose* of the WTO Agreement, we note that the WTO preamble refers to the notion of "sustainable development".[202] This means that in interpreting the terms of the chapeau, we must keep in mind that sustainable development is one of the objectives of the WTO Agreement.

---

198 Original Panel Report, paras. 5.1 to 5.312.

199 Appellate Body Report, para. 168, citing the Rio Declaration, Agenda 21, the Convention on Biological Diversity, the Bonn Convention on the Conservation of Migratory Species of Wild Animals, and the Report (1996) of the CTE.

200 Appellate Body Report, para. 165, where the Appellate Body specifies that "many of those Members [of the WTO] may be differently situated".

201 Appellate Body Report, para. 168.

202 *See* the final texts of the agreements negotiated by Governments at the United Nation Conference on Environment and Development (UNCED), Rio de Janeiro, Brazil, 3-14 June, 1992, specifically the Rio Declaration on Environment and Development (hereafter the "Rio Declaration") and Agenda 21 at www.unep.org; the concept is elaborated in detailed action plans in Agenda 21 so as to put in place development that is sustainable - i.e. that "meets the needs of the present generation without compromising the ability of future generations to meet their own needs". *See* World Commission on Environment and Development, *Our Common Future* (Oxford: Oxford University Press, 1988).

5.55 How this objective is to be appreciated can further be elaborated by reference to the Marrakesh Decision establishing the Committee on Trade and Environment (CTE). The preamble of that Decision provides, *inter alia*, that:

> "there should not be, nor need be, any policy contradiction between upholding and safeguarding an open, non-discriminatory and equitable multilateral trading system on the one hand and acting for the protection of the environment and promotion of sustainable development on the other."

These terms would seem to imply that recourse to trade-related measures not based on international consensus is generally not the most appropriate means of enforcing environmental measures, since it leads to the imposition of unwanted constraints on the multilateral trading system and may affect sustainable development.

5.56 We also have evidence in the context of Article XX showing that preference must be given to a multilateral approach in terms of protection of the environment. In this respect, we note the content of the 1996 Report of the CTE, where the CTE endorsed and supported "multilateral solutions based on international cooperation and consensus as the best and most effective way for governments to tackle environmental problems of a transboundary or global nature."[203] Insofar as this report can be deemed to embody the opinion of the WTO Members, it could be argued that it records evidence of "subsequent practice in the application of the treaty which establishes the agreement of the parties regarding its interpretation" (Article 31.3(b) of the Vienna Convention) and as such should be taken into account in the interpretation of the provisions concerned. However, even if it is not to be considered as evidence of a subsequent practice, it remains the expression of a common opinion of Members and is therefore relevant in assessing the scope of the chapeau of Article XX.

5.57 Finally, we note that the Appellate Body, like the Original Panel, referred to a number of international agreements, many of which have been ratified or otherwise accepted by the parties to this dispute.[204] Article 31.3(c) of the Vienna Convention provides that, in interpreting a treaty, there shall be taken into account, together with the context, "any relevant rule of international law applicable to the relations between the parties". We note that, with the exception of the Bonn Convention on the Conservation of Migratory Species of Wild Animals (CMS)[205], Malaysia and the United States have accepted or are committed to

---

[203] Report (1996) of the Committee on Trade and Environment, WT/CTE/1, 12 November 1996, para. 171.

[204] Appellate Body Report, para. 168.

[205] However, we note that the Memorandum of Understanding on the Conservation and Management of Marine Turtles and their Habitats of the Indian Ocean and South-East Asian Region (MOU) "shall be considered an agreement under Article IV, para. 4 of the CMS" ("Basic Principles", para. 1 of the MOU). It is also our understanding that the CMS Secretariat provided assistance in the negotiation of the MOU and is the provisional secretariat for this Memorandum of Understanding.

comply with all of the international instruments referred to by the Appellate Body in paragraph 168 of its Report.[206]

5.58 To clarify the meaning of "unjustifiable discrimination" in the context of measures relating to the protection of endangered migratory species, the above-mentioned elements, to which proper weight must be given pursuant to customary norms of interpretation, influence the positioning of the line of equilibrium that the United States must respect in this case. Undoubtedly, these elements move the line of equilibrium towards multilateral solutions and non trade-restrictive measures.[207]

5.59 We therefore conclude that the fact that sea turtles are highly migratory species whose protection concerns all the States through the territories or sea zones of which they migrate and the recognition, both at the WTO level and in other international agreements that the protection of migratory species is best achieved through international cooperation, significantly move the line of equilibrium referred to by the Appellate Body towards a bilaterally or multilaterally negotiated solution, thus rendering recourse to unilateral measures less acceptable. This is in our opinion the reason why the Appellate Body established that it was necessary for the United States to engage in serious efforts in the field of sea turtle protection and conservation in order to avoid abuse or misuse of Article XX of the GATT 1994. This means that, if we were to find that the US import prohibition had been applied without serious efforts having been made to negotiate a multilateral agreement for the protection and conservation of sea turtles, the measure might constitute an abuse or misuse of Article XX.

5.60 We also note that the Appellate Body stated that "the chapeau of Article XX is but one expression of the principle of good faith".[208] The notion of good faith, in relation to the issue under examination in this section, implies a continuity of efforts which, in our opinion, is the only way to address successfully the issue of conservation and protection of sea turtles through multilateral negotiations, as demonstrated by the circumstances of this case. We therefore consider that, even though the Appellate Body only refers to "serious efforts", the notion of good faith efforts implies, *inter alia*, that the seriousness of the United States' efforts in this case must be assessed over a period of time. It is this continuity of

---

206 See footnote 199 above.

207 We note in this respect that the Appellate Body itself used the Inter-American Convention as an illustration of the positioning of the line of equilibrium which defines when a particular measure may be perceived as an abuse or misuse of Article XX:

> "170. The juxtaposition of (a) the *consensual* undertakings to put in place regulations providing for, *inter alia*, use of TEDs *jointly determined* to be suitable for a particular party's maritime areas, with (b) the reaffirmation of the parties' obligations under the *WTO Agreement*, including the *Agreement on Technical Barriers to Trade* and Article XI of the GATT 1994, suggests that the parties to the Inter-American Convention *together marked out the equilibrium line to which we referred earlier*." (Italics in the original, underlining added).

208 Appellate Body Report, para. 158.

efforts that matters, not a particular move at a given moment, followed by inaction.

5.61 On that basis, we proceed to determine whether the line of equilibrium in the field of sea turtle conservation and protection is such as to require the conclusion of an international agreement or only efforts to negotiate.

(ii) Obligation to Negotiate v. Obligation to Reach an International Agreement

5.62 We recall that the parties differ as to the extent of the obligations of the United States in relation to the negotiation and conclusion of an international agreement on the protection and conservation of sea turtles. The United States argues that it only has to make good faith efforts to negotiate an agreement whereas Malaysia claims, as a first line of argumentation, that an international agreement has to be reached before any measure can be imposed.

5.63 The Panel first recalls that the Appellate Body considered "the *failure of the United States to engage the appellees*, as well as other Members exporting shrimp to the United States, in serious across-the-board negotiations *with the objective of concluding bilateral or multilateral agreements* for the protection and conservation of sea turtles, *before* enforcing the import prohibition against the shrimp exports of those other Members"[209] bears heavily in any appraisal of justifiable or unjustifiable discrimination within the meaning of the chapeau of Article XX. From the terms used, it appears to us that the Appellate Body had in mind a negotiation, not the conclusion of an agreement. If the Appellate Body had considered that an agreement had to be concluded before any measure can be taken by the United States, it would not have used the terms "with the objective"; it would have simply stated that an agreement had to be concluded.

5.64 We also note that the Appellate Body stated that:

> "172. Clearly, the United States *negotiated seriously with some, but not with other Members* (including the appellees), that export shrimp to the United States. The effect is plainly discriminatory and, in our view, unjustifiable. The unjustifiable nature of this discrimination emerges clearly when we consider the cumulative effects of the *failure of the United States to pursue negotiations for establishing consensual means of protection and conservation of the living marine resources here involved*, notwithstanding the explicit statutory direction in Section 609 itself to initiate negotiations as soon as possible for the development of bilateral and multilateral agreements. [Footnote omitted]"

This paragraph is evidence that the Appellate Body considered that the requirement is one of "negotiation", not "conclusion" of an agreement. Moreover, we

[209] Appellate Body Report, para. 166 (emphasis added).

consider that, if the Appellate Body had intended to imply that no measure could be adopted outside the framework of an international agreement on the protection and conservation of sea turtles, it would not have continued with its review of the unilateral measure applied pursuant to Section 609. Rather, it would have reached a final conclusion once it had determined, as had the Original Panel, that no serious efforts had been made at that time by the United States to negotiate an agreement on the protection and conservation of sea turtles.

5.65 We also note that, in paragraph 121 of its Report, the Appellate Body stated that "conditioning access to a Member's domestic market on whether exporting Members comply with, or adopt, a policy or policies unilaterally prescribed by the importing Member may, to some degree, be a common aspect of measures falling within the scope of one or another of the exceptions (a) to (j) of Article XX." This seems to mean that, in the opinion of the Appellate Body, recourse to a unilateral measure cannot *a priori* be excluded under Article XX of the GATT 1994.

5.66 In the context of this section, we conclude that the United States had the following obligations in this case in order to avoid "unjustifiable discrimination":

(a) the United States had to take the initiative of negotiations with the appellees, having already negotiated with other harvesting countries (Caribbean and Western Atlantic countries);

(b) the negotiations had to be with all interested parties ("across-the-board") and aimed at establishing consensual means of protection and conservation of endangered sea turtles;

(c) the United States had to make serious efforts in good faith[210] to negotiate; and

(d) serious efforts in good faith had to take place before[211] the enforcement of a unilaterally designed import prohibition.[212]

5.67 We are consequently of the view that the Appellate Body could not have meant in its findings that the United States had the obligation to conclude an agreement on the protection and conservation of sea turtles in order to comply with Article XX. However, we reach the conclusion that the United States has an obligation to make serious good faith efforts to reach an agreement before resorting to the type of unilateral measure currently in place. We also consider that

[210] See para. 5.60 above.

[211] The Panel considers that the use of the word "before" by the Appellate Body has to be considered in the context of the original case. This does not mean that, in terms of implementation, the United States would have to go back in time to correct the original error, something obviously impossible. The question of the conformity with the DSB recommendations and rulings has to be assessed on the basis of the actions taken by the United States subsequent to the adoption of the Panel and Appellate Body reports.

[212] On this last point, the Panel considers it to be important to note that it is not sufficient formally to "initiate" negotiations before having recourse to a unilateral measure. Serious good faith efforts must take place continuously up to the satisfactory conclusion of the negotiations.

those efforts cannot be a "one-off" exercise. There must be a continuous process, including once a unilateral measure has been adopted pending the conclusion of an agreement. Indeed, we consider the reference of the Appellate Body to a number of international agreements promoting a multilateral solution to the conservation concerns subject to Section 609 to be evidence that a multilateral, ideally non-trade restrictive, solution is generally to be preferred when dealing with those concerns, in particular if it is established that it constitutes "an alternative course of action reasonably open".[213]

5.68 Having determined the context in which recourse must be made to bilateral or multilateral negotiations, we now proceed to determine the extent of the "serious good faith efforts" required in the present case.

(iii) The Inter-American Convention as a Benchmark of Serious Good Faith Efforts in this Case

5.69 As mentioned above, what is at issue at this stage is the existence of "unjustifiable discrimination" as a result of: (i) an absence of or insufficient negotiation with some Members compared with others and, in general; and (ii) the unilateral nature of the design and application of the original measure which did not allow for the particular situation of each exporting country to be taken into account. As a result, in order to remove the unjustifiable discrimination, serious good faith efforts must address these two aspects.

5.70 We note that, with respect to the Inter-American Convention, the Appellate Body stated, *inter alia*, that:

> "170. The juxtaposition of (a) the *consensual* undertakings to put in place regulations providing for, *inter alia*, use of TEDs *jointly determined* to be suitable for a particular party's maritime areas, with (b) the reaffirmation of the parties' obligations under the *WTO Agreement*, including the *Agreement on Technical Barriers to Trade* and Article XI of the GATT 1994, suggests that the parties to the Inter-American Convention together marked out the equilibrium line to which we referred earlier. The Inter-American Convention demonstrates the conviction of its signatories, including the United States, that consensual and multilateral procedures are available and feasible for the establishment of programs for the conservation of sea turtles. Moreover, the Inter-American Convention emphasizes the continuing validity and significance of Article XI of the GATT 1994, and of the obligations of the *WTO Agreement* generally, in maintaining the balance of rights and obligations

[213] Appellate Body Report, para. 171.

> under the *WTO Agreement* among the signatories of that Convention.
>
> 171. The Inter-American Convention thus provides convincing demonstration that an alternative course of action was reasonably open to the United States for securing the legitimate policy goal of its measure, a course of action other than the unilateral and *non-consensual* procedures of the import prohibition under Section 609."[214]

5.71 With respect to the absence of or insufficient negotiation with some Members compared with others, the reference of the Appellate Body to the Inter-American Convention is evidence that the efforts made by the United States to negotiate with the complainants before imposing the original measure were largely insufficient. The Inter-American Convention was negotiated as a binding agreement and has entered into force on 2 May 2001.[215] We conclude that the Inter-American Convention can reasonably be considered as a benchmark of what can be achieved through multilateral negotiations in the field of protection and conservation. While we agree that factual circumstances may influence the duration of the process or the end result, we consider that any effort alleged to be a "serious good faith effort" must be assessed against the efforts made in relation to the conclusion of the Inter-American Convention.

5.72 Regarding the unilateral nature of the design and application of the original measure which did not allow for the particular situation of each exporting country to be taken into account, we recall that the Appellate Body noted that the Inter-American Convention provided for *consensual* undertakings to put in place regulations providing for, *inter alia*, use of TEDs *jointly determined to be suitable for a particular party's maritime areas*. This is, in our view, an application to the specific context of the negotiation of an agreement on sea turtles of the requirement more generally recalled by the Appellate Body in its findings on arbitrary and unjustifiable discrimination that the United States should have taken into account the situation prevailing in the other negotiating countries.[216]

5.73 The consequence of this is, in our view, that the standard of serious good faith efforts to negotiate an agreement on the protection and conservation of sea turtles has to be understood in line with the finding of the Appellate Body that the United States should have taken into account the situation of each exporting country. Thus, efforts to negotiate should be made taking into account the situations prevailing in the other negotiating countries. We agree that, normally, it is the very *raison d'être* of a negotiation to allow all parties to try to have their situations taken into account and that adding such a requirement could seem to be

---

[214] Underlining added.

[215] As of 15 May 2001, the Convention has nine parties: Brazil, Costa Rica, Ecuador, Honduras, Mexico, The Netherlands, Peru, Venezuela, and the United States.

[216] See, e.g., Appellate Body Report, paras. 161, 163, 164, 165, 172 and 177.

superfluous. We consider, however, that this requirement is essential in the particular context at issue. We note that Section 609 has been applied to the whole world since 1996. Since then, any country exporting shrimp to the United States and entering into negotiations has done so while being subject to the requirements Section 609. The Appellate Body noted that the original measure, in its application, was more concerned with effectively influencing WTO Members to adopt essentially the same comprehensive regulatory regime as that applied by the United States to its domestic shrimp trawlers, even though many of those Members may be differently situated.[217] We consider that, in that context, negotiators may have found themselves constrained to accept conditions that they may not have accepted had Section 609 not been applied. Even if Section 609 as currently applied takes more into account the existence of different conservation programmes, it can still influence the outcome of negotiations. This is why the Panel feels it is important to take the reality of international relations into account and considers that the standard of review of the efforts of the United States on the international plane should be expressed as follows: whether the United States made serious good faith efforts to negotiate an international agreement, taking into account the situations of the other negotiating countries.

5.74 At this stage we wish to clarify that, in our opinion, the Appellate Body perceived the Inter-American Convention not as what is *required* in the field of protection of sea turtles, but as an example of an action which would meet the criteria of the chapeau of Article XX in terms of balance between the right of a Member to invoke Article XX and the duty of that same Member to respect the treaty rights of other Members. As a result, an agreement of that type would be more consistent with the objective of the chapeau of Article XX to avoid abuse or misuse of rights than a unilaterally designed import ban. This can be deduced from the comparison made by the Appellate Body between the Inter-American Convention and "an import prohibition [which] is, ordinarily, the heaviest "weapon" in a Member's armoury of trade measures."[218]

5.75 However, even though this may be only one way of dealing with the protection of sea turtles in a manner consistent with Article XX, it appears to us that, in the context of this case, it has a particular strength: the Inter-American Convention is evidence that it is feasible to negotiate a binding agreement imposing the adoption of measures comparable to those applied in the United States. Contrary to what the United States seems to claim, the conclusion of the Inter-American Convention demonstrates that the standard of serious good faith efforts imposed in relation to the negotiation of an international agreement in the field of protection and conservation of sea turtles may be quite demanding.

[217] Appellate Body Report, para. 165.
[218] Appellate Body Report, para. 171.

(iv) Conclusion

5.76 We understand the Appellate Body findings as meaning that the United States has an obligation to make serious good faith efforts to address the question of the protection and conservation of sea turtles at the international level. We are mindful of the potentially subjective nature of the notion of serious good faith efforts and of how difficult such a test may be to apply in reality. We note, however, that in the present case a number of guideposts are available. The fact that sea turtles are migratory species and that they are on the verge of extinction is unanimously acknowledged. Objectives in terms of protection and conservation of sea turtles are quite clear and largely uncontested. The means of reaching them have been identified by scientists, discussed in seminars and included in negotiation documents. The nature of sea turtles as migratory species is also important, in light of the preference expressed in a number of international conventions for a multilateral approach to the conservation of migratory species. The United States is a *demandeur* in this field and given its scientific, diplomatic and financial means, it is reasonable to expect rather more than less from that Member in terms of serious good faith efforts. Indeed, the capacity of persuasion of the United States is illustrated by the successful negotiation of the Inter-American Convention.

5.77 Of course, no single standard may be appropriate. Moreover, the particular factual circumstances prevailing in a particular negotiation may change the degree of achievement which may be expected. This is why this Panel sought to obtain as much information as possible on the negotiation of the Memorandum of Understanding on the Conservation and Management of Marine Turtles and their Habitats of the Indian Ocean and South-East Asia[219], in the negotiation of which Malaysia and the United States have been involved.

5.78 In addition, the United States, even though it is *demandeur* in this field, may not be held exclusively responsible for reaching an agreement on the protection and conservation of sea turtles. Indeed, while it may be responsible for the absence of agreement, e.g. by blocking the negotiations, it may also share the responsibility or bear no responsibility at all.

(b) Assessment of the Consistency of the Implementing Measure

(i) Serious Good Faith Efforts by the End of the Reasonable Period of Time

5.79 Both parties have provided us with a description of their efforts to negotiate an agreement on the protection and conservation of sea turtles since 1996. The Panel notes that the first tangible evidence of a good faith effort of the

[219] July 2000, hereafter the "MOU".

United States toward the conclusion of an international agreement on the protection and conservation of sea turtles is the document communicated by the US Department of State to a number of nations of the Indian Ocean and to the four original complainants in this dispute on 14 October 1998. This document contained possible elements of a regional convention for the conservation of sea turtles in the Indian Ocean. The United States subsequently contributed to the Symposium and Workshop on Sea Turtle Conservation and Biology held in Sabah, Malaysia, on 15-17 July 1999. The Sabah Symposium led to the adoption of a Declaration calling for "the negotiation and implementation of a wider regional agreement for the conservation and management of marine turtle populations and their habitat throughout the Indo-Pacific and Indian Ocean region". Finally, at the Perth Conference in October 1999, the participating governments committed themselves to develop an international agreement on sea turtle conservation for the region.

5.80 The Panel, having regard to the criteria identified by the Appellate Body, concludes that, by the end of the reasonable period of time, the United States had made substantial efforts. However, these efforts were still continuing at that time. This Panel was established only on 23 October 2000. Between the end of the reasonable period of time and that date, new events have occurred which cannot be disregarded in assessing whether serious good faith efforts have actually been made. This is why we refrain, in this particular case, from taking a position on the existence of serious good faith efforts as of the end of the reasonable period of time and prefer to determine whether good faith efforts had actually taken place at the date of establishment of this Panel under Article 21.5 of the DSU.[220]

(ii) Serious Good Faith Efforts as of the Date the Matter Was Referred to this Panel

5.81 The major event since the end of the reasonable period of time has been the conduct of a first round of negotiations toward the conclusion of a regional agreement on the conservation of sea turtles in Kuantan, Malaysia, from 11 to 14 July 2000, in which the United States participated. At Kuantan, 24 countries adopted the text of the South-East Asian MOU. The Final Act of the meeting provides that, before the MOU can be finalised, a Conservation and Management Plan must be negotiated and annexed to the MOU. The MOU, however, will not be a legally binding instrument for the time being.

5.82 The Panel is of the view that the contribution of the United States to the steps that led to the Kuantan meeting and its contribution to the Kuantan meeting itself could be considered to constitute serious good faith efforts. As mentioned

[220] This does not mean that the United States did not have to bring its legislation into conformity by the end of the reasonable period of time.

above, the standard set by the Inter-American Convention is quite high. However, the factual circumstances have to be kept in mind.

5.83 First, the Inter-American Convention was negotiated as a legally binding instrument. It is the understanding of the Panel that the United States was in favour of a legally binding agreement for the Indian Ocean and South-East Asian region too. However, it appears that a number of other parties were in favour of a non-binding text. As mentioned above, the United States' efforts must be assessed in the light of the factual context. The United States cannot be held liable for the fact that a number of other parties in the Kuantan meeting were not in favour of a binding text. This, however, cannot detract from the United States continuing obligation to make serious good faith efforts towards a binding agreement. The Panel notes, moreover, that the remaining negotiations in relation to the South-East Asian MOU could be concluded in the course of 2001.

5.84 Second, the content of the final agreement will depend on the content of the Conservation and Management Plan, which is to be annexed to the MOU but was still being drafted as this Panel was proceeding. In this respect, the Panel cannot assume that the United States, in the light of its own policy towards protection and conservation of sea turtles, would be in favour of an international agreement which would impose or promote - in the case of a non-binding agreement - insufficient protection and conservation programmes. We believe that, at least until the Conservation and Management Plan to be attached to the MOU is completed, the United States' efforts should be judged on the basis of its active participation and its financial support to the negotiations, as well as on the basis of its previous efforts since 1998, having regard to the likelihood of a conclusion of the negotiations in the course of 2001. In that context it seems reasonable to consider that the United States had, as of the date of establishment of this Panel, made serious good faith efforts to conclude a multilateral agreement.

5.85 The Panel notes the argument of the United States that the progress made in multilateral negotiations in the Indian Ocean and South-East Asian region will not necessarily translate into the achievement of the environmental goal of the US measure. In other words, according to the United States, the negotiations may, or may not, result in multilaterally agreed steps that will save sea turtles from extinction.

5.86 The Panel would like to recall that what is required from the United States according to the Appellate Body reasoning is serious good faith efforts in the negotiation of an agreement aiming at the protection and conservation of sea turtles, taking into account the situation of the other negotiating parties. In other words, the United States, in the present case, has an obligation to make efforts commensurate with its position as the country seeking the protection and conservation of sea turtles. Moreover, the obligation borne by the United States is a continuing one. In the present case, it is because the United States has demonstrated that it was making serious good faith efforts that it is, in our opinion, *provisionally* entitled to apply the implementing measure, which may be subject to further control under Article 21.5 of the DSU.

(c) Conclusion

5.87 As mentioned above, our understanding of the Appellate Body findings is that the United States would be entitled to maintain the implementing measure if it were demonstrated that it was making serious good faith efforts to conclude an international agreement on the protection and conservation of sea turtles. The Panel is of the view that the US efforts since 1998 meet the standard established by the Appellate Body Report. In this respect, the Panel notes the sustained pace of the negotiations and the prospect of their conclusion in 2001, as well as the effective contribution of the United States in the context of these negotiations. The Panel also notes the significant contrast between the situation reviewed by the Original Panel and the Appellate Body and the situation today. Finally, the Panel notes that Malaysia did not submit convincing evidence that the United States had not made serious good faith efforts in relation to the negotiation of an international agreement on the protection and conservation of sea turtles since the adoption of the reports of the Original Panel and the Appellate Body.

5.88 Finally, the Panel would like to clarify that, in a context such as this one where a multilateral agreement is clearly to be preferred and where measures such as that taken by the United States in this case may only be accepted under Article XX if they were allowed under an international agreement, or if they were taken further to the completion of serious good faith efforts to reach a multilateral agreement, the possibility to impose a unilateral measure to protect sea turtles under Section 609 is more to be seen, for the purposes of Article XX, as the possibility to adopt a *provisional* measure allowed for emergency reasons than as a definitive "right" to take a permanent measure. The extent to which serious good faith efforts continue to be made may be reassessed at any time. For instance, steps which constituted good faith efforts at the beginning of a negotiation may fail to meet that test at a later stage.

4. *Other Requirements Related to Arbitrary or Unjustifiable Discrimination Between Countries where the Same Conditions Prevail*

(a) Claims Relating to the Findings of "unjustifiable discrimination" in the Appellate Body Report

(i) Introduction

5.89 The parties seem to agree that the findings of the Appellate Body as to the existence of "unjustifiable discrimination", beyond those concerning multilateral negotiations, relate to four main aspects of the application of Section 609, namely: (i) the insufficient flexibility of the 1996 Guidelines, in particular the absence of consideration of the different conditions that may exist in the exporting nations; (ii) the prohibition of importation of shrimp caught in uncertified countries, including when that shrimp had been caught using TEDs; (iii) the length of the "phase-in" period; and (iv) the differences in the level of efforts made by the United States to transfer successfully TED technology to exporting countries.

(ii) Insufficient Flexibility of the 1996 Guidelines, in Particular the Absence of Consideration of the Different Conditions that May Exist in the Territories of Exporting Nations

5.90 The Appellate Body considered that Section 609 as implemented through the 1996 Guidelines constituted unjustifiable discrimination insofar as its certification process lacked flexibility. In particular, the measure should have taken into consideration the different conditions that may exist in the territories of the exporting Members. Because of the complexity of the issue addressed, the Appellate Body findings on this issue deserve to be quoted extensively:

> "161. [...] Perhaps the most conspicuous flaw in this measure's application relates to its intended and actual coercive effect on the specific policy decisions made by foreign governments, Members of the WTO. Section 609, in its application, is, in effect, an economic embargo which requires *all other exporting Members*, if they wish to exercise their GATT rights, to adopt *essentially the same* policy (together with an approved enforcement program) as that applied to, and enforced on, United States domestic shrimp trawlers. As enacted by the Congress of the United States, the *statutory* provisions of Section 609(b)(2)(A) and (B) do not, in themselves, *require* that other WTO Members adopt *essentially the same* policies and enforcement practices as the United States. Viewed alone, the statute appears to permit a degree of discretion or flexibility in how the standards for determining comparability might be applied, in practice, to other countries. [Footnote omitted] However, any flexibility that may have been intended by Congress when it enacted the statutory provision has been effectively eliminated in the implementation of that policy through the 1996 Guidelines promulgated by the Department of State and through the practice of the administrators in making certification determinations.
>
> 162. According to the 1996 Guidelines, certification "shall be made" under Section 609(b)(2)(A) and (B) if an exporting country's program includes a requirement that all commercial shrimp trawl vessels operating in waters in which there is a likelihood of intercepting sea turtles use, at all times, TEDs comparable in effectiveness to those used in the United States. [Footnote omitted] Under these Guidelines, any exceptions to the requirement of the use of TEDs must be comparable to those of the United States program.[Footnote omitted] Furthermore, the harvesting country must have in place a "credible enforcement effort". [Footnote omitted]

The language in the 1996 Guidelines is mandatory: certification "shall be made" if these conditions are fulfilled. However, we understand that these rules are also applied in an *exclusive* manner. That is, the 1996 Guidelines specify the *only* way that a harvesting country's regulatory program can be deemed "comparable" to the United States' program, and, therefore, they define the *only* way that a harvesting nation can be certified under Section 609(b)(2)(A) and (B). Although the 1996 Guidelines state that, in making a comparability determination, the Department of State "shall also take into account other measures the harvesting nation undertakes to protect sea turtles" [footnote omitted], in practice, the competent government officials only look to see whether there is a regulatory program requiring the use of TEDs or one that comes within one of the extremely limited exceptions available to United States shrimp trawl vessels. [Footnote omitted]

163. The actual *application* of the measure, through the implementation of the 1996 Guidelines and the regulatory practice of administrators, *requires* other WTO Members to adopt a regulatory program that is not merely *comparable*, but rather *essentially the same*, as that applied to the United States shrimp trawl vessels. Thus, the effect of the application of Section 609 is to establish a rigid and unbending standard by which United States officials determine whether or not countries will be certified, thus granting or refusing other countries the right to export shrimp to the United States. Other specific policies and measures that an exporting country may have adopted for the protection and conservation of sea turtles are not taken into account, in practice, by the administrators making the comparability determination. [Footnote omitted]

164. We understand that the United States also applies a uniform standard throughout its territory, regardless of the particular conditions existing in certain parts of the country. The United States requires the use of approved TEDs at all times by domestic, commercial shrimp trawl vessels operating in waters where there is any likelihood that they may interact with sea turtles, regardless of the actual incidence of sea turtles in those waters, the species of those sea turtles, or other differences or disparities that may exist in different parts of the United States. It may be quite acceptable for a government, in adopting and implementing a domestic policy, to adopt a single standard applicable to all its citizens throughout that country. However, it is not acceptable, in international trade relations, for one WTO Member to use an economic embargo to *require* other Members to adopt essentially the same comprehensive regulatory program, to achieve a certain policy goal, as that in force within that Member's territory, *without* taking into considera-

> tion different conditions which may occur in the territories of those other Members."[221]

5.91 The Appellate Body opposed the text of Section 609 on the one hand and the implementing guidelines and the practice of the United States authorities on the other hand; the former only providing that conservation programmes be *comparable*, whereas the latter required them to be *essentially the same* as the US programme. The Appellate Body also opposed the application of a uniform standard throughout the US territory, which was acceptable, and the application of the same uniform standard to exporting countries, which was not.[222]

5.92 In addition, in paragraph 165, the Appellate Body seems to suggest that the essential reason that Section 609 was applied in a manner which constituted "unjustifiable discrimination" was because the application of the measure at issue did not allow for any inquiry into the appropriateness of the regulatory programme for the conditions prevailing in the exporting countries.

5.93 The Appellate Body, in paragraph 165 of its Report, also found that the original measure:

> "in its application, [was] more concerned with effectively influencing WTO Members *to adopt essentially the same comprehensive regulatory regime as that applied by the United States* to its domestic shrimp trawlers, even though many of those Members may be differently situated." (Emphasis added)

It seems that whereas the Appellate Body found that requiring the adoption of essentially the same regime constituted arbitrary discrimination, it accepted - at least implicitly - that a requirement that the US and foreign programmes be "comparable in effectiveness" would be compatible with the obligations of the United States under the chapeau of Article XX. This is because it would "permit a degree of discretion or flexibility in how the standards for determining comparability might be applied, in practice, to other countries."[223] We therefore conclude that if, *in practice*, the implementing measure provides for "comparable effectiveness", the finding of the Appellate Body in terms of lack of flexibility will have been addressed.

5.94 The first step in determining whether the implementing measure does not share the same flaw as the original measure reviewed by the Appellate Body is to assess whether the United States no longer requires that the conservation programmes of exporting countries be "essentially the same" as that of the United States but only "comparable in effectiveness". We note that Section II.B.(a)(1)(i) of the Revised Guidelines provides, with respect to those programmes which require the use of TEDs, that:

---

221 Italics in the original.

222 See para. 5.72 above.

223 Appellate Body Report, para. 161.

> "[...] a requirement that all commercial shrimp trawl vessels operating in waters in which there is a likelihood of intercepting sea turtles use TEDs at all time. TEDs *must be comparable in effectiveness* to those used in the United States. Any exception to this requirement *must be comparable to those of the US program* described above."[224]

As implicitly acknowledged by the Appellate Body[225], it is not enough that the Revised Guidelines no longer provide for the "essentially the same" test. The actual practice of the US authorities must also be considered. In this respect, the United States drew the attention of the Panel to the review of the TED-based programme put into place by Australia in its Northern Prawn Fishery. The United States reviewed the information submitted by Australia and proceeded to site visits and discussions with Australian officials and industry representatives. As stated by Australia in the course of the proceedings[226], the visits and discussions "confirm[ed] that a small number of technical differences between the [Northern Prawn Fisheries] TED regulations and the US TED regulations did not render the Australian TEDs less than comparable in effectiveness to the US TEDs." Australia did not argue that the "comparable effectiveness" test found in the Revised Guidelines was applied by US officials in a restrictive manner. We therefore conclude that, having regard to the example of Australia's Northern Prawn Fishery and in the absence of other evidence to the contrary, the actual application of the "comparable effectiveness" test contained in the Revised Guidelines provides for greater flexibility than the "essentially the same" test previously applied under the 1996 Guidelines and is not applied restrictively by the US authorities responsible for assessing TED-based programmes.

5.95 We next proceed to determine whether the Revised Guidelines allow an implementation of Section 609 that provides for "inquiry into the appropriateness of that regulatory programme for the conditions prevailing in the exporting countries". We consider that a measure which would allow a Member to demonstrate that:

(a) it has a programme comparable with the US programme without providing for the mandatory use of TEDs; or

(b) that other conditions exist on its territory

would meet the requirements of the DSB recommendation in this respect. We do not consider that the term "inquiry" in the Appellate Body findings necessarily means that the United States should take the initiative of an investigation in each country applying for certification, but that it should be prepared to investigate any claim made by a harvesting country seeking certification.

---

224 Revised Guidelines, p. 36950; Annex to this Report: para. 18 (emphasis added).

225 Appellate Body Report, paras. 161 and 162.

226 Australia's third party written submission, para. 13.

5.96 First, we note that the Revised Guidelines provide for the possibility to certify programmes which do not require the use of TEDs. The Revised Guidelines, Section II.B.(a.), provide that "The Department of State shall assess regulatory programs, as described in any documentary evidence provided by the governments of harvesting nations, for comparability with the US program". We also note that Section II.B.(a)(2) provides that:

> "If the government of a harvesting nation demonstrates that it has implemented and is enforcing a comparably effective regulatory program to protect sea turtles in the course of shrimp trawl fishing without the use of TED, that nation will also be eligible for certification."[227]

5.97 The Revised Guidelines provide that such a demonstration would need to be based on empirical data supported by objective scientific studies of sufficient duration and scope to provide the information necessary for a reliable determination. The Revised Guidelines further state that:

> "in reviewing any such information, the Department of State will take fully into account any demonstrated differences between the shrimp fishing conditions in the United States and those of other nations, as well as information available from other sources."[228]

5.98 We recall that the Revised Guidelines also mention that "The Department of State is presently aware of no measure or series of measures that can minimize the capture and drowning of sea turtles in [standard otter trawl nets used in shrimp fisheries] that is comparable in effectiveness to the required use of TEDs". However, this "presumption" is limited in scope to the use of trawl nets and does not cover other ways of protecting sea turtles such as, e.g., fishing prohibition. It therefore appears to us that, on its face, the implementing measure provides for "inquiry into the appropriateness of that regulatory programme for the conditions prevailing in the exporting countries" when it comes to assess programmes that do not require the use of TEDs.

5.99 Second, we also note that the Revised Guidelines include a new category which allows the importation of "shrimp harvested in any other manner or under any other circumstances that the Department of State may determine, following consultations with the NMFS [National Marine Fisheries Service], does not pose a threat of the incidental taking of sea turtles."[229] Consequently, it appears that the Revised Guidelines provide for the possibility of taking into account situations where turtles are not endangered by shrimp trawling.

5.100 However, as for the assessment of TED-based programmes, we nonetheless need to determine whether, *in practice*, the implementing measure is applied so as to allow for "inquiry into the appropriateness of that regulatory programme

227 Revised Guidelines, p. 36950; Annex to this Report: Section II.B.(a)(2).

228 *Ibid.*

229 Revised Guidelines, p. 36949; Annex to this Report: para. 5(d).

for the conditions prevailing in the exporting countries" in relation to non TED-based programmes and to situations where shrimp trawling does not pose a threat of incidental taking of sea turtles. We recall that the United States gave the example of Pakistan, which had been certified on the basis of a programme combining the use of TEDs and shrimp trawling prohibition. We also note the example given by Australia of shrimp caught in the Spencer Gulf. The United States excluded shrimp from the Spencer Gulf from the field of application of the prohibition on the basis of the clause mentioned in the preceeding paragraph, once the extremely low incidence of sea turtles in the fishery had been established by Australia.

5.101 We also note the statement of the representative of the United States in reply to a question of the Panel that "there is no element in the Malaysian programme, [...], that would make it impossible for the United States to certify Malaysia pursuant to Section 609."[230] We also note that Malaysia has not sought certification on the basis of its programme, which does not include the use of TEDs.

5.102 We consider that we have evidence that the United States has applied effectively the Revised Guidelines in a way that allowed for "inquiry into the appropriateness of that regulatory programme for the conditions prevailing in the exporting countries" in relation to non TED-based programmes and to situations where shrimp trawling does not pose a threat of incidental taking of sea turtles.

5.103 We also recall that Malaysia claimed that the United States, by imposing a unilaterally defined standard of protection, violates the sovereign right of Malaysia to determine its own sea turtles protection and conservation policy. We are mindful of the problem caused by the type of measure applied by the United States to pursue its environmental policy objectives. We recall that Principle 12 of the Rio Declaration on Environment and Development states in part that:

> "unilateral actions to deal with environmental challenges outside the jurisdiction of the importing country should be avoided. Environmental measures addressing transboundary or global environmental problems should, as far as possible, be based on international consensus."[231]

However, it is the understanding of the Panel that the Appellate Body Report found that, while a WTO Member may not impose on exporting members to apply the same standards of environmental protection as those it applies itself, this Member may legitimately require, as a condition of access of certain products to its market, that exporting countries commit themselves to a regulatory programme deemed comparable to its own. At present, Malaysia does not have to comply with the US requirements because it does not export to the United States.

[230] See reply of the United States, footnote 105 above.

[231] See also para. 2.22(i) of Agenda 21. The Appellate Body made reference to these international instruments in its Report (see para. 168).

If Malaysia exported shrimp to the United States, it would be subject to requirements that may distort Malaysia's priorities in terms of environmental policy. As Article XX of the GATT 1994 has been interpreted by the Appellate Body, the WTO Agreement does not provide for any recourse in the situation Malaysia would face under those circumstances. While we cannot, in light of the interpretation of Article XX made by the Appellate Body, find in favour of Malaysia on this "sovereignty" issue, we nonetheless consider that the "sovereignty" question raised by Malaysia is an additional argument in favour of the conclusion of an international agreement to protect and conserve sea turtles which would take into account the situation of all interested parties.

5.104 We therefore conclude that the United States has established a *prima facie* case that the implementing measure complies with the findings of the Appellate Body concerning the insufficient flexibility of the 1996 Guidelines. We also note that Malaysia did not provide sufficient evidence to rebut this presumption.

(iii) The Prohibition of Importation of Shrimp Caught in Uncertified Countries, Including when that Shrimp Had Been Caught Using TEDs

5.105 In its Report, the Appellate Body found that:

> "165. Furthermore, when this dispute was before the Panel and before us, the United States did not permit imports of shrimp harvested by commercial shrimp trawl vessels using TEDs comparable in effectiveness to those required in the United States if those shrimp originated in waters of countries not certified under Section 609. In other words, *shrimp caught using methods identical to those employed in the United States* have been excluded from the United States market solely because they have been caught in waters of *countries that have not been certified by the United States.* The resulting situation is difficult to reconcile with the declared policy objective of protecting and conserving sea turtles. This suggests to us that this measure, in its application, is more concerned with effectively influencing WTO Members to adopt essentially the same comprehensive regulatory regime as that applied by the United States to its domestic shrimp trawlers, even though many of those Members may be differently situated. We believe that discrimination results not only when countries in which the same conditions prevail are differently treated, but also when the application of the measure at issue does not allow for any inquiry into the appropriateness of the regulatory program for the conditions prevailing in those exporting countries."

5.106 This condition is addressed separately from the broader category concerning the lack of flexibility and insufficient consideration of the conditions prevailing in the exporting countries because, in our opinion, it required a specific solution, while the other findings left more discretion to the United States.

5.107 We note that, under the Revised Guidelines, the importation of shrimp harvested by vessels using TEDs is allowed, even if the exporting nation has not been certified pursuant to Section 609. The United States has also provided evidence of instances where imports of TED-caught shrimp have been allowed even though the country of origin has not been certified.[232]

5.108 Malaysia does not contest the fact that importation of shrimp harvested by vessels using TEDs may be allowed, even when the exporting nation is not certified pursuant to Section 609. Malaysia expressed concerns that this part of the Revised Guidelines has been found illegal in a judgement of the US Court of International Trade (CIT).[233] Malaysia claims that the United States is responsible for actions of all its branches of government, including courts, and refers to the finding of the Appellate Body in paragraph 173 of its Report.

5.109 We first note that in its judgement, the CIT, while ruling that the interpretation of the Department of State was not compatible with the terms of Section 609, refrained from granting an injunction that the US Department of State modify its guidelines. As a result, the Panel is satisfied that the United States does not, for now, have to modify its Revised Guidelines. The decision has been appealed before the Court of Appeals for the Federal Circuit. At our request, the United States confirmed that the Court of Appeals could require that the Revised Guidelines be modified in accordance with the interpretation of Section 609 made by the CIT. However, until a decision is reached by the Court of Appeals, the Revised Guidelines remain applicable. Moreover, no judgement is likely to be issued for several months and an appeal before the US Supreme Court cannot be excluded. As was recalled by the Appellate Body[234], we are not supposed to interpret domestic law, which we are to treat as a fact. Even if the possibility cannot be excluded that the Revised Guidelines be modified[235], the situation before us is, for the moment, the one provided for in the Revised Guidelines, which on this point are not contested by Malaysia.

5.110 Second, we do not consider that Malaysia appropriately referred to the Appellate Body finding in paragraph 173. A State is to be presumed to act in

---

[232] The United States gave the examples of Australia and Brazil. Exports from the northern shrimp fisheries of Brazil have been authorized even though Brazil does not qualify for certification due to the lack of TED use in the southern Brazilian fisheries. Import of shrimp harvested in the Australian Northern Prawn Fisheries has also been allowed because the use of Turtle Excluder Devices has been mandatory since April 2000, even though Australia is not certified due to the lack of TED use in other fisheries.

[233] United States Court of International Trade (CIT): *Turtle Island Restoration Network et al. v. Robert L. Mallett et al.*, 19 July 2000, 2000 WL 1024797 (CIT).

[234] See India - Patent Protection for Pharmaceutical and Agricultural Chemical Products, adopted on 16 January 1998, WT/DS50/AB/R, DSR 1998:I, 9, paras. 65-68.

[235] The Revised Guidelines themselves note the possibility that they may be revised as a result of pending domestic litigation (see p. 36951; Annex to this Report: para. 24)

good faith and in conformity with its international obligations. The CIT itself did not require that the Revised Guidelines be modified. There is no reason to consider that this situation *will* inevitably change in the near future.

5.111 Therefore, we consider that the United States, by modifying its guidelines and adjusting its practice so as to permit import of TED-caught shrimp from non-certified countries complies, as long as that situation remains unchanged, with the DSB recommendations and rulings in this respect. We do not consider that Malaysia submitted sufficient evidence to rebut the *prima facie* case established by the United States in this respect.

(iv) Phase-in Period

5.112 The Appellate Body found that the United States had discriminated between exporting countries in terms of the phase-in period granted as follows:

> "173. The application of Section 609, through the implementing guidelines together with administrative practice, also resulted in other differential treatment among various countries desiring certification. Under the 1991 and 1993 Guidelines, to be certifiable, fourteen countries in the wider Caribbean/Western Atlantic region had to commit themselves to require the use of TEDs on all commercial shrimp trawling vessels by 1 May 1994. These fourteen countries had a "phase-in" period of three years during which their respective shrimp trawling sectors could adjust to the requirement of the use of TEDs. With respect to all other countries exporting shrimp to the United States (including the appellees, India, Malaysia, Pakistan and Thailand), on 29 December 1995, the United States Court of International Trade directed the Department of State to apply the import ban on a world-wide basis not later than 1 May 1996.[236] On 19 April 1996, the 1996 Guidelines were issued by the Department of State bringing shrimp harvested in *all* foreign countries within the scope of Section 609, effective 1 May 1996. Thus, all countries that were not among the fourteen in the wider Caribbean/Western Atlantic region had only four months to implement the requirement of compulsory use of TEDs. [...]
>
> 174. The length of the "phase-in" period is not inconsequential for exporting countries desiring certification. That period relates directly to the onerousness of the burdens of complying with the requisites of certification and the practical feasibility of locating and developing alternative export markets for shrimp. The shorter that period, the heavier the burdens of compliance, particularly where an applicant has a large number of trawler vessels, and the

[236] Earth Island Institute v. Warren Christopher, 913 F. Supp. 559 (CIT 1995).

greater the difficulties of re-orienting the harvesting country's shrimp exports. The shorter that period, in net effect, the heavier the influence of the import ban. The United States sought to explain the marked difference between "phase-in" periods granted to the fourteen wider Caribbean/Western Atlantic countries and those allowed the rest of the shrimp exporting countries. The United States asserted that the longer time-period was justified by the then undeveloped character of TED technology, while the shorter period was later made possible by the improvements in that technology. This explanation is less than persuasive, for it does not address the administrative and financial costs and the difficulties of governments in putting together and enacting the necessary regulatory programs and "credible enforcement effort", and in implementing the compulsory use of TEDs on hundreds, if not thousands, of shrimp trawl vessels. [Footnote omitted]"

5.113 On this issue, the United States claims that the difference in phase-in periods has been corrected by the passage of time and that Malaysia had more than four years between the first US court ruling and the end of the reasonable period of time to adopt a TED-based programme or other comparable programmes. Malaysia generally claims that the United States should have lifted its import ban whilst it engaged in negotiations for the protection and conservation of marine turtles.

5.114 We are of the opinion that this finding of the Appellate Body has to be considered in the context in which it was made, i.e. that of assessing whether unjustifiable discrimination existed at the time. We agree with the United States that it cannot travel back in time in order to grant the same phase-in period to Malaysia as it had granted the Caribbean/Western Atlantic countries. Interpreting the Appellate Body findings as requiring such a thing would be tantamount to making any compliance impossible in this case. Rather, we believe that the issue which remains relevant is that, by providing for a shorter phase-in period for the complainants, the United States made any attempt to comply more onerous in terms of "administrative and financial costs" and in terms of the difficulties for governments to put together and enact the necessary regulatory programmes and "credible enforcement effort".

5.115 We note that Malaysia has not yet attempted to be certified. It is therefore impossible to determine whether it incurred any particularly serious cost in that respect. This as such should not be a reason for concluding that the United States has complied with its obligations in this respect. However, there are elements which should allow us to assess whether Malaysia would have actually incurred such costs. More particularly, we note that Malaysia claims that it has a comprehensive programme of protection and conservation of sea turtles and that the scientific experts consulted by the Original Panel also have made reference to Malaysia's efforts at sea turtle conservation.[237] We recall that the United States stated that there were no elements in the Malaysian programme that would make it impossible for the United States to certify Malaysia pursuant to Section 609. In this respect, we have noted the changes introduced in the Revised Guidelines, which allow the US authorities to consider certain programmes that do not provide for the mandatory use of TEDs. We therefore consider that if Malaysia sought to be certified, there is no evidence that it would incur any of the costs which the Appellate Body identified as the major issue with the difference of phase-in period between the complainants in the original case and the Caribbean/Western Atlantic countries.

5.116 We therefore conclude that, for the above-mentioned reasons, the United States has made a *prima facie* case that its practice addressed the DSB recommendations and rulings with respect to the phase-in period. We also note that Malaysia did not provide sufficient evidence to rebut this *prima facie* case.

(v) Transfer of Technology

5.117 On the issue of transfer of technology, the Appellate Body found that:

> "175. Differing treatment of different countries desiring certification is also observable in the differences in the levels of effort made by the United States in transferring the required TED technology to specific countries. Far greater efforts to transfer that technology successfully were made to certain exporting countries - basically the fourteen wider Caribbean/Western Atlantic countries cited earlier - than to other exporting countries, including the appellees. [Footnote omitted] The level of these efforts is probably related to the length of the "phase-in" periods granted - the longer the "phase-in" period, the higher the possible level of efforts at technology transfer. Because compliance with the requirements of certification realistically assumes successful TED technology transfer, low or merely nominal efforts at achieving that transfer will, in all probability, result in fewer countries being able to satisfy the certification requirements under Section 609, within the very limited "phase-in" periods allowed them."

5.118 The United States argues that it has repeatedly offered technical assistance and training in the design, construction, installation and operation of TEDs to any government that requested it. The United States has provided technical assistance and training to a number of governments and other organizations in the Indian Ocean and South-East Asian region. The US National Marine Fisheries Service (NMFS) presented a paper on TEDs and technology transfer at the Sabah Sym-

---

[237] See para. 3.162 above and Original Panel Report, Annex IV, Transcript of the Meeting with the Experts, statement of Dr. Eckert, para. 69, p. 378.

posium in July 1999. US officials assisted the government of Bahrain and conducted training and workshops in Pakistan (January 2000) and Australia (July 2000). In April 2000, NMFS hosted a training session on TEDs for technical experts from the South-East Asian Fisheries Development Center. Malaysia contends that the US offer of technical assistance was of no consequence for it in light of the efficiency of its own conservation programme.

5.119 We note that the Appellate Body Report draws a link between the phase-in period and the transfer of technology: the longer the phase-in period, the higher the possible level of efforts at technology transfer. The United States proceeded to transfer technology under various forms as early as July 1999 (Sabah Symposium), providing assistance to Bahrain and Pakistan and training in Australia. We note that these countries have since been certified or allowed to export part of their production to the United States. The Panel notes that there was no discrimination *vis-à-vis* Malaysia since Malaysia did not seek any transfer of technology.

5.120 We therefore conclude that, for the above-mentioned reasons, the United States has made a *prima facie* case that its practice addressed the DSB recommendations and rulings with respect to the transfer of technology. We also note that Malaysia did not provide sufficient evidence to rebut this *prima facie* case.

(b) Claims Relating to "arbitrary discrimination"

(i) Lack of Flexibility

5.121 The Appellate Body found that:

> "[...] We have already observed that Section 609, in its application, imposes a single, rigid and unbending requirement that countries applying for certification under Section 609(b)(2)(A) and (B) adopt a comprehensive regulatory program that is essentially the same as the United States' program, without inquiring into the appropriateness of that program for the conditions prevailing in the exporting countries. [Footnote Omitted] Furthermore, there is little or no flexibility in how officials make the determination for certification pursuant to these provisions. [Footnote omitted] In our view, this rigidity and inflexibility also constitute "arbitrary discrimination" within the meaning of the chapeau."[238]

5.122 We have already addressed the question of the rigidity and inflexibility of the 1996 Guidelines and of the administrative practices of that time in relation to the identification of "unjustifiable discrimination". From the Appellate Body Report, we understand that what caused the application of Section 609 to be considered "arbitrary discrimination" was that:

---

[238] Appellate Body Report, para. 177.

(a) It imposed a single, rigid and unbending requirement that countries applying for certification adopt a comprehensive regulatory programme that is essentially the same as the United States' programme; and

(b) that this programme was imposed without inquiring into the appropriateness of that programme for the conditions prevailing in the exporting countries.

5.123 We have already found that the United States no longer requires the exporting countries' programmes to be essentially the same as the US programme, and that the United States acknowledges that other programmes may be comparable.[239] Malaysia contests the requirement of a "comparable programme" as an interference with its sovereign right to determine its environmental policy. The Panel does not read the Appellate Body Report as supporting Malaysia's view. In our opinion, the Appellate Body did not contest the right of the United States to restrict imports of shrimp for environmental reasons; it is the requirement that other Members adopt essentially the same programme as the United States which was found to constitute arbitrary discrimination because it did not take into account the appropriateness of that programme for the countries concerned.

5.124 Having regard to the ordinary meaning of the word "arbitrary" most suitable in the context[240] of the chapeau of Article XX, i.e. "capricious, unpredictable, inconsistent"[241], we note that, with the implementation of the Revised Guidelines, the United States ought to be in a better position to avoid "arbitrary" decisions. A Member seeking certification seems to have the possibility to demonstrate that its programme - even though not requiring the use of TEDs, is comparable to that of the United States. On the face of it, the implementing measure is no longer primarily based on the application of certain methods or standards, but on the achievement of certain objectives, even though the term "objective" may, in this case, have a relatively broad meaning. Some evidence of the actual degree of flexibility of the Revised Guidelines can be found in the authorisation granted to Australia to export shrimp from the Northern Prawn Fisheries and the Spencer Gulf even though Australia as such is not certified under Section 609.

5.125 We conclude that the United States has made a *prima facie* case that the implementing measure complies with the relevant DSB recommendations and rulings. We note in this respect that Malaysia did not provide sufficient evidence to the contrary.

---

[239] See, e.g., Revised Guidelines, p. 36950-51; Annex to this Report: paras. 15, 16, 18, and Section II.B.(a)(2).

[240] In this sentence, the word "context" is not used within the legal meaning of that term in the Vienna Convention, but in its more common meaning.

[241] *The New Shorter Oxford Dictionary* (1993), p. 107.

(ii) Due Process

5.126 With respect to due process, the Appellate Body found, *inter alia*, that:

> "181. The certification processes followed by the United States thus appears to be singularly informal and casual, and to be conducted in a manner such that these processes could result in the negation of rights of Members. There appears to be no way that exporting Members can be certain whether the terms of Section 609, in particular, the 1996 Guidelines, are being applied in a fair and just manner by the appropriate governmental agencies of the United States. It appears to us that, effectively, exporting Members applying for certification whose applications are rejected are denied basic fairness and due process, and are discriminated against, *vis-à-vis* those Members which are granted certification."

5.127 The Appellate Body has criticised the absence, with respect to any type of certification under Section 609(b)(2), of a transparent, predictable certification process that is followed by the competent United States government officials. In particular, the Appellate Body has contested:

(a) The *ex parte* nature of the inquiries and certifications;

(b) the absence of formal opportunity for the country under investigation to be heard or to respond to any arguments made against it;

(c) the absence of formal written reasoned decision, whether of acceptance or of rejection. In particular, countries denied certification do not receive notice of the denial; and

(d) the absence of procedure for review of, or appeal from, a denial of an application.[242]

5.128 The United States argues that it has modified its Guidelines to take these findings of the Appellate Body into account. In order to assess the changes made by the United States, we compare the findings of the Appellate Body with the text of the Revised Guidelines and the administrative practice under those Revised Guidelines.

5.129 With regard to the *ex parte* nature of investigations and to the absence of formal opportunity for the country under investigation to be heard or to respond to any arguments made against it under the 1996 Guidelines, we note that the Revised Guidelines not only provide for visits by US officials of those nations requesting certification under Section 609(b)(2)(A) and (B), but also that:

> "Each visit will conclude with a meeting between the US officials and governments officials of the harvesting nation to discuss the results of the visit and to review any identified deficiencies regard-

[242] Appellate Body Report, para. 180.

ing the harvesting nation's program to protect sea turtles in the course of shrimp trawl fishing."[243]

5.130 Moreover, the Revised Guidelines provide for two assessments by the Department of State of the exporting country programme: a "preliminary" one by 15 March of each year and a formal one by 1 May of each year. The Revised Guidelines state that, after the "preliminary" assessment,

> "If the government of the harvesting nation so requests, the Department of State will schedule face-to-face meetings between relevant US officials and officials of the harvesting nation to discuss the situation."[244]

5.131 We therefore conclude that the Revised Guidelines address the Appellate Body concerns in terms of the *ex parte* nature of the investigation and absence of formal opportunity for the country under investigation to be heard or to respond to any arguments made against it.

5.132 With respect to the Appellate Body findings on the absence of formal written reasoned decision, whether of acceptance or of rejection, we note that the Revised Guidelines provide, with respect to the "preliminary" assessment, that:

> "By March 15, the Department of State will notify in writing through diplomatic channels the government of each nation that, on the basis of available information, including information gathered during [the visits mentioned in para. 5.129 above], does not appear to qualify for certification. Such notification will explain the reasons for this preliminary assessment, suggest steps that the government of the harvesting nation can take in order to receive a certification and invite the government of the harvesting nation to provide, by April 15, any further information."[245]

and also that:

> "By May 1 of each year the Department of State will make formal decisions on certification. The governments of all nations that have requested certification will be notified in writing of the decision promptly through diplomatic channels. In the case of those nations for which certification is denied, such notification will again state the reasons for such denials and steps necessary to receive a certification in the future."[246]

5.133 We consider that these provisions of the Revised Guidelines address the problems of notification and statement of reasons identified by the Appellate Body.

---

243 Revised Guidelines, p. 36951; Annex to this Report: para. 26.

244 Revised Guidelines, p. 36951; Annex to this Report: para. 27.

245 *Ibid.*

246 Revised Guidelines, p. 36951; Annex to this Report: para. 29.

5.134 Moreover, concerning the absence of procedure for review of, or appeal from, a denial of an application, we note that the Revised Guidelines provide that:

> "The government of any nation that is denied a certification by May 1 may, at any time thereafter, request reconsideration of that decision."[247]

At our request, the United States also confirmed that, as a general matter, judicial review of a final decision by the US Department of State regarding certification of a country may be had in the US court system pursuant to the Administrative Procedure Act.[248] Thus, it is our understanding that the Revised Guidelines, together with the relevant US legislation, address the DSB recommendations and rulings on review procedures and appeal.

5.135 Finally, instances of actual application of the Revised Guidelines also tend to demonstrate that they now comply with the findings of the Appellate Body. The information provided by the United States and Australia with regard to the process which led the United States to authorize the importation of shrimp caught in the Spencer Gulf fisheries and the Northern Prawn Fisheries show that, in those particular instances, the United States appears to have applied its Revised Guidelines in conformity with the wording of those guidelines. We also note that Australia did not mention that it was at any stage deprived of the possibility to make its views known to the US investigating authorities.

5.136 We therefore conclude that evidence available supports the view that due process appears to have been respected so far.

(c) Conclusion

5.137 We therefore conclude that the United States has made a *prima facie* case that Section 609 is now applied in a manner that no longer constitutes a means of unjustifiable or arbitrary discrimination, as identified by the Appellate Body in its Report. We note that Malaysia did not submit sufficient evidence to the contrary.

5. Disguised Restriction on International Trade

5.138 The Panel notes that it is instructed by Article 21.5 of the DSU to review "the existence or consistency with a covered agreement of measures taken to comply with the recommendations and rulings" of the DSB. The fact that the Appellate Body did not have to make a finding that the original measure was a disguised restriction on trade does not mean that the measure adopted to implement the DSB recommendations and rulings is not a disguised restriction on trade. The Panel also recalls that, as the party invoking Article XX, the United

[247] Revised Guidelines, p. 36951; Annex to this Report: para. 30.
[248] 5 U.S.C. 701 *et seq.*

States bears the burden of proving that its implementing measure meets *all* the relevant requirements of the chapeau. This implies that the United States make a *prima facie* case that the implementing measure is not a disguised restriction on trade.

5.139 We first note that the United States argued that the implementing measure is narrowly tailored to achieve a *bona fide* conservation goal. The United States has also mentioned that it has expended substantial efforts to disseminate TEDs technology worldwide, thus assisting many countries in obtaining certification under Section 609. Malaysia states that the three conditions of the chapeau of Article XX, including that according to which the implementing measure must not be applied so as to constitute a disguised restriction on international trade, have to be complied with by the United States.

5.140 The Panel notes that the fact that, on its face, a law has been narrowly tailored to achieve a *bona fide* conservation plan does not mean that, when applied, it does not constitute a disguised restriction on trade. As stressed by the Appellate Body:

> "149. The policy goal of a measure at issue cannot provide its rationale or justification under the standards of the chapeau of Article XX. [...] it does not follow from the fact that a measure falls within the terms of Article XX(g) that that measure also will necessarily comply with the requirements of the chapeau. To accept the argument of the United States would be to disregard the standards established by the chapeau."

5.141 Second, the Panel notes that, in the *United States - Gasoline* case, the Appellate Body concluded that:

> "The fundamental theme is to be found in the purpose and object of avoiding abuse or illegitimate use of the exceptions to substantive rules available in Article XX."[249]

5.142 The Panel is of the view that there would be an abuse of Article XX(g) "if [the compliance with Article XX(g) was] in fact only a disguise to conceal the pursuit of trade-restrictive objectives".[250] As mentioned by the Appellate Body in *Japan - Taxes on Alcoholic Beverages*[251], the protective application of a measure can most often be discerned from its design, architecture and revealing structure. We therefore proceed to determine whether, beyond the protection which automatically results from the imposition of a ban, the design, architecture and revealing structure of Section 609 together with the Revised Guidelines, as actually

249 Appellate Body Report on *United States - Gasoline, Op. Cit.*, DSR 1996:1, 3, at p. 23.

250 Panel Report on *European Communities - Measures Affecting Asbestos and Asbestos-Containing Products*, adopted on 5 April 2001, WT/DS135/R, DSR 2001:VIII, 3305, para. 8.236. This finding was neither reversed nor modified by the Appellate Body.

251 Appellate Body Report on *Japan - Taxes on Alcoholic Beverages*, adopted on 1 November 1996, WT/DS8; DS10; DS11/AB/R, DSR 1996:I, 97, p. 120.

applied by the US authorities, demonstrate that the implementing measure constitutes a disguised restriction on international trade. An examination of the text of Section 609 and of the Revised Guidelines does not show any element leaning in that direction.

5.143 We nonetheless recall that, before the Original Panel, the question of whether Section 609 was applied so as to constitute a disguised restriction on international trade was addressed by the parties. First, the Panel recalls that the case which led to the CIT judgement which extended the scope of application of Section 609 beyond the United States and the Caribbean/Western Atlantic countries was initiated by environmental groups.[252] The attention of the Original Panel was drawn to the legislative history of Section 609.[253] The Panel notes that US fishermen harvesting shrimp are subject to constraints comparable to those imposed on exporting countries' fishermen insofar as they have to use TEDs at all times. Even though, when the application of Section 609 was extended to the whole world, US fishermen were probably in favour of a measure imposing the same requirements on foreign fishermen, they are likely to incur little commercial gain from a ban since the Revised Guidelines make it easier to export shrimp to the United States under Section 609, compared with the situation under the 1996 Guidelines. Indeed, the United States has demonstrated that the mandatory use of TEDs in certain circumstances is no longer a condition *sine qua non* for certification if other comparable programmes are applied. The Panel considers that, by allowing exporting countries to apply programmes not based on the mandatory use of TEDs, and by offering technical assistance to develop the use of TEDs in third countries, the United States has demonstrated that Section 609 is not applied so as to constitute a disguised restriction on trade.

5.144 The Panel therefore concludes that the implementing measure does not constitute a disguised restriction on international trade within the meaning of the chapeau of Article XX of the GATT 1994.

VI. CONCLUSIONS

6.1 In light of the findings above, the Panel reaches the following conclusions:

(a) The measure adopted by the United States in order to comply with the recommendations and rulings of the DSB violates Article XI.1 of the GATT 1994;

(b) in light of the recommendations and rulings of the DSB, Section 609 of Public Law 101-162, as implemented by the Revised Guidelines of 8 July 1999 and as applied so far by the US authorities, is justified under Article XX of the GATT 1994 as long as the condi-

[252] United States Court of International Trade: *Earth Island Institute v. Warren Christopher*, 913 Fed. Supp. 559 (CIT 1995).

[253] See e.g., Original Panel Report, paras. 3.272; 3.278 and 3.281.

> tions stated in the findings of this Report, in particular the ongoing serious good faith efforts to reach a multilateral agreement, remain satisfied.

6.2 The Panel notes that should any one of the conditions referred to in subparagraph 6.1(b) above cease to be met in the future, the recommendations of the DSB may no longer be complied with. This Panel believes that, in such a case, any complaining party in the original case may be entitled to have further recourse to Article 21.5 of the DSU.

VII. CONCLUDING REMARKS

7.1 The Panel reaffirms its concluding remarks in the Original Panel Report:

> "The best way for the parties to this dispute to contribute effectively to the protection of sea turtles in a manner consistent with WTO objectives, including sustainable development, would be to reach cooperative agreements on integrated conservation strategies covering, *inter alia*, the design, implementation and use of TEDs while taking into account the specific conditions in the different geographical areas concerned."[254]

7.2 The Panel urges Malaysia and the United States to cooperate fully in order to conclude as soon a possible an agreement which will permit the protection and conservation of sea turtles to the satisfaction of all interests involved and taking into account the principle that States have common but differentiated responsibilities to conserve and protect the environment.[255]

[254] Original Panel Report, para. 9.1.
[255] Principle 7 of the Rio Declaration.

ANNEX

REVISED GUIDELINES PURSUANT TO SECTION 609, 8 JULY 1999[256]

1. For the sake of clarity, the 28 August 1998 guidelines are restated below as modified to reflect the changes proposed in the Federal Register notice issued 25 March 1999, and the comments received on those proposed changes.

I. INTRODUCTORY MATERIAL

A. *The US Program*

2. Since certification decisions under Section 609(b)(2)(A) and (B) are based on comparability with the US program governing the incidental taking of sea turtles in the course of shrimp harvesting, an explanation of the components of that program follows. The US program requires that commercial shrimp trawl vessels use TEDs approved in accordance with standards established by the US National Marine Fisheries Service (NMFS), in areas and at times when there is a likelihood of intercepting sea turtles. The goal of this program is to protect sea turtle populations from further decline by reducing the incidental mortality of sea turtles in commercial shrimp trawl operations.

3. The commercial shrimp trawl fisheries in the United States in which there is a likelihood of intercepting sea turtles occur in the temperate waters of the Gulf of Mexico and the Atlantic Ocean from North Carolina to Texas. With very limited exceptions, all US commercial shrimp trawl vessels operating in these waters must use approved TEDs at all times and in all areas. The only exceptions to this requirement are as follows:

(a) Vessels equipped exclusively with wing nets, skimmer trawls, and pusher-head trawls when used in conjunction with certain restricted tow times are not required to use TEDs because their operations do not pose a threat to sea turtles. Vessels equipped with barred beam trawls and/or barred roller trawls are not required to use TEDs. Single try nets (with less than a twelve foot headrope and fifteen foot rope) are not required to use TEDs.

(b) Vessels whose nets are retrieved exclusively by manual rather than mechanical means are not required to use TEDs because the lack of

[256] This Annex contains the Revised Guidelines for the Implementation of Section 609 of Public Law 101-162 Relating to the Protection of Sea Turtles in Shrimp Trawl Fishing Operations, US Department of State, Federal Register, Vol. 64, No. 130, 8 July 1999, Public Notice 3086, pp. 36949-36952. For ease of reference, the paras. of the Revised Guidelines have been numbered in this Annex.

a mechanical retrieval system necessarily limits tow times to a short duration so as not to pose a threat of the incidental drowning of sea turtles. This exemption applies only to vessels that have no power or mechanical-advantage trawl retrieval system.

(c) In exceptional circumstances, where NMFS determines that the use of TEDs would be impracticable because of special environmental conditions such as the presence of algae, seaweed, or debris, or that TEDs would be ineffective in protecting sea turtles in particular areas, vessels are permitted to restrict tow times instead of using TEDs. Such exceptions are generally limited to two periods of 30 days each. In practice, NMFS has permitted such exceptions only rarely.

4. With these limited exceptions, all other commercial shrimp trawl vessels operating in waters subject to US jurisdiction in which there is a likelihood of intercepting sea turtles must use TEDs at all times. For more information on the US program governing the incidental taking of sea turtles in the course of commercial shrimp trawl harvesting, see 50 CFR 227.17 and 50 CFR 227.72(e).

B. Shrimp Harvested in a Manner Not Harmful to Sea Turtles

5. The Department of State has determined that the import prohibitions imposed pursuant to Section 609 do not apply to shrimp or products of shrimp harvested under the following conditions, since such harvesting does not adversely affect sea turtle species:

(a) Shrimp harvested in an aquaculture facility in which the shrimp spend at least 30 days in pond prior to being harvested.

(b) Shrimp harvested by commercial shrimp trawl vessels using TEDs comparable in effectiveness to those required in the United States.

(c) Shrimp harvested exclusively by means that do not involve the retrieval of fishing nets by mechanical devices, such as winches, pulleys, power blocks or other devices providing mechanical advantage, or by vessels using gear that, in accordance with the US program described above, would not require TEDs.

(d) Shrimp harvested in any other manner or under any other circumstances that the Department of State may determine, following consultation with the NMFS, does not pose a threat of the incidental taking of sea turtles. The Department of State shall publish any such determinations in the Federal Register and shall notify affected foreign governments and other interested parties directly.

C. Shrimp Exporter's/Importer's Declaration

6. The requirement that all shipments of shrimp and products of shrimp imported into the United States must be accompanied by a declaration (DSP-121,

revised) became effective as of 1 May 1996 and remains effective. The DSP-121 attests that the shrimp accompanying the declaration was harvested either under conditions that do not adversely affect sea turtles (as defined above) or in waters subject to the jurisdiction of a nation currently certified pursuant to Section 609. All declarations must be signed by the exporter. The declaration must accompany the shipment through all stages of the export process, including any transformation of the original product and any shipment through any intermediary nation. As before, the Department of State will make copies of the declaration readily available. Local reproduction of the declarations is fully acceptable.

7. The requirement that a government official of the harvesting nation currently certified pursuant to Section 609 must also sign the DSP-121 asserting that the accompanying shrimp was harvested under conditions that do not adversely affect sea turtles species remains effective. In order to protect against fraud, the Department will continue to conduct periodic reviews of the systems that such foreign governments have put in place to verify the statements made on the DSP-121 form.

Date of Export

8. Import prohibitions shall not apply to shipments of shrimp and products of shrimp with a date of export falling at a time in which the harvesting nation is currently certified pursuant to Section 609.

Country of Origin

9. For purposes of implementing Section 609, the country of origin shall be deemed to be the nation in whose waters the shrimp is harvested, whether or not the harvesting vessel is flying the flag of another nation.

E. Review of Information

10. The government of any harvesting nation may request that the Department of State review any information regarding the particular shrimp fishing environment and conditions in that nation, or within a distinct geographic region of that nation, in making decisions pursuant to Section 609. Such information may be presented to demonstrate, *inter alia*:

(1) That some portion of the shrimp intended to be exported from that nation to the United States is harvested under one of the conditions identified above as not adversely affecting species of sea turtles;

(2) that the government of that nation has adopted a regulatory program governing the incidental taking of sea turtles in the course of commercial shrimp trawl fishing that is comparable to the US program and, therefore, that the nation is eligible for certification under Section 609(b)(2)(A) and (B); or

(3) that the fishing environment in that nation does not pose a threat of the incidental taking of sea turtles and, therefore, that the nation is eligible for certification under Section 609(b)(2)(C).

11. Such information should be based on empirical data supported by objective scientific studies of sufficient duration and scope to provide the information necessary for a reliable determination. In addition, information submitted to support a request for any such determination should include available biological data regarding the resources in question and operational information relating to the activities of the fishing fleet that are relevant to determining whether or not the fishing environment of the harvesting nation is likely to pose a threat to sea turtles. Studies intended to show the rate of incidental taking of sea turtles in a given shrimp fishery should, at a minimum, contain data for an entire fishing season. Upon request, the United States will review and provide comments on a planned or existing study with respect to sample size, scientific methodology and other factors that affect whether such a study provides a sufficient basis for making a reliable determination.

12. The Department will fully review and take into consideration all such information and, in consultation with the NMFS, respond in writing to the government of the harvesting nation within 120 days from the date on which the information is received.

13. The Department, in consultation with the NMFS, will also take into consideration information on the same subjects that may be available from other sources, including but not limited to academic and scientific organizations, intergovernmental organizations and non-governmental organizations with recognized expertise in the subject matter.

II. GUIDELINES FOR MAKING CERTIFICATION DECISIONS

A. *Certification Pursuant to Section 609(b)(2)(C)*

14. Section 609(b)(2)(C) authorizes the Department of State to certify a harvesting nation if the particular fishing environment of the harvesting nation does not pose a threat of incidental taking of sea turtles in the course of commercial shrimp trawl harvesting. Accordingly, the Department shall certify any harvesting nation meeting the following criteria without the need for action on the part of the government of the harvesting nation:

(a) Any harvesting nation without any of the relevant species of sea turtles occurring in waters subject to its jurisdiction;

(b) any harvesting nation that harvests shrimp exclusively by means that do not pose a threat to sea turtles, e.g., any nation that harvests shrimp exclusively by artisanal means;

(c) any nation whose commercial shrimp trawling operations take place exclusively in waters subject to its jurisdiction in which sea turtles do not occur.

B. Certification Pursuant to Section 609(b)(2)(A) and (B)

15. Under Section 609(b)(2), the Department of State shall certify any other harvesting nation by May 1st of each year if "the government of (that) nation has provided documentary evidence of the adoption of a regulatory program governing the incidental taking of such sea turtles in the course of such harvesting that is comparable to that of the United States" and if "the average rate of that incidental taking by vessels of the harvesting nation is comparable to the average rate of incidental taking of sea turtles by United States vessels in the course of such harvesting."

(a) Regulatory Program

16. The Department of State shall assess regulatory programs, as described in any documentary evidence provided by the governments of harvesting nations, for comparability with the US program.

17. Where standard otter trawl nets are used in shrimp fisheries in waters where sea turtles are present, sea turtles will inevitably be captured and drowned. The Department of State is presently aware of no measure or series of measures that can minimize the capture and drowning of sea turtles in such nets that is comparable in effectiveness to the required use of TEDs.

(1) If the government of the harvesting nation seeks certification on the basis of having adopted a TEDs program, certification shall be made if a program includes the following:

(i) Required Use of TEDs

18. A requirement that all commercial shrimp trawl vessels operating in waters in which there is a likelihood of intercepting sea turtles use TEDs at all times. TEDs must be comparable in effectiveness to those used in the United States. Any exceptions to this requirement must be comparable to those of the US program described above; and

(ii) Enforcement

19. A credible enforcement effort that includes monitoring for compliance and appropriate sanctions.

(2) If the government of a harvesting nation demonstrates that it has implemented and is enforcing a comparably effective regulatory program to protect sea turtles in the course of shrimp trawl fishing without the use of TEDs, that nation will also be eligible for certification. As described above, such a demonstration would need to be based on empirical data supported by objective scientific studies of sufficient duration and scope to provide the information necessary for a reliable determination. In reviewing any such information, the Department of State will take fully into account any demonstrated differences between the

shrimp fishing conditions in the United States and those in other nations, as well as information available from other sources.

(b) Incidental Take

20. Average incidental take rates will be deemed comparable if the harvesting nation requires the use of TEDs in a manner comparable to that of the US program or, as described above, otherwise demonstrates that it has implemented a comparably effective program to protect sea turtles in the course of shrimp trawl fishing without the use of TEDs.

(c) Additional Considerations

(i) Form

21. A regulatory program may be in the form of regulations promulgated by the government of the harvesting nation and having the force of law. If the legal system and industry structure of the harvesting nation permit voluntary arrangements between government and the fishing industry, such an arrangement may be acceptable so long as there is a governmental mechanism to monitor compliance with the arrangement and to impose penalties for non-compliance, and reliable confirmation that the fishing industry is complying with the arrangement.

(ii) Documentary Evidence

22. Documentary evidence may be in the form of copies of the relevant laws, regulations or decrees. If the regulatory program is in the form of a government-industry arrangement, then a copy of the arrangement is required. Harvesting nations are encouraged to provide, to the extent practicable, information relating to the extent of shrimp harvested by means of aquaculture.

(iii) Additional Sea Turtle Protection Measures

23. The Department of State recognizes that sea turtles require protection throughout their life cycle, not only when they are threatened during the course of commercial shrimp trawl harvesting. In making certification determinations, the Department shall also take fully into account other measures the harvesting nation undertakes to protect sea turtles, including national programs to protect nesting beaches and other habitat, prohibitions on the directed take of sea turtles, national enforcement and compliance programs, and participation in any international agreement for the protection and conservation of sea turtles. In assessing any information provided by the governments of harvesting nations in this respect, the Department of State will rely on the technical expertise of NMFS and, where appropriate, the US Fish and Wildlife Service to evaluate threats to sea turtles and the effectiveness of sea turtle protection programs.

(iv) Consultations

24. The Department of State will engage in ongoing consultations with the governments of harvesting nations. The Department recognizes that, as sea turtle protection programs develop, additional information will be gained about the interaction between sea turtle populations and shrimp fisheries. These Guidelines may be revised in the future to take into consideration that and other information, as well as to take into account changes in the US program. These Guidelines may also be revised as a result of pending domestic litigation. In addition, the Department will continue to welcome public input on the best ways to implement both these Guidelines and Section 609 as a whole and may revise these guidelines in the future accordingly.

C. Timetable and Procedures for Certification Decisions

25. Each year the Department will consider for certification: (a) any nation that is currently certified, and (b) any other shrimp harvesting nation whose government requests such certification in a written communication to the Department of State through diplomatic channels prior to 1 September of the preceding year. Any such communication should include any information not previously provided that would support the request for certification, including the information specified above under Review of Information.

26. Between 1 September and 1 March, US officials will seek to visit those nations requesting certifications pursuant to Section 609(b)(2)(A) and (B). Each visit will conclude with a meeting between the US officials and government officials of the harvesting nation to discuss the results of the visit and to review any identified deficiencies regarding the harvesting nation's program to protect sea turtles in the course of shrimp trawl fishing.

27. By 15 March, the Department of State will notify in writing through diplomatic channels the government of each nation that, on the basis of available information, including information gathered during such visits, does not appear to qualify for certification. Such notification will explain the reasons for this preliminary assessment, suggest steps that the government of the harvesting nation can take in order to receive a certification and invite the government of the harvesting nation to provide, by 15 April, any further information. If the government of the harvesting nation so requests, the Department of State will schedule face-to-face meetings between relevant US officials and officials of the harvesting nation to discuss the situation.

28. Between 15 March and 1 May, the Department of State will actively consider any additional information that the government of the harvesting nation believes should be considered by the Department in making its determination concerning certification.

29. By 1 May of each year the Department of State will make formal decisions on certification. The governments of all nations that have requested certification will be notified in writing of the decision promptly through diplomatic

channels. In the case of those nations for which certification is denied, such notification will again state the reasons for such denial and the steps necessary to receive a certification in the future.

30. The government of any nation that is denied a certification by 1 May may, at any time thereafter, request reconsideration of that decision. When the United States receives information from that government demonstrating that the circumstances that led to the denial of the certification have been corrected, US officials will visit the exporting nation as early as a visit can be arranged. If the visit demonstrates that the circumstances that led to the denial of the certification have indeed been corrected, the United States will certify that nation immediately thereafter.

D. *Special Timetable for 1999*

31. The United States and the four nations that brought the WTO complaint have agreed that the United States would implement the recommendations and rulings of the DSB within 13 months of the adoption of the WTO Appellate Body report by the DSB, i.e., by 6 December 1999.

32. Accordingly, the Department of State hereby establishes the following timetable to apply in 1999 only:

33. After the date of publication of the revised guidelines, the government of any harvesting nation that was denied certification by 1 May 1999, may request to be certified in accordance with these guidelines in a written communication to the Department of State through diplomatic channels prior to 1 September 1999.

34. Not later than 15 October 1999, US officials will seek to visit to those nations requesting such certifications. Each visit will conclude with a meeting between the US officials and government officials of the harvesting nation to discuss the results of the visit and to review any identified deficiencies regarding the harvesting nation's program to protect sea turtles in the course of shrimp trawl fishing.

35. By 1 November 1999, the Department of State will notify in writing through diplomatic channels the government of any nation that, on the basis of available information, including information gathered during such visits, does not appear to qualify for certification. Such notification will explain the reasons for this preliminary assessment, suggest steps that the government of the harvesting nation can take in order to receive a certification and invite the government of the harvesting nation to provide, by 15 November 1999, any further information.

36. Between 15 November and 6 December 1999, the Department of State will actively consider any additional information that the government of the harvesting nation believes should be considered by the Department in making its determination concerning certification.

37. By 6 December 1999, the Department of State will make formal decisions on certification. The governments of all nations that have requested certification under the special 1999 timetable will be notified in writing of the decision

promptly through diplomatic channels. In the case of those nations for which certification is denied, such notification will again state the reasons for such denial and the steps necessary to receive a certification in the future.

38. The government of any nation that is denied a certification by 6 December 1999, may, at any time thereafter, request reconsideration of that decision. When the United States receives information from that government demonstrating that the circumstances that led to the denial of the certification have been corrected, US officials will visit the exporting nation as early as a visit can be arranged. If the visit demonstrates that the circumstances that led to the denial of the certification have indeed been corrected, the United States will certify that nation immediately thereafter.

39. The Department of State recognizes that a government seeking certification on the basis of the revised guidelines may not, by 1 September 1999, be able to gather sufficient information necessary to support such a request. To meet this concern, and in accordance with its existing practice, the Department will accept requests for certification at any time in 1999 and will process them as expeditiously as possible. However, the Department can only commit to making a certification determination by 6 December 1999 if it has received the necessary information by 1 September 1999.

E. Related Determinations

40. As noted above, any harvesting nation that is not certified on 1 May of any year may be certified prior to the following 1 May at such time as the harvesting nation meets the criteria necessary for certification. Conversely, any harvesting nation that is certified on 1 May of any year may have its certification revoked prior to the following 1 May at such time as the harvesting nation no longer meets those criteria.

41. As a matter relating to the foreign affairs function, these guidelines are exempt from the notice, comment, and delayed effectiveness provisions of the Administrative Procedures Act. This action is exempt from Executive Order 12866, and is not subject to the requirements of the Regulatory Flexibility Act.

Dated: 29 June 1999.

Stuart E. Eizenstat, *Under Secretary of State for Economic, Business and Agriculture Affairs.*

[FR Doc. 99-17330 Filed 7-7-99; 8:45 am]

BILLING CODE 4710-09-U

MEXICO - ANTI-DUMPING INVESTIGATION OF HIGH FRUCTOSE CORN SYRUP (HFCS) FROM THE UNITED STATES

RECOURSE TO ARTICLE 21.5 OF THE DSU BY THE UNITED STATES

Report of the Appellate Body
WT/DS132/AB/RW

Adopted by the Appellate Body on 21 November 2001

Mexico, *Appellant*	Present:
United States, *Appellee*	Feliciano, Presiding Member
European Communities, *Third Participant*	Abi-Saab, Member
	Ehlermann, Member

TABLE OF CONTENTS

I. INTRODUCTION

1. Mexico appeals certain issues of law and legal interpretations in the Panel Report, Mexico - Anti-Dumping Investigation of High Fructose Corn Syrup (HFCS) from the United States, Recourse to Article 21.5 of the DSU by the United States (the "Panel Report").[1] The Panel considered, pursuant to Article 21.5 of the Understanding on Rules and Procedures Governing the Settlement of Disputes (the "DSU"), the complaint brought by the United States with respect to the consistency with the Agreement on Implementation of Article VI of the General Agreement on Tariffs and Trade 1994 (the "Anti-Dumping Agreement") of a measure taken by Mexico to comply with the recommendations and rulings of the Dispute Settlement Body (the "DSB") in Mexico - Anti-Dumping Investigation

[1] WT/DS132/RW, DSR 2001:XIII, 6727, 22 June 2001. In this Report, we refer to the panel that considered the United States' complaint under Article 21.5 of the DSU as the "Panel", and to its report, WT/DS132/RW, as the "Panel Report".

of High Fructose Corn Syrup (HFCS) from the United States ("Mexico - High Fructose Corn Syrup").[2]

2. In *Mexico - High Fructose Corn Syrup*, the original panel concluded that Mexico's imposition of definitive anti-dumping duties on imports of high fructose corn syrup from the United States was inconsistent with certain of Mexico's obligations under the *Anti-Dumping Agreement.*[3] The original panel report was not appealed to the Appellate Body and, on 24 February 2000, the DSB adopted the original panel report, including its recommendation that Mexico bring its measure into conformity with its obligations under the *Anti-Dumping Agreement.*[4]

3. On 20 September 2000, with a view to complying with the findings and conclusions set forth in the original panel report, Mexico published a final resolution (the "redetermination") which revised the original final resolution imposing definitive anti-dumping duties on imports of high fructose corn syrup from the United States.[5] In the redetermination, Mexico's Secretariat of Commerce and Industrial Development ("SECOFI") "ratified its conclusion that during the period under investigation, there was a threat of injury to the domestic sugar industry as a consequence of imports of high fructose corn syrup under price discriminatory conditions originating from the United States of America".[6] SECOFI, thus, found "that it is appropriate to maintain the final offsetting duties established during the [original] anti-dumping investigation".[7] The factual aspects of this dispute are set out in greater detail in the Panel Report.[8]

4. The United States considered that the redetermination was not consistent with Mexico's obligations under the *Anti-Dumping Agreement* and, therefore, requested that the matter be referred to the original panel pursuant to Article 21.5 of the DSU.[9] On 23 October 2000, in accordance with Article 21.5 of the DSU, the DSB referred the matter to the original panel.[10] A member of the original

---

[2] The recommendations and rulings of the DSB resulted from the adoption, by the DSB, of the panel report in *Mexico - High Fructose Corn Syrup*, WT/DS132/R, adopted 24 February 2000 (the "original panel report"), DSR 2000:III, 1345. In this Report, we refer to the panel that considered the original complaint brought by the United States as the "original panel".

[3] *Ibid.*, para. 8.2.

[4] Panel Report, para. 1.1.

[5] Final resolution revising, on the basis of the findings and recommendations by the Panel of the World Trade Organization's Dispute Settlement Body, the final determination in the anti-dumping investigation of high fructose corn syrup imports, merchandise classified in tariff headings 1702.40.99 and 1702.60.01 of the Schedule of the General Import Duties Act, originating from the United States of America, irrespective of the country of export; published 20 September 2000 in Mexico's *Diario Oficial de la Federación*; Exhibits MEXICO-1 (Spanish version) and MEXICO-1(a) (English translation provided by Mexico) submitted by Mexico to the Panel. See also Panel Report, para. 1.2.

[6] Redetermination, para. 188.

[7] *Ibid.*

[8] See, in particular, paras. 1.1 - 1.8 of the Panel Report.

[9] WT/DS132/6, 13 October 2000. See also Panel Report, para. 1.3.

[10] Panel Report, para. 1.4.

panel was unable to participate in the proceeding and the parties therefore agreed on a new panelist on 13 November 2000.[11] The Panel Report was circulated to the Members of the World Trade Organization (the "WTO") on 22 June 2001.

5. The Panel concluded, *inter alia*, that:

> ... Mexico's imposition of definitive anti-dumping duties on imports of HFCS from the United States on the basis of the SECOFI redetermination is inconsistent with the requirements of the AD Agreement in that Mexico's inadequate consideration of the impact of dumped imports on the domestic industry, and its inadequate consideration of the potential effect of the alleged restraint agreement in its determination of likelihood of substantially increased importation, are not consistent with the provisions of Articles 3.1, 3.4, 3.7 and 3.7(i) of the AD Agreement. We therefore consider that Mexico has failed to implement the recommendation of the original Panel and the DSU to bring its measure into conformity with its obligations under the AD Agreement.[12]

6. The Panel concluded that, to the extent that Mexico has acted inconsistently with the provisions of the *Anti-Dumping Agreement*, it has nullified or impaired benefits accruing to the United States under that Agreement, and recommended that the DSB request Mexico to bring its measure into conformity with its obligations under the *Anti-Dumping Agreement*.[13]

7. On 24 July 2001, Mexico notified the DSB of its intention to appeal certain issues of law covered in the Panel Report and legal interpretations developed by the Panel, pursuant to paragraph 4 of Article 16 of the DSU, and filed a Notice of Appeal pursuant to Rule 20 of the *Working Procedures for Appellate Review* (the "*Working Procedures*"). On 3 August 2001, Mexico filed its appellant's submission.[14] On 20 August 2001, the United States filed an appellee's submission.[15] On the same day, the European Communities filed a third participant's submission.[16]

8. The oral hearing in this appeal was held on 11 September 2001. The participants and third participant presented oral arguments and responded to questions put to them by the Members of the Division hearing the appeal.

---

[11] Panel Report, para. 1.5.

[12] Panel Report, para. 7.1.

[13] *Ibid.*, paras. 7.2 and 7.3.

[14] Pursuant to Rule 21(1) of the *Working Procedures*.

[15] Pursuant to Rule 22 of the *Working Procedures*.

[16] Pursuant to Rule 24 of the *Working Procedures*.

II. ARGUMENTS OF THE PARTICIPANTS AND THE THIRD PARTICIPANT

A. *Claims of Error by Mexico - Appellant*

1. *The Panel's Treatment of Alleged Deficiencies in the Proceedings*

9. Mexico argues that the Panel made a "fatal error" because it made no ruling regarding the fact that Mexico and the United States did not engage in consultations before the redetermination was referred to the Panel and regarding Article 6.2 of the DSU.[17] Had it done so, the Panel would have been compelled to conclude that it was not properly established. Mexico also challenges the Panel's failure to address Mexico's argument that the United States had acted inconsistently with Article 3.7 of the DSU since, by "hastily" requesting the establishment of the Panel, the United States failed to exercise its judgement as to whether action under the procedures set out in the DSU would be "fruitful".[18] In remaining silent on these issues, the Panel acted inconsistently with the obligations set forth in Articles 3.4, 7.2, 12.7 and 19 of the DSU. Mexico therefore requests the Appellate Body to reverse the substantive findings made by the Panel, in particular in paragraphs 7.1 and 7.2 of the Panel Report.

10. Mexico emphasizes the importance of consultations within the GATT and WTO dispute settlement systems. Consultations must be held, unless there is an express provision to the contrary. This principle is confirmed and strengthened by Article 4.1 of the DSU. The requirement that requests for consultations be notified to the DSB benefits all WTO Members, and not just the parties to the dispute, because the only way for Members to know whether a dispute that is to be the subject of consultations will affect them is if the disputing parties officially notify the DSB of their intent to engage in consultations.

11. Mexico stresses that the rules governing consultations and the establishment of panels do not distinguish between different types of panels. Accordingly, the generally applicable rules must also be observed in proceedings under Article 21.5 of the DSU. For this reason, Mexico interprets the phrase "these dispute settlement procedures" in Article 21.5 to include the consultations procedures provided for in the DSU.

12. In Mexico's view, it is clear from GATT and WTO practice, and from Articles 4.7 and 6.2 of the DSU, that a panel may be requested and established only *after* consultations have been held and have failed to resolve the dispute. Mexico refers, in this regard, to *Korea - Definitive Safeguard Measure on Imports*

---

[17] Translation of Mexico's appellant's submission, p. 3; original Spanish version, p. 2.

[18] This statement appears in the Notice of Appeal and was repeated by Mexico in its statement at the oral hearing. However, Mexico did not elaborate upon this statement either in its appellant's submission or at the oral hearing.

of Certain Dairy Products ("*Korea - Dairy Safeguard* ")[19], and *European Communities - Regime for the Importation, Sale and Distribution of Bananas* ("*European Communities - Bananas* "),[20] to support its view that the Appellate Body attaches great importance to the fulfilment of the requirements for establishment of a panel set forth in Article 6.2 of the DSU, including that the request must indicate whether consultations have been held.

13. Mexico recalls that, in its oral statement at the meeting with the Panel, it argued that there had been no consultations regarding the redetermination and that the United States' request for the establishment of a panel failed to mention whether consultations had been held, as required by Article 6.2 of the DSU; and that the United States had acted contrary to Article 3.7 of the DSU by failing to exercise its judgement as to whether action under the procedures in the DSU would be "fruitful". Furthermore, before the Panel, Mexico agreed with the European Communities' criticism of the lack of consultations. Mexico maintains that, in remaining silent despite these arguments, the Panel failed to comply with its obligation, under Article 7.2 of the DSU, to address the relevant provisions in the covered agreements cited by the parties to the dispute. The Panel also failed to comply with the requirement of Article 12.7 of the DSU to set out the findings of fact, applicability of relevant provisions, and the basic rationale behind its findings and recommendations, and thereby effectively diminished Mexico's rights under the DSU, contrary to Articles 3.4 and 19.2 of the DSU.

2. *Article 3 of the Anti-Dumping Agreement: "Threat of Material Injury"*

14. Mexico also requests the Appellate Body to reverse the Panel's finding in paragraph 6.23 of its Report that "SECOFI's conclusion that there was a significant likelihood of increased importation is not consistent with Article 3.7(i) of the Anti-Dumping Agreement". Mexico believes that the Panel wrongly interpreted Article 3.7 of the *Anti-Dumping Agreement* and failed to comply with the standard of review prescribed by paragraphs 5 and 6 of Article 17 of that Agreement.

15. Mexico submits that the findings of the Panel under Article 3.7(i) of the *Anti-Dumping Agreement* are "limited to assertions" regarding an alleged agreement between Mexican sugar millers and soft-drink bottlers to restrain the bottlers' use of HFCS.[21] In examining the redetermination, the Panel made "exactly the same mistake" as the original panel because both considered it necessary for SECOFI to examine the impact of an agreement whose existence had not been

---

[19] Appellate Body Report, WT/DS98/AB/R, adopted 12 January 2000, DSR 2000:I, 3, paras. 120 ff.

[20] Appellate Body Report, WT/DS27/AB/R, adopted 25 September 1997, DSR 1997:II, 591, para. 142.

[21] Mexico's appellant's submission, para. 67.

proven.[22] This "agreement", therefore, did not constitute a "fact" but rather an "allegation, conjecture, or remote possibility". As a result, Mexico concludes, the Panel misinterpreted Article 3.7(i) of the *Anti-Dumping Agreement.*

16. Mexico submits that, in basing its evaluation on the alleged agreement, the Panel failed to base itself on the "facts made available ... to the authorities of the importing Member", as required by Article 17.5 of the *Anti-Dumping Agreement.* The word "facts" must mean the same thing in Articles 3.7, 17.5 and 17.6 of the *Anti-Dumping Agreement.* Panels are empowered to examine *only* those facts that were before an investigating authority, and not things that were merely *alleged* to exist. Since, in this case, the alleged restraint agreement remained merely an "allegation, conjecture or remote possibility", Mexico contends that the Panel acted inconsistently with the standard of review prescribed in Articles 17.5 and 17.6 of the *Anti-Dumping Agreement* by presuming that the alleged restraint agreement was a "fact", when SECOFI had not determined it to be so.

17. Mexico adds that the United States failed to satisfy its burden of proving the existence of the alleged restraint agreement. Notwithstanding such failure, the Panel considered that SECOFI should have evaluated the impact of this alleged agreement. Had it properly applied Article 17.6(ii) of the *Anti-Dumping Agreement,* the Panel could not have reached the conclusion that SECOFI acted inconsistently with Article 3.7(i) of that Agreement because it had never been found that the alleged restraint agreement did in fact exist. Thus, Mexico concludes that the errors made by the Panel with respect to the alleged restraint agreement invalidate its findings regarding Mexico's non-compliance with Article 3.7(i) of the *Anti-Dumping Agreement.*

18. Mexico further requests the Appellate Body to reverse the Panel's findings in paragraphs 6.24 to 6.37 of its Report and, in particular, the Panel's finding in paragraph 6.36 that "SECOFI's redetermination with respect to the likely impact of dumped imports of HFCS from the United States on the domestic industry which underlies the determination of threat of material injury to the Mexican sugar industry is not consistent with Articles 3.1, 3.4 and 3.7 of the Anti-Dumping Agreement". Since these findings are based on the Panel's earlier conclusion regarding the likelihood of increased imports, such findings are, in the view of Mexico, also based on an incorrect interpretation of Article 3.7, and constitute an improper application of Articles 17.5 and 17.6 of the *Anti-Dumping Agreement.* Accordingly, Mexico submits that these findings should also be reversed.

[22] Mexico's appellant's submission, para. 66.

3. *Article 12.7 of the DSU and Article 17.6 of the* Anti-Dumping Agreement: *"Reasoning of the Panel"*

19. Mexico submits that the Panel's findings that Mexico violated Articles 3.1 and 3.4 of the *Anti-Dumping Agreement* should be reversed too, in view of the deficiencies in the reasoning given by the Panel for those findings. The Panel's examination of the impact of imports on the domestic industry is "extraordinarily confused".[23] Mexico argues that the Panel did not comply with its obligations under Articles 3.4, 12.7 and 19 of the DSU because the Panel did not clearly identify the obligations with which Mexico had failed to comply. In one paragraph in its Report, the Panel states that the redetermination is not consistent with Articles 3.1 and 3.4 of the *Anti-Dumping Agreement.* There is, however, no analysis underpinning these conclusions. It is unclear whether the Panel found that SECOFI's findings on impact were not acceptable because they were not based on facts, because not all the Article 3.4 factors had not been examined, or because there was no *showing* of impact on the domestic industry. Mexico notes that while the Panel might have thought that a violation of Article 3.7 of the *Anti-Dumping Agreement* automatically implies a violation of Articles 3.1 and 3.4 of that Agreement, the Panel did not say so.

20. Mexico further observes that, in paragraph 6.37 of its Report, the Panel acknowledged that in the circumstances of this case it might have been possible to establish a threat of material injury, and that Mexico "apparently" complied with the DSB's recommendations and rulings. Mexico maintains that, in making these statements, the Panel recognized that SECOFI's interpretation of the relevant provisions was "permissible". Therefore, Mexico states, the Panel acted contrary to its obligation under Article 17.6(ii) of the *Anti-Dumping Agreement* by rejecting a "permissible" interpretation of that Agreement.

B. Arguments of the United States - Appellee

1. The Panel's Treatment of Alleged Deficiencies in the Proceedings

21. The United States urges the Appellate Body to dismiss Mexico's appeal regarding the absence of consultations. Mexico asserts, for the first time on appeal, that the Panel lacked authority to address this dispute because no formal consultations had been held on the redetermination. Mexico did not raise any such objection at the DSB meeting when the redetermination was referred to the Panel, nor did it object before the Panel itself. Although it made passing reference to the absence of consultations at the meeting with the Panel, Mexico gave no indication that it was seeking a ruling from the Panel on whether the dispute was properly before it. Indeed, Mexico explicitly stated that it was *not* claiming that its rights had been infringed. Furthermore, although the European Communi-

---

23 Mexico's appellant's submission, para. 111.

ties contended that the dispute was not properly before the Panel because of the absence of consultations, this claim was, correctly, not addressed by the Panel because it was not advanced by either of the parties to the dispute. Accordingly, in the view of the United States, the Panel appropriately did not address these issues in its Report, and in no way infringed or diminished Mexico's rights under the DSU in refraining from doing so.

22. The United States argues that Mexico is precluded from raising these issues for the first time on appeal. The United States refers, in this regard, to the Appellate Body Reports in *United States - Tax Treatment for "Foreign Sales Corporations"* ("*United States - FSC*")[24] and *Thailand - Anti-Dumping Duties on Angles, Shapes and Sections of Iron or Non-Alloy Steel and H-Beams from Poland* ("*Thailand - H-Beams* ").[25] Since Mexico did not object to the lack of consultations before the Panel, and since Mexico has not attempted to demonstrate that it suffered any prejudice from this lack of consultations, Mexico cannot now assert that the claims of the United States were not properly before the Panel.

23. The United States submits that Mexico's appeal should be dismissed without addressing the merits of its arguments on consultations. Should the Appellate Body reach the issue, however, the United States asks the Appellate Body to rule that formal consultations are not a prerequisite to the establishment of a panel under Article 21.5 of the DSU. While consultations are important, the meaning of Article 21.5, as well as its object and purpose, support the view that consultations are not required in proceedings under Article 21.5 of the DSU. To read a formal consultation requirement into Article 21.5 would undermine prompt compliance with DSB recommendations and rulings and extend the period during which the complaining Member suffers harm.

2. *Article 3 of the Anti-Dumping Agreement: "Threat of Material Injury"*

24. The United States submits that the Panel's finding that SECOFI's redetermination was inconsistent with Article 3.7(i) of the *Anti-Dumping Agreement* should be upheld. As the Panel found, there is no adequate factual basis for SECOFI's findings, in its redetermination, with respect to the likelihood of substantially increased imports. Furthermore, in its appeal, Mexico does not address or challenge the actual reasoning that the Panel articulated to reach this conclusion, and the United States submits that such reasoning is not, therefore, before the Appellate Body.

25. In the view of the United States, Mexico's argument that the Panel committed the same mistakes as the original panel by requiring SECOFI to analyze the effects of the restraint agreement, without at the same time requiring SECOFI

---

[24] Appellate Body Report, WT/DS108/AB/R, adopted 20 March 2000, DSR 2000:III, 1619.

[25] Appellate Body Report, WT/DS122/AB/R, adopted 5 April 2001, DSR 2001:VII, 2701.

to determine that the restraint agreement actually existed, should be dismissed. Since the DSB has adopted the original panel's findings, Mexico cannot now argue that the original panel's analysis was erroneous.

26. The United States maintains that Article 3.7(i) of the *Anti-Dumping Agreement* requires a factual basis for a determination of a likelihood of substantially increased imports. Article 3.7(i) imposes this requirement on investigating authorities, not on panels. In this case, SECOFI purported to find, as a matter of fact that, even if the alleged agreement were in effect, it "would not eliminate the likelihood" that HFCS users other than soft-drink bottlers would substantially increase their consumption of imported HFCS.[26] Both the parties and the Panel understood this "likelihood" of increased consumption of imported HFCS by "other users" to be the factual basis for SECOFI's finding of a likelihood of increased imports. Since SECOFI chose to take this approach, the Panel was entitled to review it under Articles 17.5 and 17.6 of the *Anti-Dumping Agreement.*

27. The United States observes that SECOFI itself elected to facilitate its analysis by assuming that the restraint agreement existed and would be effective. The United States did not challenge, and the Panel did not question, SECOFI's use of this assumption. Accordingly, Mexico's arguments about "burden of proof" are misplaced and irrelevant. On Mexico's logic, investigating authorities would be able to "immunize" or "insulate" their findings from panel review by basing their conclusions on assumptions rather than findings of fact.[27] This cannot be a proper interpretation of Articles 17.5 and 17.6 of the *Anti-Dumping Agreement.* The United States, therefore, urges the Appellate Body to reject Mexico's claims that the Panel misapplied the standard of review and to affirm the finding that Mexico acted inconsistently with Article 3.7(i).

3. *Article 12.7 of the DSU and Article 17.6 of the Anti-Dumping Agreement: "Reasoning of the Panel"*

28. The United States contends that the Panel properly found that SECOFI's analysis of the likely impact of HFCS imports on the Mexican sugar industry was inconsistent with Articles 3.1 and 3.4 of the *Anti-Dumping Agreement.* The Panel was not discussing the requirements of Articles 3.1 and 3.4 "on a blank slate", but rather against the background of the discussion of comparable claims in the original panel report.[28] According to the United States, the Panel Report, whether read in conjunction with the original panel report or alone, makes clear the nature of the obligations under Articles 3.1 and 3.4 that Mexico failed to satisfy.

29. The United States also contends that the Panel provided "compelling" reasons for its conclusions under Articles 3.1 and 3.4 that are not dependent on

---

[26] United States' appellee's submission, para. 38.
[27] *Ibid.*, paras. 66 and 67.
[28] *Ibid.*, para. 70.

its findings with respect to Article 3.7.[29] The Panel Report specifically identifies the nature of Mexico's obligations under Articles 3.1 and 3.4 - which were the same obligations articulated in detail in the original panel report - and explains why SECOFI's redetermination failed to satisfy those obligations. Thus, the Panel acted consistently with Article 12.7 of the DSU. In addition, since Mexico submitted no interpretation of Articles 3.1 and 3.4 of the *Anti-Dumping Agreement* during the panel proceedings, the arguments that it now makes concerning "permissible" interpretations under Article 17.6(ii) of that Agreement are irrelevant.

C. *Arguments of the Third Participant*

1. *European Communities*

30. The European Communities recalls that, in this case, no request for consultations was provided to the DSB or circulated to Members, and the United States' request for establishment of a panel did not mention whether consultations were held. If no consultations had been requested by the United States, then the Panel should have ruled that the matter was not properly before it. The Panel erred because it neither ascertained whether consultations were held, nor ruled on the consequences of the lack of consultations.

31. According to the European Communities, Article 21.5 requires that the complaining party request consultations under Article 4 of the DSU before requesting an Article 21.5 panel. The phrase "these dispute settlement procedures" in Article 21.5 refers to the panel and Appellate Body procedures laid down in the DSU, including the requirement that consultations be held on a measure before a Member may request the establishment of a panel with respect to that measure. The European Communities refers, in support of this interpretation, to Articles 4.7 and 6.2 of the DSU, and to the Reports of the Appellate Body in *Brazil - Export Financing Programme for Aircraft* ("*Brazil - Aircraft* ")[30] and *United States - Import Measures on Certain Products from the European Communities.*[31]

32. The European Communities submits that parties to an Article 21.5 dispute cannot agree to dispense with the requirement to hold consultations under Article 4 of the DSU. Members cannot deviate from the rules set forth in the DSU unless the DSU expressly authorizes them to do so. Article 4.3 and the second sentence of Article 4.7 of the DSU confirm that consultations are a mandatory prerequisite for requesting establishment of a panel. In addition, it would be inconsistent with the objectives expressed in Articles 3.7 and 4.1, as well as with the duties imposed upon parties under Article 4.5 of the DSU, if parties could agree to dis-

---

29 United States' appellee's submission, para. 8.

30 Appellate Body Report, WT/DS46/AB/R, adopted 20 August 1999, DSR 1999:III, 1161, para. 131.

31 Appellate Body Report, WT/DS165/AB/R, adopted 10 January 2001, DSR 2001:I, 373, para. 70.

pense with consultations. The European Communities is of the view that any other approach would create uncertainty about procedural guarantees for parties, and would curtail third party rights that are clearly enshrined in the DSU.

33. The European Communities submits that, since consultations are "a fundamental prerequisite for lawful panel proceedings", Article 21.5 panels have a positive duty to ascertain, if necessary on their own motion, whether consultations under Article 4 of the DSU have been requested by the complaining party. Therefore, the Panel should have addressed the issue of the lack of consultations. In support of this view, the European Communities refers to the Appellate Body Report in *United States - Anti-Dumping Act of 1916* ("*United States - 1916 Act*"), and, in particular, to the statement that: "some issues of jurisdiction may be of such nature that they have to be addressed by the Panel at any time".[32]

III. ISSUES RAISED IN THIS APPEAL

34. The following issues are raised in this appeal:

(a) whether the Panel erred because it did not address, in its Report: the lack of consultations prior to the DSB's referral of the redetermination to the Panel; the alleged failure of the United States to comply with Article 6.2 of the DSU because its communication seeking recourse to Article 21.5 of the DSU did not indicate whether consultations had been held; and the alleged failure of the United States to exercise its judgement, in accordance with Article 3.7 of the DSU, as to whether action under the DSU would be "fruitful";

(b) whether the Panel erred in its review of SECOFI's determination of a threat of material injury, and in particular whether the Panel erred:

(i) in finding, in paragraph 6.23 of the Panel Report, that SECOFI's conclusion, in the redetermination, that there existed a significant likelihood of increased imports of HFCS, was inconsistent with Mexico's obligations under Article 3.7(i) of the *Anti-Dumping Agreement*; and

(ii) in finding, in paragraph 6.36 of the Panel Report, that SECOFI's conclusion, in the redetermination, regarding the likely impact of imports of HFCS on the domestic industry, was inconsistent with Mexico's obligations under Articles 3.1, 3.4, and 3.7 of the *Anti-Dumping Agreement*;

[32] Appellate Body Report, WT/DS136/AB/R, WT/DS162/AB/R, adopted 26 September 2000, DSR 2000:X, 4793, para. 54.

(c) whether the Panel erred in the reasoning employed to reach its findings, in particular:

(i) by failing, as required under Article 12.7 of the DSU, to set out a "basic rationale behind [its] findings" that SECOFI's analysis and conclusions, in the redetermination, regarding the likely impact of imports of HFCS on the domestic industry, were inconsistent with Mexico's obligations under Articles 3.1 and 3.4 of the *Anti-Dumping Agreement*; and

(ii) by failing to apply the standard of review set out in Article 17.6(ii) of the *Anti-Dumping Agreement* in stating, in paragraph 6.37 of its Report, that SECOFI could have made a valid determination of the existence of a threat of material injury, but in nevertheless finding that Mexico had acted inconsistently with Article 3.7 of the *Anti-Dumping Agreement*.

IV. THE PANEL'S TREATMENT OF ALLEGED DEFICIENCIES IN THE PROCEEDINGS

35. Mexico asks us to reverse the substantive findings reached by the Panel on the grounds that the Panel failed to address and consider the consequences of certain alleged deficiencies in the process of referring SECOFI's redetermination to the Panel. Mexico's principal contention is that the Panel made a "fatal error"[33] because it said *nothing* in its Report regarding: the lack of consultations between Mexico and the United States before the redetermination was referred to the Panel; the alleged failure of the United States to comply with Article 6.2 of the DSU because its communication seeking recourse to Article 21.5 of the DSU did not indicate whether consultations had been held; and the alleged failure of the United States to exercise its judgement, in accordance with Article 3.7 of the DSU, as to whether recourse to dispute settlement would be "fruitful". Before the Panel, Mexico argued that there had been no consultations, and that the United States had acted contrary to Articles 3.7 and 6.2 of the DSU. Mexico also stated that it agreed with the European Communities, which had vigorously criticized the lack of consultations. Mexico contends that the Panel, by remaining silent on these issues despite the arguments raised by Mexico, acted inconsistently with Articles 7.2 and 12.7, and diminished Mexico's rights under Articles 3.4 and 19 of the DSU.

36. We observe that, because Mexico has formulated its claims of error in terms of a "failure" on the part of the Panel to speak to and resolve, in its Report, the contentions of Mexico referred to above, it is necessary for us to examine

[33] Translation of Mexico's appellant's submission, p. 3; original Spanish version, p. 2.

whether the Panel was under a duty to address or rule on those contentions. We believe that a panel comes under a duty to address issues in at least two instances. First, as a matter of due process, and the proper exercise of the judicial function, panels are required to address issues that are put before them by the parties to a dispute. Second, panels have to address and dispose of certain issues of a fundamental nature, even if the parties to the dispute remain silent on those issues. In this regard, we have previously observed that "[t]he vesting of jurisdiction in a panel is a fundamental prerequisite for lawful panel proceedings."[34] For this reason, panels cannot simply ignore issues which go to the root of their jurisdiction - that is, to their authority to deal with and dispose of matters. Rather, panels must deal with such issues - if necessary, on their own motion - in order to satisfy themselves that they have authority to proceed.

37. We observe that Mexico's appeal *explicitly* asserts only that the Panel failed to fulfill its duty in the first type of situation mentioned above. Nevertheless, the issues that Mexico raises, in particular regarding the relation between consultations and the authority of panels to deal with and dispose of matters, require us to consider also whether the Panel failed to exercise its duty in the second type of situation, namely, to consider, on its own motion, the issues now raised by Mexico on appeal.

A. *Mexico's Conduct Before the Panel and the Consequences*

38. In considering whether the Panel was required, by virtue of Mexico's conduct before the Panel, to address the issues now raised by Mexico on appeal, we begin by setting out the relevant facts.

39. The redetermination was published on 20 September 2000.[35] On 12 October 2000, the United States submitted a communication seeking recourse to Article 21.5 of the DSU with respect to the measure taken by Mexico to comply with the recommendations and rulings of the DSB.[36] The communication submitted by the United States does not refer to any consultations having been held. At the DSB meeting on 23 October 2000, which was the first occasion that the matter was raised before the DSB, the matter was referred to the original panel. Mexico did not object to this decision, but stated at that meeting that it had "decided to exercise its right not to oppose the US request at the present meeting."[37] Mexico added that "parties to the dispute were working together with a view to agreeing on the best way to proceed on the matter".[38] Mexico did not mention at that DSB meeting any of the issues which are before us now on appeal.

---

[34] Appellate Body Report, *United States - 1916 Act*, *supra*, footnote 32, para. 54.
[35] Panel Report, para. 1.2.
[36] WT/DS132/6.
[37] WT/DSB/M/91, para. 114.
[38] *Ibid.*

40. Mexico did not mention these procedural issues or raise any objection to the authority of the Panel in either of its two written submissions to the Panel. These submissions were made on 14 December 2000 and on 18 January 2001.

41. Mexico referred to these issues for the first time in its oral statement at the meeting with the Panel on 20 February 2001. In that statement, Mexico said:

> 4. Before turning to substance, we have several *observations of a general nature* that are worth mentioning in order for the Panel to *understand the context* of this matter.
>
> 5. Firstly, it should be stressed that the United States was hasty in resorting to the Dispute Settlement Body without exercising its judgement as to whether action under those procedures would be fruitful, as required by Article 3.7 of the Dispute Settlement Understanding, and without consulting Mexico in respect of the new final resolution.
>
> 6. This haste resulted in the presentation of a superficial and deficient case, as is evident as from the request for establishment of a panel. Thus, for example, the request did not indicate whether the parties had engaged in consultations, as required under Article 6.2 of the DSU.[39] (emphasis added)

42. In its first intervention following its oral statement, Mexico returned briefly to these issues, and stated that:

> ... *we are not complaining that there were no consultations*, but simply noting the haste with which the United States acted ...[40] (emphasis added)

---

[39] Translation of Mexico's oral statement at the meeting with the Panel (Guión de la exposición oral de México), 20 February 2001, paras. 4-6. The original reads:

> 4. Antes de abordar la sustancia del asunto, tenemos algunas observaciones de carácter general que ameritan ser mencionadas para que el Grupo Especial comprenda el contexto en el que nos encontramos:
>
> 5. En primer lugar, vale la pena destacar que EUA recurrió al Órgano de Solución de Diferencias de manera apresurada, sin reflexionar sobre la utilidad de actuar al amparo de los presentes procedimientos, como lo exige el articulo 3.7 del Entendimiento sobre solución de diferencias, ni consultar con México respecto de la nueva resolución final.
>
> 6. Esta premura los obligó a presentar un caso deficiente y superficial, lo cual es evidente desde su solicitud de establecimiento de este Grupo Especial. Así por ejemplo, dicha solicitud no indica si se habían celebrado consultas, como lo requiere el articulo 6.2 del ESD.

[40] This quotation is a translation of the italicised portion of the following statement made by Mexico:

> ... fue muy desafortunado que debido a las prisas del propio Estados Unidos de recurrir al 21.5 sin haber realizado consultas; *y no estamos reclamando que no haya habido consultas, simple y sencillamente, constatando la celeridad con la que se ha trabajado*, impidieron que este tipo de información y de aclaraciones, de carácter técnico se pudieran hacer en su oportunidad.

43. The European Communities did not file a written submission as a third party in the Panel proceedings. However, at the 21 February 2001 third party session of the meeting with the Panel, held a day after Mexico had presented its oral statement to the Panel, the European Communities devoted its entire oral statement to the United States' failure to circulate a request for consultations and its failure to mention, in the communication seeking recourse to Article 21.5 of the DSU, whether such consultations had been held. The European Communities stated that the Panel "should consider that the dispute is not properly before it because no consultations were requested nor held before the request for the establishment of a panel was submitted to the DSB."[41] On the same day, in its concluding remarks, Mexico stated that it agreed with the European Communities.[42]

44. The Panel did not mention any of these issues in its Report[43], and Mexico did not comment on the Panel's failure to do so during the interim review stage of the Panel proceedings.

45. In examining Mexico's conduct, we note that Mexico did not bring up the issues it now relies upon at the DSB meeting on 23 October 2000. Rather, Mexico in effect consented to refer the matter to the Article 21.5 Panel at the first DSB meeting where the matter was raised. We further note that Mexico did not refer to these issues, *at all*, in either of its written submissions to the Panel. Nor did Mexico ask the Panel to make any preliminary ruling on these issues. The alleged deficiencies in the authority of the Panel were mentioned by Mexico *only* at the meeting with the Panel on 20-21 February 2000.

46. Furthermore, at the meeting with the Panel, although Mexico referred to the issues it now relies upon before us, Mexico described these comments simply as "observations of a general nature" that were made "for the Panel to understand the context" of the matter. Mexico did not expressly ask the Panel to examine whether it had the authority to address the matter before it, or to rule on the legal consequences of any deficiencies in the process by which the redetermination was referred to the Panel. To the contrary, Mexico explicitly said, on 20 February 2000, that it was *not* complaining that there were no consultations, but simply "noting" the haste with which the United States acted. Mexico's statement, the following day, that it "agreed" with the presentation that had been made by the European Communities did not, in our view, amount to a request to the Panel to examine whether it had authority to examine the matter before it, or to rule on the legal consequences of any deficiencies in the proceedings. Nor did Mexico's statement suffice to offset Mexico's characterization of these issues as "observations of a general nature", or to negate Mexico's express statement that it was *not* complaining with respect to these issues.

---

[41] European Communities' oral statement before the Panel, 21 February 2001, para. 11.

[42] Mexico's final statement at the meeting with the Panel, (Guión para las observaciones finales de México) 21 February 2001, p. 1.

[43] The only reference to these issues is in the summary of the arguments made by the European Communities; Panel Report, paras. 4.1-4.11.

47. In sum, the "observations" raised by Mexico were not expressed in a fashion that indicated that Mexico was raising an objection to the authority of the Panel. The requirements of good faith, due process and orderly procedure dictate that objections, especially those of such potential significance, should be explicitly raised. Only in this way will the panel, the other party to the dispute, and the third parties, understand that a specific objection has been raised, and have an adequate opportunity to address and respond to it. In our view, Mexico's objection was not explicitly raised. Thus, in making its "observations", Mexico did not meet this standard.

48. Mexico's arguments that the Panel failed to address the issues on which Mexico's appeal is now based depend on the premise that Mexico had requested the Panel to do so. As we have found that Mexico did not, in fact, make such a request - that is, it did not raise an "objection" - we need not examine further the possible scope or source of a panel's duty to "address" objections raised by parties.

49. However, had we been satisfied that Mexico did, in fact, explicitly raise its objections before the Panel, then the Panel may well have been required to "address" those objections, whether by virtue of Articles 7.2 and 12.7 of the DSU, or the requirements of due process.[44] In such circumstances, however, the Panel could have satisfied that duty simply by stating in its Report that it declined to examine or rule on Mexico's "objections" due to the *untimely* manner in which they were raised. We note, in this regard that Mexico was aware of all the facts on which it now relies in arguing that the Panel had no authority to deal with and dispose of the matter as soon as the United States submitted its communication seeking recourse to Article 21.5 of the DSU on 12 October 2000. Yet Mexico mentioned these alleged deficiencies, for the first time, more than four months later, at the meeting with the Panel on 20 February 2000. Mexico did not take advantage of the opportunities it had to raise the issues at the DSB meeting of 23 October 2000, or in either of its written submissions to the Panel.

50. In our view, assuming that Mexico had explicitly raised these issues before the Panel, the Panel could reasonably have concluded that Mexico's "objections" were not raised in a timely manner. When a Member wishes to raise an objection in dispute settlement proceedings, it is always incumbent on that Member to do so promptly.[45] A Member that fails to raise its objections in a timely

---

[44] We recall that, in a different context involving judicial economy, we said that:

> ... for purposes of transparency and fairness to the parties, a panel should, ... in all cases, address expressly [even] those claims which it declines to examine and rule upon ... Silence does not suffice for these purposes.

Appellate Body Report, *Canada - Certain Measures Affecting the Automotive Industry* WT/DS139/AB/R, WT/DS142/AB/R, DSR 2000:VI, 2985, adopted 19 June 2000, para. 117.

[45] We have already said that the principles of good faith and due process require:

> ... that responding Members seasonably and promptly bring claimed procedural deficiencies to the attention of the complaining Member, and to the DSB or the Panel, so that corrections, if needed, can be made to resolve disputes ... The proce-

manner, notwithstanding one or more opportunities to do so, may be deemed to have waived its right to have a panel consider such objections.

B. *The Nature of Mexico's "Objections"*

51. Turning to the next step in our analysis, we must consider whether the issues now raised by Mexico in its appeal are of such a nature that the Panel was in any case required to address them on its own motion. To do so, we consider separately each of the three issues now raised by Mexico. We observe, in this regard, that it is unclear whether Mexico contends that the Panel should have ruled on a *single* issue, the lack of consultations, and adduces its additional arguments regarding Articles 3.7 and 6.2 of the DSU in support of its principal position that the lack of consultations deprived the Panel of its authority to deal with and dispose of the matter; or whether Mexico is arguing that the Panel should have ruled on *three* distinct issues: first, the lack of consultations; second, the failure of the United States' communication seeking recourse to Article 21.5 to indicate whether consultations were held; and, third, the alleged failure of the United States to exercise its judgement as to whether recourse to dispute settlement would be "fruitful". For the purposes of our analysis, we will assume that Mexico contends that the Panel should have ruled on three separate issues.

52. Mexico and the European Communities seem to argue that the Panel was required to address the issue of consultations because consultations are an indispensable element of proceedings under Article 21.5 of the DSU. They interpret the phrase "these dispute settlement procedures" in Article 21.5 of the DSU as referring to *all* procedures contained in the DSU, including the provisions concerning consultations under Article 4 of the DSU and the provisions concerning establishment of a panel under Article 6.[46] The United States, on the other hand, believes that the phrase refers to something *less than all* procedures contained in the DSU and, in particular, that the only prerequisite set forth in Article 21.5 is that there exist a disagreement as to whether a Member has implemented the recommendations and rulings of the DSB.[47]

53. We do not consider that we need to examine these differences of interpretation between the participants in order to decide the issues on appeal. As we have said, our task is simply to determine whether the "objections" that Mexico now raises before us are of such a nature that they could have deprived the Panel

---

dural rules of WTO dispute settlement are designed to promote, not the development of litigation techniques, but simply the fair, prompt and effective resolution of trade disputes.

Appellate Body Report, *United States - FSC*, *supra*, footnote 24, para. 166. *See also* Appellate Body Report, *Korea - Dairy Safeguard*, *supra*, footnote 19, paras. 127-131; and Appellate Body Report, *United States - 1916 Act*, *supra*, footnote 32, para. 54.

[46] Mexico's appellant's submission, para. 12; European Communities' third participant's submission, para. 16.

[47] United States' appellant's submission, para. 26.

of its authority to deal with and dispose of the matter. If so, then the Panel was bound to address them on its own motion. To fulfill this task we will assume, *arguendo*, that the same procedures apply in Article 21.5 proceedings as in original panel proceedings. If, even on our *assumption*, we find that the lack of consultations was not a defect of such a nature as to deprive the Panel of its authority to deal with and dispose of the dispute, then we need not consider the participants' arguments on the interpretation of Article 21.5 of the DSU.

54. We note that Mexico emphasizes the importance of consultations within the GATT and WTO dispute settlement systems. We agree with Mexico on the importance of consultations. Through consultations, parties exchange information, assess the strengths and weaknesses of their respective cases, narrow the scope of the differences between them and, in many cases, reach a mutually agreed solution in accordance with the explicit preference expressed in Article 3.7 of the DSU. Moreover, even where no such agreed solution is reached, consultations provide the parties an opportunity to define and delimit the scope of the dispute between them. Clearly, consultations afford many benefits to complaining and responding parties, as well as to third parties and to the dispute settlement system as a whole.

55. The practice of GATT contracting parties in regularly holding consultations is testimony to the important role of consultations in dispute settlement. Article 4.1 of the DSU recognizes this practice and further provides that:

> Members affirm their resolve to *strengthen and improve* the *effectiveness* of the consultation procedures employed by Members. (emphasis added)

56. A number of panel and Appellate Body reports have recognized the value of consultations within the dispute settlement process.[48] The United States too, in

[48] The important role of consultations in both the GATT and the WTO dispute settlement systems has repeatedly been acknowledged, both expressly and implicitly, by panels and by the Appellate Body. See, for example: Panel Report, *Uruguayan Recourse to Article XXIII*, adopted 16 November 1962, BISD 11S/95, para. 10; Panel Report, *United States - Imposition of Anti-Dumping Duties on Imports of Fresh and Chilled Atlantic Salmon from Norway*, adopted 27 April 1994, BISD 41S/Vol.I/229, para. 333; Panel Report, *Brazil - Measures Affecting Desiccated Coconut*, WT/DS22/R, adopted 20 March 1997, as upheld by the Appellate Body Report, WT/DS22/AB/R, DSR 1997:1, 189, para. 287; Panel Report, *European Communities - Bananas*, WT/DS27/R/ECU, adopted 25 September 1997, as modified by the Appellate Body Report, WT/DS27/AB/R, DSR 1997:III, 1085, paras. 7.17-7.20; Panel Report, *Korea - Taxes on Alcoholic Beverages* ("*Korea - Alcoholic Beverages* "), WT/DS75/R, WT/DS84/R, adopted 17 February 1999, DSR 1999:I, 44, as modified by the Appellate Body Report, WT/DS75/AB/R, WT/DS84/AB/R, DSR 1999:I,3, para. 10.19; Appellate Body Report, *Brazil - Aircraft*, *supra*, footnote 30, para. 132; Panel Report, *Brazil - Aircraft*, WT/DS46/R, adopted 20 August 1999, as modified by the Appellate Body Report, WT/DS46/AB/R, DSR 1999:III, 1161, para. 7.10; Panel Report, *United States - Safeguard Measures on Imports of Fresh, Chilled or Frozen Lamb Meat from New Zealand and Australia* ("*United States - Lamb Safeguard* "), WT/DS177/R, WT/DS178/R, adopted 16 May 2001, DSR 2001:IX, 4107, as modified by the Appellate Body Report, WT/DS177/AB/R, WT/DS178/AB/R, DSR 2001:IX, 4051, para 5.40. See also the discussion of the role of consultations in disputes under the *Agreement on Textiles and Clothing* in Appellate

this appeal, recognizes the importance of consultations.[49] Nevertheless, we are not persuaded that the undoubted practical importance of consultations to the WTO dispute settlement system is dispositive of the issue before us on appeal. To resolve that issue, we turn now to the relevant texts of the WTO agreements.

57. Article 4 of the DSU sets forth a number of other provisions with respect to consultations. We recall that, in our Report in *Brazil - Aircraft*, we observed that:

> Articles 4 and 6 of the DSU, as well as paragraphs 1 to 4 of Article 4 of the *SCM Agreement*, set forth a process by which a complaining party must request consultations, and consultations must be held, before a matter may be referred to the DSB for the establishment of a panel.[50]

58. The general process that we described in that case also applies in disputes brought under other covered agreements.[51] Thus, as a general matter, consultations are a prerequisite to panel proceedings. However, this general proposition is subject to certain limitations. For example, Article 4.3 of the DSU provides:

> If a request for consultations is made pursuant to a covered agreement, the Member to which the request is made shall, unless otherwise mutually agreed, reply to the request within 10 days after the date of its receipt and shall enter into consultations in good faith within a period of no more than 30 days after the date of receipt of the request, with a view to reaching a mutually satisfactory solution. *If the Member does not respond within 10 days after the date of receipt of the request, or does not enter into consultations within a period of no more than 30 days, or a period otherwise*

Body Report, *United States - Restrictions on Imports of Cotton and Man-made Fibre Underwear*, WT/DS24/AB/R, adopted 25 February 1997, DSR 1997:I, 11, at 23-24.

[49] United States' appellant's submission, para. 32.

[50] Appellate Body Report, *supra*, footnote 30, para. 131.

[51] Pursuant to Article 17.1 of the *Anti-Dumping* Agreement, the provisions of the DSU apply to consultations and dispute settlement under that Agreement "[e]xcept as otherwise provided herein". We note that, in our Report in *Guatemala - Anti-Dumping Investigation Regarding Portland Cement from Mexico*, we observed that "the rules and procedures of the DSU apply *together with* the special or additional provisions of [the *Anti-Dumping Agreement*]", and that:

> ... it is only where the provisions of the DSU and the special or additional rules and procedures of a covered agreement *cannot* be read as *complementing* each other that the special or additional provisions are to *prevail*. A special or additional provision should only be found to *prevail* over a provision of the DSU in a situation where adherence to the one provision will lead to a violation of the other provision, that is, in the case of a *conflict* between them.

Appellate Body Report, WT/DS60/AB/R, DSR 1998:IX, 3767, adopted 25 November 1998, para. 65.

Neither of the parties to this dispute has argued that there is any conflict between the provisions of the DSU relating to consultations and dispute settlement and the "special and additional rules and procedures" contained in the *Anti-Dumping Agreement*.

> *mutually agreed, after the date of receipt of the request, then the Member that requested the holding of consultations may proceed directly to request the establishment of a panel.* (emphasis added)

59. Article 4.3 of the DSU relates the responding party's conduct towards consultations to the complaining party's right to request the establishment of a panel. When the responding party does not respond to a request for consultations, or declines to enter into consultations, the complaining party may dispense with consultations and proceed to request the establishment of a panel. In such a case, the responding party, by its own conduct, relinquishes the potential benefits that could be derived from those consultations.

60. We also note that Article 4.7 of the DSU provides:

> If the consultations fail to settle a dispute within 60 days after the date of receipt of the request for consultations, the complaining party may request the establishment of a panel. The complaining party may request a panel during the 60-day period *if the consulting parties jointly consider that consultations have failed to settle the dispute.* (emphasis added)

61. Article 4.7 also relates the conduct of the responding party concerning consultations to the complaining party's right to request the establishment of a panel. This provision states that the responding party may agree with the complaining party to forgo the potential benefits that continued pursuit of consultations might bring. Thus, Article 4.7 contemplates that a panel may be validly established notwithstanding the shortened period for consultations, as long as the parties agree. Article 4.7 does not, however, specify any particular form that the agreement between the parties must take.

62. In addition, as we discuss in more detail below[52], pursuant to Article 6.2 of the DSU, one of the requirements for requests for establishment of a panel is that such requests must "indicate whether consultations were held". The phrase "*whether* consultations were held" shows that this requirement in Article 6.2 may be satisfied by an express statement that *no consultations were held.* In other words, Article 6.2 also envisages the possibility that a panel may be validly established without being preceded by consultations.

63. Thus, the DSU explicitly recognizes circumstances where the absence of consultations would *not* deprive the panel of its authority to consider the matter referred to it by the DSB. In our view, it follows that where the responding party does not object, explicitly and in a timely manner, to the failure of the complaining party to request or engage in consultations, the responding party may be deemed to have consented to the lack of consultations and, thereby, to have relinquished whatever right to consult it may have had.

---

52 *Infra*, paras. 66-70.

64. As a result, we find that the lack of prior consultations is not a defect that, by its very nature, deprives a panel of its authority to deal with and dispose of a matter, and that, accordingly, such a defect is not one which a panel must examine even if both parties to the dispute remain silent thereon. We recall that, in this case, Mexico neither pursued the potential benefits of consultations nor objected that the United States had deprived it of such benefits.

65. For these reasons, we conclude that *even if* the general obligations in the DSU regarding prior consultations were applicable in proceedings under Article 21.5 of the DSU - a matter which we do not decide - non-compliance with those obligations would not have the effect of depriving a panel of its authority to deal with and dispose of the matter. It follows that, in this case, the Panel was not required to consider, on its own motion, whether the lack of consultations deprived it of its authority to assess the consistency of the redetermination with the *Anti-Dumping Agreement.*

66. We turn to consider whether the issue raised by Mexico with respect to Article 6.2 of the DSU relates to a defect that would deprive a panel of its authority to deal with and dispose of the matter before it and, therefore, constitutes an issue that the Panel should have addressed on its own motion. In Mexico's view, Article 6.2 of the DSU requires that a communication seeking recourse to Article 21.5 of the DSU "shall indicate whether consultations were held". Since the communication circulated by the United States in this case contained no such indication, Mexico argues that the United States failed to comply with Article 6.2 of the DSU.

67. For purposes of our analysis of this issue we again assume, *arguendo*, that the same procedures apply in Article 21.5 proceedings as in original panel proceedings. If, on this assumption, we find that the failure of the United States' communication to indicate whether consultations were held would not deprive a panel of its authority to deal with and dispose of the matter before it, then we need not inquire further into the procedures that are actually required in proceedings under Article 21.5 of the DSU.

68. Article 6.2 of the DSU, which governs requests for the establishment of a panel, provides:

> The request for the establishment of a panel shall be made in writing. *It shall indicate whether consultations were held*, identify the specific measures at issue and provide a brief summary of the legal basis of the complaint sufficient to present the problem clearly. In case the applicant requests the establishment of a panel with other than standard terms of reference, the written request shall include the proposed text of special terms of reference. (emphasis added)

69. We recall that, in previous appeals, we have observed that Article 6.2 imposes four requirements on Members requesting establishment of a panel, one of

which obliges Members requesting the establishment of a panel to "indicate", in that request, "whether consultations were held".[53] The issue which we examine here is not whether Members come under such an obligation, for it is clear that they do. Rather, we must consider the nature of that obligation, and the consequences that ensue when a requesting Member does not "indicate whether consultations were held" in its request for establishment of a panel and a responding Member does not object to that omission. We stress that, in so doing, we neither examine nor interpret the other three requirements for requests for establishment of a panel set forth in Article 6.2 of the DSU.

70. In assessing the importance of the obligation "to indicate whether consultations were held", we observe that the requirement will be satisfied by the inclusion, in the request for establishment of a panel, of a statement as to whether consultations occurred *or not*. The purpose of the requirement seems to be primarily informational - to inform the DSB and Members as to whether consultations took place. We also recall that the DSU expressly contemplates that, in certain circumstances, a panel can deal with and dispose of the matter referred to it even if no consultations took place. Similarly, the authority of the panel cannot be invalidated by the absence, in the request for establishment of the panel, of an indication "whether consultations were held". Indeed, it would be curious if the requirement in Article 6.2 to inform the DSB whether consultations were held was accorded more importance in the dispute settlement process than the requirement actually to hold those consultations.

71. Thirdly, Mexico also challenges the silence of the Panel regarding the alleged failure of the United States to satisfy its obligation under the first sentence of Article 3.7 of the DSU to exercise its judgement as to whether dispute settlement proceedings would be "fruitful". Although Mexico has not elaborated its interpretation of the scope of this obligation we, nevertheless, consider whether a failure to comply with the first sentence of Article 3.7 of the DSU would deprive a panel of its authority to deal with and dispose of a matter.

72. The first sentence of Article 3.7 of the DSU provides:

> Before bringing a case, a Member shall exercise its judgement as to whether action under these procedures would be fruitful.

73. In our view, this sentence reflects a basic principle that Members should have recourse to WTO dispute settlement in good faith, and not frivolously set in motion the procedures contemplated in the DSU. We recall that, when we examined the language of Article 3.7 of the DSU in our Report in *European Communities - Bananas*, we stated that:

> ... a Member has broad discretion in deciding whether to bring a case against another Member under the DSU. The language of Article XXIII:1 of the GATT 1994 and of Article 3.7 of the DSU

[53] Appellate Body Report, *Korea - Dairy Safeguard*, *supra*, footnote 19, para. 120.

> suggests, furthermore, that a Member is expected to be *largely self-regulating* in deciding whether any such action would be "fruitful".[54] (emphasis added)

74. Given the "largely self-regulating" nature of the requirement in the first sentence of Article 3.7, panels and the Appellate Body must presume, whenever a Member submits a request for establishment of a panel, that such Member does so in good faith, having duly exercised its judgement as to whether recourse to that panel would be "fruitful". Article 3.7 neither requires nor authorizes a panel to look behind that Member's decision and to question its exercise of judgement. Therefore, the Panel was not obliged to consider this issue on its own motion.

75. We have already found that, before the Panel, Mexico did not explicitly raise its "objections" relating to the lack of consultations, the failure of the communication seeking recourse to Article 21.5 of the DSU to indicate whether consultations were held, and the alleged failure of the United States to comply with the requirement in the first sentence of Article 3.7 of the DSU. Having considered the nature of these "objections", we also find that the Panel did not err in refraining from addressing them on its own motion. We, therefore, dismiss Mexico's appeal on these issues.

V. ARTICLE 3 OF THE *ANTI-DUMPING AGREEMENT*: "THREAT OF MATERIAL INJURY"

76. In this appeal, Mexico also asks us to reverse the Panel's findings regarding, first, the likelihood of increased HFCS imports and, second, the likely impact of these imports on the Mexican sugar industry. We will deal with each issue separately.

A. *Likelihood of Increased Imports*

77. Regarding SECOFI's conclusion that there existed a significant likelihood of increased imports, the Panel found:

> SECOFI's determination that industries other than soft-drink bottlers would undertake a massive shift from sugar use to HFCS use, resulting in total consumption of HFCS beyond the capacity of the domestic industry to supply, and a consequent significant increase in dumped imports, is not, in our view, one that could be reached by an unbiased and objective investigating authority in light of the evidence relied upon and the explanations given in the redetermination. While in its redetermination, SECOFI did set out additional information concerning the points identified by the Panel as problematic in its original report, SECOFI failed to provide a reasoned

[54] Appellate Body Report, *supra*, footnote 20, para. 135.

> explanation of how that information supports the conclusion that there was a significant likelihood of increased imports. We therefore determine that SECOFI's conclusion that there was a significant likelihood of increased importation is not consistent with Article 3.7(i) of the AD Agreement.[55]

78. We start by making certain preliminary observations on the scope of these Article 21.5 proceedings. Mexico argues that the original panel erred in its treatment of the alleged restraint agreement and that the Panel "made *exactly the same mistake as the original Panel*".[56] (emphasis added) The only difference, Mexico asserts, is that "in this case, the Panel focused on whether or not SECOFI had complied with [the findings and recommendations of the original panel as adopted by the DSB], and compliance with Article 3.7(i) of the Anti-Dumping Agreement became secondary".[57] There appear to us to be two elements to Mexico's assertion. First, Mexico seems to seek to have us revisit the original panel report. Second, Mexico is claiming that the Panel should have analysed the consistency of the new measure with Mexico's obligations under the *Anti-Dumping Agreement* rather than simply verifying whether Mexico had followed the original panel's recommendations as adopted by the DSB.

79. With respect to the first element, we note that the original panel report, regarding the *initial* measure (SECOFI's original determination), has been adopted and that these Article 21.5 proceedings concern a *subsequent* measure (SECOFI's redetermination). We also note that Mexico did not appeal the original panel's report, and that Articles 3.2 and 3.3 of the DSU reflect the importance to the multilateral trading system of security, predictability and the prompt settlement of disputes. We see no basis for us to examine the original panel's treatment of the alleged restraint agreement.

80. With respect to the second element, we note that Mexico argues that the Panel confined itself inappropriately to an examination of whether the new measure complied with the rulings and recommendations of the DSB relating to the original measure. However, we note that at the outset of its reasoning the Panel considered that it was "faced principally with determining whether SECOFI's conclusion in the redetermination ... is consistent with Articles 3.1, 3.4 and 3.7(i) of the *Anti-Dumping Agreement*".[58] In our view, making this determination is exactly what the Panel went on to do, as is clear from the rest of its analysis. Similarly, our review of the Panel Report will focus on the Panel's reasons for finding that the redetermination was not consistent with Mexico's obligations under the *Anti-Dumping Agreement*.

---

55 Panel Report, para. 6.23.

56 Mexico's appellant's submission, para. 66.

57 Mexico's appellant's submission, para. 66.

58 Panel Report, para. 6.5.

81. Returning to the substance of Mexico's appeal, we observe that Mexico asks us to reverse the finding of the Panel regarding the likelihood of increased imports on the grounds that the Panel wrongly interpreted Article 3.7 of the *Anti-Dumping Agreement* and incorrectly applied the standard of review prescribed by Articles 17.5 and 17.6 of that Agreement. In its appellant's submission, Mexico focuses its arguments on errors that it considers the Panel made in its treatment of an alleged restraint agreement between Mexican sugar millers and Mexican soft-drink producers. Article 3.7 provides, among other things, that "a determination of a threat of material injury shall be based on facts and not merely on allegation, conjecture or remote possibility". Mexico maintains that, since SECOFI never determined that this alleged agreement existed as a matter of "fact", it was only "allegation, conjecture or remote possibility". Thus, Mexico asserts that the Panel erred in relying on "allegation, conjecture or remote possibility" to find that the redetermination was inconsistent with Article 3.7(i) of the *Anti-Dumping Agreement.* Mexico also argues that the Panel erred in examining the alleged restraint agreement since Article 17.5 of the *Anti-Dumping Agreement* authorizes panels to examine only the "*facts* made available" (emphasis added) to national investigating authorities.

82. Article 3.7 of the *Anti-Dumping Agreement* provides, in relevant part:

> A determination of a threat of material injury shall be based on facts and not merely on allegation, conjecture or remote possibility. The change in circumstances which would create a situation in which the dumping would cause injury must be clearly foreseen and imminent.[10] *In making a determination regarding the existence of a threat of material injury, the authorities should consider, inter alia,* such factors as:
>
> (i) a significant rate of increase of dumped imports into the domestic market indicating the likelihood of substantially increased importation; (emphasis added)
>
> [10] One example, though not an exclusive one, is that there is convincing reason to believe that there will be, in the near future, substantially increased importation of the product at dumped prices.

83. In previous anti-dumping cases, we have emphasized the importance of distinguishing between the different roles of panels and investigating authorities.[59] We note, in this regard, that Article 3.7 of the *Anti-Dumping Agreement* sets forth a number of requirements that must be respected in order to reach a valid determination of a threat of material injury. The third sentence of Article 3.7 explicitly recognizes that it is the *investigating authorities* who make a de-

[59] Appellate Body Report, *United States - Anti-Dumping Measures on Certain Hot-Rolled Steel Products from Japan* ("*United States - Hot-Rolled Steel*"), WT/DS184/AB/R, adopted 23 August 2001, DSR 2001:X, 4697, para. 55.

termination of threat of material injury, and that such determination - by the investigating authorities - "must be based on facts and not merely on allegation, conjecture or remote possibility". Consequently, Article 3.7 is not addressed to panels, but to the national investigating authorities which determine the existence of a threat of material injury.

84. The *Anti-Dumping Agreement* imposes a specific standard of review on *panels*. With respect to facts, Articles 17.5 and 17.6(i) of the *Anti-Dumping Agreement*, together with Article 11 of the DSU[60], set out the standard to be applied by panels when assessing whether a Member's investigating authorities have "established" and "evaluated" the facts consistently with that Member's obligations under the covered agreements.[61] These provisions do not authorize panels to engage in a new and independent fact-finding exercise. Rather, in assessing the measure, panels must consider, in the light of the claims and arguments of the parties, whether, *inter alia,* the "establishment" of the facts by the investigating authorities was "proper", in accordance with the obligations imposed on such investigating authorities under the *Anti-Dumping Agreement.*[62]

85. In our view, the "establishment" of facts by investigating authorities includes both affirmative findings of events that took place during the period of investigation as well as assumptions relating to such events made by those authorities in the course of their analyses. In determining the existence of a *threat* of material injury, the investigating authorities will necessarily have to make assumptions relating to "the "occurrence of future events" since such *future* events "can never be definitively proven by facts".[63] Notwithstanding this intrinsic uncertainty, a "proper establishment" of facts in a determination of threat of material injury must be based on events that, although they have not yet occurred, must be "clearly foreseen and imminent", in accordance with Article 3.7 of the *Anti-Dumping Agreement.*[64]

86. Bearing in mind the role assigned to panels under Articles 17.5 and 17.6 of the *Anti-Dumping Agreement* and Article 11 of the DSU, we turn to examine

---

[60] Article 11 of the DSU provides in relevant part that "a panel should make an objective assessment of the matter before it, including an objective assessment of the facts of the case and the applicability of and conformity with the relevant covered agreements".

[61] Appellate Body Report, *United States - Hot-Rolled Steel, supra,* footnote 59, paras. 50-62.

[62] *Ibid.*, para. 56.

[63] Appellate Body Report, *United States - Lamb Safeguard*, WT/DS177/AB/R, WT/DS178/AB/R, adopted 16 May 2001, DSR 2001:IX, 4051, para 136.

[64] As we noted in United States - Hot-Rolled Steel:

> Article 17.6(i) ... defines when investigating authorities can be considered to have acted inconsistently with the Anti-Dumping Agreement in the course of their "establishment" and "evaluation" of the relevant facts. In other words, Article 17.6(i) sets forth the appropriate standard to be applied by panels in examining the WTO-consistency of the investigating authorities' establishment and evaluation of the facts under other provisions of the Anti-Dumping Agreement. (original emphasis)
> Appellate Body Report, *supra,* footnote 59, para. 56.

how the Panel dealt with the treatment of the alleged restraint agreement by SECOFI in its redetermination.

87. We recall that the United States asserted, before the original panel that, during the anti-dumping investigation, United States' exporters had learned of the existence of an agreement between Mexican sugar millers and Mexican soft-drink bottlers. Under that alleged agreement, Mexican soft-drink bottlers had undertaken to limit their consumption of HFCS while Mexican sugar millers had, in turn, agreed to reduce the prices at which sugar was supplied to these bottlers.[65] In its original determination, SECOFI did not determine whether the alleged restraint agreement actually existed, but nevertheless concluded that, "*in any event*, the alleged agreement 'does not eliminate the possibility that bottlers as well as other sectors that use HFCS in multiple applications [will continue to import] it under conditions of price discrimination to replace sugar.'" [66] (emphasis added)

88. We note that, in order to arrive at this conclusion, SECOFI must have considered the potential consequences of the alleged restraint agreement and found that they were not sufficient to eliminate the threat of material injury to the sugar industry. The original panel found that SECOFI had inadequately evaluated the impact of dumped imports on the domestic industry and the potential effects of the alleged restraint agreement and that, by doing so, had acted inconsistently with Articles 3.1, 3.2, 3.4, 3.7 and 3.7(i) of the *Anti-Dumping Agreement*. As we have already observed, this original panel report was not appealed and was subsequently adopted by the DSB.

89. By way of implementation, SECOFI then carried out a new investigation, the results of which are set forth in the redetermination. In the analysis leading to its new conclusion that there existed a "well-founded likelihood that a signficant increase in [imports of HFCS from the United States] would occur in the immediate future"[67], SECOFI explained:

> The Secretariat determined that even if there was an agreement to restrict the use of high fructose corn syrup in September 1997, between the sugar mills and the soft drink bottlers, it would not eliminate the threat of injury to the domestic sugar industry.[68]

---

[65] On 23 September 1997, Secretary Blanco Mendoza of SECOFI appeared before the Mexican Senate and stated that he had "been informed" of the existence of the alleged restraint agreement, and declared that he took "great satisfaction" in this "private arrangement". However, the text of the alleged agreement was never produced to the original panel and, in response to a written inquiry from SECOFI during the course of the anti-dumping investigation, the Mexican Sugar Chamber (which had filed the application for the anti-dumping investigation and was said to be one of the parties to the alleged agreement) denied the existence of such an agreement. (Original Panel Report, para. 5.529, footnote 425 to para. 5.532 and footnote 433 to para. 5.544)

[66] Original Panel Report, para. 7.173, quoting from para. 547 of SECOFI's original determination.

[67] Redetermination, para. 61.

[68] *Ibid.*, para. 56.

...

> For purposes of determining the likelihood of an increase in imports of high fructose corn syrup originating from the United States of America, *assuming without admitting that the alleged agreement existed (and in addition that it was strictly honoured by the parties)*, the Secretariat based on projections of total sugar consumption for 1997 and 1998, estimated the consumption by industrial sector users other than soft drink bottlers.[69]
>
> ...
>
> This allowed the Secretariat to conclude that, *even if the assumed agreement existed and was complied with*, the demand for imports of high fructose corn syrup based on price levels prevailing in the domestic market would provide an incentive for an increase in its consumption by the consuming industries other than soft drink bottlers. Such an increase would be at such a magnitude as to [be] consider[ed] a significant increase in imports over the levels noted during the period under investigation ...[70] (emphasis added)

90. In stating that "even if the assumed agreement existed and was complied with" the likelihood of the threat of injury to the domestic sugar industry would not be eliminated, SECOFI - *arguendo* - treated the existence of the agreement and its effectiveness *as if they were facts* and concluded that, even if those assumptions were correct, the threat of material injury to the sugar industry remained. We note that SECOFI could have made affirmative factual findings concerning the alleged agreement. However, the above reasoning clearly indicates that SECOFI *chose* to assume the existence and effectiveness of the alleged restraint agreement for purposes of its analysis of the likelihood of increased imports. We further note that none of the parties to this dispute challenged, before the Panel, SECOFI's decision to make such assumptions. In these circumstances, it was logical for the Panel to examine SECOFI's conclusions using the same premises. Indeed, we consider that it would have been improper for the Panel to have sought, on its own initiative, to go behind the assumptions made by SECOFI.[71]

91. In challenging the Panel's finding regarding SECOFI's determination of a significant likelihood of increased imports, Mexico confines its arguments to the Panel's treatment of the alleged restraint agreement. Notably, Mexico's appel-

---

[69] Redetermination, para. 58.

[70] *Ibid.*, para. 60.

[71] We note, in this context, that Articles 17.5 and 17.6(i) contemplate precisely that panels will examine antidumping measures on the *same* factual basis as that before the investigating authorities. In *Thailand - H-Beams*, we found that "Articles 17.5 and 17.6 clarify the powers of review of a panel established under the *Anti-Dumping Agreement*. These provisions place limiting obligations on a panel, with respect to the review of the establishment and evaluation of facts by the investigating authority". (Appellate Body Report, *supra*, footnote 25, para 114)

lant's submission does not allege any legal error in the Panel's analysis leading to its conclusions with respect to SECOFI's projections of increased demand for HFCS from users *other* than soft-drink bottlers.

92. Notwithstanding the narrow scope of Mexico's arguments on this issue, we believe that it is useful to observe that the Panel (like the original panel) considered that the relevant question was *not* whether the alleged agreement existed, but "whether SECOFI's analysis provide[d] a reasoned explanation for its conclusion that, assuming [a restraint] agreement existed, there was nonetheless a likelihood of substantially increased importation".[72] In answering this question, the Panel found that SECOFI's projection of increased HFCS imports depended on the finding that *users other than soft-drink bottlers* (i.e., those that purportedly were *not* parties to the alleged restraint agreement) *could and would* replace sugar with HFCS, resulting in an increase in consumption of HFCS by those users of more than 400 per cent in 1997.[73] This projection was based on SECOFI's view of the ability and willingness of that segment of the domestic industry to substitute HFCS for sugar.[74] The Panel observed that SECOFI's projection relied on the supposition that, due to price differentials between domestic sugar and imported HFCS, substitution of HFCS for sugar would take place.[75] The Panel considered that this supposition was not supported by the evidence in the record concerning the use of HFCS and sugar in 1996.[76] The Panel also observed that SECOFI had not addressed the "critical question"[77] of the degree to which companies, which had not used HFCS during the period of investigation (1996), could, as a technical matter (taking into account production processes and equipment), use HFCS in place of sugar in 1997 and 1998. It was these defects underlying SECOFI's projection of increased imports, and *not* any assumption used by the Panel relating to the existence of the alleged restraint agreement, that led the Panel to conclude that SECOFI's determination of the likelihood of increased imports was inconsistent with Article 3.7 (i) of the *Anti-Dumping Agreement.*

93. In conclusion, we find that the Panel did not err in using the same assumption with respect to the alleged restraint agreement that SECOFI used in the redetermination for purposes of the analysis leading to its conclusion that there existed a likelihood of substantially increased imports. We, therefore, uphold the Panel's finding, in paragraph 6.23 of its Report, that "SECOFI's conclusion that there was a significant likelihood of increased importation is not consistent with Article 3.7(i) of the AD Agreement."

---

[72] Panel Report, para. 6.14, referring in footnote to para. 7.175 of the Original Panel Report.

[73] *Ibid.*, para. 6.16.

[74] *Ibid.*

[75] *Ibid.*

[76] *Ibid.*, para. 6.17.

[77] *Ibid.*, para. 6.18.

B. Likely Impact of Imports on the Domestic Industry

94. Following its examination of SECOFI's analysis of the likely impact of imports on the domestic industry, the Panel concluded:

> ... that SECOFI's redetermination with respect to the likely impact of dumped imports of HFCS from the United States on the domestic industry which underlies the determination of threat of material injury to the Mexican sugar industry is not consistent with Articles 3.1, 3.4, and 3.7 of the AD Agreement.[78]

95. Mexico requests that this finding be reversed on appeal. In Mexico's view, it is clear, in particular from paragraphs 6.34 and 6.35 of the Panel Report, that the Panel's findings regarding the likely impact of imports on the domestic industry depend on its findings on the likelihood of increased imports. Since, as Mexico argued above, the Panel erred in rejecting SECOFI's conclusion regarding the likelihood of an increase in imports, Mexico submits that it follows that the Panel's finding regarding the likely impact of dumped imports on the domestic industry is similarly flawed and must be reversed. This is the sole substantive argument raised in Mexico's appellant's submission relating to the Panel's finding concerning the impact of imports on the domestic industry.

96. In the previous section, we upheld the Panel's finding that SECOFI did not determine the existence of a significant likelihood of increased imports in accordance with Article 3.7(i) of the *Anti-Dumping Agreement.* We agree with Mexico that the Panel's finding on SECOFI's determination of the impact of imports on the domestic industry depends on the Panel's finding on the likelihood of increased imports. We note, however, that despite this logical inter-dependence, the Panel also considered SECOFI's evaluation of a number of economic factors leading to its determination of threat of material injury, and we consider it useful to examine its reasoning in this regard.

97. In reviewing the information included in SECOFI's redetermination, the Panel found that SECOFI's own analysis indicated that, despite increased levels of imports, and despite increased margins of underselling by HFCS relative to sugar, "the domestic sugar industry's performance improved in 1996 over 1995, with increased operating margins, net margins, and return on investment, as well as increased production and capacity utilisation".[79] The Panel thus concluded that, in the light of the evidence and explanations provided in the redetermination, there was insufficient justification for SECOFI's conclusion that imports of HFCS had had "adverse effects" on the domestic industry during the period of investigation (1996).[80]

---

[78] Panel Report, para. 6.36.

[79] *Ibid.*, para. 6.31.

[80] Panel Report, para. 6.31.

98. With respect to SECOFI's projections concerning the likely condition of the Mexican sugar industry in 1997, the Panel found that these depended on "a projected decline in industry revenues in 1997 based on declining prices for sugar caused by increased dumped imports of HFCS".[81] As we have seen, however, the Panel also found that "SECOFI's conclusions regarding the projected increase in imports [of HFCS] are not supported by the evidence"[82] and that this "undermines the projected decline in [domestic industry] revenues for 1997 which is at the core of SECOFI's redetermination".[83]

99. The Panel further found that "SECOFI has failed to provide a reasoned explanation for why the performance of the industry will suddenly decline significantly in 1997"[84], in particular given that "SECOFI's projections of price levels and profitability for 1997 are contrary to the trends observed during the period of investigation".[85] In sum, the Panel provided a number of reasons in support of its finding that there was insufficient evidence and explanations to justify SECOFI's conclusion that the projected substantial increase in dumped HFCS imports (which, as we have seen, the Panel did not accept) would cause material injury to the domestic sugar industry in 1997.

100. As the Panel observed, several of the relevant economic factors analysed in the redetermination indicate a positive performance by the sugar industry during the period of investigation. We note that Article 3.7 of the *Anti-Dumping Agreement* provides that a determination of a threat of material injury must be based on a change in circumstances that must be "clearly foreseen and imminent". Bearing in mind this high standard set by Article 3.7, and having reviewed the reasoning of the Panel, we see no reason to question the Panel's finding, in paragraph 6.36, that "SECOFI's redetermination with respect to the likely impact of dumped imports of HFCS from the United States on the domestic industry ... is not consistent with Articles 3.1, 3.4 and 3.7 of the *Anti-Dumping Agreement*".

101. We, therefore, dismiss this part of Mexico's appeal relating to the Panel's review of SECOFI's analysis of the impact of imports on the domestic industry. We note, however, that Mexico also requests us to reverse the Panel's finding that SECOFI's analysis of the impact of imports on the domestic industry was inconsistent with Articles 3.1 and 3.4 of the *Anti-Dumping Agreement* on other grounds, to which we now turn.

---

81 Panel Report, para. 6.34.
82 *Ibid.*
83 *Ibid.*
84 *Ibid.*, para. 6.35.
85 *Ibid.*

VI. ARTICLE 12.7 OF THE DSU AND ARTICLE 17.6 OF THE *ANTI-DUMPING AGREEMENT*: "REASONING OF THE PANEL"

102. In its appeal, Mexico also challenges certain aspects of the reasoning used by the Panel in finding that SECOFI's analysis of the likely impact of the dumped imports was inconsistent with Mexico's obligations under the *Anti-Dumping Agreement.* Mexico argues, first, that the Panel failed to set out a "basic rationale", as required by Article 12.7 of the DSU, for its findings that Mexico acted inconsistently with its obligations under Articles 3.1 and 3.4 of the *Anti-Dumping Agreement.* Second, Mexico argues that the Panel erred in its application of Article 17.6(ii) of the *Anti-Dumping Agreement.*

A. Article 12.7 of the DSU: "Basic Rationale"

103. In the penultimate paragraph of the section of its Report examining SECOFI's analysis of the likely impact of dumped imports of HFCS on the domestic industry, the Panel reached the following conclusion:

> We conclude that SECOFI's redetermination with respect to the likely impact of dumped imports of HFCS from the United States on the domestic industry which underlies the determination of threat of material injury to the Mexican sugar industry is not consistent with Articles 3.1, 3.4, and 3.7 of the AD Agreement.[86]

104. On appeal, Mexico points out that this is the only paragraph in the relevant part of the Panel Report where the Panel states that the redetermination is inconsistent with Articles 3.1 and 3.4 of the *Anti-Dumping Agreement.* Mexico asserts that this section of the Panel Report lacks *any* analysis revealing how the Panel reached such conclusions, and does not identify the specific obligations that Mexico was found to have violated. Mexico notes that while the Panel may have taken the view that a violation of Article 3.7 of the *Anti-Dumping Agreement* automatically implies a violation of Articles 3.1 and 3.4 of that Agreement, the Panel Report actually contains no such explanation. Mexico argues, therefore, that the Panel failed to set out a "basic rationale" as required under Article 12.7 of the DSU.

105. Article 12.7 of the DSU provides, in relevant part, that:

> Where the parties to the dispute have failed to develop a mutually satisfactory solution, the panel shall submit its findings in the form of a written report to the DSB. In such cases, *the report of a panel shall set out the findings of fact, the applicability of relevant provisions and the basic rationale behind any findings and recommendations that it makes.* ... (emphasis added)

[86] Panel Report, para. 6.36. This conclusion is also reflected in para. 7.1 of the Panel Report.

106. In considering the scope of the duties imposed on panels under Article 12.7, we turn first to the dictionary meaning of "basic", which includes both "fundamental; essential" and "constituting a minimum ... at the lowest acceptable level".[87] "Rationale" means both "a reasoned exposition of principles; an explanation or statement of reasons" and "the fundamental or underlying reason for or basis of a thing; a justification".[88] The "basic rationale" which a panel must provide is directly linked, by the wording of Article 12.7, to the "findings and recommendations" made by a panel. We, therefore, consider that Article 12.7 establishes a minimum standard for the reasoning that panels must provide in support of their findings and recommendations. Panels must set forth explanations and reasons sufficient to disclose the essential, or fundamental, justification for those findings and recommendations.

107. In our view, the duty of panels under Article 12.7 of the DSU to provide a "basic rationale" reflects and conforms with the principles of fundamental fairness and due process that underlie and inform the provisions of the DSU.[89] In particular, in cases where a Member has been found to have acted inconsistently with its obligations under the covered agreements, that Member is entitled to know the reasons for such finding as a matter of due process. In addition, the requirement to set out a "basic rationale" in the panel report assists such Member to understand the nature of its obligations and to make informed decisions about: (i) what must be done in order to implement the eventual rulings and recommendations made by the DSB; and (ii) whether and what to appeal. Article 12.7 also furthers the objectives, expressed in Article 3.2 of the DSU, of promoting security and predictability in the multilateral trading system and of clarifying the existing provisions of the covered agreements, because the requirement to provide "basic" reasons contributes to other WTO Members' understanding of the nature and scope of the rights and obligations in the covered agreements.

108. We do not believe that it is either possible or desirable to determine, in the abstract, the minimum standard of reasoning that will constitute a "basic rationale" for the findings and recommendations made by a panel.[90] Whether a panel has articulated adequately the "basic rationale" for its findings and recommendations must be determined on a case-by-case basis, taking into account the facts of the case, the specific legal provisions at issue, and the particular findings and recommendations made by a panel. Panels must identify the relevant facts and the

---

[87] *The New Shorter Oxford English Dictionary*, Lesley Brown (ed.) (Clarendon Press, 1993), Vol. I, p. 188.

[88] *Ibid.*, Vol. II, p. 2482.

[89] We have also examined these principles in other contexts. See, for example, Appellate Body Report, *United States - Hot-Rolled Steel, supra*, footnote 59, paras. 101 and 193; Appellate Body Report, *United States - Import Prohibition of Certain Shrimp and Shrimp Products*, WT/DS58/AB/R, adopted 6 November 1998, DSR 1998:VII, 2755, para. 158; and Appellate Body Report, *United States - FSC, supra*, footnote 24, para. 166.

[90] Appellate Body Report, *Korea - Alcoholic Beverages*, WT/DS75/AB/R, WT/DS83/AB/R, adopted 17 February 1999, DSR 1999:I, 3, para. 168.

applicable legal norms. In applying those legal norms to the relevant facts, the reasoning of the panel must reveal how and why the law applies to the facts. In this way, panels will, in their reports, disclose the essential or fundamental justification for their findings and recommendations.[91]

109. This does not, however, necessarily imply that Article 12.7 requires panels to expound at length on the reasons for their findings and recommendations. We can, for example, envisage cases in which a panel's "basic rationale" might be found in reasoning that is set out in other documents, such as in previous panel or Appellate Body reports - provided that such reasoning is quoted or, at a minimum, incorporated by reference. Indeed, a panel acting pursuant to Article 21.5 of the DSU would be expected to refer to the initial panel report, particularly in cases where the implementing measure is closely related to the original measure, and where the claims made in the proceeding under Article 21.5 closely resemble the claims made in the initial panel proceedings.

110. Turning to examine whether the Panel in this case satisfied its duty to set forth a "basic rationale" for its findings under Articles 3.1 and 3.4 of the *Anti-Dumping Agreement*, we note that the relevant section of the Panel Report, entitled "Analysis of Likely Impact of Imports on the Domestic Industry", is contained in paragraphs 6.24 to 6.37 of the Panel Report. At the end of this section, the Panel found that Mexico had acted inconsistently with its obligations under Articles 3.1, 3.4 and 3.7. of the *Anti-Dumping Agreement.*

1. The Panel's Finding Concerning Article 3.4 of the Anti-Dumping Agreement

111. We first consider Mexico's argument, on appeal, that the Panel failed to set out a "basic rationale", as required by Article 12.7 of the DSU, for its finding that Mexico had acted inconsistently with its obligations under Article 3.4 of the *Anti-Dumping Agreement.*

112. In reviewing SECOFI's analysis of the likely impact of imports on the domestic industry, the Panel began by recalling the original panel's view that, in a case involving a determination of a threat of material injury, investigating authorities must "consider, among other relevant factors, all the factors set out in Article 3.4".[92] The Panel then recalled the conclusion of the original panel that SECOFI's initial determination "reflected 'no meaningful analysis of a number of the Article 3.4 factors'".[93] It appears to us that, without expressly saying so, the Panel considered, in assessing the consistency of an injury determination with Article 3.4, that it was necessary to examine, first, whether all listed and other

---

[91] Appellate Body Report, *Chile - Taxes on Alcoholic Beverages*, WT/DS87/AB/R, WT/DS110/AB/R, adopted 12 January 2000, DSR 2000:I, 281, para. 78.

[92] Panel Report, para. 6.24.

[93] *Ibid.*

relevant factors were evaluated, and second, whether the evaluation of each factor by the investigating authorities was adequate.

113. The Panel then restated the applicable standard of review, found in Article 17.6(i) of the *Anti-Dumping Agreement*, and observed that the determination of threat of material injury must "as well" satisfy the elements of Article 3.7 of the *Anti-Dumping Agreement*.[94] Having identified the relevant legal standards - Articles 3.4, 3.7 and 17.6(i) - the Panel turned to apply them to the redetermination.

114. In reviewing the evidence that was before SECOFI, the Panel's analysis relating to the claim under Article 3.4 of the *Anti-Dumping Agreement* is intertwined with its analysis relating to the claim under Article 3.7 of that Agreement. For this reason, it is not always easy to ascertain whether the Panel's review of specific facts was undertaken pursuant to Article 3.4, to Article 3.7, or to both provisions. While the Panel did not itself discuss the relationship between those two provisions, it did reproduce three lengthy passages from the original report that reflect the original panel's view of the close relationship between the obligations under Articles 3.4 and 3.7 of the *Anti-Dumping Agreement* in cases involving a determination of a threat of material injury.[95]

115. The United States acknowledged that SECOFI's redetermination contained "information" on factors relevant under Article 3.4[96] and the Panel stated that, "[i]n the redetermination, SECOFI did provide information on the elements that were not addressed in the original determination".[97] Thus, it seems that the Panel found that the redetermination did address all the relevant factors under Article 3.4 of the *Anti-Dumping Agreement*.

116. The Panel then considered the adequacy of SECOFI's analysis of a number of economic factors. Although it did not refer explicitly to Article 3.4, the economic factors analysed by the Panel are among those listed in Article 3.4, including profits, production, capacity utilisation and prices.[98] As we discussed in the previous section of this Report, the Panel found that SECOFI's analysis of these factors was not supported by the evidence that was before SECOFI.[99]

117. It appears to us that, while this part of the Panel Report might not reflect an exemplary degree of clarity in all respects, it can fairly be read as setting out the Panel's "basic" explanations and reasons for considering that SECOFI's

---

94 Panel Report, para. 6.27.

95 Panel Report, paras. 6.24 and 6.28, referring to the Original Panel Report, paras. 7.132, 7.140 and 7.141. We note, also, that the preceding paras. of the original panel report set out in detail that panel's view of the relationship between the obligations set forth in Articles 3.4 and 3.7 of the *Anti-Dumping Agreement*. (Original Panel Report, paras. 6.118-6.131)

96 Panel Report, para. 6.25.

97 *Ibid.*, para. 6.29.

98 Panel Report, paras. 6.30-6.34.

99 The Panel found deficiencies, for example, in the conclusions that SECOFI drew in its analysis of the domestic industry's projected revenues, production levels and capacity utilisation, and in SECOFI's analysis of projected domestic prices. (Panel Report, paras. 6.31-6.35)

evaluation of certain Article 3.4 factors was not adequate. Thus, we find that the Panel satisfied its duty, under Article 12.7 of the DSU, to provide a "basic rationale" for its finding that Mexico acted inconsistently with its obligations under Article 3.4 of the *Anti-Dumping Agreement.*

118. For these reasons, we dismiss Mexico's appeal concerning the Panel's alleged failure to provide a "basic rationale" for its finding concerning Article 3.4 of the *Anti-Dumping Agreement.* We also recall that, in the previous section of this Report, we dismissed Mexico's appeal regarding the substance of that finding.[100] We, therefore, uphold the Panel's finding, in paragraph 6.36 of its Report, that Mexico acted inconsistently with its obligations under Article 3.4 of the *Anti-Dumping Agreement.*

2. *The Panel's Finding Concerning Article 3.1 of the Anti-Dumping Agreement*

119. As regards the Panel's finding that Mexico acted inconsistently with Article 3.1 of the *Anti-Dumping Agreement*, we recall that the Panel found, in paragraph 6.36 of its Report, that the redetermination "is not consistent with Articles 3.1, 3.4, and 3.7 of the AD Agreement".

120. Turning again to the section of the Panel Report reviewing SECOFI's analysis of the likely impact of imports on the domestic industry, we note that it does not contain any quotation or discussion of the text of Article 3.1, or explanation of how Mexico failed to comply with the obligations set out in that provision. Nevertheless, in examining whether the Panel provided a "basic rationale" for its finding with respect to Article 3.1, we believe that we must take account of the circumstances particular to this case.

121. The Panel was charged, under Article 21.5 of the DSU, with assessing the claims made by the United States with respect to the consistency of the redetermination with Mexico's obligations under the *Anti-Dumping Agreement.* In proceeding under Article 21.5 of the DSU, the Panel conducted its work against the background of the original proceedings, and with full cognizance of the reasons provided by the original panel. The original determination and original panel proceedings, as well as the redetermination and the panel proceedings under Article 21.5, form part of a continuum of events. We consider that the Panel Report cannot be read in isolation from those events.

122. In addition, in this case, the redetermination was not a stand-alone measure, but rather one that, in the words of Mexico, "complements and amends" the original determination.[101] The United States' claims under Articles 3.1, 3.4 and 3.7 closely resembled the claims that it had made under Articles 3.1, 3.4 and 3.7 with respect to SECOFI's original determination.

---

[100] *Supra,* footnote 99, para. 101.

[101] Panel Report, para. 3.78.

123. We recall that, in its Report, the Panel provided reasons in support of its findings that the redetermination was inconsistent with Mexico's obligations under Articles 3.4 and 3.7 of the *Anti-Dumping Agreement*. There is, as we have ourselves observed, a close relationship between the various paragraphs of Article 3 of the *Anti-Dumping Agreement*.[102] In its assessment of SECOFI's original determination, the original panel explained, at length, its views as to the relationship between Articles 3.1, 3.4 and 3.7.[103] Based on its view of the relationship between these three provisions, the original panel found a violation of Article 3.1 as a consequence of having found violations of Articles 3.4 and 3.7.[104]

124. Having regard to these circumstances, we are of the view that the Panel Report, read together with the original panel report, leaves no doubt about the reasons for the Panel's additional finding under Article 3.1 of the *Anti-Dumping Agreement*. We, therefore, find that the Panel did not fail to provide a "basic rationale" for that finding.

125. For these reasons, we dismiss Mexico's appeal concerning the Panel's alleged failure to provide a "basic rationale" for its finding with respect to Article 3.1 of the *Anti-Dumping Agreement*. We recall that, in the previous section of this Report, we dismissed Mexico's appeal regarding the substance of that finding.[105] We, therefore, uphold the Panel's finding, in paragraph 6.36 of its Report, that Mexico acted inconsistently with its obligations under Article 3.1 of the *Anti-Dumping Agreement*.

126. We wish to add that for purposes of transparency and fairness to the parties, even a panel proceeding under Article 21.5 of the DSU should strive to present the essential justification for its findings and recommendations in its own report. In this case, in particular, we consider that the Panel's finding under Article 3.1 of the *Anti-Dumping Agreement* would have been better supported by a direct quotation from or, at least, an explicit reference to, the relevant reasoning set out in the original panel report.

B. Article 17.6(ii) of the Anti-Dumping Agreement: "Permissible Interpretation"

127. In paragraph 6.37 of its Report, the Panel stated:

> *We do not mean to suggest that it would not be possible to make a finding of threat of material injury in the circumstances of this case.* Such a conclusion would be beyond the scope of our standard

---

[102] See, in particular, Appellate Body Report, *Thailand - H-Beams, supra*, footnote 25, paras. 106-108; and Appellate Body Report, *United States - Hot-Rolled Steel, supra*, footnote 59, paras. 192-197.

[103] Original Panel Report, paras. 7.118-7.131.

[104] We also note that, in their responses to questioning at the oral hearing before us, both Mexico and the United States accepted that a measure that was inconsistent with Article 3.4 of the *Anti-Dumping* Agreement would also be inconsistent with Article 3.1 of that Agreement.

[105] *Supra*, footnote 104, para. 101.

> of review, as it would involve us in analysing the facts *de novo*. However, we do conclude that an unbiased and objective investigating authority could not reach the conclusion that the domestic sugar industry in Mexico was threatened with material injury on the basis of the evidence and explanations provided by SECOFI in the notice of redetermination. ... (emphasis added)

128. Mexico argues that this paragraph demonstrates that the Panel in effect recognized that SECOFI's interpretation of the relevant provisions of the *Anti-Dumping Agreement* was or could be "permissible".[106] Since Article 17.6(ii) of the *Anti-Dumping Agreement* requires panels not to disturb "permissible" interpretations by national investigating authorities - even if the panels prefer alternative "permissible" interpretations - Mexico concludes that the Panel erred in nevertheless finding the redetermination to be inconsistent with Mexico's obligations under the *Anti-Dumping Agreement*.

129. We recall that Article 17.6 of the *Anti-Dumping Agreement*, which sets out the standard of review for panels examining claims under that Agreement, contains two separate sub-paragraphs, which read:

> In examining the matter referred to in paragraph 5:
>
> (i) in its assessment of the facts of the matter, the panel shall determine whether the authorities' establishment of the facts was proper and whether their evaluation of those facts was unbiased and objective. If the establishment of the facts was proper and the evaluation was unbiased and objective, even though the panel might have reached a different conclusion, the evaluation shall not be overturned;
>
> (ii) the panel shall interpret the relevant provisions of the Agreement in accordance with customary rules of interpretation of public international law. Where the panel finds that a relevant provision of the Agreement admits of more than one permissible interpretation, the panel shall find the authorities' measure to be in conformity with the Agreement if it rests upon one of those permissible interpretations.

130. We recently examined this standard of review in *United States - Hot-Rolled Steel*. In our Report in that case, we observed that, pursuant to Article 17.6(i), "the task of panels is simply to review the investigating authorities' 'establishment' and 'evaluation' of the facts".[107] Under Article 17.6(ii), panels must "determine whether a measure rests upon an interpretation of the relevant provisions of the *Anti-Dumping Agreement* which is *permissible under the rules of treaty interpretation* in Articles 31 and 32 of the *Vienna Convention*."[108] The

---

[106] Mexico's appellant's submission, para. 127.

[107] Appellate Body Report, *supra*, footnote 59, para. 55.

[108] *Ibid.*, para. 60.

requirements of the standard of review provided for in Article 17.6(i) and 17.6(ii) are cumulative. In other words, a panel must find a determination made by the investigating authorities to be consistent with relevant provisions of the *Anti-Dumping Agreement* if it finds that those investigating authorities have properly established the facts and evaluated those facts in an unbiased and objective manner, *and* that the determination rests upon a "permissible" interpretation of the relevant provisions.

131. Before considering whether the Panel properly applied the standard of review set forth in Article 17.6(ii) of the *Anti-Dumping Agreement*, we first examine Mexico's characterization of paragraph 6.37 of the Panel Report and, in particular, its contention that the Panel found that SECOFI's interpretation of the relevant provisions of the *Anti-Dumping Agreement* could be "permissible". In the first sentence of paragraph 6.37, the Panel cautioned that it did "not mean to suggest that it would not be possible to make a finding of threat of material injury in the circumstances of this case." In our view, the Panel was not suggesting, in this sentence, that SECOFI's interpretation of the applicable legal provisions was "permissible". Rather, the Panel was simply declining to exclude the possibility that, *had certain factual circumstances been sufficiently substantiated and properly evaluated by SECOFI in its redetermination*, SECOFI could have made a determination of threat of material injury that would have been consistent with Mexico's obligations under the *Anti-Dumping Agreement*. However, in the same paragraph, the Panel considered that, on the basis of the evidence and explanations actually provided, it was not possible to make such a finding of threat of material injury:

> … we *do conclude* that an unbiased and objective investigating authority *could not* reach the conclusion that the domestic sugar industry in Mexico was threatened with material injury on the basis of the evidence and explanations provided by SECOFI in the notice of redetermination. (emphasis added)

132. We are satisfied that, in paragraph 6.37, the Panel was acting according to the standard of review set forth in Article 17.6(i) of the *Anti-Dumping Agreement*. The Panel reviewed what SECOFI had done and found that SECOFI's *establishment and evaluation of the facts* did not support its determination of a threat of material injury.[109] This finding was sufficient for the Panel to find the redetermination to be inconsistent with Articles 3.1, 3.4 and 3.7 of the *Anti-Dumping Agreement*.

133. We are further satisfied that the Panel was *not*, in this paragraph, dealing with any issue of legal interpretation of the relevant provisions of the *Anti-*

[109] We recall that the findings of the Panel were based on its review of the *factual* basis for SECOFI's projected increases in demand for HFCS from users other than soft-drink bottlers, and on the resulting projected increase in HFCS imports and projected impact on the Mexican sugar industry.

Dumping Agreement.[110] The Panel did not consider whether SECOFI's determination of the existence of a threat of material injury rested on a "permissible" legal interpretation of Articles 3.1, 3.4 and 3.7 of the *Anti-Dumping Agreement* because the Panel found that SECOFI's establishment and evaluation of *the facts* did not support that determination. Thus, the Panel did not need to apply the standard of review in Article 17.6(ii).

134. For these reasons, we are unable to accept Mexico's assertion that the reasoning used in paragraph 6.37 indicates that the Panel found that SECOFI's legal interpretation of the relevant provision of the *Anti-Dumping Agreement* could be "permissible". As Mexico's appeal concerning the standard of review in Article 17.6(ii) of the *Anti-Dumping Agreement* depends on this premise, we dismiss this part of Mexico's appeal.

VII. FINDINGS AND CONCLUSIONS

135. For the reasons set out in this Report, the Appellate Body:

(a) finds that the Panel did not err in refraining from addressing in its Report: the lack of consultations between the United States and Mexico prior to the DSB's referral of the redetermination to the Panel; the alleged failure of the United States to comply with Article 6.2 of the DSU because its communication seeking recourse to Article 21.5 of the DSU did not indicate whether consultations had been held; and the alleged failure of the United States to exercise its judgement, in accordance with Article 3.7 of the DSU, as to whether action under the DSU would be "fruitful";

(b) upholds the Panel's finding, in paragraph 6.23 of the Panel Report, that SECOFI's conclusion, in the redetermination, that there existed a significant likelihood of increased imports was inconsistent with Mexico's obligations under Article 3.7(i) of the *Anti-Dumping Agreement*;

(c) upholds the Panel's finding, in paragraph 6.36 of the Panel Report, that SECOFI's conclusion, in the redetermination, with respect to the likely impact of dumped imports of HFCS from the United States on the domestic industry, was inconsistent with Mexico's obligations under Articles 3.1, 3.4, and 3.7 of the *Anti-Dumping Agreement*;

[110] The Panel itself noted that neither Mexico nor the United States "made any arguments concerning the interpretation of the applicable provisions of the AD Agreement." (Panel Report, footnote 66 to para. 6.5)

(d) finds that the Panel satisfied its duty, under Article 12.7 of the DSU, to set out a "basic rationale behind [its] findings" with respect to Articles 3.1 and 3.4 of the *Anti-Dumping Agreement*; and

(e) finds that the Panel did not act inconsistently with the standard of review set out in Article 17.6(ii) of the *Anti-Dumping Agreement*.

136. The Appellate Body *recommends* that the DSB request that Mexico bring its anti-dumping measure found in this Report, and in the Panel Report as upheld by this Report, to be inconsistent with the *Anti-Dumping Agreement*, into conformity with its obligations under that Agreement.

MEXICO - ANTI-DUMPING INVESTIGATION OF HIGH FRUCTOSE CORN SYRUP (HFCS) FROM THE UNITED STATES

RECOURSE TO ARTICLE 21.5 OF THE DSU BY THE UNITED STATES

Report of the Panel
WT/DS132/RW

Adopted by the Dispute Settlement Body on 21 November 2001 as Upheld by the Appellate Body.

TABLE OF CONTENTS

I. INTRODUCTION AND FACTUAL BACKGROUND

1.1 On 24 February 2000, the Dispute Settlement Body ("the DSB") adopted the report and recommendations of the Panel in *Mexico - Anti-dumping Investigation of High Fructose Corn Syrup (HFCS) from the United States* (WT/DS132/R). In that report, the Panel concluded that Mexico's imposition of the definitive anti-dumping duties on imports of high fructose corn syrup, grades 42 and 55, from the United States was inconsistent with the requirements of the Agreement on Implementation of Article VI of the General Agreement on Tariffs and Trade 1994 (AD Agreement). The panel and the DSB accordingly recommended that Mexico bring its measure into conformity with its obligations under the AD Agreement.

1.2 On 20 September 2000, the Government of Mexico published a final resolution in which it stated that it had revised the original final resolution imposing definitive anti-dumping duties on imports of high fructose corn syrup, grades 42 and 55, from the United States to comply with the Panel report's conclusions and recommendations.[1] Mexico determined to repay provisional duties on entries and guarantees granted for the payment of provisional anti-dumping duties, with interest, for the period 26 June 1997 to 23 January 1998. Mexico also "ratified its conclusion that during the period under investigation, there was a threat of harm to the domestic sugar industry as a consequence of imports of high fructose corn syrup under price discriminatory conditions originating from the United States of America".[2] The revised final resolution confirmed "the final offsetting duties established during the antidumping investigation".[3]

1.3 On 12 October, the United States submitted a communication seeking recourse to Article 21.5 of the DSU (WT/DS132/6). In that communication, the United States indicated its view that the measures taken by Mexico to comply with the recommendations and rulings of the DSB were not consistent with the AD Agreement. In particular, in the view of the United States, Mexico's redetermination of a threat of material injury, including its consideration of the impact of dumped imports on the Mexican sugar industry, its consideration of the potential effect of the alleged restraint agreement in its determination of a likelihood of substantially increased importation, and its explanation of the findings and conclusions it reached on all material issues of fact and law, failed to comply with the recommendations and rulings of the DSB and was inconsistent with Articles 3.1, 3.2, 3.4, 3.5, 3.7, 12.2, and 12.2.2 of the AD Agreement. The United States further stated that because there was "a disagreement as to the existence or consistency with a covered agreement of measures taken to comply with the recommendations and rulings of the DSB" between the United States and Mexico, within the terms of Article 21.5 of the DSU, the United States sought recourse to Article 21.5 in the matter and requested that the DSB refer the disagreement to the original panel, if possible, pursuant to Article 21.5 of the DSU.

1.4 At its meeting on 23 October 2000, the DSB decided, in accordance with Article 21.5 of the DSU, to refer to the original panel the matter raised by the United States in document WT/DS132/6. The DSB further decided that the Panel should have standard terms of reference as follows:

> "To examine, in the light of the relevant provisions of the covered agreements cited by the United States in document WT/DS132/6, the matter referred to the DSB by the United

[1] Final resolution revising, on the basis of the conclusion and recommendation of the Panel of the World Trade Organization's Dispute Settlement Body, the final resolution of the anti-dumping investigation into imports of high fructose corn syrup, merchandise classified in tariff headings 1702.40.99 and 1702.60.01 of the General Import Tariff, originating in the United States of America, irrespective of the country of provenance, 20 September 2000, MEXICO-1 (hereinafter "Notice of Redetermination"). MEXICO-1 is the official Spanish version of the text, MEXICO 1(a) is the English translation provided by Mexico in this proceeding.

[2] *Ibid.* at para. 188.

[3] *Ibid.*

States in that document and to make such findings as will assist the DSB in making the recommendations or in giving the rulings provided for in those agreements."

1.5 A member of the original Panel was unable to participate in this proceeding. The parties agreed on a new panellist on 13 November 2000. As a result, the Panel is composed as follows:

Chairman:	H.E. Mr. Christer Manhusen
Members:	Mr. Gerald Salembier
	Mr. Paul O'Connor

1.6 The European Communities (EC), Mauritius and Jamaica reserved their rights to participate in the Panel proceedings as third parties to the dispute.

1.7 The Panel met with the parties on 20-21 February 2001, and with the third parties on 21 February 2000.

1.8 The Panel submitted its interim report to the parties on 11 May 2001.

II. FINDINGS AND RECOMMENDATIONS REQUESTED BY THE PARTIES

2.1 The **United States** requests the Panel to "review Mexico's redetermination and conclude that Mexico has failed to comply with the conclusions and recommendations of the DSB and Mexico's obligations under the AD Agreement".

2.2 **Mexico** requests the Panel to "find that the measures adopted by Mexico to comply with the recommendations and rulings of the DSB are consistent with the AD Agreement".

III. MAIN ARGUMENTS OF THE PARTIES

A. *First Written Submission of the United States*

3.1 The United States argues that, in its decision of January14, 2000, the Panel concluded that the Government of Mexico's imposition of a definitive anti-dumping measure on imports of high fructose corn syrup ("HFCS") from the United States was inconsistent with the requirements of the Agreement on Implementation of Article VI of the General Agreement on Tariffs and Trade 1994 (the "AD Agreement"). In particular, the Panel concluded that in making a threat of material injury determination, Mexico inadequately considered (a) the potential effect of a restraint agreement between Mexican sugar refiners and soft drink bottlers, and (b) the impact of HFCS imports on the domestic sugar industry. The Panel recommended that the Dispute Settlement Body ("DSB") request Mexico to bring its measure into conformity with its obligations under the AD Agreement.

3.2 In the view of the United States, Mexico has failed to do so. Instead, Mexico has issued a new determination that, while purporting to comply with the Panel's conclusions and recommendations, is essentially a restatement of its original determination. The United States asserts that the new gloss that Mexico has put on its original determination cannot hide the fact that Mexico's threat of material injury determination continues to be based on "conjecture" and "remote possibility," is contradicted by fundamental facts in the record, and is inadequately explained. Mexico's new determination, therefore, fails to meet the standards required by the Panel and the AD Agreement.

3.3 Specifically, the United States argues, Mexico's redetermination falls far short of what the Panel Report and the AD Agreement require in three important respects.

3.4 First, there is still no basis for the Mexican authority's conclusion that there is a likelihood of substantially increased imports of HFCS from the United States. The United States recalls that the Panel Report concluded that the original determination's finding in this respect violated Article 3.7(i) of the AD Agreement because the Mexican authority gave inadequate consideration to an agreement between Mexican sugar refiners and soft drink bottlers to restrain the soft drink bottlers' use of HFCS. Moreover, argues the United States, the redetermination largely repeats the same information that was previously submitted and again fails to explain how a substantial increase in imports is likely given the fact of the restraint agreement. Consequently, the United States maintains that redetermination suffers from the same defects the Panel identified in its review of the original determination, making the redetermination inconsistent with Article 3.7 of the AD Agreement.

3.5 Second, the redetermination still fails adequately to address the factors set forth in Article 3.4 of the AD Agreement. The Panel Report found that the Mexican authority's original determination violated Articles 3.1, 3.4, and 3.7 of the AD Agreement because it failed meaningfully to analyze both several individual Article 3.4 factors and the overall condition of the Mexican sugar industry. According to the United States, the redetermination merely presents more data concerning the individual Article 3.4 factors without providing the necessary analysis and explanation of these factors. Moreover, argues the United States, the redetermination mischaracterizes pertinent information concerning the condition of the Mexican sugar industry and fails to provide a reasoned and fact-supported explanation concerning why improvements in important industry trends during the period of investigation were not probative in ascertaining the likely future condition of the industry. Consequently, in the view of the United States, the redetermination fails to conform to the requirements of Articles 3.1, 3.4, and 3.7 of the AD Agreement.

3.6 Third, the redetermination is inconsistent with Articles 12.2 and 12.2.2 of the AD Agreement because it relies on analytical models and forecasts without adequate explanation of the inputs on which those methodologies were based.

3.7 The United States recalls that Mexico has had two opportunities to make a threat of material injury determination that is consistent with its obligations under the AD Agreement. The United States asserts that Mexico has done so on neither occasion. Indeed, according to the United States, the facts found by the Mexican authority sufficiently contradict its conclusions on redetermination so as to suggest that it cannot on its record provide a basis for finding threat of material injury. Accordingly, the United States respectfully requests that this Panel review Mexico's redetermination and conclude that Mexico has failed to comply with the conclusions and recommendations of the DSB and Mexico's obligations under the AD Agreement.

1. SECOFI Disregarded the Panel's Conclusion that it Made an Insufficient Finding of the Likelihood of Increased Imports

3.8 In its report, the United States notes, the Panel found that SECOFI's conclusion that there was a "likelihood of substantially increased importation" was inconsistent with the requirements of Article 3.7(i) of the AD Agreement.

3.9 In particular, the United States argues, the Panel agreed with the argument of the United States that SECOFI did not adequately consider an agreement between Mexican sugar refiners and soft drink bottlers to restrain the soft drink bottlers' use of HFCS. The United States recalls that it demonstrated to the Panel that the US exporters participating in the investigation informed SECOFI during the pendency of its investigation as to the existence of this agreement, which was publicly revealed by SECOFI Secretary Herminio Blanco Mendoza to the Mexican Senate in September 1997.

3.10 The United States further recalls that the Panel stated that "[t]he question before us is whether SECOFI's analysis provides a reasoned explanation for its conclusion that, assuming [the restraint] agreement existed, there was nonetheless a likelihood of substantially increased importation." According to the United States, the Panel provided several grounds for answering this question in the negative.

3.11 One ground was that SECOFI improperly premised its analysis on alleged increases in import levels from 1996, the time of the conclusion of its period of investigation, rather than from the third quarter of 1997, the latest period for which its record contained data on the volume of imports from the United States. The United States notes that the Panel concluded that "[t]he question for purposes of analysis of threat of material injury is not the level of imports already reached, but the likelihood of **increased** imports." The United States further notes that the Panel criticized SECOFI for "conclud[ing] that such imports would have continued increasing by inertia."

3.12 An additional ground was SECOFI's finding that the restraint agreement does not "rule out the possibility" that soft drink bottlers and other users would continue their purchases of imported HFCS. The United States recalls that the

Panel concluded that "not ruling out the possibility that imports would continue does not support the finding that there is a '**likelihood** of substantially **increased** importation' (emphasis added), as provided for in Article 3.7(i)."

3.13 The United States points out that the Panel also found that SECOFI's determination did not provide any discussion to support a conclusion that there was a likelihood that users other than soft drink bottlers would increase their importation of HFCS. The Panel found this omission to be critical in light of information in the record indicating that the restraint agreement affected purchasers accounting for 68 per cent of imports and that most other purchasers' ability to substitute HFCS for sugar was limited.

3.14 Consequently, according to the United States, SECOFI could not implement the Panel's findings merely by reiterating on redetermination the same arguments and information that Mexico presented to the Panel. Instead, the United States argues, for SECOFI again to conclude that there was a likelihood of increased imports notwithstanding the restraint agreement, it was obliged either to furnish additional explanation or to generate additional data that would support such a conclusion.

3.15 In the view of the United States, SECOFI failed to do so in its redetermination. Instead, it merely repeated the same information and recitation of conclusions that Mexico had previously presented to the Panel.

3.16 In particular, according to the United States, SECOFI made findings in its redetermination that the restraint agreement "does not mean that in periods subsequent to the one under investigation [non-soft drink bottlers'] share in the consumption of high fructose corn syrup would not increase" and that "[b]oth the beverage industry and other industries could acquire the imported product at low prices." Such findings, the United States asserts, are indistinguishable from the ones in the original SECOFI determination that the Panel rejected. As the United States previously noted, the Panel clearly concluded that findings based on "possible" propensity to increase purchases of imports do not satisfy the requirement of Article 3.7(i) of the AD Agreement that there be a "likelihood of substantially increased importation." Indeed, the United States argues that Article 3.7 requires that "a determination of threat shall be based on facts and not merely on allegation, conjecture, or remote possibility." Yet, according to the United States, SECOFI's continued emphasis on what purchasers other than soft drink bottlers **could** do is clearly based on conjecture and does not provide an adequate basis for the required fact-supported determination on their **likely** behavior.

3.17 In the view of the United States, SECOFI's redetermination is not flawed merely because it fails to frame its conclusions in the proper language. To the contrary, SECOFI's redetermination record provides no more support than its original record for any finding that HFCS purchasers other than soft drink bottlers would be likely to increase purchases of HFCS and that these increased purchases would result in substantially increased importations. The redetermination does make two findings that the United States anticipates, based on its arguments to the original Panel, Mexico will argue support such a conclusion. However, according to the United States, neither finding actually provides such support.

3.18 First, SECOFI postulated that increased imports are likely because imports from the United States increased between the time SECOFI's period of investigation concluded in 1996 and the latest period for which SECOFI had import data, January-September 1997. However, continues the United States, this finding is **precisely** the same finding from the original determination that the Panel specifically rejected in paragraph 7.176 of its Report as inconsistent with Article 3.7(i). In the view of the United States, the finding is equally invalid in the redetermination. Moreover, the United States claims, SECOFI did not relate the 1997 increases to purchasers that were not subject to the restraint agreement.

3.19 Second, SECOFI concluded that HFCS is theoretically substitutable for sugar in a variety of products. The United States believes, however, that this finding is based on the same data that SECOFI submitted to the Panel.

3.20 The United States recalls that the Panel did not find that this material provided adequate support for SECOFI's original determination that there was a likelihood of increased imports and it should not do so here. The United States asserts that the material does not demonstrate that HFCS users other than soft drink bottlers, which accounted for only 32 per cent of HFCS consumption in 1996, actually **were** substituting HFCS for sugar during SECOFI's period of investigation. It merely indicates that these users were theoretically capable of doing so in varying degrees depending on the type of product. The United States further asserts that finding that HFCS users **were likely to** substitute HFCS for sugar merely because they **could** do so as a theoretical matter is sheer conjecture as is SECOFI's unsupported and unexplained assumption of a 50 per cent substitution rate for all HFCS users other than soft drink bottlers. Under Article 3.7, the United States recalls, a threat determination may not be premised on such conjectural assumptions.

3.21 The United States argues that the conjectural basis of this finding is underscored by the magnitude of the substitution into HFCS from sugar that SECOFI projected users other than soft drink bottlers would make. The United States notes that SECOFI projected that HFCS imports from the United States would increase to 350,000 tons in 1998. The United States also notes that SECOFI projected that none of these imports would be by soft drink bottlers, which SECOFI assumed would obtain from Mexican sources whatever HFCS that they were permitted to consume under the restraint agreement.

3.22 Finally the United States recalls that SECOFI reported that HFCS imports from the United States in 1996, the final year of its period of investigation, were 192,906 tons. Based on SECOFI's own data, the amount of these imports attributable to users other than soft drink bottlers was 61,729 tons.

3.23 Consequently, according to the United States, SECOFI in effect projected that imports of HFCS from the United States by purchasers other than soft drink bottlers would increase by **467** per cent in just two years. The United States maintains that SECOFI's redetermination provides absolutely no information on the actual purchasing patterns of HFCS users other than soft drink bottlers that would support the conclusion that they were likely to increase their imports at such an astonishing rate. Moreover, according to the United States, the rate at which SECOFI projected these users would increase their purchases from 1996 to 1998 is not supported by the relevant facts of record. The projected rate of increase is far greater than the rate by which total HFCS imports from the United States - including those purchased by soft drink bottlers - actually increased from 1994 to 1996.

3.24 In the view of the United States, SECOFI thus disregarded the Panel's rulings concerning an appropriate analysis of the restraint agreement. The United States asserts that it engaged in conjecture, made conclusions that have absolutely no basis in the record before it, and failed to address meaningfully the question the Panel deemed pertinent - whether, notwithstanding the restraint agreement, imports of HFCS from the United States were likely to increase substantially from the levels prevailing at the time SECOFI made its original determination. Accordingly, the United States maintains that SECOFI's analysis of the restraint agreement in its redetermination suffers from the same flaws the Panel identified in its review of the original SECOFI determination. Because there is still no basis for the conclusion that there is a likelihood of substantially increased imports of HFCS from the United States, SECOFI's redetermination violates Article 3.7 of the AD Agreement.

2. *SECOFI did not Address the DSB's Rulings Regarding the Analysis of the Likely Impact of the Dumped Imports*

3.25 The United States recalls that the Panel stated that SECOFI's original determination reflected no meaningful analysis of a number of Article 3.4 factors such as the Mexican sugar industry's profits, output, productivity, utilization of capacity, employment, wages, growth, and ability to raise capital. The United States further recalls that Panel also criticized the determination for providing no analysis of the condition of the Mexican sugar industry during the period of investigation, and no projected analysis of its condition for the near future.

3.26 The United States acknowledges that SECOFI's redetermination, in contrast to its original determination, does provide a recitation of data concerning the Article 3.4 factors discussed by the Panel.

3.27 Nevertheless, according to the United States, the Panel did not indicate that Mexico could satisfy its obligations under the AD Agreement merely by having SECOFI recite data in its record concerning the current condition of the Mexican sugar industry.

3.28 The United States maintains that SECOFI did not perform this analysis in its redetermination. Instead, its analysis (i) repeatedly mischaracterizes pertinent information on the condition of the Mexican sugar industry; (ii) fails to provide a reasoned and fact-supported explanation concerning why improvements in important industry trends during the period of investigation were not probative in ascertaining the likely future condition of the industry; and (iii) makes erroneous or unsupported factual findings and calculations.

3.29 In the United States' view, SECOFI mischaracterized the data before it in several instances. For instance, it found a "decreasing trend in employment," although its data indicated that employment actually increased during each year of its period of investigation. Similarly, it characterized "the use of installed industry capacity" as a negative trend demonstrating the sugar industry's sensitivity to competition from imports. In fact, the United States points out, capacity utilization increased by 16 per cent from 1994 to 1995, and by an additional 3 per cent from 1995 to 1996.

3.30 The United States argues that SECOFI's mischaracterization of positive trends as signs of industry weakness cannot be justified as an unbiased and objective evaluation of the facts and cannot properly serve as the basis for an affirmative threat determination.

3.31 With respect to other factors, SECOFI's redetermination cites facts indicating improved industry performance over the period of investigation. Significantly, according to the United States, the redetermination demonstrates that the domestic sugar industry was profitable in 1996 and that profitability in 1996 increased substantially over 1995 - despite the increase in imports of HFCS from the United States. The United States notes that the determination also indicates that in 1996 the price of domestically-produced sugar in Mexico increased by a much higher percentage than prices for HFCS imported from the United States - notwithstanding that the volume of these imports more than doubled that year. According to the United States, these positive trends in profitability and prices, combined with the other positive evidence on the record - capacity utilization increasing, employment increasing, productivity increasing, operating costs decreasing, sales costs as a per cent of revenue decreasing, and debt level remaining constant - all weigh against a conclusion that the Mexican sugar industry was threatened with material injury.

3.32 The United States recalls that the Panel specifically stated that "[m]erely that dumped imports will increase, and will have adverse price effects, does not, *ipso facto*, lead to the conclusion that the domestic industry will be injured - if the industry is in very good condition, or other factors are at play, dumped imports may not threaten injury." In light of data showing that prices were increasing and operating performance was improving during a time when HFCS imports from the United States were increasing, the United States argues that there clearly were "other factors at play" besides the imports in determining the condition of the Mexican sugar industry.

3.33 The United States asserts that SECOFI thus was obliged to provide fact-based analysis sufficient to show why the improving trends relating to Mexican sugar industry performance it observed in 1996 would reverse in the near future or why other considerations would render these rising trends insignificant. According to the United States, it did not do so. Instead of analyzing the historical data concerning the industry's condition, as the Panel concluded was required by the AD Agreement, the United States asserts that SECOFI relied on a variety of assumptions contrary to the data.

3.34 One such assumption was that the projected increase in HFCS imports would cause a 9 per cent decline in prices for domestically-produced sugar in 1997. According to the United States, SECOFI's projection appears to be based on its view that "in order to avoid greater displacement in sales, the sugar industry would be required to reduce sugar prices to cut the price differential with respect to high fructose corn syrup." However, the United States asserts that SECOFI's assumption was contrary to the observed data during 1996, the final year of its period of investigation, when increased HFCS imports caused neither a decline in the price of sugar nor a decline in the price differential between sugar and HFCS. SECOFI has not shown that domestic sugar prices "had been 'forced downward' during the period of investigation" and SECOFI nowhere demonstrates why increased imports in 1997 were likely to cause price declines when increased imports in 1996 had opposite effects. Consequently, in the view of the United States, SECOFI's assumptions and conclusions regarding likely price declines remain "in the realm of speculation" and must be rejected as the type of allegation or conjecture insufficient to support a threat determination under Article 3.7.

3.35 Similarly, SECOFI assumed that further imports would cause domestic sales revenues to decline in 1997. The United States points out that this was contrary to what occurred during 1996. The United States further notes that SECOFI calculated that this decline would in turn cause the domestic industry to incur an operating loss. Again, according to the United States, this was contrary to the actual experience during 1996, when the industry's operating margins and profits increased. The United States asserts that SECOFI nowhere explains in its redetermination why it was reasonable to make such assumptions premised on facts contrary to those observed during the period of investigation. Thus, according to the United States, these assumptions as well must be rejected as premised on allegation or conjecture.

3.36 The United States maintains that there are several additional findings in the redetermination relating to Article 3.4 factors that are not adequately explained, or do not reconcile with other factual findings. The United States notes that the 5 per cent decline in "sales" that SECOFI calculates for the **entire** Mexican sugar industry in its redetermination is precisely the same as the decline in the **industrial sector only** that Mexico originally reported to the Panel. In its redetermination, SECOFI attributes this "sales" decline to the imports of HFCS. Because HFCS does not compete with sugar used in the household sector, argues the United States, any **overall** decline in sugar sales quantities attributable to HFCS imports should have been considerably less for the sugar industry overall than for the industrial sector alone.

3.37 Moreover, the United States notes, SECOFI emphasizes that the share of the Mexican sweetener market held by the Mexican sugar industry declined from 98 per cent in 1994 to 93 per cent in 1996, apparently suggesting to SECOFI that

HFCS imports were responsible for the decline. However, the United States further notes that SECOFI also states that the market share held by HFCS imports increased from 1.17 per cent in 1994 to 4 per cent in 1996. Consequently, in 1994, the Mexican sugar industry and imported HFCS combined for a 99.17 per cent share of the sweetener market, whereas in 1996, they combined for only a 97 per cent share. Furthermore, according to the United States, information in the redetermination indicates that Mexican HFCS production accounted for 0.82 per cent of the sweetener market in 1996 and imports from sources other than the United States accounted for less than 0.1 per cent of the sweetener market in 1996. Therefore, the United States asserts, SECOFI's redetermination fails to account for 2.18 per cent of the sweetener market in 1996. Given the small share of the market held by HFCS imports, the United States asserts that this gap indicates that SECOFI did not adequately explain its conclusions regarding market share. Moreover, the United States continues, any effects from this gap should not be attributed to HFCS imports.

3.38 Additionally, the United States notes, the redetermination indicates that between 1995 and 1996, employment increased 1 per cent, productivity rose six per cent, but production fell 2 per cent. The United States argues that the 2 per cent decline in production cannot be reconciled with SECOFI's findings of increasing employment and increasing productivity, given that productivity is calculated by dividing production by employment. In order for productivity to increase while employment is also increasing, the United States continues, production must increase and the increase must be by an amount greater than the increase in employment.

3.39 In the view of the United States, SECOFI's pattern of mischaracterizing data in the record concerning the Mexican sugar industry's condition and failing to explain how its assumptions on the likely condition of the industry may be reconciled with contrary information in the record demonstrates that it did not meaningfully account for all factors that might support a negative determination, as instructed by the Panel and as required by Articles 3.4 and 3.7 of the AD Agreement. Nor, according to the United States, did SECOFI in any way demonstrate why there was a clearly foreseen and imminent change in circumstances that threatened injury to an industry not currently injured, as the Panel ruled was required by Article 3.7.

3. *SECOFI did not Adequately Explain its Analysis in Critical Respects*

3.40 The United States notes that SECOFI's analysis of the likely impact of HFCS imports on the Mexican sugar industry focuses heavily on economic models and forecasts developed by that agency for use in its proceeding. SECOFI used models and forecasts to calculate likely imports, likely prices, and likely financial results for the Mexican sugar industry. As United States previously argued, the results generated by these methodologies were based on unexplained inputs concerning conditions in the Mexican sugar industry contrary to observed data for 1996 in the record. Hence, argues the United States, the findings SECOFI made based on these models and forecasts must be rejected as conjectural. Additionally, notes the United States, SECOFI failed to provide an adequate explanation of its analysis as required by Articles 12.2 and 12.2.2 of the AD Agreement.

3.41 When an investigating authority chooses to base its determination on the results of an economic model or forecast, argues the United States, information concerning the data used as inputs in the model or forecast is clearly "relevant information" for purposes of the determination.[4]

3.42 Yet, according to the United States, SECOFI consistently failed to explain its use of projections of industry behavior that were either contrary to or unsupported by the observed data during its period of investigation as inputs in these models and forecasts. The examples that the United States cites include its use of a 50 per cent substitution rate of HFCS for sugar, its projection that sugar prices would decline by 9 per cent[5] and its projection that the Mexican sugar industry's sales revenues would decline by 15 per cent.

B. *First Written Submission of Mexico*

1. *Introduction*

3.43 Mexico first notes its deep concern regarding the presentation of "US Exhibit 1" which contains an inadequate translation of the revised final resolution, published in the *Diario Oficial de la Federación* (DOF) of 20 September 2000. Mexico points out that as most members of the Panel, like the WTO Secretariat, are English-speaking, it is reasonable to assume that they will regularly consult this United States exhibit during the proceeding.

3.44 Mexico further points out that the above-mentioned translation was made by translators who, to all appearances, are not experts in the field, since the translation contains a series of inaccuracies, omissions and serious mistakes which, at best, tend to create confusion and, at worst, completely reverse the meaning of the revised final resolution. The many translation errors are set forth in detail in the First Written Submission.

3.45 Mexico asserts that on the basis of the findings and conclusions of the Panel in its report, adopted by the DSB on 24 February 2000 (WT/DS132/4 and

---

[4] According to the United States, it is not challenging the ability of investigating authorities to use economic models as an aid to their analysis of material injury and threat of material injury. Instead, the United States' argument concerns the data pertaining to a specific investigation that must be inputted into any model to yield a result specific to that investigation

[5] According to the United States, the projected 9 per cent decline in sugar prices itself appears to be the result of two unexplained models that SECOFI used to analyze pricing behavior. These are the "Granger causality test," and a "system of simultaneous equations." By failing to explain these models, argues the United States, SECOFI failed to provide relevant information on how it derived its predicted price decline data.

WT/DS132/4/Corr.1) and considering that Mexico, during the ordinary DSB meeting of 20 March, indicated its intention to comply with the Panel's recommendations and rulings, and that on 19 April the United States and Mexico, pursuant to Article 21.3(b) of the DSU, notified the Chairman of the DSB that on 22 September 2000 the reasonable period of time for implementation would expire, Mexico decided to revise the original final resolution by initiating a proceeding under a decision published in the DOF on 15 May 2000.

3.46 Mexico recalls that this procedure ended on 20 September 2000 with the publication in the DOF of the "*Final resolution revising, on the basis of the conclusion and recommendation of the Panel of the World Trade Organization's Dispute Settlement Body, the final resolution in the anti-dumping investigation of high fructose corn syrup imports, merchandise classified in tariff headings 1702.40.99 and 1702.60.01 of the Schedule to the General Import Duties Act, originating in the United States of America, irrespective of the country of export*".[6]

3.47 In the course of this proceeding, Mexico recalls, the investigating authority requested further information from the interested parties for the explicit purpose of implementing the Panel's recommendation.[7] In particular, given the Panel's findings and conclusions concerning the inadequacies of the analysis of the impact of imports on the domestic industry, Mexico notes that the investigating authority considered it appropriate to obtain additional information on this particular aspect in order to bring the measure into conformity with the AD Agreement. Mexico points out that several of the parties responded to these requests and the information they provided is set out in the revised final resolution.[8]

3.48 Mexico notes that, with regard to the alleged restraint agreement which, according to the Panel's findings and conclusions, Mexico did not take adequately into account in its determination of the likelihood of substantially increased importation, SECOFI considered it appropriate, in order to comply with the Panel's recommendation in this respect, legally to incorporate in the record of the proceedings (it was already physically present) the information from the *Corn Refiners Association* which had previously been rejected and legally dismissed by the investigating authority for having been submitted too late (on 22 January 1998, one day before the publication of the original final resolution).

3.49 Mexico argues that its revised final resolution complies with the Panel's recommendation insofar as it brings the definitive measure into conformity with Mexico's obligations under the AD Agreement in each and all of the instances in which it was found by the Panel to be inconsistent with that Agreement:

---

6 Notice of Redetermination, MEXICO-1.

7 *Ibid.*, para. 11.

8 *Ibid.*, paras. 13, 14, 15 and 16.

(a) By making good the inadequacies of SECOFI's threat of injury analysis, in accordance with the Panel's findings, to bring it into conformity with Article 3 of the AD Agreement in respect of the following:

(i) Consideration of the impact of the dumped imports on the domestic industry.

(ii) Determination of threat of material injury on the basis of the domestic industry as a whole.

(iii) Adequate consideration of the potential effect of the alleged restraint agreement on the likelihood of substantially increased importation.

(b) By ordering the refunding of the anti-dumping duties levied beyond the period of application of the provisional measure, in the light of the Panel's finding and conclusion with respect to Article 7.4 of the AD Agreement.

(c) By ordering the refunding of the anti-dumping duties levied retroactively for the period of application of the provisional measure, in the light of the Panel's findings and conclusions with respect to Articles 10.2, 10.4, 12.2 and 12.2.2 of the AD Agreement.

3.50 Mexico therefore requests that, in accordance with Article 21.5 of the DSU, the Panel find that the measure adopted by Mexico to comply with the recommendations and rulings of the DSB is consistent with the AD Agreement.

2. *Mexico has Complied with the Recommendations and Rulings of the Dispute Settlement Body*

(a) SECOFI Has Examined the Probable Impact of HFCS Imports on the Domestic Industry and Has Determined Threat of Injury on the Basis of the Industry as a Whole

3.51 In order to comply with the Panel's findings, Mexico argues that it examined in greater detail the economic factors mentioned in Article 3.4, basing its examination on the domestic industry as a whole. In the revised final resolution, Mexico describes the state of the domestic industry during the investigation period and the two previous years, as well as the impact of dumped imports and the state of the industry in a subsequent period, on the basis of projections.

3.52 In particular, in relation to the performance of the economic indicators, Mexico claims that it analysed the economic variables affecting the state of the domestic industry, both actual (period analysed 1994-1996) and potential (1997), as described in paragraphs 128 to 139 of the revised final resolution.

3.53 According to Mexico, threat of injury was determined for the whole of the domestic standard and refined sugar industry on the basis of reasonable methodologies, using information supplied by the National Chamber of Sugar and Alcohol Industries (hereinafter CNIAA) and working documents in the administrative record of the investigation.

3.54 With respect to price analysis, Mexico asserts that it has adequately complied with the Panel's findings in paragraphs 7.141, 7.151, 7.152 and 7.153 of the Panel report. In particular, Mexico points out that in paragraphs 80 to 126 of the revised final resolution the trends in the prices of HFCS imports from the United States and the prices of domestically produced sugar, during the investigation period and the two comparable previous periods, are analysed, together with the projected future trends.

3.55 Mexico explains that the analysis was based on the average selling prices on the domestic sugar market calculated from the sales volumes and values for the domestic industry as a whole. That is to say, sales of standard and refined sugar to both industrial and household sectors were considered. Mexico further explains that fluctuations in the prices of the imports investigated and in domestic prices were also analysed over a three-year period, which included the investigation period.

3.56 In particular, the level and trend of weighted average prices of HFCS-42 and HFCS-55 imports from the United States were examined in relation to the weighted average prices for sales on the domestic standard and refined sugar market in 1994, 1995 and 1996.

3.57 Mexico asserts that actual proof of the adverse impact of the price of the imports investigated on the domestic price during the investigation period was obtained on the basis of a detailed analysis of the month-by-month behaviour of both prices, the calculated margins of undercutting and dumping, statistical evidence of causality and the prevailing economic environment, and account was taken, in particular, of the existence of a "natural difference" between the prices of the two products.

3.58 In addition, Mexico notes that it estimated the prices of both products for 1997, taking into account the analysis made and on the basis of the monthly trend in the price of HFCS imports from the United States and the domestic selling price for sugar for the period 1994 to 1996. Mexico explains that the method of estimation employed relied on a system of simultaneous equations and the result was compared with the observed trend in the values of the variables incorporated (prices and volumes) and checked by considering the consistency of the forecasts with the economic context and conditions in the industry during the period analysed.

3.59 In conducting the financial analysis in its revised final resolution of 20 September 2000, Mexico argues that it took account of the Panel's findings and conclusions, and on the basis of audited financial information for 85 per cent of the Mexican sugar industry and information on debt amortization from that industry, SECOFI examined the financial factors set forth in Article 3.4 of the AD Agreement. Also, according to Mexico, SECOFI made a projection of the financial performance of the sugar industry in 1997 assuming HFCS imports from the United States had continued to increase, varying only the revenue from domestic sales of sugar, and selling costs and operating expenses - in proportion to the predicted volume of domestic sales - in their variable component only.

3.60 On this basis, SECOFI determined that in 1996, the domestic industry would perform positively in terms of profits and profitability owing to an improvement in selling costs and operating expenses. However, continues Mexico, SECOFI considered that owing to the specific characteristics of the industry, profits would be highly sensitive to changes in income, and with a reduction in income predicted for 1997, profits would be affected to a greater extent than income in percentage terms, and that therefore operating profits would be reduced to such an extent that the domestic sugar industry would be running at a loss and the possibility of achieving operational profitability would be wiped out.

3.61 At the same time, SECOFI concluded that in 1996 the sugar making industry had maintained its short-term credit worthiness and had seen an improvement in its accounts payable and receivable indicators. However, according to Mexico, the ratio of total liabilities to net worth of 4.6 had placed the industry in a situation of high levels of debt and saddled it, in 1996, with a high level of risk. Similarly, Mexico continues, SECOFI concluded that based on the debt service as a proportion of projected revenue, if the increasing trend in dumped HFCS imports were to continue, then the domestic industry would be unable to meet its debt servicing obligations, especially if operating losses were predicted for 1997.

3.62 Mexico argues that a joint evaluation of the above considerations led SECOFI to the justified conclusion that dumped HFCS imports from the United States have had a negative impact, as reflected in domestically produced sugar's loss of internal market share, declining sales, falling employment trends, earnings sensitivity, lower profitability, higher levels of debt and reduced ability to raise capital, which indicates that if a definitive anti-dumping measure had not been introduced, given increased importation at dumped prices, the injury to the domestic industry would have manifested itself in the other indicators as well.

(b) SECOFI Has Analysed the Potential Effects of the Alleged Restraint Agreement on the Likelihood of Substantially Increased Importation in a Manner Consistent with Article 3.7(I) of the AD Agreement

3.63 Mexico recalls that the Panel concluded that SECOFI's "consideration of the potential effects of the alleged restraint agreement [between the sugar refiners and soft drink bottlers] was inadequate"[9] and therefore determined that SECOFI's conclusion that there was a "likelihood of substantially increased importation" was inconsistent with the requirements of Article 3.7(i) of the AD Agreement[10],

[9] Notice of Redetermination, MEXICO-1, para. 7.178.

[10] Idem.

recommending that, *inter alia*, in this respect the measure be brought into conformity with the Agreement.[11]

3.64 Mexico argues that in order to comply with the Panel recommendation adopted by the DSB, SECOFI considered it appropriate and sufficient to incorporate in the record of the review the information submitted by the *Corn Refiners Association* in the course of the original investigation. On the basis of this information, Mexico asserts, SECOFI found that the alleged restraint agreement would apparently have the potential effect of limiting consumption of HFCS by the soft drink bottlers to 350,000 tons.[12] Mexico further asserts that this information on the terms of the alleged restraint agreement was considered sufficient since, according to paragraph 7.175 of the Panel report, the question was not whether an alleged restraint agreement existed, but whether its potential effects on the likelihood of dumped imports increasing in the near future had been adequately considered in the analysis.

3.65 Thus, in accordance with the Panel's findings, particularly those in paragraphs 7.175 to 7.178, Mexico claims that it carried out a detailed analysis and determined by reasoned explanation the likelihood of substantially increased importation of HFCS from the United States, taking into account the evidence of the effects of the alleged restraint agreement and the arguments relating thereto contained in the file on the anti-dumping investigation.

3.66 In determining the likelihood of substantially increased importation, Mexico argues that it considered, in accordance with subparagraphs (i) and (ii) of Article 3.7 of the AD Agreement, the existence of a significant rate of increase of dumped imports and freely disposable capacity of the HFCS-producing industry in the United States. In that context, Mexico notes that it also explored the effects of the alleged restraint agreement on the basis of the arguments and the information at its disposal. Mexico concluded that the potential effects of the said alleged restraint agreement did not preclude the likelihood of increased importation.

3.67 Mexico asserts that in the revised final resolution, SECOFI did not confine itself to repeating the arguments it made before the Panel, as claimed by the United States. Although it is true that in the new analysis, SECOFI also considered the information previously submitted to the Panel, Mexico claims that this was because this information formed part of the requested explanation of how Mexico had proceeded in its original final resolution. In Mexico's opinion, there is nothing to prevent the use of previously provided information in a subsequent proceeding intended to ensure that a panel's findings and recommendations have been correctly implemented.

3.68 In Mexico's view, the question which had to be settled was whether in the near future relative to the investigation period, even if the bottlers' HFCS consumption were limited, the likelihood of substantially increased importation

[11] Notice of Redetermination, MEXICO-1, para. 8.4.
[12] See "Informe Económico del Grupo Financiero Bancomer" of October 1997, MEXICO2.

would persist. On the basis of a comprehensive analysis of the situation which, in accordance with the observations made in the investigation period, would prevail in the near future, Mexico concluded that this likelihood would indeed persist.

3.69 Mexico argues that in an analysis of this kind, special consideration should be given to the fact that the likelihood of substantially increased importation depends not exclusively on a single factor such as the alleged limitation on the consumption of one group of users but also on a concurrence of other factors which must be taken into account in determining probable future import trends. To this end, Mexico claims that it is necessary to introduce into the analysis the trends, observed during the investigation period and comparable previous periods, in prices, volumes, actual and potential consumption, economic context and conditions in the industry and, in the light of these data for the period investigated, to determine whether in the situation envisaged there is still good reason to believe that there will be substantially increased importation in the near future.

3.70 Thus, according to Mexico, in its determination, SECOFI based itself on the figures for the consumption of sugar between 1994 and 1996 by sectors other than the soft drink bottlers and on the actual rates of utilization of HFCS recorded in 1996 by those manufacturers from whom it had requested information on the sweeteners consumed in their production processes. Mexico notes that it also considered the rates of substitution of HFCS for sugar supplied by the main importer for the investigation period, obtained from a recognized firm of economic consultants.

3.71 Similarly, according to Mexico, SECOFI determined the likelihood of increased importation by considering the effects of the alleged restraint agreement, on the basis of an estimate of the potential HFCS consumption of sectors other than the bottlers in 1997 and 1998, using as input data projections of the total sugar consumption for these years made by experts and applying those sectors' share of total consumption as recorded in 1994, 1995 and 1996.

3.72 Mexico asserts that, in this context, it is reasonable to assume that the demand from the bottlers, allegedly limited to 350,000 tons, would be met from domestically produced HFCS and not imports, due to geographical proximity and lower transport costs, together with other advantages. Mexico further asserts that this would lead to full utilization of the installed capacity of the domestic HFCS producers, so that any additional demand from other users would necessarily have to be met by imports.

3.73 Mexico explains that the underlying economic reasoning is that, in a context in which HFCS prices are depressed relative to sugar prices and in the absence of any distortions of trade flows, such as those caused by anti-dumping investigations, sectors other than the soft drink bottlers would have incentives to substitute imports for the domestically produced product. In the limit, according to Mexico, these sectors would substitute HFCS for all their sugar consumption, even though this process would depend on relative prices and the rate of substitution. Mexico notes that, in 1996, the weighted average rate of utilization in consumer industries other than soft drink bottling was 84 per cent and, on the basis of a conservative assumption, it was determined that if only 50 per cent of potential consumption was substituted and the rate of substitution remained constant, the demand for HFCS thus generated would be equivalent to increased imports as compared with the investigation period.

3.74 Mexico argues that, contrary to the claims of the United States, SECOFI's determination was not based on conjecture or remote possibility but on a forward-looking analysis of the situation observed during the investigation period. Mexico considers that it would not be consistent with Article 3.7 of the AD Agreement to determine the likelihood of increased importation on the basis of a single factor or from trade flows already distorted by the effects of an anti-dumping investigation, or repeatedly to update such a determination in the light of the latest data available to the investigating authority.

3.75 In the light of the above, Mexico respectfully requests the Panel to take into account all the factors analysed and reasons given in the revised final resolution which led the authority to make an affirmative determination of the likelihood of a substantial increase in the imports investigated, since no one of these factors by itself can necessarily give decisive guidance in this respect.

3.76 To recapitulate, in compliance with the findings and conclusions of the Panel report, in its revised final resolution Mexico argues that it has adequately considered the potential effects of an alleged restraint agreement on the likelihood of substantially increased importation, so that its determination is consistent with Article 3.7 (i) of the AD Agreement.

(c) Mexico Has Complied with the Provisions of Articles 12.2 and 12.2.2 of the AD Agreement

3.77 Mexico asserts that SECOFI's revised final resolution[13] is consistent with the provisions of Articles 12.2 and 12.2.2 of the AD Agreement. Mexico asserts that SECOFI made available in sufficient detail the findings and conclusions reached by the authority on all the issues of fact and law that SECOFI considered material.[14] Moreover, according to Mexico, SECOFI disclosed all relevant information on the matters of fact and law and reasons which led it to confirm the imposition of the final anti-dumping measure, while paying due regard to the protection of confidential information.[15]

---

[13] Notice of Redetermination, MEXICO-1.

[14] Under Article 12.2 of the AD Agreement, final public notices shall "set forth ... in sufficient detail the findings and conclusions reached on all issues of fact and law considered material by the investigating authorities."

[15] Likewise, under Article 12.2.2, the final notice shall "contain, or otherwise make available through a separate report, all relevant information on the matters of fact and law and reasons which have led to the imposition of final measures ... due regard being paid to the requirement for the protection of confidential information."

3.78 Similarly, in this context, in considering the consistency of SECOFI's actions with Articles 12.2 and 12.2.2, Mexico argues that the Panel should take particular account of the fact that the revised final resolution, which concludes the procedure followed by SECOFI for the *specific purpose of complying with the recommendation adopted by the DSB*, complements and amends the original final resolution (of 23 January 1998) in all those aspects that were reviewed by the investigating authority after the Panel had found them to be inconsistent with the AD Agreement.

3.79 At the same time, as usual in the anti-dumping practice of Mexico and other countries, Mexico asserts that the authority's relevant findings and conclusions that were included in the final notice of 20 September, like all the relevant information on matters of fact and law and the reasons which led SECOFI to confirm the imposition of the final anti-dumping measure, are based in their turn on more data, information and working documents than, for reasons of confidentiality, scope or relevance, are contained in the administrative record on the investigation, without this creating any inconsistency with the provisions of Articles 12.2 and 12.2.2 of the AD Agreement.

3.80 Thus, in Mexico's view, the Panel should consider that the revised final resolution constitutes a public notice and, in having as its specific purpose the implementation of the DSB's recommendation, complements in various respects the original final resolution, while being based to some extent on more information and documents than contained in the administrative record, without Mexico having thereby breached the provisions of Articles 12.2 and 12.2.2 of the AD Agreement.

3.81 With the specific purpose of complying with the conclusions and recommendation expressed in the Panel report, Mexico claims that SECOFI's revised final resolution:

(a) Orders the refunding of the anti-dumping duties levied retroactively for the period of application of the provisional measure, in strict compliance with the findings and conclusions of the Panel report (paragraphs 7.194 to 7.198 and 8.2 (e)) in relation, *inter alia*, to Articles 12.2 and 12.2.2 of the AD Agreement;

(b) Contains, in sufficient detail, explanations of the findings and conclusions on the issues considered material, as well as all relevant information on the matters and reasons which led SECOFI to confirm the imposition of the final measure in accordance with the analysis made by the investigating authority.

3.82 In the light of all the above considerations, Mexico maintains that it has duly complied with the provisions of Articles 12.2 and 12.2.2 of the AD Agreement.

3. *Conclusion*

3.83 On the grounds set out above, Mexico urges the Panel to declare that its revised final resolution on threat of material injury, including: (i) its examination of the impact of HFCS imports on the Mexican sugar industry as a whole; (ii) its examination of the potential effects of the alleged restraint agreement on the likelihood of substantially increased importation; and (iii) its explanation in the revised final resolution of the findings and conclusions reached by SECOFI with respect to these issues, complies fully with the recommendations and rulings of the DSB and is consistent with Articles 3.1, 3.4, 3.7, 12.2 and 12.2.2 of the AD Agreement.

C. *Second Written Submission of the United States*

3.84 The United States notes that, in its First Written Submission, it provided three grounds why the redetermination of Mexico's Secretariat of Commerce and Industrial Development ("SECOFI") does not comply with the requirements of either the report of the Panel in this proceeding or the Agreement on Implementation of Article VI of the General Agreement on Tariffs and Trade 1994 ("the AD Agreement"):

(a) SECOFI's redetermination, according to the United States, fails to explain how there is a likelihood of substantially increased imports of high fructose corn syrup ("HFCS") from the United States in light of an agreement between Mexican sugar refiners and soft drink bottlers limiting the bottlers' use of HFCS. Consequently, the redetermination, like the original determination, violates Article 3.7 of the AD Agreement.

(b) The United States further argues that the redetermination fails adequately to address the factors set forth in Article 3.4 of the AD Agreement concerning the likely impact of the imports on the Mexican sugar industry. According to the United States, the redetermination mischaracterizes pertinent information concerning the condition of the Mexican sugar industry and fails to provide a reasoned and fact-supported conclusion why improvements in industry trends during the period of investigation were not probative in ascertaining the future condition of the industry. As a result, the United States claims, the redetermination violates Articles 3.1, 3.4, and 3.7 of the AD Agreement.

(c) Finally the United States asserts that the redetermination is inconsistent with Articles 12.2 and 12.2.2 of the AD Agreement because it relies on analytical models and forecasts without adequate explanation of the inputs used within the models.

3.85 According to the United States, Mexico's First Written Submission, for the most part, does not directly address the arguments of the United States concerning the specific respects in which SECOFI's redetermination is inconsistent with the conclusions and recommendations of the Dispute Settlement Body ("DSB") and the AD Agreement. Instead, the United States continues, Mexico largely has done no more than summarize the redetermination and contend in a *pro forma* manner that it satisfies the requirements of the DSB and the AD Agreement.

3.86 In the view of the United States, Mexico's arguments only serve to confirm that SECOFI's redetermination is inconsistent with the Panel Report and the AD Agreement. Comparing Mexico's explanations of the redetermination with the redetermination itself demonstrates that SECOFI did not correct the serious deficiencies in explanation and consideration of pertinent factors critical to its determination of threat of material injury that led the Panel to conclude that the original SECOFI determination violated the AD Agreement.

1. SECOFI's Finding of Likelihood of Increased Imports was Based on Conjecture Rather than Evidence

3.87 The United States notes that in attempting to justify SECOFI's finding that there was a likelihood of increased imports of HFCS notwithstanding the restraint agreement, Mexico asserts that SECOFI based its redetermination "on facts and evidence corresponding to the investigation period and two comparable previous periods, as well as on estimates obtained using objective and reasonable methodologies."

3.88 In fact, according to the United States, this is precisely what SECOFI *failed* to do in its redetermination. The United States argues that SECOFI premised its finding that there is a likelihood of substantially increased imports not on facts and evidence corresponding to the period of investigation, but on conjecture and on projections that have no factual basis in the record and that are contrary to the facts that are in the record.

3.89 In particular, the United States argues, SECOFI's finding is premised on a projection that imports of HFCS from the United States by purchasers other than soft drink bottlers would increase from 1996 to 1998 by over twice the rate that purchases by all HFCS users increased from 1994 to 1996 (when soft drink bottlers consumed 68 per cent of HFCS imports and all other users consumed only 32 per cent of HFCS imports). The United States points out that although SECOFI's projection deviates markedly from the observed data during the period of investigation, its redetermination provides no basis why such a deviation is likely. Nor, according to the United States, does Mexico's First Written Submission explain how one can discern from the redetermination that SECOFI's projection is based either on "facts or evidence corresponding to the investigation periods" or on "objective and reasonable" methods of calculation.

3.90 Similarly, Mexico's First Written Submission does not explain how the redetermination justifies SECOFI's use of a 50 per cent substitution rate for all HFCS users other than soft drink bottlers.

3.91 According to the United States, the only information in the record pertaining to rate of substitution is information pertaining to the *theoretical* rate at which HFCS could be substituted for sugar in various products. The United States argues that a finding that HFCS users were likely to substitute HFCS for sugar merely because they could do so as a theoretical matter is sheer conjecture.

3.92 Even with respect to theoretical rates of substitution, the 50 per cent and 84 per cent substitution rates referenced by Mexico are not based on evidence in the record. The United States notes that the 84 per cent rate does not appear in the redetermination and Mexico provides no explanation of where the rate originated. Although the 50 per cent rate does appear in the redetermination, the United States asserts that it is not one based on evidence. Instead, asserts the United States, the 50 per cent rate appears to be something selected arbitrarily by SECOFI.

2. *SECOFI did not Adequately Analyze the Likely Impact of the Dumped Imports*

3.93 The United States does not dispute that SECOFI's redetermination provides a recitation of data concerning the Article 3.4 factors specified by the Panel. However the United States argues that this recitation alone is insufficient to satisfy Mexico's obligations under Article 3. The United States notes that the Panel Report, consistent with the findings of other panels, indicates that the AD Agreement requires an analysis of the pertinent information, not merely a reference to it. According to the United States, in its First Written Submission, Mexico neither challenges the reasoning of the prior panel decisions presented by the United States nor offers any of its own that would indicate that its mere recitation of data was sufficient.

3.94 The United States maintains that Mexico confirms that SECOFI's projections as to the likely levels of prices and profitability in the Mexican sugar industry are central to its analysis of likely impact. According to the United States, SECOFI's projections lead to results that are *directly contrary* to the actual experience of the Mexican sugar industry during SECOFI's period of investigation. SECOFI projected that increased HFCS imports would cause prices for domestically-produced sugar to decline in 1997. However, the United States notes, sugar prices actually increased during 1996 from their levels in 1995, notwithstanding increased imports. The United States points out that SECOFI also projected that the domestic sugar industry would incur an operating loss in 1997 because of the increased HFCS imports. By contrast, in 1996 the Mexican sugar industry was profitable, and profitability increased substantially over 1995. According to the United States, Mexico neither acknowledges nor explains the serious discrepancies between SECOFI's projections for 1997 and the observed data for 1996.

3.95 Mexico also emphasizes its affirmative threat determination is justified by the Mexican sugar industry's need to generate operating profits to allow it to service its high level of indebtedness. In the view of the United States this argument overlooks the fact that SECOFI made several findings in its redetermination that the domestic industry's positive operating results in 1996 improved the sugar industry's cash flow, thus enhancing its ability to obtain short-term financing and permitting it to improve its debt service indices. Thus, by SECOFI's own analysis, asserts the United States, the presence of increased volumes of imported HFCS does not necessarily impair the domestic industry's ability to raise capital and finance debt.

3.96 Consequently, the only support for Mexico's conclusion that SECOFI properly found that "given increased importation at dumped prices, the injury to the domestic industry would have manifested itself in the other indicators as well," is SECOFI's unexplained and seemingly conjectural projections. The projections, continues the United States, simply cannot be reconciled with the actual 1996 data for the Mexican sugar industry showing that indicators of industry performance improved while HFCS imports increased.

3. *SECOFI did not Adequately Explain its Analysis in Critical Respects*

3.97 In the view of the United States, Mexico's First Written Submission reinforces the problems caused by SECOFI's lack of explanation. For example, Mexico emphasizes that SECOFI's conclusion that an increase in import volume was likely notwithstanding the restraint agreement is premised on a projection which uses as an input a 50 per cent substitution rate of HFCS for sugar by purchasers other than soft drink bottlers. The United States asserts that nothing in SECOFI's redetermination or the administrative record explains how the 50 per cent figure was derived. According to the United States, it appears that SECOFI simply chose this figure arbitrarily. Similarly, Mexico refers to SECOFI's use of "simultaneous equations" for projecting sugar prices. But, according to the United States, Mexico provides no reference to anything in the record that would indicate either what data SECOFI inputted into these "simultaneous equations" or what the equations purport to represent.

3.98 In the view of the United States, Mexico's argument is not advanced by its statement that all material supporting SECOFI's redetermination need not be in the redetermination itself if it is available elsewhere in the administrative record. It is true, notes the United States, that under Article 12.2.2, an investigating authority may choose to make the matters of fact and law supporting the imposition of final measures available through a separate report. But, the United States asserts, Mexico has failed to identify any separate report, or even any portion of the administrative record, that provides the required explanation of the inputs it used for its projections.

D. *Second Written Submission of Mexico*

1. *Introduction*

3.99 Mexico recalls that its first written submission in this proceeding set out the facts and arguments which show that Mexico strictly complied with the conclusions and recommendation of the Dispute Settlement Body (DSB) in accordance with the report of the Panel that examined the case concerning *Mexico - High Fructose Corn Syrup (HFCS) from the United States* of 14 January 2000[16] (Panel Report). Accordingly, Mexico responded in general terms to the position taken by the United States in its first written submission.

3.100 However, inasmuch as this second written submission is a rebuttal, Mexico asserts that its fundamental purpose is to provide a more specific reply to the United States arguments by presenting facts and counter-arguments which will confirm for the Panel that Mexico has strictly complied with the DSB's conclusions and recommendations by:

(a) Adequately considering the impact of dumped imports on the domestic industry and determining threat of injury to the industry as a whole; and

(b) adequately analysing the potential effect of the alleged restraint agreement on the likelihood of substantially increased importation, in accordance with Article 3.7(i) of the AD Agreement.

3.101 According to Mexico, it has remedied the deficiencies in SECOFI's threat of injury analysis, bringing it into conformity with the requirements of Article 3 of the AD Agreement, in addition to adequately fulfilling the requirements of Articles 12.2 and 12.2.2 of the AD Agreement.

3.102 Thus, Mexico argues that it has brought its final anti-dumping measure into conformity with the obligations imposed on Mexico by the AD Agreement in respect of each and all of the aspects found to be inconsistent with the Agreement in the Panel Report.

3.103 Moreover, in its first written submission Mexico recalls that it expressed its concern at the inadequate translation into English of the revised final resolution[17], which was submitted by the United States as exhibit "US-1". However, bearing in mind that it is a document of key importance for an understanding of the actions taken by SECOFI, Mexico notes that it has made an effort to revise and submit as an annex to this second submission a more adequate translation of the revised final resolution of 20 September 2000[18], specifically to avoid errors or confusion and to facilitate the work of some English-speaking members of the Panel and of the WTO Secretariat.

---

16 *Mexico-Anti-dumping Investigation of High Fructose Corn Syrup (HFCS) from the United States*, WT/DS132/R, adopted 24 February 2000 (hereinafter "Panel Report, WT/DS132/R"), DSR 2000:III, 1345.

17 Notice of Redetermination, MEXICO-1.

18 See MEXICO-1(a).

2. *Mexico Complied with the Conclusions and Recommendation of the Panel and the Dispute Settlement Body*

(a) SECOFI Examined the Probable Impact of HFCS Imports on the Domestic Industry and Has Determined Threat of Injury on the Basis of the Industry as a Whole

3.104 According to Mexico, SECOFI revised and conducted a new review of the resulting impact of HFCS imports on the domestic industry, including an adequate assessment of the economic factors referred to in Articles 3.4 and 3.7 of the AD Agreement and on the basis of a variety of positive evidence and facts, which led to confirmation of the determination of threat of injury.

3.105 Mexico rejects the United States arguments, for the revised final resolution includes all relevant issues and findings of the new SECOFI analysis of trends in economic factors in order to determine the resulting impact of HFCS imports on the domestic industry as a whole, in both real and potential terms and was not confined to reciting data, as suggested by the United States.[19]

3.106 In Mexico's view, SECOFI did not mischaracterize the data at its disposal, since the analysis of employment and use of installed capacity was conducted objectively, without hiding or mischaracterizing the increase in those variables. Moreover, the fact that in the period of investigation, the sugar industry's sales declined to the same extent as did sales to the industrial sector is coincidental, since the variations in volume are different.[20] Similarly, if the United States cannot reconcile 100 per cent of the sweetener market or the increase in productivity in the industry, it is because it used the wrong data for its calculations.[21]

3.107 Again, Mexico is of the view that no attempts should be made to minimize the analysis of the variables which already showed in the period of investigation the genuinely adverse impact of HFCS imports from the United States, as in the case of sugar sales to the domestic market, the market loss of production oriented to the domestic market and trends in stocks; given the likelihood of increased imports, these factors would be projected as being more seriously affected, to the detriment of the other factors affecting the domestic industry.

3.108 Mexico asserts that it adequately complied with the Panel's findings concerning price analysis, particularly those contained in paragraphs 7.141, 7.151, 7.152 and 7.153 of the Panel Report. According to Mexico, paragraphs 80 to 126

---

[19] See Notice of Redetermination, MEXICO-1, *inter alia* paras. 128 to 166.

[20] See "Table of industrial sector indicators" MEXICO-3, and "Table of total standard and refined sugar sales (household and industrial sector)" MEXICO-4.

[21] See "Productivity table" MEXICO-5, and "Methodology employed in statistical calculations (analysis of imports and economic indicators)" MEXICO-6, as well as para. 26 of Mexico's first written submission.

of the revised final resolution contain a review of trends in the prices of HFCS imports from the United States and the prices of domestically produced sugar during the investigation period and the two comparable earlier periods, together with the projected future trends in the price of both products.

3.109 Mexico notes that the United States alleges that SECOFI's projections of future trends in sugar prices for 1997 were based on assumptions contrary to the data observed in 1996 and that SECOFI did not show that sugar prices declined during the investigation period as a result of dumped HFCS imports. In addition, the United States indicates that, although the increased price differentials in the case of very close substitutes might support a finding of injury or threat of injury, but that SECOFI acknowledged that HFCS and sugar are not close substitutes.[22]

3.110 In this connection, Mexico asserts that *no* such acknowledgement exists and that, even though there are differences in the degrees of substitution, both products are substitutes in a range of industrial applications. In Mexico's view, the United States is trying to divert the Panel's attention to a topic which was fully documented in the determination of likeness in the original final resolution and one which - it is important to recall - was *not* the subject of a challenge by the United States.

3.111 Again, according to Mexico, SECOFI demonstrated to the Panel - and this is fully documented in the administrative record of the anti-dumping investigation - that in the period of investigation, such substitution occurred in the reproduction processes in the baking, beverages (other than soft drinks), dairy and processed food industries, in addition to the soft drink industry. Moreover, asserts Mexico, there is a consensus among experts on the sweetener industry that, precisely because of the existing substitution between sugar and HFCS in the industrial sector, the prices of both goods are linked, and that both the existing differentials between them and the movements in one or other price have proven effects on the conditions of competition in the industry.

3.112 Mexico argues that SECOFI also demonstrated the adverse impact of the prices of the investigated imports on the domestic prices during the investigation period, on the basis of a detailed analysis of month-by-month trends in the prices of sugar and HFCS, the margins of undercutting and dumping calculated for the imports investigated, statistical evidence of causality and the prevailing economic environment, and particularly the "natural difference" between the prices of the two products.[23]

---

[22] Mexico notes that, according to the United States, Mexico so acknowledged in paras. 5.568 and 5.569 in the Panel Report, WT/DS132/R. See footnote 51 to the first written submission of the United States.

[23] See the "Summary tables on annual and monthly margins of undercutting between HFCS and sugar from 1994 to 1996", MEXICO-7, the "Table of HFCS and sugar prices in the United States from 1991 to 1996", MEXICO-8, the translation of the relevant part of the note on "Trade in Sweeteners in the North America Region" published in *Sugar and Sweetener Yearbook*, MEXICO-9, and the translation of the relevant parts of the publication *Sugar and Sweeteners* for various dates be-

3.113 Mexico points out that the price trends observed in 1996 show that greater import penetration was connected with increased undercutting and declining HFCS prices in relation to sugar. While average prices in 1996 were higher than the year before, according to Mexico, this development is explained by the adverse economic conditions observed in 1995. Consequently, Mexico argues, the basis of comparison highlighted by the United States in its argument fails to note that in 1996, compared with 1994, as well as during the investigation period, sugar prices declined in a context of growing imports, lower prices and an increase in the price differential between the two products.[24]

3.114 Furthermore, SECOFI estimated the prices of both products for 1997 on the basis of the analysis carried out and the recorded monthly trend from 1994 to 1996 in the prices of HFCS imports from the United States and the domestic selling price for sugar. Mexico claims that the method of estimation employed was a system of simultaneous equations using a vector autoregressive model, and the result was compared with the observed trend in the values of the variables incorporated (prices and volumes), and checked by reference to the consistency of the forecasts with the economic context and the conditions in the industry during the period analysed.[25]

3.115 In short, according to Mexico, the arguments put forward by the United States concerning SECOFI's price analysis in the revised final resolution are completely unfounded and should be rejected. According to Mexico, it has been shown that Mexico's determination was based, *inter alia*, on positive evidence and an objective examination of past trends and of projections of prices of the investigated imports and their actual and potential impact on the prices of domestically produced sugar, in conformity with the Panel's findings and conclusions in this respect.

3.116 Mexico points out that the United States argues that the positive trends in industry profitability and other factors determined by SECOFI contradict the conclusion that the sugar industry faced a threat of material injury. Mexico rejects the United States arguments because it claims that SECOFI conducted an objective analysis of the probable impact on the industry's profits[26] without confining itself merely to including data on that factor, as suggested by the United

tween 1995 and 1996, MEXICO-10. According to Mexico, these documents, together with other working papers, support SECOFI's conclusion set out in the revised final resolution.

24 In this connection, Mexico claims that SECOFI examined the level and trends in the weighted average prices of HFCS-42 and HFCS-45 imports from the United States in relation to the weighted average prices of standard and refined sugar sold on the domestic market in 1994, 1995 and 1996. Pursuant to the finding contained in para. 7.153 of the Panel Report, WT/DS132/R, Mexico asserts that the average sales prices of sugar on the domestic market were calculated on the basis of sales volumes and values for the whole of the domestic industry. In other words, according to Mexico, consideration was given to sales of standard and refined sugar to both the industrial and the household sectors. See the table on sugar sales to the domestic market in MEXICO-11.

25 See "Methodological note on the projection of sugar and HFCS prices for 1997", MEXICO-12.

26 See MEXICO-13.

States. In fact, notes Mexico, SECOFI's analysis recognizes the positive trend in profits, whereas the United States fails to mention that SECOFI carried out a sensitivity analysis of the Mexican sugar industry[27], which was done on the basis of established methodologies such as the degree of operational and financial leverage, which are amply explained in the "*Methodological Note on the Financial Report on Injury (HFCS)*".[28]

3.117 In this regard, it was determined that a 1 per cent change in sales revenue involves a 7 per cent variation in the industry's operating profits, which shows that sensitivity was very high in 1996. Using projections of sugar prices and volumes, SECOFI obtained a projection of domestic sugar industry earnings which showed that sales revenue for 1997 would decline by 15 per cent, and operating profits by 118 per cent. Similarly, according to Mexico, its calculation of projected profitability for 1997 indicated a 12 percentage points decline in the operating margin compared with the previous period.

3.118 In Mexico's view, another matter which conclusively demonstrates the Mexican sugar industry's high sensitivity is the ability to raise capital, since the analysis of the industry's leverage[29] showed an excessively high debt level in 1996, with a ratio of total liability to book capital of 4.6 times, placing the industry in a situation of low net investment and high debt levels exposing it to high financial risk. SECOFI acknowledged that the industry's debt is a structural problem and not a consequence of revenue from dumped imports; in other words, it took account of the prevailing situation of domestic production in 1996 and its sensibility, concluding that with such a debt level the risk to the industry is high and, hence, the financial situation is vulnerable, so that any future change might alter the profits trend of earlier periods by directing more resources to debt servicing.

3.119 On the basis of the matters set out in this section, Mexico emphatically rejects the United States arguments that Mexico did not conduct an analysis in conformity with the provisions of Articles 3.1, 3.4 and 3.7 of the AD Agreement. On the contrary, Mexico reiterates that SECOFI acted in strict compliance with each and every one of the Panel's findings and conclusions so as to bring its measure into conformity, *inter alia*, with those provisions of the AD Agreement.

---

[27] See MEXICO-15.

[28] See MEXICO-14.

[29] See MEXICO-13 and MEXICO-16.

(b) SECOFI Analysed the Potential Effects of the Alleged Restraint Agreement on the Likelihood of Substantially Increased Importation, in a Manner Consistent with Article 3.7(I) of the AD Agreement

3.120 In accordance with the findings of the Panel Report, particularly those contained in paragraphs 7.176 and 7.177, Mexico maintains that it adequately considered the potential effects of the alleged restraint agreement on the likelihood of substantially increased importation, thereby making its determination consistent with Article 3.7 of the AD Agreement.

3.121 Mexico rejects the United States allegation that SECOFI confined itself to repeating the same information and the same conclusions that it had previously submitted to the Panel. According to Mexico, SECOFI, in this new analysis, considered the information provided previously to the Panel, that it was not the only information considered by the investigating authority. In fact, the Panel's finding obliged Mexico to take more elements into account and to provide an additional explanation to that contained in the original final resolution and not, as the United States suggests, that the explanation or additional data in question should be relative to the information previously submitted to the Panel.

3.122 Mexico argues that, according to the finding contained in paragraph 7.175 of the Panel Report, the question to be resolved by Mexico was whether, in the near future relative to the investigation period, even if the soft drink bottlers' HFCS consumption were limited, the likelihood of substantially increased importation would persist. Mexico considered that determination of the prospects concerning the future behaviour of imports does not depend exclusively on one single factor, such as the alleged restraint on consumption by one group of users, but that it is also necessary to take account of competing factors.

3.123 Therefore, Mexico asserts that SECOFI considered the trends observed during the investigation period and comparable earlier periods in prices, volumes, actual and potential consumption, economic context and conditions in the industry. In the light of these data for the period investigated, Mexico claims that SECOFI found that, in the situation envisaged, there was still good reason to believe that there would be substantially increased importation in the near future.

3.124 Mexico rejects the United States interpretation that the likelihood of increased imports is determined from the date of publication of the original final resolution. Mexico argues that SECOFI's determination is based not only on the increase in imports already recorded in 1997, as the United States suggests. Mexico adopted the point made by the Panel in paragraph 7.176 of the report so as to determine the existence of such a likelihood on the basis of anticipated import trends in the near future relative to the period investigated, i.e. in 1997, using a forward-looking analysis of a present situation, i.e. the period investigated,

1996.[30] In Mexico's view[31], if such a determination were based on import trends observed during the conduct of the investigation itself, inadequate consideration would be given both to trade flows and to consumption forecasts distorted by the effects of the initiation of the anti-dumping investigation.[32]

3.125 Mexico claims that it based its case on the actual situation observed among industrial users of HFCS and sugar in 1996 and the result of the review carried out in the original investigation on the commercial interchangeability, uses and functions of both products.[33] Mexico argues that the United States is trying to disregard its own experience in substituting HFCS for sugar in applications other than soft drink bottlers, such as milk, confectionery and bakery products and various beverages and foods.[34]

3.126 Mexico asserts that its determination was based on actual sugar consumption figures from 1994 to 1996 of industrial users other than soft drink bottlers, and on the actual rates of utilisation of HFCS recorded in 1996 by those industrial users, who were requested to provide information on the consumption of sweeteners in their production processes.[35] Mexico also asserts that SECOFI considered rates of HFCS substitution for sugar supplied by the main importer for the period investigated, which were obtained from a recognized economic consultancy firm. Mexico argues that SECOFI determined the likelihood of increased importation by considering the effects of the alleged restraint agreement, on the basis of an estimate of potential HFCS consumption by sectors other than soft drink bottlers in 1997 and 1998, using as an input projections by specialists

---

30 According to Mexico, it is obvious that, in the circumstances of an anti-dumping investigation, a forward-looking analysis of this nature by the investigating authority with regard to imports beyond or outside the period investigated cannot be extended indefinitely and must have a certain cut-off point, although the AD Agreement lays down no specific requirement in this respect.

31 When the analysis of imports within the investigation period and the forward-looking analysis outside the investigation period show not only an increasing trend but substantial increases compared with previous levels (combined with the proven buoyancy of those levels), Mexico asserts that they should be considered for purposes of a determination of the likelihood of substantially increased importation.

32 Mexico notes that the effect of reduced imports as a result of anti-dumping investigations was analysed and documented by *Staiger and Wolak* in the articles mentioned in MEXICO-18.

33 See paras. 400 to 422 of the original final resolution as well as the note on "Substitution of HFCS for sugar in the USA", MEXICO-19.

34 See in MEXICO-19 the note on substitution of HFCS for sugar in the United States. In addition, Mexico claims that the administrative record includes various studies and analyses on development of the HFCS in the United States that fully document the pattern of demand and replacement of sugar by HFCS in industries other than soft drink bottlers.

35 Paragraphs 65 to 93 of the original final resolution refer to the industrial users other than soft drink bottlers who were asked for information on their sugar and HFCS consumption during the period investigated, as well as the replies of those users, on the basis of which the **actual** rates of substitution in 1996 were calculated. See the information and summary tables describing the degrees of substitutability between HFCS and sugar documented by SECOFI in MEXICO-20.

of total sugar consumption for those years, and applying those sectors' share of total consumption as recorded in 1994, 1995 and 1996.[36]

3.127 According to Mexico, the main aspects of the economic context in which the determination of the likelihood of increased imports was made include: (a) the growth rate of the imports investigated from 1994 to 1996; (b) the export potential of the United States HFCS industry; (c) the price differential recorded during the investigation period between HFCS and sugar, which is an incentive for substitution; (d) the non-existence of trade restrictions on imports and a decline in tariff rates of such imports; and (e) the proven functionality of HFCS as a sugar substitute in a variety of industries in the Mexican market, further supported by the accumulated experience of the development of the United States market.

3.128 Furthermore, contrary to the United States contention, Mexico notes that it *did not* state that HFCS consumption in 1996 by soft drink bottlers and by other industries was similar, which does not mean that potential consumption by those industries is insignificant. While soft drink bottlers stand out as the main sugar consumers, Mexico points out that the other industries, particularly those which already consumed HFCS in the period of investigation, demand a substantial volume of sugar likely to be displaced by a low-cost substitute product.[37] Thus, in a context in which HFCS prices are depressed relative to sugar prices and in the absence of any distortion of trade flows, industrial users other than soft drink bottlers would have economic incentives to substitute dumped-cost HFCS imports for sugar.

3.129 According to Mexico, the United States erroneously alleges that SECOFI did not have at its disposal information to demonstrate that HFCS users other than soft drink bottlers were actually substituting HFCS for sugar during the period of investigation.[38] Mexico rejects this argument, because it claims that it did in fact obtain information, *directly* from industrial users on HFCS consumption in their production processes, and it is attached to this written submission.[39]

3.130 Mexico recalls that the United States argued that the conjectural basis for the SECOFI determination is reflected in the scale of the estimated substitution and in the assumption that soft drink bottlers would not consume imported HFCS. Mexico categorically rejects the United States interpretation. First of all, according to Mexico, SECOFI's estimate relies on an objective and admissible economic analysis, taking into account the actual conditions prevailing in the Mexican market, which provided reasonable grounds for the likelihood of HFCS

---

[36] Mexico notes that MEXICO-21 contains the projections of total sugar consumption for 1997 and 1998 on which SECOFI based its work and which were obtained from a paper by Peter Bazanall, a recognized expert on sweeteners, and from an estimate contained in a report by the United States Department of Agriculture (USDA).

[37] See in MEXICO-21 the "Table on actual sugar consumption by sector".

[38] See para. 31 of the first written submission by the United States.

[39] See MEXICO-20.

being substituted for sugar, as shown, *inter alia*, by the trend observed during the period analysed, 1994-1996. In Mexico's view, under a forward-looking hypothesis for 1997, the restrictive effect of the alleged agreement would not be crucial in curbing the increase in demand for HFCS imports by soft drink bottlers. Furthermore, Mexico claims it has been shown that HFCS demand from other industries would be strengthened and they would increasingly substitute HFCS for their sugar consumption.[40]

3.131 Mexico argues that the elements in support of SECOFI's conclusion are stronger than those that might support a conclusion of the kind the United States is seeking to impose[41], *i.e.*, that, given the existence of the alleged agreement and notwithstanding the probable economic framework for substitution, the other sugar-consuming industries would simply abandon the market or, if necessary, revert to their consumption pattern under the conditions existing before the introduction of HFCS in their production processes.

3.132 On the basis of the points made in this section, Mexico maintains before this Panel that SECOFI's review and final conclusion about its analysis of the potential effects of the alleged restraint agreement on the determination of the likelihood of increased importation was based not on conjecture or remote possibility, but on a forward-looking analysis of the situation observed during the period under investigation, following an objective, legitimate and reasonable examination of the information contained in the administrative record.[42] According-

---

[40] Taking into account the key characteristics of the foreseeable economic context for 1997 in accordance with the points made in para. 51 of the second written submission.

[41] Mexico argues that the United States is attempting to impose a standard of analysis and a conclusion that would absurdly require the authority to obtain information concerning the alleged restraint agreement, which neither Article 3 nor any other provision of the AD Agreement requires for a determination of threat of injury, since this would imply that SECOFI should have precise knowledge and information concerning the validity, compulsory nature and actual application of the alleged agreement. Mexico claims that knowledge of these elements and possession of information based thereon is impossible in both practical and legal terms, given the time-scale of the investigation and the powers of the investigating authority. Hence, according to Mexico, SECOFI could not simply make arbitrary and vague assumptions about them outside the period investigated. In fact, in Mexico's opinion, an analysis of the type suggested as appropriate by the United States would have been possible if it had been shown that authority should arrive at a determination based on conjecture and remote possibility, rather than on facts as required by the AD Agreement.

[42] Mexico points out that, as it indicated in its first written submission, in order to comply with the Panel recommendation adopted by the DSB, SECOFI considered it appropriate and sufficient to incorporate in the review file the information submitted in the course of the original investigation by the Corn Refiners Association. According to Mexico, despite the fact that the information in question had been submitted too late (one day before publication of the original final resolution) and could not therefore be taken into account in the ordinary investigation, it was appropriate in the circumstances to incorporate it legally in the record of this proceeding so that it could be taken into account and the terms of the alleged restraint agreement could thus somehow be ascertained. On the basis of that information, Mexico asserts that SECOFI observed that the alleged restraint agreement would apparently have the potential effect of limiting HFCS consumption by soft drink bottlers to 350,000 tons (MEXICO-2). Mexico notes that this information on the terms of the alleged restraint agreement was considered adequate, since para. 7.175 of the Panel Report, WT/DS132/R, stated that

ingly, Mexico contends that its determination is consistent with Article 3.7 of the AD Agreement and that it strictly complies with the findings and recommendation of the Panel Report.

(c) Mexico Complied with the Provisions of Articles 12.2 and 12.2.2 of the AD Agreement

3.133 Mexico notes that the United States alleges that SECOFI's revised final resolution is inconsistent with the provisions of Articles 12.2 and 12.2.2 of the AD Agreement, based on the erroneous assumption that SECOFI analysed the probable impact of imports on the domestic industry using economic models and projections of industry trends, the results of which were based on unexplained data relating to the state of the industry. In this connection, Mexico firstly rejects the United States argument that SECOFI does not provide adequate information about its analysis and the data on which the methodology employed was based. Similarly it categorically opposes the United States suggestion that SECOFI's findings, based on various economic models and projections should be rejected because of their allegedly "conjectural" nature.[43]

3.134 In this same context, Mexico totally rejects the interpretation by the United States in paragraph 54 of its first written submission, where, with reference to Articles 12.2 and 12.2.2 of the AD Agreement, it states that "[...] When an investigating authority chooses to base its determination on the results of an economic model or forecast, information concerning the data used as inputs in the model or forecast is clearly 'relevant information' for purposes of determination".[44]

3.135 Mexico maintains that the relevant information referred to in these articles, particularly Article 12.2.2, does not necessarily have to consist of the data used by the investigating authority in the economic models and projections on which its analysis and determination were based. In fact, Mexico asserts that Article 12.2 does not lay down any precise formulas or specific terms in which an authority is required to express its findings or conclusions in the public notice. On the contrary, it simply states in general terms that these will relate to the issues considered material by the investigating authority. Nor does Article 12.2.2 lay down any specific formulas or terms, and even though it does in fact require the inclusion of all relevant information on the matters of fact and law and reasons which have led to the imposition of final measures, it does not specify what

---

the question was not whether an alleged restraint agreement existed, but whether its potential effects on the likelihood of dumped imports increasing in the near future had been adequately considered in the analysis. Nevertheless, Mexico claims that, from the United States' standpoint, no information that could have been available to any authority under international anti-dumping practice in a case of this kind would have been sufficient for the purposes of the analysis suggested as appropriate by the United States.

43 See paras. 6 and 53 of the first written submission of the United States.

44 *Ibid.*, para. 54.

that information should be. Rather, according to its own wording, it takes as limiting factors the relevance and confidentiality of the information.

3.136 Mexico argues that it is clear that the United States is once again attempting to base its argument on an excessive and inadmissible interpretation of Articles 12.2 and 12.2.2 of the AD Agreement when it suggests that the notice should include the data that were used by the investigating authority in the economic models and projections on which its analysis and determination were based. In Mexico's opinion, this interpretation and the absurd suggestion by the United States is even contrary to the spirit of the last sentence of Article 12.2.2, which expressly calls for due regard to be paid by the authority to "the protection of confidential information". Mexico maintains that this means that the authority is entitled to consider that certain information should be left out of the notice and be included in the administrative record in such a way as to protect the confidentiality of that information.

3.137 It is therefore clear, according to Mexico, that no valid interpretation of the AD Agreement could warrant the view that the scope of these provisions implies that the final public notice must contain explanations concerning the data on which the methodology used by the authority in its models and projections is based.

3.138 Nor do any of the Panel Report's findings and conclusions contain this implication, argues Mexico. Mexico points out that, despite the fact that the findings and conclusions of the Panel Report in this connection did not deal directly with Article 12, since the United States arguments related not to this provision but to Article 3, the Panel, in finding that Mexico had failed to comply with its obligations under Article 3, also simultaneously concerned itself with establishing what requirements had to be met by a final determination, and it even referred expressly to Article 12.2.2.[45] However, according to Mexico, none of the relevant findings or conclusions of the Panel is consistent with the United States position and its inadmissible interpretation of Article 12.2.2.

3.139 Mexico maintains that is has complied with the standard established by the Panel, particularly with paragraphs 7.128[46] and 7.140[47] as follows:

- SECOFI carried out a review of the impact of HFCS imports on the domestic industry, which, included an adequate evaluation of the economic factors referred to in Articles 3.4 and 3.7 of the AD

[45] See footnote 610 of the Panel Report, WT/DS132/R.

[46] In this connection, in the last part of para. 7.128 of the Panel Report, WT/DS132/R, the Panel stated that "[...] the consideration of each of the Article 3.4 factors must be apparent in the final determination of the investigating authority" (footnote omitted).

[47] Apart from what was stated in para. 7.140, footnote 610 of the Panel Report, WT/DS132/R, indicated that: "[...] the mere recitation of data does not constitute explanation, or findings and conclusions, sufficient to satisfy the requirements of Article 12.2 of the AD Agreement [...]" and it adds that "[...] unless consideration of a factor is reflected in the final determination, we do not take cognizance of underlying evidence in the record [...]".

Agreement. On the basis of a variety of positive evidence and facts - not conjecture as suggested by the United States - that review led it to confirm its determination of a threat of injury to the domestic sugar industry.

- The final notice of 20 September was not confined to reciting data, as asserted by the United States. Paragraphs 128 to 166, *inter alia*[48], of the revised final resolution provide sufficiently detailed explanations of the findings, conclusions and relevant information contained in the new analysis of trends in economic factors conducted by SECOFI in ascertaining the resulting impact of HFCS imports on the domestic industry as a whole, in both real and potential terms, as well as the reasons which led SECOFI to confirm the final measure, with due regard for the protection of confidential information.
- SECOFI's findings related to the whole of the domestic industry, based on data and information duly documented in the record, as well as on models and projections constituting reasonable methodologies which were also justified in the record by means of methodological notes explaining how SECOFI proceeded in various calculations.[49]

3.140 Mexico also maintains that, in accordance with the findings and conclusions of the Panel Report, particularly those contained in paragraphs 7.176 and 7.177[50], SECOFI took into account additional items of relevant information in order to analyse the potential effects of the alleged restraint agreement and arrive at an adequate determination of the likelihood of a substantial increase in HFCS imports. Thus, from paragraph 55 onwards, the revised final resolution includes a more detailed explanation than that contained in the original final resolution, which sets forth in adequate detail the findings and conclusions which led SECOFI to determine that the potential effects of the alleged restraint agreement did not eliminate the well-founded likelihood of substantially increased HFCS imports. Mexico asserts that that determination is not based on conjecture, allegation or remote possibility, as contended by the United States, but on facts and

---

48 In this connection, Mexico points out once again that the revised final resolution closing the procedure followed by SECOFI for the specific purpose of complying with the recommendation adopted by the DSB complements and amends the original final resolution (of 23 January 1998) in all those aspects reviewed by the investigating authority, because the Panel had considered them to be inconsistent with the AD Agreement.

49 See, *inter alia*, exhibits MEXICO-6 "Methodology employed in statistical calculations (analysis of imports and economic indicators"), MEXICO-12 "Methodological note on 1997 price forecasts for sugar and HFCS", MEXICO-14 "Methodological note on the financial report on injury (HFCS)" and MEXICO-21 "Methodological note on analysis of the likelihood of increased importation".

50 As mentioned earlier, Mexico asserts that on this point the United States raised no argument concerning the requirements of Article 12 of the AD Agreement. It is for this reason that the conclusions of the Panel Report refer to inconsistency with Article 3.7(i). Nevertheless, on this subject, Mexico also considered that, in order to implement the DSB recommendation, it was essential to bear in mind that, in its findings, the Panel had also dealt with this aspect of the required content of the final determination.

evidence which support the conclusion of a well-founded likelihood of increased importation despite the existence of the alleged restraint agreement.

3.141 Mexico also refutes three specific examples mentioned by the United States in an attempt to justify its argument that SECOFI did not adequately explain the use of projections of industry trends.[51]

- the United States questions the alleged use by SECOFI of a 50 per cent substitution rate in respect of industrial users other than soft drink bottlers[52], so as to conclude that there was a likelihood of increased importation. On this point, Mexico claims that the United States confuses the degree of substitution in the various industries with the potential consumption of sugar liable to substitution by HFCS, to which Mexico refers in paragraph 59 of the revised final resolution.[53]
- the United States suggests that SECOFI did not adequately explain the use of data in pricing models and projections or the methodology used and that SECOFI's sugar price projections for 1997 were based on assumptions contrary to the data observed in 1996.[54] Mexico contends that, on the basis of the analysis carried out and the recorded monthly trend from 1994 to 1996 in the prices of HFCS imports from the United States and the domestic selling prices for sugar, SECOFI estimated the prices of both products for 1997. The method of estimation employed was a system of simultaneous equations using a vector autoregressive model. The result was compared with the observed trend in the values of the variables incorporated and checked by reference to the consistency of those forecasts with the economic context and conditions in the industry during the period analysed.[55] Mexico points out that paragraph 98 of the revised final resolution clearly sets out the information used in the projections. The source of the information and the way it was obtained are described in paragraphs 85 and 86 of the resolution.
- Finally, the United States questions SECOFI's use of the projection that industry sales revenue would decline by 15 per cent.[56] Mexico

---

[51] See para. 55 and, in part, para. 53 of the first written submission of the United States.

[52] *Ibid.*, second part of para. 55.

[53] See MEXICO-21 which, according to Mexico, shows that the 1996 substitution rate was applied to the estimated consumption of sugar-consuming industries for 1997 and 1998 so as to calculate each industry's potential consumption, and a 50 per cent reduction rate was applied to the total of such potential consumption in order to obtain an objective yet conservative estimate of potential demand. See also paras. 63 and footnote 48 of Mexico's second submission.

[54] See the second part of para. 55 of the first written submission by the United States and footnote 68.

[55] See "Methodological note on projected sugar and HFCS prices for 1997", MEXICO-12. See also paras. 20 to 24 of Mexico's second submission.

[56] See para. 55 and footnote 68 of the first written submission of the United States.

asserts that the United States is mistaken in stating that the revised final resolution does not provide data on projected sales revenue. In fact, paragraph 152 of the revised final resolution contains a detailed explanation of how the investigating authority calculated projected revenue. The United States assertion is therefore totally false.[57]

3.142 On the basis of all the arguments set forth herein, Mexico rejects the United States position, which Mexico claims is clearly based on an excessive and inadmissible interpretation of Articles 12.2 and 12.2.2 of the AD Agreement, and reiterates to the Panel that Mexico has adequately complied with those provisions.

3. Conclusions

3.143 On the basis of the foregoing, and in accordance with the timetable established for this proceeding, Mexico submits its rebuttal of the arguments put forward by the United States in its first written submission, with the aim of adequately establishing the facts and setting forth the counter-arguments which will confirm to the Panel that Mexico has strictly complied with the conclusions and recommendations of the Panel and the DSB, inasmuch as it has remedied the shortcoming in the threat of injury analysis and brought its final determination into conformity with the requirements of Article 3 of the AD Agreement, while at the same time complying with Articles 12.2 and 12.2.2 of the Agreement.

3.144 Mexico also requests the Panel to declare that its revised final determination concerning the threat of material injury to the domestic sugar industry, including (i) its consideration of the impact of HFCS imports on the Mexican sugar industry as a whole; (ii) its consideration of the potential effects of the alleged restraint agreement on the likelihood of substantially increased importation; and (iii) its explanation, in the revised final resolution, of the findings and conclusions reached by SECOFI with regard to those questions, fully complies with the conclusions and recommendations of the Panel and the DSB and is consistent with Articles 3.1, 3.4, 3.7, 12.2 and 12.2.2 of the AD Agreement.

E. Oral Statement of the United States

3.145 The United States argues that there are three specific grounds on which SECOFI's redetermination violates the AD Agreement.

---

[57] See paras. 36 and 37 of Mexico's second submission, as well as the tables "Projected income for 1997" MEXICO-16, "Calculation of fixed and variable costs in accordance with the degree of operating leverage" MEXICO-17, and "Methodological note on the financial report on injury" MEXICO-14, and paras. 153, 154 and 166 of the revised final resolution.

1. The Restraint Agreement and Article 3.7(i)

3.146 According to the United States, the redetermination, like the original determination, violates Article 3.7 of the AD Agreement because it provides no basis for the conclusion that there is a likelihood of substantially increased importation of HFCS from the United States.

3.147 In this respect, the United States considers it noteworthy that the redetermination's analysis of the restraint agreement between Mexican soft drink bottlers and sugar refiners contains almost exactly the same flaws as the arguments Mexico presented in the original Panel proceeding.

3.148 Specifically, according to the United States, the Panel rejected SECOFI's original analysis because SECOFI improperly premised its analysis on alleged increases in imports from 1996, the time of the conclusion of its period of investigation, rather than from the third quarter of 1997, the latest period for which its record contained data on the volume of imports from the United States. The United States notes that the Panel concluded that "the question for purposes of analysis of threat of material injury is not the level of imports already reached, but the likelihood of **increased** imports" and criticized SECOFI for "conclud[ing] that such imports would have continued increasing by inertia."

3.149 Yet, the United States argues, SECOFI's redetermination provides the same flawed analysis. The United States notes that SECOFI concluded that increased imports were likely in part because imports from the United States during the first three quarters of 1997 exceeded the levels of the previous year. Moreover, SECOFI did not claim that these increases were attributable to purchasers not subject to the restraint agreement. The restraint agreement was not announced until September 1997. Therefore, increased imports of HFCS by soft drink bottlers between January and September 1997 would not be likely to continue after September 1997 because of the existence of the restraint agreement. Indeed, the United States recalls, SECOFI assumed that after the restraint agreement took effect all of the soft drink bottlers' consumption of HFCS would be supplied from Mexican HFCS production.

3.150 The United States notes that the Panel also found SECOFI's original analysis to be improper because SECOFI found merely that the restraint agreement "does not rule out the possibility" of future imports.

3.151 In paragraph 56 of the redetermination, SECOFI again makes conclusions regarding the possibility of increased imports notwithstanding the restraint agreement.

3.152 The United States points out that the Panel also found SECOFI's analysis to be improper on a third ground. It found that SECOFI's determination did not provide any analysis to support a conclusion that there was a likelihood that users other than soft drink bottlers would increase their importation of HFCS.

3.153 According to the United States, the information on which SECOFI relies in its redetermination is not materially different from the information the Panel previously considered and rejected.

3.154 SECOFI has projected that imports of HFCS by purchasers other than soft drink bottlers would increase by 467 per cent, from approximately 62,000 tons in 1996 to 350,000 tons in 1998. According to the United States, this rate of increase is more than double the rate by which total HFCS imports from the United States - including those by the soft drink bottlers now covered by the restraint agreement - increased during SECOFI's period of investigation. SECOFI provides no information in its redetermination why purchases by these HFCS users, which only accounted for approximately one-third of HFCS consumption in 1996, would be likely to increase at such an astonishing rate.

3.155 SECOFI's estimate of the likely volume of HFCS imports by purchasers other than soft drink bottlers is based on a series of computations. According to the United States, a careful examination of these computations reveals that notwithstanding Mexico's claims to the contrary, they are not based on the actual purchasing patterns of users of HFCS. Instead, the United States asserts, they are based on speculation and conjecture.

3.156 In the view of the United States, there are two fundamental flaws with SECOFI's computations. The first relates to Mexico's claim that: "In 1996, the weighted average rate of utilization in consumer industries other than soft drink bottling was 84 per cent."

3.157 This 84 per cent figure appears nowhere in SECOFI's redetermination. It appears that the 84 per cent figure is a weighted average of theoretical or technical substitution rates of HFCS for sugar for the various types of industries listed in Exhibit Mexico-21.

3.158 It is noteworthy, the United States argues, that the list of purchasing industries and substitution rates in Mexico-21 is not identical to the only listing of substitution rates in the redetermination. That listing appears at paragraph 57 of the redetermination. According to the United States, Mexico claims that this rate reflects data obtained directly from industrial users on HFCS consumption in their purchasing process. The United States further asserts that Mexico apparently would like the Panel to believe that this data reflects the actual rate that these users substituted HFCS for sugar in 1996.

3.159 This is not the case, argues the United States. The data in Mexico-20, insofar as used by SECOFI as the basis for the substitution rates used in Mexico-21, pertain merely to purchasers' technical *ability* to substitute HFCS for sugar. Indeed, Mexico-20 describes these substitution rates as the "technical" degrees of substitution. The United States asserts that this information is different from the material that Mexico submitted in the original Panel proceeding only insofar as it came from purchasers. According to the United States, both this material and the material in the original proceeding merely concern whether a purchaser has the theoretical or technical ability to substitute HFCS for sugar. There is a critical distinction, however, between the theoretical or technical ability to substitute and actual substitution. The United States notes that the Panel rejected data on theoretical substitution during the prior proceedings and it argues that the

Panel should do so here. According to the United States, SECOFI's redetermination provides no information pertaining to actual substitution rates.

3.160 The Unites States argues that, to the extent that there is information in Mexico-20 that reflects substitution rates of individual purchasers, SECOFI did not use it in either Mexico-21 or its redetermination. Instead, claims the United States, for purposes of Mexico-21, SECOFI simply selected the highest technical substitution rate reported to it from any source. The United States notes that SECOFI did so despite the fact that several industrial users - such as juice producers and jam makers - reported substitution rates below the maximum.

3.161 The second fundamental flaw in SECOFI's redetermination, the United States argues, relates to SECOFI's assumption that purchasers other than soft drink bottlers would substitute HFCS for 50 per cent of their potential sugar consumption in 1997 and 1998. The 50 per cent assumption is not based on record evidence, alleges the United States. It is a number that SECOFI selected arbitrarily.

3.162 In the view of the United States, it is not surprising, therefore, that neither the redetermination nor Mexico's two submissions to this Panel provides any reasoned explanation of how this 50 per cent figure was derived. According to the United States, careful scrutiny of Exhibit Mexico-21, however, reveals how Mexico used the 50 per cent figure.

3.163 Mexico-21 indicates that SECOFI went through several steps. First, SECOFI calculated the percentage of HFCS that purchasers other than soft drink bottlers could substitute for sugar in their operations. This, claims the United States, was based on theoretical or technical substitution rates. Second, SECOFI estimated the volume of sugar that would be consumed by these industries in 1997 and 1998 by taking an estimate of total Mexican sugar consumption in those years and allocating a share to each industry. The United States claims that these shares were not based on actual consumption patterns but on assigning weights based on the share of the consumer price index allocable to each industry. *See* Mexico-20. Then, SECOFI applied these technical substitution rates to each industry's total estimated consumption of sugar in 1997 and 1998 to derive SECOFI's estimate of the total amount of HFCS that industries other than the soft drink bottling industry could, theoretically, substitute for sugar in 1997 and 1998. Lastly, SECOFI reduced this number by 50 per cent and concluded that this amount represented these users' likely HFCS purchases. In other words, the United States argues, SECOFI assumed that these purchasers *would* substitute 50 per cent of the HFCS that they *could* substitute for sugar.

3.164 In the view of the United States, a careful examination of Mexico-21 confirms that SECOFI's assumption had utterly no basis in reality. The United States further claims that Mexico-21 indicates that, during the 1994-96 period, sugar purchases by industrial users other than soft drink bottlers were generally stable or increasing slightly despite the fact that: (1) these users could theoretically substitute HFCS for sugar to varying degrees and (2) imported HFCS was available from the United States. The United States notes that these purchasing patterns, incidentally, confirm that the substitution rates in Mexico-20 were theoretical, not actual. If the substitution rates were actual, argues the United States, one would have seen significant declines in the amount of sugar these industrial users purchased.

3.165 According to the United States, SECOFI, however, projected that these users would cut their use of sugar by as much as 50 per cent within a two-year period. The United States claims that this projection was not an extrapolation of the historical trends and was not in any way based on these trends. Instead, continues the United States, the projection was totally contrary to the observed data during SECOFI's period of investigation.

3.166 In the view of the United States, this confirms that SECOFI's projections were not, as Mexico claims, obtained using objective and reasonable methodologies. SECOFI's analysis was not premised on the situation observed during its period of investigation, argues the United States, nor was it based on facts. Instead, the United States claims, its conclusion that substantially increased imports were likely notwithstanding the restraint agreement is based on conjecture.

2. *Analysis of Likely Impact and Article 3.4*

3.167 According to the United States, SECOFI's redetermination does not provide a reasoned and fact-supported analysis concerning why improvements in important industry trends during its period of investigation were not probative in ascertaining the likely future condition of the industry.

3.168 SECOFI's redetermination indicates that the Mexican sugar industry's performance improved in several critical respects during 1996, a year when imports of HFCS from the United States increased. In particular, the domestic industry was profitable in 1996, and its profitability increased substantially over 1995 levels. Additionally, in 1996 the price of domestically-produced sugar in Mexico increased by a much higher percentage than prices for HFCS imported from the United States. According to the United States, the evidence also shows that, in 1996, the Mexican sugar industry had increasing capacity utilization, rising employment and productivity, declining operating costs, declining sales costs as a percentage of revenue, and stable debt levels.

3.169 In the view of the United States, SECOFI was thus obliged to provide a fact-based analysis demonstrating why such positive trends for the Mexican sugar industry in 1996 would reverse in the near future or why other considerations would make these rising trends insignificant. The United States argues that SECOFI did not do so.

3.170 Indeed, as confirmed by Mexico's written submissions to the Panel, SECOFI relied on its projections of the likely levels of sales, prices and profitability in the Mexican sugar industry in conducting its analysis of likely impact. According to the United States, these projections cannot support SECOFI's determination. They are not fact-based and they yield results that are directly contrary to the experience of the Mexican sugar industry during the period of investigation.

3.171 The United States notes that SECOFI projected a 10 per cent decline in sales volume and a 9 per cent decline in sales prices for the domestic sugar industry in 1997. However, paragraphs 60, 100, 138, 151, and 166 of the redetermination indicate that SECOFI's projections of declines in domestic sales volumes and prices were tied to SECOFI's flawed assumptions regarding likely import volumes. The United States asserts that SECOFI's projections of likely import volumes were based on conjecture contrary to fact. These same defects make SECOFI's projections of likely sales volumes for the Mexican sugar industry invalid. The United States further argues that SECOFI's pricing projections, because they are dependent on the volume projections, also cannot serve as the basis for an affirmative threat determination.

3.172 Moreover, the model used by SECOFI to project sugar prices is a "vector autoregression" analysis. This meant that SECOFI projected future values of variables such as price and volume based on the historical relationship between these variables during its period of investigation. Underlying this type of model are two critical assumptions, notes the United States. One is that the variables historically moved in a consistent manner. The second is that the variables would continue to move in the future in the manner that they had in the past.

3.173 According to the United States, neither of these assumptions was valid with respect to the Mexican sugar industry. First, there was no consistent relationship between import volumes, sales quantities of domestically-produced sugar, and the prices of domestically-produced sugar during SECOFI's period of investigation. The United States notes that import volumes increased throughout the period of investigation. The United States further notes that the quantity of domestic sugar sales declined slightly during the period of investigation. By contrast, sugar prices declined in 1995, but increased sharply in 1996. In particular, the price of refined sugar increased by 48 per cent in 1996, while the price of HFCS-55 increased by only 5 per cent that year. The United States observes that HFCS-55 was the product that constituted the bulk of the imports and that SECOFI asserted competed most directly with refined sugar. In light of this historical experience, and in light of the agreement of industry participants reported in paragraphs 111 and 112 of the redetermination that sugar prices had been "highly unstable" during its period of investigation for reasons having nothing to do with HFCS imports, the United States argues that SECOFI was obliged to explain why it was justified in relying on a model whose assumptions were not based on fact. According to the United States it did not do so.

3.174 With respect to the second assumption, because of the restraint agreement and the other reasons discussed above, the United States maintains that there was no basis to conclude that import volumes would increase in the future in the manner that they did during SECOFI's period of investigation. With respect to this issue as well, the United States asserts that SECOFI did not satisfy its obligation to explain why its reliance on its "vector autoregression" analysis was reasonable.

3.175 Finally, according to the United States, the internal documents from SECOFI's administrative record presented by Mexico to the Panel are inconsistent with the results of SECOFI's pricing projections. Exhibit Mexico-16 contains the projection used in SECOFI's redetermination, namely that sugar prices would decline by 9 per cent from 1996 to 1997. According to the United States, exhibit Mexico-12, in which SECOFI described the basis for its pricing projections, does not support SECOFI's use of the 9 per cent figure. The third page of Mexico-12 contains a chart indicating projected 1997 prices for standard sugar. The chart in Mexico-12 indicates that standard sugar prices would be stable, not declining, in 1997. Indeed, the prices projected for 1997 are at the same levels under which the Mexican sugar industry operated profitably in 1996. SECOFI acknowledges this fact about the standard sugar pricing projections at paragraph 98 of its redetermination. But, the United States argues, SECOFI's projections of stable standard sugar prices and declining overall sugar prices for 1997 are irreconcilable, given that SECOFI's record indicates that: (1) standard and refined sugar shared identical pricing trends for 35 of the 36 months in 1994, 1995, and 1996, and (2) standard sugar accounted for the majority of Mexican sugar volumes. In the view of the United States, SECOFI has failed to explain why it was justified in relying on pricing projections that were both internally inconsistent and irreconcilable with historical data.

3.176 The United States argues that SECOFI's projections of sharp declines in profitability in 1997 are based entirely on its flawed projection of declines in sugar sales volumes and sugar sales prices. Thus, according to the United States, SECOFI's projections of the sugar industry's financial performance are equally invalid. Moreover, the record data contradicts SECOFI's projections. In 1996, sugar industry profits increased substantially despite increasing volumes of imported HFCS. According to the United States, SECOFI has failed to explain why it relied on projections contrary to the facts observed during its period of investigation.

3.177 The United States notes that Mexico contends that SECOFI's conclusions on industry profitability are justified in light of the "financial sensitivity" of the Mexican sugar industry. It asserts that this "financial sensitivity" makes the sugar industry particularly susceptible to losses in revenue. Losses in revenue may be caused either by losses in sales volume or reductions in price. However, according to the United States, SECOFI's record provides no basis - apart from the results yielded by SECOFI's defective models - for the conclusion that the Mexican sugar industry was likely to face either lower sales volumes or reduced prices. Consequently, the record also contains no basis for any conclusion that losses in revenue are likely.

3.178 Moreover, the notion that the "financial sensitivity" of the Mexican sugar industry will cause its performance to deteriorate whenever imports increase is contrary to the data in the SECOFI record. According to the United States,

SECOFI's own analysis indicates that the presence of increased volumes of imported HFCS does not necessarily impair the Mexican sugar industry's ability to raise capital and finance debt. Indeed, the United States continues, SECOFI found that, notwithstanding increasing HFCS imports in 1996, the sugar industry's cash flow improved, thus enhancing its ability to obtain short-term financing and permitting it to improve its debt service indices.

3.179 In sum, the United States argues that Mexico has not satisfied its obligation to analyze the Article 3.4 factors as to impact. The United States further argues that Mexico has not provided any fact-based analysis; it has merely manipulated data from projections. Finally, the United States argues that the projections cannot serve as a substitute for analysis because they are based on conjecture and yield results contrary to the actual data observed during the course of the investigation. Th United States claims that Mexico has not attempted to explain or reconcile its projections with the contrary data.

3. Notice and Article 12

3.180 In the view of the United States, Mexico violated Articles 12.2 and 12.2.2 of the Agreement because SECOFI consistently failed to explain its use of inputs for its projection of industry behavior that yielded results either contrary to or unsupported by the observed data during its period of investigation.

3.181 The United States argues that SECOFI's failure to explain the inputs that it used in its projections makes it impossible for one reading the determination to ascertain how SECOFI derived its projections of industry behavior. The necessary explanation is not in the determination, nor is it in the type of separate report referenced in Articles 12.2 and 12.2.2. Indeed, Mexico has informed this Panel that SECOFI's analysis of the restraint agreement was premised on substitution rates of HFCS for sugar for various industries. According to the United States, the substitution rates Mexico now states that SECOFI used are different from the substitution rates set forth in paragraph 57 of the redetermination. Moreover, their derivation cannot be traced from anything in the redetermination or any separate report made available to the parties.

F. Oral Statement of Mexico

3.182 Firstly, according to Mexico, it should be stressed that the United States was hasty in resorting to the Dispute Settlement Body without exercising its judgement as to whether action under those procedures would be fruitful, as required by Article 3.7 of the Dispute Settlement Understanding, and without consulting Mexico in respect of the new final resolution.

3.183 Secondly, Mexico recalls that since this procedure concerns the implementation of the AD Agreement, the work of this Panel is governed by the standard of review in Article 17.6 of that Agreement. In other words, given that the dispute between the parties involves detailed discussions concerning the implementation of the various provisions of the AD Agreement, the Panel must bear in mind that Mexico's arguments cannot be disregarded, unless it can be demonstrated that they are based on an inadmissible interpretation of that Agreement.

1. *SECOFI Examined the Probable Impact of Corn Syrup (HFCS) Imports on the Domestic Industry and Determined Threat of Injury on the Basis of the Industry as a Whole*

3.184 On the basis of the Panel's findings and conclusions, Mexico asserts that SECOFI undertook a fresh examination of the impact of HFCS imports on the domestic industry as a whole, including an adequate actual and potential evaluation of the economic factors and indicators mentioned in Article 3.4 of the AD Agreement. On the basis of various positive evidence and facts, the investigating authority confirmed its determination of threat of injury to the whole domestic sugar industry.

3.185 With respect to price analysis, Mexico claims that it adequately complied with the Panel's findings. The revised final resolution fully sets out the trends in the prices of HFCS imports from the United States and the prices of domestically produced sugar during the investigation period and the two comparable earlier periods, together with the projected trends for the near future.

3.186 The fundamental argument of the United States is that SECOFI's determination is not supported by "factual materials" and that the results of the projections are *directly contrary* to the actual experience of the Mexican sugar industry during the investigation period. According to Mexico, that argument is based on a partial examination of isolated aspects of the revised final resolution. Mexico further claims that the United States has not examined all the information which was available to SECOFI when it made its determination.

3.187 In Mexico's view, actual proof of the adverse impact of the price of the investigated imports on the domestic price during the investigation period was obtained on the basis of a detailed analysis of the month-by-month trends in both prices, the calculated margins of undercutting and dumping, statistical evidence of causality and the prevailing economic environment, with special emphasis on the "natural difference" between the prices of the two products.

3.188 Mexico asserts that the price trends observed in 1996 showed that greater import penetration was connected with increased undercutting and declining HFCS prices in relation to sugar. In other words, given the process of substitution between the two products, an increase in the price differential stimulates demand for the alternative product at a lower price. In the circumstances, the sugar industry adjustment mechanism, given the conditions of competition imposed by imports and the structural restraints in the industry, is geared to preventing greater market displacement, by containing or reducing domestic prices.

3.189 On the basis of the monthly trends for 1994 to 1996 observed in the price of HFCS imports and the domestic selling price for sugar, Mexico notes that SECOFI estimated the prices of both products for 1997. Mexico also notes that the method of estimation employed was a system of simultaneous equations using a vector autoregressive model. The result was compared with the observed trend in prices and volumes and checked by reference to the consistency of the forecasts with the economic context and conditions in the industry during the period analysed.

3.190 According to Mexico, the reasoning behind the SECOFI determination was consistent with observed price trends during 1996. Indeed, average prices in that year were higher than the year before, even allowing for HFCS imports. This development is explained by the adverse conditions observed in 1995, which unduly depressed both the consumption and the prices of practically all goods on the domestic market.

3.191 Mexico argues that the United States' argument concerning price trends ignores the fact that sugar prices declined from 1994 to 1996, as well as during the January-December 1996 investigation period, which was characterized by growth in dumped imports at lower prices with higher undercutting margins.

3.192 Mexico points out that it determined from the original final resolution that, although sugar and HFCS are not perfect substitutes, since they are not identical products, in no way can it be inferred that they are not close substitutes. According to Mexico, this aspect is fully documented in the administrative record. Experts on the sweeteners industry agree that, precisely because of the existing substitution between HFCS and sugar in the industrial sector, the prices of the two goods are related, and both the existing differentials between them and the movements of one price or the other have a proven impact on the industry's competitiveness.

3.193 Mexico considers that its determination should not be evaluated in isolation, for in order to arrive at a determination of threat of injury all elements must be considered together, because they are interrelated. In addition, Mexico claims that even though not all the factors supported the determination of threat of injury, the negative effects already observed in the period analysed made for a positive determination in this respect.

3.194 SECOFI determined that the high rate of growth in HFCS imports at significantly low prices caused a reduction in sugar sales on the Mexican market of 2.5 and 5 per cent in 1996 compared with 1994 and 1995 respectively, given the substitution of HFCS for sugar in a wide variety of industrial products. This drop in sales, according to Mexico, resulted in the fact that in 1996 production for the domestic sugar market recorded a 4.2 percentage points reduction in its share of domestic consumption compared with 1994, while the share of HFCS imports from the United States increased by 2.76 percentage points. In Mexico's view, this shows an important link between the share lost by the sugar industry in the domestic market and the proportionately greater share gained by HFCS imports, for in the investigation period alone 60 per cent of the domestic sugar industry's loss of market share was absorbed by HFCS from the United States.

3.195 Mexico claims that the industry's 16 per cent increase in the use of installed capacity and 2 per cent increase in productivity in 1995 compared with

1994, as well as the corresponding 3 and 6 per cent increases for 1996 compared with 1995, are explained by the rising levels of domestic production, because although the installed capacity and the number of employees rose from 1994 to 1996, domestic sugar production recorded greater increases as a result of having to increase the cultivated surface area, yields per hectare and factory efficiency. Mexico further claims that the trends in employment, wages and stocks described in the revised final resolution are explained by the labour and production conditions of the Mexican sugar industry.

3.196 Moreover, the investigating authority determined that during the investigation period the sugar industry's profits and profitability indicators had shown a positive trend attributable to improved selling and operating costs. However, Mexico notes that owing to the specific characteristics of the Mexican sugar industry, operating profits and net profits remain highly sensitive to changes in sales revenue, as reflected in the fact that a decline in sales revenue would result in a disproportionately sharp fall in operating profits and net profits.

3.197 Mexico does not deny that in the period analysed, 1994-1996, the sugar industry faced structural problems. However, dumped HFCS imports from the United States did not allow the sugar industry to recover in the investigation period, in view of the fact that in 1996, compared with 1994, the drop in domestic market sales prices, the fall in domestic market sales, the loss of market share for domestic production in apparent domestic consumption and the increase in stocks indicated that, should the increasing trend in HFCS imports continue, economic factors would be affected in accordance with projections.

3.198 In accordance with those projections, SECOFI determined that, if imports continued, domestic market sales prices would fall by 9 per cent, while sugar sales on the Mexican market would drop by 10 per cent compared with those recorded in the investigation period, and this would result in a 4 point loss of share in apparent domestic consumption. A projection of the domestic sugar industry's earnings was also obtained in which sales revenue in 1997 would fall by 15 per cent and operating profits by 118 per cent, with an operational profitability indicating an operating margin of 12 percentage points with respect to 1996.

3.199 In Mexico's view, the conclusions concerning the significant rate of growth recorded in imports at prices significantly lower than those of the domestic sugar industry during the period analysed, the sufficient freely available capacity, the high export potential of the United States HFCS industry and the joint evaluation of economic factors led SECOFI to the determination that, if the final anti-dumping measure had not been adopted, the domestic industry would have suffered injury.

3.200 On the basis of the points set out above and the contents of the first submission and the rebuttal, Mexico maintains that it has complied with the Panel's findings and conclusions and with its obligations under the AD Agreement, since the revised final resolution fully considered all the facts concerning the prevailing state of the domestic industry based on the information in the administrative record of the investigation.

2. *Effects of the Restraint Agreement on the Likelihood of Substantially Increased Importation*

3.201 Mexico claims that its findings in its revised final resolution support the fact that the potential effects of an alleged restraint agreement on the likelihood of substantially increased importation were sufficiently examined. Therefore, the determination on this matter meets the requirements of paragraphs 7.176 and 7.177 of the Panel Report and is consistent with Article 3.7 of the AD Agreement.

3.202 In its determination, Mexico asserts that it took into account, in addition to the effects of the alleged restraint agreement, competition from other factors such as observed trends during the 1994-1996 investigation period in prices, volumes, actual and potential consumption, the economic context and conditions in the industry. Similarly, the revised final resolution was based on all the information at the investigating authority's disposal when the authority made its determination.

3.203 In Mexico's view, the United States has not considered the entire basis of the authority's determination in making its argument; it simply pinpoints aspects which it evaluates outside the context of the anti-dumping investigation, without relating them to various items of information at the authority's disposal. According to Mexico, the United States arguments are not based on an examination of all the information at the disposal of the investigating authority and are founded on an incorrect reading of the revised final resolution, and consequently do not demonstrate that Mexico acted inconsistently with the AD Agreement.

3.204 In its first written submission, the United States argued that the findings used by Mexico in the revised final resolution do not support its conclusion and it questions the estimates of the likely increase in imports, asserting as well that those estimates were based on the same information and were made in the same way as in the original final resolution.

3.205 In this respect, Mexico reiterates that its determination considered, but was not based on, import trends observed subsequent to the period investigated, i.e. imports effected during the course of the investigation itself, since consideration would then be given to both trade flows and consumption forecasts distorted by the effects of initiating the investigation. In most cases, this would be tantamount to concluding that there was no likelihood of increased importation, since imports tend to decrease substantially as a result of the investigation effect.

3.206 In addition, Mexico notes, the analysis was not restricted to a single factor but considered observed trends in the period under investigation and comparable earlier periods, in prices, volumes, actual and potential consumption, the economic context and the conditions of the industry. SECOFI evaluated the effects of the alleged restraint agreement on the basis of estimates of potential HFCS consumption in 1997 and 1998, for sectors other than the soft drink bottlers, taking as an input projections of total sugar consumption for those years undertaken by specialists, and applying the share of those sectors in total consumption in accordance with figures recorded in 1994, 1995 and 1996.

3.207 According to Mexico, the determination of the likelihood of increased imports was made by taking into account the following context: (a) the growth rate of the imports investigated from 1994 to 1996, (b) the export potential of the United States HFCS industry, (c) the price differential recorded during the investigation period between HFCS and sugar, which is an incentive for substitution, (d) the non-existence of trade restrictions on imports and a decline in tariff rates for such imports, and (e) the proven functionality of HFCS as a sugar substitute in a variety of industries in the Mexican market, further supported by the accumulated experience of development of the United States market.

3.208 Mexico claims that the United States fails to take into account the whole of Mexico's findings, so it does not consider the facts as a whole but simply isolated aspects that do not reflect the general picture considered by the investigating authority when it made its determination of the likelihood of increased importation.

3.209 On all the above grounds, Mexico maintains that the analysis of the potential effects of the alleged restraint agreement on the likelihood of increased imports made in the revised final resolution complied with the Panel's findings and conclusions and was consistent with the AD Agreement.

3. Mexico Complied with the Provisions of Articles 12.2 and 12.2.2 of the AD Agreement

3.210 Throughout the proceeding, Mexico maintained - and reiterates once again - that SECOFI acted in a manner that was fully consistent with Articles 12.2 and 12.2.2 of the AD Agreement.

3.211 Similarly, Mexico argues, the final notice of 20 September did not confine itself simply to presenting more data concerning the factors specified in Article 3.4 "without providing the necessary analysis and explanation of these factors", as claimed by the United States.[58] On the contrary, the notice included all the relevant findings, conclusions and information which show clearly that SECOFI's analysis significantly evaluated all the economic factors listed in Article 3.4 of the AD Agreement which influenced both the state of the sugar industry during the investigation period and the situation in the near future according to projections, in order to determine the resulting impact of imports on the domestic industry as a whole.

3.212 Mexico asserts that SECOFI also took into account more elements of relevant information in order to analyse the potential effects of the alleged restraint agreement and arrived in an appropriate manner at its determination of the likelihood of a substantial increase in HFCS imports.

3.213 According to Mexico, no admissible interpretation of Articles 12.2 and 12.2.2 implies that "relevant information" must necessarily consist of data used

---

[58] Essentially in para. 5 of its first written submission.

by the investigating authority in the economic models and projections on which its analysis and determination were based. Nor do any of the findings and conclusions of the Panel Report contain this implication.

3.214 Similarly, Mexico continues, Article 12.2 does *not* lay down precise formulas or specific terms in which an authority is required to express its findings or conclusions in the public notice. It only states in general terms that these will relate to the issues considered material by the investigating authorities. Again, Article 12.2.2 also lays down no specific formulas or terms. Even though it does in fact require the inclusion of all relevant information on the matters of fact and law and reasons which have led to the imposition of final measures, it does *not* specify what that information must be but rather takes as limiting factors the relevance and confidentiality of the information.

3.215 Accordingly, Mexico argues that SECOFI's findings related to the whole of the domestic industry, based on data and information duly documented in the administrative record, as well as on models and projections constituting reasonable methodologies which were also justified in the record by means of methodological notes explaining how SECOFI proceeded.

3.216 On the other hand, Mexico is not unaware of the findings and conclusions of the Panel which examined the *Thailand - Angles* case. Indeed, despite the fact that no specific allegation of a breach of Article 12 had been made either, the latter Panel, like the one concerned with *Mexico - HFCS*, concerned itself with emphasizing the connection of Article 12 with the context of Article 3 (paragraph 7.151 of the *Thailand - Angles* Panel Report).

3.217 However, according to Mexico it should be made clear that the circumstances of that investigation differed from the circumstances in this case. Among other things, unlike the *Thailand - Angles* case, which examined an ordinary anti-dumping investigation, the case before the Panel now concerns a review procedure for complying with a DSB recommendation, where the interested parties had the opportunity during the proceeding, at the time of and subsequent to the revised final determination, to obtain access to both the public and the confidential version of the record, by means of the appropriate procedures.

3.218 Mexico also points out that, so far, no representative of the United States has asked for access to the administrative record, either to the public or the confidential version. As regards the interested parties, they had access to the public version of the record on various occasions during the proceeding and only *one* of the interested parties, via its legal representative, asked for access to the confidential version of the administrative record, and this was granted in accordance with established procedures for access to confidential information.

3.219 Thus, having set out its arguments on this subject, Mexico rejects once again the stance of the United States and reiterates before the Panel that Mexico has duly complied with the requirements of Articles 12.2 and 12.2.2 of the AD Agreement.

4. *Conclusion*

3.220 On the basis of all the arguments set forth throughout its written submissions and which have been expressed this morning, Mexico reiterates its respectful request to the Panel to declare that SECOFI's actions, including:

(a) its consideration of the impact of HFCS imports on the Mexican sugar industry as a whole;

(b) its consideration of the potential effects of the alleged restraint agreement on the likelihood of substantially increased importation, and;

(c) the revised final resolution of 20 September;

fully comply with the Panel's findings and conclusions and are sufficient to bring Mexico's final anti-dumping measure into conformity with, *inter alia*, Articles 3.1, 3.4, 3.7, 12.2 and 12.2.2 of the AD Agreement, as recommended by the DSB in its ruling of 24 February 2000.

IV. ARGUMENTS OF THE THIRD PARTIES

A. *Oral Statement of the European Communities*

4.1 The European Communities (the "EC") notes with considerable concern that, contrary to the requirement contained in Article 6.2 of the *Understanding on Rules and Procedures Governing the Settlement of Disputes* (the "DSU"), the request for the establishment of a panel in the present proceedings does not mention whether consultations were held between Mexico and the United States before the disagreement on the compatibility of the Mexican measures with a covered agreement was referred to the Panel[59].

4.2 Furthermore, the notice concerning the request for consultations foreseen in Article 4.4 of the DSU was not provided to the Dispute Settlement Body ("DSB") and was not circulated to the WTO Members. The EC asserts that there is thus no indication whether such consultations were held in the present case.

4.3 The EC notes in this context that an inconsistent and contradictory practice has developed in a number of cases in which parties had recourse to procedures pursuant to Article 21.5 of the DSU with regard to the requirement of first entering into consultations under Article 4 of the DSU before filing a request for the establishment of a panel.

4.4 In the context of the *Bananas* dispute, the EC recalls that it has made it clear[60] that it considers consultations pursuant to Article 4 of the DSU to be necessary before the establishment of a panel can be requested pursuant to Article

59 Cf. Doc. WT/DS132/6.

60 Cf. the statement of the EC representative at the DSB meeting of 22 September 1998, Doc. WT/DSB/M/48, p. 7.

21.5 of the DSU. The reason, according to the EC, is the reference contained in Article 21.5 that any dispute on implementation "shall be decided through recourse to *these dispute settlement procedures*". In the view of the EC, "these dispute settlement procedures" include consultations and a right to an appeal. This is so for reasons related to the multilateral character of the procedures, which include procedural rights of other WTO Members, particularly potential third parties, and a standardised dispute settlement procedure the basic features of which may not be amended simply because that pleases the parties in an individual case.

4.5 In the view of the EC, if the parties to a dispute were entirely free to develop procedures of their own choice (*quod non*), this would jeopardise third party rights enshrined in the DSU (particularly in Articles 4.11 and 10). Nothing would stop the parties from agreeing bilaterally not only to jump the procedural step of consultations, but also to jump other procedural steps such as the panel stage and to submit their dispute to the Appellate Body straight away (e.g. in order to "gain time" and to exclude third parties who cannot participate in Appellate Body procedures if they did not reserve their right to participate in the preceding panel procedure). It would also mean that the parties would be free to agree among themselves that a panel report pursuant to Article 21.5 of the DSU is not binding and that it may be subjected to some kind of review by another international body outside the WTO.

4.6 The EC believes that these scenarios are not compatible with the multilateral nature of the procedures under the DSU, the procedural rights of third parties and indeed the general matrix of procedural checks and balances built into the dispute settlement system. The DSU contains sufficient flexibility to adapt the basic procedural requirements to the needs of the parties in individual disputes. As an example, Article 4.7 (second sentence) of the DSU allows the parties to shorten the 60-day period on the basis of a bilateral agreement. If the parties to the dispute agree, the EC argues, a panel under Article 21.5 of the DSU may be established at the first meeting where the request is considered by the DSB (Article 6.1 of the DSU). Panels may propose special working procedures after consultations with the parties (Article 12.1 of the DSU). The EC asserts that all these provisions indicate that there is some flexibility in the procedures, which is largely dependent on the agreement of the parties to the dispute. None of these provisions, however, allows the parties to the dispute to simply omit one of the essential procedural steps before requesting the next one.

4.7 The EC argues that the procedural step of holding consultations is of fundamental importance for the dispute settlement system. Consultations give the parties an opportunity to resolve their differences without an adjudication of the dispute and will, at the very least, allow the parties to clarify on what precise issues their disagreement continues. In this way, consultations contribute to discharging panel proceedings from issues on which there is no real and serious disagreement. In addition, any request for consultations under Article 4 of the DSU must be circulated to the entire WTO membership in order to identify and circumscribe the dispute, thus allowing potential third parties to prepare their request to participate in the procedure. In this regard, the EC recalls that third parties may participate in consultations requested under any of the provisions cited in Article 4.11 and footnote 4 of the DSU. Thus, argues the EC, third party rights are clearly impaired by the omission of the formal consultation stage in a dispute settlement procedure.

4.8 According to the EC, all these important functions of the consultations are undermined if the parties to the dispute are considered to be free to "jump the gun" and go to a panel procedure without holding formal consultations under Article 4 of the DSU first. Moreover, consultations must anyhow take place in order to agree on the procedure to be followed, and it is obvious that this is also an occasion to consult on substantive issues. Thus, in reality no time is gained in jumping this procedural step, except that third parties are put at a disadvantage and that the panel may have to address issues on which there is no real disagreement.

4.9 In conclusion, the EC is of the view that the existing rules of the DSU do not allow parties to a dispute to bilaterally agree simply to dispense with consultations under Article 4 of the DSU. Any other approach leads to unbearable procedural uncertainty about the limits of the procedural guarantees for both parties and to curtailing third party rights clearly enshrined in the DSU.

4.10 If the parties to the dispute do not respect their obligations under Article 4 of the DSU, argues the EC, the Panel should draw the consequence and make a ruling that the dispute is not properly before it (or inadmissible, to use a term of art), since all the procedural steps that are required before a dispute may be submitted to a panel have not been followed in the present case

4.11 On the basis of the foregoing considerations, the EC is of the view that the Panel should consider that the dispute is not properly before it because no consultations were requested nor held before the request for the establishment of a panel was submitted to the DSB.

B. Joint Statement of Jamaica and Mauritius

4.12 Jamaica and Mauritius as third parties in the original dispute had made a joint oral statement before the panel to highlight the potential impact this dispute could have on the trade in sugar by Jamaica, Mauritius and other suppliers in securing continued, predictable and increased opportunities for access to the United States market in accordance with the provision of Article XIII of GATT 1994.

4.13 Jamaica and Mauritius noted that they were aware at the time that the issue at hand concerned imports of High Fructose Corn Syrup (HFCS) into the Mexican market. They also recognise that since then, the panel has ruled that Mexico's imposition of the definitive anti-dumping measures on imports of HFCS for the United States is inconsistent with the requirements of the AD Agreement on several scores and that Mexico has been requested by the DSB to bring its measures into conformity. They are aware that the current case must be concerned with whether the new determination made by Mexico does indeed comply with the Panel's recommendations.

4.14 Jamaica and Mauritius understand that the primary duty of this panel is to assess whether Mexico's revised final determination is in conformity with the panel's conclusions and recommendations in respect of Mexico's obligations under the AD Agreement.

4.15 They nonetheless believe that in making their assessment of the issue at hand the panel should not lose sight of the broader disagreement over sweetener trade between these two countries and the impact that a resolution of this new dispute may have on third parties which are traditional suppliers of sugar to the US market.

4.16 Jamaica and Mauritius note previous statements made by representatives of the Mexican sugar industry in the press and other public fora to the effect that HFCS and sugar disputes are inter-related and that one cannot be resolved without resolving the other.

4.17 They note that this new dispute arises at a crucial time of the NAFTA time table for sugar trade. They recall that prior to the entry into force of the NAFTA Agreement in 1994, Mexico was a net sugar importer. However, under the NAFTA Agreement, Mexico has since seen its initial market share of 7,258 tonnes per annum for the period 1994 - 1996 increase to 25,000 tonnes for the 2000 - 2001 quota year.

4.18 This amount may after this date increase to as much as 250,000 tonnes per annum until 2008 at which time NAFTA would allow Mexico unlimited access at zero tariff for its sugar exports.

4.19 Jamaica and Mauritius, as traditional suppliers, have already seen their access reduced in the US market as sugar imports have declined since 1985. They are concerned that an increase in Mexico's sugar exports to the United States as a direct or indirect result of the resolution of this new dispute or indeed other proceedings will increasingly exacerbate the existing prejudice to the traditional suppliers to the US market. They wish to recall that the diminution of opportunity for access to the US sugar market will particularly impact on single commodity producers like Jamaica and Mauritius.

4.20 They note in this regard the assurances given by the United States delegation at the WTO Committee on Agriculture in responding to queries that:

(a) Raw cane sugar tariff quotas are allocated according to Article XIII of GATT 1994.

(b) Mexico's NAFTA allocations do not count in a country's share allocation in the TRQ (G/AG/N/USA/15 at pp. 22 and G/AG/R/16) and

(c) Mexico does not receive additional access if there are subsequent tariff quota allocations (G/AG/N/USA/13 at pp. 18 of G/AG/R/14).

4.21 Jamaica and Mauritius remain nonetheless pre-occupied by the possible serious erosion of their share as traditional sugar suppliers as a result of substantial increase of Mexico's access under NAFTA as from the 2000 - 2001 quota year and any other settlement arising from the present dispute and request that any finding of this Panel not impact negatively on the trade of traditional suppliers, particularly single commodity producers like Mauritius and Jamaica.

V. INTERIM REVIEW

5.1 On 11 May 2001, the Panel issued its interim report to the parties. On 18 May 2001, the parties filed written requests regarding review of review precise aspects of the interim report. Neither party requested a further meeting with the Panel. Therefore, in accordance with the working procedures adopted by the Panel, the parties were given the opportunity to file further written comments, which they did on 1 June 2001.

5.2 The original comments of the United States were limited to typographical and stylistic corrections, which we have incorporated in the Report, as appropriate. Mexico's further written comments were limited to certain asserted translation errors, which we took into consideration.

5.3 Mexico's original comments requested review of our consideration of SECOFI's determination of likelihood of increased imports, stating that our analysis is incomplete because it does not take account of various analytical elements of Mexico's arguments. The United States responded to these substantive points in its further written comments.

5.4 Mexico notes that in this dispute, it stressed that the quantitative scenario regarding demand for HFCS by industries other than soft drink bottlers was not the only basis for its conclusion with respect to the likelihood of increased imports. Mexico reiterates that SECOFI's determination of the likelihood of increased imports was based on a comprehensive analysis of concurrent factors, including, *inter alia*, the increase in imports during the investigation period and the most recent period for which data was available, the freely disposable capacity of the United States industry, the trend in and level of import prices, and the foreseeable economic context, together with the existence of the alleged restraint agreement. Mexico maintains that SECOFI's conclusion of a likelihood of increased imports is supported by the analysis of the mentioned factors. In Mexico's view, our decision was based only on consideration of the calculation of projected demand for HFCS.

5.5 Mexico also asserts that even if the already increased level of imports were merely maintained, the presence of these imports would suffice to cause a threat of material injury to the domestic industry. In this regard, Mexico refers to the findings of the Panel in *United States - Safeguard Measures on Imports of Fresh, Chilled or Frozen Lamb Meat from New Zealand and Australia* (WT/DS177/R and WT/DS178/R, 21 December 2000) at paragraph 7.187:

> " ... Moreover, we also deem it possible that imports continuing on an elevated level for a longer period without further increasing at the end of the investigation period may, if unchecked, go on to

cause serious injury (i.e. may threaten to cause serious injury). That is, if increased imports at a certain point in time cause *less than* serious injury, it is not necessarily true that a threat of serious injury can only be caused by a *further* increase, i.e., *additional* increased imports. In our view, in the particular circumstances of a case, a continuation of imports at an already recently increased level may suffice to cause such threat."

5.6 We considered carefully Mexico's comments on the interim report, but did not make any changes to the report in connection with the points made by Mexico on interim review. These arguments were fully expressed during the course of the proceedings, and considered in making our decision. We recognized, in paragraph 6.9 of our findings, that there was evidence concerning the rate of increase in imports during the period of investigation, as well as the available capacity in the United States and the existence of other markets, which was considered by SECOFI in making its determination of likelihood of increased imports. However, whether this evidence indicated a likelihood that imports would continue was not the issue with which we were concerned. Our concern was with SECOFI's analysis of the effects of the alleged restraint agreement on the likelihood of increased imports, which had been faulted by the original panel in its Report. It is in that connection that we considered the projected demand for HFCS by users other than the soft-drink bottlers affected by the alleged restraint agreement, and concluded that an unbiased and objective investigating authority could not have reached the conclusions reached by SECOFI. In our view, it is clear that SECOFI's finding of threat of material injury rested on the determination that imports would increase significantly despite the alleged restraint agreement, and that this conclusion rested on the projected levels of HFCS demanded by users other than soft-drink bottlers.

5.7 We note in addition that, in the redetermination, SECOFI did not conclude that there was a threat of injury to the Mexican sugar industry even if imports did not increase, but merely continued at the levels already reported during the period of investigation. Therefore, we consider Mexico's reliance on the findings of the Panel in *United States - Safeguard Measures on Imports of Fresh, Chilled or Frozen Lamb Meat from New Zealand and Australia*, WT/DS177/R and WT/DS178/R, adopted as modified in WT/DS177/ABR and WT/DS178/ABR, 16 May 2001 to be inapposite. Since SECOFI's decision was not based on this rationale, it is not appropriate for us to consider whether a decision based on this rationale should be sustained.

5.8 Mexico also requested a change to the text of paragraph 6.21 of the Report. We did not make this change, as Mexico's proposed language did not correctly convey the import of our analysis as reflected in that paragraph.

5.9 Mexico argues that our finding in paragraph 6.31does not refer to changes in factors such as sugar prices, sales, domestic market share and inventories between 1994 and 1996, and requests that we include a statement to the effect that the increase in dumped HFCS imports from the United States meant that the industry could not recover during the investigation period, since 1996, as compared to 1994, saw a decrease in domestic sugar prices, a fall in domestic sales, a loss of market share and an increase in inventories. Mexico maintains that the evaluation of these factors made it possible for SECOFI to project an adverse effect on the industry.

5.10 Mexico's arguments concerning the condition of the domestic industry regard are reflected in, *inter alia*, paragraphs 3.113 - 3.114 and 3.187 - 3.197 above, and our conclusions in paragraphs 6.26, 6.29, and 6.30 reflect our consideration of those arguments. We recognize that the domestic sugar industry did not, in 1996, show levels of performance equal to those of 1994 in some respects. However, this does not detract from our conclusion that SECOFI's analysis and conclusion failed to explain why, when the condition of the industry improved significantly from 1995 to1996 despite significantly increased imports, it was threatened with material injury in 1997. We therefore did not make the change requested by Mexico, as paragraph 6.31 accurately reflects our views.

VI. FINDINGS

A. *Introduction*

6.1 On 24 February 2000, the Dispute Settlement Body ("the DSB") adopted the report and recommendations of the Panel in *Mexico - Anti-dumping Investigation of High Fructose Corn Syrup (HFCS) from the United States* (WT/DS132/R). In that report, the Panel concluded that Mexico's imposition of definitive anti-dumping duties on imports of high fructose corn syrup, grades 42 and 55, from the United States was inconsistent with the requirements of the Agreement on Implementation of Article VI of the General Agreement on Tariffs and Trade 1994 (AD Agreement). The Panel concluded, *inter alia*, that the determination of threat of material injury was inconsistent with the requirements of the AD Agreement in that the Mexican investigating authority, SECOFI, had inadequately considered the potential effect of an alleged agreement between Mexican soft-drink bottlers and sugar producers to limit the amount of HFCS used by the bottlers, and had inadequately considered the impact of HFCS imports on the Mexican sugar industry. The Panel and the DSB accordingly recommended that Mexico bring its measure into conformity with its obligations under the AD Agreement.

6.2 The United States and Mexico having agreed on a reasonable period for implementation, Mexico decided to revise the original final determination underlying the imposition of anti-dumping duties following a newly initiated proceeding. On 20 September 2000, the Government of Mexico published the final resolution in that proceeding. In that resolution, SECOFI stated that it had revised the original final resolution imposing definitive anti-dumping duties on imports of

HFCS from the United States to comply with the Panel report's conclusions and recommendations.[61] Mexico determined to repay provisional duties on entries and guarantees granted for the payment of provisional anti-dumping duties, with interest, for the period 26 June 1997 to 23 January 1998.[62] Mexico also "ratified its conclusion that during the period under investigation, there was a threat of harm to the domestic sugar industry as a consequence of imports of high fructose corn syrup under price discriminatory conditions originating from the United States of America".[63] The revised final resolution confirmed "the final offsetting duties established during the antidumping investigation".[64]

6.3 The United States asks us to determine whether the redetermination by SECOFI in the HFCS anti-dumping case complied with the ruling of the original Panel, and the recommendation of the Panel and the DSB to "bring the measure into conformity". The United States also asks us to determine whether the redetermination is consistent with the provisions of the AD Agreement, specifically, Articles 3.1, 3.4, 3.7, 12.2 and 12.2.2 thereof. The United States maintains that the answer to both questions is no. In the United States' view, while the redetermination sets out additional evidence and discussion relevant to the findings of likelihood of increased importation and threat of material injury, these merely add a gloss to the original determination without remedying the errors found by the original Panel.

6.4 Mexico argues that SECOFI complied fully with the original Panel's ruling and recommendation in issuing the redetermination underlying this dispute. Mexico further asserts that the redetermination is fully consistent with the specific provisions of the AD Agreement cited by the United States in its claims of error. In Mexico's view, SECOFI in the redetermination provided all the information and analysis necessary to bring the measure into conformity with the AD Agreement with respect to the errors identified by the original Panel in its ruling. Mexico argues that SECOFI requested additional information from interested parties, in particular concerning the impact of imports on the domestic industry.[65] Mexico further argues that SECOFI carefully analyzed the information before it, and concluded that, first, even assuming the alleged restraint agreement existed, imports would increase significantly, and second, these dumped imports would depress domestic sugar prices, and as a consequence dumped imports threatened material injury to the domestic industry.

---

[61] Final resolution revising, on the basis of the conclusion and recommendation of the Panel of the World Trade Organization's Dispute Settlement Body, the final resolution of the anti-dumping investigation into imports of high fructose corn syrup, merchandise classified in tariff headings 1702.40.99 and 1702.60.01 of the General Import Tariff, originating in the United States of America, irrespective of the country of provenance, 20 September 2000, MEXICO-1(a) (hereinafter "Notice of Redetermination").

[62] The United States raised no issue concerning this aspect of Mexico's implementation.

[63] Notice of Redetermination, MEXICO-1(a) at para. 188.

[64] *Ibid.*

[65] *Ibid.* at para 11.

6.5 We are thus faced principally with determining whether SECOFI's conclusion in the redetermination, that dumped imports of HFCS from the United States threaten material injury to the Mexican industry producing sugar, is consistent with Articles 3.1, 3.4 and 3.7(i) of the AD Agreement. Were we to find the redetermination consistent with the provisions of the AD Agreement, we would conclude that Mexico complied with the recommendation to bring its measure into conformity.[66] However, as is discussed in detail below, we conclude that SECOFI's redetermination is not consistent with Articles 3.1, 3.4 and 3.7(i) of the AD Agreement. Therefore, we conclude that Mexico has failed to bring its measure into conformity with the requirements of that Agreement. In addition, we address below the question whether the public notice of the SECOFI redetermination is consistent with the requirements of Articles 12.2 and 12.2.2 of the AD Agreement.

B. *Finding of Likelihood of Increased Imports*

6.6 In its original determination, the Panel had concluded that SECOFI failed to adequately address the likelihood of substantially increased imports by failing to properly evaluate the facts concerning, and provide a reasoned explanation of its conclusions regarding, the potential effects of the alleged restraint agreement.[67] Consequently, the Panel found that SECOFI's conclusion that there was a "likelihood of substantially increased importation" was inconsistent with the requirements of Article 3.7(i) of the AD Agreement. In addressing this issue, the Panel noted that the question was not whether such an agreement actually existed, but "whether there was evidence of and arguments concerning the effect of the alleged restraint agreement, which, if it existed, would be relevant to the analysis of the likelihood of increased dumped imports in the near future."[68] The Panel posed the relevant question as "whether SECOFI's analysis provides a reasoned explanation for its conclusion that, assuming such an agreement existed, there was nonetheless a likelihood of substantially increased importation."[69]

6.7 The Panel concluded that Mexico had not provided such an explanation, observing:

> "7.177 Mexico's contention that users of imported HFCS other than soft-drink bottlers could have increased their consumption in

---

66 We note that neither party made any arguments concerning the interpretation of the applicable provisions of the AD Agreement. Neither did the United States question that a redetermination of the type undertaken by SECOFI in this case is an appropriate means of implementing the Panel's and the DSB's recommendation. We therefore have not addressed these matters in resolving the issues between the parties in this dispute.

67 *Mexico - Anti-dumping Investigation of High Fructose Corn Syrup (HFCS) from the United States* WT/DS132/R, adopted 24 February 2000, DSR 2001:XIII, 6727, at paras. 7.173-7.178 (hereinafter "Panel Report, WT/DS132/R")

68 *Ibid.* at para. 7.174.

69 *Ibid.* at para. 7.175.

amounts sufficient to constitute a substantial increase in imports is in our view questionable.[645] However, even assuming this to be the case, there is no discussion in the final determination of the share of imports and domestic production consumed by soft-drink bottlers, other beverage manufacturers, and other industrial users, and the degree of substitutability of HFCS and sugar in their products. Moreover, the alleged restraint agreement affected purchasers accounting for 68 per cent of the imports, suggesting that it would at least slow any further increases in imports. In addition, most other purchasers' ability to substitute HFCS for sugar was limited, suggesting that, if the alleged restraint agreement existed, any further increases in imports would be less than they had been in the past. None of these elements is addressed in SECOFI's final determination. We note, moreover, that the final determination states that the alleged restraint agreement does not "rule out the possibility" (emphasis added) that bottlers and other users would continue their purchases of imported HFCS. However, not ruling out the possibility that imports would continue does not support the conclusion that there is a "likelihood of substantially increased importation" (emphasis added), as provided for in Article 3.7(i).

7.178 We conclude that SECOFI's consideration of the potential effects of the alleged restraint agreement was inadequate. Therefore, we determine that SECOFI's conclusion that there was a "likelihood of substantially increased importation" is inconsistent with the requirements of Article 3.7(i) of the AD Agreement.

[645] We note that the distinction between soft-drink bottlers and other beverage producers is not clear from the final determination. However, we have relied on the information Mexico provided from the underlying record in this regard."[70]

6.8 SECOFI's original determination had been that, "even if Mexican soft-drink bottlers limited their consumption of HFCS, threat of injury to the domestic industry still remained." This conclusion was based on the following considerations:

"(a) imports during the period of investigation showed a significant rate of increase, which together with other factors - such as low prices, increasing substitution, freely disposable and increasing capacity in the United States, and the genuine importance of Mexico as a destination for United States' exports - indicated a likelihood that there would be a substantial increase in the future,[638]

[70] *Mexico - Anti-dumping Investigation of High Fructose Corn Syrup (HFCS) from the United States* WT/DS132/R, adopted 24 February 2000, DSR 2001:XIII, 6727, at paras. 7.177-78.

(b) SECOFI's threat of injury determination was based on information for 1996. However, SECOFI also considered import information for the period January to September 1997, which showed that imports of HFCS rose 75 per cent over the same period in 1996,[639] further demonstrating a likelihood of a substantial increase in imports,

(c) Other industries, in addition to the soft-drinks industry, use imported HFCS in their activities and they would not be subject to the restrictions in the alleged restraint agreement. These industries accounted for approximately 46 per cent of the industrial sector's total sugar consumption.[640]

(d) Both the soft-drinks industry and the other industries could purchase the imported product at low prices as a result of dumping, thereby causing sugar prices to shift and deteriorate.

[638] *Id.*, paras. 449-470.

[639] *Id.*, para. 460, *see* import statistics, MEXICO-40.

[640] Final Determination, para. 465."[71]

6.9 In the redetermination, SECOFI found that imports had shown "a high rate of growth during the period of investigation, indicating a well-founded likelihood that a significant increase in such imports would occur in the immediate future."[72] SECOFI then considered the export capacity of the United States, and the existence of alternative markets for US HFCS exports. SECOFI concluded that the available capacity in the United States "indicates a well-founded likelihood of a significant increase in exports to the Mexican market..."[73]

6.10 SECOFI next considered the effect of the alleged restraint agreement, and determined that:

> "even if there was an agreement to restrict the use of high fructose corn syrup on September 1997, between the sugar mills and the soft-drink bottlers, it would not eliminate the threat of injury to the domestic sugar industry. This is because even if Mexican soft-drink bottlers limit their consumption of high fructose corn syrup, it does not eliminate the likelihood that soft-drink bottlers as well as other sectors of the beverage industry and other industries that use high fructose corn syrup in multiple applications will continue

[71] *Mexico - Anti-dumping Investigation of High Fructose Corn Syrup (HFCS) from the United States* WT/DS132/R, adopted 24 February 2000, DSR 2001:XIII, 6727, at para 7.170.

[72] Notice of Redetermination, MEXICO-1(a), at para. 61.

[73] *Ibid.* at para. 78.

to acquire the imported product under conditions of price discrimination..."[74]

6.11 In support of this conclusion, SECOFI noted that users of sugar could use HFCS in varying degrees, and that consumers of HFCS other than soft-drink bottlers accounted for almost one-third of HFCS imports. SECOFI observed that "this does not mean" that users other than soft-drink bottlers would not increase their consumption of HFCS in the future, "given the increase in the value of [dumped] imports". SECOFI also relied on information concerning the substitution of HFCS for sugar by users other than soft-drink bottlers. SECOFI stated that the degree of substitution should not be considered a technical limit, but merely the level reached to date.

6.12 SECOFI concluded that, assuming the restraint agreement existed, soft-drink bottlers would, in 1997, consume the maximum amount of HFCS permitted under the alleged agreement, 350,000 tons, which would equal the entirety of projected domestic production. SECOFI further concluded that users other than soft-drink bottlers would consume 334,000 tons of HFCS in 1997, which would be supplied by imports.[75] Thus, SECOFI projected that dumped imports would increase from 192,906 tons in 1996 to 334,000 tons in 1997 and projected an additional increase to 350,000 tons in 1998.[76]

6.13 Mexico contends that, in the redetermination, SECOFI set out additional facts and analysis which provide a reasoned explanation for its conclusion that, assuming that the restraint agreement existed, there was nonetheless a likelihood of substantially increased importation. The United States, on the other hand, argues that Mexico's explanation and analysis are essentially the same as in the original determination, and that the redetermination is based on conjecture and projections that have no basis in the facts that were before SECOFI.[77]

6.14 Our task in this proceeding is to consider the factual determination of likelihood of substantially increased imports made by SECOFI in the redetermination. Pursuant to Article 17.6 (i), in a dispute under the AD Agreement,

> "in its assessment of the facts of the matter, the panel shall determine whether the authorities' establishment of the facts was proper

[74] Notice of Redetermination, MEXICO-1(a), at para. 56.

[75] Mexico argued before us that it was immaterial whether users other than soft-drink bottlers consumed imports or domestic production. See Answer to Question 5, Mexico's answers to the Panel's Questions, Annex A. Thus, it was apparently the total volume of HFCS consumption by Mexican users projected for 1997, 684,000 tons (based on 334,000 tons of imports and 350,000 tons of domestic production) that was relevant.

[76] Notice of Redetermination, MEXICO-1(a), at para. 59.

[77] Mexico did not respond in detail to the arguments in the US first submission until it filed its second submission brief. The United States was thus precluded from responding to the more detailed explanation of the SECOFI redetermination and the underlying evidence provided by Mexico in its second submission in writing, as its own second submission was filed simultaneously with Mexico's. The United States did respond to Mexico's second submission orally at the meeting of the Panel with the parties.

> and whether their evaluation of those facts was unbiased and objective. If the establishment of the facts was proper and the evaluation was unbiased and objective, even though the panel might have reached a different conclusion, the evaluation shall not be overturned."

Thus, in assessing the redetermination, we must judge whether, in light of the explanations given in the redetermination, an unbiased and objective investigating authority could reach the conclusions reached by SECOFI on the evidence before it. As stated by the Panel in the original dispute, the relevant question is "whether SECOFI's analysis provides a reasoned explanation for its conclusion that, assuming [a restraint] agreement existed, there was nonetheless a likelihood of substantially increased importation."[78] We note in this regard that Article 3.7 of the AD Agreement specifically provides that:

> "A determination of a threat of material injury shall be based on facts and not merely on allegation, conjecture or remote possibility. The change in circumstances which would create a situation in which the dumping would cause injury must be clearly foreseen and imminent." (footnote omitted)

The reasoned explanation required to satisfy us under the standard of review must respect these elements of Article 3.7 as well.

6.15 The logic underlying SECOFI's redetermination is, in our view, the same as that in the original determination. What SECOFI has done is respond to the specific criticisms of the Panel, concerning the lack of discussion of the share of imports consumed by various users of HFCS, the degree of substitutability, and the effects of the restraint agreement. However, while the redetermination discusses these elements, and recites facts concerning them, the basic analysis and conclusion of the redetermination, that there is a likelihood of substantially increased importation despite the potential effects of the alleged restraint agreement because users of HFCS other than soft-drink bottlers would increase their consumption of dumped imports of HFCS, remains the same.

6.16 SECOFI's determination that there was a likelihood of significantly increased imports depends on the conclusion that demand for HFCS by users other than soft-drink bottlers would increase by more than 400 per cent in 1997. SECOFI reached this conclusion on the basis of an analysis of projected demand for HFCS by users other than soft-drink bottlers. In its analysis, SECOFI had before it evidence of the utilisation of HFCS and sugar by consuming industries.[79] This information consisted of three tables, two labelled "Grado de sustituibilidad técnica del azúcar por JMAF", and the third showing "posibilidades de sustitución entre JMAF y azúcar". SECOFI considered that this evidence demonstrated the rate at which users other than soft-drink bottlers could substitute

[78] Panel Report, WT/DS132/R at para. 7.175.

[79] MEXICO-20.

HFCS for sugar in their production operations in 1997. SECOFI then projected the amount of HFCS that users of sugar other than soft-drink bottlers **could** consume in 1997, reduced it by 50 per cent, and determined that the result, 334,000 tons, was the amount of HFCS that users other than soft-drink bottlers **would** consume in 1997.[80] SECOFI projected that the amount of HFCS soft-drink bottlers could consume under the alleged restraint agreement, 350,000 tons, would be supplied by the domestic industry. Consequently, the entire 334,000 tons of demand projected for producers of products other than soft-drinks would, SECOFI concluded, be supplied by imports, principally dumped imports from the United States. Thus, SECOFI concluded that the alleged restraint agreement "would not eliminate the threat of injury to the domestic sugar industry" because it does not eliminate the likelihood that soft-drink bottlers, as well as industries other than soft-drink bottlers, would continue to acquire dumped imports.[81]

6.17 In our view, an objective and unbiased investigating authority could not have reached the conclusion that industries other than soft-drink bottlers would increase their consumption of HFCS to the extent projected by SECOFI on the basis of the evidence that was before SECOFI, in light of the explanations set out in the redetermination. The evidence in the record concerning the use of HFCS and sugar in 1996 does not support SECOFI's conclusion as to the rate at which all producers in industries other than soft-drink bottling **would** consume HFCS in 1997 and 1998. Absent some explanation as to why there would be this sudden and massive increase in HFCS consumption by industries other than soft-drink bottlers, SECOFI's conclusion of a likelihood of significant increase in imports cannot be sustained.

6.18 Mexico relies on Exhibit Mexico-20 to support the analysis of and conclusions regarding projected demand for HFCS by industries other than soft-drink bottling. Exhibit Mexico-20 contains the three tables mentioned above in paragraph 6.16. The rates of substitution set out in the three tables are different and the sources of information for the three tables are different. As we understand it, SECOFI relied principally on the information gathered in a market survey conducted during the course of the original investigation. However, that market survey reports the relative proportions of use of sugar and HFCS by a limited sample of producers in the manufacture of specific products. These companies, which already used both HFCS and sugar in their production operations, simply reported the relative rates of usage of the two sweeteners for 1996 and 1997. SECOFI considered this information to represent the degree to which HFCS could be substituted for sugar by the industries represented by the reporting companies. This information does not, however, address the critical question of the degree to which companies which had not, to date, used HFCS in their production operations **could**, as a technical matter (taking into account production proc-

[80] MEXICO-21.

[81] Notice of Redetermination, MEXICO-1(a) , at para 56.

esses and equipment) use HFCS in place of sugar.[82] Thus, for instance, evidence that some producers of marmalade had used HFCS as a sweetener in 70 per cent of their production in 1996 does not support the conclusion that all producers of marmalade will use HFCS in the same proportion in 1997.

6.19 SECOFI did not rely exclusively on the survey information, but also relied on the information in the other two tables in Exhibit Mexico-20.[83] SECOFI appears to have selectively relied on the available information in using the higher figures in most cases. Thus, while two of the tables report a degree of substitutability of HFCS for sugar in marmalade production of 33 per cent, SECOFI's calculation of projected demand for HFCS by all marmalade producers for 1997 rested on a substitution rate of 70 per cent, which is in fact information reported by one company in the SECOFI market survey.[84] Mexico provided no reasoned explanation, and in some cases, no explanation at all, of why one source was used in projecting demand for HFCS in some cases, and another in others.[85]

6.20 Mexico asserts that SECOFI discounted by 50 per cent the projected volume of demand in order not to overestimate the likelihood of increased imports. The 50 per cent "discount" factor was calculated by taking a simple average of the rates of utilisation for each product group of users providing information in the market survey, and calculating an overall average, 52.31 per cent, which SECOFI rounded to 50 per cent.[86] While this had the effect of reducing the figure projected for HFCS use by industries other than soft-drink bottlers in 1997, it is not relevant to the important question of the degree to which these industries were capable, as a technical matter, of making the change to HFCS use between 1996 and 1997. Assuming that the rates of utilisation for each product group represented the rate of substitutability, an average of those figures would be an average rate of substitutability. We cannot see how an average rate of substitutability or an "average rate of utilisation" can meaningfully operate as a factor to discount the projected demand for HFCS in the manner described by Mexico.

6.21 We see nothing in SECOFI's redetermination, or even in the explanations provided by Mexico in this proceeding, which would support the conclusion that industries other than soft-drink bottlers **would** switch to HFCS use in 1997 to the

---

82 Mexico appears to acknowledge the importance of technical limits on the ability to substitute HFCS for sugar, stating:

> "The issue of whether the use of HFCS by the new companies entering the market would match the rate at which other companies use HFCS basically depends on the specific production operations and products concerned. Conditions can vary substantially from one sector or one product to another within a given industry".

Answer to Question 8, Mexico's answers to the Panel's Questions, Annex A.

83 See answer to Question 7, Mexico's answers to the Panel's Questions, Annex A.

84 *Ibid.*

85 *Ibid.*

86 See answer to Question 11, Mexico's answers to the Panel's Questions, Annex A.

extent projected by SECOFI, even assuming the technical capability to do so.[87] Mexico argues that the lower price of HFCS, as compared with sugar prices, supports the conclusion that producers of products other than soft-drinks would switch to HFCS use as overall demand for their products increased. However, during the period of investigation, despite a similar difference in HFCS and sugar prices, nothing like this projected increase was observed, in any of the industrial sectors using both sugar and HFCS. Indeed, while the price of HFCS was lower than the price of sugar in 1996, those margins of underselling were projected by SECOFI to decrease slightly in 1997.[88] HFCS use by producers other than soft-drink bottlers had not in the past shown increases of the magnitude predicted by SECOFI for 1997, even in periods of **increasing** margins of underselling. SECOFI's determination provides no explanation for the conclusion that, despite the projection of no significant change in relative prices for 1997, use of HFCS by industries other than soft-drink bottlers would increase by over 400 per cent, when there had not been increases of this magnitude in the past.

6.22 Finally, we note that the redetermination states that the alleged restraint agreement "would not eliminate the threat of injury to the domestic sugar industry" because it does not eliminate the likelihood that both soft-drink bottlers and other users would continue to acquire dumped imports.[89] As in the original Panel's report, we do not consider that this in itself supports the conclusion that there is a likelihood of substantially increased importation, as provided for in Article 3.7(i) of the AD Agreement. A conclusion that the likelihood of further dumped imports **is not eliminated** does not demonstrate that there is a likelihood of substantially increased importation and consequent threat of material injury.

6.23 SECOFI's determination that industries other than soft-drink bottlers would undertake a massive shift from sugar use to HFCS use, resulting in total consumption of HFCS beyond the capacity of the domestic industry to supply, and a consequent significant increase in dumped imports, is not, in our view, one that could be reached by an unbiased and objective investigating authority in

---

[87] In this regard, we note that the SECOFI market survey on use of HFCS and sugar by some industrial users in MEXICO-20 also reported information for 1997. The 1997 information shows little or no increase in relative usage by the surveyed companies, some of which continued to report proportionate use below the levels relied on by SECOFI in its projection of demand for 1997. That is, even companies that had already demonstrated the ability to use HFCS to some degree did not increase their usage to the proportions relied on by SECOFI to project demand for HFCS by industries other than soft-drink bottlers. This further undermines the conclusion that producers who did not already use HFCS in their production operations would switch to doing so, in the proportions predicted by SECOFI.

[88] We note that SECOFI's redetermination continues to fail to address adequately the "natural difference" between HFCS and sugar prices. Paragraphs 91 and 92 of the redetermination (MEXICO-1(a)) report that in the US market, while the price difference between sugar and HFCS remained stable from 1991 to 1995, it increased in 1995 and 1996. It is not clear how this relates to the "natural gap" in HFCS and sugar prices in the Mexican market, which bears on the significance of the margins of underselling.

[89] Notice of Redetermination, MEXICO-1(a), at para. 56.

light of the evidence relied upon and the explanations given in the redetermination. While in its redetermination, SECOFI did set out additional information concerning the points identified by the Panel as problematic in its original report, SECOFI failed to provide a reasoned explanation of how that information supports the conclusion that there was a significant likelihood of increased imports. We therefore determine that SECOFI's conclusion that there was a significant likelihood of increased importation is not consistent with Article 3.7(i) of the AD Agreement.

C. Analysis of Likely Impact of Imports on the Domestic Industry

6.24 The second element of error alleged by the United States is the insufficiency of SECOFI's analysis of the likely impact of imports on the domestic industry. The Panel had originally concluded that, in a case involving threat of material injury, an investigating authority was required to consider, among other relevant factors, all the factors set out in Article 3.4 of the AD Agreement The Panel observed that:

> "With respect to the question of threat of material injury, we believe an investigating authority cannot come to a reasoned conclusion, based on an unbiased and objective evaluation of the facts, without taking into account the Article 3.4 factors relating to the impact of imports on the domestic industry. These factors all relate to an evaluation of the general condition and operations of the domestic industry - sales, profits, output, market share, productivity, return on investments, utilisation of capacity, factors affecting domestic prices, cash flow, inventories, employment, wages, growth, ability to raise capital. Consideration of these factors is, in our view, necessary in order to establish a background against which the investigating authority can evaluate whether imminent further dumped imports will affect the industry's condition in such a manner that material injury would occur in the absence of protective action, as required by Article 3.7."[90]

The Panel went on to consider whether SECOFI had provided an analysis of the impact of the dumped imports consistently with this obligation, and found it had not. Specifically, the Panel concluded that the final determination reflected "no meaningful analysis of a number of the Article 3.4 factors". The Panel also concluded that there was

> "no analysis of the condition of the Mexican sugar industry during the period of investigation, or projected for the near future. It is therefore not possible, by reading the final determination, to understand the overall condition of the domestic industry with respect to

[90] Panel Report, WT/DS132/R, DSR 2000:III, 1345, at para. 7.132.

the Article 3.4 factors. Yet without an understanding of the condition of the industry, it is not possible, in our view, for SECOFI to have come to a reasoned conclusion, based on an objective evaluation of the facts, concerning the likely impact of dumped imports. Such a conclusion must, in our view, reflect the projected impact of further imports on the particular domestic industry, in light of its condition. In order to conclude that there is a threat of material injury to a domestic industry that is apparently not currently injured, despite the effects of dumped imports during the period of investigation, it is necessary to have an understanding of the current condition of the industry as a background."[91]

6.25 The United States acknowledges that the redetermination contains information on the Article 3.4 factors that were not discussed in the original determination. However, in the United States' view, this consists of a mere recitation of facts, and is insufficient to satisfy the obligation to provide a reasoned analysis of the condition of the industry during the period of investigation or projected for the near future. The United States argues that SECOFI's redetermination mischaracterizes information on the condition of the domestic industry, fails to provide a reasoned explanation why improvements in trends reflecting the industry's condition during the period of investigation were not probative of the likely future condition of the industry, and relies on erroneous or unsupported factual findings. The United States points in particular to SECOFI's projections as to likely price levels and profitability of the industry, which the United States argues lead to results contrary to those actually occurring during the period of investigation, without explanation.

6.26 Mexico asserts that SECOFI's conclusions in the redetermination are well-founded, based on the evidence and the application of standard economic tests and projections. Mexico maintains that SECOFI assessed the information concerning the factors set out in Articles 3.4 and 3.7, finding that during the period of investigation, HFCS imports had had an adverse impact on the Mexican sugar industry, as seen in declining market share and increased inventories. Moreover, SECOFI reviewed the trends in prices for sugar and HFCS during the period of investigation, finding that sugar prices declined in 1996 as compared with 1994, in a context of increasing imports, and projecting stable prices for standard sugar and a decline in refined sugar prices for 1997. SECOFI projected the effects of these projected prices on the domestic industry's profits, concluding that, in light of the industry's level of debt, and its high sensitivity to price declines, projected price levels would yield declining revenues and leave the industry unable to service debt. Therefore, SECOFI concluded that there was a threat of material injury to the domestic industry.

[91] Panel Report, WT/DS132/R, DSR 2000:III, 1345, at para. 7.140.

6.27 In evaluating the redetermination in this regard, we are again faced with the question of the adequacy of SECOFI's factual redetermination, in light of the standard of review under Article 17.6.(i). Thus, in assessing the redetermination, we must judge whether, in light of the explanations given in the notice of redetermination, an unbiased and objective investigating authority could reach the conclusions reached by SECOFI on the evidence before it. We continue to keep in mind the requirements of the first two sentences of Article 3.7 of the AD Agreement, that:

> "A determination of a threat of material injury shall be based on facts and not merely on allegation, conjecture or remote possibility. The change in circumstances which would create a situation in which the dumping would cause injury must be clearly foreseen and imminent." (footnote omitted)

As noted above, the reasoned explanation required to satisfy us under the standard of review must respect these elements of Article 3.7 as well.

6.28 In the original report, the Panel observed that

> "Merely that dumped imports will increase, and will have adverse price effects, does not, *ipso facto*, lead to the conclusion that the domestic industry will be injured - if the industry is in very good condition, or if there are other factors at play, dumped imports may not threaten injury. Such a conclusion thus requires the investigating authority to analyze, based on the information before it, the likely impact of further dumped imports on the domestic industry. SECOFI concluded that imports were likely to increase, based on the increases during the period of investigation, and the available capacity of the exporting producers, but there is no meaningful analysis, based on facts, concerning the likely impact of further dumped imports on the domestic industry in the final determination, e.g., whether such increased imports are likely to account for an increased share of the growing Mexican market, have an effect on production or sales of sugar, or affect the profits of the domestic producers, etc, in such a manner as to constitute material injury. SECOFI also concluded that the dumped imports undersold the domestic product during the period of investigation, and that the dumping margins were responsible for the low prices of the dumped imports. SECOFI therefore concluded that a jump in demand for dumped imports could be expected, forcing sugar prices downward. However, there is no discussion of movements in prices of either Mexican sugar or the dumped imports - that is, there is no discussion of whether sugar prices had been "forced downward" during the period of investigation, which in our view leaves the conclusion that dumped imports in the future would force prices down in the realm of speculation. Merely that imports are likely to continue to be priced below the domestic product does not neces-

sarily lead to the conclusion that there is a threat of injury.[611] If the price level of the domestic product generates sufficient revenues and profits, injury may be unlikely."[92]

[611] This is particularly true since it appears that there is a "natural" price difference between sugar and HFCS, with HFCS priced below sugar. Notice of Initiation, US-3, MEXICO-1, para. 79. Although this price difference was mentioned in the preliminary determination, US-2, MEXICO-2, para. 277, there is no mention of it in the final determination. Nor is there any analysis as to the extent of any such "natural" price difference as compared with the observed price undercutting.

6.29 In the redetermination, SECOFI did provide information on the elements that were not addressed in the original determination. Thus, SECOFI discussed indicators of the industry's performance for the period of investigation, 1996, and the previous year, and projects trends for 1997 and in some cases 1998.[93] SECOFI noted, *inter alia*, that domestic industry market share declined, domestic sales declined, and exports increased during the period of investigation.[94] Inventories increased.[95] Productivity improved.[96] The number of workers increased 16 per cent from 1994 to 1995, and by 1 percentage point over the 1995 figure to 1996, while salaries (denominated in US dollars) declined from 1994 to 1995.[97] Capacity utilisation increased 16 per cent from 1994 to 1995, and by 3 per cent from 1995 to 1996.[98] SECOFI also analyzed the financial indicators of the industry, and found that in 1996, operating margins were 9 per cent, an increase from 5 per cent in 1995, due in large part to a decline in operating expenses.[99] The industry's net margin increased from negative 1 per cent in 1995 to 5 per cent in 1996. Return on investment increased 2 percentage points in 1996, to 5 per cent.[100]

6.30 SECOFI also addressed the movements in prices for sugar and HFCS. SECOFI noted that prices of dumped imports of HFCS declined from 1994 to 1995, then increased in 1996, although they remained below the 1994 levels.[101] Similarly, domestic sugar prices declined from 1994 to 1995, then increased in 1996, although they remained below the 1994 levels.[102] Margins of underselling

[92] Panel Report, WT/DS132/R, DSR 2000:III, 1345, at para. 7.141.

[93] The United States has made no argument that factors are not addressed *per se*; rather, the United States argues that the conclusions reached are not reasonable in light of the information addressed.

[94] We note that the notice of redetermination states that the domestic industry "was required to increase its sugar exports at prices lower than those prevailing on the domestic market". Notice of Redetermination, MEXICO-1(a), at para. 130.

[95] *Ibid.* at para. 131.

[96] *Ibid.*

[97] *Ibid.* at para. 132.

[98] *Ibid.* at para. 133.

[99] *Ibid.* at para. 143.

[100] *Ibid.* at paras. 144-45.

[101] *Ibid.* at paras. 80-81. SECOFI discusses the price changes in percentage terms, rather than actual price levels.

[102] *Ibid.* at para. 83.

for HFCS-42 compared to standard sugar were 39 per cent in 1994, 41 per cent in 1995, and 43 per cent in 1996. Margins of underselling for HFCS-55 compared to refined sugar were 48 per cent in 1994, 37 per cent in 1995, and 55 per cent in 1996.[103] SECOFI concluded that the declining trend in Mexican sugar prices was explained by competition from dumped imports, whose lower price and dynamic growth pressured the domestic industry to adapt, leading to price depression, especially in sales to the industrial sector. SECOFI concluded that this effect was confirmed by application of the Granger test.[104]

6.31 SECOFI's own analysis indicates that despite increasing levels of imports, and increasing margins of underselling by HFCS as compared to sugar prices, the domestic industry's performance improved in 1996 over 1995, with increased operating margins, net margins, and return on investment, as well as increased production and capacity utilisation. Sugar prices increased from 1995 to 1996, reflecting the general improvement in the Mexican economy. Yet despite the observed improvements in the indicators of the industry's performance, SECOFI concluded that imports of HFCS had had "adverse effects" on the domestic industry during the period of investigation. SECOFI further concluded that the projected substantially increased dumped HFCS imports would cause material injury to the domestic industry. We consider that a unbiased and objective investigating authority could not reasonably have reached these conclusions in light of the evidence and explanations in the redetermination.

6.32 In its analysis of the likely impact of dumped imports, SECOFI projected price levels for 1997, concluding that the price of HFCS 42 would increase by 2 per cent, while the price of HFCS 55 would decline by 1 per cent, the price of standard sugar would remain stable, and the price of refined sugar would decline by 10 per cent. SECOFI then projected margins of underselling for 1997, concluding that HFCS 42 would undersell standard sugar by 42 per cent, while HFCS 55 would undersell refined sugar by 52 per cent.[105] SECOFI concluded

> "The price adjustment required by domestic industry to address the estimated increase in imports under price discriminatory conditions would consequently be reflected in a decline of 9 per cent in the average selling price of sugar on the domestic market. In other words, both sugar sold to the industrial sector as well as that intended for household consumption, combined with the decline in sales, particularly to the industrial sector, because of direct substitution by high fructose corn syrup, would result in a negative impact on operating profits and margins."[106]

---

[103] Notice of Redetermination, MEXICO-1(a), at para. 87.

[104] *Ibid.* at para. 89. The Granger causality test is a standard test in economics, which measures the correlation between variables on a lagged basis.

[105] *Ibid.* at paras. 98-99.

[106] *Ibid.* at para. 100.

SECOFI also calculated that, despite an increase in demand for sweeteners, domestic industry sales would decline 10 per cent in 1997.[107]

6.33 SECOFI carried out a sensitivity analysis of the sugar industry's profits to changes in sales revenue. SECOFI found that the industry would suffer an adverse effect of 7 per cent on operating profits in response to a decline of one per cent in total revenue. Combining this with the sensitivity of the industry due to the high degree of financial leveraging, SECOFI calculated that a 1 per cent change in sales revenue would cause a 27 per cent change in net profits. Based on projected sales and prices for 1997, SECOFI projected a decline of 15 per cent in industry revenue, causing operating profits to decline by 118 per cent, which SECOFI concluded would cancel any possibility of operating profits, result in a decline in the operating margin to negative 2 per cent, and leave the industry unable to service its debt or attract capital.

6.34 As with the redetermination of likelihood of increased imports, while SECOFI has cited more information concerning the condition of the domestic industry, the underlying rationale is the same as in the original determination. SECOFI's conclusion that the industry is threatened with material injury depends on a projected decline in industry revenues in 1997 based on declining prices for sugar caused by increased dumped imports of HFCS. As discussed above, in our view, SECOFI's conclusions regarding the projected increase in imports are not supported by the evidence. This undermines the projected decline in revenues for 1997 which is at the core of SECOFI's redetermination.

6.35 Moreover, SECOFI has failed to provide a reasoned explanation for why the performance of the industry will suddenly decline significantly in 1997. SECOFI's projections of price levels and profitability for 1997 are contrary to the trends observed during the period of investigation. Thus, for instance, SECOFI projected that for 1997, prices for refined sugar would decline, while prices for standard sugar would remain the same. Yet in 1996, despite significantly increased imports, sugar prices increased. Similarly, SECOFI projected steep operating losses for the domestic industry, despite the fact that in 1996, the industry's profitability improved at the same time as imports were increasing. The projected reduction in income on which SECOFI relies in making this projection depends on the projected increase in imports, which, as discussed above, is a conclusion we do not consider could be reached by an unbiased and objective investigating authority on the evidence before SECOFI in this case.

6.36 We conclude that SECOFI's redetermination with respect to the likely impact of dumped imports of HFCS from the United States on the domestic industry which underlies the determination of threat of material injury to the Mexican sugar industry is not consistent with Articles 3.1, 3.4, and 3.7 of the AD Agreement.

[107] Notice of Redetermination, MEXICO-1(a), at para. 138.

6.37 We do not mean to suggest that it would not be possible to make a finding of threat of material injury in the circumstances of this case. Such a conclusion would be beyond the scope of our standard of review, as it would involve us in analysing the facts *de novo*. However, we do conclude that an unbiased and objective investigating authority could not reach the conclusion that the domestic sugar industry in Mexico was threatened with material injury on the basis of the evidence and explanations provided by SECOFI in the notice of redetermination. Part of the difficulty with SECOFI's redetermination in this case is that while SECOFI apparently undertook to respond to the specific criticisms set out in the original Panel's report, and has set out additional information relevant to the specific points made by the Panel in that report, there does not appear to have been an overall reconsideration and analysis of the information in light of the requirements of the AD Agreement, as clarified by the original Panel.

D. *Adequacy of Notice of Redetermination*

6.38 The United States argues that Mexico's notice of redetermination does not satisfy the requirements of Articles 12.2 and 12.2.2.[108] Mexico, on the other hand, argues that SECOFI's notice fully explains the decision on redetermination, and is backed by additional information in the record of the investigation which is referred to or underlies the analysis and conclusions set out in the notice. Essentially, Mexico argues that the United States has misunderstood the notice, or is reading Article 12 too strictly.

6.39 Article 12 of the AD Agreement requires, in pertinent part, that public notice of any final determination shall set forth

> "in sufficient detail the findings and conclusions reached on all issues of fact and law considered material by the investigating authorities. ...sufficiently detailed explanations for the ... determinations on dumping and injury and shall refer to the matters of fact and law which have led to arguments being accepted or rejected. ...all relevant information on the matters of fact and law and reasons which have led to the imposition of final measures ... as well as the reasons for the acceptance or rejection of relevant arguments or claims made by the exporters and importers...."

6.40 In this case, we have determined that SECOFI's findings and conclusions in the redetermination were not consistent with Articles 3.1, 3.4, and 3.7 of the AD Agreement. Our conclusion is based not on a failure to explain the redetermination in the notice, but on the fact that, in our view, the findings and conclusions set out in that notice, in light of the evidence in the record brought to our

---

[108] These provisions govern the contents of notices of final determinations. Mexico does not dispute that these provisions apply to the notice of redetermination, and therefore we do not address that question.

attention and as argued by Mexico in this proceeding, are not such as could reasonably be reached by an unbiased and objective investigating authority on the evidence that was before SECOFI. In light of the substantive violations found, the question of whether the notice of the ultimate determination is "sufficient" under Article 12.2 is immaterial. It is, in our view, meaningless to consider whether the notice of a decision that is substantively inconsistent with the requirements of the AD Agreement is, as a separate matter, insufficient under Article 12.2. We therefore make no findings with respect to the claim of insufficiency of the notice of redetermination.

VII. CONCLUSIONS AND RECOMMENDATION

7.1 In light of the findings above, we conclude that Mexico's imposition of definitive anti-dumping duties on imports of HFCS from the United States on the basis of the SECOFI redetermination is inconsistent with the requirements of the AD Agreement in that Mexico's inadequate consideration of the impact of dumped imports on the domestic industry, and its inadequate consideration of the potential effect of the alleged restraint agreement in its determination of likelihood of substantially increased importation, are not consistent with the provisions of Articles 3.1, 3.4, 3.7 and 3.7(i) of the AD Agreement. We therefore consider that Mexico has failed to implement the recommendation of the original Panel and the DSU to bring its measure into conformity with its obligations under the AD Agreement.

7.2 Under Article 3.8 of the DSU, in cases where there is infringement of the obligations assumed under a covered agreement, the action is considered *prima facie* to constitute a case of nullification or impairment of benefits under that agreement. Accordingly, we conclude that to the extent Mexico has acted inconsistently with the provisions of the AD Agreement, it has nullified or impaired benefits accruing to the United States under that Agreement.

7.3 We recommend that the Dispute Settlement Body request Mexico to bring its measure into conformity with its obligations under the AD Agreement.

ANNEX A

Contents	Page

ANSWERS OF MEXICO TO QUESTIONS FROM THE PANEL

1. It seems that there are two questions to be answered with respect to the possible changeover from use of sugar to use of HFCS by a particular consuming industry and a particular consuming company. First, whether such a switch is technically possible in the light of the product in question and the manufacturing process, and second, the incentive to do so in the short term and long term. What evidence supports the conclusion that the predicted increase in HFCS use by industries other than soft drink bottlers, over 400 per cent in 1997 over their actual use in 1996, is likely? Is there any information on the rate of increase of HFCS use by these industries during the period of investigation?

The basis of Mexico's determination of the likelihood of increased imports included a prospective analysis backed by the pattern observed in the period under investigation. In addition, this examination included estimates of the potential consumption of sugar likely to be switched as a result of competition from dumped HFCS imports, so as to demonstrate that, even on the assumption that there was indeed an alleged restraint agreement between soft drink bottlers and the sugar industry, the potential demand from other consuming industries pointed to the existence of a likely increase in dumped imports.

As part of its determination and in the context of the analysis of the threat of injury factors listed in Article 3.7 of the WTO Anti-Dumping Agreement, Mexico quantified the probable volume of potential demand for HFCS that industries other than soft drink bottlers might generate, so as to illustrate the convincing reasons for believing that in the immediate future there would be a substantial increase in dumped imports. Nevertheless, the United States of America (USA) boiled down Mexico's entire determination to specifying the figures which, in its opinion, ought to be included in the analysis. In particular, the crucial problem the USA identified in Mexico's determination was the size of the rate of increase, which, according to its own calculations, would be obtained from the estimate.

In its second written submission, Mexico rejected the USA's emphasis in demonstrating that the calculations were incorrect and asserting, from its own interpretation of the SECOFI determination, that the determination was inconsistent with the terms of the Anti-Dumping Agreement. In this regard, Mexico reiterates that the determination of the likelihood of increased dumped imports should not be reduced to the results of a mathematical calculation and above all when the calculation includes an estimate of future events. Since the Anti-Dumping Agreement *does not* establish quantitative parameters for compliance with the Agreement's provisions regarding a substantial increase in imports or the assumed magnitude of the likelihood of the occurrence of a future event, objecting to an investigating authority's determination on the basis of the validity of one figure goes beyond the provisions of the Agreement itself, and in no sense can obligations that *do not* stem from the Anti-Dumping Agreement be imposed on Mexico.

Again, as part of the reply, Mexico would point out that the commercial interchangeability and substitution of HFCS and sugar was amply analysed by SECOFI in the course of the anti-dumping investigation. The investigating authority's conclusions and findings, as well as the basis for arriving at the determination, were sufficiently documented in the record and established in the original preliminary and final resolutions.

In particular, the evidence on the functions and applications of HFCS and sugar were analysed in paragraphs 187 to 206 of the preliminary resolution[1] and 400 to 422 of the original final resolution. The evidence analysed by the investigating authority included more particularly: specialized literature on sweeteners, opinions of technical and industrial experts, promotional catalogues of HFCS producers and information obtained from industrial users in different production sectors.

Similarly, from an analysis of the information provided by importers of HFCS originating in the US on their sales lists, as well as information from industrial users of HFCS and sugar, the investigating authority concluded that the imports under investigation were competing on the Mexican market for the same consumers as those of domestic sugar producers.

Specifically, on the basis of sales of imported HFCS by the three main importing firms, the investigating authority found that they went to the following consumer sectors different from soft drink bottlers: food, juices and concentrates, non-carbonated beverages, wines and spirits, bread-making, biscuits, sweets and pastry, pharmaceuticals and dairy products.

From the analysis of all the information described, the investigating authority determined the commercial interchangeability and substitution of HFCS for sugar in various industrial applications. Such substitution, which obviously

---

[1] "Preliminary resolution of the anti-dumping investigation into imports of high fructose corn syrup, merchandise classified in tariff headings 1702.40.01, 1702.40.99, 1702.60.01 and 1702.90.99 of the General Import Tariff, originating in the United States of America, irrespective of the country of provenance", published in the Official Journal of the Federation, 25 June 1997.

varies depending on the product and production process, began when HFCS started to be imported from the USA.

Again, the economic context predicted for 1997 was broadly in favour of increased use of HFCS over both the long and the short term. In the three years from 1994 to 1996, the position of HFCS import prices relative to domestic sugar prices was marked by more and more undercutting. Similarly, the tariff reductions on HFCS imports from the USA as a result of the North American Free Trade Agreement, the absence of non-tariff barriers and the excess production capacity of the industry in the USA made for greater incentives to use an abundant low cost substitute. Obviously, for a producer of goods using nutritional sweeteners, the lower production cost using HFCS compared to sugar was a crucial element in deciding which sweetener to use, since both products were commercially interchangeable in the production process.

The likelihood of increased use of HFCS by industries other than soft drink bottlers is also based on the sales performance of those industries observed in 1996, as can be seen from the information supplied in exhibit MEXICO-39[2] - summarized in the following table - pertaining to the analysis of sales of HFCS imports on the Mexican market by two of the main importers, Almidones Mexicanos, S.A. de C.V. and Arancia, C.P.C., S.A. de C.V., which together account for 81 per cent of the imports investigated.[3]

High Fructose Corn Syrup (HFCS-42 and HFCS-55)/Wet Base
Import Sales
Market Segment/1996

Industry	Tons		
	Almex	**Arancia, CPC.**	**Total**
Soft drinks	96,093,060	17,173,661	113,266,721
Other industries	18,711,717	37,984,593	56,696,310
Total	**114,804,777**	**55,158,254**	**169,963,031**

Source: Sales by importing firms: written statement by Almidones Mexicanos, S.A. de C.V., sheet 1654 of 28 May 1997 and reply by Arancia CPC, S.A. de C.V., by sheet 2627 of 5 August 1997 to investigating authority request UPCI.310.97.114 of 16 July 1997.

In addition, from information on sales of imported HFCS for 1994 supplied by Arancia Corn Products, S.A. de C.V. (previously Arancia CPC, S.A. de C.V.) and information given in the previous paragraph, it was found that from 1994 to 1996 HFCS sales to industries other than soft drink bottlers showed a significant increase. Also, from January to December 1996, monthly sales of imported HFCS by that enterprise to industries other than soft drink bottlers re-

2 It should be noted that MEXICO-39 was supplied as an annex in the dispute settlement procedure brought before the previous Panel, and hence the WTO Secretariat has that annex.

3 See para. 42 of the revised final resolution.

vealed a rise, particularly in the second half of the year. The sales pattern in the two periods indicated showed increasingly larger substitution and consumption of HFCS in those industries.

High Fructose Corn Syrup (HFCS-42 and HFCS-55)/Wet Base Import Sales by Arancia CPC, S.A. de C.V.

Industry	1994 (kg.)	1996 (kg.)	1996/1994 (%)
Soft drinks	750,660	17,173,661	2,188
Other industries	17,555,457	37,984,593	116
Food	3,855,744	10,045,261	161
Beverages (not soft drinks)	3,561,994	12,611,743	254
Marketing company	560	2,539	353
Pharmaceuticals	91,404	150,070	64
Milk products	1,151,560	4,296,570	273
Bread-making and biscuits	8,894,195	10,878,410	22
Total	**18,306,117**	**55,158,254**	**201**

Source: Reply by Arancia CPC, S.A. de C.V., in sheet 2803 of 15 August 1997 to investigating authority request UPCI.310.97.1325 of 28 July 1997 (includes changes as a result of *in situ* verification of information on 23 to 26 September 1997).

The growing HFCS use and consumption in industries other than soft drink bottlers, as well as the existence of consumption of sugar that could be replaced, revealed that, if the conditions under which HFCS had been imported from 1994 to 1996 continued, an increased displacement of sugar in those industries was imminent. While the pace of such a substitution differed among industrial users, from the outlook at the time of the investigation period there was no obstacle to prevent the situation moving faster in the immediate future.

High Fructose Corn Syrup (HFCS-42 + HFCS-55)/Wet Base Import Sales by Type of Activity by Arancia CPC, S.A. de C.V. First Half of 1996

Industry	Jan	Feb	Mar	Apr	May	Jun	Jan-Jun
Soft drinks	197,886	253,205	297,640	85,190	189,010	113,045	1,135,976
Other industries	2,084,590	1,667,870	1,574,600	2,398,176	3,786,474	4,091,382	15,603,092
Food	404,140	454,203	576,250	779,099	1,263,684	1,179,876	4,657,252
Beverages (not soft drinks)	862,710	526,347	625,205	702,072	1,022,605	1,571,091	5,310,030
Marketing company	0	0	0	0	0	0	0
Pharma-ceuticals	11,075	18,530	13,535	13,705	10,550	4,200	71,595
Milk products	175,735	115,910	25,010	292,165	546,525	470,735	1,626,080

Industry	Jan	Feb	Mar	Apr	May	Jun	Jan-Jun
Bread-making and bis-cuits	630,930	552,880	334,600	611,135	943,110	865,480	3,938,135
Total	**2,282,476**	**1,921,075**	**1,872,240**	**2,483,366**	**3,975,484**	**4,204,427**	**16,739,068**

Source: Reply by Arancia CPC, S.A. de C.V., in sheet 2803 of 15 August 1997 to investigating authority request UPCI.310.97.1325 of 28 July 1997 (includes changes as a result of *in situ* verification of the information on 23 to 26 September 1997).

High Fructose Corn Syrup (HFCS-42 + HFCS-55)/Wet Base Import Sales by Type of Activity by Arancia CPC, S.A. de C.V. Second Half of 1996

Industry	Jul	Aug	Sep	Oct	Nov	Dec	Jul-Dec
Soft drinks	836,400	1,490,815	1,993,597	2,512,333	4,461,440	4,743,100	16,037,685
Other industries	3,125,040	2,769,807	3,673,645	4,378,471	4,487,479	3,947,059	22,381,501
Food	1,254,105	728,547	984,840	856,635	834,970	728,912	5,388,009
Beverages (not soft drinks)	1,039,915	1,195,295	965,965	1,460,551	1,739,784	900,203	7,301,713
Marketing company	0	0	0	0	1,120	1,419	2,539
Pharma-ceuticals	1,960	14,365	0	32,460	16,350	13,340	78,475
Milk products	398,160	383,500	349,350	441,770	559,805	537,905	2,670,490
Bread-making and bis-cuits	430,900	448,100	1,373,490	1,587,055	1,335,450	1,765,280	6,940,275
Total	**3,961,440**	**4,260,622**	**5,667,242**	**6,890,804**	**8,948,919**	**8,690,159**	**38,419,186**

Source: Reply by Arancia CPC, S.A. de C.V., in sheet 2803 of 15 August 1997 to investigating authority request UPCI.310.97.1325 of 28 July 1997 (includes changes as a result of *in situ* verification of the information on 23 to 26 September 1997).

High Fructose Corn Syrup (HFCS-42 + HFCS-55)/Wet Base
Import Sales by Type of Activity by Arancia CPC, S.A. de C.V.
1996

Industry	Jan-Jun	Jul-Dec	Jan-Jun/Jul-Dec (%)
Soft Drinks	1,1135,976	16,037,685	1,312
Other Industries	15,603,092	22,381,501	43
Food	4,657,252	5,388,009	16
Beverages (not soft drinks)	5,310,030	7,301,713	38
Marketing company	0	2,539	n/a
Pharmaceuticals	71,595	78,475	10
Milk products	1,626,080	2,670,490	64
Bread-making and biscuits	3,938,135	6,940,275	76
Total	**16,739,068**	**38,419,186**	**130**

Source: Reply by Arancia CPC, S.A. de C.V., in sheet 2803 of 15 August 1997 to investigating authority request UPCI.310.97.1325 of 28 July 1997 (includes changes as a result of *in situ* verification of the information on 23-26 September 1997).

2. There is no reference in paragraph 57 of the redetermination to the degree of technical substitutability of HFCS for sugar in bread-making. Nor is there any information on the proportionate use of HFCS and sugar in bread-making in exhibit MEXICO-20. Bread accounts for 86 per cent of the projected volume of sugar consumption in 1997 that SECOFI concludes could be substituted for by HFCS. Could Mexico point to any evidence in the record on the actual use of HFCS in bread-making in Mexico? Could Mexico indicate specifically where in the redetermination this information, if any, was considered?

First of all it is necessary to point out that exhibit MEXICO-20 does contain information on the use of HFCS and sugar in the bread-making industry. It includes, in particular, the data on the enterprises Marinela de Occidente, S.A. de C.V., Productos Marinela, S.A. de C.V., and Panificación Bimbo, S.A. de C.V. Secondly, as evidence of the actual use of HFCS in the bread-making industry in Mexico, the Panel is referred to the information contained in exhibit MEXICO-39 which shows imported HFCS sales in 1996 by the main importers mentioned in the reply to question 2. The information notes that, in 1996, enterprises in the bread-making industry that consumed HFCS in Mexico were, among others, the following:

Sales of High Fructose Corn Syrup Originating in the United States of America 1996

Name of Client	Sales by Arancia kg.	Sales by Almex kg.
Bimbo de Baja California, S.A. de C.V.	189,420	-
Bimbo de Chihuahua, S.A. de C.V.	47,320	-
Bimbo de Occidente, S.A. de C.V.	78,685	-
Bimbo de Puebla S.A. de C.V.	24,080	-
Bimbo de San Luis Potosi S.A. de C.V.	17,640	-
Bimbo de Yucatan, S.A. de C.V.	92,960	-
Bimbo del Centro S.A. de C.V.	18,200	-
Bimbo del Norte, S.A. de C.V.	98,825	-
Bimbo del Pacifico, S.A. de C.V.	37,520	-
Bimbo del Golfo, S.A. de C.V.	-	41,630
Bimbo del Noroeste, S.A. de C.V.	-	56,500
Continental de Alimentos, S.A.	110,440	-
Complementos Alimenticios, S.A.	-	59,780
Marinela de Baja California S.A. de C.V.	632,320	-
Marinela de Occidente S.A. de C	663,145	190,120
Marinela del Norte, S.A. de C.V.	409,488	220,545
Marinela del Sureste S.A. de C.V.	140,030	41,930
Panificacion Bimbo, S.A. de C.V.	421,480	-
Panificadora el Panque, S.A. de C.V.	1,680	-
Paniplus S.A. de C.V.	445,920	-
Paniplus de Occidente, S.A. de C.V.	-	28,290
Productos Lamar, S.A. de C.V.	-	71,030
Productos Marinela, S.A. de C.V.	2,124,905	223,906
Suandy Mexico, S.A. de C.V.	91,000	-
Tia Rosa, S.A. de C.V.	506,935	78,140
TOTAL	6,151,993	1,011,871

Source: Exhibit MEXICO-39, reply by Arancia CPC, S.A. de C.V., in sheet 2803 of 15 August 1997 to investigating authority request UPCI.310.97.1325 of 28 July 1997 and reply by Almidones Mexicanos, S.A. de C.V., in sheet 2770 of 13 August 1997 to investigating authority request UPCI.310.97.1193 of 16 July 1997.

Again, in relation to the last part of the question, it should be noted that, although paragraph 57 of the revised final resolution failed to mention the degree of substitution of HFCS for sugar in the bread-making industry, the explicit reference to that information is made in paragraphs 122 and 123 of the revised final resolution. It should also be noted that the information on the use of HFCS in the bread-making industry was considered in the analysis described in paragraph 53 of the resolution.

3. Could Mexico clarify what is meant, in paragraph 144 of the redetermination, by the net financial burden as a percentage of overall cost of financing? Specifically, could Mexico explain what elements make up the numerator, what is netted out of the numerator, and what elements make up the denominator.

Mexico wishes to clarify that in paragraph 144 of the revised final resolution SECOFI did not state that the net financial burden corresponds to a percentage of the overall cost of financing, but that the investigating authority said:

> "144 What is more ... the industry's net financial burden viewed as a percentage of the overall cost of financing remained unchanged in 1996 compared to 1995" (Emphasis added)

In this respect it is important to note that, in keeping with Mexican accountancy rules, the overall cost of financing[4] is defined as the sum of: (1) the interest on an enterprise's loans; (2) the profit or loss from foreign exchange fluctuations[5]; and (3) the result of the monetary position known as *Repomo*.[6]

Since interest, foreign exchange fluctuations and the monetary position have a direct impact on the amounts paid for debt use, it is necessary to add them in accordance with the following formula

$$cif = i \pm gpc \pm repomo$$

Where **cif** is the overall cost of financing, **i** represents the net interest of the period, **gpc** is equal to the period's foreign exchange profits or losses and ***repomo*** is the difference between monetary assets and monetary liabilities, as multiplied by the period's rate of inflation[7]; as will be seen, the arithmetical sign ± means in fact that the variables in the equation are net variables.

As for **i**, it is a net variable because it represents the balance of the financial *revenue and expenses* account[8]; **gpc** is a net variable because it involves the *profits or losses* from foreign currency operations and ***repomo*** represents the *net inflationary profits or losses* due to maintaining monetary positions of credits with creditors and debts with debtors, in Mexican pesos.

---

4 Paragraph 116 of Bulletin B-10 of the Generally Accepted Accountancy Principles (GAAP) MEXICO-22.

5 For further details see paras. 122 to 139 of GAAP Bulletin B-10. MEXICO-22.

6 For further details see paras. 140 to 155 of GAAP Bulletin B-10. MEXICO-22.

7 Monetary assets means cash, customers, accounts payable, amounts realisable, i.e., liquid assets. Monetary liabilities means suppliers, loans, creditors, the circulating part of long-term liabilities and similar accounts of a circulating nature.

8 Point 5.1 of the first updated document in GAAP Bulletin B-10. MEXICO-22.

Because of this, SECOFI calculated the industry's net financial burden as the sum of the overall cost of financing of 48 sugar mills[9] and not as a percentage, as can be seen from the following equation:

$$cfn_{ind} = \sum_{n=1} cf_{n}$$

Where $\mathbf{cfn}_{ind}$ represents the sugar industry's net financial burden, $\mathbf{cif}_{n}$ is the overall cost of financing each sugar $\text{mill}_{\mathbf{n}}$, which is shown on the corresponding statement of interest, immediately after the operating profit or EBIT. Hence, the net financial burden is not a quotient or a percentage, for which reason there are no numerators or denominators in the calculations of any of the variables in the above equation.

4. It appears from paragraph 17 of Mexico's second submission that SECOFI chose to exclude production for export markets when considering changes in production volumes. The redetermination refers, at paragraph 129, to the fact that the production volume oriented toward the domestic market declined by 2 per cent in 1996 with respect to 1995, but does not refer to the absolute increase in production. Could Mexico explain why? How can consideration only of production oriented to the domestic market be justified in light of the fact that the productivity of the industry included production for both the domestic and export markets?

Mexico wishes to clarify that in paragraph 129 of the revised final resolution, SECOFI analysed the pattern of domestic sugar production oriented towards the domestic market in terms of volume (percentage variation) and in relation to apparent domestic consumption (ADC). In other words, it is *the proportion of the domestic market that corresponded to domestic sugar production* and *not* the part intended for the export market.[10]

Where:

> The percentage share of domestic production oriented to the domestic market in apparent domestic consumption = [((domestic sugar production - sugar exports) / ADP)* 100]

---

9 See MEXICO-14.

10 See para. 129 of the revised final resolution "... the share of apparent domestic consumption declined by 4 percentage points with respect to the level in 1995; this loss of market share for the sugar industry was not limited to the period under investigation, since it changed from a share of apparent domestic consumption of 98 per cent in 1994 to 93 per cent in 1996. In absolute terms as well, the production volume oriented to the domestic market declined by 2 per cent in 1996 with respect to 1995".

ADP = (domestic sugar production + domestic HFCS production + sugar imports + HFCS imports - sugar exports)

If the share of domestic sugar production intended for the export market had been included, the factors making up apparent domestic consumption *would not total 100 per cent*, since sugar exports were deducted in calculating domestic consumption of sweeteners. Furthermore, Mexico considers that when a share of domestic production is intended for the export market, the market performance of the domestic industry will be shown by production oriented to the domestic market.

It is important to mention that SECOFI *did not* fail to evaluate domestic sugar exports, since the Ministry examined it as another of the factors with an impact on the situation of the domestic industry, so that paragraph 130 of the revised final resolution said that, in view of the loss of domestic sales, the industry was obliged to increase its exports of sugar.

Again, it is important to point out that SECOFI *did not* deny the increase in total domestic sugar production, nor did it deny the increased employment, resulting in increased productivity in the sugar industry.[11] However, the increased productivity is explained by the increase in domestic sugar production as a result of dynamic exports, *which does not detract from the loss of market share for domestic sugar.*

5. Mexico's conclusion that the soft drink industry will supply the entirety of HFCS consumption allowed under the restraint agreement, 350,000 tons, from domestic production implies an increase of 128 per cent in HFCS use by soft drink bottlers. What is the evidence to support this projected level of HFCS use? This increase refers to domestically produced HFCS. Does this not suggest that the problem is not HFCS imports, but simply increasing use of HFCS *per se*?

First, it should be noted that the consideration that all of the consumption permitted under the alleged restraint agreement would be supplied by domestic production was not a conclusion reached by Mexico but a working hypothesis. Under this hypothesis, it could be established that, even if the alleged restraint agreement was not strictly complied with and the consumption level to which

---

[11] See paras. 131 and 135 of the revised final resolution.

"131. ... the sugar industry's productivity, measured as the ratio of production to the number of workers employed, improved during the period under investigation by 6 percentage points compared to 1995."

"135. It is also significant that the behaviour of wages, inventory and productivity in the sugar industry can be explained by the condition in which the sugar industry was found during the period under investigation, since it needed to improve its production levels in order to meet internal demand, maintain a stock of inventory so as not to generate charges, and be able to export its surplus."

bottlers were allegedly confined was not supplied by imports (as had traditionally been the case) but by domestic production, an increase in imports would have proved necessary to satisfy the growing demand by industries other than bottlers.

In fact, as Mexico established in its second written submission with regard to the USA's assertions in its first submission, that hypothesis could be discarded. The information that Mexico considered in respect of the alleged agreement and supplied by the parties did not establish the source of supply nor did it indicate a requirement to comply strictly with the level of consumption or penalties in the event of non-compliance. Nevertheless, Mexico considered as a hypothesis, for the purpose of determining the existence of a likelihood of increased imports, that both conditions might exist, so as not to overestimate the demand for further imports.

Indeed, a consumption level limited to 350,000 tons for soft drink bottlers could be supplied by imports, whereas the demand from other industries would have to be met by domestic production. Actually, the decision as to which HFCS is to supply a particular industry or enterprise would depend on the importer-producer in terms of costs, prices and commercial agreements with his customers. The fact is that, regardless of the decision, domestic production, even if it worked at 100 per cent capacity, would not be enough to supply total demand. As an example, it should be noted that, from January to September 1997, imports stood at nearly 260,000 tons wet base, even though the anti-dumping investigation had been initiated in January 1997 and domestic HFCS production was operating to the full.

Again, with the information available to it, Mexico was able to estimate that annual domestic HFCS production for 1997 had not exceeded 250,000 tons, which in terms of the alleged restraint agreement alone left 100,000 tons to be supplied by imports, plus additional demand by industries other than soft drink bottlers. Nevertheless, Mexico made both of these restrictive assumptions so as not to overestimate the likelihood of increased imports, in other words, that the limit on consumption by bottlers would be strictly complied with and that consumption would be supplied by domestic production.

The increased use of HFCS by soft drink bottlers is to be seen in the growing trend in sales to such users during the period of investigation, namely January-December 1996[12], as well as in the information available in the investigation's administrative record on HFCS consumption forecasts for such users that are based on the estimated performance of soft drinks production and, hence, on demand for sweeteners, particularly HFCS. This is supported by two attached studies (MEXICO-23) by recognized specialists in the sweetener industry on the outlook for HFCS demand in Mexico by the soft drinks industry, and they form part of the administrative record of the anti-dumping investigation.

---

12 See MEXICO-39.

Mexico rejects the scenario estimated for 1997 which suggests that the problem lies in increased use of HFCS *per se* and not in imports. In fact, Mexico considered in its estimate that part of HFCS consumption would be met by domestic production and not only by imports. This does not imply that the increase in imports stemming from greater use can be qualified as negligible or that its adverse effects on the domestic industry can be minimized. It should be emphasized that greater use of HFCS supplied by domestic production, while it would gradually displace the use of the sugar, the effects would differ from those of dumped imports. Furthermore, domestic HFCS production and sugar would compete on a basis that was not distorted by unfair practices and, therefore, at higher prices, whereas the reason for the increase in imports is attractive dumping prices on the Mexican market, which may have the effect of speeding up substitution and increasing demand for further imports. The momentum of the substitution and the price effects of greater HFCS use differ significantly as between domestically produced HFCS and HFCS obtained from dumped imports.

6. In paragraph 162 of the redetermination, Mexico refers to the 4.6 times ratio of total liabilities to book capital as a negative indication of the condition of the industry. Could Mexico explain what the benchmark is against which it is concluded that this particular ratio is high?

In conducting its financial analysis, SECOFI considered that borrowing capacity relates to the additional debts an enterprise may contract without running the risk of failing to pay off a loan, in other words, lenders can recover their loans only when the borrower's repayment capacity is equivalent to or higher than the sum of repayments of principal and payment of interest.

In view of the above, it is important for every enterprise to maintain a suitable balance between debt and capital in order to ensure that the capital or the viability of the organization are not at risk, i.e. enterprises must make sure that they do not borrow beyond their payment capacity.

Broadly speaking, financial leverage ratios measure the protection of creditors against the probable insolvency of a borrowing enterprise, as well as the enterprise's ability to obtain financing for investment. In fact, leverage ratios show what is the enterprise's capital structure, and therefore allow us to understand the link between that capital structure and the operating risk associated with a leveraged enterprise.

If the leverage is significantly high, this means that to continue financing itself at similar levels, economic viability will depend on stable growth in expected income; otherwise, the enterprise is likely to become insolvent in repaying its commitments to creditors or perhaps it may incur net losses.

This reasoning is fully applicable to the ratio of total liabilities to book capital. However, this ratio reveals a further situation: the autonomy of shareholders over their investment depends on the level of borrowing; in other words, as this ratio rises, the shareholders' net investment value falls proportionately, which gradually leads to lost decision-making ability regarding the financing strategy to be followed.[13]

In view of these considerations, in paragraph 162 of its revised final resolution, SECOFI stated that in 1996 the domestic industry showed a ratio of total liabilities to book capital of 4.6 times, in other words, the sugar industry's debt was at least 3.6 times higher than shareholders' investment in the industry. This reveals that shareholders technically lost their investments to creditors and lost autonomous decision-making powers.

In short, Mexico is of the view that the very significance of the leverage ratios obtained gives enough of an idea to appreciate when a debt level is unmistakably high. Mexico recognises that SECOFI did not compare the resulting debt to book capital ratio with the average in other industries. However, a ratio of 4.6 times (460 per cent) for the industry in 1996 showed a debt level that is excessive.

Further considerations

Mexico considers it of the utmost importance to expatiate on the significance, in terms of the present procedure, of the concepts of overall cost of financing and financial leverage, since they involve, on the one hand, net payments by the sugar industry for the use of debts in its operations, and on the other, the industry's capital structure and the risk it runs.

In this respect, it should be borne in mind that the debt level has a direct impact on the amount of the financial burden, for which reason, as already pointed out, the industry must in future be able to generate stable income and operating profits at least for an amount identical to its financing cost, so as not to incur losses. What is more, it must generate profits that can guarantee its economic viability.

In this connection, Mexico recognizes that an enterprise with low debt levels should increase the debt in order to back investment for higher profits. However, this means that it has to cope with greater payments for interest, foreign exchange fluctuations and a better monetary situation, which will increase its overall cost of financing. It can be deduced from this that the outstanding issues for deciding to increase borrowings and the overall cost of financing are: how risky is it to borrow more and how far can it be done?, and how is the risk of insolvency viewed in the light of the decision to change the existing capital structure for one that is more leveraged?[14] From this it can be inferred that the decision to increase the debt is not a straight forward decision and involves a thorough-going analysis to define an enterprise's financial strategy.

---

[13] This is because creditors will not want the enterprise to borrow more, for they must protect their interests.

[14] It should be borne in mind that capital structure is defined as a percentage mixture of own capital and total liabilities, because 100 per cent of the investment is accounted for by total assets.

7. Can Mexico reconcile the substitution rates provided in the Almex market survey and by the consultants GEA that are set out in exhibit MEXICO-20 with the substitution rates relied on by SECOFI in exhibit MEXICO-21? What is the evidence for the conclusion that manufacturers of products other than soft drinks who had not in the past used HFCS would do so in 1997 in the amounts implied by the figures in exhibit MEXICO-21, i.e., in the case of marmalade, 35 per cent of total predicted 1997 sugar consumption, or 6,900 tons. In particular, why would this occur when the price differential between sugar and HFCS was projected to lessen, slightly, as compared to 1996, a year in which such volumes of HFCS were not consumed by industries other than soft drink bottlers?

The substitution rates set out in exhibit MEXICO-21 derive in part from the substitution rates established in the Almex market survey and in part from the evidence available on the use of HFCS in products included in the sugar consuming sectors, as explained in the following table:

Industry	Degree of substitution mentioned in exhibit MEXICO-21	Degree of substitution mentioned in the Almex survey	Comments
Bread	100%	100%	Nominally, it was decided to use the same percentage substitution for bread-making as indicated by Almex, although effectively a degree of substitution of 50% was relied upon.
Juices and concentrates	100%	100%	The Almex survey concerns non-carbonated beverages - i.e. beverage industries other than the soft drink bottlers.
Marmalades	70%	33%	In this case, the degree of substitution relied upon was the degree to which HFCS had already been used instead of sugar in accordance with the information supplied by the company Mermeladas Mago, S.A. de C.V. Reducing the 70% by half, a degree of substitution of 35% was in fact used, which is lower than the average degree of substitution of other producers of marmalades such as Frexport, S.A. de C.V.
Canned fruit	52%	3%	In this case, the degree of substitution relied upon was the degree to which HFCS had already been used instead of sugar in accordance with the information supplied by the company Confituras La Florida, S.A. de C.V. Reducing the 52% by half, the degree of substitution used in reality was 26%. It should be pointed out that in the case of Almex, it concerns the heading "Canned fruit". The reference in exhibit MEXICO-21, is to "fruit in syrup" from the food segment. This segment also contains products such as orange segments,

Industry	Degree of substitution mentioned in exhibit MEXICO-21	Degree of substitution mentioned in the Almex survey	Comments
			grapefruit segments, pineapple cubes, papaya cubes, melon cubes and mango slices, which correspond generically to canned fruit, and already showed a rate of substitution of 100% according to the information supplied by the company Industrias Citrícolas de Montemorelos, S.A. de C.V.
Milk products	50%	0-50%	In the case of Almex, the milk products heading corresponds to yoghurt. In this case, the degree to which HFCS had already been substituted for sugar in accordance with the information supplied by the companies Chantilly, S.A. de C.V., Helados Bing, S.A. de C.V. and Helados Holanda, S.A. de C.V. was considered to provide evidence to suggest that the rate could average about 25%.
Biscuits	10%	0-10%	The degree of substitution relied upon was the maximum that could be reached according to the Almex survey, since the information supplied by the companies Fabrica de Galletas La Moderna, S.A. de C.V. and Gamesa, S.A. de C.V. confirmed that that degree had already been attained.
Sweets	50%	0-5%	36. With respect to sweets, the information relied upon was that supplied by the company Anderson Clayton & Co., S.A. de C.V., which showed a degree of substitution of 100% for liquid caramel. However, in view of the wide range of products that could be considered in this industry, it was in fact decided to use a degree of substitution of 25%.

The elements supporting Mexico's conclusion that industries other than soft drink bottlers that had not used HFCS would do so in 1997 are as follows:

Imports of HFCS from the United States increased significantly during the second half of 1996 as compared to the first half of the year, spurred on by the growing margin of price undercutting by competitors on the Mexican market with respect to domestically produced sugar.

This increase in sales of imported HFCS took place in an economic context marked by the recovery of domestic demand. In other words, industrial users already using HFCS were taking advantage of the increase in demand by using a substitute supplied at a price significantly lower than that of sugar used by their competitors.

This meant that those already using HFCS benefited from a reduction in the cost of sweetener inputs, ranging from 43 to 56 per cent, on average, with respect to the sugar consumed by the other producers. This cost advantage inevitably meant that they were more competitive with their goods on the market than those that did not use HFCS or, alternatively, that they could increase their profits, or both.

Persistence of these conditions would clearly mean that eventually, the industrial producers that did not consume HFCS would lose their market share, or else suffer a loss of profitability. If dumped HFCS imports were to continue competing on the market, undercutting sugar prices, the expansion of the customer base resulting from the demonstration effect of users already utilizing HFCS would accelerate substitution of HFCS for sugar in production operations, even assuming that the rate of substitution of a given industry constituted a technical limitation.

This is corroborated by the behaviour of industrial users during 1996. Exhibit MEXICO-39 shows that during the second half of 1996, importers considerably expanded their customer base in practically all of the industries other than the soft drink bottling industry.

In other words, many companies which did not consume HFCS during the months from January to June 1996 began to use it in their production operations starting in July of that year. In the specific case of the HFCS import sales of Arancia CPC, S.A. de C.V., the number of industrial users other than soft drink bottlers that began to use HFCS in the second half of 1996 rose to 48 enterprises. In fact, the increase in imported HFCS sales by that company in the above-mentioned sectors between the first half and the second half of the year was 43 per cent.

These facts, added to what was already said by Mexico in its first and second written submissions concerning the economic context foreseen for 1997, support the determination that *the substitution of HFCS for sugar in industries other than the soft drink bottling industry would accelerate if competition from dumped imports continued.* The repercussions of this substitution on sugar consumption were assessed by using an estimate, based on an accepted methodology, of what could reasonably be expected in the immediate future if the incentives to use HFCS in the different production operations remained unchanged.

The reason for the conclusion that in 1997 the increase in the use of HFCS would accelerate in this way considering the predicted evolution of prices, in addition to the considerations set forth in the reply to question 1, lies in the fact that for that year the pre-market phase could already be considered to have ended (i.e. a potential demand had already been created and the necessary conditions for market expansion had been met). It should be recalled that an embryonic market had already begun to form before 1994, but the process had been interrupted by the sharp fall in consumption in 1995, and it was only in the second half of 1996 that the market growth recovered its momentum. Thus, by the end of 1996 it was reasonable to expect a significant growth in demand for 1997, especially considering that the economic context was far more favourable for the industry than during the three preceding years.

Thus, in spite of the fact that the price forecasts for HFCS suggested that there would be a slight variation with respect to 1996, the margin of price undercutting by HFCS imports with respect to sugar would continue to be sufficiently high to constitute an economic incentive that would strengthen the increase in consumption by the enterprises using HFCS, and would hence increase the pressure on competitors that continued to consume sugar, obliging them in the short term to adjust to the conditions of competition imposed by their rivals. This in turn, would put pressure on the domestic sugar industry to reduce its prices for those users so as to make them competitive with HFCS prices. However, since the magnitude of the adjustment that would be needed to compete on an equal footing implied a significant decline in sugar prices, the only realistic option would be substitution, and the resulting displacement of sugar from the market.

8. Could Mexico please clarify what is meant by "grados de sustitución" in the table "Consumo real de azúcar por sector" in exhibit MEXICO-21. Do those figures not indicate the proportions in which the surveyed companies actually used HFCS and sugar in their production operations in 1996? If so, on what basis can it be concluded that other companies both can and will, in 1997, switch from using sugar to using sugar and HFCS in the same proportions in their own production operations. It appears that the survey information in exhibit MEXICO-20 is from companies that already use HFCS in their production operations. How can conclusions about the likely rate of use of HFCS by companies that have not in the past used HFCS be justified on the basis of information provided by companies that already use HFCS.

The degrees of substitution (*grados de sustitución*) mentioned in exhibit MEXICO-21 refer, as explained in the reply to question 7, to the extent to which industrial users could substitute HFCS for sugar in their production operations, calculated on the basis of the percentage of substitution already used in certain sectors and the extent to which it was technically feasible to substitute sugar consumption for a given product or in a given sector.

Thus, we are not speaking of volumes of sugar actually displaced, but of potential sugar consumption likely to be substituted for by dumped imports; otherwise the situation of the domestic sugar industry would have been one of injury rather than threat of injury.

The basis for concluding that companies that had not used the imported product would in fact use it in the immediate future is the unquestionable economic benefit they would derive from using an input that was cheaper because it was imported at dumped prices, given that it had already proven to be commercially interchangeable with sugar.

The issue of whether the use of HFCS by the new companies entering the market would match the rate at which other companies use HFCS basically depends on the specific production operations and products concerned. Conditions can vary substantially from one sector or one product to another within a given industry. However, at the level of each consumer industry there are common conditions of competition which would imply that new HFCS users would try at least to equal the average rate of use prevailing in the market in order to maintain their competitive position.

Obviously, not all of the industrial users would substitute HFCS for sugar at the same time, at the same rate, or to the same extent. That is why Mexico estimated that the potential consumption of sugar under threat would amount to 33 per cent of estimated consumption for industries other than soft drink bottlers in 1997 (i.e. the proportion of potential consumption of other industries liable to substitution was 334.2 thousand tons in the subtotal covering other industries in the real sugar consumption table by sector: 1,015.1 thousand tons. However, according to the information in the investigation's administrative record, in 1996 HFCS consumption by industries other than soft drink bottlers (108,523 tons), including domestic production and imports already stood at 11 per cent of sugar consumption in those sectors in 1996 (974.9 thousand tons), so that the additional increase in the estimated share for Mexico for 1997 was 22 per cent.

9. The information in exhibit MEXICO-19 indicates that HFCS-55 is used predominantly in the soft drink bottling industry, while HFCS-42 is used predominantly in other industries, such as baking, beverages other than soft drinks, processed foods, and milk products. According to the data in paragraphs 39 and 44 of the redetermination, imports of HFCS-55 increased far more rapidly from 1995 to 1996 than did imports of HFCS-42 (increase of 179 per cent as compared with 5 per cent), and imports of HFCS-55 accounted for the vast majority of imports in 1996, 81 per cent. Does Mexico's predicted increase in usage by industries other than soft drink bottlers not imply that these trends and levels in the distribution of imports between HFCS-55 and HFCS-42 will be reversed in 1997? What is the evidence to suggest such a reversal is likely? Mexico's oral response to this question seemed to indicate that those companies that already use HFCS-55 to manufacture products other than soft-drinks would increase their purchases of HFCS-55. However, since these producers are only a subset of all manufacturers of products other than soft drinks, this would imply an even larger rate of increase in their purchases than the over 400 per cent calculated as the increase in HFCS consumption by all producers of products other than soft drinks. Could Mexico clarify? In addition, Mexico referred to the information in exhibit MEXICO-20 to support its statement that manufacturers of products other than soft drinks used HFCS-55 in their products. This seems to conflict with the information in exhibit MEXICO-19. Could Mexico reconcile this apparent conflict in the evidence?

The information contained in exhibit MEXICO-19 indicates that in the United States market, although HFCS-42 is used predominantly in industries other than soft drink bottlers, those industries also consume HFCS-55, although to a lesser degree. Similarly, while soft drink bottlers consume mainly HFCS-55, they also use HFCS-42.

This does not contradict the information contained in exhibit MEXICO-20 referred to in the oral reply, in which it was stated that industrial users other than soft drink bottlers also use HFCS-55. The point of what Mexico said in its oral response with respect to the performance of HFCS-42 imports in 1996 as indicated by the Panel was to stress that the predicted increase in HFCS consumption by industries other than bottlers would not be limited exclusively to HFCS-42, but would also include HFCS-55. Nor does this mean that all of the increase in imports would be attributable to companies from industries other than the soft drink bottlers already using HFCS-55.

Similarly, the figures available to the investigating authority on HFCS consumption in Mexico for 1996 are consistent with the information contained in exhibit MEXICO-19. That exhibit shows that, of total HFCS consumption by industries other than soft drink bottlers, 61 per cent concerned HFCS-42 and 39 per cent concerned HFCS-55, while in the case of soft drink bottlers, 84 per cent of HFCS consumption concerned HFCS-55 and 16 per cent concerned HFCS-42.

At the same time, the slower growth and smaller share of HFCS-42 imports in the 1996 total was explained by the fact that the product was already manufactured domestically. In that year, sales of HFCS-42 produced domestically amounted to 54,207 tons while sales of locally produced HFCS-55 totalled 4,254 tons. This is because practically the only company to manufacture HFCS in Mexico in 1996 was Almex, which did not have the necessary facilities for producing HFCS-55, but only HFCS-42, while Arancia CPC did not begin its production until December of that year.

Distribution of HFCS Consumption in Mexico by Origin and Grade 1996

Industry	HFCS-42	HFCS-55	Total	42-Total (%)	55-Total (%)
		Domestic			
Soft drinks	12,200	1,002	13,202	92	8
Other industries	42,007	3,252	45,258	93	7
Total	54,207	3,252	45,258	93	7
		Imported			
Soft drinks	12,073	130,621	142,694	8	92
Other industries	23,995	39,269	63,264	38	62
Total	36,068	169,269	205,958	18	82
		Total			
Soft drinks	24,273	131,623	155,896	16	84
Other industries	66,002	42,521	108,522	61	39
Total	90,275	174,143	264,418	34	66

Source: Replies of Arancia CPC, S.A. de C.V., (in sheet 2627 of 5 August 1997 and sheet 2803 of 15 August 1997) to investigating authority requests UPCI.310.97.1194 and UPCI.310.97.1325 of 16 and 28 July 1997 respectively (with changes resulting from the *in situ* verification as from 23-26 September 1997); and letter from Almidones Mexicanos, S.A. de C.V., (in sheet 1654 of 28 May

1997) and reply of 13 August 1997 (folio 2770) to investigating authority request UPCI.310.97.1193 of 16 July 1997.

In fact, it is important to note that HFCS-42 is used as an input in manufacturing HFCS-55 either by using a chromatographic separation tower to enrich the HFCS-42 until the required grade has been attained, or by physically mixing HFCS-42 with an enriched form of HFCS, generally HFCS-90, to obtain HFCS-55. In any case, the producer must determine which proportion of HFCS-42 production is intended for the market and which proportion to be consumed in the manufacturing of HFCS-55.

During 1996, 97 per cent of Almex's production of HFCS-42 went to domestic market sales, while 3 per cent was used to manufacture HFCS-55, which was produced only in the month of December of that year using the abovementioned mixing process. Of its sales of domestically produced HFCS-42, 77 per cent went to other industries, while the remaining 23 per cent went to soft drink bottlers.

Bearing this in mind, the predicted increase in the use of HFCS by industries other than the soft drink bottlers would in fact imply an investment in the distribution of imports in 1997 as compared to 1996, assuming that the source of supply for the allegedly restrained consumption by the bottlers was domestic production, since local producers would not have enough HFCS-42 to meet the demands of the market (other industries and soft drink bottlers) and to produce, in addition, HFCS-55.

Thus, if all of the domestic HFCS production were distributed to the bottlers in the same proportions as the bottlers had consumed HFCS during 1996, 85 per cent of the 350,000 tons of the alleged restraint agreement would be HFCS-55 and 15 per cent would be HFCS-42. Likewise, according to this scenario, the potential sugar consumption liable to substitution with HFCS in 1997 corresponding to industries other than the bottling industry, i.e. 334.2 thousand tons according to exhibit MEXICO-21, would have to be supplied by imports and, if distributed in line with HFCS consumption by those industries in 1996, 39 per cent of the imports would be HFCS-55 and 61 per cent would be HFCS-42.

However, as Mexico stated in its reply to question 5, the hypothesis that the consumption limited by the alleged restraint agreement would be supplied through domestic production alone could be dropped in a less stringent scenario, thereby possibly balancing the distribution of imports as between HFCS-42 and HFCS-55.

10. If one adds together the share of the market accounted for by imports of HFCS from the United States and Mexican production of sugar in 1994 and 1996, the total is not 100 per cent. For 1994, it is 99.7 per cent, while for 1996, it is 98 per cent. Could Mexico answer the following:

(a) What makes up the remainder of the 100 per cent? Sugar imports? Imports of HFCS from other sources? Domestic production of HFCS? What per cent of the market was accounted for in 1994 and 1996 by each of these elements?

The market is made up 100 per cent of domestic production for the domestic sugar market, domestic production of HFCS, sugar imports and HFCS imports, based on the calculation of apparent domestic consumption.

ADC = (domestic sugar production + domestic HFCS production + sugar imports + HFCS imports - sugar exports)

The percentages of each one of these elements are set forth in the annexed table entitled "Apparent Domestic Consumption" (MEXICO-24), which shows that the different shares add up to 100 per cent of the market.

(b) Does the remainder of the 100 per cent consist of the same elements in 1994 as in 1996?

Apparent domestic consumption was calculated on the basis of the same factors. However, it should be noted that in 1994-1995, *no* HFCS was produced in Mexico, which is why it does not form part of domestic consumption for those years.

(c) If domestic production of HFCS is included in the total market, could Mexico explain why, given that all Mexican producers of HFCS were excluded from the industry as related parties?

For the purposes of defining the relevant domestic industry, Mexico excluded Arancia and Almidones Mexicanos, since these companies were the main importers of HFCS from the United States and had benefited directly from the dumped HFCS imports. However, since domestic production of HFCS formed part of the demand, SECOFI included it in its calculation of apparent domestic consumption so as not to overestimate the relative shares of imports and of the domestic production of sugar.

(d) Regardless of what makes up the remainder of the market, the share of the market attributable to these other elements increased from 1994 to 1996, from 0.3 per cent to 2 per cent, an increase almost equal to the increase in HFCS imports from the United States. Did Mexico take this into account in its analysis?

The share of the market attributable to the remaining elements making up apparent domestic consumption other than imports of HFCS from the United States and production for the domestic sugar market grew from 0.74 per cent in 1994 to 2.21 per cent in 1996. However, it should be noted that, although the remaining elements (sugar imports, HFCS imports from countries other than the United States and domestic HFCS production) increased their market shares, the share of dumped HFCS imports in domestic consumption increased to a greater extent, rising from 1.68 per cent in 1994 to 4.44 per cent in 1996.[15]

Similarly, while the market share of production for the domestic market fell by 4.22 per cent in 1996 as compared with 1994, the share of HFCS imports from the United States increased by 2.76 per cent and the share of the remaining elements gained 1.47 per cent during the same period.

On the basis of the above, the Panel will be able to confirm that Mexico took account of all the factors making up 100 per cent of the market for sweeteners, and that while the market share of the other elements (sugar imports, HFCS imports from sources other than the United States and domestic HFCS production) increased, the increase in the share of HFCS imports from the United States was greater; in other words, the loss in market share suffered by domestically produced sugar is attributable more to the investigated imports than to the other elements making up consumption.

11. Could Mexico please explain how it derived the 50 per cent figure by which it discounted the projected volume of sugar consumption in 1997 and 1998 that could be substituted for by HFCS? A simple average of the substitution rates set out in exhibit MEXICO-20 yields a result of approximately 30. A simple average of the substitution rates used in exhibit MEXICO-21 yields a result of approximately 62. What is the basis for the 50 per cent discount rate?

In estimating the likelihood of an increase in imports considering the effects of the alleged restraint agreement, Mexico took account of the information available in the administrative record of the investigation concerning the use of HFCS in various sectors, supplied by the industrial users, as well as the degrees of substitution provided by the main HFCS importer for the period investigated. However, the information supplied both by the users and the importer was either limited to very specific products or, in some cases, covered very broad sectors, so that it was decided to calculate a simple average of the percentage of utilization of the products contained in each group for which data had been provided by the industrial users, and then to calculate an average of the different groups.

The percentage obtained through this procedure was 52.31 per cent, which it was decided to round off to 50 per cent. It was thought that this 50 per cent discounting of the percentages used in the calculation of potential consumption would reflect the variations within each sector and between sectors.

[15] See MEXICO-24.

Rate of Utilization of HFCS by industrial users other than soft drink bottlers in 1996

No.	Product	Segment	HFCS (%)	Average
1	*Jumex* (can)	Juices	63.00	
2	*Jumex* (bottle)	Juices	56.00	
3	*Jumex* (minibrik)	Juices	53.00	
4	*Jumex* (tetrabrik)	Juices	58.00	
5	*Ami*	Juices	68.00	
6	*Sonrisa* juice	Juices	100.00	
7	*Confruta* juice	Juices	100.00	
8	*Nectars*	Juices	100.00	
9	Uncarbonated beverages	**Juices**	100.00	**77.56%**
10	*Caribe Cooler* (peach)	Wines	50.00	
11	*Caribe Cooler* (lemon)	Wines	50.00	
12	*Caribe Cooler* (mandarin)	Wines	50.00	
13	*Caribe Cooler* (grapefruit)	Wines	50.00	
14	*Caribe Cooler* (strawberry)	Wines	50.00	
15	*Caribe Cooler* (tropical)	Wines	50.00	
16	*Presidencola*	Wines	50.00	
17	*Cubaraima*	Wines	50.00	
18	*Sidra Valle Redondo*	Wines	50.00	
19	*Sidra Campanario*	**Wines**	50.00	**50.00%**
20	Uncarbonated beverages	Other beverages	25.00	
21	Pau-pau	Other beverages	64.00	
22	*Chupifruit*	Other beverages	68.00	
23	*Chocoloco*	Other beverages	97.00	
24	Natural syrup	**Other beverages**	50.00	**60.80%**
25	Marmalades	Food	41.00	
26	Ketchup	Food	96.00	
27	Liquid caramel	Food	100.00	
28	Marmalades	Food	8.03	
29	Fruit jellies	Food	16.10	
30	Canned fruit	Food	52.00	
31	Topping	Food	100.00	
32	Glazes	Food	100.00	
33	*Cajeta DIF c/*nut	Food	29.75	
34	*Babar* pastry cream	Food	27.79	
35	Grape jelly 51	Food	44.69	
36	Raspberry marmalade 340	Food	53.26	
37	Blueberry marmalade 340	Food	51.30	
38	Cherry marmalade 340	Food	40.93	

No.	Product	Segment	HFCS (%)	Average
39	Peach marmalade 340	Food	53.30	
40	Peach marmalade 510 gr.	Food	46.99	
41	Raspberry marmalade 142	Food	36.80	
42	Raspberry marmalade 510 gr.	Food	49.05	
43	Strawberry marmalade 340	Food	38.58	
44	Strawberry marmalade 40 gr.	Food	40.67	
45	Blueberry marmalade	Food	35.48	
46	Apricot marmalade 340	Food	46.70	
47	Apricot marmalade 510 gr.	Food	50.27	
48	Peach marmalade 142 gr.	Food	35.07	
49	Strawberry marmalade 440 gr.	Food	14.90	
50	Orange marmalade 142 gr.	Food	39.28	
51	Pineapple marmalade 340 gr.	Food	48.44	
52	Blackberry marmalade 142 gr.	Food	36.46	
53	Strawberry marmalade 142 gr.	Food	26.73	
54	Strawberry marmalade 510	Food	38.33	
55	Orange marmalade 440	Food	27.94	
56	Orange marmalade 510 gr.	Food	50.65	
57	Pineapple marmalade 142	Food	35.38	
58	Blackberry marmalade 510 gr.	Food	48.75	
59	Strawberry pie filling	Food	20.61	
60	Pineapple pie filling	Food	27.83	
61	Nut pie filling	Food	11.02	
62	*Multi*strawberry filling	Food	20.61	
63	Tamarind for drinks 52 kg.	Food	21.73	
64	Marmalade	Food	43.70	
65	Orange segments	Food	100.00	
66	Grapefruit segments	Food	100.00	
67	Pineapple cubes	Food	100.00	
68	Papaya cubes	Food	100.00	
69	Melon cubes	Food	100.00	
70	Mango slices	Food	100.00	
71	Salads	Food	100.00	
72	Crystallized fruit	Confectionery	9.32	
73	Marmalades	Food	70.00	
74	Glaze	Food	46.00	
75	Sweet syrup	**Food**	99.00	51.73%
76	*Trompadita*	Bakery products	1.75	
77	*Trompada* (long) *Marve*	Bakery products	2.63	
78	*Huesito* (vanilla flavour)	Bakery products	2.63	

No.	Product	Segment	HFCS (%)	Average
79	*Huesito* (special)	Bakery products	10.13	
80	*Base betunada* (strawberry)	Bakery products	6.86	
81	*Base betunada* (lemon)	Bakery products	6.86	
82	*Base bombom*	Bakery products	5.40	
83	*Base betunada* (export)	Bakery products	6.86	
84	*Base chiocolina*	Bakery products	5.37	
85	*Base* (chocolate)	Bakery products	5.49	
86	*Base deportigrillo*	Bakery products	7.14	
87	*Base Garrillas*	Bakery products	7.03	
88	*Base Glorias*	Bakery products	7.88	
89	*Base Laura Castellanos*	Bakery products	5.38	
90	*Base Laura* (chocolate)	Bakery products	5.39	
91	*Base Marcela* (chocolate)	Bakery products	6.86	
92	*Base Magdalenas*	Bakery products	7.87	
93	*Base Malvavisco*	Bakery products	5.40	
94	*Base Rosalia Dif.*	Bakery products	5.27	
95	*Base Sandwich* (lemon)	Bakery products	7.86	
96	*Base* (vanilla)	Bakery products	7.63	
97	*Base Wond* (vanilla)	Bakery products	7.63	
98	*Base Wond* (export)	Bakery products	7.63	
99	*Granel Azucena*	Bakery products	8.25	
100	*Granel Animalitos*	Bakery products	5.51	
101	*Granel Alejandrinas*	Bakery products	4.67	
102	*Granel Azucena Lyconsa*	Bakery products	8.38	
103	*Granel Animalitos*	Bakery products	10.12	
104	*Granel Barra de Coco*	Bakery products	5.64	
105	*Granel Bing* (chocolate)	Bakery products	5.56	
106	*Granel Club Crema*	Bakery products	2.51	
107	*Granel Esmeraldas*	Bakery products	5.60	
108	*Granel Grageas* (chocolate)	Bakery products	4.94	
109	*Granel Grageas* (vanilla)	Bakery products	7.89	
110	*Granel Jarochas*	Bakery products	5.61	
111	*Granel María*	Bakery products	8.76	
112	*Granel Mordisko*	Bakery products	2.10	
113	*Granel Minigalleta* (chocolate)	Bakery products	3.85	
114	*Granel Marianitas*	Bakery products	5.52	
115	*Granel Pescaditos*	Bakery products	2.77	
116	*Granel Rikis Ajonjolí*	Bakery products	5.85	
117	*Granel Rikis*	Bakery products	2.40	

No.	Product	Segment	HFCS (%)	Average
118	*Granel Rikis* (butter)	Bakery products	1.99	
119	*Granel Tostada*	Bakery products	9.29	
120	*Marías*	Bakery products	8.63	
121	*Animalitos*	Bakery products	6.31	
122	*Sabrosas*	Bakery products	2.53	
123	*Sw. Emperador ch.*	Bakery products	11.03	
124	*Sw. Emperador v.*	Bakery products	8.15	
125	*Sw. Emperador n.*	Bakery products	7.47	
126	*Populares*	Bakery products	10.00	
127	*Ricanelas*	Bakery products	14.83	
128	*Pancrema*	Bakery products	3.91	
129	*Arco Iris*	Bakery products	5.27	
130	*Maravillas*	Bakery products	3.83	
131	*Frutana*	Bakery products	10.00	
132	*Mamut*	Bakery products	6.93	
133	*Ovaladas*	Bakery products	6.11	
134	*Flipy*	Bakery products	6.63	
135	*Delicias*	Bakery products	4.75	
136	*Marinas betunadas*	Bakery products	4.83	
137	*Grageitas*	Bakery products	3.89	
138	*Barra de coco*	Bakery products	9.15	
139	*Sw. de merengue*	Bakery products	8.39	
140	*Roscas de canela*	Bakery products	4.52	
141	*Chokis*	Bakery products	2.45	
142	*Hawaianas* (pineapple)	Bakery products	4.09	
143	*Dóro*	Bakery products	6.08	
144	*Chocolatines*	Bakery products	9.69	
145	*Zoo*	Bakery products	14.00	
146	*Flups v.*	Bakery products	6.44	
147	*Flups ch.*	Bakery products	6.38	
148	*Flor de naranjo*	Bakery products	7.00	
149	*Marías* (chocolate)	Bakery products	8.51	
150	*Gansito*	Bakery products	22.05	
151	*Submarino* (strawberry)	Bakery products	52.15	
152	*Submarino* (vanilla)	Bakery products	52.14	
153	*Pingüinos*	Bakery products	35.69	
154	*Chocorroles* (2)	Bakery products	36.56	
155	Strawberry roll	Bakery products	41.23	
156	*Napolitano*	Bakery products	2.73	
157	*Triki trakes*	Bakery products	33.96	

No.	Product	Segment	HFCS (%)	Average
158	*Plativolos*	Bakery products	7.40	
159	*Pipucho*	Bakery products	6.59	
160	*Minipríncipe*	Bakery products	6.25	
161	Toffee rolls	Bakery products	13.37	
162	*KG*	Bakery products	15.20	
163	*Polvoron* (chocolate)	Bakery products	22.63	
164	*Shok* (vanilla)	Bakery products	8.80	
165	*Shok* (chocolate)	Bakery products	6.61	
166	Pancakes with raisins	Bakery products	0.88	
167	Pancakes with nuts	Bakery products	0.91	
168	*Mantecadas* (4)	Bakery products	0.74	
169	Cinnamon rolls (6)	Bakery products	3.50	
170	*Glass* rolls (6)	Bakery products	3.27	
171	Cinnamon rolls (2)	Bakery products	3.51	
172	*Glass* rolls (2)	Bakery products	3.26	
173	*Panquecitos* (2)	Bakery products	2.29	
174	*Triki trakes*	Bakery products	16.20	
175	*Principe*	Bakery products	6.30	
176	*Plativolos*	Bakery products	10.20	
177	*Chocorroles* (2)	Bakery products	30.30	
178	Strawberry rolls	Bakery products	31.10	
179	Toffee rolls	Bakery products	13.40	
180	*KG*	Bakery products	14.90	
181	*Rocko*	Bakery products	5.20	
182	*Hit*	Bakery products	15.30	
183	*Sponch*	Bakery products	19.00	
184	*Pingüinos*	Bakery products	22.10	
185	*Submarinos*	Bakery products	52.50	
186	*Napolitano*	Bakery products	1.70	
187	*Gansito*	Bakery products	11.20	
188	*Pipucho*	Bakery products	41.50	
189	*Dalmata*	Bakery products	2.10	
190	Cakes	Bakery products	17.00	
191	Cake "8"	Bakery products	19.15	
192	*Rosca de reyes*	**Bakery products**	21.77	**10.30%**
193	Whipped cream	Milk products	100.00	
194	*Media crema*	Milk products	100.00	
195	*Helado*	Milk products	17.90	
196	Yoghurt *helado*	**Milk products**	36.00	**63.48%**
TOTAL				**52.31%**

12. The information in exhibit MEXICO-20 for 1997 shows almost no increases in the rate of usage of HFCS over that reported by the same companies for 1996. Could Mexico reconcile this with its projection of a significant increase in the use of HFCS in 1997?

Indeed, the information contained in exhibit MEXICO-20 for 1997 as compared to 1996 *does not* show any increases in the rate of usage of HFCS. This can be explained by the fact that during the period concerned, the anti-dumping investigation initiated in January 1997 was still under way, and this made consumers more cautious and prevented substitution from taking place or at least slowed it down. However, the fact that the rate of usage remained the same does not mean that a greater quantity of HFCS was not being used in absolute terms to the detriment of domestically produced sugar, since imports had already increased.

At the same time, Mexico's estimate as to the probability of an increase in imports was not supported by the real performance of the market in 1997 alone, but also by the fact that based on the information available for the period under analysis it was reasonable to predict that such increase would take place in the near future if the circumstances remained the same. Thus, one cannot compare what actually happened in reality with what was likely to happen, since each situation involved different factors. Obviously, any estimate of what is likely to happen in the future, seen with the benefit of hindsight in the light of what happened in reality, particularly when there are a number of elements which significantly alter the course of events, could turn out to be erroneous and even meaningless.

ANSWERS OF THE UNITED STATES TO QUESTIONS FROM THE PANEL

13. Could the United States please specify the portions of the original panel determination referred to in paragraph 9 of the United States' oral submission?

1. Paragraph 9 of the Oral Statement of the United States was based on paragraphs 24-27 of the First Written Submission of the United States. In that discussion, the United States cited paragraphs 7.177 and 7.178 of the original Panel Report in support of the proposition that the Panel found that SECOFI's original determination did not provide any analysis to support the conclusion that there was a likelihood that users other than soft drink bottlers would substantially increase their importation of HFCS.

14. In paragraph 5 of its oral statement, the United States seems to express concern that SECOFI failed to focus on 1997 data in its analysis. Does the United States contend that SECOFI was obligated to base its determination on 1997 data? If so, on what basis in the AD Agreement does the United States makes this contention?

2. The concern that the United States expressed in paragraph 5 of its Oral Statement simply repeats a concern that the Panel expressed in its original report. In its original determination, as in its redetermination, SECOFI relied on the fact that HFCS imports were higher in January-September 1997 than in January-September 1996 in finding that there was a likelihood of increased importation. Because the January-September 1997 data do not reflect the operation of the restraint agreement - which was not announced until September 1997 - the Panel concluded that this data did not support SECOFI's conclusion, under Article 3.7(i) of the AD Agreement, that substantial increases in HFCS imports were likely after September 1997. As the Panel stated in paragraph 7.176 of its original report:

> "Mexico's references to the increasing trend of HFCS imports suggest that somehow SECOFI concluded that such imports would have continued increasing by inertia, given the significant increases recorded during the period of investigation and through September 1997, even if they were not demanded in significantly increased quantities by soft-drink bottlers, the leading consumers of imported HFCS. Mexico points out that the alleged restraint agreement was made after the period of investigation, and thus any limitation on imports started from the already significantly increased levels that had been reached. However, the question for purposes of analysis is not the level of imports already reached, but the likelihood of **increased** imports."(Emphasis in original).

3. As the United States indicated in paragraphs 5 and 6 of its Oral Statement and paragraph 29 of its First Written Submission, one reason that the analysis of the restraint agreement in SECOFI's redetermination is inadequate is because it fails to address these concerns of the Panel. As the Panel previously recognized, the fact that imports of HFCS increased prior to September 1997, predominantly because of increased purchases by soft drink bottlers, cannot serve as a basis for finding that purchasers other than soft drink bottlers are likely to substantially increase imports after September 1997.

15. Based on the reported 75 per cent increase of imports in January-September 1997 as compared to the same period in 1996, it might be extrapolated that total imports for 1997 would increase by 75 per cent over total imports for 1996, to a level of 338,000 tons. This is approximately the same level of imports predicted by SECOFI for 1997. Similarly, it appears that under the alleged restraint agreement, soft-drink bottlers could purchase 350,000 tons of HFCS, presumably all from imports, which would again be an increase of about 74 per cent from 1996 levels. Putting aside the question of who would purchase these imports, does the United States maintain that the level of 1997 imports *per se* would not support a conclusion that there was a likelihood of substantially increased imports? That is, is the United States' objection to SECOFI's conclusion of substantially increased imports based on the projected level of imports or on the methodology used on the projection?

4. The United States has not made any arguments, either in the original Panel proceedings or the current proceedings, that any particular increase in import level or penetration can or cannot be substantial *per se*. The United States argues that SECOFI's methodology is not fact-based and, hence, could not serve as the basis for SECOFI's conclusion that substantially increased imports are likely. As the United States argued in paragraph 7 of its First Written Submission, the facts found by SECOFI sufficiently contradict its conclusions on redetermination so as to suggest that SECOFI cannot on its record provide a basis for finding a threat of material injury.

5. The original Panel decision, as well as Article 3.7(i) of the AD Agreement, obligated SECOFI to examine whether substantial increases in HFCS imports were likely notwithstanding the restraint agreement. SECOFI attempted to satisfy the Panel's concern by focusing on users other than soft drink bottlers. SECOFI projected that soft drink bottlers would obtain from Mexican production all quantities of HFCS that they were permitted to use under the restraint agreement, and that all Mexican HFCS production capacity would be used to supply soft drink bottlers. Redetermination, para. 58.

6. SECOFI projected that imports of HFCS by purchasers other than soft drink bottlers would increase from approximately 62,000 tons in 1996 to 350,000 tons in 1998. As the United States indicated at paragraphs 11 through 24 of its Oral Statement, as well as in responses to questions the Panel asked orally at the Meeting on February 20 and February 21, the methodology that SECOFI used to

project this increase must be rejected because it is not based on data reflecting either actual HFCS purchases by users other than soft drink bottlers or the actual rates at which these users substituted HFCS for sugar during SECOFI's period of investigation and because it is not consistent with historical trends.

16. Does the United States consider its arguments under Article 12 to constitute an independent claim of violation of the AD Agreement? In this regard, could the United States please comment on the findings of the Panel in *European Communities - Anti-Dumping Duties on Imports of Cotton-Type Bed Linen from India*, WT/DS141/R, circulated 30 October 2000 (appeal on other issues pending) at paragraphs 6.257 and 6.259.

7. The United States considers its arguments under Article 12 to constitute an independent claim of violation of the AD Agreement. We note that in its original decision, this Panel concluded that Mexico acted inconsistently with the substantive requirements of Article 10.2, when it applied dumping duties retroactively, and with the notice requirements of Articles 12.2 and 12.2.2. *See* Panel Report, paras. 7.194 - 7.198. Nevertheless, we believe it is within a Panel's discretion to decide, as a matter of judicial economy, not to reach the question of whether there has been an Article 12 violation when it has found a violation of a related substantive obligation. This appears to have been the basis for the *Bed Linen* decision. However, we would disagree with the *Bed Linen* Panel to the extent that it was suggesting that Article 12 is not an independent obligation under the AD Agreement or that there will always be an overlap between a Member's substantive obligations and its obligations under Article 12. The United States considers the transparency obligations created by Article 12 to be critical to the effective operation of the AD Agreement.

COMMENTS BY THE UNITED STATES ON NEW FACTUAL INFORMATION SUBMITTED BY MEXICO

1. Mexico 39

1. At several points in its responses to the Panel's questions, Mexico refers to material from exhibit MEXICO-39 in the original Panel proceedings. Because Mexico had never previously referred to this information during the current proceeding, MEXICO-39 is "new information" for purposes of this Article 21.5 proceeding.

2. The MEXICO-39 material concerns import sales data from Arancia CPC, S.A. de C.V., one of two importers of HFCS from the United States during SECOFI's period of investigation. Mexico contends that this material shows that Arancia's sales of HFCS to users other than soft drink bottlers were increasing throughout SECOFI's period of investigation, particularly during 1996.

3. It is noteworthy that Mexico never referenced the MEXICO-39 material in either of its two written submissions or during the meeting with the Panel. Instead, in all of its previous submissions, Mexico has attempted to demonstrate the accuracy of SECOFI's projections of likely purchases of HFCS by users other than soft drink bottlers. Indeed, SECOFI's redetermination clearly relied on these projections, rather than any material concerning actual purchasing patterns, in finding that the restraint agreement "would not eliminate the likelihood" of further increased imports of HFCS. *See* SECOFI Redetermination, paras. 55-59. Consequently, Mexico's current reliance on MEXICO-39 is another example of Mexico attempting to defend SECOFI's redetermination on the basis of reasoning not discernible from, or even consistent with, the determination itself.

4. In any event, Mexico's characterization of the material from MEXICO-39 is inaccurate.

5. The MEXICO-39 material does not show, as SECOFI contends, that Arancia's sales to purchasers other than soft drink bottlers increased sharply during 1996. The monthly sales data included after paragraph 4(viii) of Mexico's response do not show steadily increasing sales during the course of the year to non-soft drink bottlers. Instead, these data indicate sharp fluctuations in sales volumes from month to month. Thus, Arancia's sales to purchasers other than soft drink bottlers during June 1996 were greater than its monthly sales to such purchasers for four of the six subsequent months.

6. Although MEXICO-39 reflects that Arancia increased its sales to purchasers other than soft drink bottlers from 1994 to 1996, the rate of increase in such sales is far smaller than the 2188 per cent increase in sales to soft drink bottlers during the same period. Additionally, this increase is from a small base: Arancia's 1994 sales to HFCS users other than soft drink bottlers were under 20,000 tons. By contrast, SECOFI projected that these users would purchase 350,000 tons of HFCS in 1998. The 1994 to 1996 increase is also far smaller than the over 400 per cent increase in sales to purchasers other than soft drink

bottlers SECOFI projected from 1996 to 1998 in an effort to show that overall imports would increase notwithstanding the restraint agreement.

7. Finally, Arancia was neither the sole nor even the principal importer of HFCS from the United States. The MEXICO-39 material included in Mexico's response indicates that the other importer, Almex, was responsible for 67.5 per cent of all HFCS imports in 1996. Almex's sales were much more heavily oriented to soft drink bottlers than Arancia's. There is consequently no basis for concluding that Arancia's data are representative of all HFCS importers.

2. "Rate Of Utilization" Chart

8. After its response to question 11, Mexico has submitted a chart purporting to demonstrate how it derived the 50 per cent figure by which it discounted the amount of projected sugar consumption in 1997 and 1998 that could be substituted for HFCS. Because Mexico has never previously disclosed this material, this chart is also new factual information.

9. Mexico claims that the chart demonstrates that SECOFI derived the 50 per cent figure by taking a simple (not weighted) average of actual utilization rates in various sectors. Absent data - which Mexico does not provide - concerning the volume of HFCS used by the each of the industries listed in the chart, there is no basis for concluding that Mexico's technique of computing a simple average of utilization rates provides reliable information concerning the actual average rate of utilization. In this regard, it is noteworthy that the chart contains no information showing actual HFCS usage in the production of bread, which SECOFI predicts will account for 86 per cent of the consumption of HFCS in the near term.

10. Although Mexico maintains, at least for purposes of its answer to question 11, that the 50 per cent rate reflects the rate that HFCS was actually substituted for sugar, the redetermination and its answer to question 6 suggest that SECOFI viewed the 50 per cent figure differently. The redetermination and Mexico's answer to question 6 suggests that the 50 per cent figure was simply a figure SECOFI arbitrarily chose to reduce theoretical substitution rates that were unrealistically high. We maintain that the redetermination and the answer to question 6, rather than the answer to question 11, indicate the true derivation and purpose of the 50 per cent figure.

CANADA - MEASURES AFFECTING THE IMPORTATION OF MILK AND THE EXPORTATION OF DAIRY PRODUCTS

RECOURSE TO ARTICLE 21.5 OF THE DSU BY NEW ZEALAND AND THE UNITED STATES

Report of the Appellate Body
WT/DS103/AB/RW, WT/DS113/AB/RW

Adopted bythe Appellate Body on 18 December 2001

Canada, *Appellant*	Present:
New Zealand, *Appellee*	Taniguchi, Presiding Member
United States, *Appellee*	Abi-Saab, Member
European Communities, *Third Participant*	Ganesan, Member

TABLE OF CONTENTS

I. INTRODUCTION

1. Canada appeals certain issues of law and legal interpretations in the Panel Report, Canada - Measures Affecting the Importation of Milk and the Exportation of Dairy Products - Recourse to Article 21.5 of the DSU by New Zealand and the United States (the "Panel Report").[1] The Panel was established to consider a complaint by New Zealand and the United States that certain measures taken by Canada to comply with the recommendations and rulings of the Dispute Settlement Body (the "DSB") in Canada - Measures Affecting the Importation of Milk and the Exportation of Dairy Products ("Canada - Dairy ")[2] were not consistent with Canada's obligations under the Agreement on Agriculture and the Agreement on Subsidies and Countervailing Duties (the "SCM Agreement ").

[1] WT/DS103/RW, WT/DS113/RW, DSR 2001:XIII, 6875, 11 July 2001.

[2] The recommendations and rulings of the DSB resulted from the adoption, by the DSB, of the panel report in *Canada - Dairy*, WT/DS103/R, WT/DS113/R (the "original panel report"), DSR 1999:VI, 2097, as modified by the Appellate Body Report, WT/DS103/AB/R and Corr.1, WT/DS113/AB/R and Corr.1, DSR 2001:XIII, 6839, both adopted 27 October 1999. In this Report, we refer to the panel that considered the original complaint brought by New Zealand and the United States as the "original panel".

2. In *Canada - Dairy*, the original panel and the Appellate Body found, *inter alia*, that Canada had acted inconsistently with its obligations under Articles 3.3 and 8 of the *Agreement on Agriculture*, through its scheme of Special Milk Classes 5(d) and 5(e), by providing "export subsidies" within the meaning of Article 9.1(c) of that Agreement, in excess of the quantity commitment levels specified by Canada in its Schedule of Commitments under the *Marrakesh Agreement Establishing the World Trade Organization* (the "*WTO Agreement* "). On 27 October 1999, the DSB adopted the original panel and Appellate Body reports.

3. On 23 December 1999, pursuant to Article 21.3(b) of the *Understanding on Rules and Procedures Governing the Settlement of Disputes* (the "DSU"), Canada, New Zealand and the United States agreed that the reasonable period of time for Canada to implement the recommendations and rulings of the DSB would expire on 31 December 2000.[3] On 11 December 2000, the parties agreed to extend this period of time until 31 January 2001.[4] On 19 January 2001, Canada affirmed that it would complete its implementation of the recommendations and rulings of the DSB by 31 January 2001.[5]

4. The measures taken by Canada to comply with the recommendations and rulings of the DSB included the elimination of Special Milk Class 5(e) and the restriction of exports of dairy products under Special Milk Class 5(d) to Canada's export subsidy commitment levels. Canada otherwise maintained its pre-existing milk supply management scheme, including the establishment of an annual Market Sharing Quota for industrial milk and its allocation to milk producers, as well as regulation of supplies and prices of milk through Milk Classes 1 to 4 and Special Milk Classes 5(a) to 5(d).[6] Canada also created a new class of domestic milk, Class 4(m), under which any over-quota milk could be sold only as animal feed. In addition, Canada introduced a new category of milk for export processing known as "commercial export milk" ("CEM"). Under pre-commitment contracts, that is, contracts concluded in advance of production, Canadian producers can sell any quantity of CEM to Canadian processors for export processing on terms and conditions freely negotiated between the producer and the processor. Sales of CEM do not require a quota, or any other form of permit, from the Canadian government or its agencies, and the revenues derived by the producer from sales of CEM are collected directly by it without government involvement. However, if a processed dairy product, which is produced using CEM, is sold on the domestic market, the processor is liable to financial penalties for diverting the

---

[3] WT/DS103/10, WT/DS113/10.

[4] WT/DS103/13, WT/DS113/13.

[5] WT/DS103/12/Add.6, WT/DS113/12/Add.6.

[6] For a description of the pre-existing milk supply management scheme, *see*, Appellate Body Report, *Canada - Dairy*, *supra*, footnote 2, paras. 6-16, and the original Panel Report, *Canada - Dairy*, *supra*, footnote 2, paras. 2.1-2.66.

dairy product into the domestic market.[7] The factual aspects of the new scheme are set out in greater detail in the Panel Report.[8]

5. Taking the view that certain of the measures taken by Canada to comply with the recommendations and rulings of the DSB were not consistent with its obligations under the *Agreement on Agriculture* and the *SCM Agreement*, New Zealand and the United States requested, on 16 February 2001, that the matter be referred to a panel pursuant to Article 21.5 of the DSU.[9]

6. On the same day, New Zealand and the United States also requested authorization from the DSB to suspend concessions and other obligations, as provided for in Article 22.2 of the DSU.[10] Canada objected to the level of suspension proposed, and the matter was referred to arbitration, pursuant to Article 22.6 of the DSU.[11] However, the parties agreed to request the arbitrator to suspend its work pending the outcome of the Article 21.5 proceeding.[12]

7. Before the Panel, New Zealand and the United States claimed that Canada had acted inconsistently with Articles 3.3, 8, 9.1(c) and 10.1 of the *Agreement on Agriculture* through the creation of a CEM market and the continued operation of Special Milk Class 5(d). The United States also claimed that through these measures, Canada had acted inconsistently with its obligations under Articles 1.1 and 3.1 of the *SCM Agreement*. Before the Panel, Canada denied that the provision of CEM involved export subsidies under either the *Agreement on Agriculture* or the *SCM Agreement*.

8. In its Report, the Panel concluded that:

> ... Canada, through the CEM scheme and the continued operation of Special Milk Class 5(d), has acted inconsistently with its obligations under Articles 3.3 and 8 of the *Agreement on Agriculture*, by providing export subsidies within the meaning of Article 9.1(c) of the *Agreement on Agriculture* in excess of its quantity commitment levels specified in its Schedule for exports of cheese, for the marketing year 2000/2001.[13]

---

7 Panel Report, para. 6.77.

8 *Ibid.*, paras. 3.1-3.9.

9 WT/DS103/16 and WT/DS113/16. Two of the three members of the Panel had previously served on the original panel. Panel Report, para. 1.10 and the original Panel Report, para. 1.8.

10 WT/DS103/17 and WT/DS113/17.

11 WT/DS103/18 and WT/DS113/18.

12 Panel Report, para. 1.7; WT/DS103/14, para. 9 and WT/DS113/14, para. 9.

13 Panel Report, para. 7.1. Having found that Canada had acted inconsistently with its obligations under Article 9.1(c) of the *Agreement on Agriculture*, the Panel declined to address the claims relating to Article 10.1 of that Agreement and to Articles 1.1 and 3.1 of the *SCM Agreement*. (Panel Report, paras. 6.88 and 6.102)

9. The Panel recommended that the DSB request Canada to "bring its dairy products marketing regime into conformity with its obligations in respect of export subsidies under the *Agreement on Agriculture*." [14]

10. On 4 September 2001, Canada notified the DSB of its intention to appeal certain issues of law covered in the Panel Report and certain legal interpretations developed by the Panel, pursuant to paragraph 4 of Article 16 of the DSU, and filed a Notice of Appeal pursuant to Rule 20 of the *Working Procedures for Appellate Review* (the "*Working Procedures*"). On 14 September 2001, Canada filed its appellant's submission. [15] On 1 October 2001, New Zealand and the United States each filed an appellee's submission. [16] On the same day, the European Communities filed a third participant's submission. [17]

11. The oral hearing in the appeal was held on 26 October 2001. The participants and the European Communities, as third participant, presented oral arguments and responded to questions put to them by the Members of the Division hearing the appeal.

II. ARGUMENTS OF THE PARTICIPANTS AND THIRD PARTICIPANT

A. *Claims of Error by Canada - Appellant*

1. *Article 9.1(c) of the Agreement on Agriculture - "payments"*

12. Canada appeals the Panel's finding that CEM sales by producers to processors constitute "payments" within the meaning of Article 9.1(c) of the *Agreement on Agriculture*.

13. Canada relies upon the finding of the Appellate Body in *Canada - Dairy* that "payments" under Article 9.1(c) are made to the recipient "[i]f goods or services are supplied ... at reduced rates (that is, at below market-rates)". [18] In the present case, there is no such "payment", since the CEM scheme does not involve any government control over the price of milk destined for export processing, in contrast with the former scheme where the Canadian government was found to set lower prices for export milk through the Special Milk Classes and price-pooling mechanisms. Accordingly, the prices freely determined for CEM on a willing-buyer, willing-seller basis, outside the domestic price classification system, are prices at "market-rates", and not prices below "market-rates". The

---

[14] Panel Report, para. 7.3.
[15] Pursuant to Rule 21 of the *Working Procedures*.
[16] Pursuant to Rules 22 and 23(3) of the *Working Procedures*.
[17] Pursuant to Rule 24 of the *Working Procedures*.
[18] Appellate Body Report, *supra*, footnote 2, para. 113.

Panel's failure to consider the changes in market conditions as a result of the deregulation of CEM thus amounts to an error of law.

14. Canada further submits that in determining whether there was a "payment", the Panel incorrectly used domestic regulated prices as the benchmark for comparison with the "market-determined" prices of CEM. A benchmark analysis is neither appropriate nor necessary in a situation where the alleged discounted price is a market-determined price. In Canada's view, it is not rational to use as a benchmark a "government-regulated" price to establish the "trade-distorting potential" of a "market-determined" price.

2. *Article 9.1(c) of the Agreement on Agriculture - "financed by virtue of governmental action"*

15. Canada also appeals the Panel's finding that the "payments" were "financed by virtue of governmental action", within the meaning of Article 9.1(c) of the *Agreement on Agriculture.*

16. According to Canada, the Panel erred by applying a standard "less stringent" than the one contemplated by Article 9.1(c) of the *Agreement on Agriculture.* The ordinary meaning of the three elements of Article 9.1(c), that is, "financed", "by virtue of ", and "governmental action", read individually and collectively, support Canada's view that there should be a "strong affirmative and positive linkage between the governmental action and the financing of the payments". [19] On the contrary, the Panel's interpretation suggests that Article 9.1(c) applies even when government is "merely involved" in export markets or where private action is "simply encouraged" by government. The Panel also misapplied the legal reasoning of the Appellate Body in *Canada - Dairy* where the Appellate Body found that "'governmental action' [was] not simply involved; it [was], in fact, indispensable to enable the supply of milk to processors for export, and hence the transfer of resources, to take place." [20] Under the new CEM scheme, where the government has deregulated the export transactions, there is no "strong affirmative and positive linkage" between the governmental action and the financing of the payments.

17. Canada argues that the "but for" test, applied by the Panel to determine whether the payments are "financed by virtue of governmental action", overlooks the word "financed" and falls short of the concept of "indispensability" referred to by the Appellate Body in *Canada - Dairy.* Canada submits that the Panel interpreted the word "financed" merely to mean that a payment is "made". [21] The word "financed", in its ordinary meaning, requires that a government "provide[]

[19] Canada's appellant's submission, paras. 7, 49 and 52.
[20] Appellate Body Report, *supra*, footnote 2, para. 120.
[21] Canada's appellant's submission, para. 8.

funds" or "perform[] functions of raising, furnishing or managing funds".[22] Canada finds support for this interpretation in the levy example in Article 9.1(c), in the object and purpose of the *Agreement on Agriculture*, and in the Appellate Body Report in *Canada - Dairy*.

18. Canada also submits that the Panel misread Article 9.1(c) to mean that payments need not be "directly financed", provided that governments "*establish the conditions which ensure that* the payment ... takes place".[23] (emphasis in original) Even if this standard were applicable under Article 9.1(c) of the *Agreement on Agriculture*, Canada submits that the CEM scheme would not fall within its scope, since Canada has not taken any measure to "ensure" or "compel" the provision of CEM to processors. CEM is provided by producers to processors of their own volition and at freely negotiated prices.

19. Furthermore, in the view of Canada, the Panel should have used the *SCM Agreement* as relevant context and interpreted the word "subsidy" as used in that Agreement. Canada argues that the *Agreement on Agriculture* and the *SCM Agreement* should be interpreted consistently, to the extent permitted by their wording, in order to determine whether subsidies are involved. In particular, Canada refers to the concept of "financial contribution" as a "cornerstone" in the meaning of "subsidy" under the *SCM Agreement*, and to the panel report in *United States - Measures Treating Exports Restraints as Subsidies* ("*US - Export Restraints*")[24] which provides an analysis of the fourth kind of "financial contribution " described in Article 1.1(a)(1) of the *SCM Agreement*. Canada explains that in *US - Export Restraints*, the panel rejected the proposition that the focus should be on the effects or results of governmental action, suggesting instead, that the focus should be on the nature of that action.[25]

20. Canada criticizes the "two-part" test used by the Panel to establish whether payments are "financed by virtue of governmental action". In the view of Canada, the Panel erroneously concentrated upon the alleged effects of the domestic regulation measures on commercial export transactions, while commercial export transactions by themselves should have been the real focus for an analysis under Article 9.1(c) of the *Agreement on Agriculture*. In particular, Canada submits that quotas which prevent producers "from selling more milk on the regulated domestic market at a higher price, than to the extent of the quota allocated to them"[26] do not constitute "governmental action" that "finances" payments on the export of dairy products manufactured with CEM. Quotas for the domestic market have no bearing on a producer's decision to produce or sell CEM, since this decision is made before, not after, the production. Moreover, penalties for

---

[22] Canada's appellant's submission, paras. 10 and 49.
[23] Panel Report, para. 6.38.
[24] Panel Report, WT/DS194/R and Corr.2, adopted 23 August 2001.
[25] Canada's appellants's submission, para. 77.
[26] Panel Report, para. 6.42.

diversion of milk cannot be considered as "governmental action" that "finances" payments, since they occur once the transaction between the producer and processor is completed.

21. Canada stresses further that the Panel failed to take account of its deregulation of the export market for milk, of the existence of a regulated domestic market and a deregulated export market in Canada, and of the commercial nature of the transactions for the provision of CEM, namely, that the transactions are negotiated exclusively by private parties of their own free will. Canada recalls that the original panel noted that the mere existence of parallel markets with lower export prices did not, by itself, create an export subsidy, and that the issue was rather the extent of government involvement in providing the lower-priced product for export. As a result of this approach, the Panel effectively "collapsed" the domestic support disciplines and the export subsidy disciplines of the *Agreement on Agriculture*.

22. Canada challenges the Panel's conclusion that producers are "driven by governmental action to sell milk produced outside their quota into the export market".[27] Producers and processors are under no control or compulsion of the government; they now freely choose to sell or purchase CEM at prices and terms based on market forces. The Panel's conclusion that producers are "driven" to sell milk for export is premised on the assumption that producers behave in a "profit-maximizing" manner. Such an assumption is not a proper basis for identifying WTO-inconsistent subsidies. Article 9.1(c) does not equate export subsidies with choices between "profit-maximizing" options or "unfettered commercial freedom". Canada finds it "illogical" that the very act of "deregulating" was interpreted by the Panel to be governmental "intervention" that restricts producers' commercial freedom. The mere fact that markets exist within a legal framework established by the government does not imply that producers' choices are not free in those markets.

23. Canada also emphasizes that the standard developed by the Panel for Article 9.1(c) of the *Agreement on Agriculture* is more stringent than the one applicable for an export subsidy under the *SCM Agreement*, whereas the subsidy disciplines in the agricultural sector are designed to reduce agricultural support and protection over time, and are yet to achieve the level of disciplines imposed by the *SCM Agreement*.

24. Accordingly, in the view of Canada, there is no "governmental action" which "finances" payments through the supply of CEM within the meaning of Article 9.1(c) of the *Agreement on Agriculture*.

---

[27] Panel Report, para. 6.48.

3. *Article 10.1 of the Agreement on Agriculture and Article 3.1 of the SCM Agreement*

25. In the event that the Appellate Body deems it necessary to complete the Panel's analysis, Canada presents the following arguments with respect to Article 10.1 of the *Agreement on Agriculture*. In essence, Canada claims that there is no subsidy provided to processors within the meaning of Article 1(e) of the *Agreement on Agriculture* and Article 1.1 of the *SCM Agreement*, including item (d) of the Illustrative List of Export Subsidies (the "Illustrative List") in Annex I of the *SCM Agreement*. Accordingly, Canada's measures are not inconsistent with Article 10.1 of the *Agreement on Agriculture*.

26. Canada asserts further that it is not circumventing its export subsidy commitments within the meaning of Article 10.1 of the *Agreement on Agriculture*, since there is no export subsidy involved in CEM transactions; neither is it circumventing its export subsidy commitments by "non-commercial transactions" so as to attract application of Article 10.1 of the *Agreement on Agriculture*.

27. Finally, Canada argues that, as there are no "subsidies" conferred on processors within the meaning of Article 1.1 of the *SCM Agreement*, there can be no "export subsidy" within the meaning of Article 3.1 of the *SCM Agreement*.

B. *Arguments of New Zealand - Appellee*

1. *Article 9.1(c) of the Agreement on Agriculture - "payments"*

28. New Zealand submits that Canada's new measures also are "payments" within the meaning of Article 9.1(c) of the *Agreement on Agriculture*. Although prices are determined through negotiations between producers and processors under the CEM scheme, producers only sell and negotiate prices for CEM because they are prevented from selling that milk into the domestic market. Canada's contention that prices are determined by "arm's length private transactions" is based on the erroneous assumption that these transactions are genuinely voluntary and are purely market-based. Processors are the beneficiaries of an artificially constructed market which provides them with milk for export processing at prices lower than those applicable to the domestic market.

29. New Zealand argues that Canada incorrectly assumes that there are two separate markets. The domestic and the export markets are, in reality, identical in terms of participants and products, and they differ only with regard to the degree of government involvement. Should Canada's argument on "separate markets" be accepted, it would allow Members with domestic supply management schemes to evade their export subsidy commitments by simply creating a "separate" artificial market through which processors for export would have access to inputs at subsidized prices. Even if the CEM market were to be treated as a "separate" market, there would still be "payments" within the meaning of Article 9.1(c) of the *Agreement on Agriculture*, because the determinative question is whether proces-

sors for export obtain milk at reduced rates, not whether milk is obtained through one market or another.

2. *Article 9.1(c) of the Agreement on Agriculture - "financed by virtue of governmental action"*

30. New Zealand submits that Canada erroneously restricts the interpretation of Article 9.1(c) of the *Agreement on Agriculture* to mean that only "overt" action by government, such as the setting of prices or the imposition of a levy, would satisfy the requirement that payments are "financed by virtue of governmental action". New Zealand contends that such an approach is not supported by the Appellate Body's ruling in *Canada - Certain Measures Concerning Periodicals* [28], or by the negotiating history of the *Agreement on Agriculture*. Canada improperly isolates the word "financed" from the other words of the phrase "financed by virtue of ". Furthermore, the phrase "by virtue of " indicates that Article 9.1(c) cannot be read to mean that it is limited to measures with "levy-type characteristics". New Zealand contends that Canada overlooks the ordinary meaning of "by virtue of " by substituting its own standard of "a strong affirmative and positive linkage between the government action and the financing of the payments". New Zealand supports the Panel's view that the degree of government involvement is not a decisive factor, and that "indispensability" is the appropriate standard to be applied under Article 9.1(c), in this case, although it is not necessarily the only standard applicable under this article.

31. New Zealand argues further that the Panel rightly used the "but for" test as it is grounded in the ordinary meaning of "indispensable". In applying the "but for" test, the Panel did not use "less than a stringent standard", nor is it founded on mere or incidental governmental involvement.

32. With regard to "governmental action", New Zealand criticizes Canada's argument that its involvement is not "indispensable" for the financing of payments in this case because it has eliminated many of the specific factors that were found to be violative in the Appellate Body Report in *Canada - Dairy*. Canada's view implies that Article 9.1(c) of the *Agreement on Agriculture* would be violated only if the types of action that previously existed under Special Milk Classes 5(d) and 5(e) were present in the new scheme also. The application of the Appellate Body's ruling in *Canada - Dairy* cannot be restricted to such narrowly defined circumstances.

33. Citing the facts of this case, New Zealand argues that governmental action is clearly indispensable to the financing of payments made from producers to processors, as concluded by the Panel by using correctly its "two-part" test.

---

[28] Appellate Body Report, WT/DS31/AB/R, adopted 30 July 1997, DSR 1997:I, 449.

34. New Zealand expresses its deep reservations on Canada's reference to the *SCM Agreement* as contextual support for interpreting Article 9.1(c) of the *Agreement on Agriculture*. There is insufficient similarity between the terms of Article 1.1(a)(1) of the *SCM Agreement* and of Article 9.1(c) of the *Agreement on Agriculture* for the *SCM Agreement* to be of any decisive guidance. Moreover, Canada, by relying on the panel report in *US - Export Restraints*, creates an unwarranted dichotomy between the nature of governmental action and its "effects".

35. New Zealand also believes that Canada is seeking to re-argue the facts of this case by asserting that producers make free decisions, and that this question falls outside the scope of appellate review. No rational, profit-maximizing producer would voluntarily forego the opportunity of using high-priced sales in the domestic market to make additional profits, albeit by low-priced sales in the export market. Canada seeks to reinterpret Article 9.1(c) incorrectly by trying to restrict its application only to governmental action that, by itself, finances the transfer of resources.

36. Finally, New Zealand disagrees with Canada's view of the Panel's decision as one that penalizes governments that decide to deregulate.

3. *Article 10.1 of the Agreement on Agriculture*

37. In the alternative, New Zealand argues that, should the Appellate Body find that Canada's schemes are not export subsidies within the meaning of Article 9.1(c), the Appellate Body should conclude that the schemes constitute export subsidies within the meaning of Article 10.1 of the *Agreement on Agriculture.*

38. New Zealand argues that the CEM scheme, under which Canada enables processors for export to obtain milk at prices that are lower than those on the domestic market, constitutes an "export subsidy" within the meaning of item (d) of the Illustrative List of the *SCM Agreement*. Accordingly, it constitutes an "export subsidy" within the meaning of Article 1(e) of the *Agreement on Agriculture*, and, hence, within the meaning of Article 10.1 of that Agreement. The CEM scheme also results in non-commercial transactions being used to circumvent Canada's export subsidy commitments. Finally, New Zealand asserts that CEM transactions are "non-commercial transactions" that fall within Article 10.1 of the *Agreement on Agriculture*. Therefore, even if the Appellate Body were to conclude that the CEM scheme does not constitute an "export subsidy" under Article 9.1(c), it is in a position to complete the analysis and conclude that the schemes have been applied in a manner that is contrary to Article 10.1 of the *Agreement on Agriculture*.

C. *Arguments of the United States - Appellee*

39. At the outset, the United States emphasizes that Article 10.3 of the *Agreement on Agriculture* shifts the burden of proof to Canada to establish that,

through its milk management scheme, including CEM, Canada has not subsidized exports of milk in excess of its export subsidy commitment levels specified in its Schedule of commitments under the *WTO Agreement.* According to the United States, the Panel rightly concluded that Canada has failed to carry its burden.

1. Article 9.1(c) of the Agreement on Agriculture - "payments"

40. The United States rejects Canada's argument that the processors do not receive a "payment" within the meaning of Article 9.1(c) of the *Agreement on Agriculture.* The Panel properly concluded that a "payment" is conferred upon the processors through the provision of discounted milk for export, whether the price of export milk is compared with the price of domestic milk or with the terms of imported milk under the Import for Re-export Program ("IREP"), which are the only other sources of milk available to exporters in Canada.

41. In the view of the United States, the Panel's benchmark analysis is necessary and applicable to the present case. The Panel did not fail to consider Canada's argument that the deregulated CEM prices cannot be compared with the regulated prices for milk in the domestic market. In determining whether there is a "payment" within the meaning of Article 9.1(c) of the *Agreement on Agriculture*, the Panel considered Canada's assertion, and found that the degree of government intervention is not relevant at this stage of the analysis. The United States notes that this approach is consistent with the Appellate Body Reports in *Canada - Measures Affecting the Export of Civilian Aircraft* ("*Canada - Aircraft* ")[29] and *Canada - Dairy*, and that the Panel correctly relied upon the context of Articles 9.1(b) and 9.1(e) of the *Agreement on Agriculture* for determining the appropriate benchmark, and the object and purpose of the *Agreement on Agriculture*, as support for its conclusion.

42. The United States agrees with the Panel that the CEM market is not a market in which transactions occur "privately at arm's length." This market for export milk would cease to exist absent government intervention. The only difference between Canada's so-called "two" markets is the degree of government regulation in each. The buyers, the sellers and the product, are all the same. Other than price, there is no distinction between milk destined for the export market and milk destined for the domestic market. Canada has confirmed, during the Panel proceedings, that milk destined for the export market is not stored or processed separately from other milk. [30]

43. The United States rejects Canada's argument that no benchmark is necessary and that no benchmark should be used other than the price of CEM itself. The correct approach in analyzing "payments" under Article 9.1(c) of the *Agree-*

---

[29] WT/DS70/AB/R, adopted 20 August 1999, DSR 1999:III,1377.

[30] Panel Report, footnote 105 to para. 6.16.

ment on Agriculture requires a comparison between what is received by the processor and what is otherwise available to it as an alternative source, and this comparison remains unaffected by government intervention. Therefore, there is no reason to disregard domestic price as the appropriate benchmark, particularly because of the fact that the "two" markets are in reality "one" that has been partitioned by government for differential pricing purposes. The Appellate Body in *Canada - Dairy* never suggested to exclude the use of a benchmark and, more particularly, the use of the domestic market price (or the IREP price). Moreover, the Appellate Body's interpretation of the term "benefit" in Article 1.1 of the *SCM Agreement* in *Canada - Aircraft*, provides context for the interpretation of "payment" in Article 9.1(c) of the *Agreement on Agriculture* and further support for the use of a benchmark.

44. The United States emphasizes that even under the new scheme, exporters still receive milk that is priced lower than what is otherwise available to them either on the domestic market or through the IREP. Producers are providing milk for export at a substantial discount to the market price for milk delivered for domestic consumption. Thus, even under the replacement measures, producers are foregoing revenue and processors are receiving a benefit in the same manner that the Appellate Body in the original proceeding found to constitute a "payment" within the meaning of Article 9.1(c).

45. Finally, the United States submits that Canada cannot dispute that the payment (that is, the provision of lower-priced milk) is only available in the case of milk purchased for the manufacture of dairy products destined for the export market. Consequently, the payment constitutes a payment "on the export of an agricultural product" under Article 9.1(c) of the *Agreement on Agriculture.*

2. *Article 9.1(c) of the Agreement on Agriculture - "financed by virtue of governmental action"*

46. According to the United States, the Panel properly concluded that the payments are "financed by virtue of governmental action" within the meaning of Article 9.1(c) of the *Agreement on Agriculture.*

47. In particular, the United States is of the view that the Panel rightly referred to the Appellate Body's analysis in *Canada - Dairy* in applying what it terms as the "'indispensability' test" in order to determine whether the payments are "financed by virtue of governmental action." The United States considers that the "but for" test of the Panel is only an alternative formulation for the "'indispensability' test", and that this standard, in this case, is grounded in treaty language. Thus, the Panel did not erroneously equate "by virtue of " with "merely influences" or "encourages" as asserted by Canada, and the Panel only applied the same "'indispensability' test" that the Appellate Body applied in *Canada - Dairy*. Canada attempts to restrict unduly the scope of Article 9.1(c) to the specific levy example. Moreover, the standard proposed by Canada, that is, a "strong affirmative and positive linkage between the government action and the financing of the

payments", seems less stringent than the one applied by the Panel, which requires governmental action to be "necessary" or "vital" to the transfer of economic resources in determining whether payments are "financed by virtue of governmental action".

48. The United States also refers to Canada's argument that the Panel should have considered the context of the *SCM Agreement*. The fact that the Panel did not consider the *SCM Agreement* as context does not invalidate the Panel's otherwise valid conclusion regarding the proper standard and that Agreement, in fact, supports the Panel's conclusion. However, the United States disagrees with Canada's argument relating to Article 1.1(a)(1)(iv) of the *SCM Agreement*, based on the panel's interpretation of that article in its report in *US - Export Restraints*. The United States is of the view that the panel's finding in that report is "irrelevant" and that the passages quoted by Canada are "of decidedly questionable validity given their hypothetical and advisory nature". Furthermore, the panel's analysis of Article 1.1(a)(1)(iv) in that case only constitutes "*obiter dictum* at best and therefore [is] of no legal effect." [31]

49. The United States further argues that the Panel properly applied the "'indispensability' test" to the facts of the case by articulating its "two-part" test, and by applying the test, examined whether the governmental actions oblige producers to forego revenue and to sell to the export market. Having correctly found that these two facts are established in the present case, the Panel concluded that the governmental action is indispensable to the transfer of resources from the producers to the processors. The United States supports the Panel's finding that, in the absence of either of the governmental measures described in its "two-part" test, lower-priced milk could not be provided by the producers to the processors. Without quotas on the volume of milk that a producer can sell in the higher-priced domestic market, an "economically rational producer" would not choose to sell in a lower-priced export market. Without the governmental requirement that milk contracted for export be exported and the governmental enforcement of that requirement, export milk would be diverted into the domestic market thereby undermining the low export price as well as the high domestic price.

50. The United States claims that Canada's response to the "two-part" test in this appeal is to "re-argue the facts". This falls outside the scope of appellate review. Furthermore, the Panel rightly found that Canada had not discharged its burden of proof. Therefore, the Appellate Body should uphold the Panel's conclusion that processors are receiving payments "financed by virtue of governmental action".

51. The United States disagrees with Canada that the Panel, through its "two-part" test, improperly focused on the effects of domestic regulation instead of on the measures taken to comply with the recommendations and rulings of the DSB.

---

[31] United States' appellee's submission, paras. 44 and 45.

The governmental action guarantees that milk in excess of the quota will be exported and available for exports at a lower price. The "domestic regulation" referred to by Canada is nothing more than an "artificial segregation" of the milk market into a "domestic" market and an "export" market. By examining the segregation of the markets, the Panel analyzed government intervention in the export market, not only in the domestic market, and considered government action as a whole before concluding that governmental action is indispensable to the producers providing lower-priced milk to processors. The United States rejects Canada's view that the Panel failed to take into account the "deregulation" of the export market.

52. Finally, the United States argues that the factual record establishes that processors are provided milk at discounted prices, contingent on export, only through governmental action. Therefore, the Panel's conclusion that processors are receiving payments "financed by virtue of government action" should be upheld.

3. *Article 10.1 of the Agreement on Agriculture and Article 3.1 of the SCM Agreement*

53. Should the Appellate Body decide to complete the legal analysis of the Panel, the United States submits that, in the alternative, Canada's revised export schemes constitute export subsidies within the meaning of Article 10.1 of the *Agreement on Agriculture*. In the view of the United States, such a finding would be supported by the fact that the revised schemes satisfy each of the criteria identified in item (d) of the Illustrative List of the *SCM Agreement*. The United States further argues that Canada's revised export schemes result in subsidized exports without any limitation, and threaten to lead to circumvention of Canada's export reduction commitments on milk products, within the meaning of Article 10.1 of the *Agreement on Agriculture*. The United States also emphasizes that, in this case, there is actual circumvention of Canada's export commitment levels as shown by the fact that Canada's exports of cheese have in fact already exceeded the limitations set out in Canada's Schedule of Commitments.

54. Finally, should the Appellate Body deem it necessary to complete the analysis of the Panel, the United States submits that Canada's revised export schemes are prohibited export subsidies under Article 3.1 of the *SCM Agreement* as well.

D. *Arguments of the European Communities - Third Participant*

55. The European Communities supports Canada's contention that the Panel erroneously broadened the reach of Article 9.1(c) of the *Agreement on Agriculture* to include a measure which is not a subsidy within the meaning of that article. The European Communities also agrees with Canada that Article 9.1(c) can and should be interpreted against the background of the general concept of "subsidy" as defined under the *SCM Agreement*. The concept of "subsidy" should not

be subject to diverging interpretations, and it should be interpreted consistently like the concept of "export contingency". In the view of the European Communities, there are compelling arguments that support a consistent approach to the interpretation of a subsidy, in particular, the consideration that the objective of the *Agreement on Agriculture* is only to limit subsidization of agricultural products, not to create stricter disciplines on agricultural subsidies than those applicable to industrial products.

1. *Article 9.1(c) of the Agreement on Agriculture - "payments"*

56. The European Communities considers that the ordinary meaning of the word "payment", read together with the term "financed", and the levy example contained in Article 9.1(c) of the *Agreement on Agriculture*, suggests a transfer of money. In the event that the Appellate Body reaffirms that the word "payments" includes "payments-in-kind", the European Communities argues that the Panel erred in finding that the regulated domestic market price constitutes the correct benchmark to determine whether a "payment" exists. Unlike Articles 9.1(b) and 9.1(e), Article 9.1(c) does not indicate that the domestic market is the decisive benchmark. The decisive benchmark must be what is otherwise commercially available to processors on the market, as supported by the immediate context of Article 9.1(c) as well as Article 14 of the *SCM Agreement* and item (d) of the Illustrative List of the *SCM Agreement*. Since the domestic market in milk is not available to processors for export, the world market should be used in this case.

57. With regard to the Panel's finding on the requirement that "payments" be "on the export", the European Communities considers that the Appellate Body should declare this finding to be "moot and without legal effect" because the Panel erroneously "decoupled" the term "on the export" from the term "payment" and then equated it with the concept of export contingency, although the notion of "payment *on* the export" involves a more direct and strict link with the export operation.

2. *Article 9.1(c) of the Agreement on Agriculture - "financed by virtue of governmental action"*

58. The European Communities considers that the Panel erroneously developed the "but for" test to determine whether the payment is "financed by virtue of governmental action". The Panel's approach cannot be supported by the term "financed" and the levy example contained in Article 9.1(c). The European Communities also submits that the Panel's reasoning fails to take account of the interpretative guidance provided by Article 1.1 of the *SCM Agreement*, notably, the phrase "financial contribution".

59. According to the European Communities, the element "financial contribution" in the *SCM Agreement* is an "important filter" to "sift" WTO-inconsistent subsidies from any other governmental measure that may have trade-distorting effects. The test for determining the element "financial contribution", as developed by the panel in *US - Export Restraints*, indicates that Article 9.1(c) should be limited to cases where governments address a clear command to agricultural producers to transfer a certain amount of economic resources at a certain price.

60. Finally, the European Communities is of the view that the Appellate Body should not uphold the Panel's conclusion that "payments" were "financed by virtue of governmental action" because the Panel incorrectly based its conclusion solely on the two governmental actions set out in its "two-part" test. Although these actions, if established, may encourage producers to sell CEM, the European Communities fails to see how the provision of lower-priced milk to processors can be said to be "imposed" on producers by the government in the circumstances of the present case.

III. ISSUE RAISED IN THIS APPEAL

61. The issue raised in this appeal is whether the Panel erred in finding, in paragraph 6.79 of the Panel Report, that the supply of "commercial export milk" ("CEM") by domestic milk producers to domestic dairy processors involves "payments" on the export of milk "that are financed by virtue of governmental action" within the meaning of Article 9.1(c) of the *Agreement on Agriculture*.

IV. ARTICLE 9.1(c) OF THE AGREEMENT ON AGRICULTURE

62. Before the Panel, New Zealand and the United States claimed that the supply of CEM by Canadian milk producers to Canadian dairy processors, as an input for exports of processed dairy products, involved export subsidies under Article 9.1(c) of the *Agreement on Agriculture*. The Panel addressed this claim by: first, examining whether sales of CEM involve "*payments*"; second, having found that they do, whether those payments are "*financed by virtue of governmental action*". [32] (emphasis added); and third, examining whether the payments are made "on the *export* of an agricultural product", and concluded that they are. [33] (emphasis added)

63. Canada appeals the Panel's findings on the first and second of these three elements, but does not appeal the Panel's finding on the third. In our examination of these issues raised by Canada's appeal, we will follow the same order of analysis, examining, first, the Panel's finding that the measure involves "payments"

[32] Panel Report, paras. 6.27 and 6.77.
[33] *Ibid.*, para. 6.78.

and, second, the Panel's finding that those payments are "financed by virtue of governmental action".

A. *"Payments"*

64. The Panel recalled our statement in the original proceedings:

> ... the word "payments" in Article 9.1(c) denotes a transfer of economic resources, and ... the ordinary meaning of the word "payments" in Article 9.1(c) encompasses "payments" made in forms other than money, including revenue foregone. [34] (footnotes omitted)

65. The Panel also referred to the following passage from our Report in *Canada - Dairy*:

> In our view, the provision of milk at discounted prices to processors for export under Special Classes 5(d) and 5(e) constitutes "payments", in a form other than money, within the meaning of Article 9.1(c). If goods or services are supplied to an enterprise, or a group of enterprises, at reduced rates (that is, at below market-rates), "payments" are, in effect, made to the recipient of the portion of the price that is not charged. Instead of receiving a monetary payment equal to the revenue foregone, the recipient is paid in the form of goods or services. But, as far as the recipient is concerned, the economic value of the transfer is precisely the same. [35]

66. The Panel took the view that a determination that CEM is sold by producers at "discounted" or "reduced" rates, which are "below market", requires a comparison between the prices of CEM and a "benchmark" that provides a basis for comparison. The Panel found that the "right benchmark", in this dispute, is the price at which milk is sold by producers in the *domestic* market. [36] In reaching this conclusion, the Panel relied, *inter alia*, on sub-paragraphs (b) and (e) of Article 9.1 of the *Agreement on Agriculture* as context.

67. The Panel also examined a second, alternative benchmark based on world market prices. Canadian processors wishing to export processed dairy products may import raw milk, or milk derivatives, under Canada's Import for Re-Export Programme ("IREP"), provided that the processed products are exported. The Panel did not examine the parties' arguments regarding the "competitive relation-

---

[34] Panel Report, para. 6.12; Appellate Body Report, *Canada - Dairy, supra*, footnote 2, paras. 107 and 112.

[35] Panel Report, para. 6.12; Appellate Body Report, *supra*, footnote 2, para. 113.

[36] Panel Report, para. 6.22.

ship" between CEM and dairy products imported under IREP. [37] Instead, the Panel examined only the terms and conditions on which dairy products may be imported under IREP. The Panel held that imports under IREP depend upon the exercise by government of "wide and untrammelled discretion", as an import permit is required. [38] In addition, the Panel found that an administrative fee must be paid to obtain an import permit under IREP. On this basis, and without comparing the prices of CEM with the prices of dairy products imported under IREP, the Panel concluded that IREP imports are not "effectively" available on "equally favourable terms" as those offered for commercial export milk. [39]

68. The Panel concluded that "the provision of milk at discounted prices to processors for export under the CEM scheme constitutes 'payments', in a form other than money, within the meaning of Article 9.1(c) of the *Agreement on Agriculture*." [40]

69. On appeal, Canada argues that the Panel failed to take sufficient account of the fact that supplies of CEM are "no longer subject to government regulation". [41] Canada points out that we stated in *Canada - Dairy* that "payments" are made when goods are supplied at "below market-rates" and for "less than full consideration". [42] Canada emphasizes that the price of CEM is freely negotiated in the marketplace between the producer and the processor, on a willing-buyer, willing-seller basis and, accordingly, it represents both market price and full consideration for the milk. Consequently, Canada contends that no comparison with any benchmark is required. [43] In Canada's view, there is, therefore, no "payment" when a producer sells CEM to a processor.

70. Article 9.1(c) of the *Agreement on Agriculture* reads:

> The following export subsidies are subject to reduction commitments under this Agreement:
>
> ...
>
> payments on the export of an agricultural product that are financed by virtue of governmental action, whether or not a charge on the public account is involved, including payments that are financed from the proceeds of a levy imposed on the agricultural product concerned or on an agricultural product from which the exported product is derived;

---

[37] Panel Report, para. 6.26. Imports under IREP, generally, involve whole milk powder, while CEM involves fluid milk. The Panel noted in this para. that the parties had submitted "conflicting evidence" regarding fluid milk equivalent prices of whole milk powder.

[38] Panel Report, para. 6.25.

[39] *Ibid.*

[40] *Ibid.*, para. 6.27.

[41] Canada's appellant's submission, para. 40.

[42] Appellate Body Report, *supra*, footnote 2, paras. 87 and 113.

[43] Canada's appellant's submission, para. 46; *see also*, para. 36 and footnote 28 thereto.

...

71. We observe, first, that the "payment" which the Panel found to exist in this dispute is effected through the supply of goods - commercial export milk or CEM. The alleged payment is, thus, not a monetary payment but a payment-in-kind. As the Panel observed, we held in the original proceedings that the word "payments" in Article 9.1(c) "encompasses 'payments' made in forms other than money, including revenue foregone." [44] It is not contested, in this appeal, that "payments" can include payments-in-kind in Article 9.1(c) of the *Agreement on Agriculture*.

72. In the original proceedings, in order to identify whether there were "payments" in Article 9.1(c), through the supply of milk under Special Milk Classes 5(d) and 5(e), the panel identified two benchmarks against which to compare the price of milk sold under these Special Milk Classes. These two benchmarks were (1) domestic prices and (2) the price of milk available to processors from world markets through imports under IREP. The original panel found that supplies under Special Milk Classes 5(d) and 5(e) were available on terms and conditions more favourable than those applicable under both of the two benchmarks on which it relied. [45] The original panel's findings regarding the benchmarks under Articles 9.1(a) and 9.1(c) were not challenged on appeal and we merely based our examination on the fact that Special Milk Classes 5(d) and 5(e) were supplied to processors at "discounted" prices or at "below market-rates". In this appeal, Canada's challenge to the Panel's finding focuses squarely upon the Panel's use of a benchmark as a basis for determining whether there are "payments" in this dispute. [46]

73. Although we did not have to examine whether the benchmarks used by the panel in the original proceedings were appropriate, our findings in those proceedings provide guidance in identifying when "payments" are made under Article 9.1(c). We recall that we upheld the original panel's finding that "the provision of *discounted* milk to processors or exporters under Special Classes 5(d) and 5(e) involves 'payments' within the meaning of Article 9.1(c) of the *Agreement on Agriculture*." [47] (emphasis added) In reaching this conclusion, we noted that, where milk is sold at "*reduced* rates (that is, at *below market-rates*), 'payments' are, in effect, made to the recipient of the portion of the price that is not

44 Appellate Body Report, *Canada - Dairy*, *supra*, footnote 2, para. 112. We note that the *Agreement on Agriculture* and the *SCM Agreement* both use the word "foregone", which can also be spelled "forgone".

45 Original Panel Report, *Canada - Dairy*, *supra*, footnote 2, para. 7.58. The original panel's analysis of the benchmarks forms part of its examination of the claims made in those proceedings regarding "payments-in-kind" under Article 9.1(a) of the *Agreement on Agriculture*. In examining the claims made regarding payments-in-kind under Article 9.1(c), the panel relied on its earlier findings under Article 9.1(a). *See*, original Panel Report, paras. 7.90 and 7.101.

46 *See*, *supra*, para. 69.

47 Appellate Body Report, *Canada - Dairy*, *supra*, footnote 2, para. 114.

charged." [48] (emphasis added) We noted that the producer of the milk "foregoes" the uncharged portion of the price. [49] In short, we indicated that there are "payments" under Article 9.1(c) when the price charged by the producer of the milk is less than the milk's *proper value* to the producer. [50]

74. Thus, the determination of whether "payments" are involved requires a comparison between the price actually charged by the provider of the goods or services - the prices of CEM in this case - and some objective standard or benchmark which reflects the proper value of the goods or services to their provider - the milk producer in this case. We do not accept Canada's argument that as the producer negotiates freely the price with the processor, and CEM prices are, therefore, market-determined, it is not necessary to compare these prices with an objective standard.

75. Article 9.1(c) of the *Agreement on Agriculture* does not expressly identify any standard for determining when a measure involves "payments" in the form of payments-in-kind. The absence of an express standard in Article 9.1(c) may be contrasted with several other provisions involving export subsidies which do provide an express standard. Thus, for instance, even within Article 9.1 itself, sub-paragraphs (b) and (e) expressly provide that the domestic market constitutes the appropriate basis for comparison. [51]

76. We believe that it is significant that Article 9.1(c) of the *Agreement on Agriculture* does not expressly identify a standard or benchmark for determining whether a measure involves "payments". It is clear that the notion of "payments" encompasses a diverse range of practices involving a transfer of resources, either monetary or in-kind. Moreover, the "payments" may take place in many different factual and regulatory settings. Accordingly, we believe that it is necessary to scrutinize carefully the facts and circumstances of a disputed measure, including the regulatory framework surrounding that measure, to determine the appropriate basis for comparison in assessing whether the measure involves "payments" under Article 9.1(c).

77. We turn now to examine the factual and regulatory setting of the disputed measure in this appeal. We note that, in these proceedings, certain aspects of the measure at issue are substantially different from those of the measure at issue in the original proceedings.

---

48 Appellate Body Report, *Canada - Dairy*, *supra*, footnote 2, para. 113.

49 *Ibid.*

50 We will examine below the concept of the proper value of goods to the producer, in the context of these proceedings. *See, infra*, paras. 86 to 96.

51 *See also*, items (c), (d), (f), (g), (h), (j) and (k) of the Illustrative List of the *SCM Agreement*, each of which expressly identifies one or more benchmarks to be used as a basis for comparison in determining whether a measure involves export subsidies. *See further*, paras. 8 and 13 of Annex 3, and para. 2 of Annex 4, of the *Agreement on Agriculture*, which expressly identify one or more benchmarks for calculating the amount of domestic support.

78. In the original proceedings, sales of milk under Special Milk Classes 5(d) and 5(e) were entirely regulated by the Canadian government or its agencies. The government granted permits for these sales, and also negotiated the sales price with the processors on a transaction-by-transaction basis. The government also collected the revenues from the sales transactions and allocated them to producers. The role of the government in regulating the export sales of producers mirrored the role of the government in regulating sales in the domestic market, where supplies were strictly controlled by the government through a quota system and where prices were determined by the provincial marketing boards, which were found by us to be government agencies under the *Agreement on Agriculture.*[52]

79. While continuing to regulate the domestic market in the same way, the Canadian government has now altered its role in regulating export sales by the producers. At present, there are two categories of export sales of milk by producers. First, under the Special Milk Classes 5(a) to 5(d), the Canadian government continues to require that export sales be made within a quota and under government permit. As in the original proceedings, prices for export sales under these Special Milk Classes, including in particular Special Milk Class 5(d), are regulated by the government. However, besides abolishing Special Milk Class 5(e), Canada has now established a second category of export milk, known as commercial export milk or CEM. Sales of CEM do not require any permit from the government, and the volume and price of CEM sales are freely negotiated between the producer and the processor. Each producer decides for itself whether, and when, to produce and sell milk as CEM. Many producers may find that the production of additional milk for sale as CEM is not profitable and they are free to decide not to produce such additional milk for export sale. This is borne out by the fact that many producers do choose not to produce and sell CEM.[53] Milk sold as CEM cannot be diverted into the domestic market and dairy products produced with CEM must be exported.

80. With these factual and regulatory circumstances of the new measure in mind, we now examine the appropriate standard for determining whether the measure at issue involves "payments" under Article 9.1(c) of the *Agreement on Agriculture*. In so doing, we begin by reviewing the Panel's finding that the domestic market provides the "right benchmark" for this dispute.

81. The domestic price in this case is an administered price fixed by the Canadian government as part of the regulatory framework established by it for managing the supply of milk destined for consumption in the domestic market. As with administered prices in general, this price expresses a government policy

52 Appellate Body Report, *Canada - Dairy*, *supra*, footnote 2, para. 102.

53 Canada asserted before the Panel that about 30 percent of Canadian producers had participated in CEM transactions since deregulation measures were introduced in August 2000. (Panel Report, para. 4.24)

choice based, not only on economic considerations, but also on other social objectives. The Canadian regulatory framework for managing domestic milk supply, including the establishment of the administered price, is not in dispute in this case. There can be little doubt, however, that the administered price is a price that is favourable to the domestic producers. Consequently, sale of CEM by the producer at less than the administered domestic price does not, necessarily, imply that the producer has foregone a portion of the proper value of the milk to it. In the situation where the producer, rather than the government, chooses to produce and sell CEM in the marketplace at a price it freely negotiates, we do not believe it is appropriate to use, as a basis for comparison, a domestic price that is fixed by the government.

82. We, therefore, reverse the Panel's finding, in paragraph 6.22 of the Panel Report, that the "right benchmark" in these proceedings is the "domestic market price".[54]

83. The alternative "benchmark" which the Panel relied upon to determine whether CEM prices involve "payments" was the terms and conditions on which alternative supplies are available to processors on world markets, through IREP.[55] In reviewing this benchmark, we recall that, in these proceedings, the standard used to determine whether there are "payments" under Article 9.1(c) must be based on the proper value of the milk to the producer, in order to determine whether the producer foregoes a portion of this value. If a producer wishes to sell milk for export processing, it is obvious that the price of the milk to the processor must be competitive with world market prices. If it is not, the processor will not buy the milk, as it will not be able to produce a final product that is competitive in export markets. Accordingly, the range of world market prices determines the price which the producer can charge for milk destined for export markets.[56] World market prices do, therefore, provide one possible measure of the value of the milk to the producer.

---

[54] *See also,* our reasoning, *infra*, in para. 90.

[55] Panel Report, paras. 6.22 ff. *See, supra*, para. 67. We note that, in examining the terms and conditions on which IREP is available, the Panel focused exclusively on the requirements to obtain a discretionary permit and to pay an administrative fee. In assessing whether alternative sources of supply are available on more favourable terms, we consider that panels should take account of all the factors which affect the relative "attractiveness" in the marketplace of the different goods or services. The primary consideration must be price, while the importance of administrative formalities will depend on their nature and characteristics. For instance, if an import permit were granted to importers as a matter of course, in the context of straightforward import procedures, and if import fees were only administrative charges to cover expenses, these formalities would be unlikely, on their own, to mean that imports were available on less favourable terms and conditions.

[56] New Zealand acknowledged, before the Panel, that the price of CEM "will be essentially world market prices". (New Zealand's first submission to the Panel, para. 4.05) Canada also argued that the processor offers producers a price for CEM that is based on world market conditions. (Canada's first submission to the Panel, para. 37; Canada's second submission to the Panel, para. 13; Canada's oral

84. However, world market prices do not provide a valid basis for determining whether there are "payments", under Article 9.1(c) of the *Agreement on Agriculture*, for, it remains possible that the reason CEM can be sold at prices competitive with world market prices is precisely because sales of CEM involve subsidies that make it competitive. Thus, a comparison between CEM prices and world market prices gives no indication on the crucial question, namely, whether Canadian export production has been given an advantage. Furthermore, if the basis for comparison were world market prices, it would be possible for WTO Members to subsidize domestic inputs for export processing, while taking care to maintain the price of these inputs to the processors at a level which equalled or marginally exceeded world market prices. There would then be no "payments" under Article 9.1(c) of the *Agreement on Agriculture* and WTO Members could easily defeat the export subsidy commitments that they have undertaken in Article 3 of the *Agreement on Agriculture*.[57]

85. We do not, therefore, accept that world market prices are an appropriate basis for determining whether sales of CEM by producers involve "payments" under Article 9.1(c) of the *Agreement on Agriculture*.

86. We turn now to determine the appropriate standard for assessing whether sales of CEM by producers involve "payments" under Article 9.1(c) of the *Agreement on Agriculture*. We reiterate that the standard must be objective and based on the value of the milk to the producer.

87. Although the proceeds from sales at domestic or world market prices represent two possible measures of the value of milk to the producer, we do not see these as the only possible measures of this value. For any economic operator, the production of goods or services involves an investment of economic resources. In the case of a milk producer, production requires an investment in fixed assets, such as land, cattle and milking facilities, and an outlay to meet variable costs, such as labour, animal feed and health-care, power and administration. These fixed and variable costs are the total amount which the producer must spend in order to produce the milk and the total amount it must recoup, in the long-term, to avoid making losses. To the extent that the producer charges prices that do not recoup the total cost of production, over time, it sustains a loss which must be financed from some other source, possibly "by virtue of governmental action".

88. In our view, reliance upon the total cost of production, in this dispute, as a basis for determining whether there are "payments" within the meaning of Article 9.1(c), is in harmony with the domestic support and export subsidies disciplines of the *Agreement on Agriculture*. Under Article 3 of the *Agreement on Agricul-*

---

statement before the Panel, paras. 21, 30, 49 and 51; Canada's appellant's submission, para. 39 and footnote 32 thereto)

[57] We note that none of the participants in these proceedings argued that world market prices are the appropriate benchmark for determining whether supplies of CEM involve "payments" within the meaning of Article 9.1(c) of the *Agreement on Agriculture*. *See also*, *supra*, footnote 43.

ture, WTO Members are entitled to provide "*domestic support* " to agricultural producers within the limits of their domestic support commitments. The same Article establishes separate disciplines on *export subsidies* which prohibit WTO Members from providing such subsidies in excess of their export subsidy commitments.

89. It is possible that the economic effects of WTO-consistent domestic support in favour of producers may "spill over" to provide certain benefits to export production, especially as many agricultural products result from a single line of production that does not distinguish whether the production is destined for consumption in the domestic or export market.

90. We believe that it would erode the distinction between the domestic support and export subsidies disciplines of the *Agreement on Agriculture* if WTO-consistent domestic support measures were automatically characterized as export subsidies because they produced spill-over economic benefits for export production. Indeed, this is another reason why we do not agree with the Panel that sales of CEM at any price below the administered domestic price for milk can be regarded as "payments" under Article 9.1(c) of the *Agreement on Agriculture*. Such a basis for comparison would tend to collapse the distinction between these two different disciplines.

91. However, we consider that the distinction between the domestic support and export subsidies disciplines in the *Agreement on Agriculture* would also be eroded if a WTO Member were entitled to use domestic support, without limit, to provide support for exports of agricultural products. Broadly stated, domestic support provisions of that Agreement, coupled with high levels of tariff protection, allow extensive support to producers, as compared with the limitations imposed through the export subsidies disciplines. Consequently, if domestic support could be used, without limit, to provide support for exports, it would undermine the benefits intended to accrue through a WTO Member's export subsidy commitments.

92. In our view, by relying upon the total cost of production in this dispute, to determine whether there are "payments", the integrity of the two disciplines is best respected. The existence of "payments" is determined by reference to a standard that focuses upon the motivations of the independent economic operator who is making the alleged "payments" - here the producer - and not upon any government intervention in the marketplace. More importantly, using this basis for comparison, the potential for WTO Members to export their agricultural production is preserved, provided that any export-destined sales by a producer at below the total cost of production are not financed by virtue of governmental action. The export subsidy disciplines of the *Agreement on Agriculture* will also be maintained without erosion.

93. Our approach is supported by the standards used in items (j) and (k) of the Illustrative List of the *SCM Agreement*. Item (j) is concerned with export subsidies that arise through the provision by the government of a variety of export credit guarantee and insurance programmes. Under item (j), the provision of such

services by the government involves export subsidies when the premium rates charged do not "cover the *long-term operating costs and losses* of the programmes". (emphasis added) Thus, the measure of value under item (j) is the overall cost to the government, as the service provider, of providing the service. Likewise, in item (k), where the government provides export credits, the measure of the value of the service provided by the government is the amount "which [governments] actually have to pay for the funds so employed (or would have to pay if they borrowed on international capital markets...)". Again, the measure of value is by reference to the cost to the government, as the service provider, of providing the service. Therefore, items (j) and (k) give contextual support and *rationale*, for using the cost of production as a standard for determining whether there are "payments" under Article 9.1(c) of the *Agreement on Agriculture* in these proceedings.

94. A producer's cost of production may be measured in, at least, two ways. First, for any given unit of production, for instance a hectolitre of milk, there is an average total cost of production, which is the total cost of production divided by the total number of units produced, regardless of whether the production is destined for the domestic or export markets. The total cost of production includes *all* fixed and variable costs incurred in the production of all the units in question. Second, there is also the marginal cost of production which includes only the additional costs incurred by the producer in producing an extra unit of production. Generally, the marginal cost of production does not include any amount for the fixed costs of production. Although a producer may very well decide to sell goods or services if the sales price covers its marginal costs, the producer will make losses on such sales unless all of the remaining costs associated with making these sales, essentially the fixed costs, are financed through some other source, such as through highly profitable sales of the product in another market.

95. In the ordinary course of business, an economic operator chooses to invest, produce and sell, not only to recover the total cost of production, but also in the hope of making profits.

96. Accordingly, in the circumstances of these proceedings, where the alleged payment is made by an independent economic operator and where the domestic price is administered, we believe that the average total cost of production represents the appropriate standard for determining whether sales of CEM involve "payments" under Article 9.1(c) of the *Agreement on Agriculture*. The average total cost of production would be determined by dividing the fixed and variable costs of producing *all* milk, whether destined for domestic or export markets, by the total number of units of milk produced for both these markets.

97. We observe that, in this part of our findings, we are examining only whether there are "*payments*" within the meaning of Article 9.1(c) of the *Agreement on Agriculture*. Although sales by a producer below average total cost of production might involve "payments", this does not, by itself, mean that such sales involve *export subsidies*. The export subsidy described in Article 9.1(c) comprises of several elements, the first of which is that there must be "pay-

ments". But the "payments" will be an export subsidy only when they are financed by virtue of governmental action. Thus, on the basis of the standard of average total cost of production, there will be an export subsidy only if the below-cost portion of an export sale is "financed by virtue of governmental action".

98. As we have reversed the Panel's findings regarding the standard for determining the existence of "payments" and have, instead, identified the appropriate standard for these proceedings, namely, the average total cost of production, we now consider whether we can resolve this aspect of the dispute by completing the analysis. The Panel found that, in these proceedings, Article 10.3 of the *Agreement on Agriculture* reverses the burden of proof so that Canada must establish "that no export subsidy ... has been granted".[58] Although the burden of proof is on Canada, we must nonetheless complete the analysis solely on the basis of factual findings made by the Panel and uncontested facts in the Panel record.

99. As regards the cost of production, New Zealand submitted evidence from the Canadian Dairy Commission (the "CDC") that the cost of production of milk in Canada was C$56.83 per hectolitre.[59] The United States argued that "less than 30 percent of Canadian farmers cover their cost of production at an average price of C$57.41/hl and less than 1 percent could cover costs at export market prices of around C$30/hl."[60] The United States submitted a graph illustrating producers' costs of production.[61] According to this graph, it appears that the lowest cost of production of any producer is around C$30 per hectolitre. However, the data in the graph and the assumptions behind the data are not clear.

100. Canada contested these figures before the Panel. It argued that the figures relied upon by New Zealand and the United States were too high because they included "imputed returns to labour, management and equity - costs that are additional charges not generally associated with costing for production decisions".[62] Canada submits that a "far more relevant" figure would be based on "direct input costs (such as costs for feed and supplies) and costs associated with fixed costs (such as interest payments on debt and depreciation on buildings and equipment)."[63] In addition, Canada stated that the cost of production would also include "all cash costs of production" but would exclude "imputed or assigned"

---

58 Panel Report, para. 6.6. Canada has not appealed this finding.

59 New Zealand's second submission to the Panel, footnote 9 to para. 2.05, and Exhibit NZ-21 submitted by New Zealand to the Panel. In support of this figure, New Zealand cited a speech given by the Chairman of the CDC in January 2000 in which he said that a CDC study "estimated the cost of production for milk in Canada to be C$56.83/hl at that time." New Zealand also provided an exhibit containing the publicly-available speaking notes of the Chairman for that speech. In these notes, it is said that the CDC determined a "new [cost of production] of $58.89 per hL".

60 United States' second submission to the Panel, para. 13, and Exhibit US-24 submitted by the United States to the Panel.

61 Exhibit US-24 submitted by the United States to the Panel.

62 Canada's oral statement before the Panel, para. 19.

63 *Ibid.*, para. 20.

amounts that "do not represent actual expenses".[64] Canada submitted its own graph illustrating the cost of production based on generally accepted accounting principles ("GAAP").[65] According to this graph, it appears that the lowest cost of production of any producer is around C$19 per hectolitre. However, the data in the graph and the assumptions behind the data are not clear.

101. The Panel record contains data relating to the prices of CEM and domestic market milk. Canada submitted to the Panel that sales of CEM have been made in the price range of C$19.06 to C$36.86 per hectolitre, and New Zealand and the United States submitted figures which appear to be consistent with this range of prices.[66] New Zealand submitted to the Panel that the price of milk in the domestic market is between C$49.48 and C$56.06 per hectolitre, while the United States gave an average figure of C$52.92 per hectolitre. Canada did not contest these figures.[67] We note, as did the Panel, that there is a "clear differential" between the prices of CEM and the domestic market price.[68] This suggests the possibility that the prices of CEM might be below the average total cost of production and, thus, might involve "payments" under Article 9.1(c).

102. However, the Panel did not find it necessary to make any factual findings on the costs of production and the facts relating to this issue were not the subject of agreement between the parties. Moreover, the Panel proceedings were conducted without the parties arguing their case, or the Panel making enquiries, from the perspective of the average total cost of production standard we have adopted.

103. In these circumstances, we are unable to complete the analysis by determining whether the supply of CEM involves "payments" under Article 9.1(c) of the *Agreement on Agriculture*. Yet, we do not wish to be understood as holding that the supply of CEM does *not* involve "payments" under Article 9.1(c). We are simply not in a position to make a ruling on this issue.

104. In conclusion, we have reversed the Panel's finding, in paragraph 6.22 of the Panel Report, that the "right benchmark" in this dispute is the domestic market price, and we have also rejected the Panel's alternative benchmark based on world market prices. Instead, we have adopted as a standard, for these proceedings, the average total cost of production of the milk producers.[69] In the light of the factual record before us, we are unable to determine whether supplies of CEM involve "payments" under Article 9.1(c) of the *Agreement on Agriculture*. In these circumstances, we reverse the Panel's finding, in paragraph 6.27 of the

---

[64] Canada's oral statement before the Panel, footnote 1 to para. 20.

[65] Exhibit CDA-26 submitted by Canada to the Panel.

[66] Panel Report, para. 6.10. At the oral hearing, Canada stated that the weighted-average price for sales of CEM, for the period of 1 August 2000 to 31 July 2001, in Manitoba, Ontario and Quebec, was C$29 per hectolitre.

[67] Panel Report, para. 6.10. At the oral hearing, Canada stated that the price for Class 3 domestic industrial milk in Canada, for the period of 1 August 2000 to 31 July 2001, was C$58 per hectolitre.

[68] Panel Report, para. 6.10.

[69] *Supra*, para. 96.

Panel Report, that the provision of CEM "constitutes 'payments', in a form other than money, within the meaning of Article 9.1(c) of the *Agreement on Agriculture.*" As a result, we also reverse the Panel's finding, in paragraph 6.79 of the Panel Report, that the measure at issue involves export subsidies under Article 9.1(c) of the *Agreement on Agriculture* and its finding, in paragraph 7.1 of the Panel Report, that Canada acted inconsistently with its obligations under Articles 3.3 and 8 of that Agreement "through the CEM scheme and the continued operation of Special Milk Class 5(d)". This does not amount to a finding that the measure at issue is WTO-consistent, but simply that the Panel's findings are vitiated by error of law.

B. "Financed by Virtue of Governmental Action"

105. We turn now to examine Canada's appeal of the Panel's findings on the phrase "financed by virtue of governmental action". In so doing, we recognize that the Panel's findings were predicated on the existence of "payments", under Article 9.1(c) of the *Agreement on Agriculture*, in the form of supplies of milk at prices below the domestic market prices and that we have found that this is not the appropriate basis for determining whether there are "payments". We also recognize that the factual record does not allow us to determine whether there are "payments" under the measure at issue based on the standard we have adopted of average total cost of production.

106. The Panel took the view that the phrase "financed by virtue of governmental action" implies "a certain degree of causality". [70] Recalling our Report, the Panel considered that governmental action has to be "indispensable" for the payment to take place. [71] The Panel found that it is not required that a government "force", "direct", or "compel" producers to sell into the commercial export market. [72]

107. Having examined the general meaning of the phrase "financed by virtue of governmental action", the Panel formulated the issue before it in the following way: "would milk processors for export have access to lower priced commercial export milk in Canada *but for* governmental action? " [73] (emphasis in original) The Panel opined that this "but for" standard would be met if the following two elements were demonstrated:

> ... that governmental action, *de jure* or *de facto*: (i) prevents Canadian milk producers from selling more milk on the regulated domestic market, at a higher price, than to the extent of the quota allocated to them; and (ii) obliges Canadian milk processors to ex-

70 Panel Report, para. 6.35.
71 *Ibid.*, paras. 6.37, 6.40-6.41 and 6.44.
72 *Ibid.*, para. 6.44.
73 *Ibid.*, para. 6.41.

> port all milk contracted as lower priced commercial export milk, and, accordingly, penalizes the diversion by processors of milk contracted as commercial export milk to the domestic market.[74]

108. The Panel explained that underlying this analysis was the assumption that milk producers are "economically rational" and will "try to maximize [their] profits".[75] In the light of this assumption, the Panel concluded that, if the two elements above were demonstrated, "the choice left to the Canadian producer is *not a real choice*."[76] (emphasis added) In those circumstances, the Panel found that "the 'reason' [for producers to sell CEM] would be the governmental action *driving* producers to the economically second-best option of producing for export."[77] (emphasis added) Moreover, demonstrating these circumstances "would establish that producers choose the economic second-best option as a totally rational and predictable reaction to government action taking away the first-best option [that is, sale in the domestic market at higher prices]."[78] The Panel also insisted that, to satisfy its standard, governmental "anti-diversion measures" be in place to "ensure" that export milk is not diverted back to the domestic market.[79]

109. Applying this reasoning, the Panel found, relying on Canadian federal and provincial governmental action, that the two elements, set forth in the passage cited above from paragraph 6.42 of the Panel Report, were established.[80] This, the Panel said, meant that CEM "would not be available to Canadian processors *but for* the ... federal and provincial actions ... *obliging* producers, at least *de facto*, to sell outside-quota milk for export".[81] (emphasis in original, underlining added) Accordingly, the Panel found that "payments" under CEM are "financed by virtue of governmental action".[82]

110. On appeal, Canada argues that the Panel applied a standard that fails to ensure "a strong affirmative and positive linkage between governmental action and financing of payments."[83] Canada contends that the Panel erred by interpreting "financed" to mean simply that a payment is "made".[84] Instead, the word "financing" requires that a "government performs functions of raising, furnishing or managing funds".[85] In this case, supplies of CEM do not involve any such funding either by the government or by a government mandate.

---

74 Panel Report, para. 6.42.

75 Panel Report, paras. 6.43 and 6.45.

76 *Ibid.*, para. 6.45.

77 *Ibid.*

78 *Ibid.*

79 *Ibid.*, paras. 6.42 and 6.48.

80 *Supra*, para. 107.

81 Panel Report, para. 6.77.

82 *Ibid.*, para. 6.79.

83 Canada's appellant's submission, paras. 7, 49 and 52.

84 *Ibid.*, para. 8.

85 Canada's appellant's submission., paras. 10 and 49.

111. We begin with Article 9.1(c) of the *Agreement on Agriculture*, which covers "payments ... *financed by virtue of governmental action*, whether or not a charge on the public account is involved". (emphasis added) We recall that, in the original proceedings, the role of the government in managing the supply of milk for export was manifest. We stated that:

> "[G]overnmental action" is not simply involved; it is, in fact, *indispensable* to enable the supply of milk to processors for export, and hence the transfer of resources, to take place. In the regulatory framework, "government agencies" stand so completely between the producers of the milk and the processors or the exporters that we have no doubt that the transfer of resources takes place "by virtue of governmental action". [86] (emphasis added)

112. Although the phrase "financed by virtue of governmental action" must be understood as a whole, it is useful to consider separately the meaning of the different parts of this phrase. Taking the words "governmental action" first, we observe that the text of Article 9.1(c) does not place any qualifications on the types of "governmental action" which may be relevant under Article 9.1(c). In the original proceedings, we stated that "[t]he essence of 'government' is ... that it enjoys the effective power to 'regulate', 'control' or 'supervise' individuals, or otherwise 'restrain' their conduct, through the exercise of lawful authority." [87] In our opinion the word "action" embraces the full-range of these activities, including governmental action regulating the supply and price of milk in the domestic market.

113. Mere governmental action is not, however, sufficient for a finding that there is an export subsidy under Article 9.1(c). The words "by virtue of " indicate that there must be a demonstrable link between the *governmental action* at issue and the *financing* of the payments, whereby the payments are, in some way, financed as a result of, or as a consequence of, the governmental action. In our view, the link between governmental action and the financing of payments will be more difficult to establish, as an evidentiary matter, when the payment is in the form of a payment-in-kind rather than in monetary form, and all the more so when the payment-in-kind is made, not by the government, but by an independent economic operator. In any event, it will not be sufficient simply to demonstrate that a payment occurs as a consequence of governmental action because the word "financed", in Article 9.1(c), must also be given meaning.

114. The word "financed" might be given a rather specific meaning such that it would be confined to the financing of "payments" in monetary form or to the funding of "payments" from government resources. However, we have already recalled that "payments", under Article 9.1(c), include payments-in-kind, so the

---

[86] Appellate Body Report, *Canada - Dairy*, *supra*, footnote 2, para. 120.
[87] *Ibid.*, para. 97.

word "financed" needs to cover both the financing of monetary payments and payments-in-kind. [88] In addition, Article 9.1(c) explicitly excludes a reading of the word "financed" whereby payments must be funded from government resources, as the provision states that payments can be financed by virtue of governmental action "whether or not a charge on the public account is involved". Thus, under Article 9.1(c), it is not necessary that the economic resources constituting the "payment" actually be paid by the government or even that they be paid from government resources. Accordingly, although the words "by virtue of " render governmental action essential, Article 9.1(c) contemplates that payments may be financed by virtue of governmental action even though significant aspects of the financing might not involve government.

115. It is extremely difficult, however, to define in the abstract the precise character of the required link between the governmental action and the financing of the payments, particularly where payments-in-kind are at issue. Governments are constantly engaged in regulation of different kinds in pursuit of a variety of objectives. For instance, we can envisage that governmental action might establish a regulatory framework merely enabling a third person freely to make and finance "payments". In this situation, the link between the governmental action and the financing of the payments is too tenuous for the "payments" to be regarded as "*financed* by virtue of governmental action" (emphasis added) within the meaning of Article 9.1(c). Rather, there must be a tighter nexus between the mechanism or process by which the payments are *financed*, even if by a third person, and governmental action. [89] In our opinion, the existence of such a demonstrable link must be identified on a case-by-case basis, taking account of the particular governmental action at issue and its effects on payments made by a third person.

116. Although the Panel addressed this issue in different ways, we consider that the Panel's reasoning, taken as a whole, was directed towards establishing the demonstrable link between governmental action and the financing of the payments. [90] We quoted earlier the Panel's statement, in paragraph 6.42 of its Re-

---

[88] *Supra*, para. 71.

[89] Where "payments" *do* involve a "charge on the public account", the link between the financing of the payments and governmental action is clearly less difficult to establish.

[90] We observe that the Panel stated: (i) that governmental action need "only *establish the conditions which ensure that* the payment ... takes place. The governmental action is, in that sense, a necessary condition for the transfer to take place" (emphasis in original, Panel Report, para. 6.38); (ii) "the Panel considers that for a payment to be 'financed by virtue of governmental action', it must be established that a payment would not be financed, i.e. resources would not be transferred from grantor to recipient, *but for* governmental action" (emphasis in original, Panel Report, para. 6.39); (iii) there must be "action which is '*indispensable*' to the financing of [the] payment" (emphasis in original, Panel Report, paras. 6.40 and 6.44); and (iv) "[t]he question which the Panel needs to address is the following: would milk processors for export have access to lower priced commercial export milk in Canada *but for* governmental action? Put another way, have the Canadian government

port, of the two elements which, if demonstrated, would, according to the Panel, establish that the payments are "financed by virtue of governmental action".[91] In determining that these two elements were demonstrated, the Panel concluded that governmental action "*obliges*" or "*drives*" producers to sell CEM.[92]

117. It is true that Canadian governmental action establishes a regulatory regime whereby some milk producers can make additional profits only if they choose to sell CEM.[93] However, even though Canadian governmental action prevents further domestic sales[94], we do not see how producers are obliged or driven to produce additional milk for export sale. As we said above, each producer is free to decide whether or not to produce additional milk for sale as CEM.[95] Furthermore, as we also said, the majority of Canadian milk producers choose not to sell CEM.[96] For these reasons, we disagree with the Panel's characterization of the measure as "obliging producers, at least *de facto*, to sell outside-quota milk for export".[97]

118. In view of our findings on "payments" above, it is not necessary for us to consider further the Panel's findings on the phrase "financed by virtue of governmental action".

V. ARTICLE 10.1 OF THE AGREEMENT ON AGRICULTURE

119. New Zealand and the United States claim, in the alternative, that, if the measure at issue were not an export subsidy under Article 9.1(c) of the *Agreement on Agriculture*, it would be an export subsidy under Article 10.1 of that Agreement.

120. Article 10.1 of the *Agreement on Agriculture* reads:

> *Export subsidies not listed in paragraph 1 of Article 9* shall not be applied in a manner which results in, or which threatens to lead to,

---

and its agencies taken action which is *indispensable* for the lower priced milk to be available to processors for export?" (emphasis in original, Panel Report, para. 6.41)

91 *See*, *supra*, para. 107.

92 *See*, Panel Report, paras. 6.42, 6.45, 6.48 and 6.77.

93 We note that milk sold as CEM could also be sold as animal feed under Milk Class 4(m). The price of milk sold under Class 4(m) is approximately C$10 per hectolitre and is, therefore, commercially unattractive when compared with the prices of CEM. *See*, Panel Report, paras. 4.25 and 6.52.

94 According to Canada, the sole purpose of obliging processors to export dairy products manufactured with commercial export milk and penalizing diversion of this milk into the domestic market, is to protect quota-holding producers' entitlement to the higher regulated price. (Canada's statement at the oral hearing)

95 *Supra*, para. 79.

96 Canada asserted before the Panel that about 30 percent of Canadian producers had participated in CEM transactions since deregulation measures were introduced in August 2000. (Panel Report, para. 4.24)

97 *Ibid.*, para. 6.77.

> circumvention of export subsidy commitments; nor shall non-commercial transactions be used to circumvent such commitments. (emphasis added)

121. It is clear from the opening clause of Article 10.1 that this provision is residual in character to Article 9.1 of the *Agreement on Agriculture*. If a measure is an export subsidy listed in Article 9.1, it cannot simultaneously be an export subsidy under Article 10.1. In light of the facts available to us, we have found that we are unable to determine whether the measure at issue is an export subsidy listed in Article 9.1(c). However, it remains possible that the measure *is* such an export subsidy. Clearly, in that event, the opening clause of Article 10.1 means that the measure could not also be an export subsidy under Article 10.1. In these circumstances, where we are unable to determine the legal character of the measure under Article 9.1 of the *Agreement on Agriculture*, we are similarly unable to rule upon the legal character of the measure under Article 10.1 of that Agreement.

VI. ARTICLE 3.1 OF THE *SCM AGREEMENT*

122. In these proceedings, the United States also claims that the measure is a prohibited export subsidy under Article 3.1 of the *SCM Agreement*. The United States reiterates the arguments it made to the Panel concerning this claim in its appeal.[98]

123. The relationship between the *Agreement on Agriculture* and the *SCM Agreement* is defined, in part, by Article 3.1 of the *SCM Agreement*, which states that certain subsidies are "prohibited" "[e]xcept as provided in the Agreement on Agriculture". This clause, therefore, indicates that the WTO-consistency of an export subsidy for agricultural products has to be examined, in the first place, under the *Agreement on Agriculture*.

124. This is borne out by Article 13(c)(ii) of the *Agreement on Agriculture*, which provides that "export subsidies that conform fully to the [export subsidy] provisions of Part V" of the *Agreement on Agriculture*, "as reflected in each Member's Schedule, shall be ... exempt from actions based on Article XVI of GATT 1994 or Articles 3, 5 and 6 of the Subsidies Agreement."

125. In this appeal, we are unable to determine whether the measure at issue "conforms fully" to Articles 9.1(c) or 10.1 of Part V of the *Agreement on Agriculture*. In these circumstances, we decline to examine the claim made by the United States that the measure is inconsistent with Article 3.1 of the *SCM Agreement*.

98 United States' appellee's submission, para. 82.

VII. FINDINGS AND CONCLUSIONS

126. For the reasons set forth in this Report, the Appellate Body reverses the Panel's findings, in paragraph 6.79 of the Panel Report, that the supply of CEM by domestic milk producers to domestic dairy processors involves "payments" on the export of milk "that are financed by virtue of governmental action" under Article 9.1(c) of the *Agreement on Agriculture*, and, in consequence, reverses the Panel's finding in paragraph 7.1 of the Panel Report.

127. However, in the light of the factual findings made by the Panel and the uncontested facts in the Panel record, the Appellate Body is unable to complete the analysis of the claims made by New Zealand and the United States under Articles 9.1(c) or 10.1 of the *Agreement on Agriculture*, or the claim made by the United States under Article 3.1 of the *SCM Agreement*.

CANADA - MEASURES AFFECTING THE IMPORTATION OF MILK AND THE EXPORTATION OF DAIRY PRODUCTS

RECOURSE TO ARTICLE 21.5 OF THE DSU BY NEW ZEALAND AND THE UNITED STATES

Report of the Panel
WT/DS103/RW, WT/DS113/RW

Adopted by the Dispute Settlement Body on 18 December 2001 as reversed by the Appellate Body Report

TABLE OF CONTENTS

I. INTRODUCTION

1.1 On 23 December 1999, pursuant to Article 21.3(b) of the DSU, Canada, New Zealand and the United States agreed (WT/DS103/10; WT/DS113/10) on the reasonable period of time for implementation of the recommendations and rulings of the Dispute Settlement Body (the DSB) in the matter of "Canada - Measures Affecting the Importation of Milk and the Exportation of Dairy Products". According to the terms of the 23 December 1999 agreement, as amended on 11 December 2000 (WT/DS103/13; WT/DS113/13), the staged implementation process, "including any new measures for the export of " dairy products, was to be completed by 31 January 2001.

1.2 On 19 January 2001, Canada circulated to all Members of the DSB (WT/DS103/12/Add.6, WT/DS/113/12/Add.6) its "final status report", pursuant to Article 21.6 of the Understanding on Rules and Procedures Governing the Settlement of Disputes (the DSU). In that report Canada affirmed "that it will be in full compliance with the rulings and recommendations of the DSB by the conclusion of the implementation period" on 31 January 2001.

1.3 New Zealand and the United States consider that Canada has failed to comply with the above mentioned recommendations and rulings of the DSB by 31 January 2001.

1.4 Without prejudice to their rights under the WTO, and in accordance with paragraph 1 of the 21 December 2000 "Agreed Procedures between Canada, New Zealand and the United States under Articles 21 and 22 of the Dispute Settlement Understanding in the follow-up to the dispute in "Canada - Measures Affecting the Importation of Milk and the Exportation of Dairy Products" (WT/DS113/14 and 103/14, respectively) (Agreed Procedures), New Zealand and the United States requested consultations with Canada on 2 February 2001. Consultations were held on 9 February 2001, but failed to resolve the dispute.

1.5 Pursuant to Article 21.5, and as envisaged in the Agreed Procedures, New Zealand and the United States on 16 February 2001 accordingly requested the establishment of a panel in this matter and requested that the DSB refer the matter to the original panel, if possible (WT/DS113/16 and 103/16, respectively.)

1.6 On 16 February 2001, New Zealand and the United States also requested authorization from the DSB, pursuant to Article 22.2 of the DSU, to suspend the application to Canada of tariff concessions and other obligations under the General Agreement on Tariffs and Trade 1994 (GATT 1994) covering trade in the amount of US$35 million for each complainant. Pursuant to Article 22.6 of the Understanding on Rules and Procedures Governing the Settlement of Disputes (DSU), Canada objected on 28 February 2001 to the level of suspension of tariff concessions and other obligations under the GATT 1994 proposed by New Zealand and the United (document WT/DS113/17 and 103/17, respectively). In accordance with the provisions of Article 22.6 of the DSU and as envisaged in the "Agreed Procedures, Canada therefore requested that this matter be referred to arbitration.

1.7 In accordance with the Agreed Procedures, the complainants did not object to the referral of the level of suspension of concessions or other obligations to arbitration pursuant to Article 22.6 of the DSU. In this case, New Zealand and the United States agreed to request the arbitrator to suspend its work until either (a) the adoption of the Article 21.5 compliance panel report; or (b) if there were an appeal, the adoption of the Appellate Body report.

1.8 At its meeting on 1 March 2001, the Dispute Settlement Body (DSB) decided, in accordance with Article 21.5 of the DSU, to refer to the original Panel, if possible, the matter raised by New Zealand and the United States in documents WT/DS113/16 and WT/DS103/16, respectively.

(i) Terms of Reference

1.9 At that DSB meeting, it was also agreed that the Panel should have standard terms of reference as follows:

> "To examine, in the light of the relevant provisions of the covered agreements cited by the United States in document WT/DS103/16 and by New Zealand in document WT/DS113/16, the matter referred to the DSB by the United States and New Zealand in those documents and to make such findings as will assist the DSB in making the recommendations or in giving the rulings provided for in those agreements."

(ii) Composition of Panel

1.10 The Panel was composed on 12 April 2001 as follows:[1]

Chairperson: Mr. Ernst-Ulrich Petersmann

Members: Mr. Guillermo Aguilar Alvarez

Mr. Peter Palečka

1.11 Australia, the European Communities and Mexico reserved their third party rights.

1.12 The Panel held a meeting with the parties on 29-30 May 2001 and with the third parties on 30 May 2001. The report of the Panel was submitted to the parties on 5 July 2001.

II. PRELIMINARY RULINGS

1. Canada's Request Concerning Business Confidential Information

2.1 On 15 May 2001, **Canada,** pursuant to paragraph 12 of the Panel's working procedures, requested a preliminary ruling from the Panel regarding the adoption of procedures governing business confidential information (BCI) that may be submitted to Canada in the course of these proceedings. Canada proposed that such procedures form part of the Panel's working procedures pursuant to paragraph 14 thereof and Article 12.1 of the DSU.

2.2 Canada indicated that Canadian producers and processors proposing to submit BCI to the Canadian litigation group in the context of these proceedings need BCI procedures to be in place before disclosure is made.[2] Currently, Canada

---

[1] The Chairperson of the original Panel, Mr. Tommy Koh, was not available for these proceedings. The parties agreed to his replacement by Mr. Peter Palečka as a member of the Panel.

[2] Canada indicated that within the Canadian delegation and wider consultative group itself, procedures similar to those requested here would govern the handling of BCI.

did not have access to certain BCI and would not be in a position to obtain, assess and provide such BCI to the Panel or to the other Parties unless adequate procedures are in place to govern its handling and the access thereto in the course of these proceedings. That is why Canada requested BCI procedures and proposed procedures that are built upon those adopted in the *Brazil and Canada Aircraft* cases, the *Australia - Automotive Leather* case and the *United States - Wheat Gluten* case.[3] The objective is to provide the Panel and all parties involved in the dispute, including third parties, with all relevant factual information necessary to arrive at correct factual and legal conclusions. Canada contended that it would not be able to do so without these procedures in place.

2.3 Canada submitted that the confidentiality provisions already applicable to this dispute are paragraph 3 of the model working procedures set out in Annex 3 of the DSU[4] and Article 18.2 of the DSU. In many cases these provisions may provide sufficient protection for information which a Member may want to form part of the factual record of the proceedings. In some cases, these provisions may suffice even to protect BCI from being disclosed beyond the parties to a dispute.

2.4 Article 12.1 of the DSU, Canada submitted, explicitly allows the Panel to adapt its working procedures to the circumstances of the case before it. Under the procedures proposed in Appendix I, a Member party to this dispute would not be denied access to BCI. While specific persons within the Member's delegation or larger consultative group would be excluded from access to specific numerical and other BCI, they would be provided with a summary form of the information which would enable them to draw the appropriate analytical conclusions. In light of the considerations set out above, Canada respectfully requested that the Panel adopt the BCI procedure, as proposed by Canada, as part of its working procedures.

2.5 **New Zealand** did not see a need for additional working procedures for BCI in relation to the current proceedings. Article 18 and Appendix 3 of the DSU already provide sufficient coverage for the concerns that Canada has expressed and, in any event, New Zealand did not believe that Canada has adequately demonstrated the need for stepping beyond the parameters of these provisions.

2.6 As Canada recognised, the DSU already contains provisions which deal with the issue of ensuring confidentiality in dispute settlement proceedings. In New Zealand's view, Article 18 and Appendix 3 of the DSU adequately ensure that, when a party to a dispute submits information which it designates as "confi-

---

[3] *Brazil - Aircraft,* panel report, DSR 1999:III, 1221; *Canada - Aircraft,* panel report, DSR 1999:IV, 1443; *Australia - Automotive Leather* panel report, DSR 1999:III, 951; *United States - Wheat Gluten,* panel report, DSR 2001:III, 779.
Please note that the full title of all cases referred to here and in the rest of the report can be found in the Annex on page 6952.

[4] By virtue of Article 12.1 of the DSU and para. 1 of Annex 3 of the DSU, para. 3 of Annex 3 of the DSU is also para. 3 of the Working Procedures of this Panel.

dential", all other parties to the dispute are under an obligation to treat such information as confidential. This is confirmed *inter alia* by the Appellate Body in *Canada - Aircraft* where the Appellate Body noted, *inter alia*, that Article 18.2 obliges Members to "maintain the confidentiality of any submissions or information submitted, or received" in a dispute settlement proceeding.[5] The Appellate Body went on to observe that such a provision also "oblige[s] Members to ensure that such confidentiality is fully respected by any person that a Member selects to act as its representative, counsel or consultant."[6]

2.7 New Zealand also observed that there is no precedent for BCI procedures being imposed on a party to a dispute under the DSU. Additionally, and most importantly, there is no precedent for the working procedures of a panel being substantively modified over the objections of one of the principal parties to a dispute.

2.8 New Zealand noted that on the only occasion when the Appellate Body has been asked to consider the issue of BCI procedures (in Canada-Aircraft), it declined the request of the parties, who had agreed such procedures at the panel stage, to apply those procedures *mutatis mutandis* to proceedings before the Appellate Body. Moreover, it refused to agree to impose those procedures on third participants in the appeal.[7] New Zealand also submitted that in the circumstance where there is no precedent for BCI procedures to be imposed on a party to a dispute, the burden on Canada to justify its proposal is a heavy one which Canada has by no means met.

2.9 New Zealand considered that if Canada's concerns are being driven by domestic considerations whereby some parts of its industry want to protect information from other parts of the Canadian industry, then this is an internal matter for Canada and is of no concern to New Zealand or the Panel. In New Zealand's view, pertinent information in relation to the so-called "commercial export milk" is already before the Panel. As a result, New Zealand was unclear as to what additional information Canada believes is "necessary" for the Panel to resolve this dispute.

2.10 In light of the above, New Zealand requested that the Panel decline Canada's request for additional working procedures in relation to BCI. Such additional procedures would be unnecessary and would serve no useful purpose in the upcoming hearing.

2.11 The **United States** shared some of New Zealand's concerns and was not advocating the adoption of such procedures. At the same time, the United States would not object to the inclusion of BCI procedures in this case as long as they adequately address the concerns raised by the United States. The United States

5 *Canada - Aircraft*, Appellate Body report, DSR 1999:III, 1377, para. 145.
6 *Ibid.*
7 *Ibid.*, para. 147.

opposed the adoption of Canada's proposal without modifications based on its objection to the following provisions: 1) the definition of "business confidential information", 2) the inclusion of outside legal counsel or other advisor or consultant to a party in the definition of "representative", 3) the exclusion of government employees involved in the dairy field from the definition of "representative", and 4) the inclusion of provisions for the submission of BCI to third parties. The United States was concerned that if the Panel were to adopt the procedures proposed by Canada without modification, the systemic ramifications could be severe. For example, other panels could use the procedures as a model in other disputes. These procedures have a number of flaws and may be particularly inappropriate, or even inconsistent with WTO obligations, if used in another context such as a dispute brought under the Agreement on Safeguards or the Anti-dumping Agreement.

2.12 With regard to outside legal counsel, although the United States understood that a party may include outside legal counsel in its delegation, the United States did not believe that the sanctions in place under the DSU and WTO rules are sufficient to ensure that BCI is adequately protected if access is permitted for outside legal counsel. Moreover, there is too great a potential for a conflict of interest. The situation in *Thailand - Steel* demonstrates the danger of submitting BCI to outside legal counsel who may also represent a domestic stakeholder. In that case, different representatives of the same law firm represented the government and the private sector association. Despite the fact that the law firm, as a representative or counsel to the government, was bound by the same confidentiality obligations under the DSU as Poland, the private sector association somehow came into possession of Thailand's brief. For *inter alia* these reasons, the United States proposed striking "legal counsel or other advisor or consultant of a party" from the definition of "representative " and striking entirely the provision for submission of BCI to third parties.

2.13 Furthermore, the United States considered that information other than business proprietary information does not need protection as business confidential information. Such a broad definition imposes an even greater burden on the Panel and parties and is not consistent with the restrained use of the BCI designation. Also, this definition is not consistent with the rationale provided by Canada in support of its need for BCI procedures.

2.14 As concerns the definition of "representatives", the United States considered that the proposal for exclusion of government employees involved in the dairy field is overly broad. The United States would propose striking "government" from the exclusion in the definition of "representative", or at least making it clear that the exclusion only applies to government entities that are actual market participants. The United States accordingly requested that if the Panel decides that the adoption of BCI procedures is warranted in this case, that it adopt the Canadian procedures as BCI procedures with the modifications proposed by the United States. And in any event the procedures should specify that they are applicable only to BCI submitted by Canada.

(i) The Panel's Decision

2.15 After having reviewed Canada's request and the comments by New Zealand and the United States, the **Panel** decided to decline, at the time of its preliminary ruling[8], Canada's request to adopt the procedures governing BCI proposed by Canada. The Panel reached this conclusion on the basis of the following considerations.

2.16 The Panel considers that Article 18.2 of the DSU[9] and paragraph 3 of the Panel's Working Procedures[10] already provide substantial protection to parties regarding treatment of BCI.[11]

2.17 The Panel notes that New Zealand does not see the need for BCI procedures[12], and that the United States does not intend to submit BCI.[13] The Panel considers that it has the authority to amend the Working Procedures, after consulting the parties, including the possibility to adopt procedures governing BCI, pursuant to Article 12.1 of the DSU and paragraph 14 of the Working Procedures. It also considers that it would not be prevented from doing so because the parties to the dispute are in disagreement regarding such a proposed amendment, provided that requirements of due process are respected. Article 12.1 of the DSU only provides that the Panel should consult with the parties.

2.18 The Panel considers that it needs to examine Canada's request in the light of a panel's obligation under Article 11 of the DSU to make an objective assessment of the facts of the case. If certain information is required to allow the Panel to make an objective assessment of the facts and such information cannot rea-

---

8 23 May 2001.

9 Written submissions to the panel of the Appellate Body shall be treated as confidential, but shall be available to the parties to the dispute. Nothing in this Understanding shall preclude a party to a dispute from disclosing statements of its own positions to the public. Members shall treat as confidential information submitted by another Member to the panel or the Appellate Body which that Member has designated as confidential. [...]

10 The deliberations of the Panel and the documents submitted to it shall be kept confidential. Nothing in the DSU shall preclude a party to a dispute from disclosing statements of its own positions to the public. Members shall treat as confidential information submitted by another Member to the Panel which that Member has designated as confidential. [...]

11 See the Appellate Body report on *Canada -Aircraft*, para. 145, where the Appellate Body notes, with approval, the following statement made by the Panel in *Indonesia -Automobiles*, para. 14.1.:

> "We would like to emphasize that *all members of parties' delegations - whether or not they are government employees - are present as representatives of their governments, and as such are subject to the provisions of the DSU and of the standard working procedures, including Articles 18.1 and 18.2 of the DSU and paras. 2 and 3 of those procedures.* In particular, parties are required to treat as confidential all submissions to the Panel and all information so designated by other Members; and, in addition, the Panel meets in closed session. *Accordingly, we expect that all delegations will fully respect those obligations and will treat these proceedings with the utmost circumspection and discretion.* [...]." (emphasis added by the Appellate Body).

12 Paragraph 2 of the response by New Zealand, 21 May 2001.

13 Paragraph 2 of the response by the United States, 21 May 2001.

sonably be expected to be disclosed to the Panel and the parties in the absence of additional procedures governing BCI, the Panel would need to accommodate a party's concerns regarding treatment of BCI. A panel's decision not to do so in such circumstances might very well affect that party's due process rights, as that party might find itself unable to disclose information necessary to its defence, and hence, make it impossible for the Panel to make an objective assessment of the facts.

2.19 At the same time, the Panel considers that a party requesting the adoption of BCI procedures should clearly explain to the Panel what kind of information it may be unable to obtain and disclose but for the adoption of BCI procedures, in order to enable the Panel to assess the need for such BCI procedures. In this respect, the Panel notes that Canada does not provide any indication as regards the nature of the information which it may consider necessary or desirable to disclose during the proceedings, and which it considers it could not disclose in the absence of BCI procedures. Rather, Canada limits itself to stating that:

> "One of the provisions that may form part of a commercial transaction involving milk for use in products destined for export [...], is the confidentiality of terms of the contract, or indeed, of the entire contract itself. Confidentiality covenants along these lines are commonplace in commercial transactions. [...][14]
>
> [...] Canadian producers and processors proposing to submit BCI to the Canadian litigation group in the context of these proceedings need BCI procedures to be in place before disclosure is made.[15] Currently, Canada does not have access to certain BCI and will not be in a position to obtain, assess and provide such BCI to the Panel or to the other Parties unless adequate procedures are in place to govern its handling and the access thereto in the course of these proceedings."[16]

2.20 While the Panel understands that confidentiality clauses may prevent private entities from disclosing certain or all information contained in a contract[17], it notes that certain data in connection with such contracts, albeit not on an individual basis, has already been made available by the parties to the dispute, including Canada.[18] The Panel does not, and, of course, cannot, exclude that there may be

---

14 Paragraph 3 of Canada's request for a preliminary ruling, 15 May 2001.

15 [Footnote omitted]

16 Paragraph 4 of Canada's request for a preliminary ruling, 15 May 2001.

17 The Panel notes that none of the "Examples of Commercial Export Milk Contracts" provided by Canada in Exhibit 15 to its First Submission contain any obligations as regards confidentiality of their terms and conditions.(Exhibit 15 erroneously referred to as Exhibit 14 in the original ruling) The Panel is aware, however, that those examples may not necessarily constitute a representative sample in this respect.

18 Including average prices, traded volumes and supply terms. See paras. 42 and 51 of Canada's first submission, 15 May 2001.

other factual information which Canada may wish to provide and which would assist the Panel in making an objective assessment of the facts. The Panel considers, however, that for BCI procedures to be put in place, with the associated burden imposed on the Panel and the parties, Canada would, at least, need to describe to the Panel the nature of that information, and why the existing confidentiality requirements are insufficient. Only then would the Panel be able to assess the need to adopt BCI procedures.

2.21 In conclusion, Canada's request has not enabled the Panel to assess the need for the proposed procedures governing BCI. The Panel is therefore not persuaded at this time that it should adopt BCI procedures, as proposed by Canada. The Panel, however, does not exclude that it may need to revisit the issue at a later time, if and when Canada provides additional justification and clearly establishes the need for additional arrangements regarding BCI.[19] The Panel is committed to protecting the due process rights of all parties to the dispute and will take any appropriate action for that purpose in the course of the proceedings, after consulting the parties.

2. *The European Communities Request Concerning Access to the Rebuttals for Third Parties*

2.22 On 18 May 2001 the **European Communities** (EC) made the following request concerning third party access to the rebuttals. The EC noted that paragraph 8 of the Working Procedures of the Panel provides in relevant part that "Third parties shall receive copies of the parties' first written submissions". In the view of the EC, this regulation conflicts with Article 10. 3 of the DSU which states that "Third parties shall receive the submissions of the parties to the dispute to the *first meeting* of the Panel". (emphasis added)

2.23 The EC argued that it had continuously objected to similar Working Schedules of previous compliance panels. The DSU Article 21.5 panel in *Australia - Automotive Leather* justified its approach solely with the following argument: "If it had decided to hold two meetings, with the parties, as in the normal situation envisioned in Appendix 3 of the DSU, third parties would have received only the written submissions made prior to the first meeting, but not the rebuttals or other submissions made subsequently."[20] The EC considered that this reasoning is not tenable. The argument is based on the assumption that two substantive meetings are the "normal situation" in DSU Article 21.5 proceedings. The EC recalled that, due to the expedited nature of compliance panels, *all* DSU Article

[19] The Panel is fully aware that Canada's request for adoption of BCI procedures needs to be assessed in the light of Article 10.3 of the *Agreement on Agriculture*.

[20] *Australia - Automotive Leather,* recourse to Article 21.5, panel report, *supra*, footnote 3, para. 3.9.

21.5 panels so far have only held *one* substantive meeting.[21] This is, thus, the normal situation.

2.24 The practice of giving third parties only the first submissions, the EC continued, deprives them of their participatory rights under the DSU. Article 10.1 of the DSU emphasises that the "interests of the parties to a dispute and those of other Members under a covered agreement at issue in the dispute shall be fully taken into account during the panel process". The EC believed that its systemic interest in the correct interpretation of the *Agreement on Agriculture* can only be protected if it can contribute meaningfully to the Panel proceedings by giving its views on all arguments exchanged by the parties before the first and only substantive meeting of the Panel, as foreseen by Article 10.3 of the DSU.

2.25 The EC submitted that Article 12.1 of the DSU grants each panel the authority to adapt the Working Procedures "after consulting the parties to the dispute". However, Article 12.1 of the DSU does not grant any panel the authority to "*limit* the right of third parties under Article 10.3 to receive the submissions of the parties to the dispute to the first meeting to copies of the first submissions of the parties".[22] The Appellate Body, in *United States - 1916 Act* has only acknowledged the discretionary authority of panels to grant *extended* third party rights.[23]

2.26 The EC noted that even if previous DSU Article 21.5 panels have similarly excluded the third parties from the second set of submissions, such a practice, which is, in the opinion of the EC, in conflict with the express provisions and the objectives of the DSU, cannot be considered as being justified because it has also been followed in some other procedures. On the basis of the foregoing considerations, the EC was of the view that this Panel should ensure that the third parties receive the second set of submissions to be exchanged before its substantive meeting.

2.27 **Canada** noted that its general policy is to make available, upon request, a public version of the submissions it has filed. Accordingly, the EC can receive Canada's rebuttal submission, as can the other third parties, as of 25 May 2001, if they so request. Canada's response in this case is without prejudice to Canada's position on the broader question of whether third parties have a right under the DSU to receive the rebuttal submissions of disputing parties before the hearing, in the context of dispute settlement proceedings under Article 21.5 of the DSU.

2.28 **New Zealand** did not oppose the EC request but noted that any decision by the Panel to accede to the EC request should be seen as being confined to this

---

21 *Australia - Automotive Leather*; *Australia - Salmon*; *United States - DRAMS*; *Canada - Aircraft*; *Brazil - Aircraft*; *EC - Bananas (Ecuador)*; *United States - FSC*; *United States - Shrimps*; *Mexico - High Fructose Corn Syrup*; *Brazil - Aircraft - Second Recourse to Article 21.5 of the DSU.*

22 This was expressly done in the Article 21.5 panel report, *Australia - Salmon"*, para. 7.5.

23 *United States - 1916 Act,* Appellate Body report, DSR 2000:X, 4793, paras. 139-150.

dispute and without prejudice to the rights and obligations contained under the DSU.

2.29 The **United States** noted that the EC has made similar arguments in other Article 21.5 proceedings in which a panel has held only a single meeting with the parties and third parties, and in each such proceeding, the panel has rejected the EC argument. The first in this line of cases is *Australia - Automotive Leather*, in which the panel rejected the EC request.[24] The panel in *Australia- Salmon - f*aced a similar argument by the EC and also found that third parties are not entitled to rebuttal submissions in Article 21.5 panel proceedings where there is only one substantive meeting of the panel.[25] More recently, the panel in *United States - DRAMS* also rejected the EC's position.[26] In the view of the United States, the reasoning of these prior panels is sound, and should be followed by this Panel.

2.30 The United States also urged the Panel to reject the EC's assertion that Article 12.1 of the DSU requires that the EC be consulted regarding the provisions of the Working Procedures in this case involving third party rights. Article 12.1 states clearly that panels are to consult the parties to the dispute, not the third parties. The United States noted that, with the exception of business confidential information, it routinely makes its submissions to WTO panels available to the public by placing its submissions on the Internet Web page of the Office of the US Trade Representative. Thus, as a practical matter, third parties (along with the rest of the world) have access to the US rebuttal submission. The United States understood that both Canada and New Zealand may also make their rebuttal submissions public. In any event, the working procedures make it clear that the other parties to the dispute have the option to provide copies of their rebuttal submissions to the EC. In conclusion, the United States asked that the Panel follow the consistent positions of past panels on this issue and reject the EC's request.

2.31 **Mexico** submitted that although it recognized the right of panels to deviate from the working procedures set forth in Appendix 3 to the DSU, a panel may not act in a manner contrary to the actual provisions of the DSU, in particular when this affects the rights of third parties. According to Mexico, Article 10.3 of the DSU clearly stipulates that third parties shall receive the submissions of the parties to the dispute to the first meeting of the panel. Thus, if in the case of an accelerated procedure the panel decides to conduct its first meeting after receiving the rebuttal submissions, this must not affect the rights of third parties to have their interests fully taken into account, including the right to receive all of the

[24] *Australia - Automotive Leather*, Recourse to Article 21.5, panel report, *supra*, footnote 3, para. 3.9. This decision was followed in *Australia - Salmon*, Recourse to Article 21.5, panel report, DSR 1998:VIII, 3407, paras. 7.5-7.6.

[25] *Australia- Salmon*, Recourse to Article 21.5, panel report, *supra*, footnote 24, paras. 7.5 and 7.6.

[26] *United States - DRAMS* - Recourse to Article 21.5, Decision of the panel concerning the EC request for access to the parties' rebuttal submissions, 27 June 2000 (footnotes omitted).

submissions of the parties to the first meeting of the panel. Pragmatic arguments such as the fact that the parties to the dispute have a policy of making their rebuttals public are, in Mexico's view, not acceptable. Mexico put forward three general observations in this respect: (i) the right of third parties includes the right to receive submissions from the parties without having to seek them; (ii) certain Members only publish the actual texts of their submissions, and not the annexes; (iii) the third parties are not necessarily always English speaking. In view of the above, Mexico supported and associated itself with the EC's request that the rebuttal submissions of the parties be provided.

(i) The Panel's Decision

2.32 After having reviewed the EC's request and the comments by the parties, the **Panel** decided[27] to accept the EC's request, and accordingly amend its Working Procedures. The Panel reached this conclusion on the basis of the considerations presented hereafter. Appendix 3 to the DSU requires this Panel to "follow the relevant provisions of this Understanding" (paragraph 1) subject to the power of the Panel to adopt "any additional procedures specific to the panel" (paragraph 11). In this case, all parties and third parties agree that Article 10.3 of the DSU remains applicable and requires that "(t)hird parties shall receive the submissions of the parties to the dispute to the first meeting of the Panel". The disagreement relates as to whether the third party rights under Article 10.3 of the DSU have been inappropriately limited by the Panel when it adopted, in accordance with the practice of previous Article 21.5 panels and in agreement with the parties to this dispute, the following rule in paragraph 8 of this Panel's Working Procedures: "Third parties shall receive copies of the parties' *first* written submissions".[28] (emphasis added)

2.33 Referring to the EC's claims in paragraphs 2.22 - 2.26 above, as supported by Mexico in paragraph 2.31, the Panel noted that the text of Article 10.3 is clear and requires this Panel to make available to third parties "*the* submissions of the parties to the dispute to the first meeting of the panel" (emphasis added). In the particular context of Article 21.5, panels which, as in this case, request both parties to submit also their rebuttal submissions prior to the first meeting with the parties, the literal reading of Article 10.3 clearly requires to make available to third parties also these rebuttal submissions. Even in the different context of normal Article 12 panel proceedings with two meetings with the parties, nothing in the text of Article 10.3 and in the different context of normal Article 12 panel proceedings justifies ignoring the clear textual requirement of Article 10.3 to enable third parties to participate in the first panel meeting with access to *all* "the

---

[27] Decision dated 25 May 2001.

[28] The Panel notes that its Working Procedures were adopted consistently with past practice of Article 21.5 Panels.

submissions" of the parties made up to this point of the panel process. In the particular context of this Article 21.5 Panel proceeding, the term "submissions" in Article 10.3 of the DSU must therefore include the parties' rebuttal submissions.

2.34 In the view of the Panel, only this strict compliance with the unequivocal text of Article 10.3 secures that the interests and rights of third parties are "fully taken into account during the panel process" (Article 10.1) in a manner enabling the Panel to "make an objective assessment of the matter before it" (Article 11.1). In the Panel's view, the object and purpose of Article 10.3 of the DSU is to allow third parties to participate in an informed and, hence, meaningful, manner in a session of the meeting with the parties specifically set aside for that purpose. Third parties can only do so if they have received all the information exchanged between the parties before that session. Otherwise, third parties might find themselves in a situation where their oral statements at the meeting become partially or totally irrelevant or moot in the light of second submissions by the parties to which third parties did not have access. Without access to all the submissions by the parties to the dispute to the first meeting of the panel, uninformed third party submissions could unduly delay panel proceedings and, as rightly emphasised by the EC and supported by Mexico, could prevent the Panel from receiving "the benefit of a useful contribution by third parties which could help the Panel to make the objective assessment that it is required to make under Article 11 of the DSU".[29]

2.35 The Panel therefore concludes that nothing in the DSU authorises this Panel to restrict the right of third parties to only receive the "first" submissions made on 4 May 2001, and to withhold from the third parties the rebuttal submissions due for 25 May 2001 (i.e. before the first meeting of the panel on 29-31 May 2001). The Panel decides that, pursuant to Article 10.3 of the DSU, third parties have the right to receive all written submissions "to the first meeting," including rebuttal submissions made before that first meeting. Accordingly, the Panel replaces the current sentence in paragraph 8 of its Working Procedures ("Third parties shall receive copies of the parties' first written submissions") by the text in Article 10.3 of the DSU: "Third parties shall receive the submissions of the parties to the dispute to the first meeting of the panel." The Panel notes that, pursuant to Article 12.1 of the DSU and paragraph 14 of its Working Procedures, the Panel can amend the Working Procedures after consulting the parties. The Panel considers that, having invited and received comments by the parties regarding the European Communities' request, it has duly consulted with them.

[29] EC request for ruling, 18 May 2001.

III. FACTUAL ASPECTS

(i) Previous System

3.1 Under the previous Canadian supply management system, introduced on 1 August 1995, a processor had to obtain a permit from the Canadian Dairy Commission (CDC), allowing it to buy milk under Special Milk Class 5(d) and (e). Class 5(e), referred to as "surplus removal", was made up of both in-quota and over-quota milk. Class 5(d) referred to specific negotiated exports including cheese under quota destined for the markets of the United States and the United Kingdom, as well as evaporated milk, whole milk powder and niche markets. The permit also specified the dairy products to be exported. The CDC only issued Special Milk Class 5(e) permits when all demand for milk in the domestic market was met. Once the processor had obtained the CDC permit, it approached the local marketing board, which made milk available to the processor at the regulated price and with a guaranteed margin. Prices for Classes 5(d) and (e) were negotiated and established on a case-by-case basis with the processors/exporters. The CDC conducted these negotiations in accordance with the criteria agreed upon in the Canadian Milk Supply Management Committee (CMSMC).

(ii) Previous Panel and Appellate Body Judgements

3.2 In its decision of 17 May 1999, the original panel in *Canada - Dairy* concluded that Canada "through Special Milk Classes 5(d) and (e) ... has acted inconsistently with its obligations under Article 3.3 and Article 8 of the *Agreement on Agriculture* by providing export subsidies as listed in Article 9.1(a) and Article 9.1(c) of that Agreement in excess of the quantity commitment levels specified in Canada's Schedule; ... "[30] In its report of 23 September 1999 the Appellate Body upheld the findings in the original panel report with respect to Articles 3.3, 8 and 9.1(c) of the *Agreement on Agriculture.*[31] In respect of Article 9.1(a), the Appellate Body did not uphold the reasoning of the Panel, but it reserved its judgement on the question of whether Classes 5(d) and 5(e) conferred export subsidies within the meaning of Article 9.1(a).[32] The Appellate Body recommended that Canada bring those measures found to be inconsistent with its obligations under the *Agreement on Agriculture* into conformity with that agreement.[33] Canada's implementation of the Appellate Body ruling has resulted in the elimination of Special Milk Class 5(e) and the restriction of Class 5(d) to the export of dairy products within Canada's export subsidy commitment levels.[34]

---

30 Paragraph 8.1(a).

31 *Canada - Dairy*, Appellate Body report, DSR 1999:V, 2057, para. 144(b).

32 *Ibid.*, para. 144(a).

33 *Ibid.*, para. 145.

34 Canada Gazette Part II, Vol.135, No.1: Regulatory Impact Analysis Statement for the Regulations under the Canadian Dairy Commission Act amending the Dairy Products Marketing Regula-

(iii) Canada's Implementation Measures

3.3 In Canada, regulatory jurisdiction over the marketing and trade of dairy products is divided between the federal and provincial governments. Implementation of the recommendations and rulings of the DSB in *Canada-Dairy* therefore required action by the federal and provincial governments, and their agencies.

3.4 Milk destined for the commercial export market is referred to under federal regulations as commercial export milk or cream.[35]

3.5 Under the domestic supply management scheme, milk can be marketed either on the domestic market subject to a quota, or as Class 4(m) (animal feed) for any amount above the quota. Milk produced in Canada can also be pre-committed for sale outside the quota system and be sold to processors for export as commercial export milk (CEM). Regulations relating to health considerations and auditing continue to apply to export milk.

3.6 Pursuant to the *Canadian Dairy Commission Act*[36], the *Dairy Products Marketing Regulations*[37] have been modified to exclude commercial export milk and cream from federal licensing,[38] quota[39] and levy requirements[40] and from the requirement to market this milk through the provincial marketing boards. Furthermore, the milk delegation orders issued to provinces pursuant to *the Agricultural Products Marketing Act*, R.S.C. 1985, c. A-6, have been amended to remove provincial authority regarding commercial export milk or cream.[41] As a consequence of the changes made under *the Dairy Products Marketing Regulations* and the *Ministerial Direction*,[42] the regional pooling agreements (the P-9, P-6 and P-4 Agreements) do not apply to commercial export milk. The national pooling agreement, the P-9, provides for a domestic surplus management Class, Class 4(m).

---

tions. The amendment to section 7.1 "provides that export subsidies for Canadian dairy products will be provided only by a program established under para. 9(1)(i) of the CDC Act (Special Milk Class 5(d))." (Exhibit NZ-6)

[35] Canada Gazette Part II, Vol.135, No.1. (Exhibit CDA-1A)

[36] R.S.C. 1985, c. C-15 (Exhibit CDA-1C).

[37] SOR/94-466 (Exhibit CDA-1B). The Dairy Products Marketing Regulations were amended by *the Regulations Amending the Dairy Products Marketing Regulations*, C. Gaz. 2001.II.57 (Exhibit CDA-1A).

[38] *Supra*, footnote 31, s. 3(3) and s. 7.

[39] *Ibid.*, s. 4, 5 and 6.

[40] *Ibid.*, s. 3(3).

[41] See Order Amending Milk Orders Under the *Agricultural Products Marketing Act*, SOR/2001-16, C. Gaz. 2001.II.67. (Exhibit CDA-1A)

[42] Published in Canada Gazette, 3 January 2001.

(iv) Regulatory Amendments at the Provincial Level

3.7 As a consequence of the original Canada - Dairy panel and Appellate Body reports, legal frameworks in nine of the Canadian provinces have been modified to exclude export milk from the domestic management scheme.

3.8 In British Columbia, Alberta, Saskatchewan, Manitoba, New Brunswick, Nova Scotia, and Prince Edward Island as well as in Ontario and Quebec, individual producers and processors participating in the commercial export market agree on the terms of commercial export transactions. The governments in Ontario and Quebec require that all export participants operate through a single commercial export exchange. These "bulletin boards" are part of the operational framework within which commercial export transactions take place.[43]

3.9 If milk is not marketed as CEM, it is domestic milk and accordingly subject to existing domestic regulations.

IV. MAIN ARGUMENTS

4.1 **New Zealand** and the **United States** claimed that the new measures' established by Canada, enable processors for export to obtain milk at prices that are lower than domestic prices, providing those processors with export subsidies within the meaning of Article 9 or of Article 10 of the *Agreement on Agriculture*. Accordingly, any exports of dairy products produced from milk accessed under Canada's new schemes must be within Canada's export subsidy reduction commitments. The complainants requested the Panel to recommend to the DSB that Canada bring its export subsidies into conformity with its obligations under the Agreement on Agriculture.

4.2 **Canada** requested that the Panel reject the claims of New Zealand and the United States and find that Canada's measures, including federal measures and the provincial measures of British Columbia, Alberta, Saskatchewan, Manitoba, Ontario, Quebec, Nova Scotia, New Brunswick and Prince Edward Island, fully implement the recommendations and rulings of the DSB and are thus consistent with Canada's WTO obligations.

1. Burden of Proof

4.3 **New Zealand** submitted that as specified by Article 10.3 of the *Agreement on Agriculture*, Canada bears the burden of establishing that its dairy management measures, including those putatively taken to comply with the DSB's recommendations, have not subsidised dairy exports in excess of its commitment levels under that *Agreement*. Canada has demonstrably failed to meet this burden.

---

[43] For details of the pertinent legislation in the provinces, please see the exhibits referred to by Canada, New Zealand and the United States, respectively, in their submissions to the Panel.

4.4 **Canada** responded that while Canada recognised the presence of Article 10.3, it noted that reports issued by panels and the Appellate Body under Article 21.5 of the DSU uniformly confirm that a Member's measure is presumed to comply with WTO obligations and, thus, any Member challenging that measure bears the burden of proof.[44] In any case, Canada's submissions provide more than sufficient evidence and legal arguments to show that it does not subsidise any quantities exported in excess of its export subsidy commitment levels.

4.5 **New Zealand** and the **United States** replied that none of the cases Canada cited dealt with the *Agreement on Agriculture* and Article 10.3. In cases involving the allegation that subsidisation in excess of export subsidy reduction commitments has occurred, Article 10.3 reverses the normal rule relating to burden of proof. The conclusion applies equally to cases brought under Article 21.5.

2. *General*

4.6 **New Zealand** noted that Canada has put in place new measures in substitution for the measures that were ruled in contravention of Canada's WTO commitments by the panel and Appellate Body in the original Canada - Dairy proceedings. Canada has developed schemes designed to continue the exportation of dairy products at previous levels by creating a new means of access to lower-priced milk for processors for export. The effect of these schemes is that Canada will continue to export subsidised dairy products in excess of its export subsidy reduction commitment levels. Canada has thus put in place measures that are not in conformity with the *Agreement on Agriculture* and is therefore in violation of its obligations under Article 21 of the DSU. Canada's implementation of the original ruling, New Zealand continued, has involved the elimination of Special Milk Class 5(e) and the limitation of the use of Class 5(d). Replacement measures have been adopted by Canada on a province-by-province basis.

4.7 New Zealand submitted that the new schemes have not eliminated an essential governmental presence and role. Federal and provincial governments have enacted the relevant amendments to existing regulatory schemes. They retain auditing functions over contracts between producers and processors and over exports by processors. The new schemes rest on the basic requirement, imposed by government, that milk surplus to the needs of the domestic market must be sold for export or not sold at all. Producers of such non-quota milk cannot sell into the domestic market, but are compelled to sell to processors for export. The effect of the creation of this separate market for non-quota milk is that processors for export can obtain milk at prices that are significantly lower than the price for

[44] See, *e.g.*, *Canada - Aircraft*, Recourse to Article 21.5, *supra*, footnote 3, para. 5.14; *Australia - Salmon*, Recourse to Article 21.5, *supra*, footnote 24, para. 7.37; *EC - Bananas*, Recourse to Article 21.5 by the EC para. 4.13, DSR1999:II, 783; *EC Bananas*, Recourse to Article 21.5 by Ecuador, DSR 1997:II, 803, para. 6.133 and n.225; *Brazil - Aircraft*, Recourse to Article 21.5, *supra*, footnote 3, para. 66.

milk sold on the domestic market with the sole proviso that the resulting product is exported.

4.8 In New Zealand's view, Canada's new schemes have implications for the exportation of dairy products from other countries. If Canada's schemes are allowed to stand, there will be no limit on the exportation of subsidised dairy products by countries with domestic supply management schemes, thereby undermining the export subsidy disciplines in the *Agreement on Agriculture*. The new dairy export mechanisms put in place by Canada all involve "payments on the export of an agricultural product, financed by virtue of governmental action" within the meaning of Article 9.1(c) of the *Agreement on Agriculture*. Alternatively, the schemes involve export subsidies "applied in a manner which results in, or which threatens to lead to, circumvention" of Canada's export subsidy commitments within the meaning of Article 10.1 of the *Agreement on Agriculture*. Hence, Canada continues to be in violation of Article 3.3 and Article 8 of the *Agreement on Agriculture*.

4.9 **The United States** submitted that while the programmes introduced in August 2000 are in some regards different from the Special Milk Class 5(e) which they replace, their objective, the provision of low priced milk to exporters to make dairy exports commercially viable, is precisely the same. The new programmes vary somewhat from province to province, but possess several common elements. Specifically, the provincial programmes allow exporters to purchase milk at prices that are below prevailing market levels for milk used in dairy products sold into Canada's domestic market. The low-priced milk made available to dairy processors and exporters can only be used to manufacture dairy products for export. Thus, the availability of such discounted milk is contingent on export. Furthermore, any person that diverts the low-priced milk, products made from it, or components of the milk, into Canada's domestic market faces severe sanctions.

4.10 Because Ontario and Quebec account for the vast majority (approximately 80 per cent) of dairy product exports from Canada, the United States has focused on the fundamental aspects of the provincial regimes that have been established there. There are four core elements to those provincial regimes. First, any milk produced above the level of the domestic quota must be sold for export- processing only (or relegated to use in the production of animal feed). The milk that is committed to export may not be introduced into the domestic market; such milk (or the resulting dairy products) must be exported. Second, the price paid by exporters for milk produced outside of the domestic quota is not regulated; this is in contrast to milk produced within the domestic quota, for which prices are specifically established by the provincial authorities. Third, any milk producer desiring to contract to provide milk for export must do so through a single, mandatory offer-and-acceptance process established by the provincial milk marketing board in conjunction with dairy processors in each province. Fourth, the export contracts are policed and enforced by the federal and provincial governments through a comprehensive array of mechanisms. While the contracts can be enforced by the private parties themselves, they are also subject to audit and enforcement by both provincial and federal authorities. For example, in Quebec a substantial monetary penalty is imposed on any entity diverting into Canada's domestic market any milk or milk products committed to an export contract.

4.11 The separate market for discounted export milk, the United States claimed, exists in all provinces solely by virtue of the government requirement that milk produced above or outside of domestic quota must be sold for export. By mandating the separation of the two markets, the Canadian government ensures that reduced price milk will be offered to processors for export. The producers have no real choice if they produce over-quota or without quota. They can either: (i) sell their milk into the export market for a lower price; (ii) sell their milk into the animal feed market under Class 4(m) for an even lower price which has been set by government; or (iii) destroy the extra milk which would have obvious political ramifications. The only real commercial option is to sell any over-quota or non-quota milk into the export market. By restricting the choice of the producer, the government enables the transfer of lower-priced milk to the processor. Absent these restrictions, the processor would have to pay the higher price applicable to milk for dairy products sold into the domestic market.

4.12 The government further secures the supply of discounted milk for the export market, the United States continued, by requiring that producers "pre-commit" their milk destined for the export market and that export milk must be delivered "first out of the tank." This ensures that, by law, producers cannot abandon their obligations to supply milk for export at a discount from the domestic price. These requirements further demonstrate that the export market is not a true commercial market but rather a contrived market created and controlled by the Canadian government. While creating the impression that producers are making a commercial decision to produce for the export market, these two requirements help ensure that export milk is not redirected into the domestic market. In reality, producers are doing exactly what they did under the Special Milk Class programme - arranging for the disposition of any milk not permitted to be sold in the domestic market

4.13 The CDC, the United States further submitted, also continues to play a central role in the export of dairy products. Although Canada has eliminated Special Milk Class 5(e), the CDC is still involved in the issuance of permits and the negotiation of milk prices for Class 5 (d) and 5(a), 5(b) and 5(c). Also, the CDC remains heavily engaged both in the operation of Canada's supply management system, as well as in the enforcement of the export mechanisms recently created by the provinces. For example, pursuant to section 10 of the federal regulations, the CDC possesses the authority to audit the books and records of both producers and processors to determine whether milk committed for export has in fact been exported. In addition, under new section 11(1), the CDC's inspectors have the authority to seize any dairy product that the inspector believes on reasonable grounds was marketed in inter-provincial or export trade in contravention of the federal regulations.[45]

4.14 **Canada** submitted that it has fully implemented the recommendations and rulings of the DSB in *Canada -Dairy* through federal measures and provincial measures in British Columbia, Alberta, Saskatchewan, Manitoba, Ontario, Quebec, Nova Scotia, New Brunswick and Prince Edward Island. First, Canada has limited exports of dairy products manufactured with milk purchased under Special Milk Class 5(d) to Canada's export subsidy commitment levels and has abolished Special Milk Class 5(e) (surplus removal through exports). The function of surplus removal performed by Special Milk Class 5(e) has been replaced by measures internal to the domestic system. Second, federal regulations and regulations in nine separate provinces have been changed to eliminate government control over the commercial decisions by producers and processors to participate in the commercial export market. As a result of these regulatory changes, there are now two separate markets for milk in Canada: a regulated supply-managed market and an unregulated commercial export milk market.

4.15 Canada argued that the dairy regime has been fundamentally altered so that neither the CDC nor the provincial marketing boards can control commercial export transactions in the commercial export milk market. Decisions to produce milk for the commercial export milk market are left to the sole commercial discretion of individual producers. Likewise, decisions to purchase this milk are left to the sole discretion of processors. The characteristics of the previous regime which were found by the panel and Appellate Body to give rise to export subsidies, Canada continued, no longer exist with respect to commercial export transactions. Due to regulatory changes at both the federal and provincial levels, among other things: (i) milk producers have complete freedom to independently allocate some, none or all of their milk to the commercial export market; (ii) producers do not need to hold quota to produce milk for the commercial export market; (iii) neither the CDC nor the provincial marketing boards determine when and what quantity of commercial export milk may be processed for export; (iv) individual producers and processors determine the sale price of commercial export milk; not the CDC or provincial boards; (v) processors do not have to obtain a permit form the CDC or appeal to the provincial marketing boards to obtain commercial export milk; (vi) the CDC does not negotiate or guarantee the processors' profit margins on sales of commercial export milk; (vii) provincial marketing boards do not regulate the collection of commercial export milk revenues from processors for payment to producers; (viii) there is no pooling of commercial export returns by government; and (ix) market forces, not governments, determine the effective selling price of commercial export milk.

---

[45] "Regulations Amending the Dairy products Marketing Regulations", Canada Gazette Part II, Vol.135, No.1.

4.16 The limited powers retained by the CDC and the provincial milk marketing boards, Canada continued, relate to licensing for the purpose of ensuring compliance with health, sanitary and quality standards and the post-transaction power to require the disclosure of records relating to milk utilisation and verification for the purpose of regulating and protecting the domestic market. There is nothing in these powers that enables the CDC or the provincial marketing boards to control commercial export transactions. Indeed the CDC is subject to clear and mandatory Direction from the Minister of Agriculture and Agri-Food stipulating that: "The Commission shall not act in any manner so as to influence, directly or indirectly, the terms, conditions or formation of contracts for the sale of commercial export milk or cream."

4.17 As a result of the implementation measures adopted by Canada, transactions for the sale of commercial export milk are *market driven at every stage* according to Canada. From the processor's determination of its volume and price requirements and issuance of an offer to purchase, to the decision by a producer to produce milk for the commercial export market, and his or her commitment under a contract to provide the milk, to the payment to the producer by the processor, these transactions are strictly a matter of private contract.

4.18 Canada submitted that processors make individual choices regarding the price that they are willing to pay for commercial export milk and the quantity of this milk that they wish to purchase, based on the commercial export business that they are able to secure. The prices offered for the milk are influenced by the prices at which the processors are able to sell their finished products, which are in turn influenced by international competition for these foreign sales, currency fluctuations and world-market conditions. In the deregulated commercial export milk marketplace, processors seek an assured supply of milk so that they can plan their export business, maximize revenue opportunities and respect their commitments to foreign buyers. Processors therefore seek commercial export milk supply commitments well in advance of production, and in some cases up to twelve months in advance. Referring to the United States arguments in paragraph 4.12, Canada submitted that pre-commitment does not provide, through governmental action, security of supply to processors. Security of supply is a function of the private contractual commitment by producers to deliver a specified volume of milk at a specified price.

4.19 Canada further contended that individual producers for their part, make production and marketing choices based on commercial grounds (i.e., on an allocation of sales to the two markets with a view to maximising revenue) and make calculated pre-planned production decisions. In response to identified market opportunities, processors make offers to purchase commercial export milk in advance of production and producers decide whether to take up those opportunities and in what quantities. Referring to the complainants argument that producers produce milk beyond their quota and then enter into export contracts after the fact to get rid of this milk, Canada submitted that, on the contrary, the commercial practice of the dairy industry throughout Canada is that processors arrange their milk supply for export in advance of production. Pre-commitment and its corollary, the first milk out of the bulk tank principle, are the operational realities of contracted production.

4.20 Referring in particular to New Zealand's arguments in paragraph 4.8, Canada submitted that New Zealand is attempting to have the Panel establish new rules applying to two-price systems and their relationship to export subsidy commitments - rules that have not yet been the subject of agreement between WTO Members. Collapsing domestic support disciplines into export subsidy disciplines would have consequences extending far beyond the reach of the disciplines carefully negotiated by WTO Members and, therefore, should be rejected. The right to export while maintaining tariffs and domestic support was clearly built into the decisions incorporated into the results of the Uruguay Round. Any re-negotiation of WTO obligations is the responsibility of Members, and this is being pursued by Members in the current negotiations on agriculture.

4.21 **New Zealand** responded that a producer wishing to produce in excess of current quota must purchase quota if the milk is to go into the domestic market. But the total amount of quota is finite, and quota costs are substantial. Faced with such limitations, the producer who produces non-quota milk either has to negotiate a contract with a processor for export at a price less than the domestic market price or has to have the milk disposed of under Class 4(m). This is not the functioning of a voluntary, commercially-based market as Canada would have it. It is a case of individual producers making less than optimal choices because they are constrained by the regulatory system established and administered by governments. Accordingly, Canada's replacement schemes provide export subsidies within the meaning of Article 9.1(c) of the *Agreement on Agriculture*. But even if this is not the case, they nevertheless provide export subsidies within the meaning of Article 10.1 of the *Agreement on Agriculture*.

4.22 **Canada** submitted further that the evidence clearly demonstrates that producers have a number of very real choices in the marketplace and manage their production based on the choices that they make. Evidence submitted by Canada illustrates the range of pre-production choices available to a producer, the quota and production management requirements associated with those choices and the post-production consequences of those choices. Producers are no longer required to hold domestic quota to produce milk in Canada. A producer, therefore, can choose not to hold domestic quota and can produce exclusively for the commercial export milk market. A producer can also choose to purchase or lease quota and sell into the domestic market. The data presented by Canada demonstrates there is an active commercial trade in quota.

4.23 Where a producer chooses to produce commercial export milk through a private contract with a processor, Canada argued, the producer decides how much of his or her production to allocate to this market and makes a contractual commitment to do so prior to producing the milk. It is then the responsibility of the producer to manage his or her production in order to meet the contractual commitment. Where a quota-holding producer does not want to sell into the commercial export market the producer can maintain production at levels within his or her quota range and will receive the Special Class 4(m) price for any production that exceeds that range (see paragraph 4.25 below).

4.24 Nothing prevents producers from producing milk and selling it to a processor under a commercial export contract instead of selling it into the regulated market, and nothing requires them to do so. Canada was of the view that if, as New Zealand and the United States suggested, producers were forced into the commercial export market by governmental measures, one would expect to see a very high proportion of producers, if not all, participating in commercial export transactions but as of April, 2001, only about 30 per cent of Canadian producers had participated in commercial export contracts since deregulation measures were introduced in August 2000.

4.25 Canada considered that it has demonstrated that producers manage variations in production and respond to changes in quota levels within the flexibility provided by the administration of the domestic system. However, if in aiming to fill domestic quota, a producer over produces, the over-quota production cannot be sold into the commercial export market. Over-quota milk must be sold by the producer into the domestic system through internal pricing arrangements (at the Class 4(m) price of approximately $10 per hectolitre). About one half of Canadian producers have sold a small volume of milk at the Class 4(m) price. This small volume of sales (less than 1 per cent of total Canadian production) shows that producers are able to manage their production effectively so as to minimise the amount of milk that will be sold at this low price. The large number of producers selling at the Class 4(m) price demonstrates that this Class is effective in dealing with over-quota production and that producers do not and cannot divert over-quota milk into the commercial export market. Canada was of the view that if it were possible to sell over-quota milk on the commercial export market there would not be such a high degree of participation in Class 4(m).

4.26 **New Zealand** responded with respect to Canada's assertion in paragraphs 4.17 - 4.19 above that this is a misleading statement of the system under which the sale of milk for processing for export takes place. Given a real choice, producers would not sell to processors for export at all but rather in the higher priced domestic market. But that market is available only for milk produced under a government-set quota, and its existence protects processors for export from having to purchase milk at the higher domestic market price. Commercial export milk cannot be sold on the domestic market without "financial consequences", which are designed to "prevent the flow of commercial export milk into the domestic market, as admitted by Canada. This prohibition on the sale of non-quota milk on the domestic market results in the transfer of economic resources to processors for export that allows them to enter the international market.

4.27 As concerns the possibility of selling non-quota milk at the Class 4(m) price, in New Zealand's view the information presented by Canada (see paragraph 4.25), including the "small" volume of sales involved, confirms that Class 4(m) is not a realistic alternative for producers of non-quota milk. While producers may have been forced to use Class 4(m) in the past, the $10 per hectolitre average price received could not even cover a producer's marginal costs of production. This means that producers of non-quota milk are effectively compelled by governmental action to sell, at a price discount, to processors for export. New Zealand was of the view that the economic incentives that govern Canada's "commercial export milk market" are not the prices offered by processors for export, but the requirement that non-quota milk be sold for export. The commercial export milk market is ancillary to the domestic system and its existence is completely dictated by the constraints in that system. It is an artificial market which would not exist if individual producers were allowed to choose where they place their production.

4.28 With respect to Canada's claim that the notion of "surplus milk" no longer applies to the milk sold under export contracts, New Zealand submitted this is a matter of words, not substance. The fundamental nature of the system has not changed. The milk that producers now have to pre-plan and pre-commit is still "surplus milk" in the sense that it is deemed to be surplus to the needs of the domestic market. The way in which processors for export gain access to milk has not changed in its fundamental respects. Canada's replacement schemes still provide processors for export with access to lower-priced milk than that available in the domestic market. These schemes continue to constitute an export subsidy under Article 9.1(c) of the Agreement on Agriculture. Alternatively, they violate Article 10.1 of that Agreement.

4.29 New Zealand contended that Canada does not address the consequences for the agricultural trading system if its view were to be accepted. Export subsidies are fundamentally a means used by governments to maintain domestic prices at levels higher than world prices. The existence of a price difference is, therefore, an indicator that an export subsidy may exist, even if it is not the only element needed to establish an export subsidy. It is not possible to ignore the comparator domestic market when looking at whether an export subsidy exists under Article 9.1. Canada claims that its creation of separate "markets" with producers acting "commercially" in each means that the price difference somehow disappears. But the implications of such an argument are clear. A government could claim no export subsidy existed by simply creating in law a separate "market" for export with lower prices than those in the domestic market.

4.30 The **United States** submitted that cost of production data used to set prices in the domestic system contradict the claim in Canada's first submission that farmers freely supply this milk based on normal commercial factors. According to data from the official cost of production survey, less than 30 per cent of Canadian farmers cover their cost of production at an average price of C$57.41/hl and less than 1 per cent could cover costs at export market prices of around C$30/hl. Why would the average farmer choose to produce for this market?

4.31 As concerns the complainants arguments with respect to the cost of production and the price at which the milk is sold in the commercial export market,

Canada submitted that the relevant facts show that profitable participation in the commercial export milk market is feasible for many producers. Furthermore, Canada considered that it has demonstrated that the CDC and provincial marketing boards have no role in individual producer and processor decisions to participate in the commercial export milk market and thus cannot be said to be compelling producers to sell their milk under commercial export contracts. Although the precise details of how each provincial industry now operates vary, they share a crucial feature: producers and processors decide, free of government control, whether to engage in commercial export transactions, the volume of milk to commit to produce and the price for the milk. As in any private contract, the responsibilities for enforcing the contractual obligations rest with the parties to the transaction (i.e., the producer and the processor).

4.32 In British Columbia, Alberta, Saskatchewan, New Brunswick, Nova Scotia and Prince Edward Island, Canada continued, terms and conditions regarding commercial export contracts are agreed to directly and privately between producers and processors. In Manitoba, Ontario and Quebec, export contract offers and acceptances are communicated through commercial exchanges using electronic bulletin boards. The exchange format allows processors to post contract offers to which producers respond by phone. The results or confirmations are then posted on the web site. The exchanges are administrative constructs operated by independent, reputable, private firms and are particularly effective in provinces with market places having numerous participants. In Manitoba, processors and producers can also contract directly and there is nothing to preclude the establishment of other bulletin boards.

4.33 **New Zealand** responded with respect to Canada's arguments in paragraph 4.32, that governmental action remains indispensable to the transfer of economic resources from producers to processors for export because the decision to produce milk for export is a decision that is dictated by the fact that milk for the domestic market is regulated by quota. The decision to sell is equally trammelled. No profit-maximising producer would sell into the commercial export milk market in the absence of the prohibition against selling non-quota milk into the domestic market. This prohibition is by virtue of governmental action. Equally, the decision of a processor for export to purchase milk in the commercial export milk market is a product of governmental action. In the absence of a prohibition on the selling of non-quota milk into the domestic market, a processor for export would only be able to access milk from the higher priced domestic market.

4.34 The **United States** submitted that the fundamental obligation of the *Agreement on Agriculture* concerning export subsidies is contained in Article 8, which provides that: "Each Member undertakes not to provide export subsidies other than in conformity with this *Agreement* and with the commitments as specified in that Member's Schedule." Article 3.3 of the *Agreement*, in turn, provides that a Member shall not provide export subsidies listed in paragraph 1 of Article 9 in excess of the budgetary outlay and quantity commitment levels specified in Section II of Part IV of that Member's Schedule. To ensure, moreover, that the disciplines on export subsidies contained in Article 3.3 are not circumvented, Article 10.1 of the *Agreement* directs that any export subsidy not identified in Article 9.1 may "not be applied in a manner which results in, or which threatens to lead to, circumvention of export subsidy commitments . . ." Thus, a Member may use export subsidies not listed in Article 9.1 only within the limits of its scheduled reduction commitments.

4.35 Given this framework, the United States continued, any export subsidy that falls either within the scope of the export subsidy descriptions contained in Article 9.1 or within the broader reach of Article 10.1 of the *Agreement* is subject to the limitations, both budgetary and quantitative, included in each Member's Schedule. The United States considered that Canada's provincial export measures are export subsidies within the meaning of Article 1(e) of the *Agreement* and, therefore, must be confined within the quantitative limits prescribed in Canada's Schedule. Canada's failure to respect its Schedule limitations on export subsidies is, in turn, a failure to comply with the DSB's recommendations to bring its milk export subsidies into conformity with the *Agreement*.

3. *Article 9(1)(c) of the Agreement on Agriculture*

(i) "payments"

4.36 **New Zealand** and the **United States** submitted that two elements are required in order to establish the existence of an export subsidy under Article 9.1(c). First, there must be a "payment", and second, that payment must be "financed by virtue of governmental action".

4.37 In the original Canada - Dairy proceeding, **New Zealand** submitted, the Appellate Body held that the term "payments" "denotes a transfer of economic resources." In the Appellate Body's view, whether "payments" had been made in the context of Special Milk Classes 5(d) and 5(e) depended upon whether processors for export were obtaining milk at prices that were discounted from the prices that applied in the domestic market.[46] New Zealand considered that this reasoning applies equally to Canada's new measures. Milk continues to be available to processor for export at prices that are lower than domestic market prices.

4.38 The **United States** submitted that the new provincial export schemes fulfil both of the conditions set forth in paragraph 4.36 above and, thus, constitute Article 9.1(c) export subsidies. The Appellate Body articulated the standard for determining whether a "payment" exists as follows:

> If goods or services are supplied to an enterprise, or a group of enterprises, at reduced rates (that is, at below market-rates), "payments" are, in effect, made to the recipient of the portion of the price that is not charged. Instead of receiving a monetary payment

[46] *Canada - Dairy*, Appellate Body report, *supra*, footnote 31, para. 107.

equal to the revenue foregone, the recipient is paid in the form of goods or services. But as far as the recipient is concerned, the economic value of the transfer is precisely the same.[47]

4.39 Under the new provincial programmes, the United States continued, the export contract prices offered are significantly below the market prices paid for milk entering Canada's domestic market for final consumption. For example, the average price for Class 3 milk sold into the Canadian market for ultimate consumption within Canada was about C$56 per hectolitre for the period August to December 2000, i.e. about 85 per cent above the price offered in export contracts reported for the same month. Thus, just as in the case of the earlier Special Milk Class system, the new provincial export measures result in milk producers providing milk for export at a substantial discount to the prevailing market price for milk delivered for ultimate consumption in Canada. Milk producers are now foregoing revenue in the same manner that the original panel and Appellate Body found to constitute a "payment" for purposes of Article 9.1(c) under the Special Milk Class system.

4.40 **Canada** responded that the complainants arguments disregard the finding of the Appellate Body on what constitutes a 'payment' under Article 9.1(c). The Appellate Body held that "[i]f goods or services are supplied to an enterprise, or a group of enterprises, at *reduced rates* (that is, at below *market rates*), 'payments' are, in effect, made to the recipient of the portion of the price that is not charged".[48] The corollary of this proposition, Canada continued, is that where the recipient of goods or services pays market-rates or market value[49] for those goods or services, there can be no "payment" under Article 9.1(c)[50] as no "advantage" or "benefit" is conferred on the recipient.[51] Sales at fair market value through arm's length transactions in a private commercial context cannot be considered to confer a benefit.[52]

4.41 Applying the facts to the text of the *Agreement on Agriculture*, Canada continued, there is no export subsidy provided to processors within the meaning of Article 9.1(c) of the *Agreement on Agriculture.* There are no "payments" on the export of dairy products manufactured with commercial export milk, since commercial export milk is sold *at,* not *below* market rates. Even if "payments" were provided to processors in commercial export transactions, an export subsidy would not exist because those "payments" would not be financed by virtue of governmental action.

---

47 *Canada - Dairy*, Appellate Body report, *supra* footnote 31, para. 113.

48 *Ibid.* (emphasis added).

49 "Market-rate" and "market value" are synonymous. See the *New Shorter Oxford English Dictionary* (Clarendon Press: Oxford, 1993) page 1699.

50 See also *Canada-Dairy,* Appellate Body report, *supra* note 1, para. 107.

51 See also *Canada-Dairy*, Appellate Body report, supra note 1, para. 87. This reasoning equally applies to Article 9.1(c). See *Canada - Dairy*, Appellate Body report, *supra* note 1, para. 107.

52 See for example, *United States -Hot-Rolled Lead and Carbon Steel*, paras. 72-74.

4.42 **New Zealand** responded that Canada's whole argument rests on the assumption that its commercial export milk market can be considered in isolation from its domestic market. But the so-called commercial export milk market exists only because of the ban of non-quota milk from the domestic market. Processors for export receive a transfer of economic resources because they are able to access milk at a price that would not be available to them if producers were permitted to sell non-quota milk into the domestic market. In the absence of any requirement that producers sell non-quota milk into the "commercial export milk market", processors for export would have to purchase their product from the domestic market at the higher domestic price. The implication of Canada's argument would be that governments that were not permitted to make payments directly to processors for export, nor were entitled to do so by the provision of payments-in-kind or revenue forgone, could provide such payments indirectly by effectively forcing producers to sell milk for export into a separate "export market" at a lower price.

4.43 The **United States,** responding to the arguments by Canada in paragraph 4.56 above, argued that these arguments should be rejected because the original panel did not consider the *SCM Agreement* in analysing Article 9.1(c) of the *Agreement on Agriculture*. It was only when pondering the claim under Article 10.1 of the *Agreement on Agriculture* that the panel considered the *SCM Agreement* as *context* and then the panel determined that it was more appropriate to analyse paragraph (d) of the Illustrative List of Export Subsidies than to analyse the general concepts of Article 1 of the *SCM Agreement*. As well, Canada's interpretation of Article 9.1(c) is not supported by the language of the agreement itself or the negotiating history cited by Canada.

4.44 **Canada** submitted that whether or not there exists "payments" on the exports of agricultural products must be determined in the light of the prevailing market conditions. At the time of the findings of the original panel and Appellate Body, there was only one market for milk in Canada: a regulated market. Government set the prices of all milk under this market. It is in light of these market conditions that the difference between the domestic and the export price was found to constitute a "payment" under Article 9.1(c).

4.45 The market conditions which presently exist are completely different, Canada contended. Hence the fact that there exists a difference between the export price and the regulated domestic price is, in Canada's view, irrelevant. Producers and processors now have access to two markets: a regulated market and a commercial export market. Market forces, not government, now determine the price at which commercial export milk is purchased and sold. More particularly, the price at which commercial export milk is bought and sold reflects the price at which the seller (a private producer) is ready and willing to sell and a buyer (the private processor) is willing to buy. The prices are determined through mutual agreement, without regulatory control or compulsion of any kind. Processors are not paying less than adequate remuneration for commercial export milk. Rather, they are paying prices determined by the competitive forces of supply and demand in international markets. Moreover, Canada noted that New Zealand conceded that commercial export milk prices were global or world market prices. For these reasons, there are no "payments" on the exports of dairy products manufactured with commercial export milk. Canada therefore considered that since the first element of Article 9.1(c) has not been met, there is no violation of this export subsidy discipline.

4.46 **New Zealand** submitted that the Appellate Body did not hold that since government no longer sets prices in its export market, somehow this means the difference in prices between the export market and the domestic market is no longer relevant. Instead it held that the provision of lower-priced milk constitutes a payment. It did not say that the lower price has to be set by government. Canada's argument is based on a confusion between the question of whether lower-priced milk is made available and the question of whether this is done by virtue of governmental action. The first question under Article 9.1(c) is one of fact - are "payments" being made, that is, is lower-priced milk being provided? It is not a question of whether government is setting prices. The answer to the first part of this question is self-evident. The price for milk paid by processors for export is substantially less than the price paid for milk accessed in the domestic market. That fact is not denied by Canada, and it constitutes a payment within the meaning of Article 9.1(c). Furthermore, such a transfer of economic resources from producers to processors is provided by virtue of governmental action, because producers of non-quota milk cannot sell their milk into the domestic market at domestic market prices. That prohibition results from the action of governments.

4.47 The **United States,** referring to Canada's arguments in paragraphs 4.40 and 4.45 above, responded that Canada's approach to analysing whether a "payment" is conferred assumes that the appropriate benchmark is the export market price. However, this approach is inconsistent with the legal standard that the Appellate Body and the original panel in this case applied in determining the existence of a subsidy under Article 9. In determining whether a "payment" is made within Article 9.1(c), the United States considered that this Panel must assess what would have been *otherwise available* to processors/exporters in the marketplace. For all practical purposes, the only source of milk otherwise available to Canadian processors/exporters is milk produced *in* Canada. And that milk is sold at a high price pursuant to regulation (unless, of course, the milk is destined for export). Just as in the case of the Special Milk Class 5(e) scheme, the processor is accessing milk for export at a price that is lower than would be paid by the same processor purchasing the same milk for use in manufacturing dairy products destined for the domestic market. Likewise, producers are providing milk for export at a substantial discount to the market price for milk delivered for domestic consumption.

(ii) "financed by virtue of governmental action"

4.48 **New Zealand** considered that, in the present case, Canada's new measures equally meet the test of whether "governmental action" is "indispensable"[53] to the transfer of resources that amounts to a "payment". Canada's new schemes provide milk to processors for export at prices lower than domestic prices because of the requirement that 'non-quota' milk be sold for export. It is the governmental segregation of the 'market' for export milk from the domestic market that allows processors to access milk at prices that are lower than domestic prices. The Appellate Body held that "payments" were "financed by virtue of governmental action" because the "governmental action" in question was "indispensable to the transfer of resources that takes place as a result of the operation of Special Milk Classes 5(d) and 5(e)."[54] The standard was whether processors for export would be able to gain access to milk at prices lower than those available on the domestic market in Canada were it not for the actions of the Canadian government or its agencies.

4.49 If Canadian governments and their agencies did not make a distinction between "domestic" and "export" markets, New Zealand continued, processors for export would not have access to lower-priced milk for export production. They would simply have access to milk available on a single Canadian market at whatever price was current in that market. It would be up to processors to decide whether to sell the resultant product domestically or for export. No export subsidisation would be involved. As a result, the new Canadian measures clearly provide "payments on the export of an agricultural product financed by virtue of governmental action" within the meaning of Article 9.1(c) of the *Agreement on Agriculture*. Such subsidies are subject to Canada's reduction commitments.

4.50 With regard to the analysis of the second prong of Article 9.1(c), the **United States** submitted, it is clear from a review of the government's involvement that the payments to the processors under the provincial export programmes are made by "virtue of governmental action." There are three primary indicia of the government's involvement in the new provincial export programmes. These include: (i) the fact that Canada artificially segregates the market for milk that is exported and milk that is consumed domestically; (ii) that provincial regulations require that any milk committed for export contracts through the new export schemes be exported, and that the federal and provincial governments have sanction authority to enforce this requirement; and (iii) that in Ontario and Quebec all milk destined for export must be sold through an exclusive mandatory bulletin board system.

4.51 Furthermore, the United States argued, the panel in the original proceeding recognized the role of the domestic quota system in the transfer of resources from the producer to the processor under the Special Milk Class system as "gov-

---

53 *Canada - Dairy*, Appellate Body report, DSR 1999:V, 2057, para. 120.

54 *Ibid.*

ernment action" within Article 9.1(c).[55] Its analysis of this issue is directly applicable to the role of the domestic quota system and hence the government under the new provincial export programmes. In sum, the United States submitted, Canada has not refuted that the overall action of Canadian governments in establishing domestic production quotas, in excluding over-quota and non-quota milk from the domestic market, in exempting export contract milk from domestic pricing requirements, in instituting mandatory and exclusive export contracting mechanisms, and in enforcing the various obligations arising from these regulatory requirements, constitutes pervasive government intervention. It is only through the exercise of these government powers that exporters are provided milk at discounted prices. Not only is government action involved, but it is indispensable. Accordingly, the requirement under Article 9.1(c) that payments are financed "by virtue of government action" is satisfied in this case.

4.52 The United States contended further that Canada insists that there must be a "direct connection" or there must be evidence that the government has "affirmatively instructed or directed someone to provide a financial contribution" under Article 1.1(a)(1)(iv) and that this standard must be satisfied to fall within Article 1 of the *SCM Agreement* and therefore Article 9.1(c) of the *Agreement on Agriculture*. This interpretation is, in the opinion of the United States, not legally sound as it ignores the phrase "by virtue of" in Article 9.1(c) which suggests an indirect connection and essentially writes the language in paragraph (d) of the Illustrative List referring to the provision of subsidies "indirectly" through "government mandated-schemes" out of the *SCM Agreement*.

4.53 Finally, with respect to Canada's reference to the negotiating history, the United States submitted that under the Vienna Convention on the Law of Treaties, negotiating history should only be considered if the plain meaning of the text is ambiguous. Canada has not established this and, indeed, it is not. In any event, a review of the negotiating history does not strengthen Canada's arguments. The quote referred to by Canada[56] simply supports the principle that it is the extent of government action that is important. The United States agreed and believed that it had established that government action is indispensable to the payment to the exporters in this case.

4.54 **Canada** submitted that even if "payments" were found to exist, they would not be financed by virtue of governmental action. All of the factors relied upon by the original panel and Appellate Body related directly to the determina-

---

[55] *Canada - Dairy*, panel report, *supra*, footnote 53, para. 7.100.

[56] "[T]here was no doubt that there was an obligation to notify all schemes of levy/subsidy affecting imports or exports in which the government took a part either by making payments into the common fund or by entrusting to a private body the functions of taxation and subsidisation with the result that the practice would in no real sense differ from those normally followed by governments. In view of these considerations the Panel feels that the question of notifying levy/subsidy arrangements depends upon the source of the funds and the extent of government action, if any, in their collection." Panel report, *Review Pursuant to Article XVI:5*, BISD, 9S/189.

tion of the volume of milk for export or to decisions regarding prices, including the pooling of revenues.[57] Each involved some form of affirmative or positive action on the part of governments or their agencies by virtue of which the payments were financed. As the panel in *Canada-Dairy* reasoned, the existence of parallel markets for domestic use and for export with different prices does not necessarily constitute an export subsidy. What is key is the government involvement in providing the "payment". In particular, there must be a direct connection between the "governmental action" on the one hand and the "payments" on the other. Governments need not be the actual source of the funds. However, the financing must be by virtue of governmental action, as opposed to commercial decisions by private individuals or companies. The very text of Article 9.1(c) provides an illustration of this point. The financing need not involve a "charge on the public account". However, as shown by the example of a mandatory levy "imposed" on an agricultural product, in Canada's view, the financing of the payment must be directly connected to "governmental action". The ordinary meaning of the words "by virtue of"[58] also support this proposition.

4.55 The complainants, Canada continued, had not demonstrated this connection, and therefore argued that measures relating to the regulated market effectively force producers to provide commercial export milk to processors. Canada submitted that no support for such a test can be found in either the findings of the original panel or of the Appellate Body. Nor can any support be found in the ordinary meaning of the words under Article 9.1(c), interpreted in their context and in the light of their object and purpose, or in the negotiating history of Article 9.1(c) and other export subsidy disciplines.

4.56 In this respect Canada submitted that the words in Article 9.1(c) must also be read in light of basic subsidy principles and disciplines that both the *Agreement on Agriculture* and the *SCM Agreement* contain. Canada's interpretation of Article 9.1(c) is informed by the important context provided in the *SCM Agreement*. Under Article 1.1(a)(1)(iv) of the *SCM Agreement*, an "indirect subsidy" arises when governments affirmatively instruct or direct someone to provide a financial contribution, for example in the form of goods. There must be an affirmative action of delegation or command on the part of government. Absent this, there is no government action and no subsidy. Since no such governmental action exists in Canada with respect to CEM, there can be no subsidy under Article 9.1(c) of the *Agreement on Agriculture*. Canada considered that its interpretation is confirmed by the negotiating history of Article 9.1(c) which contemplates

---

[57] For instance, after describing the mandatory pooling arrangements in respect of Class 5(d) and the more limited form of pooling in respect of Class 5(e), the Appellate Body described these arrangements as involving "governmental action" that remains an essential aspect of the financing of "payments" to processors. *Canada - Dairy*, Appellate Body report, *supra* footnote 1, para. 121.

[58] *Black's Law Dictionary*, *supra* note 88, page 201, defines "by virtue of " as follows: "[b]y force of, by authority of, by reason of."

that "indirect subsidies" exist when governments instruct or direct someone else to provide a financial contribution that they would normally provide themselves.

4.57 Canada submitted that it had removed any possibility of any payments "financed by virtue of governmental action". In particular, the CDC and provincial marketing boards have no authority over the decision to produce, purchase or sell commercial export milk. They do not set the price of commercial export milk nor do they control processor margins or pool revenues, impose quantitative limits, issue transaction-specific permits, calculate returns or dictate means of payment in commercial export transactions. In short, commercial export transactions have been deregulated.

4.58 **New Zealand** responded that Canada misconstrues the clear wording of Article 9.1(c), and confuses the requirement that there be a "direct subsidy" under Article 9.1(a) with the requirement that the "payment" must be financed "by virtue of" governmental action under Article 9.1(c). The word "direct" stands in contrast to the phrase "by virtue of" which is not confined to a relationship that is "direct". If the drafters of Article 9.1(c) had intended the connection between "governmental action" and "payment" to have been "direct", they would have used words that provided that meaning and not the more generic phrase "by virtue of".

4.59 **Canada** submitted that as a result of its deregulation, the factors relied upon by the original panel and Appellate Body to find "governmental action", all of which involved some form of positive action on the part of government, have been eliminated with respect to commercial export transactions. According to Canada, governments do not provide commercial export milk to processors, nor have they mandated that someone else provide commercial export milk to processors in their place. Licensing and auditing do not constitute financing by virtue of governmental action. These activities have nothing to do with the decision to produce, sell or purchase milk for commercial export markets. Similarly, the fact that in certain provinces commercial export transactions must be concluded on a bulletin board does not meet the test under Article 9.1(c), as producers in these provinces also decide of their own volition whether or not to provide commercial export milk to processors. Whether or not Canada's measures prohibit, penalise or impede the diversion of commercial export milk into the domestic market is also irrelevant to the question of the existence of an export subsidy. Those measures are maintained to support or protect the regulated market, not to support, force or mandate exports.

4.60 **New Zealand** responded that whether the prohibition to sell export contract milk into the domestic market results from a directive with a formal sanction imposed at either the federal or provincial level, or whether it results from financial consequences for the processor who diverts milk under a commercial export contract into the domestic market, the result is the same. There is, effectively, a prohibition on the sale of non-quota milk into the domestic market.

4.61 **Canada** submitted that the ordinary meaning of the words "by virtue of" does not support the positions of New Zealand and the United States. "By virtue of" means "by force of, by authority of, by reason of". Governments must therefore direct or require the provision of goods. Governments have done no such thing with respect to commercial export milk. Rather, producers voluntarily choose to provide commercial export milk to processors. Canada considered that the complainants erroneously present as direct action the very actions necessary to deregulate the export market and measures to ensure health and safety standards for all milk and auditing of the regulated market. Given the absence of direct governmental action, Canada continued, their efforts must fail because they present no evidence of impermissible government action - direct or indirect.

4.62 Canada considered the assertion by the complainants that, by precluding the sale of commercial export milk into the domestic market, Canada effectively forces producers to provide processors with commercial export milk as incorrect. First, producers *choose* to produce for this market, just as they choose to produce for the regulated market. Second, an export subsidy is not defined by the *effects* of government measures related to the domestic regulated market. The complainants' assertions are not based on the legal standards that actually exist in either the *Agreement on Agriculture* or the *SCM Agreement*. In Canada, government does not provide commercial export milk to processors, nor does it instruct or direct producers to provide this milk to processors or mandate that they do so.

4.63 **New Zealand** responded that Canada's reliance on the ordinary meaning of the words "by virtue of" is unduly selective. Canada ignores one of the meanings given - "by reason of". In the view of New Zealand, such an extrapolation bears no relation to the dictionary definitions provided for either in *Black's Law Dictionary*, or in the *Oxford English Dictionary*, which indicates that it means "by the power or efficacy[59] of (something aiding or justifying); hence, in later use, by the authority of, in reliance upon, in consequence of, because of",

4. *Article 10.1 of the Agreement on Agriculture*

4.64 **New Zealand** and the **United States** submitted that even if the new Canadian measures did not provide export subsidies within the meaning of Article 9.1(c) of the *Agreement on Agriculture*, they nevertheless provide export subsidies within the meaning of Article 10.1 of that Agreement. **New Zealand** considered that the first part of this Article requires two elements to be established: there must be "export subsidies not listed in paragraph 1 of Article 9"; and those export subsidies must be "applied in a manner which results in, or which threatens to lead to, circumvention of export subsidy commitments." Alternatively, if it can be shown that "non-commercial transactions" have been used to circumvent export subsidy commitments, this too will constitute a violation of Article 10.1. Measures which meet some but not all the definitional elements of the individual export subsidy practices listed in Article 9.1 would be covered by Article 10.1,

[59] Exhibit NZ-27.

provided that they meet the basic requirement of Article 1(e) of the *Agreement on Agriculture* that they are "subsidies contingent upon export performance".

4.65 The product that is sold to processors for export under Special Milk Classes 5(d), **New Zealand** submitted, and the product that is sold to processors for export under Canada's replacement schemes is identical. In each case, processors for export are provided with access to lower-priced milk. In the one case, Canada recognises that the exported product is subsidised and keeps it within its export subsidy reduction commitments. In the other case, Canada claims that the exported product is not subsidised and that it is entitled to exclude it from its reduction commitments. However, a measure that mirrors in all respects a measure that provides an export subsidy and is treated as such by Canada under Special Milk Classes 5(d), must itself be an export subsidy.

4.66 The drafters of Article 10.1, New Zealand submitted, were trying to capture measures that did not technically fall within the definitions of Article 9.1, but which had the same economic effect as measures that did. A key element of the subsidisation that occurs in this case relates to the price difference between the domestic market and the so-called "commercial export milk market". The relevance of price differences in establishing the existence of an export subsidy is noted particularly in Article 9.1(b) of the *Agreement on Agriculture*. The presence of a price difference becomes, in a sense, a "warning factor" of the existence of an export subsidy.

4.67 The **United States** referred to the Appellate Body which stated in the *United States - FSC* case that the obligations under Article 10.1 come into play when three factors are present: (i) there is a subsidy not identified in Article 9.1 of the *Agreement*, (ii) that subsidy is contingent on export, and (iii) the subsidy results in, or threatens to lead to, circumvention of a Member's export subsidy commitments. The Appellate Body has drawn upon the definition of a "subsidy" in the *SCM Agreement* as context for construing that same term for purposes of the *Agreement on Agriculture*. A subsidy arises where the grantor makes a "financial contribution" which confers a "benefit" on the recipient as compared with what would have been otherwise available to the recipient in the marketplace.[60]

4.68 Here, the United States continued, exporters obtain milk on a discounted basis, at a lower price than would otherwise be available to them in their domestic market, which is, practically speaking, the only market for milk in Canada. The exporters thus receive a benefit comprised of the cost savings resulting from the availability of lower priced milk. Second, it is undisputed that the availability of discounted milk is dependent on use of the milk in the manufacture of dairy exports. Thus, it is a subsidy contingent on export. Third, the subsidy results in, or threatens to lead to, the circumvention of Canada's reduction commitments. Because there is no constraint on the availability of the export subsidy created by

60 *United States - FSC*, Appellate Body report, para. 135-154.

the new export schemes, those export subsidies are unlimited in scope as are the exports they foster.

4.69 **Canada** noted that the *Agreement on Agriculture* does not define the term "subsidy". However, as the Appellate Body has indicated in the *United States - FSC* report,[61] the definition of "subsidy" in Article 1.1 of the *SCM Agreement* provides important contextual guidance in defining the scope of an "export subsidy" under Article 1(e) of the *Agreement on Agriculture*.[62] Both the United States and New Zealand implicitly recognize this in their submissions.[63] In assessing whether Canadian measures fall under Article 10.1 (*i.e.*, whether there is a transfer of economic resources and whether that transfer involves a benefit to the recipient[64]), reference is therefore made to the definition of a "subsidy" under the *SCM Agreement*. As such, the definition of "subsidy" under the *SCM Agreement* consists of two discrete elements: (i) a financial contribution by a government ; and (ii) conferral of a benefit thereby. [65] The nature of the government action, Canada continued, is determinative as to whether a "financial contribution" exists under Article 1.1(a)(1). If a government has not acted in a manner enumerated in Article 1.1(a)(1), then a "financial contribution" does not exist and there can be no "subsidy". As stated before, Canada's measures adopted to implement the recommendations and rulings of the DSB do not provide "subsidies" within the meaning of Article 1.1(a)(1)(iii) or (iv). Furthermore, since there is no subsidy and no export subsidy involved in commercial export milk transactions, there can be no circumvention of Canada's export subsidy commitment within the meaning of Article 10.1 of the *Agreement on Agriculture*.

4.70 **New Zealand** noted that to "circumvent" means to "find a way round" or "evade". A Member finds a way around or evades its obligations if it transfers by another means the very economic resources that it would be prohibited from providing in another form under Article 3.3 and Article 9.1 of the *Agreement on Agriculture*. In the view of New Zealand, Canada has done precisely this. Through the combined exercise of federal and provincial authority, mechanisms have been established to provide processors for export with lower-priced milk. Equally, where a Member has taken measures that will enable the export of subsidised products in excess of reduction commitments, those measures threaten to lead to circumvention, even though no quantities in excess of reduction commitments may have yet been exported. New Zealand further noted that Article 10.1 also provides that non-commercial transactions shall not be used to circumvent export subsidy commitments. A non-commercial transaction is one in which private profit-maximising individuals would not, from choice, engage. In the present

61 *United States - FSC,* Appellate Body report, para. 136.

62 *Ibid.*

63 Submission by New Zealand, para. 7.28 and Submission of the United States, para. 96.

64 *United States - FSC,* Appellate Body report, *supra* note 107, para. 137.

65 *Canada -Aircraft,* panel report, para. 156. See also *Brazil - Aircraft,* Appellate Body report, DSR 1999:III, 1161, para. 157.

case, the market in which these transactions take place is completely constructed. Producers of non-quota milk are compelled to sell to processors for export. Such are thus "non-commercial transactions" within the meaning of Article 10.1[66].

4.71 New Zealand considered that Canada has failed to meet the burden of showing that no export subsidies within the meaning of Article 10.1 have been provided and thus Canada is circumventing its export subsidy commitments. Referring to Canada's argument that as a result of the Import for Re-Export Program access to imported milk is unrestricted and depends on commercial considerations only, New Zealand contended that Canada does not answer the concerns expressed by the Panel, such as the fact that permits under the programme are discretionary and that volumes imported suggest that terms of access are less favourable.

4.72 **New Zealand** and the **United States** were of the view that the export subsidy provided by Canada's replacement schemes falls within the definition of export subsidy contained in paragraph (d) of the Illustrative List of Export Subsidies in Annex I to the *SCM Agreement*. The *SCM Agreement*, the complainants submitted, is relevant to determining the meaning of "export subsidy" in Article 10.1. Specific guidance can be obtained from paragraph (d) of the Illustrative List of Export Subsidies in Annex I of the *SCM Agreement*. The new Canadian dairy exporting schemes fulfil all of the elements of paragraph (d): first, dairy processors continue to have access to milk through the electronic export contract bulletin boards which is priced on more favourable terms than would otherwise be available to such processors for milk in the domestic market; second there has been the provision of a product "for use in the production of exported goods, on terms more favourable than for provision of like or directly competitive products ... for use in the production of goods for domestic consumption" as the price for export milk is much lower than that for milk to be sold for domestic uses; third, the lower-priced milk has been provided "by governments or their agencies directly or indirectly through government-mandated schemes" as it is made available to processors for export as a result of the prohibition, imposed and enforced by government, on the selling of non-quota milk into the domestic market; and fourth, the terms and conditions on which milk is made available for processors for export are more favourable than those available to them on world markets. Therefore, New Zealand and the United States continued, the Canadian schemes provide "subsidies" within the meaning of Article 1 of the *SCM Agreement*, and hence are "export subsidies" within the meaning of Article 10.1 of the *Agreement on Agriculture* as they are subsidies "contingent upon export performance".

4.73 **Canada** reiterated that since governments do not affirmatively instruct or direct producers to provide commercial export milk to processors, no "subsidy" exists such as under Article 1.1(a)(1)(iv) of the *SCM Agreement*. Nor are gov-

[66] Submission by New Zealand, paras. 7.43 to 7.47.

ernments providing a "subsidy" in a manner such as that described under Article 1.1(a)(iii) of the *SCM Agreement*, which contemplates a direct provision of goods by government. Applying the facts to the text of the *SCM Agreement* itself, there is no export subsidy provided to processors in commercial export transactions. In particular, there is no export subsidy within the meaning of paragraph (d) of the Illustrative List of Export Subsidies in Annex I of the *SCM Agreement*, contrary to the complainants' arguments under that Agreement.

4.74 Canada noted that three conditions must be met in order for a measure to constitute an export subsidy under paragraph (d) of the Illustrative List. The first of these conditions (i.e. that governments must provide goods either directly or indirectly through government mandated schemes) is clearly not met. Since every export subsidy in the Illustrative List is by definition an Article 1.1 "subsidy" that is contingent on export performance, the words "indirectly through a government mandated scheme" must have a meaning consistent with Article 1.1(a)(1)(iv). To hold otherwise would render the words "i.e. where" in paragraph 1.1(a)(1) completely meaningless and would amount to grafting a new type of "financial contribution" onto the definition of "subsidy" in the *SCM Agreement*. Accordingly, for the same reason discussed previously regarding governmental action under Article 9.1(c) of the *Agreement on Agriculture*, governments do not provide milk to processors, either directly or indirectly through a government mandated scheme.

4.75 Given that the first requirement in paragraph (d) is not met, Canada continued, the other two conditions under paragraph (d) are irrelevant. In any event, processors can and do source milk for use in the manufacture of exported dairy products under the Import for Re-Export Program. IREP serves as a competitive alternative source to commercial export milk. At the time the original panel report was issued, there were no guidelines in respect of the Import for Re-Export Program to structure the discretionary authority associated with the Program. Canada has recently issued a set of guidelines.[67] Although, technically, the issuance of IREP permits is still discretionary, what is important is how that discretion is actually exercised. In practice, IREP requests that meet the guidelines are granted automatically. Indeed, every single one of the over 500 requests since 1 August 2000 to import milk or milk products for re-export has been granted. Moreover, once an IREP request is approved, import permits for individual transactions are electronically issued online. IREP users are free to import any quantity of milk or milk products they wish and to decide the export use to which the imported product will be put. Thus, in reality, access by Canadian processors through IREP to milk and milk products is unrestricted and depends on commercial considerations only.

[67] See Notice to Importers, Export and Import Permits Act, Serial no 616, 17 April 2001 (Exhibit CDA-33).

4.76 In addition, Canada noted, it has been repeatedly held by the Appellate Body that, absent evidence that discretionary legislation is being applied in a manner contrary to WTO obligations, there can be no presumption of inconsistency: "Only legislation that mandates a violation of GATT obligations can be found, as such, to be inconsistent with those obligations."[68]

4.77 In answer to a question by the Panel, Canada indicated that the average weighted price for fluid milk during the period August 2000-February 2001 was $0.44 per kilogram. However, Canada considered that this average price is significantly inflated by imports under the programme of pasteurised milk for ships' stores use. Canada noted that imported raw milk is bought at prices reflective of US market conditions for such milk. As concerns the average price of imported whole milk powder during this period, on a per hectolitre equivalent basis, it was $20.46.[69] Canada was of the view that whole milk powder is competitive with raw milk in industrial processing. The differences between the two products relate mainly to issues of transportation and storage. Indeed, in many cases the rehydration of whole milk powder for a number of end uses is more cost effective than paying the transportation and storage costs associated with the use of raw milk. Imports of whole milk powder have almost tripled since the previous Panel proceedings and now account for approximately half of total imports under the programme.

4.78 In **New Zealand's** opinion, Canada's response to the question by the Panel concerning the IREP does not change the essential nature of the IREP scheme. The programme remains discretionary in nature and the "guidelines" appear to be nothing more than a listing of the substantial number of requirements that need to be met. In addition, it appears from information provided by Canada [70]that the "within access commitment" tariff continues to apply to IREP as it did in earlier years. A tariff is itself a form of restriction and thus, in New Zealand's view, imports under the IREP do not depend only on commercial considerations. Moreover, a "permit fee" is also applicable for each permit under the scheme, fees which are not applied to commercial transactions.

4.79 Referring to Canada's answer to a question by the Panel with respect to the IREP (see paragraph 4.75 above), the **United States** contended that it is irrelevant whether or not all requests for permits have actually been granted, for the purposes of the issues before this Panel. The question with regard to IREP is whether fluid milk is available on terms that are as favourable as those available for commercial export milk. The United States was of the view that the terms are not as favourable since a permit which is subject to the government's discretion must be obtained. This is not changed by the new guidelines. These do not

---

[68] *United States - Act of 1916* Appellate Body report, DSR 2000:X, 4793, para. 60.

[69] @ 11 kg. per hectolitre.

[70] Notice to Importers, Export and Import Permits Act, Serial no 616, 17 April 2001 (Exhibit CDA-33).

change or circumscribe the Minister's discretion. Indeed, in paragraph 4.3 of the guidelines, it states simply that "the Minister *may* issue to any resident of Canada applying therefore a permit ..."[71] In other words, although the government has granted the last 500 requests, it is within the Minister's discretion to deny the next 500 requests. As concerns Canada's answer to another question by the Panel (see paragraph 4.77 above), the United States responded that the price of imported fluid milk under the IREP is too high to be as favourable as milk obtained trough domestic sources for export contracts. Secondly, in the opinion of the United States the price of whole milk powder and that of fluid milk are not equally favourable since the whole milk powder price is almost double that of fluid milk according to US calculations when certain corrections have been applied to Canada's calculations. Third, even if whole milk powder were available at the same price as fluid milk, it would still be available on less favourable terms since it would need to be re-hydrated for most end-uses, implying additional time and expense in spite of technological advances.

4.80 **Canada** indicated that every one of the over 500 requests had been granted since 1 August 2000. Thus, the mere presence of discretion does not, in reality, render the choice between domestic and imported products "restricted" or "not dependant only on commercial considerations". Canada also submitted that the United States incorrectly revised Canada's calculation of the milk-equivalent average price of whole milk powder imported under the IREP. Using appropriate conversion factors, milk-equivalent prices remain within the range of commercial export milk prices even if one were to use the average value of imported whole milk powder cited by the United States.

4.81 The **United States** submitted that Canada's argument with respect to Article 10.1 is without legal support and should be rejected by the Panel. Canada's argument that there must be a "direct connection" is not supported by the language of Article 10.1 of the Agriculture Agreement or paragraph (d) of the Illustrative List of Export Subsidies contained in Annex 1 to the *SCM Agreement*. The United States reiterated that the original panel concluded that it was more appropriate to consider paragraph (d) of the Illustrative List than the general concepts of Article 1 of the *SCM Agreement* when analysing the context of Article 10.1 of the *Agreement on Agriculture*. The new provincial export programmes satisfy each of the elements of paragraph (d). Accordingly, the new export programmes constitute export subsidies for purposes of the *SCM Agreement*. Because the *SCM* Agreement is part of the context of the *Agreement on Agriculture*, the fact that the provincial programmes constitute a subsidy under the Illustrative List supports a finding that the programmes are export subsidies under Article 10.1 of the *Agreement on Agriculture*. Additionally, Canada does not dispute that there are no restraints on the availability of the export subsidies under the new

[71] Notice to Importers, Export and Import Permits Act, Serial no 616, 17 April 2001 (Exhibit CDA-33).

export programmes. Consequently, the export programmes have already resulted in or threaten to lead to the circumvention of Canada's reduction commitment within the meaning of Article 10.1.

5. *Articles 3.3 and 8 of the Agreement on Agriculture*

4.82 **New Zealand** submitted that, any export of dairy products by Canada under Special Milk Class 5(d) and the new schemes in excess of its reduction commitment levels constitutes a violation of Canada's obligations under Article 3.3 and Article 8 of the *Agreement on Agriculture.*

4.83 A review of available export data, the **United States** submitted, shows that, when the volume of exports made pursuant to Special Milk Class 5(d) is combined with exports made under the provincial marketing schemes, the total aggregate volume of exports of cheese already exceed Canada's reduction commitments and exports of other milk products are barely below the quantity of subsidised exports that may be permitted consistent with Canada's reduction commitments. Consequently, because the new provincial export schemes constitute export subsidies, Canada's exports of cheese and other dairy products breach its obligations under Articles 3.3, 8 and 9 of the *Agreement on Agriculture.*

4.84 **Canada** contended that since it has not exported in excess of its reduction commitment levels, there was no violation of Articles 3.3 and 8 of the *Agreement on Agriculture.*

6. *Articles 1 and 3 of the SCM Agreement*

4.85 The **United States** submitted that, in addition to constituting violations of Articles 9.1(c), or in the alternative, Article 10 of the *Agreement on Agriculture,* Canada's measures affecting the exportation of dairy products constitute prohibited export subsidies pursuant to Articles 1.1 and 3.1 of the *SCM Agreement.* These measures -i.e. Canada's new provincial export subsidy programmes as well as the maintenance of Special Class 5(d) - provide discounted milk to milk dealers on the condition that the milk is exported to foreign markets. They do so by allowing exporters to purchase milk at prices that are below prevailing market-levels as compared to milk used in dairy products sold in Canada's domestic market. Access to this low-priced product is contingent on the product being exported, because should a milk dealer divert the low-priced milk or products made from it to the domestic market, the milk dealer must pay a severe penalty. The result is that milk sold for export is often half the price of milk sold on the domestic market. Therefore, Canada's measures constitute subsidies contingent upon export performance in violation of Article 3.1(a) of the *SCM Agreement.*

4.86 In demonstrating a violation of Article 3 of the *SCM Agreement,* the United States submitted that it relied upon paragraph (d) of the Illustrative List of Export Subsidies in Annex 1 to the SCM Agreement. Canada criticised this approach as inappropriately abbreviated. However, Canada adopted and indeed championed the same approach in another subsidies case. In *Brazil - Aircraft*, Canada argued that a measure that satisfies the requirements of the Illustrative List is *ispo facto* an export subsidy and therefore prohibited.[72] Just as in *Brazil - Aircraft*, the Panel in this dispute is confronted with a *per se* violation of Article 3 of the *SCM Agreement*.

4.87 The United States therefore claimed that Canada's measures constitute subsidies contingent upon export performance in violation of Article 3.1(a) of the *SCM Agreement*, and the appropriate remedy shall be withdrawal of the subsidy without delay pursuant to Article 4.7 of the *SCM Agreement*.

4.88 **Canada** responded that since there is no "subsidy" conferred to processors within the meaning of Article 1.1(a)(1)(iii) or (iv), there can be no "prohibited export subsidy" under Article 3 of the *SCM Agreement*. The arguments of the United States under this provision should, therefore, also be rejected.

V. THIRD PARTIES ARGUMENTS

A. *Australia*

1. *General*

5.1 Australia considered that creating a separate regime for milk used in the export of dairy products ensures that processors/exporters have access to inexpensive milk. Whether labelled as special milk class 5(e) or excluded from quota milk for domestic consumption, the effect is the same. The replacement measures continue to provide milk at a price below an adequate level of remuneration, are contingent on the export of the manufactured product, and therefore would constitute an export subsidy under both the *Agreement on Agriculture* and the *SCM Agreement*. Milk for export is excluded from the domestic market; the only way that producers can sell above-quota or non-quota milk is if it is exported. And the only way that processors can receive lower price discounted milk is if it is for export. Without the prohibition on selling milk for export in the domestic market, processors for export would not have access to milk at discounted prices.

5.2 The fact that milk is "pre-committed" and "first-out-of-the-tank"[73] ensures that processors receive discounted milk. This does not alter the fact that a producer would not produce commercially for export (that is non-quota milk) where the returns are so low compared to milk for domestic consumption while the domestic milk supply management system is maintained and a producer can secure high prices for milk for domestic consumption. In the view of Australia, export milk is surplus to Canada's domestic supply management needs.

---

[72] *Brazil - Aircraft*, panel report, DSR 1999:III, 1221, para. 4.48.

[73] Documents describing provincial dairy export mechanisms, dated 22 September from Canada's Department of Foreign Affairs and International Trade.

2. *Article 9.1 (c) of the Agreement on Agriculture*

5.3 Australia noted that there are two requirements under Article 9.1(c): (i) "payments on the export of an agricultural product"; and (ii) the payments must be "financed by virtue of governmental action".

(i) "payments"

5.4 Australia referred to the Appellate Body report which upheld the original panel's finding in relation to the meaning and definition of "payment" in the context of Article 9.1 (c).[74] The Appellate Body found that the word "payments" "denotes a transfer of economic resources"; further, "a 'payment' could be made in a form, other than money, that confers value, such as by way of goods or services."[75] The provision of milk at discounted prices to processors for export constitutes "payments" in a form other than money within the meaning of Article 9.1(c) of the *Agreement on Agriculture*. As the milk is supplied at below market rates, "'payments' are, in effect, made to the recipient of the portion of the price that is not charged".[76]

5.5 Just as under the Special Milk Classes system, Australia continued, the replacement measures provide a benefit to processors/exporters since the processors/exporters receive milk at a price that enables them to export the processed product concerned. Despite export milk being "excluded" from the domestic market, it is only non-quota milk that is available to processors for export. Milk for export cannot be redirected to the domestic market.

5.6 Processors receive milk for export at below the price for milk destined for domestic consumption. The very fact, Australia argued, that Canada has deemed by legislation that there are "separate" markets provides a benefit or advantage to processors not otherwise available in the (domestic) marketplace.[77] Milk for export could not be obtainable at such a low price to processors without the existence of domestic price support. The Canadian supply management system/regulatory scheme is underpinned and implemented by Federal and provincial legislation and regulations and milk marketing boards.

(ii) "financed by virtue of governmental action"

5.7 Australia noted that in examining the second element of Article 9.1(c), namely whether payments are "financed by virtue of governmental action", the Appellate Body observed that "it is appropriate to look to the "governmental" involvement as a whole and not just to the role of the provincial milk marketing

---

74 *Canada - Dairy*, Appellate Body report, DSR 1999:V, 2057, paras. 107, 112-113.

75 *Ibid.*, para. 107.

76 *Ibid.*, para. 113.

77 Submission by Canada, paras. 83 ff.

boards"[78]. The Appellate Body further noted that "the price paid for the milk by the *processors* is not, in any way, dependent on whether milk is part of in-quota or over-quota production".[79]

5.8 The domestic milk supply management system is managed, monitored and supervised by agencies of the Canadian federal or provincial governments, Australia continued. The volume and pricing of milk is still determined by these agencies. Regulatory schemes are enacted at both the federal and provincial levels. The provincial governments and the CDC still control the "separate" domestic and export markets. They determine the size of the quota for the domestic market. Export milk is still licensed by provincial milk marketing boards[80] and producer levies are still required to be paid regardless of the destination of the milk.[81] All the control in relation to the pooling, pricing, volume of milk etc continues to be regulated through the CDC and the provincial milk marketing boards. Australia considers that the replacement measures which create a 'separate' export milk regime continue to provide "payments" within the meaning of Article 9.1(c) of the *Agreement on Agriculture* by virtue of governmental action.

5.9 In summary, Australia considered that the replacement measures continue to provide "payments" on the export of dairy products within the meaning of Article 9.1(c) of the *Agreement on Agriculture* by virtue of governmental action. Accordingly, Canada should bring its replacement measures for dairy products into conformity with its WTO obligations.

3. *Article 3 and 8 of the Agreement on Agriculture*

5.10 Since the replacement measures are export subsidies within the meaning of Article 9.1(c) of the *Agreement on Agriculture* and to the extent that Canada's dairy exports exceed Canada's annual quantity commitments, Australia considered that Canada is in breach of Article 3.3 of the *Agreement on Agriculture* not to provide export subsidies in excess of its budgetary outlay and quantity commitments levels specified in Section II of Part IV of its Schedule and in breach of Article 8 of the *Agreement on Agriculture* not to provide export subsidies otherwise than in conformity with the Agreement and with the commitments specified in its schedule.

4. *Article 10.1 of the Agreement on Agriculture*

5.11 In the alternative, Australia argued, if the replacement measures are not found to be a 9.1(c) export subsidy under the *Agreement on Agriculture*, the measures would still amount to an export subsidy, as defined under Article 1(e)

[78] *Canada - Dairy*, Appellate Body report, *supra*, footnote 74, para. 119.
[79] *Ibid.*, para. 121.
[80] Dairy Farmers of Ontario Milk General Regulation 09/00, Section 5.
[81] *Ibid.*, Section 7.

of the *Agreement on Agriculture,* [82] as captured by Article 10.1 of the *Agreement on Agriculture.* The object and purpose of that Article is to prevent the circumvention of export subsidy commitments. As there is no limitation or restraint on Canada's export subsidies on dairy products, Canada's replacement measures threaten to lead to circumvention of its export subsidy commitments. This is reinforced by Article 10.3 which places the onus on an exporting Member to demonstrate that any exports in excess of its scheduled commitments are not subject to export subsidies. As noted above, in Australia's view, the replacement measures provide an export subsidy and so the onus is on Canada to demonstrate that it is not in breach of its export subsidy commitments.

5. *Article 3 of the SCM Agreement*

5.12 Australia argued that the replacement measures in question fall under Article 3.1(a) of the *SCM Agreement.* Since Canada is in breach of its export subsidy commitments under the *Agreement on Agriculture*, it does not receive cover through Article 13(c) of the *Agreement on Agriculture*, and so is in breach of Article 3 of the SCM. In the alternative, if the Panel finds that the replacement measures are not an export subsidy within the meaning of the *Agreement on Agriculture* but are an export subsidy under Article 3.1(a) of the SCM, then again Canada would receive no cover from Article 13(c) of the *Agreement on Agriculture*, and so would be in breach of Article 3 of the *SCM Agreement.*

5.13 Australia noted that Canada claims that export milk is not "surplus" to domestic requirements but is pre-planned and pre-committed production. However, Canada does not address the fact that the ability of a producer to acquire additional quota (essentially through trading of quota) is determined by a system of legislation and regulations which set the quota volumes. The fact that the quota volumes are being adjusted more frequently by government suggests greater manipulation of product available for the export market.

5.14 As concerns the benchmark price advocated by Canada, Australia considered that the point of comparison is the domestic or regulated market. This is the basis on which it is determined whether milk is supplied at or below market rates. By virtue of Canada's supply management system and consequent high domestic prices, the price of milk to processors is below market rates and therefore constitutes a payment. Further, through regulatory control of a "separate" export market, Canada has assured processors that they will not have to pay the domestic price by "preventing" export milk being diverted into the domestic market.

---

82 ""[E]xport subsidies" refers to subsidies contingent upon export performance, including the export subsidies listed in Article 9 of this Agreement."

B. *European Communities*

1. *Article 9.1 (c) of the Agreement on Agriculture*

(i) "financed by virtue of governmental action"

5.15 The **EC** was of the view that the complainants' citation to the test developed by the Appellate Body for "by virtue of governmental action" is incomplete and therefore misleading. The United States and New Zealand only purport to show that governmental action is "indispensable to the occurrence of the payment".[83] However, the Appellate Body differentiates in a more nuanced manner whether governmental action "is not simply involved", but whether it is "in fact, indispensable" for "the transfer of resources, to take place".[84]

5.16 Referring to the complainants' arguments concerning the segregation of the market for contracted export milk from the domestic market[85], the EC submitted that these arguments imply that all kinds of purely regulatory government measures could amount to export subsidies within the meaning of Article 9.1(c) of the *Agreement on Agriculture* simply because, by affecting market conditions, they necessarily have an impact on the conduct of certain economic operators and "may" have incidentally a trade distorting effect.

5.17 The EC noted that Article 9.1(c) departs from the general notion of subsidy laid down in Article 1.1 of the *SCM Agreement* by not requiring that a payment must involve a charge on the public account. This wording does not prevent producer-financed payments on the export of an agricultural product to qualify as export subsidy. However, the condition is that such payments must be "financed by virtue of governmental action". The key question, therefore, is to determine the extent of governmental involvement in the transfer of economic resources between agricultural producers and export processors.

5.18 The EC, referring to Canada's arguments that there must be a direct connection between governmental action and payments and relying on the dictionary meaning of the term "by virtue of", submitted that that expression, when compared to the notion of "government-*mandated*" schemes in item (d) of the Illustrative List of export subsidies annexed to the *SCM Agreement*, does not establish a particular degree of government involvement. The EC considered rather that the term "financed" provides important guidance in that respect. To finance

---

[83] First Written Submission of New Zealand, para. 7.11; First Written Submission of the United States, para. 82.

[84] *Canada -Dairy,* Appellate Body report, *supra,* footnote 74, para. 120.

[85] First Written Submission of the United States, paras. 79, 83, 86 and 90; Second Written Submission of the United States, paras. 9, 16 and 55; First Written Submission of New Zealand, paras. 7.12-7.16; Second Written Submission of New Zealand, paras. 1.03, 2.10, 3.01 and 4.13. See also Third Party Submission of Australia, para. 3 as well as the panel report in *Canada - Dairy,* as modified by the Appellate Body report, para. 7.62.

means, to "engage in or manage financial operations".[86] Moreover, the term "financed" implies that money is being paid, i.e., a financial contribution is being made. The immediate context of the expression "financed by virtue of governmental action" is also relevant to its interpretation. Article 9.1(c) illustrates its scope by laying down an example, i.e., "payments that are *financed* from the proceeds of a levy *imposed* on the agricultural product concerned". This suggests that the transfer of economic resources under Article 9.1(c) must (i) be imposed by the government, and (ii) involve a kind of zero sum situation, where the exporters win what the producers lose.

5.19 In the opinion of the EC, neither the example of a protective duty, as cited by the panel in its original report, nor a double-pricing system as such can fulfil the conditions set by Article 9.1(c), if producers can still freely determine whether to sell over-quota products at cost plus margin or not to produce them at all. Under such conditions, the decision of farmers is only an incidental effect of a general regulatory measure which may have trade distortive effects, but still does not fulfil all conditions to be a WTO incompatible export subsidy.

5.20 Such a strict reading of "financed by virtue of governmental action" is further buttressed by the purpose of Article 9.1 of the *Agreement on Agriculture* which, in the view of the EC, was intended to provide a "careful, specific list of the principal categories of export subsidies that were known to be provided to the agricultural sector at the time the *Agreement on Agriculture* was drafted."[87]

5.21 The EC therefore submitted that the major argument of the complainants regarding the exclusion of contracted export milk from the domestic market is not, in itself, sufficient to establish that payments were "financed by virtue of governmental action".

2. *Article 10.1 of the Agreement on Agriculture*

5.22 The EC took issue with the broad interpretation of the concept of "export subsidies not listed in paragraph 1 of Article 9", advocated by the complainants. In particular, New Zealand argues that "all measures that do not technically meet the strict letter of Article 9.1, but have the same economic effect", must fall within Article 10.1.[88] The United States asserts that any argument whereby the standard for finding a subsidy under Article 10 is the same as under Article 1 of the *SCM Agreement* is without legal support.[89]

86 Shorter Oxford Dictionary, Volume I, at 950.

87 Appellant's Submission of the United States in *United States - FSC*, paras. 321-322, agreed to by the EC in its Appellee's submission, para. 258.

88 First Written Submission of New Zealand, para. 7.27. See also, Second Written Submission of New Zealand, para. 4.22.

89 Second Written Submission of the United States, paras. 51, 52.

5.23 Referring to the text of Article 1(e) of *Agreement on Agriculture,* the EC submitted that it leaves open the question of whether the definition of subsidy under the *Agreement on Agriculture* is the same as under the *SCM Agreement.* The Appellate Body has not yet clarified the precise notion of export subsidy applicable under Article 10.1 of *the Agreement on Agriculture*. In *United States - FSCs*, the Appellate Body developed a general definition of subsidy whereby "a 'subsidy' involves a transfer of economic resources from the grantor to the recipient for less than full consideration", but drew heavily on the general context of the *SCM Agreement.*[90] The Appellate Body also saw no reason to read the requirement of "contingent upon export performance" in the *Agreement on Agriculture* differently from the same requirement imposed by the *SCM Agreement*, because "the two agreements use precisely the same words to define export subsidies".[91]

5.24 Although not attempting to develop a comprehensive analytical framework of the precise relationship between the notion of export subsidy under Article 1(e) of the *Agreement on Agriculture* and Article 1.1 of the *SCM Agreement,* the EC put forward the following: the term "subsidy" is the same under both agreements, as is the expression "contingent upon export performance". Secondly, several provisions directly bear on the relationship between the concept of export subsidy under Article 1(e) and 10.1 of the *Agreement on Agriculture* and that under the *SCM Agreement.* Thus, Article 21 of the *Agreement on Agriculture* provides that "the provisions of the GATT 1994 and of other multilateral trade agreements shall apply subject to the provisions of this Agreement". Article 3.1 of the *SCM Agreement*, in turn, prohibits export subsidies "except as provided in the Agreement on Agriculture". This suggests a co-extensive application of the notion of subsidy, unless the *Agreement on Agriculture* explicitly provides otherwise, as, e.g., through the specific list of export subsidies in Article 9.1.

5.25 Another argument, the EC continued, can be gleaned from Article 13 of the *Agreement on Agriculture*, entitled "due restraint", which foresees that export subsidies which conform fully to the provisions of Part V of this Agreement shall be "subject to countervailing duties only upon determination of injury or threat thereof based on volume, effect on prices, or consequent impact in accordance with Article VI of the GATT 1994 and Part V of the Subsidies Agreement". This reference implies that a Member wishing to impose countervailing duties could determine the existence of a subsidy on the basis of Article 9.1 of the *Agreement on Agriculture* in addition to Articles 1-3 of the *SCM Agreement* and therefore requires a co-extensive application of the basic concept of subsidy. The EC did not see any provision in the *Agreement on Agriculture* that mandates the use of different concepts of subsidies. The chapeau of Article 1.1 of the *SCM Agreement,* which states that "[f]or the purpose of this Agreement, a subsidy shall be

[90] *United States - FSC,* Appellate Body report, DSR 2000:III, 1619, para. 136.
[91] *Ibid.*, para. 141.

deemed to exist" does not exclude that other agreements refer back to this basic definition of subsidy which is the only one agreed on by the Members. Like the expression "contingent upon export performance", the term "subsidy" is the same under both agreements.

5.26 In conclusion, the EC failed to understand how one of those concepts can be subject to a diverging interpretation depending on whether it arises in the context of the *SCM Agreement* or the *Agreement on Agriculture*, while the other is consistently interpreted. Such an approach is certainly not justified on the basis of the language and context of Articles 1(e) and 10.1 of the *Agreement on Agriculture*. To the contrary, the EC considered that a pick and choose approach resulting in an oscillating notion of subsidy under the anti-circumvention provision does not provide security and predictability to trade in agricultural products.

VI. FINDINGS

A. *Agreement on Agriculture*

1. *Burden of Proof*

6.1 New Zealand and the United States argue that pursuant to Article 10.3 of the *Agreement on Agriculture*, Canada must establish that no export subsidy has been granted in respect of exports exceeding Canada's reduction commitments. Canada "recognises the presence of Article 10.3", but submits that "it is important to note that reports issued by panels and the Appellate Body under Article 21.5 of the DSU uniformly confirm that a Member's measure is presumed to comply with WTO obligations and, thus, any Member challenging that measure bears the burden of proof."

6.2 Article 10.3 of the *Agreement on Agriculture* provides,

> Any Member which claims that any quantity exported in excess of a reduction commitment level is not subsidized must establish that no export subsidy, whether listed in Article 9 or not, has been granted in respect of the quantity of exports in question.

6.3 The Panel considers that, when reduction commitments have been exceeded, Article 10.3 has the effect of reversing the usual burden of proof with regard to claims made under Articles 3.3, 9 and 10 of the *Agreement on Agriculture*.[92] Thus, in the case before the Panel, if dairy exports exceed Canada's reduction commitments, and Canada claims that any quantity of exports exceeding its commitment levels is not subsidized, then it is for Canada to present evidence which is sufficient in terms of Article 10.3 to establish a presumption that no ex-

---

[92] As acknowledged by Canada in the original panel proceedings. See report of the panel on *Canada - Dairy*, *supra* footnote 3, para. 7.33.

port subsidy has been granted in respect of the quantities exported in excess of its reduction commitment levels.

6.4 The Panel does not consider that the rules on the allocation of the burden of proof change simply because a claim is made in the context of Article 21.5 DSU proceedings. The Panel notes in that respect the following statement by the Appellate Body in its report in *Brazil - Aircraft (21.5)*:

> We recall that, before the original panel in *Brazil - Aircraft*, Brazil conceded that it had the burden of proof in demonstrating its alleged "defence" under item (k). However, in these Article 21.5 proceedings, Brazil argues that this burden of proof, under item (k), is on Canada. In our view, *the fact that the measure at issue was "taken to comply" with the "recommendations and rulings" of the DSB does not alter the allocation of the burden of proving* Brazil's "defence" under item (k). (emphasis added)

The Panel considers that this reasoning equally applies to the allocation of the burden of proof pursuant to Article 10.3 of the *Agreement on Agriculture*.

6.5 It is clear from the text of Article 10.3, however, that the burden of proof with regard to Articles 3.3, 9 and 10 is only reversed *if* reduction commitment levels have been exceeded. The exceeding of reduction commitment levels triggers the reversal of burden of proof pursuant to Article 10.3. The Panel must therefore turn to the question whether reduction commitment levels have indeed already been exceeded by Canadian dairy exports.[93]

6.6 The Panel notes in this respect that, according to Canada, total cheese exports from Canada between August 2000 and February 2001 amounted to 10,026 metric tons.[94] Canada's reduction commitment level for the marketing year 2000/2001 was set at 9,076 metric tons. The Panel thus finds that Canada's reduction commitment level for cheese has been exceeded. The Panel notes that Canada claims that a quantity of those excess exports is not being subsidized. The Panel, therefore, concludes that, with regard to the claims made under Articles 3.3, 9 and 10 of the *Agreement on Agriculture*, Canada has the burden of proof.

[93] The Panel considers that the ordinary rules on burden of proof apply to a claim that reduction commitment levels have been exceeded, and, accordingly, that it is in the first instance up to the complainants to establish a *prima facie* case that exports of the product are in excess of the commitment level relating to that product.

[94] Canada's reply to Question 22.

2. *Article 9.1(c)*

(a) Introduction

6.7 In deciding on the Article 9.1(c) claim, the Panel will address the following questions on the basis that a measure or arrangement which meets all of the substantive requirements of Article 9.1(c) constitutes an export subsidy for the purposes of the *Agreement on Agriculture*:

(a) Are there "payments"?

(b) If so, are such payments "financed by virtue of governmental action"?

(c) If so, are those payments made "on the export of an agricultural product"?

(b) "Payments"

6.8 New Zealand and the United States argue that the prices at which Canadian milk processors source commercial export milk ("CEM") are significantly below the prices at which Canadian milk processors source milk for the domestic market, and that Canadian milk producers are therefore foregoing revenue in the same manner that the Panel and the Appellate Body have found to constitute a payment. In their view, in determining whether a "payment" is made within Article 9.1(c), the Panel must assess what would have been otherwise available to processors/exporters in the marketplace.

6.9 Canada refers to paragraph 113 of the Appellate Body report in *Canada - Dairy*, the second sentence of which states that

> [i]f goods or services are supplied to an enterprise, or a group of enterprises, at reduced rates (that is at below market rates), "payments" are, in effect, made to the recipient of the portion of the price that is not charged.

According to Canada, the corollary of this proposition is that where the recipient of goods or services pays market rates or market value, there can be no "payment." Since the commercial export milk market has been deregulated, processors are paying "market value" for the milk. Therefore, in Canada's view, commercial export milk in Canada is being sold at, not below, market rates, and, in line with the aforementioned Appellate Body citation, there could be no "payment."

6.10 Before assessing the parties' arguments, the Panel notes that there appears to be no disagreement between the parties as to whether the prices paid for domestic market milk and those paid for what is described as commercial export milk show a clear differential. On the one hand, New Zealand provides data indicating that current commercial export milk prices per hectolitre are within the range of C$25.03 to C$35.09. The United States provides an average value of C$31.53 per hectolitre for Ontario and C$29 per hectolitre for Quebec. Canada states that prices range from C$19.06 to C$36.86 per hectolitre of commercial export milk. According to New Zealand and the United States, domestic market milk, on the other hand, sells for anywhere between C$49.48 and C$56.06 per hectolitre (New Zealand), or, at an average, for C$52.92 per hectolitre (the United Stataes). Canada has not disputed the latter figures.

6.11 The parties, however, clearly differ over what the Appellate Body meant by the supply of goods "at below market rates". According to New Zealand and the United States, the market rate is the higher price of milk in the regulated domestic market. According to Canada, the lower CEM price resulting from "arm's length transactions in a private commercial context"[95] is the market rate. Consequently, in order to decide whether a "payment", within the meaning of Article 9.1(c), is made to processors for export through the provision of commercial export milk at lower prices than domestic milk, the Panel needs to determine against what *benchmark* the commercial export milk prices have to be compared.

6.12 The Panel first recalls that the ordinary meaning of "payment" has already been examined by both the Panel and the Appellate Body in the original proceedings. The Appellate Body considered that the word "payments" in Article 9.1(c) denotes a transfer of economic resources,[96] and agreed with the panel that the ordinary meaning of the word "payments" in Article 9.1(c) encompasses "payments" made in forms other than money, including revenue foregone.[97] The Appellate Body concluded that,

> In our view, the provision of milk at discounted prices to processors for export under Special Classes 5(d) and 5(e) constitutes "payments", in a form other than money, within the meaning of Article 9.1(c). If goods or services are supplied to an enterprise, or a group of enterprises, at reduced rates (that is, at below market-rates), "payments" are, in effect, made to the recipient of the portion of the price that is not charged. Instead of receiving a monetary payment equal to the revenue foregone, the recipient is paid in the form of goods or services. But, as far as the recipient is concerned, the economic value of the transfer is precisely the same.[98]

6.13 The Panel notes that the ordinary meaning of "payments" in Article 9.1(c), as determined by the Appellate Body, does not provide *explicit* guidance as regards the benchmark which is to be applied when determining whether goods are being provided at "discounted", "reduced" or "below market" rates. It is clear that, *in casu*, the regulated export price was considered "discounted", "reduced" or "at below market rates" as compared with the regulated price of milk destined for the domestic market. Canada argues, however, that when the export price is

---

95 Canada's First Submission, para. 84.

96 Report of the Appellate Body on *Canada - Dairy*, *supra*, footnote 74, para. 107.

97 *Ibid.*, para. 112.

98 *Ibid.*, para. 113.

no longer regulated, the benchmark would change from the regulated domestic market price to the deregulated export market price. Canada bases this assertion, *inter alia*, on the Appellate Body's reference to "at below market rates", arguing that the "market rate" can only be the price resulting from "arm's length transactions in a private commercial context".

6.14 The Panel is not persuaded by Canada's argument. The Appellate Body did indeed equate "reduced rates" with "below market rates" in paragraph 113 of its report. However, it can not be inferred from that statement that the Appellate Body meant to exclude from the meaning of "market rates" prices which were not the result of "arm's length transactions in a private commercial context" but, rather, the result of a certain degree of governmental intervention. On the contrary, the opposite conclusion is borne out by the very facts of the case which provide the context of the Appellate Body's statement. In the original dispute the export milk price was considered "discounted" in reference to a price which was clearly not the result of "arm's length transactions in a private commercial context". The "market rate" in that case was a price regulated by the government. The Appellate Body statement itself cited by Canada clearly allows for the possibility that the "market rate" is a price regulated by the government, and not the result of "arm's length transactions in a private commercial context". The Appellate Body statement therefore does not prejudge the question before the Panel whether, for the purpose of Article 9.1(c), the appropriate benchmark is the domestic regulated price or, as claimed by Canada, the price resulting from "arm's length transactions in a private commercial context".

6.15 Canada asserts along the same lines that "[t]he fact that prices in the regulated market are higher than the prices in the commercial export market is irrelevant",[99] and explains in its oral statement the reasons underlying that assertion:

> To understand the Appellate Body's ruling [in *Canada - Dairy*], it is important to examine the market conditions that were prevailing in Canada at that time. The Panel determined that *there was only one market* for milk in Canada: a regulated market (other markets were considered not to be viable alternatives for sourcing milk for export in Canada).
>
> [...]
>
> As a result of Canada's implementation of the recommendations and rulings of the DSB, governments no longer set the prices for milk for export. *The domestic regulated market and the commercial export market now respond to different conditions of competition.*[100] (emphasis added)

99 Canada's Rebuttal Submission, para. 13.
100 Canada's Oral Statement, paras. 43-47.

Thus, according to Canada, there would now be two distinct milk markets, domestic and export, and, consequently, the domestic price benchmark to determine whether export prices are discounted can no longer be relevant. Canada notes that by deregulating the export milk market, it "has not created this market," but, rather, has "given producers and processors access to an existing market."[101]

6.16 The Panel is not convinced by Canada's argument. The Panel does not agree with the market definition which Canada proposes in order to determine whether a "payment" exists within the meaning of Article 9.1(c). Pursuant to Canada's argument, for the purposes of Article 9.1(c), a "transfer of economic resources" from the grantor to the recipient can not take place in a given market if there is a different degree of government intervention in that market, depending on whether a good is destined by the buyer for export or not. In this case, the Canadian government intervenes extensively with regard to dairy transactions when the milk is destined for the domestic market, and intervenes less extensively[102] with regard to dairy transactions when the milk is destined for export. The Panel notes, however, that the "commercial export market" is not any different from the domestic market in terms of sellers,[103] buyers[104] and the products[105] which they trade. The only difference between these "two" markets is Canada's degree of government intervention, depending on whether the buyer purchases milk for export or not. Thus, Canada makes a distinction between these domestic and export dairy markets on the sole basis of the degree of its own regulatory intervention in transactions between producers and processors. This distinction between markets, for the purposes of determining against what benchmark the existence of a "discount" needs to be assessed, solely according to the degree of regulatory intervention by government, is not warranted by either the text and context of Article 9.1(c), or the object and purpose of the *Agreement on Agriculture*.

6.17 First, with regard to the text, as noted earlier, nothing in the wording of Article 9.1(c) suggests that the degree of government intervention, in function of the destination of the processed product, should affect the interpretation of "pay-

---

101 Canada's Oral Statement, para. 49.

102 See, for instance, paras. 6.46-6.47 below.

103 This conclusion is not affected by the fact that there are currently 74 producers in Canada who do not hold quota and produce milk exclusively for export. This group accounted for 0,08 per cent of total Canadian milk production between August 2000 and February 2001 (Canada's reply to Question 21), and constitutes less than 0,5 per cent of Canadian dairy producers (Canada's reply to Question 3).

104 The Panel understands that Canadian milk processors can engage in marketing activities both on the domestic and export markets.

105 Canada confirms that "[a]ll milk in a producer's bulk tank is collected. The quantity of commercial export milk is specified in the contract between the producer and the processor. Producers and processors identify commercial export milk deliveries through the commercial export milk contracts and processors' monthly plant utilization reports. As milk is fungible, commercial export milk is not stored or processed separately from other milk." (Canada's reply to Question 14)

ment". The question of government intervention is, of course, highly relevant under Article 9.1(c), but only in the analysis of the "financed by virtue of government action" requirement.

6.18 Second, as regards context, other paragraphs of Article 9.1 indicate that the proper comparison to be made in order to assess the existence of a "payment" is between the price charged for the domestic market and the price charged for export. According to Article 9.1(b), for instance, the sale for export by governments of agricultural goods *at a price lower than the comparable price charged for the like product to buyers in the domestic market* constitutes an export subsidy. Similarly, under Article 9.1(e), the provision by government of transport services for export shipments at *prices lower than the price charged for domestic shipments* is also an export subsidy. Nothing in the text of these paragraphs specifies to what extent the higher domestic price may result from government intervention. The only benchmark which is stipulated is the price for the domestic market, *independently of* the extent of government intervention in the formation of that price.

6.19 Third, Article 9.1(c), and the associated reference by the Appellate Body to the "market", should be read having regard to the object and purpose of the *Agreement on Agriculture*. The Panel considers that the Preamble of the *Agreement on Agriculture* provides useful guidance to identify the object and purpose of that Agreement. According to the Preamble, Members

> [...] decided to establish a basis for initiating a process of reform of trade in agriculture [...],

and recalled that

> their long-term objective [...] "is to establish a fair and market-oriented agricultural trading system and that a reform process should be initiated through the negotiation of commitments on support and protection and through the establishment of strengthened and more operationally effective GATT rules and disciplines",

and that

> [...] "the above-mentioned long-term objective is to provide for substantial progressive reductions in agricultural support and protection sustained over an agreed period, resulting in correcting and preventing restrictions in world agricultural markets.

6.20 This language makes clear that the working assumption in agricultural trade is not that of a market free of government intervention. The establishment of a fair and market-oriented agricultural trading system, through progressive reductions in agricultural support and protection, is the long-term objective, and the *Agreement on Agriculture* has established a "basis for initiating the process of reform" aimed at achieving that long-term objective. In the meantime, markets subject to a certain degree of government regulation would appear to be rather the rule in agricultural trade, and regulation-free markets the exception. Claiming that, under Article 9.1(c), the right benchmark to determine whether a "payment" exists is the extent to which government has decided to intervene in the market, depending on whether a good is destined by the buyer for export or not, ignores that fundamental economic reality, as reflected in the object and purpose of the *Agreement on Agriculture*.

6.21 Finally, even assuming, for the sake of argument, that the Panel would agree with Canada that the "reduced" or "market" price is the price of those transactions in which government intervention is absent, Canada's argument would be self-defeating. The fundamental reason for this is that the commercial export milk price itself is, in reality, not a mere product of "arm's length transactions in a private commercial context".[106] At least part of that context is clearly government-regulated. At this stage, the Panel does not need to look further than Canada's oral statement that it has "given producers and processors access to" another market. Thus, by its own admission, the Canadian government has *intervened* for producers and processors to "have access to" that market. Thus, the very existence of - or, as Canada puts it - "access to" that market is premised on some degree of government intervention. As a result, should the Panel consistently apply Canada's argument, the benchmark for the comparison with the export price would not be that same export price, but the price which a processor would pay to a milk producer *but for any intervention by the Canadian government relating to supply and price management in the dairy market*. If the Canadian government were not to maintain a quota-system on the domestic market, and, hence, if the Canadian producers were able to produce more for the domestic market than they can now, supply for the domestic market would increase. The resulting market equilibrium milk price is likely to be lower than current domestic market prices, but higher than current export prices. In conclusion, even under Canada's "deregulated market" analysis, there would still be a difference, albeit less extensive, between current export prices and the counterfactual benchmark which would result from a consistent application of its argument.

6.22 Canada alludes to the "concession" by New Zealand that the current commercial export milk prices reflect "world prices", apparently suggesting that when the "market price" would be taken to mean the "world price", there would still be no "payment".[107] The Panel disagrees with Canada in two respects. First, for the reasons set out above,[108] the Panel considers that the domestic market price constitutes the right benchmark for the purpose of determining the existence of a payment under Article 9.1(c). Second, even assuming, for the sake of argument, that the Panel were to accept that world prices constitute the right benchmark, Canada's argument would fail.

---

[106] Canada's Oral Statement, para. 49.

[107] Canada's Oral Statement, paras. 21 and 51.

[108] See paras. 6.12-6.21 above.

6.23 The Panel notes that the panel in the original proceedings addressed the same issue when determining the existence of a payment in kind under Article 9.1(a):

> We noted above that a benefit must be conferred for a payment in kind to exist in the sense of Article 9.1(a).[109] In this case, the question thus arises whether the provision of milk to processors/exporters under Classes 5(d) or (e) confers a benefit to these processors/exporters. This, in turn, raises the question of what the appropriate *benchmark* is for determining whether the provision of a good at a certain price confers a benefit.[110] Does it suffice, as the complainants argue, that milk for export use is provided to processors at a price below the *domestic milk price* for there to be a benefit conferred to these processors (hereafter referred to as "the first benchmark", namely the domestic milk price)? Or, does one need to establish that processors/exporters receive milk under Classes 5(d) and (e) at a price which is not only lower than the domestic milk price, but also lower than the price of milk these processors/exporters can obtain from any other source, in particular the price of milk they can source from the *world market* (hereafter referred to as "the second benchmark", namely the lowest milk price to be obtained from any other source)?[111] (emphasis added)

6.24 Without making a finding on the issue of the appropriate benchmark, the original panel proceeded, in the first instance, on the assumption that the second benchmark, although more favourable to Canada, was appropriate in the circumstances. In the panel's view, if the price of milk under Classes 5(d) and (e) was lower than the price at which processors/exporters could obtain milk from any other source, a bounty or benefit - i.e., something they would otherwise not have obtained - would, indeed, be conferred.[112] Canada had argued that milk imported under its Import for Re-Export Program ("IREP") would be available under equally favourable terms and conditions as those offered under Classes 5(d) and (e). The panel, however, concluded that the fact that the Minister had to issue a permit before such imports were allowed and that the Minister disposed of a wide discretion in doing so, was proof that these imports were not effectively available under equally favourable terms and conditions as those offered under Classes 5(d) and (e).[113]

6.25 This Panel notes that nothing has basically changed under Canada's IREP as regards the terms and conditions on which milk can be imported for export

109 [footnote omitted]
110 [footnote omitted]
111 Report of the panel on *Canada - Dairy, supra*, footnote 3, para. 7.47.
112 *Ibid.*, para. 7.48.
113 *Ibid.*, para. 7.53.

processing in Canada. Data has been provided which indicates that during the period August 2000 to February 2001 imports of dairy products under the IREP increased. However, Canada has confirmed that the Minister still has to issue a permit before such imports are allowed. In the light of the evidence before it as a whole, it appears to the Panel that the Minister still disposes of wide and untrammelled discretion as regards the issue of import licences under the IREP.[114] In addition, processors who wish to import under the IREP still have to pay an administrative permit fee.[115] Therefore, *even if* (i) world prices were to constitute the right benchmark for the purpose of determining the existence of a "payment" under Article 9.1(c), and *even if* (ii) current commercial export milk prices were to reflect world prices, the fact that the Minister has to issue a permit before IREP imports are allowed, that the Minister disposes of a wide discretion in doing so, and that payment of an administrative fee is required, is proof that these imports are not effectively available under equally favourable terms and conditions as those offered for commercial export milk.[116]

6.26 The Panel notes that the parties have also presented arguments regarding the competitive relationship between fluid milk and whole milk powder imported under the IREP, and that they have submitted conflicting evidence regarding milk

---

[114] Canada's reply to Question 18. Although Canada asserts that licences are now granted automatically, the new Guidelines, dated 17 April 2001 and contained in Canada's Exhibit 33, merely confirm that

> "the Minister [...] *may* determine an import access quantity which *may* be allowed to enter at the low rate of duty and the Minister *may* allocate it to residents of Canada." (Section 4.2)(emphasis added),

and that

> "the Minister *may* issue to any resident of Canada applying therefor a permit to import goods included in an Import Control List, in such quantity and of such quality, by such persons, from such places or persons and *subject to such other terms and conditions as are described in the permit or in the regulations.*" (Section 4.3)(emphasis added)

Thus, the new Guidelines do not appear to restrict in any way the Minister's discretion, and even if the Minister were to be exercising that discretion in a certain way today, under the new Guidelines he would be free to exercise it differently tomorrow. Canada's assertion that "absent evidence that discretionary legislation is being applied in a manner contrary to WTO obligations, there can be no presumption of inconsistency" (Canada's reply to Question 18, para. 35) is in the Panel's view irrelevant. The Panel is not assessing the WTO consistency of the IREP, but is simply determining whether or not milk can be sourced at equally favourable conditions through the IREP.

[115] Canada's Exhibit 33, Section 7.1.

[116] The Panel also considers that using world market price related benchmarks under Article 9.1 (which for many if not most agricultural products would in practice be difficult to establish) would tend to eviscerate the substance of the export commitments and defeat one of the main objects and purposes of the *Agreement on Agriculture*. Clearly, to do so would open up the possibility of using benchmarks under administratively created and controlled import for re-export schemes to get around the scheduled export subsidy reduction commitment levels under which only 25 WTO Members are able at present to use export subsidies.

equivalent prices of whole milk powder.[117] The Panel takes note of the parties' arguments on the matter, but considers that the fact that imports of IREP milk are subject to the discretionary licensing authority held by the Minister is sufficient for the Panel to conclude that IREP milk is not available on equally favourable terms.

6.27 For the reasons set out above,[118] the Panel accordingly finds that the provision of milk at discounted prices to processors for export under the CEM scheme constitutes "payments", in a form other than money, within the meaning of Article 9.1(c) of the *Agreement on Agriculture.*

6.28 Having found the existence of a "payment", the Panel notes that this finding is fully consistent with the original panel's consideration in paragraph 7.62 of its report on *Canada - Dairy*, on which Canada has relied.[119] Paragraph 7.62 of the panel report reads:

> We want to stress, however, that the existence of this "payment in kind" to processors does not in and of itself establish the existence of an export subsidy within the meaning of Article 9.1(a). In our view, in particular the existence of parallel markets for domestic use and for export with different prices does not necessarily constitute an export subsidy.[120] *Whether or not the "payments-in-kind" to processors in this dispute constitute an export subsidy depends on the government's involvement in providing it.*[121] *This relates to the second condition under Article 9.1(a).* (emphasis added)

6.29 The Panel notes that this statement was made in the context of Article 9.1(a), not Article 9.1(c). Nevertheless, the Panel agrees with Canada that the

---

[117] In its reply to Question 10 from the Panel, Canada has stated that the average weighted price for fluid milk for the period examined was C$0.44/kg. According to the United States, this price would approximately be C$45/hl and would therefore not be equally favourable as the CEM price. In addition, Canada has argued that whole milk powder is competitive with fluid milk and is available on equally favourable terms. According to the United States, however, imports of whole milk powder under the IREP do not constitute a source of milk that is available on equally favourable terms as domestically purchased milk. The United States has asserted, first, that, when appropriate corrections are applied, the C$20.46/hl price provided by Canada would be nearly doubled. Second, even if the price of whole milk powder were equally favourable, the United States disagrees that whole milk powder would be directly competitive with fluid milk. Canada has responded to the United States' comment stating that if one were to use other conversion factors used by the United States, as well as the average value of C$2.55/kg for imported whole milk powder, the resulting milk equivalent prices would remain within the range of CEM prices of C$29-$33/hl. Canada has also noted that there is no "standard conversion factor" between whole milk powder and raw milk, whether it be at the Canadian, US or international level. According to Canada, while there has been limited debate within the International Dairy Federation on milk equivalents, there is neither specific agreement nor general consensus on this issue.

[118] Paragraphs 6.11-6.26 above.

[119] Canada's First Submission, para. 99.

[120] [footnote omitted]

[121] [footnote omitted]

statement merits reflection also in the context of Article 9.1(c). The Panel considers that, in the case before it, the mere "payment" would not in and of itself establish the existence of an export subsidy within the meaning of Article 9.1(c). In particular, the existence of parallel markets for domestic use and for export with different prices would not necessarily constitute such an export subsidy. This view, however, does not in any way conflict with the Panel's finding regarding the existence of a "payment".

6.30 First, the Panel draws attention to the last phrase of paragraph 7.62, which makes clear that the panel simply meant to say that a certain degree of government involvement is required for the "payment in kind" to become an export subsidy under Article 9.1(a): it must also be demonstrated that the payment in kind is "provided by governments or their agencies". The same reasoning holds true for Article 9.1(c): the existence of a "payment" is not sufficient to conclude that there is an export subsidy. The Panel must, in addition, examine whether that payment was "financed by virtue of government action".

6.31 Second, footnote 412 to paragraph 7.62 explains when the existence of parallel markets for domestic use and for export with different prices would *not* constitute an export subsidy:

> The price differential may, for example, be a consequence of high - but WTO consistent - import tariffs that can cause domestic prices to be higher than the world market price. In such scenario, efficient producers may take the decision - based on their own profitability - to also produce and sell milk for export, albeit at a lower price than the domestic price. If the decision to sell in either the domestic market or the export market is one made by the individual producer and *based on commercial grounds only* (e.g., on an allocation of sales to the two markets with a view to obtaining a maximized total revenue, taking into account the inherently limited domestic demand for milk and the lower price for export) - *not a decision by the government or its agencies taken on behalf of the producers* - such scenario would, in our view, not appear to be an export subsidy in the sense of Article 9.1. (emphasis added)

It is readily apparent, in the Panel's view, that the facts of this case do not fit with this hypothetical scenario. Domestic prices are high, not simply because of high import tariffs, but as a result of government regulation setting, *inter alia*, price floors and marketing quotas. At the same time, it confirms that only when the decision by Canadian producers to sell for either market is based exclusively on commercial considerations, the existence of parallel markets with different prices would not necessarily constitute an export subsidy. This is precisely the analysis to which the Panel will now turn.

(c) "Financed by Virtue of Governmental Action"

(i) Arguments by the Parties

6.32 Both New Zealand and the United States argue that the above payments are being financed by virtue of governmental action, in reference to paragraph 120 of the Appellate Body report on *Canada - Dairy*, according to which this condition is met if governmental action is "indispensable" to the transfer of resources. Both claimants argue that, in this case, lower priced milk would indeed not be available to processors for export, and resources not transferred, *but for* the combined effect of a set of governmental measures.

6.33 Canada argues that there must be "a direct connection" between the governmental action and the payments, an interpretation which it sees confirmed by an ordinary meaning analysis of "by virtue of". According to Canada, such a direct connection does not exist in this case.

6.34 New Zealand and the United States argue, and Canada contests, that the following governmental measures, "taken as a whole", meet the standard of "financed by virtue of governmental action" under Article 9.1(c):

(a) The regulatory distinction between the domestic milk market and the commercial export milk market, whereby the former is regulated with respect to both quantity ceilings and price floors and the latter is exempt from such regulation.

(b) The prohibition against selling over-quota or non-quota milk into the domestic market, with the exception of class 4(m) milk (animal feed).

(c) The prohibition, both on federal and provincial level, against diverting any milk committed to export into the domestic consumption market, enforced by sanctions and penalties at the federal and provincial level.

(d) The regulations granting the authority to the Canadian Dairy Commission ("CDC") to audit the books and records of producers and processors to determine whether commercial export milk has been marketed for final consumption in Canada.

(e) The requirement that commercial export milk has to be "pre-committed" for export and "first out of the tank".

(f) As regards Ontario and Quebec, the obligation to sell all commercial export milk through an exclusive, mandatory bulletin board system where processors invite offers of milk for export contracts at prices established by the processors.

(ii) Textual and Contextual Analysis of "financed by virtue of"

6.35 The Panel notes that the dictionary meaning of "by virtue of" is "*by the power or efficacy of; now, on the strength of; in consequence of; because of*",[122] and "*by force of, by authority of, by reason of*".[123] The term appears to refer to (i) a certain degree of causality between cause and effect (in consequence of, because of, by reason of), and (ii) the exercise of a power to enforce obedience or influence action[124] (by authority of, by the power of). The Panel considers that dictionary meaning (i) is subsumed under dictionary meaning (ii): when a result is said to come about by the power to enforce obedience or influence action, the exercise of that power can be considered the cause, and the obedience or action the result. This is clear when the obedience is "enforced", but also when the action is simply "influenced": in both instances, the result would not occur *but for* the power to enforce or influence. The Panel considers that these dictionary meanings provide useful guidance regarding the ordinary meaning of "by virtue of".

6.36 The dictionary meaning of "to finance" is "*pay or put to ransom; engage in or manage financial operations; provide oneself with capital; provide with money, esp. capital; provide money for*".[125] The Panel considers that the ordinary meaning of "payments financed", as used in Article 9.1(c), is therefore "payments for which money is provided".[126]

6.37 The Panel now turns to an analysis of the context of "financed by virtue of" in Article 9.1. First, the Panel notes that Article 9,1(c) itself provides an example of what may be understood as meaning "financed by virtue of": when payments are financed from the proceeds of a levy imposed on the agricultural product concerned or on an agricultural product from which the exported product is derived, those payments would be "financed by virtue of" governmental action. In this example, the governmental action would supposedly be constituted by the *imposition* of the levy on the agricultural product concerned or on an agricultural product from which the exported product is derived. When government imposes such a levy, for example, it will also be government who *allocates* the proceeds of that levy to a certain beneficiary or group of beneficiaries in society. Therefore, when Article 9.1(c) states that payments are *financed from* the proceeds of the levy, it carries with it the implicit, but clear, understanding, that government has necessarily also *allocated* those proceeds to the financing of the payments. As a result, in the example provided by Article 9.1(c), "by virtue of" clearly im-

---

[122] New Shorter Oxford English Dictionary (Lesley Brown, ed.), page 3586.

[123] Black's Law Dictionary (5th Edition), page 182.

[124] Based on the New Shorter Oxford English Dictionary meaning of "authority" (page 151).

[125] New Shorter Oxford English Dictionary, page 950.

[126] The Panel notes that none of the parties has examined in much detail how "financing" by virtue of governmental action should be interpreted.

plies the exercise of government power *with the effect of* financing payments on the export of agricultural goods, whereby the governmental action is *indispensable* for the funds to be transferred from grantor to recipient. The Panel, however, is aware that the example provided by Article 9.1(c) is merely illustrative, not exhaustive, and that, therefore, the scope of "financed by virtue of" is not necessarily restricted to the meaning imparted to it by this particular example.

6.38 Consideration should also be given to the context provided by the other paragraphs of Article 9.1. The Panel notes in this respect the prominent difference which exists as regards the nature and extent of government action required under paragraph (c) as compared with the other paragraphs of Article 9.1. Whereas paragraph (c) requires that the payment merely be "*financed by virtue of*" governmental action, other paragraphs of Article 9.1 require the "*provision by* governments or their agencies",[127] the "*sale or disposal by* governments or their agencies",[128] the "*provision of* subsidies",[129] "charges *provided or mandated by* governments".[130] The Panel considers that this difference must have some meaning. In the Panel's view, a key difference exists as regards both (i) the *nature* of the involvement and (ii) the *extent* of the involvement by government. First, governments or their agencies under paragraph (c) need not necessarily themselves directly *provide* subsidies or goods or services at reduced rates. The government or its agencies are merely involved in the *financing of* the payment which may exist as a result of the provision of goods at reduced rates. Second, the payments need not necessarily be directly financed *by* governments or their agencies under paragraph (c). Through the exercise of governmental power, they only *establish the conditions which ensure that* the payment, i.e. the transfer of resources from producer to processor, takes place. The governmental action is, in that sense, a necessary condition for the transfer to take place.

6.39 In conclusion, on the basis of the text and context of Article 9.1(c), the Panel considers that for a payment to be "financed by virtue of governmental action", it must be established that a payment would not be financed, i.e. resources would not be transferred from grantor to recipient, *but for* governmental action.

6.40 This textual and contextual meaning coincides with the Appellate Body's interpretation of this term in its report on *Canada - Dairy* as referring to action which is "*indispensable*" to the financing of the payment.[131] An action is indispensable when it is necessary or vital to a result which could not take place without it. Although it cannot be inferred from the Appellate Body report in *Canada - Dairy* that the Appellate Body meant to equate "by virtue of" with "indispensabil-

---

[127] Article 9.1(a) of the *Agreement on Agriculture*.

[128] Article 9.1(b) of the *Agreement on Agriculture*.

[129] Article 9.1(d) of the *Agreement on Agriculture*.

[130] Article 9.1(e) of the *Agreement on Agriculture*.

[131] Report of the Appellate Body on *Canada - Dairy*, para. 120.

ity" as a matter of general interpretation, the Panel does consider that, having regard to the text and context of Article 9.1(c), it does constitute an appropriate standard to be applied under Article 9.1(c) in this case, as it did in the original case.

(iii) General Analysis by the Panel

6.41 The question which the Panel needs to address is the following: would milk processors for export have access to lower priced commercial export milk in Canada *but for* governmental action? Put another way, have the Canadian government and its agencies taken action which is *indispensable* for the lower priced milk to be available to processors for export?

6.42 The Panel considers that this standard would be met if it can be demonstrated that governmental action, *de jure* or *de facto*: (i) prevents Canadian milk producers from selling more milk on the regulated domestic market, at a higher price, than to the extent of the quota allocated to them; and (ii) obliges Canadian milk processors to export all milk contracted as lower priced commercial export milk, and, accordingly, penalizes the diversion by processors of milk contracted as commercial export milk to the domestic market. As explained below,[132] only if both those requirements were to be met, governmental action could be said to be indispensable for the transfer of resources to take place: the lower priced commercial export milk would not have been available to Canadian processors for export *but for* these governmental actions, taken together.

6.43 When a producer decides whether to produce for the domestic market or the export market, it can be assumed that he will try to maximize his profits. The Panel notes in this respect that the parties have submitted conflicting data on milk producers' average costs of production and their related capability to produce profitably for export.[133] According to Canada, the information provided by the complainants is intended to convince the Panel that producers are *forced* to sell milk into the commercial export market because absent government compulsion to do so, they would not sell into that market at a loss.[134] Canada also asserts that government does not direct, compel, *or even encourage* producers to sell into the commercial export market. Thus, according to Canada, the reasons why certain producers sell into the commercial export market and other producers do not sell into that market are irrelevant.[135]

---

[132] See paras. 6.43-6.48 below.

[133] According to the United States, less than 1 per cent of Canadian producers could cover costs of production at export prices of around C$30/hl (United States' Second Submission, para. 13 and United States' Exhibit 24), whereas Canada asserts that these figures are inadequate and argues that over 30 per cent of Canadian producers could cover their costs of production at a price of C$31.53/hl (Canada's Oral Statement, paras. 17-22 and Canada's Exhibit 26).

[134] Canada's Oral Statement, para. 17.

[135] *Ibid.*, para. 18.

6.44 The Panel makes the following observations in this respect. First, under this Panel's, and the Appellate Body's, interpretation of "by virtue of governmental action" as referring to governmental action which is "indispensable to" the financing of a payment, it is not necessarily required that a government "forces", "directs", or "compels" producers to sell into the commercial export market. What is required is that producers would not sell into the commercial export market *but for* governmental action. This requirement is quite different from the one advanced by Canada. Whether the government "forces" or merely "encourages" producers to sell into the commercial export market are *qualifications* of the causal relationship required under Article 9.1(c). The "financed by virtue of" requirement, however, does not necessarily qualify the causal relationship between governmental action and payment in the way suggested by Canada. It only requires that, independently of the nature of the governmental action, it must be indispensable for the resources to be transferred. What is indispensable in terms of governmental action may vary from one case to another.

6.45 Second, the Panel disagrees with Canada that producers in this case would not be, at least, "encouraged" by government to sell into the commercial export market if the existence of the above two categories of governmental action would be established. Indeed, in the Panel's view, if the existence of the above measures were to be established, the choice left to the Canadian producer is not a real choice. Why would the economically rational producer sell other than for the domestic market at an average price of about C$53/hl in the absence of such regulation? Would the economically rational producer rather sell commercial export milk in the C$30/hl range, under class 4(m) in the C$10/hl range, or destroy his production? In the Panel's view, this is not tenable. The economically rational producer will sell for export only if he cannot sell to the domestic market, either because his quota is filled, or he anticipates that it will be filled,[136] or because he does not have any quota.[137] Arguing the opposite is disregarding the basic assumption that the economic behaviour of a producer is premised on profit-maximization. The reasons why producers in Canada sell into the commercial export market are therefore not "irrelevant", as Canada would argue: if the existence of the above measures can be established, the "reason" would be the governmental action driving producers to the economically second-best option of producing for export. This reason is, in the Panel's view, highly relevant, because it would establish that producers choose the economic second-best option as a totally rational and predictable reaction to government action taking away the first-best option.

---

136 See para. 6.47 below.

137 The Panel notes that at this time more than 99,5 per cent of Canadian producers have chosen not to sell exclusively milk for the commercial export market (Canada's reply to Question 3). The 74 producers who do not hold quota and do exclusively produce for the commercial export market, accounted for 0,08 per cent of total milk production in Canada between August 2000 and February 2001 (Canada's reply to Question 21).

6.46 Therefore, the fact that milk has to be *pre-committed* or *first-out-of-tank* for it to be exported does not affect the Panel's analysis in paragraph 6.42. Canada argues that by pre-committing milk to export, producers are required to decide how to allocate their production in advance, before knowing whether they will exceed their domestic quota. According to Canada, this demonstrates that commercial export milk is not milk produced above the domestic quota, and that the decision to produce for export is a commercially free one. In the Panel's view, however, these pre-commitment and first-out-of-tank requirements would not change the fact that the decision to sell for the export market would *not* be based on purely commercial considerations if the above governmental action can be established. A decision based on purely commercial considerations will maximize profit. Selling for export, rather than for the domestic market, does not maximize profit, *unless the first-best profit-maximizing option has been foreclosed by governmental action*. Inevitably, if a producer decides "in advance" to produce for the second-best option, it is because he knows that the first-best option will, at some point, no longer be available. According to Canada, producers can calculate and "pre-plan" their production for export.[138] If this assertion by Canada is true, then a producer who regularly - and knowingly - produced surplus-milk in the past, will know whether he will be producing milk above his quota in the future. Consequently, that producer, following Canada's assertion, would be able to anticipate whether his production will exceed the quota, and "pre-commit" that portion to export. If the decision to pre-commit for export was a truly commercial one, i.e. the first-best option, producers would produce for export rather than fill their quota. Producers in Canada who pre-commit milk for export, however, continue to meet their domestic quota.[139]

6.47 Finally, the complainants have argued that the regulatory requirement to use exclusively electronic bulletin boards for all export milk transactions in Ontario and Quebec is part of the governmental action by virtue of which the payment is made. The Panel notes that the bulletin boards physically bring together offer and demand for commercial export milk, and, in that sense, are instrumental in the conclusion of export milk contracts. The Panel does not see, however, how the use of such bulletin boards, mandatory or otherwise, could be *indispensable* to the provision of lower-priced milk. In the Panel's view, it would be the governmental action referenced at paragraph 6.42 which would be indispensable to the provision of lower-priced milk. The very assertion by the complainants that payments on export milk are financed by governmental action in the other provinces, where those bulletin boards either are not in place, or, as in the case of Manitoba, their use is not mandatory, would appear to confirm this. All other

[138] Canada's Rebuttal Submission, para. 54; Canada's First Submission, paras. 42, 53-54.

[139] The fact that 74 out of approximately 18,900 Canadian producers produce exclusively for export without having domestic quota (Canada's reply to Question 3) does not affect the Panel's conclusion. As stated earlier, these producers account for only 0,08 per cent of Canadian milk production.

things remaining the same, if a payment could be financed by virtue of governmental action in provinces where no bulletin boards are in place or their use is not mandatory, those bulletin boards could then not be said to be "indispensable" to the financing of the payment in the two provinces where they do exist and their use is mandatory. At this stage, therefore, the Panel does not consider that the mandatory and exclusive use of electronic bulletin boards for commercial export milk in Ontario and Quebec would appear to be indispensable to making commercial export milk available to processors at reduced rates.

6.48 Thus, the Panel considers that the above governmental action, if proven, would drive milk producers in Canada to sell milk produced outside their quota at a lower price into the export market. The fact, however, that *producers* are driven by governmental action to sell milk produced outside their quota into the export market would not necessarily be sufficient to ensure that such milk effectively ends up in the export stream. Anti-diversion measures need to be put in place and enforced to ensure that *processors* do not divert commercial export milk back to the domestic market. If processors were allowed to market milk contracted for export by producers on the domestic market, they would have a commercial incentive to do so. Since processors buy commercial export milk at prices approximately 40 per cent lower than domestic market prices, they could, by sourcing milk on the export market and subsequently marketing the processed product on the domestic market, reduce the cost of raw material by 40 per cent and substantially increase their profit margins. As a result, it is unlikely that the same amounts of lower priced commercial export milk would end up in the export stream. Thus, *but for* governmental action obliging Canadian milk processors to export all milk contracted for export, and, accordingly, penalizing the diversion of commercial export milk to the domestic market, there would be no payment on the export of milk. Therefore, only if the Panel were also to find that governmental action obliges Canadian milk processors to export all milk contracted as commercial export milk, and, accordingly, penalizes the diversion of commercial export milk to the domestic market, a payment on Canadian dairy exports could be said to be "financed by virtue of governmental action."

6.49 In conclusion, the two categories of governmental[140] measures referred to at paragraph 6.42 above, if proven, in and of themselves, would be considered indispensable to the financing of the payment on the export of milk. The Panel

[140] The Panel considers that the entities involved in the adoption and/or enforcement of the measures referred to in para. 6.42 above do not raise questions as regards their qualification as "governmental". These entities, i.e. the federal and provincial governments, the CDC, the CMSMC and the provincial marketing boards, were all found to meet the "governmental" requirement in the Panel report on *Canada -Dairy* (*supra*, footnote 3, paras. 7.73-7.80), and the Panel's underlying reasoning and its finding with respect to the governmental character of the provincial marketing boards was confirmed by the Appellate Body (paras. 93-102). The Panel considers that no change in the source of these entities' powers or in the functions conferred upon them can be observed which would justify changing the qualification of their action as "governmental".

will now turn to an analysis of the claims that these two categories of governmental measures do effectively exist in Canada.

(iv) Does Governmental Action Prevent Canadian Producers from Selling Milk Produced Outside their Quota on the Domestic Market?

6.50 In principle, dairy producers in Canada can only market their milk on the domestic market to the extent of the quota they have been allocated.[141] Consequently, and subject to the Panel's considerations below,[142] a Canadian dairy producer is in principle prevented from marketing his milk on the domestic market outside the quota allocated to him.

6.51 Canada argues, however, that this governmental restriction is mitigated by (i) the possibility to sell milk under Class 4(m) (animal feed), and (ii) the possibility for producers to trade and/or lease additional quota among each other.

6.52 First, as regards the Class 4(m) option, the evidence on the record shows that Class 4(m) sales are a commercially far less attractive option as compared to quota sales or commercial export sales. Canada has confirmed that the average Class 4(m) price is C$10/hl, i.e. about 20 per cent of the average quota milk price and about 30 per cent of the average commercial export price.[143] It follows that, if a rational producer were to be given the choice between selling for the domestic quota market or the commercial export market and selling under Class 4(m), he would, absent exceptional circumstances, never sell milk under Class 4(m). Not surprisingly, Class 4(m) sales constitute a very small portion of total milk sales in Canada (less than 1 per cent[144]). The theoretical choice offered to the producer under Class 4(m) is therefore not of such a nature as to mitigate the governmental restriction on production for the domestic milk market.

6.53 Second, as confirmed by Canada, the fact that producers are free to trade quota *among each other* cannot in any way affect the ceiling of *total quota volume* set by the government.[145] The trading among producers of individual quota always takes places below that ceiling, and inter-producer quota transactions do not increase the total volume of available quota. According to Canada, "quota is always available to those producers willing to purchase/lease additional quota

---

[141] This is not controversial. See, for instance, Canada's First Submission, paras. 7, 24, 31, 41. See also the report of the panel on *Canada - Dairy*, *supra*, footnote 3, para. 2.20.

[142] See paras. 6.52-6.53 below.

[143] Canada's reply to Question 2b.

[144] *Ibid.*

[145] Canada's reply to Question 4(a)(i). Only government, not inter-producer quota transactions, can change the total quota volume. The CMSMC automatically adjusts MSQ for the domestic market to reflect changes in domestic demand using an agreed formula (Canada's reply to Question 15(a)).

who bid *at or above* the market price for quota."[146] This may be true. However, if demand for a - by definition - scarce product such as quota is strong, the price of additional quota is likely to be high. When demand increases, supply remaining the same, the price can be expected to increase as well. As a result, the cost of trading additional quota would exceed the profit its use may generate, and the purchasing or leasing of additional quota would no longer be a profit-maximizing one.[147] Canada has confirmed that between August 2000 and February 2001, only about 3.85 per cent of originally allocated quota in Canada changed hands.[148] The Panel also notes that Canada had asserted, but not documented, that "over 5 per cent of quota changes hands in Canada every year."[149] The Panel considers that these small proportions may be indicative of the extent to which producers in Canada consider the purchasing or leasing of quota a commercially viable alternative. The Panel considers, therefore, that the theoretical choice offered to the producer to purchase or lease additional quota is not of such a nature as to mitigate the governmental restriction on production for the domestic milk market.

6.54 In conclusion, the Panel considers that, for the reasons set out above,[150] Canadian dairy producers are, at least *de facto*, prevented by governmental action from freely marketing outside-quota milk on the domestic market.

(v) Does Governmental Action Oblige Canadian Milk Processors to Export All Milk Contracted as Commercial Export Milk, and, Accordingly, Penalize the Diversion of Commercial Export Milk to the Domestic Market?

6.55 Arguments have been advanced by the complainants concerning both federal and provincial regulatory provisions. The Panel will first address the arguments made concerning the federal Regulations, and thereafter the arguments made concerning the various provincial provisions.

The Federal Dairy Products Marketing Regulations

6.56 The United States submits that although there is no explicit prohibition on diverting milk contracted for export into the domestic market, to do so would still constitute a violation of the federal Dairy Products Marketing Regulations (the

146 Canada's reply to Question 4(a)(ii), para. 11. Emphasis added.

147 The Panel notes that New Zealand has asserted, on the basis of New Zealand's Exhibit 15, that "the right to produce 1 kg of butterfat per day can cost over C$25.000" (New Zealand's Rebuttal Submission, para. 4.18), and that Canada has not contested this assertion.

148 Canada's reply to Question 4b.

149 Canada's Rebuttal Submission, footnote 53. Canada's Oral Statement, para. 14.

150 Paras. 6.50-6.53.

"federal Regulations"). According to the United States, this is because only milk that precisely meets the definition of "commercial export milk" is exempt from the federal Regulations. Part of the definition of "commercial export milk" under section 2(1)(b) is that the milk must be "marketed in a province set out in the schedule and *in a manner that is consistent with exclusions from the dairy product marketing laws in that province*." Thus, in the view of the United States, if commercial export milk is diverted into the domestic market in violation of provincial regulations, it would no longer fall within the exclusion for "commercial export milk" and therefore would be subject to domestic regulation and the seizure power of the federal inspectors.[151] The United States has provided the Panel two examples of situations where, in the United States' view, milk that falls out of the defined exemption for "commercial export milk" could trigger a violation of federal Regulations and, thus, seizure by the federal inspector of the milk, or the products into which it was manufactured, under section 11(1):[152]

(a) if the processor purchased milk from a producer without a federal license (since none is required under federal regulation for commercial export milk): the diversion of this milk would entail a violation of section 7(3), because, if the milk no longer meets the definition of "commercial export milk," then section 7(3) would apply and a federal license would be required.

(b) if the processor is not identifying the diversion of milk in his written records (in other words, the records are incorrect or incomplete): a violation of section 10 would arise because he would not be keeping accurate records.

6.57 Canada confirms that if milk is marketed in a province in a manner that is not consistent with exclusions from the dairy products marketing laws in that province, then it does not meet the definition of commercial export milk in the federal Regulations, and is therefore not excluded from the application of sec-

[151] United States' Second Submission, para. 49. In its First Submission, the United States had also asserted that it results from new section 7(4) of the federal Regulations that "any person who knowingly diverts commercial export milk for final consumption in Canada violates the [federal] Regulations." (footnote 62) According to the United States, Section 11(1) of the federal Regulations "empowers inspectors appointed under the Canadian Dairy Commission Act to seize any dairy product that the inspector believes on reasonable grounds was marketed in interprovincial or export trade in contravention of the [federal] Regulations. Since the [federal] Regulations prohibit the diversion into Canada's domestic market of any milk committed to export, the CDC inspectors (and their provincial counterparts) have been given authority to seize any commercial export milk or cream that based 'on reasonable grounds' is believed to have been sold into the domestic market for final consumption, rather than exported as required by the [federal] Regulations." (para. 46). Following the Panel's request to clarify its position regarding those arguments under the federal Regulations, the United States confirmed that it considered its argument regarding section 7(4) moot (United States' reply to Question 5a). The Panel will therefore not address the argument made under section 7(4) of the federal Regulations.

[152] United States' reply to Question 5c.

tions 4 to 7 and 8 and 9 of the federal Regulations.[153] As regards the possibility of seizure by federal inspectors in the two examples provided by the United States, Canada has stated that "[a] violation of [the] requirement [to keep books and records under Section 10] cannot be equated to a diversion of commercial export milk into the domestic market."[154]

6.58 The United States and Canada confirm that there is no *de jure* prohibition in the federal Regulations on diverting milk contracted as commercial export milk to the domestic market. As Canada confirms, however, if a sale of commercial export milk into the domestic market were to occur, there would be "financial consequences" for the processor. The processor would pay *twice* for milk: initially at the price contracted under the commercial export contract, and then a second time at the much higher domestic price.[155] The Panel therefore considers that the federal Regulations penalize diversion of commercial export milk to the domestic market through the application of "financial disincentives". These "financial disincentives" exceed the domestic market price and are therefore of a punitive nature. The Panel considers that this penalty, in conjunction with the CDC's auditing power,[156] constitutes an effective government-imposed deterrent to diversion of commercial export milk.

6.59 As regards the possibility of seizure by federal inspectors in the two examples provided by the United States, the Panel considers that, even if the examples were to accurately reflect the operation of the federal Regulations, their relevance to the Panel's assessment is rather limited. In the Panel's understanding, example (a) would ordinarily only apply if the diverted milk has been produced

---

[153] Canada's reply to Question 5c.

[154] Canada's Comments on the United States' and New Zealand's replies to the Questions of the Panel, para. 8.

[155] Canada's reply to Question 5c, para. 16. Although Canada does not specify that these "financial disincentives" would result from the application of the federal Regulations, the fact that (i) the information was provided in response to the Panel's specific question regarding the United States' argument under the federal Regulations, and (ii) that Canada makes no reference in its reply to provincial measures, seems to confirm, in the Panel's view, that Canada was referring to the application of the federal Regulations.

[156] The CDC has the authority, pursuant to Section 10 of the federal Regulations, to request every person who is engaged in the production or processing of a dairy product for marketing in interprovincial or export trade to make available complete and accurate books and records of all matters relating to production or processing. According to new Section 10.1, "[a]ny information made available to the [CDC] under Section 10 does not have to contain pricing or other information on commercial export milk or cream, *except information that is necessary to determine whether it has been marketed for final consumption in Canada.*" (emphasis added) If the CDC would not have this authority to verify whether milk contracted as CEM has been diverted to the domestic market, the likelihood that processors could divert CEM without paying the applicable penalties would, of course, be much greater. The assertion by Canada that a CDC audit which takes places after the transaction cannot affect decisions regarding that transaction (Canada's First Submission, para. 111) is not convincing: one would not forego the making of an income tax declaration because the tax inspector only audits one's books later on.

by a producer who does not hold a licence and, therefore,[157] would normally not hold quota. As acknowledged by the United States,[158] the number of those Canadian milk producers that produce without a quota for the export market is extremely small, and so are the quantities they produce. Example (b) does not concern a breach of the federal Regulations by the diversion of commercial export milk to the domestic market, but, rather, by not keeping accurate records. If the diversion of commercial export milk would be accurately reflected in the processor's records, the "financial disincentives" referred to by Canada are likely to kick in, but no breach of Section 10 would occur, and, thus, no milk would be seized.

Provincial Measures

6.60 Both complainants have argued that anti-diversion measures are in place at the provincial level in Canada. They have mostly focused their arguments on the provinces of Quebec and Ontario, given the importance of these provinces in terms of Canadian milk exports.[159] All parties, however, have also submitted or clarified information with regard to other milk-exporting provinces in Canada.

6.61 The Panel takes note of Canada's statement that, under each of the nine provincial regimes governing the purchase and sale of non-quota milk, "all producers and processors in Canada are subject to sanctions for breach of [certain provincial regulatory] requirements. These could include suspension or cancellation of license or in some circumstances penalties [...] *and/or financial consequences (i.e. through product re-classification or in the case of commercial export milk, if sold in the domestic market, by becoming part of the domestic classification system*)."[160] (emphasis added)

6.62 The Panel, therefore, accepts as established that diversion of commercial export milk into the domestic market will, at least, result in "financial consequences" in all nine milk-exporting provinces in Canada. The Panel will now turn to an analysis of the individual provinces to determine the level of these financial consequences and the applicability of other sanctions, such as the suspension or cancellation of licences.

[157] Section 7(1) of the federal Regulations provides that the Canadian Dairy Commission shall cause a federal licence to be issued only to a person (a) to whom a share of the federal quota has been allotted; (b) who is registered as a milk producer with, or is licensed as a cream producer by, the Manitoba Milk Producers; or (c) who is licensed as a producer under the Milk Act of Ontario.

[158] United States' Second Submission, footnote 4.

[159] The United States asserts that Quebec and Ontario together account for approximately 80 per cent of Canadian milk exports (United States' First Submission, para. 20).

[160] Canada's reply to Question 19(ii).

Quebec

6.63 Decision 7111 of the Régie des Marchés Agricoles et Alimentaires du Québec (the "Régie"), dated 28 July 2000, has amended the provisions of the Milk Marketing Agreement between the Féderation des Producteurs de Lait du Quebec and Agropur (the "MMA Agreement"). The Panel notes that Canada refers to Decision 7111 as either the "relevant legal provisions"[161] or the "relevant regulatory amendment" in Quebec.[162]

6.64 Pursuant to the amended paragraph 2.25 of the MMA Agreement

> All components of milk intended for export markets and covered by a specific commitment between an individual producer and a milk dealer must be exported. Any milk dealer who breaches this obligation is subject to the penalties stipulated in this chapter.

Pursuant to the amended paragraph 2.43 of the MMA Agreement,

> When a milk dealer is unable to show that all the quantities of components of the volume of milk received have been exported or are stored, it must, upon receiving the audit report to this effect, pay to the Federation, subject to the other remedies of the parties to the contract, an amount, per kilogram of component, equal to twice the component price payable in class $3b_2$.

According to the United States, the penalty would equal an amount that would approximately be four times the price that the processor would have paid for milk destined for export.[163] Canada has not contested this assertion.

6.65 The Panel considers that this penalty is of a punitive nature and, in conjunction with the CDC's auditing power, constitutes an effective government-imposed deterrent to diversion of commercial export milk.

Ontario

6.66 The United States has submitted a document entitled "Ontario Dairy Export Exchange Mechanism", provided by the Canadian government and "describing the dairy export mechanisms for [....] Ontario."[164] In its reply to a request for clarification by the Panel following its meeting with the parties, however, Canada has explained that this document is a draft document, and that it has been replaced by a different version,[165] which does not contain the provisions the United

161 Canada's reply to Question 19(i).
162 Canada's reply to Question 19(ii). Canada also lists Decision 7111 as such (Canada's Exhibit List, page iv).
163 United States' First Submission, para. 37.
164 United States' Exhibit 6.
165 Canada's reply to Question 6.

States referred to.[166] Notwithstanding the fact that the document submitted by the United States has never been more than a draft, the United States opines that "[i]n any event, the statements in the document should be treated as admissions by Canada for the purposes of this proceeding."[167] The Panel does not agree with the United States, and will only consider the final version of the document.

6.67 Section F.1 of the Ontario Dairy Export Contract Exchange Mechanism provides,

> All buyers will keep and provide to the auditor of the domestic market all records required to demonstrate that all components provided pursuant to an export contract have either been duly exported or are being held in inventory.

6.68 The Panel considers that this provision clearly implies the existence of an obligation for processors to export milk contracted through the Ontario Dairy Export Contract Exchange Mechanism. Although Canada has characterized the document as a "private industry agreement",[168] the Panel notes that one of the parties to this agreement is DFO (Dairy Farmers of Ontario), a provincial marketing board, which the Panel in its report on *Canada - Dairy* has characterized as an agency of the Canadian government,[169] and that the agreement, as acknowledged by Canada, "is referenced in the DFO regulations as part of the definition of milk."[170]

6.69 Second, Section 1(b) of DFO Milk General Regulation 09/00[171] sets forth the definition of "export contract milk" as "pre-committed first milk out of the producer's bulk tank that is the subject of a commercial export contract made through the export contract exchange operated by the Third Party Administrator and is deemed to be the first milk out of the tank." The parties agree that, as a result, if milk is not delivered to export it would no longer constitute export contract milk and would therefore be subject to domestic regulation.[172]

6.70 DFO Milk General Regulation 09/00 does not set forth a specific sanction on diversion, but Section 3 of DFO Milk Pricing Regulation 08/00 provides that "export contract milk" is exempt from the provisions set forth in that regulation.

---

166 "Ontario Dairy Export Contract Exchange Mechanism", contained in Canada's Exhibit 32, New Zealand's Exhibit 7.

167 United States' reply to Question 6.

168 Canada's reply to Question 6.

169 Report of the panel on *Canada - Dairy*, *supra*, footnote 3, paras. 7.76-7.78.

170 Canada's reply to Question 6.

171 The Panel takes note of Canada's statement that "DFO Milk General Regulation 15/00 is the most up-to-date version of the General Regulation, but makes no significant changes to DFO Milk General Regulation 09/00 with respect to provisions involving export contract milk." (Canada's First Submission, Annex 5, footnote 2). In view of this statement, and considering that the exchanges between the parties have drawn upon DFO Milk General Regulation 09/00, the Panel will use DFO Milk General Regulation 09/00 as a basis for its analysis.

172 United States' reply to Question 16. Canada's reply to Question 6.

If the milk no longer qualifies as "export contract milk" (because it was not exported), the processor would be subject to Section 4 which states that "[a]ll classes of milk supplied to a processor shall be sold by the DFO and bought by the processor at price equal to the total of the amount per kilogram of [milk product] as set out in [the relevant column of Schedule 1]." According to the United States, this price would be paid in addition to the export price that has already been paid by the processor, who would end up paying approximately C$90/hl. Canada has not contested this assertion.

6.71 The Panel considers that the imposition of a severe monetary penalty under DFO Regulations in case of diversion, in conjunction with the CDC's auditing power, constitutes an effective government-imposed deterrent to diversion of commercial export milk in Ontario.

6.72 Finally, the United States refers to Section 5(4) of the DFO Milk General Regulation 09/00, which provides that:

> DFO may refuse to grant or renew or may suspend or revoke a licence [...] where the applicant or licensee has failed to comply with or has contravened the Act, the Regulations, the Plan or any Order or Direction of DFO.

According to the United States, pursuant to Section 5(4) failure to export milk so committed can lead to the revocation of the licence of a milk *producer* in Ontario.[173] Canada replies by stating that the DFO "cannot use licensing as a means to enforce the terms of private commercial agreements",[174] and that "the United States is inviting the Panel to speculate that DFO will somehow use its health and safety licensing authority for extraneous and illegal purposes, namely, to somehow 'punish' for any 'breach' of the commercial export exchange."[175]

6.73 The Panel understands that, according to the United States, DFO could punish a *producer* for diversion of commercial export milk to the domestic market by a *processor*. On the one hand, the Panel has difficulty seeing how, as a practical matter, the producer of a fungible product such as milk could be identified on the basis of the processed product it was used in, and, if he can be identified, why he would be punished for a regulatory breach by a processor. On the other hand, the Panel notes that Canada's replies to the Panel's questions on the matter have not fully enabled the Panel to make its assessment in this respect.[176]

---

173 United States' First Submission, para. 80. United States' Second Submission, para. 47.

174 Canada's First Submission, para. 109.

175 Canada's Second Submission, para. 44.

176 Questions 6, 7 and 8 by the Panel, and Canada's replies to these questions. In questions 7 and 8, the Panel had asked Canada to include in its replies any regulatory instruments referenced in its reply to Question 6, regarding the "Ontario Dairy Export Exchange Mechanism". In its reply to Question 6, Canada stated, *inter alia*, that "*the exchange set out in this agreement is [...] referenced in the DFO regulations* as part of the definition of milk, the marketing of which is deregulated when marketed through that exchange." Although the Panel would therefore have expected Canada to include the relevant "DFO Regulations" in its replies to Questions 7 and 8, Canada did not do so.

The Panel is mindful of the fact that Canada has the burden of proof pursuant to Article 10.3, and that, therefore, it is up to Canada to raise a presumption that what it asserts is true. Nevertheless, the Panel will not enter into speculations as regards the interpretation and application of this aspect of Ontario law, as it already has found that the imposition of a severe monetary penalty under DFO Regulations in case of diversion, in conjunction with the CDC's auditing power, constitutes an effective government-imposed deterrent to diversion of commercial export milk in Ontario.

Other Canadian Milk-Exporting Provinces

6.74 The Panel has reviewed the evidence submitted by the parties with respect to the provincial regulatory instruments governing commercial export milk in the remaining 7 milk-exporting provinces. On the basis of that review, the Panel has found that in each of these provinces:

(a) commercial export milk is clearly defined as milk that must be exported;[177]

(b) milk that meets this definition of commercial export milk is exempted from domestic regulation;[178]

(c) milk that was contracted as commercial export milk and subsequently diverted to the domestic market becomes subject to domestic regulation, and, as a result, a processor would be obliged to pay the higher domestic price *on top of* the price already paid for the commercial export milk.[179]

6.75 The Panel considers that this penalty is of a punitive nature and, in conjunction with the CDC's auditing power, constitutes an effective government-imposed deterrent to diversion of commercial export milk.

---

[177] British Columbia Milk Marketing Board Regulation Amendments, BC Reg 167/94, section 1; Alberta Dairy Board Regulation section 1(2)(e.1); Saskatchewan Milk Control Regulations, Part I section 2 (f.1, f.2); Manitoba Milk Producers' Marketing Export Contract Milk Exemption Order, sections 1, 2; New Brunswick Milk Marketing Board Exemption Order 11, section 2; Nova Scotia Regulation Respecting Contracted Exports of Dairy Products, Schedule 13, section 1(a); Prince Edward Island Milk Marketing Regulation Amendments, EC2000-785, section 1.

[178] British Columbia Milk Marketing Board Regulation Amendments, BC Reg 167/94, section 7.1(2); Alberta Dairy Board Regulation section 1(2)(e.1); Saskatchewan Milk Control Regulations, Part II section 3, Part III section 15(2), Part V section 39.7(2); Manitoba Milk Producers' Marketing Milk General Order 301/89, Part I, section 1; New Brunswick Milk Marketing Board Exemption Order 11, section 4; New Brunswick Milk Marketing Board Milk Pricing Order, section 3; Nova Scotia Regulation Respecting Contracted Exports of Dairy Products, Schedule 13, section 2; Prince Edward Island Milk Marketing Regulations, MMB00-02, section 3, 4; Prince Edward Island Milk Marketing Regulation Amendments, EC2000-785, section 3.1(1).

[179] In certain regulatory instruments, it is explicitly stipulated which domestic market price will have to be paid by the processor: British Columbia Milk Marketing Board Regulation Amendments, BC Reg 167/94, section 7.2; Saskatchewan Milk Control Regulations, Part IV, section 39(4)(4).

6.76 The Panel has not found that diversion of commercial export milk in those provinces may lead to seizure by the provincial authorities. The United States has in that respect only drawn the Panel's attention to the seizure power of the Prince Edward Island Marketing Board pursuant to Section 3(q), Chapter N-3 of the Prince Edward Island Marketing Regulations.[180] That provision gives the Prince Edward Island Marketing Board the power "to seize and dispose of any milk marketed in violation of any order of the Board." Consequently, if diversion would constitute a violation of "an order of the Board", it would trigger the possibility of seizure. The Panel is mindful of the fact that Canada has the burden of proof pursuant to Article 10.3, but considers that it does not need to make a finding on this particular issue, as it has already found that the financial penalty for diversion is of a punitive nature and, in conjunction with the CDC's auditing power, constitutes an effective government-imposed deterrent to diversion of commercial export milk.

(vi) Conclusion

6.77 In conclusion, the Panel finds that the payment is "financed by virtue of governmental action", in that lower-priced commercial export milk would not be available to Canadian processors *but for* the above federal and provincial actions (i) restricting supply on the domestic milk market, obliging producers, at least *de facto*, to sell outside-quota milk for export, and (ii) obliging processors to export all milk contracted as commercial export milk, and penalizing diversion by processors of commercial export milk into the domestic market.

(d) Payment "on the export of an agricultural product"

6.78 The lower priced commercial export milk is only available to processors if the milk is contracted for export and effectively exported. Only by contracting for export and effectively exporting milk can producers and processors engage in transactions outside the regulatory framework of price floors and quota ceilings applicable to domestic market milk transactions in Canada. The Panel, therefore, finds that a clear export contingency exists, and that the payment is made "on the export of an agricultural product."

[180] United States' reply to Question 19.

(e) Conclusion Regarding Article 9.1(c)

6.79 For the reasons set out above,[181] the Panel finds that a payment on the export of milk is financed by virtue of governmental action in Canada, within the meaning of Article 9.1(c).

3. *Article 3.3*

6.80 Having found that CEM exports are being subsidized within the meaning of Article 9.1(c), the Panel recalls the original panel's[182] and Appellate Body's[183] finding that, as acknowledged by Canada,[184] Class 5(d) exports are also subsidized within the meaning of Article 9.1(c). Consequently, if the sum of CEM and Class 5(d) export quantities in the marketing year 2000/2001 were to exceed Canada's quantity commitment levels specified in its Schedule, the Panel would find a breach of Article 3.3.

6.81 According to data provided by New Zealand and the United States, and spanning the period August 2000 - February 2001, Canadian exports of cheese amount to 9,613 metric tons,[185] and exports of other milk products range from 25.600[186] to 28.826[187] metric tonnes. Canada's reduction commitment levels for the marketing year 2000/2001 are set at 9,076 and 30.282 metric tons, respectively. The United States contended that these figures do *not* include exports under Canada's IREP.[188] As a result, according to this data, Canadian cheese exports would already be subsidized in excess of Canada's reduction commitment levels specified in its Schedule as of February 2001. According to Canada, however, these figures *do* include exports under Canada's IREP.[189] According to Canada, Canadian exports of other milk products between August 2000 and February 2001, *excluding* IREP exports, amount to 25,538 metric tons,[190] and Canadian cheese exports for the same period, *excluding* IREP exports, 7,986 metric tons.[191] As a result, according to the Canadian data, no export subsidies would have been provided in respect of any dairy exports in excess of Canada's quantity commitment levels specified in its Schedule as of February 2001.

6.82 In the light of such conflicting evidence, the Panel requested each of the parties to explain precisely how the data they had used was arrived at and to refer

[181] Paragraphs 6.7-6.78.
[182] Report of the panel on *Canada - Dairy, supra*, footnote 3, para. 7.113.
[183] Report of the Appellate Body on *Canada - Dairy, supra*, footnote 74, para. 124.
[184] Canada's reply to Question 23a, para. 1.
[185] New Zealand's Exhibit 4. United States' Exhibit 1.
[186] New Zealand's Exhibit 4.
[187] United States' Exhibit 1.
[188] United States' Oral Statement, para. 29.
[189] Canada's Rebuttal Submission, para. 50. Reiterated in Canada's reply to Question 23a, para. 2.
[190] Canada's reply to Question 22.
[191] *Ibid.*

to the exact source and documentation which was used for its computation. The Panel also requested the parties to provide the available statistical data, as well as the source and documentation used for its computation, on total cheese exports from Canada for the months following February 2001, both including and excluding IREP exports.[192] The replies by the parties did not enable the Panel to determine whether or not the figures regarding dairy exports for the period August 2000 - February 2001 included IREP exports.[193] Canada, however, did provide the Panel with data on cheese exports for the months of March and April 2001. The Panel proceeded to include in its assessment under Article 3.3 this data, which, according to Canada, does not include IREP exports.[194]

6.83 The data provided by Canada in response to the Panel's questions shows that, as of April 2001, exports of cheese under Class 5(d) and CEM together amount to 10,666 metric tons.[195] As stated earlier, Canada's quantity commitment level for 2000/2001 was set at 9,076 metric tonnes. The Panel, therefore, finds that Canada has provided export subsidies in respect of cheese in excess of its quantity commitment level specified in its Schedule, in breach of Article 3.3.

4. *Article 10.1*

6.84 In the alternative to their claims under Article 9.1(c), both complainants have made claims under Article 10.1. The United States invokes the first phrase

---

[192] Panel's Question 23.

[193] In its reply to Question 23, New Zealand "note[d] that [9,613 tons] is the same figure used by the United States and that, according to the United States, the statistics used do not include exports derived from the IREP, although New Zealand has not been able to confirm this independently." In its reply of 22 June 2001 to Question 23 (para. 6), Canada explained that "although Statistics Canada does include IREP data [in the aggregate export data], it does *not* include data on transshipments such as products destined for ship-stores or products-in-transit, which are the data that Statistics Canada considers as re-export data." In its reply of 25 June 2001 to Question 23, the United States "note[d] that, in its June 22 supplementary answer, Canada now asserts that 're-exports' as reported by Statistics Canada does not include exports under the IREP. This is contrary to our understanding."

[194] The Panel considers that, under the terms of Article 3.3, it can and, indeed, should take into account this export data for the months of March and April 2001 to determine whether export subsidies have been provided in excess of reduction commitment levels, notwithstanding the fact that these exports took place after the matter was referred by the DSB to the original panel, i.e. after 1 March 2001. It is submitted that the Panel's finding that CEM exports are being subsidized within the meaning of Article 9.1(c) cannot be restricted to exports which took place before that date, but applies to *all* dairy exports traded under the terms and conditions of the CEM scheme. The same reasoning applies to exports which took place under the continued Class5(d) scheme. The Panel does not address claims not made or measures not included in the complainants' requests for establishment of this Panel. The Panel also notes that the United States explicitly stated in its request for establishment of this Panel that "cheese and other dairy product exports during the 2000/2001 marketing year appear to be occurring at monthly levels that, if continued for the remainder of the year, would result in an additional year of subsidized export shipments inconsistent with Canada's obligations." (WT/DS103/16, page2)

[195] Canada's reply to Question 23a.

of Article 10.1, while New Zealand invokes both the first and the second phrase of Article 10.1. The first phrase applies to "export subsidies *not* listed in paragraph 1 of Article 9". The second phrase applies to "non-commercial transactions". As the panel in the original proceedings noted, Article 9.1(c) and the first phrase of Article 10.1 are mutually exclusive, and, accordingly, export subsidies listed in Article 9.1 cannot be found to contravene the first phrase of Article 10.1.[196]

6.85 In addressing the question whether the Panel should exercise judicial economy with regard to the Article 10.1 claims, the Panel notes, on the one hand, the Appellate Body's statement in its report on *Australia - Measures Affecting Importation of Salmon*:

> The principle of judicial economy has to be applied keeping in mind the aim of the dispute settlement system. This aim is to resolve the matter at issue and "to secure a positive solution to a dispute". To provide only a partial resolution of the matter at issue would be false judicial economy. *A panel has to address those claims on which a finding is necessary in order to enable the DSB to make sufficiently precise recommendations and rulings so as to allow for prompt compliance by a Member with those recommendations and rulings in order to ensure effective resolution of disputes to the benefit of all Members.*[197] (emphasis added)

6.86 On the other hand, the Panel notes the statement by the Appellate Body in its report on *EC - Asbestos*:

> The need for sufficient facts is not the only limit on our ability to complete the legal analysis in any given case. In *Canada - Periodicals*, we reversed the panel's conclusion that the measure at issue was inconsistent with Article III:2, first sentence, of the GATT 1994, and we then proceeded to examine the United States' claims under Article III:2, second sentence, which the panel had not examined at all. However, in embarking there on an analysis of a provision that the panel had not considered, we emphasized that "the first and second sentences of Article III:2 are *closely related*" and that those two sentences are "part of a *logical continuum*."[198] (emphasis added by the Appellate Body)

6.87 Having regard to these considerations, the Panel notes that the facts underlying the Article 9.1(c) and Article 10.1 claims are, in this case, fully co-extensive. In addition, Articles 9 and 10 can be said to be "closely related" and

---

196 Report of the panel in *Canada - Dairy*, *supra*, footnote 3, para. 7.118.

197 Appellate Body report on *Australia - Salmon*, DSR 1998:VIII, 3327, para. 223.

198 Report of the Appellate Body on *EC - Asbestos*, DSR 2001:VII, 3243, para. 79. [original footnote omitted]

"part of a logical continuum".[199] As a result, should the Panel's findings regarding Article 9.1(c) be subject to appellate review, and should the Appellate Body decide to reverse one or more of the Panel's findings regarding Article 9.1(c), the Appellate Body would still be able to make findings regarding the Article 10.1 claims on the basis of the Panel record. Thus, should the Appellate Body deem it necessary to complete the analysis by making findings regarding Article 10.1 for the purpose of effectively settling this dispute, it could do so notwithstanding the Panel's decision to exercise judicial economy. Accordingly, the Panel's decision to exercise judicial economy in this instance as regards the Article 10.1 claims should not prevent the DSB from making sufficiently precise recommendations and rulings so as to allow for prompt compliance by a Member with those recommendations and rulings in order to ensure effective resolution of this dispute to the benefit of all Members.

6.88 In conclusion, having made an affirmative finding regarding the Article 9.1(c) claim, the Panel has decided to exercise judicial economy and not to address the Article 10.1 claims.

5. *Article 8*

6.89 Article 8 provides that "[e]ach Member undertakes not to provide export subsidies otherwise than in conformity with this Agreement and with the commitments as specified in that Member's Schedule."

6.90 Since the Panel has found a breach of Article 3.3 (through Article 9.1), it therefore also concludes that Canada has acted inconsistently with Article 8.

B. *SCM Agreement*

6.91 The United States has argued that, in addition to constituting export subsidies within the meaning of Article 9.1(c) of the *Agreement on Agriculture*, or in the alternative, Article 10.1 of that Agreement, Canada's measures affecting the exportation of dairy products constitute prohibited export subsidies pursuant to Articles 1.1 and 3.1 of the *SCM Agreement.*

6.92 The Panel has already noted *supra* that the facts underlying the Article 9.1(c) and Article 10.1 claims are, in this case, fully co-extensive. The Panel believes that this conclusion also applies to the facts underlying the claims made under the *Agreement on Agriculture*, on the one hand, and those made under Articles 1.1 and 3.1 of the *SCM Agreement*, on the other. In addition, the Panel considers that Article 9.1 of the *Agreement on Agriculture* and Articles 1.1 and 3.1 of the *SCM Agreement* can be said to be "closely related" and "part of a logical

[199] Article 10.1 requires Members not to apply export subsidies not listed in Article 9.1 in a manner which results in, or which threatens to result in, circumvention of export subsidy commitments, nor to use non-commercial transactions to circumvent such commitments.

continuum". Thus, the Panel's reasoning set forth *supra*[200] regarding the claims made under Article 10.1 of the *Agreement on Agriculture* is equally relevant for the claims made under Articles 1.1 and 3.1 of the *SCM Agreement.*

6.93 The Panel also recalls, however, that the panel in the original proceedings decided to exercise judicial economy with respect to the SCM claim, because (i) the United States arguments under Article 3 were minimal (in reality only one sentence);[201] and (ii) the United States never invoked or even referred to the rules and procedures contained in Article 4.[202] In addition, the original panel raised the question whether it could examine the Article 3 claim at all given that in the United States' requests for consultations and establishment of the original panel, the United States only invoked Article 30 as a legal basis for consultations and a panel on its SCM claims.[203]

6.94 In the current proceedings, the Panel notes that (i) the United States argued the Article 3 claim more extensively than before the original panel; (ii) explicitly referred in its First Submission to Article 4.7;[204] and (iii) provided a statement of available evidence in accordance with Article 4.2 in its request for consultations.[205] The question before the Panel is whether these new elements should lead the Panel to decide *not* to exercise judicial economy, despite the Panel's earlier conclusion that the facts underlying the claims made under the *Agreement on Agriculture* and the *SCM Agreement* are fully co-extensive.

6.95 The Panel considers that it should decide this question in the light of the Appellate Body statement cited above.[206] The Panel should, therefore, only address those claims on which a finding is necessary in order to enable the DSB to make *sufficiently* precise recommendations and rulings so as to allow for *prompt* compliance by a Member with those recommendations and rulings in order to ensure effective resolution of disputes to the benefit of all Members. The question before the Panel can therefore be formulated as follows: if the Panel were not to address the SCM claim made by the United States, would the DSB be prevented from making *sufficiently* precise recommendations and rulings so as to allow for *prompt* compliance by Canada?

6.96 It is submitted that an *affirmative* finding in respect of Article 3.1 of the *SCM Agreement* would affect the specificity of the recommendation to be made by the Panel. In accordance with Article 4.7, if the measure in question is found to be a prohibited subsidy, the panel shall (i) recommend that the subsidizing

---

200 See para. 6.87.
201 Report of the panel on *Canada - Dairy, supra,* footnote 3, para. 7.138.
202 *Ibid.*, paras. 7.139-7-140.
203 *Ibid.*, footnote 515.
204 United States' First Submission, paras. 116 and 122.
205 WT/DS103/15.
206 Appellate Body report on *Australia - Salmon, supra,* footnote 197, para. 223.

Member *withdraw* the subsidy without delay, and (ii) specify in its recommendation the *time-period* within which the measure must be withdrawn.[207]

6.97 First, as regards the recommendation to *withdraw* the export subsidy, the Panel notes, on the one hand, that the Appellate Body in *Brazil - Aircraft (Art. 21.5)* analyzed the meaning of the word "withdraw" as follows:

> [...] we observe first that this word has been defined as "remove", or "take away"[208], and as "to take away what has been enjoyed; to take from."[209] This definition suggests that "withdrawal" of a subsidy, under Article 4.7 of the *SCM Agreement*, refers to the "removal" or "taking away" of that subsidy."
>
> [...]
>
> In our view, to continue to make payments under an export subsidy measure found to be prohibited is not consistent with the obligation to "withdraw" prohibited export subsidies, in the sense of "removing" or "taking away".[210]

6.98 On the other hand, the Panel notes that Article 21.1 of the *Agreement on Agriculture* provides,

> The provisions of GATT 1994 and of other Multilateral Trade Agreements in Annex 1A to the WTO Agreement shall apply *subject to* the provisions of this Agreement (emphasis added),

that Article 8 of the *Agreement on Agriculture* provides,

> Each Member undertakes *not to provide export subsidies otherwise than in conformity with this Agreement* and with the commitments as specified in that Member's Schedule, (emphasis added)

and that Article 3.1 of the *SCM Agreement* provides,

> *Except as provided in the Agreement on Agriculture*, the following subsidies, within the meaning of Article 1, shall be prohibited [...]. (emphasis added)

6.99 In the Panel's view, it results from Articles 8 and 21.1 of the *Agreement on Agriculture* and Article 3.1 of the *SCM Agreement* that the Panel would not be able to recommend Canada to "withdraw" - as interpreted by the Appellate Body - measures constituting an export subsidy, exclusively in respect of agricultural

---

207 The Panel notes that, in order to make an Article 4.7 recommendation, it would first need to assess the merits of the SCM claim and make an *affirmative* finding that the measure is a prohibited export subsidy. Only if the Panel were to find that the measure is a prohibited subsidy, Article 4.7 would come into play. As a result, the Panel would need to make an affirmative finding on the SCM claim, and, hence, not exercise judicial economy, *before* it could actually determine whether its recommendation would effectively be more specific.

208 [footnote omitted]

209 [footnote omitted]

210 Report of the Appellate Body on *Brazil - Aircraft (Art. 21.5)*, DSR 2000:VIII, 4067, para. 45.

products, both within the meaning of Article 9.1(c) of the *Agreement on Agriculture* and Article 3.1 of the *SCM Agreement*. Under Articles 3.3 and 8 of the *Agreement on Agriculture*, Canada has the right to provide export subsidies in respect of products specified in its Schedule, *provided that* it does not exceed the budgetary outlay and quantity commitment levels specified therein. Accordingly, if Canada has exceeded its quantity commitment levels, the Panel can only recommend Canada to bring its measures into conformity with its obligations under the *Agreement on Agriculture*.

6.100 Since the Panel, in case it would make an affirmative finding in respect of Article 3.1 of the *SCM Agreement*, would not be able to make the withdrawal recommendation provided for in the first sentence of Article 4.7 of the *SCM Agreement*, the Panel does not need to consider the first sentence of Article 4.7 to determine whether or not it should exercise judicial economy. Having found that it would not be able make a recommendation to withdraw the subsidy, in accordance with the first sentence of Article 4.7, the Panel considers that, *a fortiori*, it would not be able to specify a *time-period for* withdrawal, in accordance with the second sentence of Article 4.7.

6.101 Alternatively, assuming *arguendo* that the Panel could make a recommendation to Canada to "withdraw" the export subsidy, it could, pursuant to Article 21.1 of the *Agreement on Agriculture* and Article 3.1 of the *SCM Agreement*, only do so with respect to that portion of the subsidized exports which exceeds Canada's reduction commitment levels under the *Agreement on Agriculture*. The Panel does not see how such a recommendation to partially withdraw would differ from a recommendation to bring the measure into conformity with the *Agreement on Agriculture*. If it could make such a recommendation of "partial" withdrawal, it could also specify the time-period within which such "partial" withdrawal was to take place. Such a specification of a time-period for "partial" withdrawal, however, would, in the Panel's view, not be necessary for Canada to know what it needs to do in order to ensure prompt compliance. In addition, the Panel notes that the practical relevance of this question should be assessed in the light of the "*Agreed Procedures under Articles 21 and 22 of the Dispute Settlement Understanding in the follow-up to the dispute in Canada - Measures Affecting the Importation of Milk and the Exportation of Dairy Products*" which the parties to the dispute have concluded.[211] Pursuant to these Agreed Procedures, it

[211] The Understanding between Canada and the United States is contained in WT/DS103/14. According to the Agreed Procedures, (i) the United States has requested authorization to suspend concessions or other obligations pursuant to Article 22.2 of the DSU against Canada; (ii) Canada has objected to the level of suspension of concessions or other obligations; (iii) the matter has been referred to arbitration pursuant to Article 22.6; (iv) the parties have requested the Article 22.6 arbitrator to suspend its work until either the adoption of the Panel's report or, if there is an appeal, the adoption of the Appellate Body report; and (v) in the event that the DSB finds that Canada has failed to comply with the recommendations and rulings of the DSB or that the measures taken by Canada to comply with the recommendations and rulings of the DSB are inconsistent with the covered

is envisaged that, if the Appellate Body were to confirm and the DSB to adopt the Panel's recommendations based on the Panel's findings under Article 9.1(c) of the *Agreement on Agriculture*, an Article 22.6 arbitrator would, in any case, relatively soon thereafter decide what level of suspension of concessions or other obligations should be authorized against Canada.

6.102 For the reasons set out above,[212] the Panel considers that, by not making findings on the SCM claims, it will not prevent the DSB from making sufficiently precise recommendations and rulings so as to allow for prompt compliance by Canada. Consequently, having made an affirmative finding regarding the claim made under Article 9.1(c) of the *Agreement on Agriculture*, the Panel has decided to exercise judicial economy and not to address the claims made under Articles 1.1 and 3.1 of the *SCM Agreement*.

VII. CONCLUSIONS AND RECOMMENDATIONS

7.1 In light of the findings contained in Section VI above, the Panel therefore concludes that Canada, through the CEM scheme and the continued operation of Special Milk Class 5(d), has acted inconsistently with its obligations under Articles 3.3 and 8 of the *Agreement on Agriculture*, by providing export subsidies within the meaning of Article 9.1(c) of the *Agreement on Agriculture* in excess of its quantity commitment levels specified in its Schedule for exports of cheese, for the marketing year 2000/2001.

7.2 Since Article 3.8 of the DSU provides that "[i]n cases where there is an infringement of the obligations assumed under a covered agreement [including the *Agreement on Agriculture*], the action is considered *prima facie* to constitute a case of nullification or impairment", the Panel concludes that - to the extent Canada has acted inconsistently with its obligations under the *Agreement on Agriculture* - it has nullified or impaired benefits accruing to New Zealand and the United States under this Agreement.

7.3 The Panel *recommends* that the Dispute Settlement Body request Canada to bring its dairy products marketing regime into conformity with its obligations in respect of export subsidies under the *Agreement on Agriculture*.

---

agreements as referred to in the Article 21.5 compliance panel request, the arbitrator will automatically resume its work.

[212] Paragraphs 6.95-6.101.

VIII. ANNEX

1. *Abbreviations Used for Dispute Settlement Cases Referred to in the Report*

Australia - Salmon: Australia - Measures Affecting Importation of Salmon, recourse to Article 21.5 of the DSU, (WT/DS18/RW), adopted 20 March 2000;

Australia - Automotive Leather: Australia - Subsidies Provided to Producers and Exporters of Automotive Leather (WT/DS126/R) , adopted 16 June 1999;

Australia - Automotive Leather: Australia - Subsidies Provided to Producers and Exporters of Automotive Leather, recourse to Article 21.5 of the DSU (WT/DS126/RW), adopted 11 February 2000;

Brazil - Aircraft: Brazil - Export Financing Programme for Aircraft (WT/DS46/R), adopted 20 August 1999;

Brazil - Aircraft: Brazil - Export Financing Programme for Aircraft, second recourse to Article 21.5 of the DSU, (WT/DS46/RW), established 16 February 2001;

Canada - Aircraft: Canada - Measures Affecting the Export of Civilian Aircraft (WT/DS70/R), adopted 20 August 1999;

Canada - Aircraft: Canada - Measures Affecting the Export of Civilian Aircraft (WT/DS70/AB/R), adopted 20 August 1999;

Canada - Dairy: Canada - Measures Affecting the Importation of Milk and the Exportation of Dairy

Products, (WT/DS103/R, WT/DS113/R), adopted 27 October 1999;

Canada - Dairy: Canada - Measures Affecting the Importation of Milk and the Exportation of Dairy

Products, (WT/DS103/AB/R, WT/DS113/AB/R), adopted 27 October 1999;

EC - Bananas (Ecuador): European Communities—Regime for the Importation, Sale and Distribution of Bananas - recourse to Article 21.5 of the DSU (WT/DS27/RW/ECU), adopted 6 May 1999;

EC - Bananas (European Communities): European Communities - Regime for the Importation, Sale and Distribution of Bananas, recourse to Article 21.5 of the DSU, /WT/DS27/RW/EEC), panel report circulated 12 April 1999.

EC - Asbestos: European Communities - Measures Affecting the Production of Asbestos and Asbestos Products (WT/DS/135/ABR), adopted 5 April 2001;

Indonesia - Automobiles: Indonesia - Certain Measures Affecting the Automobile Industry, (WTDS54, 55, 59,63/R), adopted 23 July 1998;

Mexico - High Fructose Corn Syrup: Mexico - Anti-dumping Investigation of High-Fructose Corn Syrup from the United States, recourse to Article 21.5 of the DSU (WT/DS132/RW), circulated 22 June 2001;

United States - FSC : United States - Tax Treatment for "Foreign Sales Corporations, (WT/DS108/AB/R), adopted 20 March 2000;

United States - Steel: United States - Hot-Rolled Lead and Carbon Steel: Imposition of Countervailing Duties On Certain Hot-Rolled Lead and Bismuth Carbon Steel Products Originating in the United Kingdom, (WD/DS138/AB/R), adopted 7 June 2000;

United States - Shrimp; United States - Import Prohibition of Certain Shrimp and Shrimp Products, Recourse to Article 21.5 of the DSU (WT/DS58/RW), circulated 15 June 2001;

United States - Wheat Gluten: United States - Definitive Safeguard Measures on Imports of Wheat Gluten from the European Communities (WT/DS166/R), adopted 19 January 2001;

United States - 1916 Act: United States - Anti-Dumping Act of 1916, (WT/DS136/AB/R, WT/DS162/AB/R), adopted 26 September 2000;

United States - DRAMs: United States - Anti-Dumping Duty on Dynamic Random Access Memory Semiconductors of One Megabit or Above from Korea, Recourse to Article 21.5 of the DSU (WT/DS99/RW), mutually agreed solution notified 20 October 2000, panel report circulated 7 November 2000;

Thailand - Steel: Thailand - Antidumping Duties on Angles Shapes and Sections of Iron or Non-Alloy Steel and H-Beams from Poland, (WT/DS122/R), adopted 5 April 2001.